PEOPLE IN THE NEWS
1991
by

David Brownstone

People in the News

People in the News

David Brownstone

Irene Franck

MACMILLAN PUBLISHING COMPANY
NEW YORK
Maxwell Macmillan Canada
TORONTO
Maxwell Macmillan International
NEW YORK OXFORD SINGAPORE SYDNEY

Acknowledgements for illustrative materials are on pp. 353–354, which shall be considered a continuation of the copyright page.

Macmillan Publishing Company
866 Third Avenue
New York, NY 10022

Maxwell Macmillan Canada, Inc.
1200 Eglinton Avenue East, Suite 200
Don Mills, Ontario M3C 3N1

Macmillan, Inc., is part of the Maxwell
Communication Group of Companies

Library of Congress Catalog Card Number: 91–14962

Printed in the United States of America

printing number

1 2 3 4 5 6 7 8 9 10

Library of Congress Cataloging-in-Publication Data

Brownstone, David M.
People in the news / David Brownstone Irene Franck.
p. Cm.
Includes bibliographical references and index.
Summary: Presents clear, up-to-date biographical information on a wide selection of the most newsworthy people in the world.
ISBN 0–02–897073–X
1. Celebrities—Biography—Juvenile literature.
2. Biography—20th century—Juvenile literature. [1. Celebrities.
2. Biography.] I. Franck, Irene M. II. Title.
CT120.B76 1991
920—dc20 91–14962
CIP

Contents

Preface

This is the first edition of **People in the News.** Our aim in this work is to present clear, up-to-date biographical information on a wide selection of the most newsworthy people in the world, stressing their current activities, including brief biographies on each of them, and backing each entry with further reading for those who want to dig deeper into their current and past histories.

To those ends, we have identified and present here profiles of 700 people, the world's key political leaders and trend-setters—the presidents, prime ministers, generals, musicians, film stars, directors, scientists, doctors, business leaders, spies, criminals, victims, writers, judges, and the rest who are the main stuff day-to-day reportage on screen and in print throughout the year. Please also note that these profiles include a selection of a little over 200 key obituaries, offering a capsule overview of the person's life.

Our thanks to Philip Friedman president and publisher of Macmillan's reference division, to editorial assistants Elizabeth Halleron and Melissa Solomon, and to managing editor Michael Sander, who have so capably seen this book through the publishing process. We also thank the staff of the Chappaqua Library, and their colleagues throughout the northeastern library network, who have once again been so helpful in fulfilling our research needs. Our thanks also to our expert photo researchers: Susan Hormuth, visual resource consultant, and Joan Carroll of Wide World Photos.

David Brownstone
Irene Franck
Chappaqua, New York

Abdul, Paula (1962–) Suddenly, dancer-singer-choreographer Abdul seemed to be everywhere. In 1990 alone, she appeared on the Grammys, the Academy Awards, the Emmys, the People's Choice Awards, the Soul Train Awards, Dance Music Awards, and America's Dance Honors, among others. Frequently a presenter, sometimes also a performer or choreographer (as of the two main musical numbers at the 1990 Oscars), Abdul often won awards herself, such as an Emmy for her choreography of the American Music Awards. At the American Classic Awards given in May 1990 by ASCAP (American Society of Composers, Authors, and Publishers), Abdul's "Straight Up" (1988) was named the most performed song of 1989. With this and a string of other singles from her album *Forever Your Girl* (1988), including "(It's Just) The Way That You Love Me," "Knocked Out," "Forever Your Girl," "Cold-Hearted," and "Opposites Attract," Abdul was on the top 40 pop charts for well over a year, much of it in the number one spot for singles, albums, or (unusually) both. The popular, widely played video versions of the songs were an important part of her success. In *Rolling Stone's* Readers and Critics Poll, released in February 1990, Abdul was voted best female singer, as well as the best-dressed and sexiest female singer.

In 1990, Abdul released her second album, *Shut Up and Dance (The Dance Mixes)*, made up of her previous hits remixed for dancing. Some people faulted the quality of the dance remixing, and others criticized her for releasing a second album containing only recycled hits. But Abdul's fans did not seem to mind, because the album promptly shot up to the top ten on the Billboard pop album charts. During 1990, she also worked on several other projects, including the choreography for Oliver Stone's new film *The Doors*, scheduled for 1991 release.

Of Syrian, Brazilian, and French-Canadian descent, California-born Abdul studied tap and jazz dancing as a child, performing summers in a traveling group. She began her work as a choreographer during her six-year engagement as one of the Laker Girls, cheerleaders at the Los Angeles Lakers basketball games. In 1984, she also began to choreograph for Michael Jackson and his brothers, then for Janet Jackson and other entertainment figures, including the Pointer Sisters, Eddie Murphy in *Coming to America*, and Tracey Ullman, winning an Emmy for her choreography of the "Tracey Ullman Show." In 1988, her career took an entirely new turn, as her first album, *Forever Your Girl,* hit the top of the bestseller charts. She attended California State University.

FURTHER READING

"Janet Jackson and Paula Abdul. . . ." *Jet*, May 7, 1990.
"The many talents of Paula Abdul. . . ." LYNN NORMENT. *Ebony*, May 1990.
"Paula Abdul." *People*, Spring 1990.
"Straight up . . . and up and up." JEANNIE PARK. *People*, Mar. 12, 1990.
Paula Abdul: Forever Yours. GRACE CATALANO. New American Library-Dutton, 1990.
"Paula Abdul." *Teen Magazine*, June 1989.
"Paula Abdul." *Seventeen*, Feb. 1989.

Abe, Shintaro (1924–) A leader of Japan's ruling Liberal Democratic Party, Abe was secretary-general of his party and widely regarded as the probable successor to Prime Minister Noburu Takeshita during the late 1980s. But Abe publicly admitted that his wife had taken "gifts" of millions of yen from the Recruit Company. He was therefore accused of deep involvement in the Recruit scandal of 1989 that forced Takeshita's resignation. Abe continued to lead a faction of his party in the Diet (parliament), but he did not attempt to become prime minister. Instead, he supported Toshiki Kaifu, who replaced Sosuke Uno in August 1989, after Uno resigned in another scandal. Yet, Japanese voters returned Abe and many other scandal-tainted Liberal Democratic Party leaders to office in the February 1990 elections. After the elections, Abe was frozen out of the Kaifu cabinet, which was composed of politicians not involved in the scandals that had rocked Japanese politics during the 1980s. Abe remained a powerful faction leader and a potential future prime minister.

After his graduation from Tokyo University in 1949, Abe became a newspaper reporter, leaving journalism to become private secretary to Foreign Minister Nobosuke Kishi, who became prime minister a year later. In 1958, Abe entered parliament, beginning a long political career that included key cabinet posts in the 1970s. He became foreign minister in 1982 and became the Liberal Democratic Party's secretary-general in 1987. He married Yoko Abe in 1951; they have two sons.

FURTHER READING

"Year of constant surprises." *Economist,* Jan. 27, 1990.
"Now appearing in the role. . . ." ROBERT NEFF and PAUL MAGNUSSON. *Business Week*, Aug. 21, 1989.
"Fresh Recruits for the scandal." *Economist*, Nov. 12, 1988.
"Tee time for threesome." BARRY HILLENBRAND. *Time*, Oct. 19, 1987.
"Political poker game. . . ." MARY LORD. *U.S. News and World Report*, July 20, 1987.
"Soothing talks, troubled times. . . ." BARBARA RUDOLPH. *Time*, May 4, 1987.
"The political rivals. . . ." BARBARA BUELL et al. *Business Week*, Apr. 20, 1987.

Abernathy, Ralph David (1926–90) Reverend Abernathy was a key civil rights leader, the man who cradled in his arms the dying Martin Luther King, Jr. Grandson of a slave and one of 12 children raised on a 500-acre Alabama farm, Abernathy met King in the 1950s in Montgomery, Alabama, and with him organized the 1955 bus boycott there. In 1957, they formed the Southern Christian Leadership Conference (SCLC), for which Abernathy worked full time from 1961 and which he led from King's death in 1968 until 1977. Afterward he returned to the Baptist ministry. Abernathy and his former SCLC colleagues later diverged over his 1980 support of Ronald Reagan for president and over the "warts-and-all" portrait of King in

Abernathy's 1989 autobiography *And the Walls Came Tumbling Down*. (d. Atlanta, Georgia; April 17, 1990)

FURTHER READING

Obituary. *Current Biography*, June 1990.
Obituary. *Jet,* May 7, 1990.
"Torchbearer." *U.S. News and World Report*, Apr. 30, 1990.
Obituary. *The Times* (of London). Apr. 19, 1990.
Obituary. RICHARD SEVERO. *New York Times*, Apr. 18, 1990.
Voices of Freedom: An Oral History of the Civil Rights Movement from the 1950s Through the 1980s. HENRY HAMPTON and STEVE FAYER. Bantam, 1990.
"Tattletale memoir. . . ." *Time*, Oct. 23, 1989.
Parting the Waters: America in the King Years, 1954-63. TAYLOR BRANCH. Simon and Schuster, 1988.

Aiello, Danny (Danny Louis Aiello, Jr., 1935–) Aiello won an Oscar nomination for his leading role as Sal, the Italian pizza parlor owner, in a racially troubled Brooklyn neighborhood, in Spike Lee's *Do the Right Thing* (1989). He also won best supporting actor awards from the Los Angeles and Chicago film critics. Later in 1989, he played opposite Eddie Murphy as the White gangster in *Harlem Nights*. Forthcoming are a starring role opposite Lainie Kazan in *29th Street*, set in a New York Italian neighborhood during the 1970s, and *Hudson Hawk*, starring Bruce Willis.

New York City-born Aiello played modest supporting roles on stage and screen from the early 1970s, appearing in such films as *The Godfather Part II* (1974), *The Front* (1976), *Fort Apache, the Bronx* (1981), and *The Purple Rose of Cairo* (1984). He emerged in substantial roles in the late 1980s, beginning with his lead opposite Cher in *Moonstruck* (1987). He married Sandy Cohen in 1955; they have four children.

FURTHER READING

"Danny Aiello." LORENZO CARCATERRA. *People*, Feb. 19, 1990.
"His bus came in." MICHAEL NORMAN. *New York Times Magazine*, Jan. 21, 1990.

Ailey, Alvin (1931–89) Dancer, director, and choreographer Ailey was a major figure in popularizing modern dance. Born poor in Rogers, Texas, and fatherless from infancy, Ailey was introduced to modern dance only in his early teens in Los Angeles, where he made his dance debut in 1950. Moving on to the New York stage in 1954, he founded the Alvin Ailey American Dance Theatre four years later. Though he choreographed for a wide range of settings, his most characteristic works were those like *Blues Suite* (1958), and *Revelations* (1960), which illuminated the Black experience through gospel songs, spirituals, and jazz, and became known worldwide through the company's international tours. (d. New York City; December 1, 1989)

FURTHER READING

Obituary. *Current Biography*, Jan. 1990.
Black Dance in America: A History Through Its People. JAMES HASKINS. HarperCollins, 1990.
"With dances deeply rooted. . . ." *People*, Dec. 18, 1989.
Obituary. *Jet*, Dec. 18, 1989.
"Dance Master." *U.S. News and World Report*, Dec. 11, 1989.
Obituary. *Variety*, Dec. 6, 1989.
Obituary. *The Times* (of London), Dec. 4, 1989.
Obituary. JENNIFER DUNNING. *New York Times*, Dec. 2, 1989.
Reaching for Dreams: A Ballet from Rehearsal to Opening Night. SUSAN KUKLIN. Lothrop, 1987.

Akihito (1933–) The son of former emperor Hirohito, Akihito succeeded to the throne on January 7, 1989, after the death of his father. Like Hirohito, he is mostly a ceremonial figure, though one of great significance to many in Japan. He finished the long process of installation as emperor on November 23, 1990, in the religious ceremony called "daijosai," a Shinto Buddhist religious ceremony that historically has been thought to complete the process of transforming him into a living god. The government-funded event cost $20 million and was attended by prime minister Kaifu and other members of his government. Many Japanese sharply criticized the ceremony for violating the constitutional separation of church and state, and for continuing the kind of belief and practice that led Japan into imperialism and the disaster of World War II. The Kaifu government and many other Japanese disagreed, upholding the ceremony as a traditional event and government payments as customary. Akihito married Michiko Shoda in 1959; they have three children.

FURTHER READING

"Japan's imperial present." Steven R. Weisman. *New York Times Magazine*, Aug. 26, 1990.

"The longest reign. . . ." Pico Iyor and Michael Walsh. *Time*, Jan. 16, 1989.

"'I can't imagine another way of life.'" Dorian Benkoil. *Newsweek*, Jan. 16, 1989.

Alda, Alan (1936–) As director, writer, and actor, Alda wore three hats for his latest film, *Betsy's Wedding*, which opened in the summer of 1990. Betsy, played by Molly Ringwald, is a fashion design student about to be married; Alda is Betsy's father, faced with the possibility of losing his youngest daughter and perhaps being overwhelmed by the wedding, as his business also rides on shaky ground. Reviews were mixed, with some suggesting that Alda had spread his talents too thin among his various responsibilities. Alda the actor won considerable praise for his work in Woody Allen's *Crimes and Misdemeanors* (1989); the role won Alda the Directors Guild of America's award for best supporting actor. Rumors that Alda might be joining NBC for the 1990–91 season came to nought. He was honored this year for his lifetime achievement by the National Italian-American Foundation.

New York-born Alda, the son of actor Robert Alda, appeared on the New York stage from the late 1950s in such plays as *Purlie Victorious* (1961), *The Owl and the Pussycat* (1964), and *The Apple Tree* (1966). He became a major television star during the 1970s, appearing in *The Glass House* (1972), and then starring as Korean War surgeon Benjamin Franklin "Hawkeye" Pierce in the long-running "M*A*S*H" (1972–83). He has also starred in such films as *The Moonshine War* (1970), *California Suite* (1978), *Same Time Next Year* (1978), and *The Seduction of Joe Tynan* (1979), and has written, directed, and appeared in the films *The Four Seasons* (1981) and *Sweet Liberty* (1986). He married Arlene Weiss in 1957; they have three children. Alda attended Fordham University.

FURTHER READING

"Alan Alda. . . ." Cliff Jahr. *Ladies Home Journal*, Mar. 1985.

The Last Days of Mash. Arlene Alda and Alan Alda. Unicorn, 1984.

Alan Alda: A Biography. RAYMOND STRAIT. St. Martin's, 1983.

Alan Alda: An Unauthorized Biography. JASON BONDEROFF. New American Library-Dutton, 1982.

Alexander, Jane (Jane Quigley, 1939–) Alexander had a tough row to hoe in early 1990, in the most unsympathetic role of a self-righteous social activist mother who fails to see her own daughter's needs, in the television film *Daughter of the Streets*. Her character was even more difficult to bear when, discovering that the daughter had turned hooker on the streets, she ties her to her bed to "bring her back to her senses." Alexander's stage roles were perhaps more satisfying and successful. Late in 1989, she starred in the Los Angeles production of Manuel Puig's two-hander, *Mystery of the Rose Bouquet*, as a psychiatric nurse not sure she can handle wealthy Argentinian patient Anne Bancroft. In December 1990, she opened on Broadway in *Shadowlands* as Joy Davidman, an American admirer and, later, wife of reclusive Oxford don and writer C.S. Lewis, played by Nigel Hawthorne. The play tells their brief time together before her death from cancer. Alexander also continued to use her celebrity in aid of causes she supports. During the controversy over censorship by the National Endowment of the Arts, she was one of numerous artists to testify before Congress on the importance of freedom in the arts. She also appeared in a series of TV announcements on the threat of global warming.

Alexander played in regional theater in the mid-1960s. She emerged as a major dramatic actress on Broadway in 1968 in her Tony-winning role opposite James Earl Jones in *The Great White Hope*. Some of her most notable stage roles were in *6 Rms Riv Vu* (1972), *Find Your Way Home* (1974), *The Heiress* (1976), *First Monday in October* (1978), *Hedda Gabler* (1981), *Old Times* (1984), and *Night of the Iguana* (1988). On screen, she was nominated for a Best Actress Oscar for the film version of *The Great White Hope* (1970), and she also appeared in such films as *All the President's Men* (1976), *Kramer vs. Kramer* (1979), *Testament* (1983), and *Glory* (1989). She has also made several telefilms, most notably in *Eleanor and Franklin* (1976) as a classic Eleanor Roosevelt, in *Playing For Time* (1980), and in *Calamity Jane* (1984). Alexander attended Sarah Lawrence College and the University of Edinburgh. She has been married twice, last to Edwin Sherin in 1975, and has one child.

FURTHER READING

"Liz and Jane. . . ." BILL DAVIDSON. *TV Guide*, Apr. 20, 1985.

"Jane Alexander launching. . . ." JIM ROBBINS. *Variety*, Jan. 30. 1985.

Alia, Ramiz (1925–) As democratic reform swept Eastern Europe and the Soviet Union, the Communist leader of Albania bent—a little—in May 1990, and introduced such reforms as opening more phone lines abroad and loosening rigid restraints on the right to practice religion. These minor concessions merely encouraged the pro-democracy forces. Demonstrations broke out in Tirana, the capital, in late June and early July, and were broken up when police fired on the demonstrators. Alia did give way to international pressure in early July, though, allowing an estimated 4,000 to 5,000 Albanians who had taken refuge in foreign embassies to leave the country unharmed. In an attempt to placate rebellious Albanians, he also announced wage increases and government changes that were said to have retired some hardline government ministers. But in the early winter of 1990–91, Albania under Alia was the only hardline Communist state left in Europe, though perhaps only for a little while longer.

Born of a Muslim family, Alia, as a teenager, joined the anti-German Albanian Communist partisans led by Enver Hoxha during World War II, and joined the Communist Party in 1943, when he was 18. He became a member of his party's Central Committee in 1948, when 23, and was a nonvoting member of its Politburo in 1956. From 1960, he was a key aide to dictator Hoxha, deeply involved in the 1960 break with the Soviet Union and the long-term, hardline anti-Soviet relationship with Maoist China that followed. He became state president in 1982 and leader of the Communist Party in 1985, after Hoxha's death. His wife, Semirani Xhurani, died in 1986.

FURTHER READING

"Next to fall?" *Time*, July 16, 1990.

"Leaping to freedom. . . ." SAM SEIBERT. *Newsweek*, July 16, 1990.
"The Albanian exodus." *Economist*, July 14, 1990.
"Tirana too?" *Economist*, July 7, 1990.
"Fortress Albania." STAFFAN BRUUN. *World Press Review*, May 1990.
"Closet-talk." *Economist*, Mar. 31, 1990.

Allen, Woody (Allen Stewart Konigsberg, 1935–) Director-writer-actor Allen's *Crimes and Misdemeanors*, which opened in late 1989, played around the country to mixed reviews, winning a best-director nomination from the Directors Guild of America, but being passed over in the Oscar nominations. Some reviewers thought the bittersweet story (which includes an intellectual who commits suicide) pretentious, while others found it both humorous and profound, tending to confirm Allen's status as America's "most original filmmaker." Allen's next film, *Alice*, opened to critical praise for Christmas 1990, with Mia Farrow in the title role as the Upper-East-Side, upper-middle-class Manhattan lady who discovers aspects of New York—and herself—she did not know existed. Late in the year, Allen himself was working as an actor opposite Bette Midler in Paul Mazursky's *Scenes from a Mall*, released in early 1991.

A New Yorker, Allen emerged as a leading television comedy writer in the late 1950s, and during the 1960s also worked in cabaret and theater, beginning a long series of hit films as the writer and star of *What's New Pussycat?* (1965). He then became one of the leading filmmakers of the 1970s and 1980s, with such films as his Oscar-winning *Annie Hall* (1977), *Manhattan* (1979), and *Hannah and Her Sisters* (1984). Allen attended City College in New York, and New York University. He was formerly married to Louise Lasser. He and Mia Farrow have two children.

FURTHER READING

Woody Allen. GRAHAM MCCANN. Basil Blackwell, 1990.
Love, Sex, Death, and the Meaning of Life: The Films of Woody Allen, rev. ed. FOSTER HIRSCH. Limelight, 1990.
Everything You Always Wanted to Know about Woody Allen: The Ultimate Quiz Book. FRANK WEIMANN. Shapolsky, 1990.
"'Crimes' story." MARCIA PALLY. *Film Comment*, Nov.–Dec. 1989.
"Play it again, Woody." THOMAS A. SANCTON. *Time*, Oct. 23, 1989.
Schickel on Film: Encounters—Critical and Personal—with Movie Immortals. RICHARD SCHICKEL. Morrow, 1989.
Woody Allen: His Films and Career. DOUGLAS BRODE. Carol, 1987.
Woody Allen on Location. T. DE NAVACELLE. Morrow, 1987.
Woody Allen. NANCY POGEL. G.K. Hall, 1987.

Alley, Kirstie (1955–) Alley made her major breakthrough in 1987, when she joined the cast of television's very popular and long-running *Cheers*. Her film breakthrough came opposite John Travolta in the film comedy *Look Who's Talking* (1989). The film, which also featured the voice of Bruce Willis, became a surprise hit and spawned a sequel, *Look Who's Talking, Too* (1990), with the voices of Willis, Damon Wayans, and Roseanne Barr. Also in 1990, she starred in the film comedies *Madhouse* and *Sibling Rivalry*.

Kansas-born Alley worked as an interior decorator before taking up an acting career in the early 1980s. Her most notable earlier work was in the Lieutenant Saavik role in *Star*

Trek II: The Wrath of Khan (1982), which was followed by supporting roles in several other theater and television films. She attended Kansas State University. Alley is married to actor Parker Stevenson.

FURTHER READING

"Feisty, funny Kirstie Alley." GREGG KILDAY. *Cosmopolitan*, Dec. 1990.
"The tears behind the Cheers." J.D. REED. *People*, Oct. 29, 1990.
"Kirstie Alley." RICHARD BLAINE. *Good Housekeeping*, Mar. 1990.
"Chez Alley." FRED ROBBINS. *Saturday Evening Post*, Jan.–Feb. 1990.
"The vulcan's revenge. . . ." TOM GREEN. *Los Angeles Magazine*, Dec. 1989.

Altman, Robert (1925–) Writer-director-producer Altman came up with a new and different approach to the life of artist Vincent van Gogh, best-known for the great, swirling yellows and blues of his paintings—and for the madness signaled by his cutting off his own ear. *Vincent and Theo* (1990) focuses on the complex relationship between van Gogh (Tim Roth) and his brother Theo (Paul Rhys), an art dealer who tried unsuccessfully to interest buyers in the now much-prized paintings. Originally intended as a four-hour television miniseries, though definitely not a traditional bio-picture, the film was cut for general release in theaters, and won much praise for its intensity and raw energy, with many critics citing it as among Altman's best work.

In late 1990, Altman was working on putting together a new film, tentatively titled *L.A. Short Cuts*, based on a series of short stories by Raymond Carver. The film is an ensemble work set in the Pacific Northwest and planned as a set of intertwined story lines, as in *Nashville*. Financing was still being arranged, always a complicated process for an out-of-mainstream filmmaker. Meanwhile, Altman and Gary Trudeau were already looking ahead to the 1991 presidential election for a possible new version of their innovative pseudo-documentary series, *Tanner* (1988), in which Michael Murphy ran for president.

Altman directed in television and films from the late 1950s, emerging as a major film director in the 1970s, with such films as *M*A*S*H* (1970), *Brewster McCloud* (1971), *McCabe and Mrs. Miller* (1972), *California Split* (1974), *Nashville* (1975), and *Buffalo Bill and the Indians* (1976). He received best picture and best director nominations for *M*A*S*H* and *Nashville*. But his film career sagged as the American film industry moved toward the theater of spectacle, and away from his kind of social commentary. During the 1980s, he directed a variety of films, plays, and telefilms, most notably *Come Back to the Five and Dime, Jimmy Dean, Jimmy Dean* (1982), and *Streamers* (1983). He has been married three times, and has five children. He attended the University of Missouri.

FURTHER READING

Robert Altman: Jumping Off the Cliff. PATRICK MCGILLIGAN. St. Martin's, 1989.
A Cinema of Loneliness: Penn, Kubrick, Scorsese, Spielberg, Altman, 2nd ed. ROBERT P. KOLKER. Oxford University Press, 1988.

Amis, Martin Louis (1949–) Amis's most recent novel, *London Fields* (1989, in the U.S. 1990), appeared to considerable critical acclaim, though it was passed over at award time. Amis himself toured the United States promoting the black comedy murder mystery set in a world speeding toward self-destruction, with the end of the millennium at hand. Mid-year also saw the paperback release of his *Einstein's Monsters* (1987), a work a *Los Angeles Times* reviewer described as "five nightmarish stories and a darkly brooding essay" about humanity facing possible nuclear destruction.

The son of writer Kingsley Amis, Martin Amis has made his reputation as an angry young satirist who focuses on what he perceives as the decline and fast-approaching end of British society and the poisoning of the environment. Among his other works are *The Rachel Papers* (1973), *Dead Babies* (1975), *Success* (1978), *Other People* (1981), *Money* (1984), and *The Moronic Inferno* (1986). He married Antonia Phillips in 1984; they have two children. He attended Exeter College, at Oxford, and lives in England.

FURTHER READING

"Amis, Martin Louis." *Current Biography*, June 1990.
"The wit and the fury. . . ." SUSAN MORRISON. *Rolling Stone*, May 17, 1990.
"Novelist Martin Amis. . . ." KIM HUBBARD. *People*, Apr. 23, 1990.
"Amis looking ahead in anguish." HELLE BERING-JENSEN. *Insight*, Apr. 16, 1990.
"English accents." MARK MATOUSEK. *Harper's Bazaar*, Apr. 1990.
"Martin Amis." BRENDAN LEMON. *Interview*, Mar. 1990.
"Martin Amis. . . ." *New York Times Magazine*, Feb. 4, 1990.

Andreotti, Giulio (1919–) The Italian prime minister, a Christian Democratic Party leader, came to power in July 1989, succeeding Christian Democratic prime minister Ciriaco De Mita. In power, Andreotti, as had previous prime ministers, focused on attempts to reduce the enormous Italian budget deficit and to solve Italy's recurrent financial crises. At the same time, much of his attention was taken up by Italian plans to become part of the coming economic union of Europe, part of which was scheduled to go into effect in 1992. His government faced an embarrassing financial scandal in September 1989, when officials of the mostly government-owned Banca Nazionale del Lavoro were accused of taking large bribes for arranging almost $3 billion in improper loans to Iraq. As some of the money was allegedly for military purchasing purposes, the scandal became especially notable after the August 1990 outbreak of the Persian Gulf Crisis. After initial coolness, Andreotti expressed support for American and allied actions in the crisis, and sent token forces in support.

Rome-born Andreotti began his long political career just after World War II. He entered the Italian parliament in 1947 and was parliamentary chairman of the Christian Democratic Party from 1954 to 1972. He has held many cabinet posts from the 1950s through the early 1990s, and has been prime minister three times (1972–73, 1976–79, and 1989–). He married Livia Danese in 1945; they have four children. He attended the University of Rome. When out of office, he has been a leading Italian journalist.

FURTHER READING

"Andreotti, Italian Prime Minister." *Business Week*, Dec. 24, 1990.

Andrew Albert Christian Edward (1960–) and **Sarah Margaret Ferguson** (1959–), **the Duke and Duchess of York** Prince Andrew is the third child and second son of Elizabeth II. He is a Royal Navy helicopter pilot and flight instructor, and a photographer who has published and exhibited his work. The former Sarah Ferguson, known as "Fergie" in the media, worked in publishing before her marriage. In 1986, the couple married; from then on, they became worldwide, media-created celebrities. They spend much of their public time in ceremonial appearances, and must otherwise pay a great deal of attention to avoiding the media—although in September 1990, their invitation of a photographer into their home and the subsequent informal pictures caught much attention. She visited Houston, Texas, in early November 1989, at the invitation of the Houston Grand Opera, then celebrating 300 years of British opera. After one of the most highly publicized pregnancies in recent history, she gave birth to their second daughter, Eugenie, on March 23, 1990; their older daughter is Beatrice. The Duke of York is a serving naval officer and attended the Royal Naval College, seeing active service in the Falklands War. The Duchess of York attended secretarial college.

FURTHER READING

"First photos. . . ." GENE NOCON. *Life*, Oct. 1990.
The Princess & the Duchess: A Behind the Scenes Biography of the Princess of Wales & the Duchess of York. JANE ARTHUR. State Mutual, 1990.
"Fergie at 30." INGRID SEWARD. *Woman's Day*, Oct. 24, 1989.
"Royal revenge." RAE CORELLI. *Maclean's*, July 24, 1989.
The Princess & Duchess. JOSEPHINE FAIRLEY. St. Martin's, 1989.
Duchess: An Intimate Portrait of Sarah, Duchess of York. ANDREW MORTON. Contemporary, 1989.
"Andrew, Duke of York." *Current Biography*, Mar. 1987.

"Sarah, Duchess of York." *Current Biography*, Mar. 1987.
Sarah Ferguson: The Royal Redhead. DAVID BANKS. Dillon, 1987.
Their Royal Highnesses the Duke & Duchess of York. CHRISTOPHER WARWICK and VALERIE GARNER. Salem House, 1986.

Angelo, Richard (1962–) After an eight-week trial, a Suffolk County, New York jury on December 14, 1989, found ex-nurse Angelo guilty of murder, manslaughter, and criminally negligent homicide. After eight days of deliberation, the jurors found that in 1987, Angelo, then a nurse at Good Samaritan Hospital in West Islip, Long Island, had injected seven patients with the muscle relaxant Pavulum. Of the six that died, the injections were found to have caused four of the deaths. In the other three cases, Angelo was convicted only of assault; the jury found not enough evidence to convict him of murder in those instances.

FURTHER READING

"Long Island's 'angel of death'. . . ." DAVID GATES, et al. *Newsweek*, Nov. 30, 1987.
"The angel of death." *Time*, Nov. 30, 1987.

Angelou, Maya (1928–) Angelou ventured into far different territory than usual this year, as she worked on *King*, the $4 million musical about the life of Martin Luther King, Jr. It was apparently a troubled project from early on, and various writers and directors—Angelou among them—left the project and asked to be disassociated from it. Angelou said she was unhappy because of the way King was portrayed. When it finally opened in London, critics blasted it as oversimplified and "an insult to adults," though the opening night audience gave it a four-minute standing ovation; in the end it ran less than two months. Angelou was also one of the eulogists at the emotional memorial for dancer-choreographer Alvin Ailey, a moving ceremony seen by many in a televised tribute, *Going Home: Alvin Ailey Remembered*.

St. Louis-born Angelou became a national figure in 1970, with publication of her autobiographical *I Know Why the Caged Bird Sings*, dealing with her life as a Black woman, and by extension, with the lives of many other Black women in the United States. Her works, mostly autobiographical, include such books as *Just Give Me a Cool Drink of Water B'fore I Die* (1971), *Georgia, Georgia* (1972), *Gather Together in My Name* (1974), *Singin' and Swingin' and Gettin' Merry Like Christmas* (1976), *The Heart of a Woman* (1986), and *All God's Children Need Traveling Shoes* (1987). She has one child.

FURTHER READING

"Maya Angelou and Billie Holiday." NANCY CALDWELL SOREL. *Atlantic*, Sept. 1990.
Conversations with Maya Angelou. JEFFREY M. ELLIOTT, ed. University Press of Mississippi, 1989.
"Maya Angelou. . . ." CHERYL MCCALL. *People*, Mar. 8, 1982.
"Why I moved. . . ." MAYA ANGELOU. *Ebony*, Feb. 1982.

Annenberg, Walter Hubert (1908–) Annenberg caught the nation's attention in March 1990, when he donated $50 million to the United Negro College Fund (UNCF), making the largest single gift ever to Black higher education. Annenberg made the announcement at a ceremony with President George Bush, kicking off in a big way the UNCF's $250-million fund-raising campaign. Among his other philanthropic gifts in 1990 was over $20 million to Northwestern University, $15 million of which was for the university's Annenberg Washington Program in Communication Policy Studies, in Washington, D.C. In January 1990, however, his Annenberg Foundation withdrew its support of the Corporation for Public Broadcasting's program to provide courses for college credit over public and cable television channels. He had pledged $150 million in 1981, $90 million of which had been received by the program for the courses that began in 1984.

Annenberg's notable collection of Impressionist and Post-Impressionist paintings, including works by Gauguin, Renoir, and van Gogh, was being shown in a traveling exhibition, opening at the Los Angeles County Museum of Art late in 1990. One of the works was Picasso's *Au Lapin Agile,* purchased in

November 1989 for $40.7 million, at the time the third-highest price ever paid for a work of art.

Milwaukee-born Annenberg is the son of publisher M. L. (Moe) Annenberg, who founded Triangle Publications, the large publishing company that Walter Annenberg built into an even larger communications empire. He is also a very active Republican Party fundraiser and contributor, and an intimate friend of Presidents Richard Nixon and Ronald Reagan. Annenberg was U.S. ambassador to Britain from 1969 to 1975. He is also a major philanthropist, most notably as the founder of the Annenberg School of Communicationsat the University of Pennsylvania. After selling his interest in Triangle Publications to Rupert Murdoch for approximately $3 billion, he further developed his philanthropic interests. Annenberg attended the University of Pennsylvania and its Wharton School. He has been married twice, and has one child.

FURTHER READING

"Strength of vision." HUNTER DROHOJOWSKA. *Harper's Bazaar*, Apr. 1989.
"Guiding TV. . . ." ERIC NADLER. *Mother Jones*, Apr. 1984.
"An unlikely American friend." *Time*, Mar. 14, 1983.
The Annenbergs: The Salvaging of a Tainted Empire. JOHN COONEY. Simon and Schuster, 1982.

Antall, József (1932–) The Hungarian historian and political leader led the Hungarian Democratic Forum to electoral victory in April 1990, and on May 3rd became the premier of Hungary, succeeding Socialist Miklos Nemeth. Antall was elected on a platform that called for a move away from state planning and toward a market-driven economy, while at the same time supporting the kinds of social services that had been developed during Hungary's Communist years. Like Mikhail Gorbachev, whose policies he supported, he called for far closer ties with the new European Community, and saw Hungary's future as identified with that of the new Europe. Like many other new leaders in Eastern Europe, he called for the end of the Warsaw Pact, which had bound together the Soviet-satellite nations of Eastern Europe during the now-finished Cold War. In the months that followed his election, Antall moved toward privatization of many formerly state-owned companies. He introduced some economic austerity measures to attract foreign investors and World Bank loans, and encouraged such measures as the opening of the Budapest Stock Exchange, the first such organization in the new Eastern Europe.

During the electoral campaign, after an anti-Semitic broadcast by one of his leading supporters, Antall denied that he or his party were anti-Semitic. He pointed to his own record and the record of his father, József Antall, Sr., who was refugee commissioner during World War II. Antall Sr. was credited with saving from the Nazis many Jews, as well as Poles and other persecuted nationalities. The younger Antall was active in the right-of-center Smallholders Party before the 1947 Communist takeover, was mostly out of politics until 1956, and was arrested after joining the failed Hungarian revolution against Soviet domination. He stayed in Hungary after the revolution and was barred from travel abroad until 1973. His earned his doctorate at Budapest's Eokvos University.

FURTHER READING

"Antall, József, Jr." *Current Biography*, Sept. 1990.
"Good, but not yet. . . ." *Economist*, May 26, 1990.
"A historic decision. . . ." MARY NEMETH. *Maclean's*, Apr. 23, 1990.
"Easy does it." *Economist*, Apr. 14, 1990.

Appiah, Joe (Joseph Emmanuel Appiah, 1918–90) Born in Kumasi, Ghana, Appiah was a leader of the Ghanian independence movement. He was Kwame Nkrumah's London representative before independence came in 1957. In 1953, while studying law in London, he married Peggy Cripps, the daughter of Sir Stafford Cripps, in a pioneering, long-lasting interracial marriage that was a sensation in its time. Returning home as a barrister, Appiah went into political opposition to Nkrumah. He campaigned against the Preventive Detention Act of 1958, and he was imprisoned by Nkrumah from 1961 to 1962. He left politics on his release and returned to politics after Nkrumah was deposed in 1966. In the late 1960s, he formed his own short-lived Justice Party, and in the mid-1970s was a roving ambassador for his country. His books include *Joe Appiah: The Life of an African Patriot* (1990). (d. Accra; July 8, 1990)

FURTHER READING

"Former diplomat. . . ." *Jet*, July 30, 1990.
Obituary. *The Times* (of London), July 14, 1990.
Obituary. *New York Times*, July 12, 1990.

Aquino, Corazon (Maria Corazon Cojuangco, 1933–) The president of the Philippines led her country through a continuing series of major problems during 1989 and 1990. The most serious by far was the nearly successful sixth attempt to overthrow her government by force, in the armed forces revolt of the first week in December 1989. Before the fighting was over, rebel troops and government forces had fought hard for control of Manila, and also in several other locations around the country. During the rebellion, Aquino declared a state of emergency and called for and received critically important American air and weapons support. Ten months later, from October 4–6, 1990, her forces put down the seventh attempt to topple the democratic government by force, defeating an army revolt led by Colonel Alexander Noble on the island of Mindanao.

Aquino also faced a continuing left-wing armed rebellion, in spite of her efforts to bring the long Philippines civil war to an end by negotiation. Small-scale guerrilla warfare continued in the countryside, while a series of terrorist bombings and attacks on Americans drew great attention as she began the long process of negotiating the phaseout and eventual closing of American bases in her country. She also faced continuing economic problems, as the weak economy of her country became even weaker, and as American aid came in much smaller amounts than she felt had been promised.

But Corazon Aquino is quite used to solving major problems. In 1980, she went into exile with her husband, opposition leader Benigno Aquino. He was assassinated by agents of then-dictator Ferdinand Marcos on their return to the Philippines in 1983. She took her husband's place as head of the Liberal Party and three years later, in 1986, swept Marcos from power and into exile in the elections and following series of events that became the Philippine Revolution. She then introduced a new democratic constitution and government, and had survived five earlier right-wing coup attempts and the continuing left-wing insurrection. Corazon Cojuangco and Benigno Aquino were married in 1954 and had five children. She attended New York's College of Mount St. Vincent.

FURTHER READING

"Cory Aquino After Four Years." DENIS MURPHY. *America*, Apr. 21, 1990.
Corazon Aquino: Leader of the Philippines. JAMES HASKINS. Enslow, 1988.

Corazon Aquino. LUCY KOMISAR. Braziller, 1987.
Picture Life of Corazon Aquino. MARGARET M. SCARIANO. Watts, 1987.
Corazon Aquino: The Miracle of a President. CECILIA K. GULLAS. Cultural House, 1987.
"Three against. . . ." MARK WHITAKER, et al. *Newsweek*, Dec. 16, 1985.

Arafat, Yasir (1929–) During 1989, Arafat seemed on the verge of a major breakthrough in the long Palestinian-Israeli conflict. His newly declared Palestinian government-in-exile continued to pick up international support, and he saw substantial support developing for Palestine Liberation Organization (PLO)–Israeli peace talks in the United States and in Israel itself, as the Palestinian Intifada (uprising) continued to focus world attention on his cause. And he toured the world, meeting with such notables as the Pope and French president Mitterand. But the Israelis resisted talks with the PLO, while elements in his own organization criticized what seemed to them Arafat's too-soft approach. As massive Soviet Jewish emigration to Israel began, the Intifada brought more Palestinian casualties and no more gains.

On May 30, 1990, Libyan-based guerrillas of the Abu Abbas-led Palestine Liberation Front (PLF) mounted a failed raid on Tel Aviv by sea. Arafat refused to condemn the raid, and in June, the United States broke off talks with the PLO. After the August Iraqi invasion of Kuwait, the PLO supported Iraq against the main body of the other Arab states; Arafat, having taken sides with Saddam Hussein, lost much of the prestige and bargaining position he so carefully built in the late 1980s. As the Persian Gulf War began, he seemed to be attempting some fence-straddling, by somewhat distancing himself from the Iraqis, while at the same time not criticizing them.

Jerusalem-born Arafat was a founder of the militant Palestinian organization Al Fatah in 1956 and of its guerrilla army in 1959. He has headed the PLO and been the top leader of the Palestinian national movement since 1969. He suffered major personal defeats when his forces were expelled from Jordan in 1970 and 1971, and from Lebanon in 1983. In the mid-1980s, he moved toward negotiation and publicly renounced terrorism, and seemed for a time all but overwhelmed by the more extreme terrorist elements within his own movement. In late 1988, he forced Palestine National Council and PLO acceptance of key United Nations (UN) resolutions 242 and 338. On November 15, 1988, he issued a Palestinian declaration of independence. Over 50 countries had recognized the new Palestinian state by the end of the year. His worldwide status as supreme Palestinian leader was greatly helped by United States refusal to grant him a visa to address the United Nations General Assembly, and the consequent moving of the meeting to Geneva: Arafat then addressed the UN at Geneva. Until he took his position beside Saddam Hussein during the Gulf Crisis, he had seemed to be an emerging statesman, capable of becoming a leader in the search for peaceful resolution of the long Arab-Israeli wars. He attended Cairo University, and was an engineer before becoming a full-time political leader.

FURTHER READING

Arafat: In the Eyes of the Beholder. JANET WALLACH and JOHN WALLACH. Carol, 1990.
"Should we trust Yassir Arafat?" DAVID REED. *Reader's Digest*, Sept. 1989.
"Next year in Jerusalem?" JULIO FUENTES. *World Press Review*, Apr. 1989.
"Saying no to Arafat. . . ." SCOTT MACLEOD. *Time*, Jan. 2, 1989.
Arafat: A Political Biography. ALAN HART. Indiana University Press, 1989.

Arden, Eve (Eunice Quedons, 1908–90) California-born Arden made most of her long career in Hollywood, although she was probably best-known as television's *Our Miss Brooks* (1948–57), for which she won a 1953 best actress Emmy. She began her career on stage in southern California in the mid-1920s, moved into films in the early 1930s, and scored her first hit on film in *Stage Door* (1937). She then appeared in scores of films, sometimes becoming typecast in brittle comedic roles, though she won an Oscar nomination for her role in *Mildred Pierce* (1945). Her later television work also included the short-lived "Eve Arden Show", and a co-starring role in "The Mothers-in-Law" (1967–69). (d. Beverly Hills, California; November 12, 1990)

FURTHER READING

"Tart-tongued Eve Arden. . . ." *People*, Nov. 26, 1990.
Obituary. *Variety*, Nov. 19, 1990.
Obituary. *The Times* (of London), Nov. 14, 1990.
Obituary. ALBIN KREBS. *New York Times*, Nov. 13, 1990.
Three Phases of Eve. EVE ARDEN. St. Martin's, 1985.

Arévalo Bermejo, Juan José (1904–90) A teacher and politician, Arévalo studied in Argentina, worked briefly in the Guatemalan education ministry in the mid-1930s, and went into exile in Argentina, there becoming a leader of the democratic opposition to Guatemalan dictator Jorge Ubico. After the 1944 revolution, he was from 1945 to 1951 the reformist president of Guatemala. When his successor, Jacobo Arbenz Guzmán, was overthrown in the right-wing coup of 1954 sponsored by the Central Intelligence Agency (CIA), Arévalo fled into Mexican exile. He returned again in 1963 to campaign for the presidency, but the Guatemalan military canceled the election, forcing him once more into exile. After two more decades of civil war and dictatorship, he came home again after the return of civilian rule in 1985. (d. Guatemala City; October 6, 1990)

FURTHER READING

Obituary. *The Times* (of London), Oct. 11, 1990.
Obituary. TIM GOLDEN. *New York Times*, Oct. 9, 1990.

Arias, Roberto Emilio (1918–89) The Panamanian politician, diplomat, and publisher was a key figure in Panamanian life from the early 1940s through the late 1960s. The child of a political family, he was the son of Hermodio Arias, a former president of Panama (1932–36). During the 1940s, he was an editor and publisher. He turned to diplomacy in the 1950s, as Panamanian United Nations delegate in 1953, and as ambassador to Britain (1955–58 and 1960–62). In 1955, he married ballerina Margot Fonteyn. Four years later, in a widely publicized incident, she was arrested and expelled from Panama after he had been accused of leading an attempted revolution. He took refuge in the Brazilian embassy, where he spent two months before being allowed to leave the country. In 1964, he was elected to the National Assembly, but was shot by a political rival, nearly killed, and was crippled for the rest of his life, though able to continue on in the assembly until 1968. (d. Panama City; November 22, 1989)

FURTHER READING

Obituary. *The Times* (of London), Nov. 25, 1989.
Obituary. *New York Times*, Nov. 23, 1989.

Arias Sánchez, Oscar (1941–) Arias Sánchez was the moderate democratic socialist president of Costa Rica from 1986 to 1990, then stepping down after one term as required by Costa Rican law. He was succeeded by conservative coalition candidate Rafael Angel Calderon Fournier in May 1990. While in office, Arias made a major contribution to the settlement of the Nicaraguan civil war and other conflicts in the area, and won a Nobel Peace Prize for his 1987 "Arias Plan." Out of office, he continues to lead Costa Rica's largest party, the National Liberation Party, and he is a major figure in Latin American political life.

Arias Sánchez became an economic adviser to the Costa Rican president in 1970, and was national planning minister from 1972 to 1977. He became a leading figure in the National Liberation Party in the mid-1970s and entered the national legislature in 1978. He attended the University of Costa Rica and Britain's University of Essex; his doctorate was in economics. He is married and has two children.

FURTHER READING

The Costa Rica Reader. MARK EDELMAN and JOANNE KENAN. Grove-Weidenfeld, 1989.
"Oscar Arias Sanchez." HANS JANITSCHEK. *Omni*, July 1988.
"Golden opportunity for Don Oscar. . . ." JILL SMOLOWE. *Time*, Oct. 26, 1987.
"Arias: is Costa Rica big enough?" NANCY COOPER. *Newsweek*, Oct. 26, 1987.
"Arias Sanchez, Oscar." *Current Biography*, Aug. 1987.

Aspin, Les (Leslie Aspin, Jr., 1938–) As the Cold War ended, House Armed Services Committee Chairman Les Aspin strongly influenced the direction and pace of planned Bush administration defense budget cuts. He developed and changed his position as American-Soviet relations continued to improve. In March 1990, he led House Democrats to agree that large defense cuts were needed, but should be spread over several years. By late April, he was leading an attack on the proposed cuts, which in his view were too small and did not sufficiently reflect the great changes then under way. By late July, he was leading an attack on the Stealth bomber program, and calling for larger and earlier defense cuts.

As the Persian Gulf Crisis developed, Aspin at first seemed to support the administration's actions, with their large additional special costs, without changing his view on the need for carrying through such programs as already-planned military base closings at home and abroad. But during the run-up to the Gulf War, he favored allowing more time for trying to make sanctions work, and for further attempts to seek a diplomatic solution.

Milwaukee-born Aspin was chairman of President John F. Kennedy's Council of Economic Advisers in 1963. In that year, he moved into his long career as a leading Wisconsin Democratic congressman, with powerful influence on military appropriations through his House committee memberships. His B.A. was from Yale University, his M.A. from Oxford University, and his Ph.D. from the Massachusetts Institute of Technology.

FURTHER READING

"The old breed strikes back." CHRISTOPHER J. MATTHEWS. *New Republic*, Mar. 2, 1987.
"The real Les Aspin story." DAVID BROOKS and PETER OSTERLUND. *National Review*, Dec. 19, 1986.
"A nation without a defense policy." RICHARD D. BARTEL. *Challenge*, July–Aug. 1986.
"Aspin, Les(lie, Jr.)" *Current Biography*, Feb. 1986.

Assad, Hafez al- (1928–) The year 1990 marked two decades of absolute power for Syrian President Assad. The year also saw a major Syrian victory in the long Lebanese civil war, as Syrian forces attacked and defeated the Christian army of general Michel Aoun, possibly bringing the 15-year-old civil war to an end on terms favored by Assad. But Assad also faced the major new threat posed by Iraq, fresh from victory in the long Iran-Iraq war, in which Syria had supported Iran against its long-term Iraqi enemy and neighbor. With Soviet military and economic aid lessening after the end of the Cold War, Assad moved to repair his relations with the moderate Arab states and the West. He met with Egyptian President Mubarak in July, the first such meeting in 13 years, and declared his willingness to join in Arab-Israeli peace talks.

At the outset of the Persian Gulf Crisis, Assad joined the anti-Iraqi alliance, pledging troops for Saudi Arabia within a week of the Iraqi invasion of Kuwait, and sending the first Syrian units a week later. In the months that followed, Assad met repeatedly with Western and moderate Arab leaders, including

George Bush, although Assad had long been linked with terrorists, and had sheltered and supplied several terrorist leaders. As the Gulf Crisis turned into the Gulf War, Assad continued to be a rather uneasy member of the allied coalition.

Assad began his political and military career as a Baath Party activist and air force officer. He became an air force general after the 1963 Baathist coup, and air force commander in chief and minister of defense in 1966. He took power in 1970 and was named president of Syria in 1971. He was closely allied with, and his armed forces were supplied by, the Soviet Union during the Cold War. His forces were badly defeated by Israel in the fourth Arab-Israeli (Yom Kippur) war in 1973. Since 1976, his forces have partially occupied Lebanon, although they were defeated again by the Israelis in Lebanon in 1982. He supported Iran against Iraq, a long-term enemy, during the Iran-Iraq war of the 1980s. Assad is married, and has five children. He attended Syria's armed forces colleges.

FURTHER READING

"Trouble in Damascus." ALAN COWELL. *New York Times Magazine*, Apr. 1, 1990.

"Following the independent course. . . ." *Time*, Apr. 3, 1989.

Hafez al-Assad. MATTHEW GORDON. Chelsea House, 1989.

Asad of Syria: The Struggle for the Middle East. PATRICK SEALE. University of California Press, 1989.

Atwood, Margaret (1939–) Canadian writer Atwood received much attention on the release of the controversial 1990 movie made from her *The Handmaid's Tale* (1986). The anti-utopian tale tells of a poisoned, partly destroyed world whose remaining fertile women are turned into baby machines for the new order, run by right-wing fundamentalists (though Atwood says she was inspired by visits to Cold-War Berlin and Eastern Europe). Her most recent work was *Cat's Eye* (1989), a painful-but-funny novel about a Canadian woman artist's professional and private retrospective, released in paperback in 1990.

Ottawa-born Atwood is a versatile poet, novelist, short story writer, essayist, and editor, whose other works include *The Edible Woman* (1969), and *Murder in the Dark* (1983). She is married to Graeme Gibson; they have one child. She attended the University of Toronto and Harvard University.

FURTHER READING

"Witch craft. . . ." CAMILLE PERI. *Mother Jones*, Apr. 1989.

"Reflected in. . . ." KIM HUBBARD. *People*, Mar. 6, 1989.

Margaret Atwood. JEROME H. ROSENBERG. G.K. Hall, 1984.

Annotated Bibliography of Canada's Major Authors, Vol. I . . . . ROBERT LECKER and JACK DAVID, eds. G.K. Hall, 1980.

Ayckbourn, Alan (1939–) The British playwright and director's 35th play, *Man of the Moment* (1990), starring Michael Gambon, delighted audiences in London's West End, and was named Britain's Comedy of the Year. Meanwhile, *The Revengers' Comedies*, paired plays developed at Scarborough in 1989, were being readied for arrival on the London stage in 1991. Broadway has been wary of Ayckbourn plays since the commercial failure of his *Bedroom Farce* in 1979, but at year's end, New York's Manhattan Theatre Club was planning a production of his *Absent Friends* (1974), and his plays are frequently done in American regional theaters.

Son of a violinist father and romance novelist mother (pen name, Mary James), Ayckbourn is a prolific playwright, who has written 39 plays, most of them light comedies set in middle-class

British life, beginning with *Relatively Speaking* (1965), and including such works as *Family Circles* (1970), *The Norman Conquests* (1973; actually three plays about the same events), *Intimate Exchanges* (1982; eight plays), and a children's play, *Invisible Friends* (1989). He married Christine Helen Roland in 1959; they had two children before separating. He has based himself in northern England's Scarborough since 1971, as artistic director of the small Stephen Joseph Theatre, which he uses to develop and show his plays.

FURTHER READING

"Bard of the British bourgeoisie." MEL GUSSOW. *New York Times Magazine*, Jan. 28, 1990.
Alan Ayckbourn, 2nd ed. MICHAEL BILLINGTON. St. Martin's, 1990.
"The swan of Scarborough." *Economist*, Aug. 19, 1989.
File on Ayckbourn. MALCOLM PAGE and SIMON TRUSSLER, eds. Heinemann, 1989.
Conversations with Ayckbourn. IAN WATSON. Faber and Faber, 1989; Humanities, 1981.
Alan Ayckbourn. SIDNEY H. WHITE. G.K. Hall, 1984.

Aykroyd, Dan (Daniel Edward Aykroyd, 1952–) Aykroyd received some unusual acclaim from his fellow artists this year, when they gave him an Oscar nomination for best supporting actor as the son in *Driving Miss Daisy*. Though he ultimately lost to Denzel Washington in *Glory*, the nomination alone honored Aykroyd's performance in a role quite different from his past work. All this was very far from the *Ghostbusters* films that helped boost Aykroyd into the second biggest box-office star of the 1980s, right behind Harrison Ford, according to *Orbit Video* magazine's survey. A different survey, this one by research firm Baseline, Inc., pronounced Aykroyd the second biggest money-maker of all the "Saturday Night Live" alumni, behind Eddie Murray.

In his more usual vein, Aykroyd appeared opposite Gene Hackman in a new police comedy, *Loose Cannons*, which turns on a West German chancellor with a Nazi past trying to murder anyone with access to a film showing him during Hitler's last minutes. Though the script was panned as just another standard story, Aykroyd and Hackman received some good reviews. Meanwhile, the versatile Aykroyd was acting, writing, and making his directing debut in a new adventure comedy, *Git*, starring his old "Saturday Night Live" colleagues, Chevy Chase and John Candy, as Wall Streeters adrift in an Atlantic seashore village. He was also planning to direct another film, tentatively titled *Valkenvania*.

Canadian-born Aykroyd became a star in television comedy as one of the original members of the "Saturday Night Live" troupe, from 1975 to 1979; he also wrote for the show. He and John Belushi created The Blues Brothers for the show, then starred in the film, *The Blues Brothers* (1980), which Aykroyd wrote. He went on to star in many other films, including *Neighbors* (1981), *Trading Places* (1983), *Ghostbusters* (1984), *Spies Like Us* (1985), *Dragnet* (1987), *The Great Outdoors* (1988), *My Stepmother Is an Alien* (1988), and *Ghostbusters II* (1989). He attended Ottawa's Carleton College. He has been married twice, and has three children.

FURTHER READING

"A haunted humorist. . . ." BRIAN JOHNSON. *Maclean's*, June 26, 1989.
The Second City. DONNA MCCROHAN. Putnam, 1987.

Aylwin Azócar, Patricio (1919–) Aylwin led the democratic coalition that replaced military dictator Augusto Pinochet Ugarte. He was elected to the Chilean presidency in December 1989, was inaugurated on March 11, 1990, and then began the long process of restoring Chilean democracy. One of his earliest acts, on March 12th, was to release many of Chile's political prisoners. In April, he set up a national commission to study and report on the human rights violations of the Pinochet government, alleged to have tortured tens of thousands and murdered thousands of Chileans in its sixteen years of power. In May, Aylwin publicly criticized Pinochet, who had stayed on as armed forces commander, for obstructing the work of the commission. In June, the new government began the long, long process of uncovering the mass graves of the victims of the dictatorship. At the same time, Aylwin began to address Chile's serious

economic problems, including a foreign debt of over $20 billion.

Aylwin, a lawyer and Christian Democrat, became a senator in 1965 and leader of his party in 1973. He opposed the socialist Allende government in the early 1970s. In the early years, he did not openly oppose the Pinochet dictatorship, but he did join other lawyers in defending some people imprisoned by the government, and later more openly opposed military rule. He married Leonor Oyarzun in 1948; they have five children.

FURTHER READING

"In the free market wake. . . ." DAVID BROCK. *Insight,* Nov. 5, 1990.

"Chile turning democracy to prosperity." ARTURO CRUZ, JR. *Insight,* Nov. 5, 1990.

"Aylwin Azocar, Patricio." *Current Biography,* Aug. 1990.

"Toward coexistence in Chile." Jose Comas. *World Press Review.* May 1990.

Aziz, Tariq (Michael Yuhanna, 1936–) The Iraqi foreign minister became a well-known face on world television screens in August 1990, as he defended the Iraqi invasion of Kuwait. It was not an unfamiliar role. Aziz had similarly defended the Iraqi invasion of Iran in 1980, claiming Iranian provocation, and had then become Iraq's chief spokesperson and negotiator in Iraq's years-long attempt to find some way out of what, until very near the end, was a losing war. In the months following the Kuwait invasion, Aziz repeatedly and unsuccessfully tried to blunt the edge of world condemnation of the Iraqi takeover, meeting rejection in Moscow, at the United Nations, and at meetings with all but a few other Arab leaders.

Aziz is one of the few Christians in the largely Muslim Iraqi leadership. He attended Baghdad University and was a journalist before the Baath Party coup of 1968. Long an associate of Saddam Hussein, he became a key media specialist for Hussein after the 1970 coup that brought Hussein to power. He was Minister of Information from 1974 to 1977, and has been a member of Hussein's small inner group, the Revolutionary Command Council, since 1977. He became a deputy prime minister in 1979.

FURTHER READING

"Tariq 'Aziz'. . ." PETER HEBBLETHWAITE. *National Catholic Reporter,* Dec. 14, 1990.

Bailey, Pearl (Pearl Mae Bailey, 1918–90) The American singer and actress Bailey was noted for her very distinctive style. Born in Newport News, Virginia, in 1918, of mixed Black and Creek Indian ancestry, she grew up in Philadelphia, singing and dancing in amateur contests and clubs from age 15. She debuted in New York clubs in 1941, toured with various bands, won a recording contract for the song "Tired," and came to Broadway in 1946. From then on she was a major star in nightclubs and variety theaters, in films such as *Carmen Jones* and *Porgy and Bess*, and on television, her biggest success being the title role in Broadway's 1967 all-Black *Hello, Dolly!* From 1975, she traveled the world for the United States and United Nations. After receiving a 1978 honorary degree from Georgetown University, she enrolled there and in 1985 received a B.A. in theology. In 1989, she published her autobiography *Between You and Me*. (d. Philadelphia; August 17, 1990)

FURTHER READING

Obituary. JOHN MCDONOUGH. *Down Beat*, Nov. 1990.
Obituary. *Current Biography*, Oct. 1990.
"'Pearl was love'. . . ." *Jet*, Sept. 10, 1990.
"The final curtain. . . . " *People*, Sept. 3, 1990.
"Pearl Bailey, 'Ambassador of Love'. . . ." *Jet*, Sept. 3, 1990.
"Farewell, Dolly. . . ." *Maclean's*, Aug. 27, 1990.
Obituary. *Variety*, Aug. 22, 1990.
Obituary. *The Times* (of London), Aug. 20, 1990.
Obituary. JOHN S. WILSON. *New York Times*, Aug. 19, 1990.

Baker, James (James Addison Baker, III, 1930–) The U.S. secretary of state, long associated with George Bush, played a key role in developing and executing United States policy during the first years of the Bush administration. He was particularly active in developing the new set of American-Soviet relations that fully ended the Cold War, meeting formally and informally with Soviet Foreign Minister Shevardnadze to end regional conflicts and to further arms control negotiations. A major attempt was the series of unsuccessful efforts to bring the long Palestinian-Israeli confrontation to an end. After the August 2, 1990, Iraqi invasion and conquest of Kuwait, he was deeply involved in the nonstop series of consultations, United

Nations resolutions, and aborted negotiations that preceded the outbreak of the Persian Gulf War.

Houston-born Baker, a lawyer, has long been a personal friend and political ally of George Bush; their alliance goes back to the early 1970s, a period in which both men moved from Texas Republican politics onto the national scene. Baker was an undersecretary of commerce from 1975 to 1976, was active in the Ford campaign of 1976, and from 1979 to 1980 managed the Bush presidential nomination campaign, from which Bush emerged as Ronald Reagan's vice-president. Baker went into the Reagan administration, too, in the central role of White House chief of staff. Then in 1985, he switched jobs with Treasury Secretary Donald Regan, and was treasury secretary from 1985 to 1988. He went on to manage the successful 1988 Bush presidential campaign, and then became secretary of state in the new Bush administration. He married Susan Garrett in 1973; they have eight children. His B.A. was from Princeton University, in 1952, and his LL.B. was from the University of Texas, in 1957.

FURTHER READING

"The tactician." JOHN NEWHOUSE. *New Yorker*, May 7, 1990.

"The tide turns our way." *American Legion Magazine*, Feb. 1990.

"James Baker. . . ." ROWLAND EVANS and ROBERT NOVAK. *Reader's Digest*, Nov. 1989.

"Playing for the edge. MICHAEL KRAMER. *Time*, Feb. 13, 1989.

"Baker, James A., III." *Current Biography*, Feb. 1982.

Barco Vargas, Virgilio (1921–) Barco Vargas was Colombian president from 1986 to 1990. He faced major problems throughout his presidency, including the continuing and developing left revolutionary movement, the increasingly powerful Medellin and other drug cartels, the growth of right-wing death squads, and the constant threat of a right-wing army takeover. During 1989, he and his government lived in what was essentially a state of siege, as they attacked the drug cartels, which responded with a wave of terror bombings and assassinations. In the autumn of 1989, he joined U.S. president George Bush and the presidents of Peru and Bolivia in an international anti-drug campaign. In February 1990, he joined in the four-president anti-drug meeting at Cartagena, Colombia. In March 1990, Barco Vargas made a historic peace agreement with the M-19 left guerrilla movement, which then laid down its arms. He was succeeded in the presidency by César Gaviria Trujillo, of his own Liberal Party.

Barco Vargas began his long career in Colombian public life in 1943. He has held a wide range of posts, including local and national elective positions, appointment to cabinet-level positions, and ambassadorships to the United States and Great Britain. He became leader of the Liberal Party and was elected to the presidency in 1985, taking office in 1986. He attended the Colombian National University, Massachusetts Institute of Technology, and Boston University. He is married to American-born Caroline Isakson; they have four children.

FURTHER READING

"Barco Vargas, Virgilio." *Current Biography*, Feb. 1990.

Bardot, Brigitte (Camille Javal, 1934–) The often-reclusive French actress came back into the public eye in 1989–90 through her long-time interests in animal rights. Although she said she was "tired of fighting windmills," in April she hosted a four-part French television series about animal abuse, including graphic film footage on animal trafficking, vivisection, and slaughter. She also spoke and traveled against such activities as a proposed kill of 30,000 seals off South Africa by Taiwanese, which she labeled a "barbaric massacre," and a French farm union's slaughter of hundreds of animals in the yard of a government office to protest importing of lower-priced livestock.

Bardot became an international film star as the "sex kitten" of the 1950s, after her appearance in *And God Created Woman* (1956), directed by her first husband, Roger Vadim. She went on to play in many other films until the early 1970s, and remained a great celebrity, but her career did not develop much beyond its first impact. She has used her celebrity to support several causes, most notably animal rights. She has been married three times, and has one child.

FURTHER READING

Bardot: A Personal Biography. GLENYS ROBERTS. St. Martin's, 1985.
"Swept away by her sadness." PETER CARLSON. *People*, Oct. 24, 1983.

Baron, Salo W. (1895–1989) A teacher, rabbi, and historian, Baron is best-known for his major work, *The Social and Religious History of the Jews*, that appeared in three volumes in 1937. At the time of his death, he was working on a new edition of the work, that had so far been partially published in eighteen volumes. His wife, Jeannette Meisel Baron, was his close collaborator from their marriage in 1934 to her death in 1985, co-authoring two books and working with him on all of his books. Born in Tarnow, Poland, Baron studied and taught in Vienna before moving to New York in the 1920s. From 1930 to 1963, he taught at Columbia University. He testified on the impact of the Holocaust at the 1961 trial of Adolf Eichmann. (d. New York City; November 25, 1990)

FURTHER READING

Obituary. *The Times* (of London), Nov. 27, 1989.
Obituary. *New York Times*, Nov. 26, 1989.

Barr, Roseanne (1952–) Barr was riding high in 1989 and 1990, with her television series, "Roseanne", at or near number one in the ratings. She returned to live standup comedy, with a new act—and a new husband, comedian and long-time collaborator Tom Arnold. She also appeared on HBO comedy specials and moved into television production, though her first feature film, *She-Devil*, was criticized by many viewers as too strident, lacking the underlying warmth of her television persona. In 1989, she also published *Roseanne: My Life as a Woman* and *Stand Up!*.

Fame can be double-edged, however. In August 1990, at a San Diego Padres baseball game, Barr sang "The Star-Spangled Banner" in a screeching, off-key style, topping off her rendition by scratching her crotch and spitting on the ground. Public reaction was strongly negative, and "Roseanne"'s ratings suffered for

a time, as many people saw her performance as insulting to the nation, the flag, baseball, or all of the above. Barr and Arnold appeared on talk shows, sometimes singing the national anthem and explaining that Barr had panicked when the audience started to boo her, and that her actions mimicked those of the baseball players.

Privately, Barr and Arnold were involved in several lawsuits, including a palimony suit by Barr's ex-husband and ex-collaborator, William Pentland; a suit to keep Pentland from discussing the divorce publicly; one against two tabloids for publishing stolen love letters written by Barr; and a charge that Arnold assaulted two photographers trying to snap the couple at an airport. The couple even seriously explored the possibility of moving production of "Roseanne" from "tabloid-infested" Los Angeles to Minneapolis.

Salt Lake City-born Barr began her career as a stand-up comedian in variety in the late 1970s. A decade later she was the star of the very popular television series "Roseanne" (1988–). Her personal style propelled her into major celebrity. She has been married twice, and has three children.

FURTHER READING

"Roseanne sings. . . ." JOBETH MCDANIEL. *Ladies Home Journal*, Jan. 1991.
"The wretched. . . ." BARBARA EHRENREICH. *New Republic*, Apr. 2, 1990.
"Roseanne unchained." JIM JEROME. *People*, Oct. 9, 1989.
"The real Roseanne." KATHRYN CASEY. *Ladies Home Journal*, Sept. 1989.

"Slightly to the left of normal." ELAINE DUTKA. *Time*, May 8, 1989.
"Barr, Roseanne." *Current Biography*, May 1989.
"Roseanne. . . ." FRED ROBBINS. *Ladies Home Journal*, Feb. 1989.
"Talking with Roseanne Barr. . . ." MONICA COLLINS. *Redbook*, Feb. 1989.
"TV's battle of the sexes. . . ." JACK HICKS. *TV Guide*, Jan. 28, 1989.

Barry, Marion Shepilov, Jr. (1936–) In January 1990, Washington, D.C., Mayor Barry attracted immense national attention when he was arrested on a drug-use charge in a Washington motel. This was the climax of a long series of drug-use and corruption charges, denials, and countercharges of discrimination made by Barry. In February and again in May, he was indicted by a Washington grand jury on a total of thirteen perjury and drug-related charges, going back to 1987. In June, he announced that he would not run for a fourth mayoral term, and later ran a poor third in the race for an at-large city council seat. In October, he received a six-month jail sentence.

Mississippi-born Barry was active in the civil rights movement of the 1960s, and moved into Washington, D.C., politics in the early 1970s as a school board member, and then in 1976 as a city council member. He began his long, highly controversial tenure as mayor of Washington in 1979. From the early years of his administration, he denied persistent charges of city government corruption and personal drug use. He married Effi Barry in 1978; they have one child. His B.S. was from Lemoyne College, in 1958; his M.S. was from Fisk University, in 1960.

FURTHER READING

"A clean sweep in the capital." WILLIAM LOWTHER. *Maclean's*, Nov. 19, 1990.
"Who can beat Barry?" BARBARA MATUSOW and JOHN SANSING. *Washingtonian*, June 1990.
"Barry and his city. . . ." JEFFERSON MORLEY. *Nation*, Feb. 19, 1990.
The Mayor Who Stayed Too Long: The Story of Marion S. Barry. JONATHAN I. AGRONSKY. British American, 1990.
"A bright, broken promise." MICHAEL RILEY. *Time*, June 26, 1989.
"Washington's mayor. . . ." MONTGOMERY BROWER. *People*, Jan. 16, 1989.

Baryshnikov, Mikhail (1948–) After Baryshnikov's abrupt departure from the American Ballet Theatre (ABT) late in 1989, speculation focused not only on how the ABT would fare without him (apparently well) but also on what direction "Misha", himself, would take. The answer surprised many observers, as the 42-year-old Baryshnikov teamed up with the ultramodern choreographer Mark Morris to form the White Oak Dance Project, a nine-member dance company that in the fall of 1990 set out on a 17-city tour, starting with a sold-out Boston concert. In the aftermath of his angry departure from the ABT, reportedly in a disagreement over his version of *Swan Lake*, Baryshnikov withdrew the rights to perform versions of his works in the ABT repertory. In 1989, Baryshnikov had also appeared on Broadway, giving a notable performance as Gregor Samsa in a stage version of Franz Kafka's *Metamorphosis*. In the business world, the line of women's exercise clothing sold under Baryshnikov's name became a leader in the "active-wear" field.

Russian-born Baryshnikov was well on his way to becoming a world figure in ballet when he defected to the West in 1974, after five years (1969–74) as a leading dancer with the Kirov Ballet. The promise came to pass: In the years that followed, he danced as a leading guest artist with most of the world's great ballet companies and was artistic director of the American Ballet Theatre (1980–89). His work included the creation of leads in such new ballets as *Vestris* (1965), *Hamlet* (1970), *Santa Fe Saga* (1978), and *Rhapsody* (1980); the choreography of new versions of *The Nutcracker* (1976), *Don Quixote* (1978), and *Cinderella* (1984); and appearances in several films, including *White Nights* (1985), and *The Dancers* (1987).

FURTHER READING

"Baryshnikov: his years at ABT." DEBORAH JOWITT. *Dance Magazine*, Jan. 1990.
Mikhail Baryshnikov. BRUCE GLASSMAN. Silver Burdett, 1990.
"Baryshnikov's transformation. . . ." JACK KROLL. *Newsweek*, Mar. 20, 1989.
"The next stage." PATRICIA CORBETT. *Connoisseur*, Jan. 1989.
Misha!: The Mikhail Baryshnikov Story. BARBARA ARIA. St. Martin's, 1989.
Private View: Behind the Scenes with American Ballet Theatre. JOHN FRASER. Bantam, 1988.
The Swan Prince. MIKHAIL BARYSHNIKOV and PETER ANASTOS. Bantam, 1987.
Baryshnikov in Russia. NINA ALOVERT. Holt, 1984.
Baryshnikov: From Russia to the West. GENNADY SMAKOV. Farrar, Straus and Giroux, 1981.
Baryshnikov. MIKHAIL BARYSHNIKOV. Abrams, 1980.

Basinger, Kim (1953–) Basinger became one of the leading Hollywood sex symbols of the 1980s as Domino in Sean Connery's last James Bond film (*Never Say Never Again*; 1983), and opposite Mickey Rourke in *9½ Weeks* (1986). She starred with Michael Keaton and Jack Nicholson in *Batman* (1989), and in the spring of 1990, she filmed Neil Simon's *The Marrying Kind*. She was also one of the hosts of the televised Academy Award ceremonies, and used the occasion to criticize the members for slighting Spike Lee's *Do the Right Thing*, which was the center of much controversy, but won no awards. Georgia-born Basinger, who went to school in Athens, Georgia, also opened another major phase of her career in 1990, purchasing (with the financial aid of a Chicago company) 1,728 acres near Athens, consisting of most of Braselton, Georgia. Her aim is to build a major film studio and recording center there.

Basinger worked as a New York model in the mid-1970s, then moved into television, most notably in *Katie—Portrait of a Centerfold* (1978), and in the 1979 remake of *From Here to Eternity*. She became a film star in the 1980s, in *Hard Country* (1980), and *Never Say Never Again*, then went on to such films as *The Man Who Loved Women* (1983), *The Natural* (1984), and *Fool for Love* (1985). Basinger attended New York's Neighborhood Playhouse. She was formerly married.

FURTHER READING

"Basinger, Kim." *Current Biography*, Feb. 1990.

Bates, Alan (1934–) One of the leading British actors of the past three decades, Bates continues to appear in a wide range of roles. He made a notable 1990 appearance as Claudius in Franco Zeffirelli's film version of *Hamlet*, in a cast that included Mel Gibson in the title role, Glenn Close, Paul Scofield, Ian

Holm and Helen Bonham-Carter. He also appeared as the police officer in *Mr. Frost* (1989), opposite Jeff Goldblum and Kathy Baker.

Bates became a star in Harold Pinter's *The Caretaker* (1960; and the 1964 film version). He went on to such plays as *Butley* (1972; he won a Tony), *Otherwise Engaged* (1975), *A Patriot for Me* (1983), and *Ivanov* (1989). He has appeared in such films as *A Kind of Loving* (1962), *King of Hearts* (1966), *Far from the Madding Crowd* (1967), *A Day in the Death of Joe Egg* (1972), *In Celebration* (1974), *An Unmarried Woman* (1977), *Nijinsky* (1979), *The Return of the Soldier* (1982), and *A Prayer for the Dying* (1987). He also appeared in such telefilms as *An Englishman Abroad* (1983) and *Pack of Lies* (1987). Bates attended the Royal Academy of Dramatic Arts. He married Victoria Ward in 1970; they have two children.

FURTHER READING

"Alan Bates returns. . . ." CAROL LAWSON. *New York Times*, Dec. 30, 1983.

Baulieu, Etienne-Emile (1926–) French biochemist Baulieu is one of the world's leading and most honored endocrinologists. He is also the inventor of RU 486, the very effective abortion pill, and he leads the worldwide campaign for distribution of the pill, while anti-abortion forces continue their attempts to bar distribution. Baulieu was an adviser to Roussel-Uclaf, the pharmaceutical company that ultimately manufactured the pill and marketed it in France. When Roussel, under pressure from anti-abortion forces, withdrew the drug from French distribution, Baulieu led the successful campaign that forced the French government to order production and distribution of the pill in France, although distribution elsewhere has been blocked. In the United States, anti-abortion groups have blocked federal approval of RU 486 testing; but in March 1990, California State Attorney General John Van de Kamp called for state testing, and in April, doctors at three California hospitals sought state permission to start human testing of the drug. Through 1990, French experience with the drug continued to seem positive as to safety and effectiveness. Pro-abortion and anti-abortion groups continued their battle over the use of the drug in 1991, while Baulieu expressed regret that the long argument would harm research into several other promising medical uses of the drug.

Baulieu received his medical degree from the University of Paris in 1955, and he taught medicine at Rheims, Rouen, the University of Paris, and Columbia University during the 1950s and early 1960s. In 1963, he became director of a hormonal research unit of the French National Institute of Health and Medical Research (Inserm), and founded the International Society for Research in the Biology of Reproduction in 1967. He led the research group that developed the abortion pill in the late 1970s, and ultimately saw the pill go into distribution in France. Baulieu married Yolande Compagnon in 1947; they have three children.

FURTHER READING

"Are you for RU 486?. . . ." Tony KAYE. *New Republic*, Jan. 27, 1986.
"Testing a better. . . ." *Newsweek*, May 3, 1982.

Beatty, Warren (Warren Beaty, 1937–) Early in 1990, the normally rather reclusive Beatty seemed to be ever-present, as he worked to gain publicity for his latest film as director, producer, and star in the title role. For his *Dick Tracy*, based on Chester Gould's comic-strip detective, Beatty had assembled a stellar cast for major roles and cameos, including Madonna (Beatty's recent companion) as Breathless Mahoney, Al Pacino as a grimly comic Big Boy Caprice, Dustin Hoffman as Mumbles, and Glenne Headly as Tess Trueheart, with James Caan, Charles Durning, Mandy Patinkin, Paul Sorvino, Dick Van Dyke, Estelle Parsons, and Michael J. Pollard appearing as other Gould grotesques. Hoping to duplicate the commercial success of 1989's *Batman*, the publicity generated a whole range of "Dick Tracy" products, everything from watches to T-shirts, with most featuring the yellow-overcoated, fedora-hatted Tracy, symbol of the film. But though *Tracy* set box-office records at its opening, it did not achieve the overall success of *Batman*. Reviews were somewhat mixed, but generally strongly favorable, praising the sure conception, direction, sense of style and fun, and method of melding living figures in a cartoon landscape. However, the film—and, audience research showed, Beatty himself—did not have as strong an appeal to young moviegoers. Also, unlike *Batman*, *Dick Tracy* was not so immediately recognizable to many moviegoers, since the comic strip is no longer so widely syndicated.

Virginia-born Beatty, the brother of actress Shirley MacLaine, acted in television and theater from the late 1950s, moving into films in the early 1960s. He starred in *Splendor in the Grass* (1961), but his breakthrough role was that of Clyde Barrow in *Bonnie and Clyde* (1961). He produced that film, and went on to produce and star in such films as *McCabe and Mrs. Miller* (1971), and *Heaven Can Wait* (1978), which he also wrote. His most substantial work, so far, has been the epic film *Reds* (1981); he produced, directed, co-wrote, starred as John Reed, and won a Best Director Oscar for the film. In the next ten years, he appeared in two films: the disastrous *Ishtar* (1987), and *Dick Tracy*. He attended the Stella Adler theater school.

FURTHER READING

The Films of Warren Beatty. Lawrence J. Quirk. Carol, 1990.
"Beds. . . ." Stephanie Mansfield. *Esquire*, May 1990.
Actors: A Celebration. Rita Gam. St. Martin's, 1988.
Warren Beatty and Desert Eyes: A Life and a Story. David Thomson. Doubleday, 1987.
"Meditations on the Angel of Sex." David Thomson. *California*, May, 1986.
Warren Beatty: His Life, His Loves, His Work. Suzanne Munshower. St. Martin's, 1983.

Beckett, Samuel Barclay (1906–89) Best-known as one of the central playwrights of the 20th century, Beckett was also a novelist, poet, essayist, screenwriter, and radio writer. The Dublin-born Irish writer lived in France in the late 1920s, there becoming close to James Joyce, returned to teach briefly in Ireland in the early 1930s, and settled in France in 1937. Afterwards, he worked mostly in French. His play *Waiting for Godot*, the first major work of what came to be known as the revolutionary Theatre of the Absurd, premiered in Paris in 1953; he translated it into English for its 1955 London premiere. It was followed by such plays as *Endgame* (1958), *Krapp's Last Tape* (1960), and *Happy Days* (1961), as well as by a wide range of other works. He was awarded the 1969 Nobel Prize for literature. (d. Paris; December 22, 1989)

FURTHER READING

"Beckett's last act." Laurence Bergreen. *Esquire*, May 1990.
Obituary. *Current Biography*, Feb. 1990.
"Sam's last. . . ." Michael J. Farrell. *National Catholic Reporter*, Jan. 19, 1990.
Obituary. H. Kenner. *National Review*, Jan. 22, 1990.
"Terrible beauty. . . ." John Bemrose. *Maclean's*, Jan. 8, 1990
"A great writer. . . ." *People*, Jan. 8, 1990.
"Giving birth. . . ." William A. Henry III. *Time*, Jan. 8, 1990.
"Merry messenger of doom." *U.S. News & World Report*, Jan. 8, 1990.
"Stories against the silence. . . ." David Gates. *Newsweek*, Jan. 8, 1990.
Samuel Beckett. Deirdre Bair. Simon & Schuster, 1990; Harcourt Brace, 1980.
Obituary. Mel Gussow. *New York Times*, Dec. 27, 1989.
Samuel Beckett. Arthur K. Kennedy. Cambridge University Press, 1989.

Belfrage, Cedric (1904–90) Belfrage, a British journalist, was deported from the United States as an alleged Communist during the McCarthy era. London-born Belfrage first visited America at age 21, and worked for several papers before becoming editor of the left-political *National Guardian* in 1948, a job he believed triggered the House Un-American Activities Committee's 1953 questioning of him. After a lengthy legal battle, including a month-long internment at Ellis Island, he was finally deported in 1955. From the 1960s he lived in Mexico. He wrote of his experiences in *The American Inquisition, 1945–1960: A Profile of the "McCarthy Era"* (1973). (d. Cuernavaca; June 21, 1990)

FURTHER READING

Obituary. *New York Times*, June 22, 1990.
Obituary. *The Times* (of London). June 5, 1990.

Bellamy, Madge (Margaret Philpott, 1900–90) On stage as a child, Bellamy became a silent film star of the 1920s, most notably in *Lorna Doone* (1922), and in John Ford's *The Iron Horse* (1924). She continued to star until the close of the silent film era, but in mediocre vehicles, and made the transition to sound, but not very successfully. Her film career ended in the mid-1930s, though she continued on in stage roles. She had just published her autobiographical *A Darling of the Twenties* (1990). (d. Upland, California; January 24, 1990)

FURTHER READING

Obituary. *The Times* (of London), Jan. 30, 1990.

Bennett, Joan (1910–90) The child of a theatrical family, Bennett was the daughter of actor Richard Bennett, and the sister of Constance and Barbara Bennett. On screen from 1916, she became a star in such films as *Bulldog Drummond* (1929), and *Little Women* (1933). She changed her image and hair color in 1939, married producer Walter Wanger in 1940, and then emerged as a leading dramatic star of the 1940s, in such films as *Man Hunt* (1941), *The Woman in the Window* (1944), *Scarlet Street* (1946), *The Macomber Affair* (1947), and *Woman on the Beach* (1947). Waning by 1951, her career was given a push downward by a scandal involving Wanger and her agent, whom Wanger shot, accusing him of having an affair with Bennett. She later made a comeback in television, as the star of the soap opera "Dark Shadows" (1967–71). Her autobiography is *The Bennett Playbill* (1970, coauthored with Lois Kibbee). (d. Scarsdale, New York; December 6, 1990)

FURTHER READING

Obituary. *The Times* (of London), Dec. 10, 1990.
Obituary. *New York Times*, Dec. 9, 1990.

Bennett, William John (1943–) Bennett became director of the U.S. Office of National Drug Control Policy in 1989, at the height of the drug crisis that was widely seen to be tearing apart the fabric of American life. In that post, he led the Bush administration campaign against drugs, stressing law enforcement and the stoppage of drug trafficking, rather than anti-drug education and treatment. Bennett had no enforcement powers or organization of his own, although he was a highly visible symbol of stated Bush administration concerns and drug control approaches. After his late 1990 resignation as "drug czar," he was named head of the Republican Party, but then withdrew, citing economic reasons, although it was suggested that some members of the White House staff had successfully objected to his outspoken, often-abrasive politically conservative style.

Brooklyn-born Bennett went to Washington in the early 1980s after spending some years in education and nonprofit organizational work, most notably as executive director and then president of the Raleigh-based National Humanities Center from 1976 to 1981. He was chairman of the National Endowment for the Humanities from 1981 to 1985, and from 1985 to 1988 was a highly controversial U.S. secretary of education in the second Reagan administration. He then practiced law in Washington, until his appointment as "drug czar" of the Bush administration. Bennett received a B.A. from Williams College in 1965, a Ph.D. in philosophy from the University of Texas in 1970, and a J.D. from Harvard Law School in 1971. He married Elayne Glover in 1982; they have two children.

FURTHER READING

"Bill Bennett can't lose. . . ." JACOB WEISBERG. *Esquire*, Sept. 1990.
"William Bennett." JANE SIMS PODESTA. *People*, June 11, 1990.
"Bill Bennett's blinders." JACOB SULLUM. *Reason*, Mar. 1990.
"Cowboy in the capital. . . ." HOWARD KOHN. *Rolling Stone*, Nov. 2, 1989.
"General Bennett." FRED BARNES. *New Republic*, Sept. 18, 1989.
"Bennett. . . ." *Newsweek*, Sept. 11, 1989.
"The drug warrior. . . ." TOM MORGANTHAU and MARK MILLER. *Newsweek*, Apr. 10, 1989.
"Bennett the drug czar. . . ." FRED BARNES. *American Spectator*, Apr. 1989.

Bergen, Candice (1946–) As television's attractive-but-tough newswoman Murphy Brown, Bergen had both commercial success and critical acclaim in 1990, with Emmys for

the show as best comedy series and for herself as best actress in a comedy series, her second in a row. She also acted as co-host (with Jay Leno and Jane Pauley) of the Fox network's Emmy Award show, appeared on the *Comic Relief* marathon at Radio City Music Hall to aid the homeless, and hosted the season finale of "Saturday Night Live", her fifth appearance on the show starting with the opening 1975–76 season. Her mother, Frances Bergen, acted in a "Murphy Brown" episode, as the groom's mother in a wedding sequence. Though real-life television newswomen say they must work much harder than Murphy Brown, they generally respect her portrait, and the Hollywood Women's Press Club even gave Bergen their Golden Apple Award as female star of the year.

Daughter of famed ventriloquist Edgar Bergen, the creator of Charlie McCarthy, California-born Bergen is a major actress in her own right, with a long series of major roles in such films as *Carnal Knowledge* (1971), *Starting Over* (1979), *Rich and Famous* (1981), and *Gandhi* (1982). In 1988, she began a whole new aspect of her career, playing the lead (reportedly modeled on Diane Sawyer, among others) in television's *Murphy Brown*. She has also written and photographed articles for several major magazines, and wrote the autobiographical *Knock Wood* (1984). Bergen is married to film director Louis Malle, and has one daughter. She attended the University of Pennsylvania.

FURTHER READING

"Where does Murphy Brown. . . ." Karen Stabiner. *Working Woman*, Dec. 1990.
"Candid Candice." Linda Ellerbee and Michael J. Bandler. *Ladies Home Journal*, June 1990.
"Candice Bergen." Tom Green. *Los Angeles Magazine,* May 1990.
"Playboy interview. . . ." David Sheff. *Playboy,* Dec. 1989.
"What TV's real. . . ." Joanna Elm and Dick Cavett. *TV Guide,* Dec. 23, 1989.
"Candice Bergen. . . ." Michael Segell. *Cosmopolitan,* Nov. 1989.
"Talking with Candice Bergen. . . ." Vicki Jo Radovsky. *Redbook,* Apr. 1989.
"Shedding a glacial identity. . . ." Harry F. Waters. *Newsweek*, Mar. 13, 1989.
"Candice Bergen. . . ." Catherine Reid. *Good Housekeeping,* Mar. 1989.
"Hard Candy." Bill Zehme. *Rolling Stone,* Jan. 26, 1989.

Berghof, Herbert (1909–90) Austrian-born Berghof studied in Vienna and played in the Austrian theater until the Nazi takeover. He fled to Britain and then the United States, and worked as an actor during World War II. He and Uta Hagen, later his wife, founded a New York acting school in 1945, while also developing such original productions as *The Andersonville Trial* (1960), and *In the Matter of J. Robert Oppenheimer* (1967). Many of his students went on to become leading stage and screen players. (d. New York City; November 5, 1990)

FURTHER READING

Obituary. *The Times* (of London), Nov. 27, 1990.
Obituary. *Variety*, Nov. 12, 1990.

Bergman, Ingmar (1918–) The Swedish director, writer, and producer is a central figure in world film history and at the same time is a major figure in the Swedish theater. From the mid-1950s, he created a series of film masterworks that have been tremendously important to all who followed. Now, very late in his career, in 1990 he was writing the next installment of his autobiography, the forthcoming *Pictures*, a sequel to *The Magic Lantern* (1987). In

March 1990, he received the D.W. Griffith award from The Directors Guild of America, for lifetime contribution to film. His son, Daniel Bergman, is also a film director, while his sister, Margareta Bergman, is a novelist, whose *Karin* was translated into English in 1990.

Bergman's work includes such film classics as *Smiles of a Summer Night* (1955), *Wild Strawberries* (1957), *The Magician* (1958), *The Virgin Spring* (1960), *Through a Glass Darkly* (1961), *Scenes From a Marriage* (1974), *Fanny and Alexander* (1982), *After the Rehearsal* (1984), and *Good Intentions* (1989). Bergman attended Stockholm University. He has been married six times, and has eight children.

FURTHER READING

The Poet at the Piano: Portraits of Writers, Filmmakers, and Performers at Work. MICHIKO KAKUTANI. Random, 1988.
Ingmar Bergman: A Guide to References and Resources. BIRGITTA STEEN. G.K. Hall, 1987.
"Ingmar Bergman. . . ." MICHIKO KAKUTANI. *New York Times Magazine*, June 26, 1983.
"God, sex and. . . ." RICHARD CORLISS and WILLIAM WOLF. *Film Comment*, May–June 1983.
Talking with Ingmar Bergman. G. WILLIAM JONES, ed. SMU Press, 1983.
Ingmar Bergman. LISE-LONE MARKER and FREDERICK J. MARKER. Cambridge University Press, 1982.
Ingmar Bergman: A Critical Biography. PETER COWIE. Macmillan, 1982.
"Ingmar Bergman." *Current Biography*, Oct. 1981.
Ingmar Bergman: An Appreciation. ROGER MANVELL. Ayer, 1980.

Bernstein, Leonard (1918–90) A wide-ranging, often spectacular, and very popular composer, conductor, and pianist, Bernstein was a major figure in both classical and popular music. He conducted symphony orchestras from 1943 and was musical director of the New York Philharmonic from 1958 to 1969. He composed such popular works as the ballet *Fancy Free* (1944), the musicals *On the Town* (1944), *Wonderful Town* (1953), and *West Side Story* (1957); and such classical works as the *Jeremiah Symphony* (1943), *The Age of Anxiety* (1949), the *Kaddish Symphony* (1963), and the opera *A Quiet Place* (1983). Among his writings about his life and works are *Findings* (1982), and *Bernstein on Broadway* (1981; with Jack Gottlieb and Paul Wittke, eds.). (d. New York City; October 14, 1990)

FURTHER READING

"Leonard Bernstein." JONATHAN COTT. *Rolling Stone*, Nov. 29, 1990.
Obituary. *Current Biography*, Nov. 1990.
"America's maestro bows out." MICHELLE GREEN. *People*, Oct. 29, 1990.
"An affair to remember. . . ." KATRINE AMES. *Newsweek*, Oct. 29, 1990.
"A rhapsodic life." PAMELA YOUNG. *Maclean's*, Oct. 29, 1990
"The best and the brightest. . . ." MICHAEL WALSH. *Time*, Oct. 29, 1990.
Obituary. MIRIAM HORN. *U.S. News & World Report*, Oct. 29, 1990.
Obituary. *New York Times*, Oct. 16, 1990.
Obituary. *The Times* (of London), Oct. 16, 1990.
Bernstein: A Biography. JOAN PEYSER. Ballantine, 1988; Morrow, 1987.
Leonard Bernstein. PETER GRADENWITZ. St. Martin's, 1987.

Bertolucci, Bernardo (1940–) For his latest film, Bertolucci chose a setting far from the crowded, pageant-like work of his *The Last Emperor*. In what he termed a "private project," *The Sheltering Sky* followed a couple on a nightmare caravan through the Sahara Desert. The film, adapted from Paul Bowles's 1949 novel by Mark Peploe, focuses on Port and Kit Moresby, played by John Malkovich and Debra Winger, as expatriate Manhattanites trying to revive their lives and marriage in exotic Africa. Campbell Scott, son of George C. Scott and Colleen Dewhurst, made his feature debut in a key supporting role. In a striking device, Bertolucci used Bowles, himself, now 80 years old, as an observer and sometime narrator. The critics had mixed reactions to *The Sheltering Sky*, with some finding it boring, others brilliant, but with many guessing that it will become a film classic.

Regarding his 1976 classic *1900*, Bertolucci had good news: The film, cut by over an hour for its original U.S. release, has been restored to its full length of 5 hours and 11 minutes, under the watchful eye of the original cinematographer, Vittorio Storaro (who also shot *The Sheltering Sky*). The version restored is the English-language version, however, not the original Italian one with English subtitles. With a new soundtrack in Dolby stereo, the restored *1900* went into limited theatrical release in early 1991.

During 1990, Bertolucci headed the jury at the prestigious Cannes Film Festival. He has also joined with many other European filmmakers to give prestige to the European Cinema Society and its new Felix Awards, hoping to make them equivalent to Hollywood's Oscars. Late in 1990, he won his fight in a London court, against a Hong Kong company's attempted injunction, to proceed with what may be his next project, a film based on the life of the religious leader Gautama Buddha.

Parma-born Bertolucci has long been one of the leading directors of the Italian cinema. He was an assistant director on Pier Paolo Pasolini's *Accatone* (1961), and then set off on his own, with *The Grim Reaper* (1962). In 1964, there came the acclaimed *Before the Revolution* and 1970 brought *The Spider's Strategem* and the classic *The Conformist*. Marlon Brando starred in Bertolucci's *Last Tango in Paris* (1972); the film, sexually explicit for a mainstream film of its time, created a worldwide controversy over its alleged pornography. His films also include *Luna* (1979), *Tragedy of a Ridiculous Man* (1982), and *The Last Emperor* (1987), for which he won a Best Director Oscar, one of nine Oscars won by the film. Bertolucci is married to filmmaker Clare Peploe, sister of Mark Peploe.

FURTHER READING

"Last tango in Tangier." BOB SPITZ. *New York Times Magazine*, May 20, 1990.
"Hollywood continues. . . ." LAWRENCE COHN. *Variety*, Oct. 25, 1989.
Bernardo Bertolucci. ROBERT P. KOLKER. Oxford University Press, 1985.

Bettelheim, Bruno (1903–90) Vienna-born child psychologist Bettelheim felt that his experiences in the Nazi camps at Dachau and Buchenwald helped him develop ways of treating severely disturbed children, many previously thought unreachable. Trained in Vienna, he began working with autistic children in 1932, but was interned by the Nazis in 1938, being released by special petition (from Eleanor Roosevelt and others) in late 1939. He then joined the University of Chicago faculty and, in 1944, became director of the Orthogenic School there, remaining until his 1973 retirement. Among his widely influential books were *Love Is Not Enough: The Treatment of Emotionally Disturbed Children* (1950), and *The Uses of Enchantment* (1976). (d. Silver Spring, Maryland; March 13, 1990)

FURTHER READING

"Bruno Bettelheim." AMY S. BERNSTEIN. *U.S. News & World Report*, Sept. 10, 1990.
Obituary. *Current Biography*, May 1990.
"Bruno Bettelheim. . . ." WILLIAM PLUMMER. *People*, Apr. 2, 1990.
"Dead by his own decision. . . ." OTTO FRIEDRICH. *Time*, Mar. 26, 1990.
"An explorer. . . ." BARBARA KANTROWITZ. *Newsweek*, Mar. 26, 1990.
"The special finesse. . . ." *U.S. News & World Report*, Mar. 26, 1990.
Obituary. *The Times* (of London), Mar. 16, 1990.
Obituary. *New York Times*, Mar. 14, 1990.

Bhutto, Benazir (1943–) After the death of military dictator Zia Ul-Haq in an August 1988 plane crash, Bhutto was elected prime minister of Pakistan in the free election of December 2, 1988. She was the second Bhutto to become prime minister. Her father, Zulfikar Ali Bhutto, had been Pakistani prime minister from 1972 to 1977; he was executed in 1979 by Zia's military government.

In office, Benazir Bhutto was hailed as one of the world's leading women; but at home, she faced increasing opposition from the Pakistani army and fundamentalist religious leaders. On August 6, 1990, she was removed from office by President Ishak Khan, acting with the support of the military; she was charged with corruption. Arrests of her supporters followed, as did further charges directed at her. She was also forbidden to leave the country. She and her party were defeated in the October 24th elections, which she called fraud-ridden. In late 1990, concern grew that she might ultimately suffer her father's fate.

Bhutto and her mother, Nusrat Bhutto, were under house arrest in Pakistan from 1977 to 1984, after the coup that deposed her father. She left Pakistan in 1984, returned for the funeral of her brother in 1985, and was rearrested and expelled from her country. She returned again in 1986 as head of the Pakistan People's Party and led the opposition to the government. She published *Daughter of Destiny: An Autobiography* in 1989. She married Asif Ali Zardari in 1987; they have two children. She attended Harvard University and Lady Margaret Hall, Oxford University.

FURTHER READING

Benazir Bhutto. KATHERINE M. DOHERTY and CRAIG A. DOHERTY. Watts, 1990.
From Prison to Prime Minister: A Biography of Benazir Bhutto. LIBBY HUGHES. Dillon, 1990.
Women and Politics in Islam: the Trial of Benazir Bhutto. RAFIG ZAKARIA. New Horizons, 1990.
"Pakistan under Benazir Bhutto." WILLIAM L. RICHTER. *Current History*, Dec. 1989.
"Dynasty's daughter." TARIQ ALI. *Interview*, Feb. 1989.

Biden, Joseph Robinette, Jr. (1942–)

Biden was a leading candidate for the 1988 Democratic presidential nomination, but withdrew after allegations that he had plagiarized some of the material in his campaign speeches from the speeches of British Labour leader Neil Kinnock. The incident still dims his presidential possibilities, although he is often spoken of as a possible Democratic candidate in 1992 or 1996. He is still the highly visible chairman of the Senate Judiciary Committee, who, in the winter and spring of 1990, repeatedly criticized the Bush administration's "war on drugs," and in September, played a central role in hearings on the nomination of David Souter to the Supreme Court. In November 1990, Delaware voters returned Biden to his fourth term in the Senate.

After briefly practicing law in Delaware, Biden became a Democratic senator from that state in 1972, moving into a key position as head of the Senate Judiciary Committee. In 1986, he played a major role in the rejection of President Reagan's nomination of Robert Bork to the Supreme Court. In early 1990, Biden survived two brain operations, both for aneurysms, then resumed his Senate career. Pennsylvania-born Biden was previously married to Neilia Hunter, and married Jill Tracy Jacobs in 1977; he has four children. He received his A.B. from the University of Delaware and his J.D. from Syracuse University.

FURTHER READING

"Biden is also reborn." MARGARET CARLSON. *Time*, Sept. 12, 1988.
"The fall of a contender." MARCI McDONALD. *Maclean's*, Oct. 5, 1987.
"Joe Biden. . . ." GARY SMITH. *Life*, Oct. 1987.
"Biden's familiar quotations. . . ." WALTER SHAPAIRO. *Time*, Sept. 28, 1987.

"Sen. Joseph Biden." CYNTHIA POLS. *Nation's Cities Weekly*, June 15, 1987.
"Orator for. . . ." LAURENCE I. BARRETT. *Time*, June 22, 1987.
"Ronald Biden. . . ." FRED BARNES. *New Republic*, June 1, 1987.
"Biden, Joseph (Robinette), Jr." *Current Biography*, Jan. 1987.
"The Democrats' point man." JERRY ADLER. *Newsweek*, May 5, 1986.
"Hot, handsome Joe. . . ." GARRY CLIFFORD. *People Weekly*, Aug. 25, 1986.

Bird, Larry Joe (1956–) As the 1980s ended, and a new decade began, Boston Celtics basketball star Bird ran into a series of injuries that hampered his play and sidelined him for long periods of time. Yet when he is healthy, he is still the key figure on his team, and he is a leading player in the National Basketball Association. That became clear all over again, as the Celtics, with the addition of several good young players, became a very strong team early in the 1990–91 season. When Bird was sidelined with an injury in January 1991, his team immediately became far less formidable, but resumed winning as he recovered.

Indiana-born Bird has been, with Magic Johnson, one of the two leading players in the game since the late 1970s, when he was the high-scoring star forward of the Indiana University team. After joining the Boston Celtics in 1979, he was National Basketball Association Rookie of the Year in 1980, and the league's Most Valuable Player in 1984, 1985, and 1986, as well as an All-Star Game starter for nine straight years, from 1980 to 1988. His autobiography, *Drive: The Story of My Life*, was published in 1989. He married Dinah Mattingly in 1989.

FURTHER READING

"A player for the ages. . . ." FRANK DEFORD. *Sports Illustrated*, Mar. 21, 1988.
"Man of the Year. . . ." PAUL ATTNER. *Sporting News*, Jan. 5, 1987.
Magic Johnson Larry Bird. BRUCE WEBER. Avon, 1986.
"Bird. . ." MIKE WEBER. *Sporting News*, May 6, 1985.
"Masters of their own game." TOM CALLAHAN. *Time*, Mar 18, 1985.
Larry Bird. MATTHEW NEWMAN. Crestwood, 1985.
Sports Star: Larry Bird. S.H. BURCHARD. Harcourt Brace, 1983.
"Bird, Larry." *Current Biography*, June 1982.
Basketball's Magnificent Bird: The Larry Bird Story. FREDERICK L. CORN. Random, 1982.
Sports Hero: Larry Bird. MARSHALL BURCHARD. Putnam, 1982.
Larry Bird: Cool Man on the Court. BERT ROSENTHAL. Childrens, 1981.

Birendra Bir Bikram Shah Deva (1945–) In 1990, the king's autocratic rule over Nepal came to an end. On February 18, mass demonstrations for multiparty democracy began in Nepal; they were met by force, and scores were killed by security forces in the two months that followed, as the king attempted to maintain the ban on political parties imposed by his father in 1960. In April, protests grew, as did the government's armed response; hundreds of demonstrators were killed or injured in Katmandu on April 6th, as an estimated 200–250,000 demonstrators attempted to storm the royal palace. The king gave way completely on April 16th. He legalized all political parties and agreed to the formation of an interim government composed of opposition leaders. The new government adopted a democratic constitution and scheduled multiparty elections for April 1991.

Birendra became king of Nepal in 1972, succeeding his father Mahendra Bir Bikram Shah Deva. Like his father, his main concern internationally was to pursue a balanced, very careful nonaligned course between Nepal's huge, often-opposed neighbors, India and China, although what India perceived as a lean toward China in the late 1980s caused strain between Nepal and India. This strain contributed to economic problems that stirred unrest. Internally, Birendra successfully resisted efforts to make Nepal more democratic for 18 years, as did his father after a brief experiment with democracy during 1959 and 1960. He married Aishwarya Rajya Laxmi Devi Rana in 1970; they have three children. He attended St. Joseph's College, Eton College, the University of Tokyo, and Harvard University.

FURTHER READING

"Royal seal of approval." *Time*, Nov. 19, 1990.
"The king's hand." *Economist*, Oct. 6, 1990.
"The top of. . . ." ROBERT CRAFT. *New York Review of Books*, May 17, 1990.
"King Birendra and his trouble and strife." *Economist*, May 5, 1990.
"Dawn of Himalayan democracy." RICHARD MACKENZIE. *Insight*, Apr. 30, 1990.
"A god-king descends." *Economist*, Apr. 14, 1990.

Bisset, Jacqueline (Jacqueline Fraser Bisset, 1944–) Bisset's recent work included the Paul Bartels film farce *Scenes From the Class Struggle in Beverly Hills* (1989), in which she played an aging situation comedy star, in a cast that included Robert Beltran, Ray Sharkey, Mary Woronow, Edith Diaz, and Arnetia Walker. The British actress also starred opposite Mickey Rourke in *Wild Orchid* (1989), a not-very-well-received film that drew a good deal of attention because of a dispute over its allegedly high sexual content.

Born in Weybridge, Bisset was a London model in her late teens, breaking into films in *The Knack* (1965), catching attention in *Casino Royale* (1967), and then appearing in such films as *The Detective* (1968), *Bullitt* (1968), *The Grasshopper* (1970), *Day for Night* (1973), *End of the Game* (1974), *The Deep* (1976), *Rich and Famous* (1981), *Under the Volcano* (1983), and *High Season* (1988).

FURTHER READING

"Jacqueline Bisset." IVOR DAVIS. *Los Angeles Magazine*, Nov. 1987.
"Bewitched, bothered. . . ." MICHELLE GREEN. *Harper's Bazaar*, Apr. 1987.
"Just your ordinary couple." DAVID WALLACE. *People*, Apr. 1, 1985.
"Jackie and Alexander." *Life*, Apr. 1985.

Blackmun, Harry Andrew (1908–) U.S. Supreme Court Justice Blackmun generally continued to vote with the liberal minority during the 1989–90 term. In the landmark *Cruzan* v. *Missouri* "right to die" case, he voted with the minority that Nancy Cruzan's family should have the right to remove her from her life support system. He also voted with the minority in a group of abortion-related cases, in which the Court majority affirmed the right of states to pass laws requiring notification of parents or a court hearing before abortions are performed. He wrote the unanimous opinion in *University of Pennsylvania* v. *EEOC*, that universities have no right to withhold certain kinds of information in a discrimination complaint case. He also wrote the majority opinion in *Sullivan* v. *Zebley*, striking down federal restrictions on aid to disabled children. He helped strike down the federal flag burning law, upheld the legality of a broadcasting industry affirmative action program, helped upset a Chicago conviction based on illegally obtained evidence, and cut the ability of politicians in power to name party sympathizers to most low-level government jobs. But he saw the more conservative view win in a series of cases involving law enforcement and defendant's rights.

Nashville-born Blackmun practiced and taught law in Minneapolis during the 1930s and 1940s, and was then counsel to the Mayo Clinic from 1950 to 1959. He was named to the 8th Circuit of the U.S. Court of Appeals in 1959, and was appointed by President Richard Nixon to the Supreme Court in 1970. His course in the liberal Warren Court of the time was generally considered moderately conservative; but in later years, Blackmun's unwavering commitment to a set of so-called "liberal" positions on civil and personal rights placed him with the liberal minority in a more conservative Court. He married Dorothy Clark in 1941; they have three children. His B.A. and LL.B. were from Harvard University, in 1929 and 1932.

FURTHER READING

"What they say it is. . . ." *Time*, July 6, 1987.
"A candid talk. . . ." JOHN A. JENKINS. *New York Times Magazine,* Feb. 20, 1983.

Blaize, Herbert A. (1918–89) Blaize was the elected prime minister of Grenada after the 1983 United States invasion ousted the previous Marxist government. Born on the nearby island of Carriacou, Blaize worked in the civil service and as an English teacher, and qualified as a lawyer, before entering politics with the Grenada National Party (GNP). He was appointed Grenada's first chief minister by the British in 1960, served again from 1962 to 1967, and remained GNP head through the island's independence in 1974 until ousted in early 1989, though continuing as prime minister. (d. St. George's, Grenada; December 19, 1989)

FURTHER READING

Obituary. *The Times* (of London), Dec. 20, 1989.
Obituary. *New York Times,* Dec. 20, 1989.
"Hot spice." *Economist,* Oct. 21, 1989.

Blakey, Art (1919–90) American drummer Blakey was a key figure in 20th-century jazz. First on the piano, then on the drums, music was Blakey's way out of Pittsburgh and its steel mills. He toured in the early 1940s with figures like Mary Lou Williams, Fletcher Henderson, Billy Eckstine, and Thelonius Monk. In the 1950s, notably with Horace Silver, Blakey developed "hard bebop," a distinctive, driving, gospel-and-blues-influenced jazz style, as in his well-known "Moanin'." Out of this work came the Jazz Messengers, an ever-changing group that for over 35 years was a school for budding talent, as it helped bring jazz to worldwide audiences. In the 1940s Blakey had converted to Islam, taking the name of Abdullah Ibn Buhaina, and worked in Africa with traditional drummers. (d. New York City; October 1, 1990)

FURTHER READING

Obituary. *The Times* (of London), Oct. 18, 1990.
Obituary. *New York Times*, Oct. 17, 1990.

Boesak, Allen (1946–) The South African clergyman and anti-apartheid campaigner, who had become a world figure as the fight for South African democracy progressed during the 1980s, was beset by personal difficulties in the summer of 1990. In July, Boesak was reported to have had an affair with journalist Elna Botha during the time when he was president of the Geneva-based World Council of Reformed Churches in 1982. In August, he resigned his position, with a public apology, and was succeeded by Princeton Theological Seminary Professor Jane Dempsey Douglass.

Boesak was a co-founder of the South African United Democratic Front in 1983, and was president of the South African Council of Churches from 1984 to 1987. Among his written works are *If This Is Treason, I Am Guilty* (1987) and *Comfort and Protest* (1987). He married Dorothy Rose Martin in 1969, and he has three children.

FURTHER READING

"An adulterous indiscretion. . . ." SUSAN HACK. *People*, Aug. 6, 1990.
"Boesak. . . ." ELAINE BROWN. *Essence Magazine,* Apr. 1988.
"Boesak, Allan (Aubrey)." *Current Biography,* Nov. 1986.

Bolet, Jorge (1914–90) Havana-born Bolet, a leading pianist and teacher of the piano, studied music in Havana and from the age of 12 at Philadelphia's Curtis Institute. He made his debut in Europe in 1935 and in the United States in 1937, but he emerged only in the 1970s as a major soloist, very highly respected for his interpretations of the romantics, and particularly for his work with Liszt. He taught at Indiana University, and in 1977 he became head of the piano department at Curtis, succeeding Rudolf Serkin. (d. San Francisco; October 15, 1990)

FURTHER READING

Obituary. *The Times* (of London), Oct. 18, 1990.
Obituary. *New York Times*, Oct. 17, 1990.

Pianists on Playing: Interviews with Twelve Concert Pianists. LINDA J. NOYLE. Scarecrow, 1987.

Boskin, Michael Jay (1945–) Since his 1989 appointment as George Bush's chairman of the Council of Economic Advisers, Boskin has functioned both as Bush administration economic adviser and as an advocate of Bush administration policies. His February 1990 annual economic report made a series of rather optimistic predictions, among them that the federal deficit would be paid off by the mid-1990s. The rest of the year was spent grappling with skyrocketing deficit figures, a sagging economy, and a continuing and worsening budget crisis, as the real size and shape of the huge deficit problem became ever more apparent.

New York-born Boskin taught economics at California's Stanford University for almost two decades before going to Washington. He had also been director of Stanford's Center for Economic Policy Research, from 1986 to 1989. He married Chris Dornin in 1981. His B.A., M.A., and Ph.D. were from the University of California at Berkeley in 1967, 1968, and 1971.

FURTHER READING

"Mr. Bush's forecaster. . . ." THOMAS G. DONLAN. *Barron's*, Nov. 12, 1990.
"Free markets. . . ." *Challenge*, May–June, 1990.
"Boskin, Michael Jay." *Current Biography*, Sept. 1989.
"The year's 25 most fascinating. . . ." *Fortune*, Jan. 2, 1989.

Bosze, Jean-Pierre (1977–90) The 13-year-old Bosze, a leukemia victim, became the center of widely publicized controversy as his father, Tams Bosze, sought desperately to find possible donors of life-saving bone marrow for him. After Tams and other relatives were found incompatible, and therefore unable to donate bone marrow, Tams sought to legally force the testing of two potential blood marrow donors—Jean-Pierre's half-siblings, the twin children of Tams and Nancy Curran—to find out if they were compatible. Curran had refused to authorize the tests. When Judge Monica Reynolds ruled that a forced test would illegally invade the privacy of the twins, Bosze appealed to a higher court. But Jean-Pierre Bosze died while the appeal was still pending. (d. Chicago; November 19, 1990)

FURTHER READING

Obituary. *U.S. News & World Report*, Dec. 3, 1990.
Obituary. *New York Times*, Nov. 20, 1990.
"The gift of life—or else. . . ." by NANCY GIBBS. *Time*, Sept. 10, 1990.

Botha, Roelof Frederik "Pik" (1932–) The South African foreign secretary failed in his February 1989 bid to succeed President Pieter William Botha as National Party leader. After the August resignation of the prime minister, Pik Botha stayed on as foreign secretary in the new De Klerk government. He was his country's chief international spokesperson throughout the De Klerk government's attempts to end the long stalemate in South Africa, and to restore normal relations with the many countries that had imposed trade sanctions on South Africa because of its racist policies. He was also a key negotiator in the long 1990 African National Congress-government talks that resulted in the August 7th ceasefire.

Botha, a lawyer, has spent his whole career in South African government service. He joined the foreign service in 1953, and he held a long series of diplomatic and legal posts at home and in Europe during the 1950s and 1960s. He was elected to parliament in 1970, serving until 1974. He was South African ambassador to the United Nations from 1974 to 1977, and to the United States, as well, from 1975 to 1977. He went home to become South African foreign minister in 1977, and was his government's chief international spokesperson during its long fight to maintain and deepen the apartheid system. He married Helen Bosman in 1953; they have four children. He attended the University of Pretoria.

FURTHER READING

"Giving as good as he got." *Time*, Nov. 21, 1988.
"How not to fight sanctions." *Fortune*, Oct. 27, 1986.

"Now hear this." *Fortune*, Sept. 1, 1986.
"'We cannot be. . . ." EDWARD L. JAMIESON and PETER HAWTHORNE. *Time*, June 9, 1986.
"Two views. . . ." RAY WILKINSON and PETER YOUNGHUSBAND. *Newsweek*, Mar.11, 1985.

Boudin, Leonard (1912–89) A noted civil liberties lawyer, Boudin defended many controversial clients. Brooklyn-born and New York-educated, Boudin entered the law in 1936. Among his best-known cases were those involving the State Department's withholding of Paul Robeson's passport, the Georgia House's denial of a seat to Julian Bond, and charges against Daniel Ellsberg relating to the theft of the Pentagon Papers. Boudin's daughter, Kathy, an activist in the Weather Underground, was involved in a 1981 armored truck robbery and killing, for which she was later jailed. Leonard Boudin was also a visiting lecturer at the law schools of Harvard University, Stanford University, and the University of California at Berkeley. (d. New York City; November 24, 1989)

FURTHER READING

Obituary. *National Review*, Dec. 22, 1989.
Obituary. *Nation*, Dec. 18, 1989.
Obituary. *New York Times*, Nov. 26, 1989.

Bowie, David (David Robert Jones, 1947–) British singer, songwriter, and actor Bowie toured in 1989 with his group The Tin Machine, and saw release of the first album of his retrospective set, titled *Sound + Vision*. In 1990, he went on a world "Sound + Vision" tour, backed by a four-piece group that included Adam Belew. The tour began in Quebec, on March 4th, and opened its U.S. portion in Miami, on April 27th. On this tour, Bowie introduced no new work, instead announcing that he would sing only his old standards, and that this was the last time he would sing the old songs in concert. Critics and fans alike reacted skeptically to Bowie's announcement, recalling his 1973 retirement announcement, after his Ziggy Stardust tour that year. The second album of the retrospective set was issued in 1990: It was *Changesbowie*, which added seven songs and 27 minutes to the original 1976 *Changesonebowie* album. Bowie will also appear in the forthcoming film *The Linguine Incident*.

Bowie became a leading rock singer and songwriter in 1969, with publication of his first song, "Space Oddity," followed by such albums as *The Man Who Sold the World* (1970), *Hunky Dory* (1971), *The Rise and Fall of Ziggy Stardust and the Spiders from Mars* (1972), *Pin Ups* (1973), *Young Americans* (1975), *Lodger* (1979), and *Let's Dance* (1983). He also starred as the alien in the film *The Man Who Fell to Earth* (1976), and appeared in such films as *Merry Christmas Mr. Lawrence* (1983) and *The Last Temptation of Christ* (1988). He appeared on Broadway in *The Elephant Man* (1980). Among his written works about his own work and experiences are *David Bowie in His Own Words* (1981), *David Bowie: Tonight* (1984), and *David Bowie Anthology* (1985). Bowie was formerly married, and has one child.

FURTHER READING

"Bowie." GLEN O'BRIEN. *Interview*, May 1990.
"Stardust memories. . . ." KURT LODER. *Rolling Stone*, Apr. 23, 1987.
Alias David Bowie. PETER GILLMAN and LENI GILLMAN. Holt, 1987.
Stardust: The David Bowie Story. TONY ZANETTA and HENRY EDWARDS. McGraw-Hill, 1986.
Bowie JERRY HOPKINS. Macmillan, 1986.
Ziggy Stardust: David Bowie, 1972–1974. MICK ROCK. St. Martin's, 1984.
David Bowie's Serious Moonlight: The World Tour. CHET FLIPPO. Doubleday, 1984.
David Bowie. KEVIN CANN. Simon and Schuster, 1984.

Brady, James Scott (1944–) and **Sarah Kemp Brady** (1942–) James Brady was President Ronald Reagan's press secretary. He was seriously wounded during John Hinckley's March 31, 1981 presidential assassination attempt, shot with a cheap $29 handgun, and remains partially paralyzed. After the incident, Sarah Kemp Brady, his wife, became an extraordinarily effective crusader for gun control, her work continuing and expanding throughout the 1980s and into the 1990s. She is chairperson of Handgun Control Inc.

James Brady continued to be presidential press secretary during the Reagan years, and spoke little on the subject of gun control until after the 1988 elections. But starting in 1989, he came forward very strongly, as in his November 1989 congressional committee testimony, in which he attacked the "evil empire" of the National Rifle Association (NRA), supported tightened handgun controls, and called many members of Congress "gutless" on handgun control. During 1990, Brady revisited his White House offices. There President Bush and his own press secretary, Marlin Fitzwater, joined Brady in giving a guided tour to actor Beau Bridges, who portrays Brady in a new television movie, *The James Brady Story,* scheduled for 1991 showing.

Grand Rapids-born James Brady practiced law in Michigan from 1969 to 1977, and was an attorney in western Michigan from 1977 to 1981, then becoming presidential press secretary. He attended the University of Western Michigan and the University of Notre Dame. Sarah Kemp Brady is an experienced political professional. She worked for the Republican Congressional Committee in the late 1960s, was an administrative assistant to two Republican congressmen from 1970 to 1974, then was an administrator with the Republican National Committee from 1974 to 1978. James and Sarah Brady have one son. He also has a daughter from a previous marriage.

FURTHER READING

"Target: the gun lobby." WAYNE KING. *New York Times Magazine*, Dec. 9, 1990.

Thumbs Up: The Jim Brady Story. MOLLIE DICKENSON. Morrow, 1987.

Brady, Nicholas Frederick (1930–)

Treasury Secretary Brady faced massive and increasing financial problems during the 1989 to 1990 period. By late 1990, it had become clear that the savings and loan bailout would cost U.S. taxpayers far more than he and others in the administration had predicted; some estimates went as high as $200 billion. At the same time, the foreign debt crisis that had been faced by U.S. banks during most of the 1980s continued, now joined by the collapse of the junk bond market, the prosecution of Drexel, Burnham, Lambert and other stock market speculators, and during 1990, the near-collapse of the real estate market and the construction industry, all causing great pressure on the whole American banking system.

With the recurrent federal budget crisis, accelerating federal deficits, and a recession looming, Brady spent much of his time attempting to reassure Congress and the American people that all was not quite as bad as it seemed. He negotiated new foreign debt arrangements and picked up the pieces after the multiple collapses that followed the high-flying 1980s. In September, as the Persian Gulf Crisis developed, he also joined President Bush in demanding more money from U.S. allies to help pay for the costs of the action.

Brady went to Washington after a long career in investment banking. He spent 28 years with Dillon, Read, ultimately becoming its chief executive officer and chairman, and leaving to become a U.S. senatorial appointee from his home state of New Jersey in 1982. He was chairman of the Purolator company from 1983 to 1988, leaving the business world again in 1989 to become treasury secretary in the Bush administration. His B.A. was from Yale University, in 1952; his M.B.A. was from Harvard University, in 1954. He married

Katherine Douglas in 1952; they have three children.

FURTHER READING

"Who is Nick Brady?. . . ." LOUIS S. RICHMAN. *Fortune*, May 22, 1989.

Branagh, Kenneth (1960–) British actor-director-producer Branagh has laid claim to the mantle of Laurence Olivier, making his film directing debut and also starring in a new film version of Shakespeare's *Henry V* (1989). His success was considerable. The film was named the British Film Institute's best film, Branagh won the Directors Guild of America's D. W. Griffith Award for best director, and both he and the film gained Oscar nominations, though ultimately losing to others.

Like Orson Welles, Branagh published his autobiography, *Beginning* (1990), very young, at the tender age of 28. It was, he explained, written partly to fund his Renaissance Theatre Company (RTC). The RTC also came to Hollywood, bringing their stage productions of Shakespeare's *Midsummer Night's Dream*, *King Lear,* and Ibsen's *Ghosts*, the latter two also starring Branagh, himself; their *Ghosts* was also presented in a television version. These, however, played to mixed reviews. Late in 1990, Branagh was directing a mainstream film for Paramount, called *Dead Again*, about a woman with amnesia, starring Branagh's wife, Emma Thompson, and Derek Jacobi.

Belfast-born Branagh was one of the most promising theater people to come out of the 1980s. He very quickly became a very notable Shakespearean actor, starring on stage as Hamlet and Henry *V* (at age 23) and directing and producing *Romeo and Juliet*, all in Britain, before doing the film of *Henry V*. On screen, his work also included the highly regarded television series "The Fortunes of War" and the film *A Month in the Country* (both 1987). Also in 1987, he founded the Renaissance Theatre Company and Renaissance Films. Branagh married actress Emma Thompson in 1989. He attended the Royal Academy of Dramatic Arts.

FURTHER READING

"The man who would be king. . . ." KIM HUBBARD. *People*, Feb. 12, 1990.
"Much ado about something." ROBERT TURNBULL. *Harper's Bazaar*, Feb. 1990.
"A rising star enlivens Shakespeare." GARY ARNOLD. *Insight*, Jan. 15, 1990.
"King Ken comes to conquer. . . ." RICHARD CORLISS. *Time*, Nov. 13, 1989.
"Kenneth." GRAHAM FULLER. *Film Comment*, Nov.–Dec. 1989.

Brandley, Clarence Lee (1952–) On October 1, 1990, the U.S. Supreme Court refused to reconsider the Brandley case, assuring that he would go free. On August 23, 1980, 16-year-old Cheryl Dee Fergeson, a student at Conroe High School, near Houston, Texas, was kidnapped, raped, and murdered. Brandley, the only Black janitor working at the school at the time, was later charged and tried for the murder. A first all-White jury was hung; a second all-White jury convicted Brandley, and he was sentenced to death. Then followed ten years of appeals, stays of execution just before Brandley was to be put to death, and exposure of much new evidence that had not been found by the prosecution. On December 13, 1989, the Texas Court of Criminal Appeals overturned Brandley's conviction 6–3, ruling that the original investigators and prosecutors had abused due process of law, were potentially racist, and that the case represented a "subversion of justice."

FURTHER READING

"Blind justice." *Economist*, Dec. 10, 1988.

"Guilty until proven innocent." Tom Curtis. *Texas Monthly*, Sept. 1987.

Brando, Marlon, Jr. (1924–) Though normally rather reclusive, Brando was the focus of attention from several quarters in 1990. On film, he starred in *The Freshman*, doing a comically twisted reprise of his "Godfather" role. He had previously been coaxed out of seclusion to play a South African barrister in Euzhan Palcy's anti-apartheid movie *The Dry White Season* (1989). In fall 1990, Brando also sparked a multimillion-dollar bidding war among prospective publishers for his projected autobiography.

Privately, however, Brando had to support his family through tragedy. In May, his son, Christian, was charged with killing Dag Drollet, the lover of his half-sister Cheyenne, reportedly during an argument at the family home over Drollet's beating of the pregnant Cheyenne. Brando confirmed the physical abuse and placed his $4 million home as bond to keep Christian out of jail. Cheyenne—a key witness in any possible murder trial—fled to Tahiti, presumably to avoid testifying against Christian; a federal judge refused a prosecution request to compel her return. In Tahiti, Cheyenne bore Drollet's child and attempted suicide, for a time being put on a respirator for life support, and later going to Paris for psychiatric care. In the end, Christian agreed to plead guilty to voluntary manslaughter, for which he faced a sentence of up to 16 years.

Omaha-born Brando is one of the leading stage and screen actors of his time. In 1947, he created the role of Stanley Kowalski in Tennessee Williams's *A Streetcar Named Desire*. This major breakthrough role also signaled the breakthrough of "method" acting, the enormously influential American version of the Stanislavski school, as taught at New York's Actors Studio. Brando's first Best Actor Oscar was for his film role in *On the Waterfront* (1951), his second for creation of another landmark role, that of Vito Corleone, in *The Godfather* (1972). He has been married to Anna Kashfi and Movita Brando.

FURTHER READING

"Marlon Brando . . . ." *Life*, Fall 1990.
"Brando's son faces murder one." James S. Kunen. *People*, June 4, 1990.
"Marlon Brando . . . ." Michael Frank. *Architectural Digest*, Apr.1990.
"Brando." Mark Kram. *Esquire*, Nov. 1989.
"Can Brando still tango?" Merrill Shindler. *Los Angeles Magazine*, Mar. 1989.
Brando: The Unauthorized Biography. Charles Higham. NAL-Dutton, 1987.
Brando: A Biography in Photographs. Christopher Nickens. Doubleday, 1987.
Marlon Brando: The Only Contender. Gary Carey. St. Martin's, 1985.
Marlon Brando. David Downing. Scarborough House, 1984.
The Films of Marlon Brando. Bruce Braithwaite. Beaufort, 1982.
Screen Greats: Marlon Brando. Alan Frank. Bookthrift, 1982.

Brennan, William Joseph, Jr. (1906–) On July 20, 1990, after 34 years on the Supreme Court, Justice Brennan resigned. In his last Court term, he continued to lead the liberal wing of the Court. He wrote the majority opinions in *U.S.* v. *Eichman*, striking down the federal law against flag burning; in *Rutan* v. *Republican Party of Illinois*, cutting the power of politicians in power to name party sympathizers to most low-level government jobs; and in *Metro Broadcasting* v. *FCC*, supporting an affirmative action program in the broadcasting industry.

He also wrote a long string of minority opinions, as in the landmark *Cruzan* v. *Missouri* "right to die" case, holding that Nancy Cruzan's family should have the right to remove her from her life support system. He also was in the minority in a group of abortion-related cases, in which the Court majority affirmed the right of states to pass laws requiring notification of parents or a court hearing before abortions are performed, and also in a series of cases involving law enforcement and defendant's rights. He was replaced on the Court by Associate Justice David H. Souter.

New Jersey-born Brennan practiced law in Newark from 1931 to 1949, became a state superior court judge in 1949, an appellate division judge in 1950, and a state supreme court judge in 1952. He was a Dwight D. Eisenhower appointee to the U.S. Supreme Court in 1956, and soon became a leading liberal on the Court, a position he maintained until his 1990 resignation. He wrote several landmark opinions, including *Baker* v. *Carr* (1962), providing for "one man, one vote"; *New York Times* v. *Sullivan* (1964), the key freedom of the press decision; and landmark opinions outlawing loyalty oaths and establishing more equal rights for women, minorities, and the aged. Brennan married Marjorie Leonard, now deceased, in 1928; they had three children. He married Mary Fowler in 1983. His B.A. was from the University of Pennsylvania, and his LL.B. was from Harvard University.

FURTHER READING

"Right turn ahead?" ED MAGNUSON. *Time*, July 30, 1990.
"A master builder." DAVID A. KAPLAN. *Newsweek*, July 30, 1990.
"The constitutionalist." NAT HENTOFF. *New Yorker*, Mar. 12, 1990.
"The most powerful liberal. . . ." LYNN ROSELLINI. *U.S. News & World Report*, Jan. 8, 1990.
Landmark Justice: The Influence of William J. Brennan on America's Communities. CHARLES M. HAAR and JEROLD S. KAYDEN. Preservation Press, 1989.

Bridges, Beau (Lloyd Vernet Bridges, III, 1941–) For Beau Bridges, acting has always been a family occupation, but he had never acted in a film with his younger brother, Jeff. That was remedied in 1989, when the two opened to general applause as the lounge-pianist brothers in *The Fabulous Baker Boys*. Early in 1990, the National Society of Film Critics named Beau Bridges best supporting actor and Michelle Pfeiffer as best actress for their roles in the film.

In mid-1990, Bridges appeared in an HBO production, *Women & Men: Stories of Seduction*, dramatizations of three short stories; in Mary McCarthy's "The Man in the Brooks Brothers Shirt," he appeared as a salesman having a one-night stand with sophisticate Elizabeth McGovern on a cross-country train. Meanwhile, Bridges was shooting *Married to It*, an ensemble movie about the lives of three contemporary couples. He also appeared on stage opposite Lesley Ann Warren as one of a series of occasional pairs doing A.R. Gurney's *Love Letters* in Beverly Hills. In late 1990, Bridges was shooting a new television movie, playing James Brady, the White House press secretary wounded and partly paralyzed in the shooting of President Reagan in 1981; in preparation for the role, Brady took Bridges on a tour of the White House, with President Bush and his own press secretary, Marlin Fitzwater, showing how it all worked from the inside.

As a child, Beau Bridges appeared in such films as *Force of Evil* (1948), and *The Red Pony* (1949). From his late teens, he emerged as a Hollywood star, in such films as *Gaily Gaily* (1969), *The Landlord* (1970), *Lovin' Molly* (1974), *The Other Side of the Mountain* (1975), *Norma Rae* (1979), *Heart Like a Wheel* (1983), and *The Iron Triangle* (1989), and in such telefilms as *The Child Stealer* (1979), *The Runner Stumbles* (1979), *Witness for the Prosecution* (1984), and *Space* (1985). Los Angeles-born Bridges is the son of actor Lloyd Bridges and the brother of actor Jeff Bridges. After an earlier divorce, Bridges remarried; he has four children. He attended the University of California at Los Angeles.

FURTHER READING

"On a movie set. . . ." KAREN DE WITT. *New York Times*, Dec. 18, 1990.

Bridges, Harry (Alfred Renton Bryant Bridges, 1901–90) The Australian-born long-time leader of America's West Coast longshoremen went to sea at age 21, lured by the writer Jack London, and arrived on the San Francisco docks in 1922. There, in 1933, he organized the International Longshoremen's Association (ILA), affiliated first with the American Federation of Labor (AFL) and later the Congress of Industrial Organizations (CIO); in 1937 he organized the International Longshoremen's and Warehousemen's Union (ILWU). Branded a Communist and an "undesirable alien" by Congress, Bridges was cleared and remained in office with support from his members and favorable rulings from the courts, twice including the Supreme Court. In the 1960s he was a leader in modernizing cargo-handling, with union agreements allowing the use of mechanical loaders and shipping containers. (d. San Francisco; March 30, 1990)

FURTHER READING

Obituary. *Current Biography*, May, 1990.
Obituary. *National Review*, Apr. 30, 1990.
Obituary. *New York Times*, Mar. 31, 1990.

Bridges, Jeff (1949–) This year Bridges returned to the site of the movie that made him a star, *The Last Picture Show* (1971), along with his director, Peter Bogdanovich, and co-stars, including Cybill Shepherd, Cloris Leachman, Timothy Bottoms, Randy Quaid, and Eileen Brennan. The result was a sequel, *Texasville*, showing their characters some 30 years on, deep in mid-life crises—for Bridges that involved gaining 35 pounds for the part of the older Duane Jackson. As *Texasville* arrived in the theaters, Bridges, himself, was shooting another film, *The Fisher King*, playing a lifelong cynic who hopes to redeem himself through the help of visionary street-person Robin Williams.

Los Angeles-born Bridges is one of the leading American film actors of the last two decades, in such films as *Hearts of the West* (1975), *Starman* (1984), the title role in *Tucker* (1989), and opposite his brother, Beau Bridges, in *The Fabulous Baker Boys* (1989). They are the sons of actor Lloyd Bridges; Jeff played his first screen role at the age of eight, in his father's television series, "Sea Hunt". He is married to Susan Bridges; they have three children.

FURTHER READING

"Lone star Bridges." Martha Frankel. *American Film*, Oct. 1990.
"How Bridges fights boredom." Richard Corliss. *Time*, Aug. 15, 1988.

Broderick, Matthew (1962–) In 1990, Broderick had the rather rare experience of playing opposite Marlon Brando—and in a comedy, too. The film was *The Freshman*, with Broderick in the title role becoming entangled with Brando, in a comically canted version of his Oscar-winning *Godfather* role, with a plot revolving around an endangered, giant Komodo dragon, a 66-inch lizard named Mzee.

In the Civil War film *Glory*, which opened in late 1989, Broderick scored a major breakthrough as a dramatic actor in playing Robert Gould Shaw, the young White colonel leading the first all-Black volunteer regiment, the Massachusetts 54th. The film, which also starred Denzel Washington and Morgan Freeman, was honored in 1990 by the Academy of Family Films and Family Television with its Special Award of Merit for Oustanding Achievement. The film *Family Business*, in which Broderick played opposite Dustin Hoffman and Sean Connery, was a three-generational caper comedy, something of a box-office disappointment after its 1989 opening. But it was a big hit in 1990 in the video rental market.

New York City-born Broderick, the son of actor James Broderick, emerged as a leading young stage and screen actor in the early 1980s. On stage, he won a Tony for *Brighton Beach Memoirs* (1983), and also appeared in such plays as *Torch Song Trilogy* (1981), *Biloxi Blues* (1985), and *The Widow Clare* (1986). On screen, he appeared in several popular films, including *Wargames* (1983), *Ladyhawke* (1985), *Ferris Bueller's Day Off* (1986), and *Project X* (1986), and in the film versions of *Torch Song Trilogy* (1988), and *Biloxi Blues* (1988).

FURTHER READING

"Glory days." John Sedgwick. *GQ—Gentlemen's Quarterly*, Jan. 1990.
"A day off with. . . ." Elizabeth Kaye. *Seventeen*, July 1988.
"The happy blues. . . ." William Wolf. *Cosmopolitan*, May, 1988.
"Blues for Matthew." Amy Engeler. *Rolling Stone*, Apr. 21, 1988.
"Broderick, Matthew." *Current Biography*, May 1987.
"Zooming in on Matthew Broderick." *Teen*, Apr. 1985.
"The kid with. . . ." Jesse Kornbluth. *New York*, Mar 25, 1985.

Brokaw, Tom (Thomas John Brokaw, 1940–) News anchor Tom Brokaw ran third in a field of three, with his "NBC Nightly News" trailing ABC's "World News Tonight" and the "CBS Evening News". But in fact, the three shows were often so close together as to be separated by only tenths of a point; Brokaw himself, put his network's position down to "statistical error." He and the National Broadcasting Company (NBC) have this to cheer about, in any case: Brokaw and the "Nightly News" are the most attractive to younger, urban viewers, and therefore can charge their advertisers more than the other networks. Nevertheless, in mid-1990, a new executive producer was brought in, to help reshape the news program.

Like his counterparts, Brokaw often traveled abroad to report the breaking international stories that have dominated the news in 1989 and 1990. He was the first, for example, to broadcast live at the tearing down of the Berlin Wall, spent a week reporting from the Middle East on the Persian Gulf Crisis, and reported from Moscow and Helsinki at the time of the September 1990 Bush-Gorbachev summit. He was barred from Iraq, however. NBC complained publicly when in late August Columbia Broadcasting System (CBS) and American Broadcasting Company (ABC) reporters were given permission to report from Iraq, charging that the censorship was in retaliation for NBC's previous reports on Iraq's military build-up and use of poison gas.

Brokaw was also seen on occasional series, like "Expose" a series of investigative reports on various stories. He and Jane Pauley also did a well-regarded end-of-the-decade retrospective, "The Eighties." When Pauley left NBC's "Today" show, rumors flew that she would be made co-anchor with Brokaw (her old "Today" partner); they proved untrue, however, and Pauley settled into her own prime-time news program, though occasionally substituting on the evening news. In April 1990, *Newsweek* reported in its "Periscope" piece that the White House found Brokaw the least impressive of the three anchors; that brought an immediate phone call from White House Chief of Staff John Sununu denying the report and labeling it as "off the wall."

South Dakota-born Brokaw began his long career in broadcasting in 1962, and anchored news shows in Atlanta and Los Angeles during the mid-1960s, before becoming NBC White House correspondent in 1973. He became a nationally known figure as the host of the "Today" show, from 1976 to 1982, and has anchored the "NBC Nightly News" since 1982. He, Peter Jennings for ABC, and Dan Rather for CBS are the key American news broadcasters of the day. He married Meredith Lynn Auld in 1962; they have three children. His B.A. was from the University of South Dakota.

FURTHER READING

"50/50: happy birthday. . . ." Joanna Elm. *TV Guide*, Feb. 3, 1990.

Anchors: Brokaw, Jennings, Rather and the Evening News. Robert Goldberg and Gerald J. Goldberg. Carol, 1990.

"NBC's power-Brokaw. . . ." John Lippman. *Variety*, Aug. 3, 1988.

"Tom Brokaw. . . ." James Kaplan. *Vogue*, Apr. 1988.

"The news about 'broadcast'. . . ." Jane Hall and Brad Darrach. *People*, Feb. 1, 1988.

"The most trusted men in America." Carol Kramer. *McCall's*, July 1987.

"NBC's catalytic anchor." Channels, May 1987.

"Hey ma, top o' the world!. . . ." Gioia Diliberto. *People*, Apr. 28, 1986.

"Country boy makes pretty good." Lynn Darling. *Esquire*, Mar. 1986.

Brower, David Ross (1912–)

Conservationist Brower was looking back over the past in 1990, with the first volume of his projected two-volume autobiography *For Earth's Sake: The Life and Times of David Brower*. The time was right. The 20th anniversary of Earth Day and the rise in concern over a whole range of environmental issues both owed much to Brower's life and indefatigable work. The Public Broadcasting System (PBS) recognized this in airing a documentary on Brower, also called *For Earth's Sake*. Among various current projects, Brower has recently focused on restricting or banning the purchase of tuna caught with methods that also kill dolphins. He scored a success in April 1990, when the three largest U.S. tuna canners agreed to stop using such tuna; Brower and various groups went to court against imports of such tuna from foreign fleets. He also was working on plans to establish a "Green Cross" to help restore devastated areas around the world.

California-born Brower has been a leading conservationist for over four decades. Active in the Sierra Club from 1935, he became a member of the club's board of directors in 1941 and was the club's executive director from 1952 to 1969. In that long period, he became a major figure who as writer, editor, and spokesperson helped lay the foundations of the modern ecological movement. In 1969, he broke with the Sierra Club over various issues, though he later returned as honorary vice-president. He founded and was until 1979 the first president of Friends of the Earth, and in 1982, he moved on to found the Earth Island Institute. He was an editor at the University of California Press from 1941 to 1952, and used his book skills to create the celebrated Sierra Club and Friends of the Earth picture book series. He also wrote many articles and several books on conservation-related matters. Since the late 1960s, he has been a leading anti-nuclear activist. Brower attended the University of California. He married Anne Hus in 1943; they have four children.

FURTHER READING

"David Brower." BILL MCKIBBEN. *Rolling Stone*, June 28, 1990.

"David Brower. . . ." MONTGOMERY BROWER. *People*, Apr. 30, 1990.

"A nasty split. . . ." PAUL RAUBER. *Mother Jones*, Nov. 1986.

Brown, Ron (Ronald Harmon Brown, 1941–) A leading Democratic politician, Brown became a major figure as Jesse Jackson's 1988 Democratic Convention manager. He was a Dukakis political adviser during the 1988 campaign, and in February 1989 he became the trailblazing first Black Democratic National Committee chairman. Brown's attempt has been to play a unifying and rebuilding role after the 1988 Michael Dukakis loss to George Bush, calling himself from the outset a chairman for all Democrats, and focusing attacks upon the Bush administration, rather than on intra-party matters. He has especially focused on such matters as Senator Moynihan's proposal to cut social security taxes, on the continuing federal budget crisis, and on attempting to place blame on the Republican administration for the savings and loan disaster. In July 1990 he announced that the 1992 Democratic National Convention would be held in New York City.

Washington, D.C.-born Brown began his career as a Washington "insider" soon after his graduation from the St. John's University School of Law in 1970. He worked in a series of increasingly responsible posts at the National Urban League (1971–79), was counsel for the Senate Judiciary Committee in 1980 and for Senator Edward Kennedy in 1981, and from 1981 to 1989 was a partner in Patton, Boggs & Blow. During the 1980s, he became a substantial figure in the Democratic Party, working in the 1979 to 1980 Kennedy presidential campaign, and working with the Democratic National Committee from 1981. Brown's B.A. was from Middlebury College, in 1962, and his 1970 J.D. was from St. John's. He married Alma Arrington in 1962; they have two children.

FURTHER READING

"From two new party chairmen. . . ." *American Visions*, June 1989.

"Brown, Ronald Harmon." *Current Biography*, July 1989.

"Ron Brown. . . ." *Ebony*, May 1989.

"Running as his own man." WALTER ISSACSON. *Time*, Jan. 30, 1989.

Broyard, Anatole (1920–90) Book critic, essayist, and editor Broyard was born in New Orleans, the son of a builder. He attended college in New York, beginning early to write articles and short stories for literary and political magazines, which he continued after serving as a troop transport officer in the Pacific during World War II. A teacher of writing for many years, Broyard worked at *The New York Times* from 1971, for 15 years as daily book critic, then as editor of the *Book Review*. After his 1989 retirement, he wrote several personal, reflective articles about the cancer that would take his life. (d. Cambridge, Massachusetts; October 11, 1990.)

FURTHER READING

Obituary. ALFRED KAZIN. *New York Times Book Review*, Nov. 25, 1990.
Obituary. ERNEST VAN DEN HAAG. *National Review*, Nov. 5, 1990.
Obituary. *New York Times*, Oct. 12, 1990.

Buckey, Raymond (1958–) On July 27, 1990, the McMartin preschool child molestation case, the longest and most expensive set of criminal trials in American history, ended when a California jury deadlocked and refused to convict on a final set of eight counts against former nursery-school teacher Raymond Buckey. In January, Buckey and his mother, Peggy McMartin Buckey, had been acquitted of 52 counts, all stemming from the alleged sexual molestation of 11 children at the Virginia McMartin Pre-School in Manhattan Beach, California, from 1979 to 1983. Then followed the retrial on eight of 13 left-over counts on which the first jury had deadlocked. The set of cases lasted six years and cost the state of California well over $17 million. Not one conviction was secured, although the case had from the start drawn huge national attention, starting as it did with sensational charges of devil worship, animal sacrifices, pornographic photo sessions, and widespread sexual abuse involving scores of young children and seven of their teachers. Buckey spent five years in jail, then was finally freed on a $3 million bond only in 1989. Along the way, Buckey's sister and grandmother and three other defendants were also charged; all charges against them had previously been dropped for lack of evidence. The school itself had been closed by the state in 1984, while the charges were pending. After their acquittals, the defendants sued the state and many of their accusers for tens of millions of dollars.

FURTHER READING

"The longest mistrial. . . ." RICHARD LACAYO. *Time*, Aug. 6, 1990.
"McMartin. . . ." *Playboy*, June 1990.
"Ray Buckey. . . ." MARY A. FISCHER. *Los Angeles Magazine*, Apr. 1990.
"Retrial ordered. . . ." *Time*, Feb. 12, 1990.
"After the verdict. . . ." SUSAN SCHINDEHETTE. *People*, Feb. 5, 1990.
"Six years of trial. . . ." MARGARET CARLSON. *Time*, Jan. 29, 1990
"The child-abuse trial. . . ." *U.S. News & World Report*, Jan. 29, 1990.
"A case of dominoes?. . . ." MARY A. FISCHER. *Los Angeles Magazine*, Oct. 1989.
"Hollywood tapes. . . ." RICHARD LACAYO. *Time*, Dec. 15, 1986.
Pity the Little Children: The Politics of Child Abuse. PAUL EBERLE. Carol, 1986.
"The McMartins. . . ." Michelle Green. *People*, May 21, 1984.

Bunshaft, Gordon (1909–90) As chief designer in the New York office of Skidmore, Owings and Merrill, Bunshaft was responsible for the design of Lever House (1952), the glass-walled box set in open space that became a model for thousands of others much like it in cities all over the world. He went on to design such major modern buildings as New York's Pepsi-Cola (1959) and Union Carbide (1961) buildings, Yale University's Beinecke Library (1963), the Lyndon Baines Johnson library at the Austin campus of the University of Texas (1971), the Hirschhorn Museum (1974), and the Jiddah, Saudi Arabia, airport buildings (1975). (d. New York City; August 8, 1990)

FURTHER READING

"One less giant. . . ." STEPHEN A. KLIMENT. *Architectural Record*, Oct. 1990.
Obituary. *Current Biography*, Oct. 1990.
Obituary. *New York Times*, Aug. 9, 1990.
"Bunshaft, Gordon." *Current Biography*, Mar. 1989.
Gordon Bunshaft of Skidmore, Owings and Merrill: Architectural History Foundation American Monograph. CAROL H. KRINSKY. MIT Press, 1988.
Gordon Bunshaft: The Life and Work of a Modern Master. FRANCES C. GRETES. Vance, 1988.

Burnett, Carol (1936–) Burnett zoomed right back to the top in 1990, with her new NBC half-hour comedy-variety series "Carol & Company", which debuted in March, jumped quickly into the top ten prime-time shows, and returned for a full season in September, becoming once again a Saturday-night staple. For Christmas 1989, Burnett had teamed with Julie Andrews for a widely viewed television special *Julie & Carol*, the two friends brought together—they reported—by shared experiences of growing up with alcoholic parents.

San Antonio-born Burnett became a highly regarded television comedian in the early 1960s, and was the enormously popular star of her own "The Carol Burnett Show" (1967–79). Through the early 1980s, she also appeared in several plays, including *Plaza Suite* (1970), and *I Do, I Do* (1973), both on Broadway, and in films such as *Pete 'n' Tillie* (1972), *A Wedding* (1977), and *Annie* (1982). Then she fell into a difficult period before her 1990 comeback. In 1986, she published the autobiographical *One More Time*. She was formerly married to Joseph Hamilton, and has three children. She attended the University of California at Los Angeles.

FURTHER READING

"Burnett, Carol." *Current Biography*, Nov. 1990.
"Carol Burnett comes home." ERIC SHERMAN. *Ladies Home Journal*, Sept. 1990.
"Carol Burnett. . ." MARK MORRISON. *Woman's Day*, Aug. 7, 1990.
"After 12 years, Carol's back. . . ." SUSAN LITTWIN. *TV Guide*, May 19, 1990.
"Carol Burnett is a legend. . . ." CHARLES BUSCH. *Interview*, Mar. 1990
Carol Burnett: The Sound of Laughter. JAMES HOWE. Puffin, 1988; Viking Penguin, 1987.
Laughing Till It Hurts. J. RANDY TARABORELLI. Morrow, 1988.
Carol Burnett. CAROLINE LATHAM. New American Library-Dutton, 1986.

Burns, Olive Ann (1917–90) Burns's one novel, *Cold Sassy Tree*, achieved wide popularity. A free-lance writer and newspaper advice columnist, under the pseudonym Amy Larkin, Burns began the novel in 1975 after a diagnosis that she had lymphoma. The novel, focusing on an unconventional May-December marriage in the early 20th-century, small Georgia town of the title, was a bestseller and a television movie. A sequel was unfinished at her death. (d. Atlanta; July 4, 1990)

FURTHER READING

Obituary. *New York Times*, July 6, 1990.
"Olive Ann Burns." BOB SUMMER. Publishers Weekly, Nov. 9, 1984.

Burrud, Bill (1925–90) A child actor in 1930s Hollywood films, Burrud formed his own production company in 1954, and was for over 35 years a leading producer of hundreds of animal, nature, and travel series and specials for television. These included his long-running, very popular "Animal World" (1968-76), the current series "Animal Odyssey", and such series as "World of the Sea" and "Animal America". (d. Los Angeles; July 10, 1990)

FURTHER READING

Obituary. *New York Times*, July 15, 1990.

Bush, Barbara Pierce (1925–   ) As U.S. First Lady, the wife of President George Bush, Barbara Pierce Bush continued to be active in a wide range of voluntary organizations, as was so when her husband was a Texas senator and a two-term vice-president, with special emphasis on fighting cancer and allied diseases and promoting literacy. Since 1983, she has been a trustee of the Morehouse School of Medicine. She uses her own celebrity and that of others to work against illiteracy; Loretta Lynn, for example, recorded two music videos to support her literacy project. Following up her earlier book, *C. Fred's Story* (1984), a dog's-eye look at life in the national capital, Bush in 1990 published *Millie's Book: As Dictated to Barbara Bush*, an updated look at life in the White House from the viewpoint of Millie, the family springer spaniel. It soon became a bestseller.

Since being in residence at the White House, Bush's life is lived in something of a fishbowl. The radiation treatments on her swollen eyes, the result of Graves' disease, a thyroid disorder, have been routinely reported in the media. And when some Wellesley students objected to Bush as the speaker at their graduation ceremonies (though she was chosen by vote of the student body), it provoked

nationwide discussion. Bush dealt with the potentially difficult situation unflappably by inviting Raisa Gorbachev to join her, and turning the occasion into an international event.

Barbara Pierce married George Bush in 1945. They have five living children—George, John, Neil, Marvin, and Dorothy; their second child, Robyn, died of leukemia in 1953, at the age of three. She attended Smith College.

FURTHER READING

Barbara Bush. ARLEEN HEISS. Chelsea House, 1991.
"Tough and tender talk. . . ." MARIA WILHELM and LANDON Y. JONES. *People*, Dec. 17, 1990.
"Barbara Bush. . . ." CINDY ADAMS. *Ladies Home Journal*, Nov. 1990.
"In the eye of the storm." PAULA CHIN. *People*, Oct. 1, 1990.
"The hidden life. . . ." KENNETH T. WALSH. *U.S. News & World Report*, May 28, 1990.
Barbara Bush: First Lady of Literacy. JUNE BEHRENS. Childrens, 1990.
Simply Barbara Bush: A Portrait of America's Candid First Lady. DONNIE RADCLIFFE. Warner, 1990.
"Barbara and George. . . ." DONNIE RADCLIFFE. *Good Housekeeping*, Nov. 1989.
"Bush, Barbara Pierce." *Current Biography*, Oct. 1989.

Bush, George (George Herbert Walker Bush, 1924–) As the second year of his administration unfolded, President George Bush found himself deeply involved in the conduct of foreign affairs. It was a time of huge opportunities, and, as it turned out, of massive hazards, as well. His first crisis came with the December 20, 1989, U.S. invasion of Panama; it resulted in a quick and easy four-day victory, and ended with Manuel Noriega's surrender on January 3, 1990.

For the next seven months, there were what seemed to be an unending series of triumphs, as the Cold War fully ended, many Eastern European nations shook themselves free of Stalinism and Soviet control, Germany was reunited, and a whole new set of worldwide relationships began to emerge. The American president played a major role every step of the way, meeting with Gorbachev at the May–June Washington summit and keeping in close touch with world leaders as the year unfolded.

But on August 2, 1990, with the Iraqi invasion and quick conquest of Kuwait, an entirely different and much darker set of possibilities emerged, as Bush ordered a huge American forces buildup in the Persian Gulf, developed a worldwide alliance and a set of United Nations resolutions demanding Iraqi withdrawal, and ultimately led the United States and the alliance into the Persian Gulf War.

At home, George Bush faced massive problems during the second year of his administration, with Congress working out a painful

and inconclusive set of budget compromises as deficits continued to soar, continuing to face an ever-expanding savings and loan bailout crisis, and seeing a much-publicized "war" on drugs slowing the American drug abuse epidemic only a little, if that, while during 1990 the nation slid further into a real estate crisis and fully into a recession.

George Bush defeated Michael Dukakis in the bitterly contested 1988 presidential race, becoming the 41st president of the United States in 1989, the climax of a political career that began in Texas in the early 1960s. He had grown up in a Republican Party family, the son of Connecticut Senator Prescott Bush, and then left New England to enter the oil business in Texas in the early 1950s. In 1953, he co-founded the Zapata Petroleum Company and in 1956, he became president and then board chairman of the Zapata Off Shore Company. He was an unsuccessful Republican senatorial candidate from Texas in 1964, and then moved to Washington as a Houston congressman in 1967, a seat he held for two terms, until 1971. In 1970, he made another unsuccessful run for the Senate on the Republican ticket.

Bush was United States ambassador to the United Nations from 1971 to 1972, during the waning days of the Vietnam War, and was Republican National Committee chairman from 1973 to 1974. He was the chief American liaison officer in Peking from 1974 to 1976, then returned to Washington as head of the Central Intelligence Agency (CIA) from 1976 to 1977. He made an unsuccessful Republican presidential nomination run in 1980, but withdrew in favor of Ronald Reagan, and subsequently became Reagan's two-term vice-president, operating in those eight years mostly ceremonially, as have most vice-presidents. He then succeeded Reagan as president. The early period of his presidency was marked by a focus on such very difficult, existing, domestic problems as the enormous federal deficit and the huge savings and loan fiscal crisis, which quite clearly was destined to cost scores of billions of dollars—and all within the framework created by the Bush campaign pledge not to raise federal taxes, the famous "read my lips" promise. Around the time of the 1988 campaign, Bush published two books, *Man of Integrity* (with Doug Wead) and *Looking Forward: The George Bush Story* (with Victor Gold).

The president, a navy pilot in World War II, has been married to Barbara Pierce Bush since 1945. Their five living children are George, John, Neil, Marvin, and Dorothy; their second child, Robyn, died of leukemia at age three. Mr. Bush's B.A. was from Yale University, in 1948.

FURTHER READING

"Men of the Year." DAN GOODGAME, et al. *Time*, Jan. 7, 1991.
"Commander. . . ." KENNETH WALSH. *U.S. News & World Report*, Dec. 31, 1990.
"Tough and tender talk. . . ." MARIA WILHELM and LANDON Y. JONES. *People*, Dec. 17, 1990.
"Deadline: Jan. 15. . . ." MICHAEL KRAMER. *Time*, Dec. 10, 1990.
"Fighting mad. . . ." MARCI MCDONALD. *Maclean's*, Nov. 19, 1990
"Bush's other summit. . . ." CARL BERNSTEIN. *Time*, Sept. 17, 1990.
"Shared goals." *Newsweek*, Sept. 17, 1990.
"Pausing at the rim of the abyss. . . ." LISA BEYER. *Time*, Sept. 10, 1990.
"Bush's balancing act." HUGH SIDEY. *Time*, Sept. 10, 1990.
"The winds of war." MARCI MCDONALD. *Maclean's*, Aug. 20, 1990.
"'Who can read the tea leaves?'" KEVIN DOYLE, et al. *Maclean's*, June 25, 1990.
George Bush: An Intimate Portrait. FITZHUGH GREEN. Hippocrene, 1990.
Our Forty-First President: George Bush. Scholastic, 1989.
George Bush: The Story of Our Forty-First President. Dell, 1989.
George Bush: Forty-First President of the United States. JUNE BEHRENS. Childrens, 1989.
Picture Life of George Bush. RON SCHNEIDERMAN. Watts, 1989.
Looking Forward: The George Bush Story. GEORGE H. BUSH and VICTOR GOLD. Doubleday, 1987.
"Bush, George Herbert." *Current Biography*, Sept. 1983.

Butcher, Susan (1955–) On March 14, 1990, dog sled racer Butcher set a new course record of 11 days, 1 hour, and 53 minutes in winning Alaska's 1,158-mile Anchorage-Nome Iditarod Trail Sled Dog Race. It was her fourth win in five years; the only other four-time winner is Rick Swenson. She had set out on March 3 from Anchorage, surviving difficult weather conditions and the need to cut out three of her dogs; she emerged at the head of

seventy contestants as the world's leading dog sled racer, and the winner of first place prizes totaling $75,000. Coming in second place was 1989 winner Joe Runyan. In the 1991 Iditarod, she lost to Swenson.

Massachusetts-born Butcher and her husband, lawyer Dave Monson, live and breed sled dogs at Trail Breaker Kennel, in Eureka, Alaska. She arrived in Alaska by way of two years spent in Colorado, and in 1977, she moved to Eureka and founded her kennels. That year, she first attracted media attention by dog sledding to the top of Mount McKinley. During the late 1980s and early 1990s, she became a symbol of endurance and accomplishment for women throughout the world, as the leading figure in what had before been viewed as a "man's" sport.

FURTHER READING

"An intense drive." CANDICE SZIRAK. *Women's Sports and Fitness*, Mar. 1989.

"Here's one musher. . . ." JOHN SKOW. *Sports Illustrated*, Feb. 15, 1988.

"Musher." *New Yorker*, Oct. 5, 1987.

Buthelezi, Mangosuthu Gatsha

(1928–) South African Zulu leader Buthelezi emerged as a powerful independent force in South African politics during 1990, as negotiations over the future of the country began between the African National Congress (ANC), led by newly-freed Nelson Mandela, and the De Klerk government. The ANC, which had tried to bypass Buthelezi, found itself engaged in a hot and growing civil war with the mostly Zulu Inkatha organization. Since 1988, Inkatha-ANC clashes had flared repeatedly in Natal, historically the center of Zulu strength. In the spring of 1990, there was widespread violence in Natal, and by summer, violence had spread to Johannesburg and other areas. As hundreds died and thousands were injured, the ANC and Inkatha, led by Mandela and Buthelezi, moved toward new relationships, though Buthelezi's aims were not yet clearly stated.

Buthelezi became chief of the Buthelezi tribe in 1963, succeeding his father, Mathole Buthelezi. He was a Zulu administrator for two decades, becoming chief minister of the Kwa-Zulu in 1976. As the long fight for South African democracy developed during the 1970s and 1980s, he became the main spokesperson and leader of the Zulus, and a third force in South African politics, for he negotiated with the white South African government on behalf of the Zulus, and often opposed the African National Congress. His followers, organized into the Inkatha movement, carried those disagreements into anti-ANC street fighting throughout the 1980s. He married Irene Audrey Thandekile Mzila in 1952; they have seven children. He attended Adams College and Fort-Hare University.

FURTHER READING

Gatsha Buthelezi: Chief with a Double Agenda. MZALA. Humanities, 1988.

An Appetite for Power: Buthelezi's Inkatha and South Africa. GERHARD MARE and GEORGINA HAMILTON. Indiana University Press, 1988.

"The chief." MICHAEL MASSING. *New York Review of Books*, Feb. 12, 1987.

"Buthelezi, Gatsha Mangosuthu." *Current Biography*, Oct. 1986.

"Zulu chief in the middle." JANICE C. SIMPSON. *Time*, May 26, 1986.

Caan, James (1939–) Actor and director Caan, the classic "tough guy" who created the role of Sonny Corleone in *The Godfather* (1972), appeared in a totally different role late in 1990, as the disabled, victimized romance novelist held hostage by an insane fan, in the Rob Reiner film *Misery*, adapted from the Stephen King novel. He will also be appearing in the forthcoming musical film *For the Boys*, completing the major comeback that followed his long retirement from active filmmaking during much of the 1980s.

New York City-born Caan played in New York theater and television in the early 1960s, and became a major player in the early 1970s, with his notable television lead in "Brian's Song" (1971), which was followed by his star-making role in *The Godfather*. He went on to such films as *Cinderella Liberty* (1974), *Funny Lady* (1975), *Rollerball* (1975), *A Bridge Too Far* (1977), *Chapter Two* (1979), *Hide in Plain Sight* (1980; he also directed), *Gardens of Stone* (1987), and *Alien Nation* (1988). Caan attended New York's Hofstra University and the Neighborhood Playhouse. He has been married three times, most recently to Ingrid Hajek, and has two children.

FURTHER READING

"James Caan. . . ." Jean Vallely. *Rolling Stone*, May 14, 1981.
"James Caan. . . ." Al Ellenberg. *New York*, May 5, 1980.
"James Caan. . . ." James Horowitz. *Cosmopolitan*, Mar. 1980.

Cage, Nicolas (Nicholas Coppola, 1965–) Cage often plays "offbeat" leads: in late 1990, as Sailor Ripley opposite Laura Dern as Lula Pace Fortune in the David Lynch film *Wild at Heart*. He played a more conventional lead opposite Tommie Lee Jones in David Green's action film *Firebirds* (1990). In 1989, he starred in Robert Bierman's film *Vampire's Kiss*, in a cast that included Elizabeth Ashley, Maria Conchia Alonso, and Jennifer Beals as the vampire. A year earlier, he had played the one-armed baker who becomes Cher's lover in *Moonstruck* (1988).

California-born Cage, the nephew of Francis Ford Coppola, began his career with strong supporting roles in such 1980s films as *Valley Girl* (1983), *Rumble Fish* (1983), *Racing with the Moon* (1984), *Birdy* (1984), and *The Cotton Club* (1984), and moved into leads with his role opposite Kathleen Turner in *Peggy Sue Got Married* (1986), and in *Raising Arizona* (1987).

FURTHER READING

"Nicolas Cage. . . ." Mark Rowland. *Cosmopolitan*, Sept. 1990.
"Nicolas Cage." John Clark. *Premiere*, Sept. 1990.
"Rebel without. . . ." Stephanie Mansfield. *GQ—Gentleman's Quarterly*, Aug. 1990.
"The beasts within. . . ." Mark Rowland. *American Film*, June 1990.
"20 questions. . . ." Robert Crane. *Playboy*, June, 1989.
"Nicolas Cage. . . ." T. Klein. *Cosmopolitan*, Oct. 1988.

Caine, Michael (Maurice Joseph Micklewhite, (1933–) Caine appeared on screen in several very different roles in 1990. In the winter, he starred in the double title roles in a new television movie, *Jekyll & Hyde*, co-starring Cheryl Ladd. In the spring, he was Graham Marshall, a marketing executive who is passed over for promotion and turns murderous, in the off-beat black comedy *A Shock to the System,* co-starring Elizabeth McGovern. In the fall he appeared in the title role of the fantasy-comedy *Mr. Destiny*, who rearranges a moment in the childhood of Jim Belushi. Also in the works was a British heist movie, *Bullseye*, co-starring Roger Moore and directed by Michael Winner. During 1989, *Dirty Rotten Scoundrels* (1988), starring Caine and Steve Martin as con men on the French Riviera, was a hit in the video rental market. In 1989, he also published a book titled *Acting in Film: An Actor's Take on Movie Making.*

London-born Caine has been a durable, versatile film star since the mid-1960s, beginning with such films as *Zulu* (1964), *The Ipcress File* (1965), *Alfie* (1966), and *Funeral in Berlin* (1966). His work also includes such films as *The Wilby Conspiracy* (1974), *The Eagle Has Landed* (1975), *California Suite* (1977), *Educating Rita* (1972), *The Holcraft Covenant* (1984), *Hannah and Her Sisters* (1975), for which he won a Best Supporting Actor Oscar, and *To Kill a Priest* (1989). He was formerly married to Patricia Haines. He married Shakira Khatoon Baksh in 1973, and has two children.

FURTHER READING

"Michael Caine; Cockney superstar." JOHN ENNIS. *Reader's Digest* (Canadian), Dec. 1988.
"Caine, Michael." *Current Biography*, Jan. 1988.

Callaghan, Morley (1903–90) Born and educated as a lawyer in Toronto, Callaghan published his first novel, *Strange Fugitive*, in 1928. That was the year he met Ernest Hemingway, who influenced Callaghan to move to Paris, a period he notably described in *That Summer in Paris: Memories of Tangled Friendships with Hemingway, Fitzgerald and Some Others* (1963). Hemingway also influenced Callaghan's lean style, but his voice and focus on the spirit, not the letter, of Christianity were his own, as in the most highly regarded of his 13 novels, *The Many Coloured Coat* (1960); this and much of his work was in the modern, liberal, Roman Catholic tradition. (d. Toronto; August 25, 1990.)

FURTHER READING

"Literary treasure. . . ." PAMELA YOUNG. *Maclean's,* Sept. 3, 1990.
Obituary. *The Times* (of London), Aug. 28, 1990.
Obituary. *New York Times*, Aug. 27, 1990.

Candy, John (John Franklin Candy, 1950–) Candy has become one of the busiest actors in Hollywood. He had one of the top box office hits of 1989 in *Uncle Buck*, which continued its winning ways when it arrived in the video rental market in 1990. Riding on the crest of this success, Candy was shooting a string of new films. In spring 1990, he was in Los Angeles starring in the fantasy-comedy *Delirious*, as a daytime soap opera scriptwriter who finds himself in the middle of one of his own stories. In the summer, he was shooting in *Git*, a film written and directed by Dan Aykroyd, in which two Wall Streeters (Candy and Chevy Chase) are set loose in an Atlantic seaside village. In late 1990, Candy was in Chicago filming *Only the Lonely*, as a Chicago cop in love with a mortician (Ally Sheedy) and not sure how to break it to his mother. After that he was scheduled to start filming a new comedy opposite Sylvester Stallone, playing feuding neighbors in *Bartholomew vs. Neff.*

Toronto-born Candy began his career as a comedian in Canadian cabaret and films, joined Chicago's Second City group in 1972, and worked with Second City groups in Toronto and Los Angeles during the rest of the 1970s, becoming a television star in the SCTV comedy show spun off from the groups. He became a leading film comedian in such movies as *1941* (1979), *The Blues Brothers* (1980), *Stripes* (1982), *Vacation* (1983), *Splash* (1984), *Brewster's Millions* (1985), *Volunteers* (1985), *Summer Rental* (1985), *Little Shop of Horrors* (1986), *Planes, Trains and Automobiles* (1987), and *The Great Outdoors* (1988).

FURTHER READING

"Candy, John." *Current Biography*, Feb. 1990.
"20 questions. . . ." *Playboy*, Aug. 1989.
The Second City. DONNA MCCROHAN. Putnam, 1987.

Capriati, Jennifer (1976–) Barely 14 and still an eighth-grade student at the Saddlebrook Tennis Academy, Jennifer Capriati turned professional in 1990 and was widely hailed as an enormously promising tennis player. Her first year as a professional did demonstrate some of that promise, though many continued to be concerned about the possible damage that might result from playing so young on the very demanding professional tennis tour. In June, she reached the semifinals of the French Open, losing to Monica Seles. In July, it was defending champion Steffi Graf who eliminated her in the third round at Wimbledon. In August, she lost to second-seeded Gabriela Sabatini in the quarter-finals of the Canadian Open. Graf once again defeated her at the U.S. Open in September. In October, she won the Puerto Rico Open.

Capriati was trained for tennis from the age of four, first by her father Stefano Capriati, and then by Florida tennis professional Jimmy Evert, father of tennis star Chris Evert. She began winning junior tennis championships at the age of 12. At 13, she won junior titles at the U.S. and French Open tournaments.

FURTHER READING

"Tennis' new legend. . . ." DAVE SCHEIBER. *Saturday Evening Post*, July–Aug. 1990.
"Capriati's debut. . . ." CINDY HAHN. *Tennis*, May 1990.
"Jennifer Capriati. . . ." ANTONIO N. FINS and FLAVIA TAGGIASCO. *Business Week*, Mar. 26, 1990.
"The next Chris Evert?" WILLIAM A. HENRY, III. *Time*, Mar. 26, 1990.
"Will she be a smash?" FRANZ LIDZ. *Sports Illustrated*, Feb. 12, 1990.
"The start of something big." CINDY SHMERLER and CHRIS EVERT. *World Tennis*, Jan. 1990.

Capucine (Germaine Lefebvre, 1933–90) French actress Capucine was best-known for her roles opposite Peter Sellers in *The Pink Panther* (1963), and *What's New Pussycat* (1964). Born in Toulon, she studied foreign languages and modeled for Dior and Givenchy, her cool, aristocratic bearing being a major asset. Her first film was *Song Without End* (1960) in which, she said, she learned to act, while also learning English. Among her other films were *A Walk on the Wild Side* (1962), *The Seventh Dawn* (1964), and *Fellini's Satyricon* (1969). She died in a fall, apparently a suicide. (d. Lausanne, Switzerland; March 17, 1990.)

FURTHER READING

Obituary. *Variety*, Mar. 28, 1990.
Obituary. *The Times* (of London), Mar. 21, 1990.
Obituary. *New York Times*, Mar. 21, 1990.
"Capucine!" *Town and Country*, Feb. 1982.

Carter, Jimmy (James Earl Carter, Jr., 1924–) Ten years after leaving the presidency, Jimmy Carter continued to take on multiple public service roles. He played a major role as a member of the international observation team in the May 1989 Panamanian elections, declaring it a fraud. He observed the key February 1989 Nicaraguan presidential election, declaring it fairly run, and then went on to help mediate the Contra-Sandinista agreements that ended the long civil war. He also observed the May 1990 Dominican Republic election, and played a mediator's role in Ethiopia and the Sudan, though with far less success. At home, he continued to work for low-income housing and housing for the homeless. In 1989, he also published a book titled, *An Outdoor Journal: Adventures and Reflections.*

Georgia-born Carter became the 39th president of the United States in 1977, the climax of a political career that began with his four years in the Georgia Senate from 1963 to 1967. He went on to become governor of Georgia from 1971 to 1975, emerged as the surprise "outsider" winner of the Democratic presidential nomination after a long series of primary campaigns, and defeated incumbent Gerald Ford in the 1976 presidential race. His earlier career included seven years as a naval officer, from 1946 to 1953, and ten years as a successful Georgia farmer and businessman at Plains, Georgia.

Jimmy Carter's very difficult presidential term was dominated by mostly adverse foreign affairs matters, including the Arab oil embargo of the mid–1970s, the Iran hostage crisis that began in late 1979 and dominated the rest of his presidency, and the worsening Soviet-American relations that began with the Soviet invasion of Afghanistan, and resulted in the American boycott of the 1980 Moscow Olympics. His major accomplishment was the 1978 Camp David Accords, which paved the way for the 1979 Egyptian-Israeli peace treaty.

He married Rosalynn Smith in 1946; they have four children. After he left office, the couple collaborated in writing *Everything to Gain: Making the Most of the Rest of Your Life* (1988).

FURTHER READING

"The Carter connection. . . ." Debbie S. Miller. *Wilderness*, Winter, 1990.
"Hail to the ex-chief. . . ." Stanley Cloud. *Time*, Sept. 11, 1989.
Jimmy Carter. Ed Slavin. Chelsea House, 1989.
The President Builds a House: The Work of Habitat for Humanity. Tom Shachtman, Simon & Schuster, 1989.
"Former presidents reflect. . . ." Michael Delon. *USA Today*, Nov. 1988.
"From Plains to the presidency." *Southern Living*, May 1988.
"Jimmy Carter. . . ." Alan M. Webber. *Harvard Business Review*, Mar.–Apr. 1988.

Carvel, Tom (Thomas Andreas Carvelas, 1906–90) The Greek-American inventor of the soft ice cream machine, which was then called frozen custard, Carvel began selling his soft ice cream machines to store owners in 1934, and then developed what ultimately grew into his franchised ice cream store chain. From 1955, he pioneered in becoming chief radio and television advertiser for his stores, a model followed by many other chief executives in the years to come—though very few ventured to follow the fractured English "common man" style Carvel developed. (d. Pine Plains, New York; October 21, 1990.)

FURTHER READING

Obituary. *New York Times*, Oct. 22, 1990.
"Tom Carvel." Chris Andersen. *Good Housekeeping*, Nov. 1986.
"Big dippers. . . ." Robert Masello. *Town and Country*, Aug. 1982.

Castro Ruz, Fidel (1926–) The long Soviet-Cuban relationship changed sharply in the Gorbachev era, leaving Castro in the early 1990s as one of the few hardline Marxist leaders left in the Western world. Soviet economic support also sharply declined, making Cuba's long economic isolation from its natural trading partners even harder to bear. Cuba's political isolation from its former allies was highlighted in June 1990, when Czech president Vaclav Havel publicly called for release of Castro's political prisoners; Castro responded angrily, and made no move to do so.

In July, over 60 Cubans sought political asylum in Havana's Czech, Spanish, Belgian, and several other embassies. The Cuban government refused to allow them to leave the country, and all ultimately surrendered; but Spanish-Cuban relations were greatly damaged. Spain and the European Community responded by stopping all Cuban aid programs, further isolating the Castro government. A defiant Castro responded by attempting to tighten his grip on Cuba and its ruling Communist Party.

Castro has been a key figure in world politics since taking power in Cuba in 1959, after leading the successful revolution against the government of Fulgencio Batista. He survived the U.S.-backed Bay of Pigs invasion of 1961, and also the Soviet missile withdrawal after the 1962 Cuban Missile Crisis came very close to igniting World War III. He remained in power as a Soviet ally and economic dependent through the late 1980s. Castro has played a major role in supplying and training leftist revolutionaries throughout Latin America, and sent tens of thousands of troops to Angola and Ethiopia in the late 1970s; withdrawal of those forces was agreed upon only in the late 1980s, under pressure from the Soviet Union. He is married to Mirta Diaz-Bilart, and has one son. He attended the University of Havana, and practiced law in Havana before beginning his political career.

FURTHER READING

"Fidel Castro's. . . ." Linda Robinson. *U.S. News and World Report,* Dec. 31, 1990.
Castro's Cuba, Cuba's Fidel. Lee Lockwood. Westview, 1990.
"After Castro. . . ." Saul Landau. *Mother Jones,* July–Aug. 1989.
"Castro's curveball." J. David Truby. *Harper's Magazine,* May 1989.
A Totally Free Man: An "Unauthorized Autobiography" of Fidel Castro. John Krich. Simon & Schuster, 1988; Creative Arts, 1981.
Fidel: A Critical Portrait. Tad Szulc. Avon, 1987.
Fidel Castro. John Vail. Chelsea House, 1986.

Ceausescu, Nicolae (1919–89) and **Elena Ceausescu** (1918–89) Former Romanian dictator Nicolae Ceausescu began to lose the ability to govern after the December 16–17, 1989, killings of many demonstrators in Timosoara. Demonstrations in Bucharest and throughout the country broke out on December 21st, quickly turning into the Romanian

Elena and Nicolae Ceausescu.

Revolution. When the army joined the revolution, the government fell. Ceausescu and his wife, Elena, were captured by the revolutionaries on December 22nd, and were executed on December 25th. She had been by far his closest colleague; together, they had ruled Romania.

Nicolai Ceausescu became head of the Romanian Communist Party in 1965, and president of Romania in 1967, after a long Communist Party political career that began in the early 1930s. In power, he deepened Romania's resistance to the Soviet Union and its allies, further developing ties with China and reaching for relationships with Western countries, as well. Internally, he became a wholly repressive, hardline dictator, and he developed both a huge "cult of personality" and a powerful secret police. During the Ceausescu period, Romania was one of the world's most repressive police states. Elena Petrescu Ceausescu had been a chemist; she attended the College of Industrial Chemistry and the Bucharest Polytechnic Institute. The couple had three children.

FURTHER READING

"Flap follows French airing. . . ." Michael Williams. *Variety*, Apr. 25, 1990.
"Ceausescu's last ride." Tira Shubart. *World Monitor,* Mar. 1990.
Obituary. *Current Biography*, Feb. 1990.
"A lingering fear." Andrew Phillips. *Maclean's*, Jan. 15, 1990.
"Lifestyle of a despot. . . ." Andrew Bilski. *Maclean's*, Jan. 8, 1990.
Obituary. *New York Times*. Dec. 26, 1989.
Nicolae Ceausescu: A Political Biography. Mary E. Fischer. Lynne Rienner, 1989.
Romanian Politics in the Ceausescu Era. Daniel N. Nelson. Gordon and Breach, 1988.

Central Park Jogger (1960–) On April 19, 1989, a 28-year-old woman, whose identity has not been published to protect her privacy, was attacked by a group of young men while she was jogging in New York City's Central Park. She was repeatedly raped and beaten, receiving injuries so severe that she had not fully recovered from the attack at the beginning of 1991, among them head injuries that caused her to lose all memory of the attack. She was, however, able to resume her work as an investment banker. A graduate of Wellesley College, she had gone on to earn an M.B.A. in business and international relations at Yale University, and was employed by the Salomon Brothers investment banking firm at the time of the attack. Some of her attackers admitted the attack soon after its occurrence, and six were ultimately indicted on multiple counts of attempted murder, rape, and sodomy, in a case that attracted national and international attention. In August 1990, three of her attackers were convicted of rape and first degree assault. In December 1990, two more were convicted, one of attempted murder, rape, and sodomy, the other on less serious charges. Their victim testified at both trials. In early 1991, a sixth defendant awaited trial.

FURTHER READING

"Her name on record. . . ." *New York Times*, July 17, 1990.
"Smart, driven' woman. . . ." M.A. Farber. *New York Times*, July 17, 1990.

Chamberlain, Richard (George Richard Chamberlain, 1935–) Sometimes dubbed "king of the miniseries," Chamberlain failed in his 1989 television series comeback attempt. The show, CBS's "Island Son," in which Chamberlain played Dr. Daniel Kulani in a Hawaiian hospital, opened with great promise in fall 1989, had rather poor ratings to start with, and then in December was moved into one of the toughest spots on the television line up: opposite the often-top-rated NBC series "Cheers." The ax fell in February 1990, though the shows already produced continued to be aired. Late in the year, Chamberlain could be heard narrating the Public Broadcasting System (PBS) series "The Astronomers."

Los Angeles-born Chamberlain's first major role was a long run as television's "Dr. Kildare" (1961–66). He went on to star in such major television productions as "Centennial" (1978), "Shogun" (1980), "The Thorn Birds" (1985), "Wallenberg: A Hero's Story" (1985), and "Dream West" (1986). He also played in many action-adventure films, including *The Three Musketeers* (1974), *The Four Musketeers* (1974), *The Slipper and the Rose* (1977), *King*

Solomon's Mines (1985), *Allan Quartermain and the Lost City of Gold* (1988), and *The Return of the Musketeers* (1989). He married Marilyn Roessler in 1949; they have three children. He attended the Los Angeles Conservatory of Music and studied acting with Jeff Corey.

FURTHER READING

"23 years after. . . ." LAWRENCE EISENBERG. *TV Guide*, Nov. 11, 1989.
Richard Chamberlain: An Actor's Life. BARBARA SIEGEL and SCOTT SIEGEL. St. Martin's. 1989.
"Richard Chamberlain's risk. . . ." MARY FIORE. *Good Housekeeping*, May 1988.
Richard Chamberlain: An Unauthorized Biography. JEFFREY RYDER. Dell, 1988.
"Chamberlain, Richard." *Current Biography*, Nov. 1987.

Chamorro, Violeta (Violeta Barrios de Chamorro, 1939–) Chamorro became the elected president of Nicaragua on February 25, 1990, after Sandinista leader Daniel Ortega had quite surprisingly agreed to a free election, and to honor the election results, which he did. Her election was the start of a new chapter in a story that began on January 10, 1978, when her husband, crusading newspaper editor Pedro Joaquin Chamorro Cardenal, a leading opponent of the dictator Anastasio Somoza Debayle, was murdered on a street in Managua. That murder made him a martyr, and helped trigger the series of events that led to the Sandinista revolution and the overthrow of Somoza.

Violeta Chamorro was a member of the first Sandinista government, but withdrew within a year, when she saw the Sandinistas moving toward a dictatorship of their own. She took her husband's place as the crusading editor of *La Prensa*, in opposition to Sandinista attacks on freedom. Then came ten years of civil war between Contra and Sandinista forces, with the United States helping the Contras, and Cuba and the Soviet Union helping the Sandinistas. After becoming president of a free Nicaragua, she spent her first year in office successfully reaching agreements to disarm the former combatants, guaranteeing the freedoms that she and her husband had fought for, and trying to set her very poor and damaged country on the road to economic recovery.

Violeta Barrios and Pedro Chamorro had four children. Carlos Fernando and Claudia became highly placed Sandinistas. Pedro Joaquin became a Contra leader, and Cristiana became an editor of *La Prensa*.

FURTHER READING

"Viva democracy." *American Legion Magazine*, Aug. 1990.
"Flowers for Violeta." DENNIS COVINGTON. *Vogue*, Aug. 1990.
"Chamorro, Violeta Barrios de." *Current Biography*, June 1990.
"Crisis of the clans. . . ." ARTURO CRUZ, JR., and CONSUELO CRUZ SEQUEIRA. *New Republic*, May 21, 1990.
"A defiant widow. . . ." RON ARIAS. *People*, Mar. 19, 1990.
"A family affair. . . ." D'ARCY JENISH. *Maclean's*, Mar. 12, 1990.
"Chamorro: more than just a name?" JOHN MOODY. *Time*, Mar. 12, 1990.
Life Stories of the Nicaraguan Revolution. DENIS L. HEYCK. Routledge Chapman and Hall, 1990.
Nicaragua Divided: La Prensa and the Chamorro Legacy. PATRICIA T. EDMISTEN. University Presses of Florida, 1990.
"Don't call her comrade . . . ." JOHN MOODY. *Time*, June 12, 1989.

Chamoun, Dany (1934–90) Chamoun, the Maronite Christian head of Lebanon's Democratic Liberal Party and of a coalition of parties backing general Michel Aoun, was assassinated with his wife and two sons eight days after Aoun was defeated by the Syrian army. Chamoun had attempted to peacefully settle his disputes with the new Syrian-backed government of Lebanese prime minister Elias Hrawi. Reunification of war-torn Lebanon and the end of the long civil war was his main goal, after his own participation in factional battles for much of his life. He was the son of former Christian Prime Minister Camille Chamoun, and was until 1980, the leader of the "Tigers," a Christian militia faction. (d. East Beirut, Lebanon; October 21, 1990.)

FURTHER READING

"Blood overlooked." *Economist*, Oct. 27, 1990.
Obituary. *New York Times*, Oct. 22, 1990.
Obituary. *The Times* (of London), Oct. 22, 1990.

Chapel, Alain (1937–90) Chapel was a celebrated French chef and restaurateur, whose restaurant at Mionnay, near Lyons, shot to prominence in 1973, when it received the *Michelin Guide's* highly prized three-star rating, one of only 19 in France. Born into a restaurant family in Lyons, Chapel began intensive training at age 15, taking over the family bistro in Mionnay in 1970, and renaming it for himself. From then until his death, his special creations made his restaurant a highlight for gourmet tourists in France. (d. Avignon, France; July 10, 1990.)

FURTHER READING

Obituary. *New York Times*, July 1, 1990.

Chapman, Tracy (1963–) Cleveland-born guitarist, singer, and songwriter Chapman emerged very suddenly in 1988 as a leading writer and singer of social protest. She won three Grammys and several other awards for her first album, *Tracy Chapman*, which eventually sold an estimated 10 million copies worldwide. In 1989, she joined the worldwide Amnesty International tour. In 1989, she also enjoyed the distinction of having her song "Freedom Now," about then-jailed African National Congress leader Nelson Mandela, banned from South African state radio and television. Her second album was *Crossroads* (1989), also an enormous popular hit. She attended Connecticut's Wooster School and Tufts University.

FURTHER READING

"Singing for herself. . . ." RICHARD STENGEL. *Time*, Mar. 12, 1990.
"Women popsters. . . ." KEVIN ZIMMERMAN. *Variety*, Sept. 20, 1989.
"Chapman, Tracy." *Current Biography*, Aug. 1989.
"Tracy Chapman." *People*, Dec. 26, 1988.
"On her own terms." STEVE POND. *Rolling Stone*, Sept. 22, 1988.
"Good 'n' gritty. . . ." JENNIFER ASH and MARY FRAKES. *Life*, Aug. 1988
"Tracy Chapman's. . . ." ANTHONY DECURTIS. *Rolling Stone*, June 30, 1988.

Charles Philip Arthur George, the Prince of Wales (1948–) The Prince of Wales is the oldest son of Elizabeth II and Prince Philip, and heir to the British throne. He has undertaken a wide range of ceremonial duties, such as an appearance at the enthronement of Japanese Emperor Akihito. He has also often spoken out on ecological issues, as well as becoming a leading critic of modern architecture. Major objects of his attack include

such massive works as Britain's National Theatre, National Gallery, and National Library. He attended Trinity College, Cambridge University, and the University College of Wales. He married Lady Diana Spencer in 1981; they have two children, William Arthur Philip, born June 21, 1982, and Henry Charles Albert David, born September 15, 1984.

FURTHER READING

Prince Charles and the Architect. St. Martin's, 1990.
"Charles III—in waiting. . . ." ANTHONY HOLDEN. *Maclean's*, Nov. 14, 1988.
"Prince Charles; a dangerous age." BRAD DARRACH. *People*, Oct. 31, 1988.
"Prince Charles. . . ." PETER DAVIS. *Esquire*, Apr. 1988.
"Wanted: less pomp. . . ." NANCY COOPER. *Newsweek*, Mar. 7, 1988.
"Defying tradition. . . ." HOWELL RAINES. *New York Times Magazine*, Feb. 21, 1988.
The Picture Life of Charles and Diana. HENRY RASOF. Watts, 1988.
Charles and Diana. RALPH G. MARTIN. Putnam, 1985.

Charleson, Ian (1949–90) Best-known for his role as Christian missionary and champion runner Eric Liddell in *Chariots of Fire* (1981), Charleson was an extraordinarily talented young Scottish actor, who had already played many major roles on stage, and was headed for much more before his encounter with AIDS. Near the end, stricken with the fatal disease, he was a very notable Hamlet at Britain's National Theatre. He was on stage with the Young Vic company in the late 1960s, and in a wide range of traditional and modern classics on stage and screen during the following two decades. Eric Liddell, too, died young, in a Japanese prison camp in China during World War II. (d. London; January 6, 1990.)

FURTHER READING

Obituary. *The Times* (of London), Jan. 9, 1990.
Obituary. *New York Times*, Jan. 8, 1990.

Chase, Chevy (Cornelius Crane Chase, 1943–) Chase continued to act out the comically terrible disasters that can befall supposedly placid citizens of middle-class suburbia. Joined by Beverly D'Angelo, Chase had another big hit with *National Lampoon's Christmas Vacation,* which opened in late 1989 and continued its success in the video rental market, although it was released in mid-summer. During 1990, Chevy Chase was shooting a new movie, *Git*, written and directed by fellow "Saturday Night Live" alumnus Dan Aykroyd, with Chase and John Candy as Wall Street types set loose in an Atlantic coastal village. After that it was off to shoot *The Memoirs of an Invisible Man*, John Carpenter's new black comedy about a Wall Streeter (again) who becomes invisible after an industrial accident.

Among his other activities, Chase and Steve Martin helped singer Paul Simon make a video this year, to accompany Simon's new album *Rhythm of the Saints*, their job being to hold down a giant "Casper the Friendly Ghost" balloon. This year, Chase was also named to the board of trustees of his alma mater, Bard College, at Annandale-on-Hudson, New York.

New York City-born Chase was a comedy writer and off-Broadway comedian in cabaret in the late 1960s and early 1970s, emerging in the mid-1970s as a nationally recognized television comedian as a member of the "Saturday Night Live" troupe. In the late 1970s, he also became a leading film comedian, in such movies as *Foul Play* (1978), *Oh Heavenly Dog* (1980),

Caddyshack (1980; and the 1988 sequel), *Modern Problems* (1981), *Deal of the Century* (1983), *Fletch* (1985; and the 1988 and 1989 sequels), *Spies Like Us* (1985), *Three Amigos* (1986), and *Funny Farm* (1988). He has been married three times, and has three children.

FURTHER READING

"Playboy interview: Chevy Chase." JOHN BLUMENTHAL. *Playboy*, June 1988.
"Mr. middle class. . . ." MYRON MEISEL. *Rolling Stone*, Oct. 13, 1983.
"Drugs and depression. . . ." JEFF JARVIS. *People*, Sept. 12, 1983.
"Chase, Chevy." *Current Biography*, Mar, 1979.

Cheney, Dick (Richard Bruce Cheney, 1941–) As the Cold War ended and the federal deficit and budget crises grew, Defense Secretary Cheney began a long series of military spending cuts and planned cuts. He often took a position somewhere between the Pentagon, which resisted sharp cuts, and the Congress, which demanded them. In November 1989, he asked the Pentagon to plan for massive spending cuts. In January 1990, he froze new military construction and civilian hiring. He began to plan the series of base closings, armed forces reductions, and project cuts that became important features of the long-range plans he announced in June, as part of the run-up to the federal budget. At the same time, he strongly resisted calls by the Congress and especially the House of Representatives for far deeper and more immediate spending and forces cuts, though the pace of change in Eastern Europe and the Soviet Union increased the pressure for cuts.

After the August 1990 onset of the Persian Gulf Crisis, however, the pressure from Congress lessened, as a new military buildup began. Yet, he did proceed with cuts previously announced and the 1991 federal defense budget cuts were not restored. He took a very active role in the Gulf Crisis, visiting the region twice in August, and continuing close day-to-day contact. On September 17, he fired Air Force Chief of Staff Michael J. Dugan, for speaking out of turn about United States plans in the event of a war with Iraq.

Nebraska-born Cheney is a long-term Washington "insider," who worked in several Washington administrative positions during the 1970s, ultimately becoming a White House assistant of President Gerald Ford (1975–77). He became a Republican congressman from Wyoming in 1979, and during the 1980s became a leading House Republican. He became defense secretary in early 1989, after the John Tower nomination had been rejected in a long, bitter Senate fight. He married Lynne Anne Vincent in 1964; they have two children. His B.A. and M.A. were from the University of Wyoming, in 1965 and 1966.

FURTHER READING

"Ready for action." BRUCE W. NELAN. *Time*, Nov. 12, 1990.
"Defense at the crossroads." *American Legion Magazine*, Mar. 1990.
"Cheney, Richard Bruce." *Current Biography*, Aug. 1989.
"On the second shot, a straight arrow." *Time*, Mar. 20, 1989.

Cher (Cherilyn LaPiere Sarkisian, 1946–) In December 1990, Cher opened in the Richard Benjamin film *Mermaids,* opposite Bob Hoskins and Winona Ryder. On the musical side of her career, Cher had a road tour coinciding with her new video and album *Hearts of Stone,* with concerts scheduled from Boston to San Diego. Though her costumes, by designer Bob Mackie, have often caused controversy, in her new video she was clothed in a miniskirt and blazer, rather than skimpy straps and nets, as in the earlier "If I Could Turn Back the Time." Cher's song "Trail of Broken Tears" was also a notable part of the soundtrack for the film *Days of Thunder.* With continuing social concern, Cher spoke at the memorial for the late homeless advocate Mitch Snyder, and she performed to raise money for a homeless shelter in Atlantic City.

California-born Cher became a popular singer in the mid-1960s, and teamed with her first husband, Sonny Bono, as Sonny and Cher. On her own from the late 1970s, she emerged as a star entertainer and recording artist, and as one of the leading celebrities of the 1980s, whose every move was news. She also became known as a leading dramatic actress, whose quite notable body of work includes *Silkwood* (1983), *The Witches of Eastwick* (1987), and her Oscar-winning lead in *Moonstruck* (1987). In addition to Bono, she was formerly married to Gregg Allman, and has one child.

FURTHER READING

"Cher the unstoppable." CLIFF JAHR. *Ladies Home Journal*, Nov. 1990.
"Seeking a private place." NORA UNDERWOOD. *Maclean's*, Mar. 6, 1989.
"Playboy interview. . . ." EUGENIE ROSS-LEMING and DAVID STANDISH. *Playboy*, Dec. 1988.
"Cher struck!" BONNIE ALLEN. *Ms. Magazine*, July 1988.
"Cheers for Cher." *Ms. Magazine*, July 1988.
"Cher." JAMES GRANT. *Life*, Feb. 1988.
"Cher. . . ." HARLAN JACOBSON. *Film Comment*, Jan.–Feb. 1988.
Cher. J. RANDY TARRABORRELLI. St. Martin's, 1986.

Childs, Marquis (1903–90) In 1970, the veteran American journalist Childs won the first Pulitzer Prize for distinguished commentary. Born and educated in Iowa, he was affiliated with the *St. Louis Post-Dispatch* for most of his working life, from 1926. Reporting from Washington for decades, as the paper's chief correspondent from 1962 to 1968, Childs interviewed many of the mid-20th-century's major world leaders, making his own trenchant analyses, such as his famous prediction of political downfall for Britain's Prime Minister Anthony Eden. His syndicated column was carried in over 200 papers before his 1974 retirement, and occasional commentaries appeared until 1989. Childs also published several books, notably *Sweden: The Middle Way* (1936). (d. San Francisco; June 30, 1990.)

FURTHER READING

Obituary. *Current Biography*, Sept. 1990.
Obituary. *The Times* (of London), July 7, 1990.
Obituary. *New York Times*, July 2, 1990.

Chissanó, Joaquim Alberto (1939–) Part of the long, complex set of peace processes at work in southern Africa during 1989 and 1990 has been the first serious attempt to end the 15-year-old Mozambique civil war, between the government forces of the Mozambique Liberation Front (FRELIMO) and the insurgent forces of the Mozambique National Front (RENAMO). Since mid-1989, Mozambique President Chissanó has moved his party away from Marxism and one-party rule, toward multiparty democracy, a market-driven economy, and a peaceful reconciliation with the RENAMO insurgents. He has been much encouraged to do so by gradual withdrawal of South African support for RENAMO, beginning in 1988 and accelerated by the De Klerk government, which has repeatedly called for an end to the war in Mozambique, as part of the general settlement of hostilities in the horn of Africa. The heads of several neighboring Black frontline governments have also attempted to mediate the conflict, and U.S. President Bush, meeting with Chissanó in March 1990, declared his support for the new peace initiatives. RENAMO, in turn, has distanced itself from its Portuguese supporters, and declared its desire for peace.

In July 1990, Chissanó declared that FRELIMO would give up its one-party rule and participate in free elections. On November 3, a new democratic constitution was adopted, establishing a multiparty system and a series of democratic safeguards. Chissanó opened new negotiations with RENAMO, as hope grew for the end of the long civil war.

Chissanó has spent his whole career as a Mozambiquan revolutionary and then as a government official. He held several responsible posts in FRELIMO during the long war against the Portuguese colonizers of his country. He was foreign minister of newly independent, one-party, Marxist Mozambique from 1975 to 1986, and he succeeded Samora Machel as president in 1986. The early years of his presidency were dominated by the long civil war and the continuing Black African-White South African confrontation in southernmost Africa, which deeply affected all the peoples of the region. He is married to Marcelina Rafael Chissanó; they have four children.

FURTHER READING

"Chissanó, Joachim Alberto." *Current Biography*, Nov. 1990.

Christy, June (1925–90) Christy began her singing career as a teenager in her hometown of Decatur, Illinois. Her first hit was "Tampico," recorded with Stan Kenton's band in 1945. She went on to become a leading popular singer of the late 1940s and 1950s, touring and recording over twenty albums with Kenton and others, including her husband, tenor saxophonist Bob Cooper. One of her most popular songs was "Misty;" she was often called "the misty Miss Christy." She worked in cabaret until the mid-1980s. (d. Los Angeles, June 21, 1990.)

FURTHER READING

Obituary. *Down Beat*, Oct. 1990.
Obituary. *Variety*, June 27, 1990.
Obituary. *New York Times*, June 24, 1990.

Chung, Connie (Constance Yu-hwa Chung, 1946–) Chung stunned television watchers in mid-1990, when she announced that she would be taking what amounted to a "conception leave," cutting back on her schedule to maximize her chances of conceiving a child, at age 44. Her "Saturday Night With Connie Chung," on the Columbia Broadcasting System (CBS) from 1989, had been so successful that it was being moved into a new Monday night time slot in August 1990, renamed "Face to Face With Connie Chung." But in late July, she announced that she would be postponing the weekly series, doing only occasional specials, while she and her husband, Fox's "A Current Affair" anchor Maury Povich, take "a very aggressive approach to having a baby," recognizing that "time is running out for me when it comes to childbearing."

Though "Face to Face" was criticized by some for being overly dependent on celebrity interviews, Chung felt that the magazine format was more varied than the promotional ads sometimes indicated. Dropping the show from the lineup left CBS with a noticeable gap to fill. Meanwhile, Chung's decision, widely explored in the media, brought to the fore discussions of the biological clock ticking for many professional women in their late 30s and 40s.

Washington, D.C.-born Chung, a leading broadcast journalist and Asian-American, began her broadcasting career in 1969, as a Washington-area television reporter, and moved through a series of increasingly responsible and highly visible jobs in the next two decades, including seven years (1976–83) anchoring KNXT in Los Angeles and a series of anchor assignments with NBC from 1983 to 1989, before moving to CBS. Her B.S. was from the University of Maryland, in 1969.

FURTHER READING

"Waking up. . . ." SUSAN SCHINDEHETTE. *People*, Aug. 20, 1990.
"Chung, Connie." *Current Biography*, July 1989.
"Two hearts. . . ." KRISTIN MCMURRAN. *People*. Apr. 10, 1989.
"CBS woos NBC's Connie Chung." *Variety*, Feb. 15, 1989.

The Imperfect Mirror: Inside Stories of Television Newscasters. DANIEL PAISNER. Morrow, 1989.
"Anchors aweigh." TIM APPELO. *Savvy*, Apr. 1988.
"The prime time of. . . ." HELEN K. CHANG. *Savvy*, Feb. 1986.
"D.C. newsman. . . ." CAROL WALLACE. *People*, June 10, 1985.

Clancy, Tom (Thomas John Clancy, 1923–90) Tipperary-born Clancy and his brother Patrick began their joint careers as Shakespearean actors in Ireland after World War II. In the 1950s, Tom worked in the New York theater, and in the mid-1950s, with Patrick, began The Clancy Brothers folk-singing group. In 1956, they were joined by brother Liam Clancy and Tommy Makem, and quickly became a popular international group, a mainstay of the folk music revival of the 1960s, and a long-running worldwide hit. In the 1970s and 1980s, Tom Clancy also appeared as an actor in such television shows as "Little House on the Prairie" and "Charlie's Angels." (d. County Cork, Ireland; November 7, 1990.)

FURTHER READING

Obituary. *The Times* (of London), Nov. 15, 1990.
Obituary. *New York Times*, Nov. 8, 1990.

Clark, Dick (1929–) Clark is best-known by far as the host of television's long-running "American Bandstand." After he retired from the show in April 1989, his Dick Clark Productions continued to produce the show, but it lasted only another six months, ending in October. Clark continued to produce a wide range of other television series and individual productions, theatrical films, and concert tours, building on over three decades as a very active independent producer. He also continued to be a television host, for example, on the June 1989 Songwriters Hall of Fame 20th Anniversary show, and of such new game shows as "The Challengers." Clark received a special Grammy award from the National Academy of Recording Arts & Sciences, and he also received the American Classic award on the American Society on Composers, Authors, and Publishers (ASCAP).

Clark worked as an announcer in radio in the early 1950s, and hosted "American Bandstand" on radio before beginning his 33-year run on television as host of the show (1956–89). He attended Syracuse University, graduating in 1951. He has been married three times, most recently to Kari Wigton, and has three children.

FURTHER READING

"Dick Clark." HENRY SCHIPPER. *Rolling Stone*, Apr. 19, 1990.
"American handstand." MICHAEL BARRIER. *Nation's Business*, Oct. 1987.
"Dick Clark grows up." ADAM SNYDER. *Channels*, May 1987.
"Clark, Dick." *Current Biography*, Jan. 1987.
"American Bandstand's Dick Clark. . . ." DALMA HEYN. *McCall's*, Jan. 1987.
"Dick Clark." CHRISTOPHER P. ANDERSEN. *People*, Jan. 27, 1986.
Dick Clark's the First Twenty Five Years of Rock and Roll. MICHAEL OLSEN and BRUCE SOLOMON. Dell, 1981.

Clark, Joseph Sill Jr. (1901–90) A wealthy Philadelphia lawyer who became a Democratic reformer, Clark broke the local Republican machine and in 1951 became Philadelphia's first Democratic mayor since 1884. A newcomer to politics, he also broke with entrenched, corrupt practices. He established a merit system in city government, bringing in skilled administrators from around the country, to the considerable dismay of local Democratic machine politicians. Five years later, in 1956, running as a reformist liberal Democrat, he won a U.S. Senate seat, and served two terms, until 1968. (d. Philadelphia; January 12, 1990)

FURTHER READING

Obituary. *Current Biography*, March 1990.
"Good guy gone." *New Republic*, Feb. 12, 1990.
Obituary. *New York Times*, Jan. 16, 1990.

Clay, Andrew Dice (Andrew Silverstein, 1957–) Clay was briefly popular as a stand-up comedian in 1989 and 1990. His act was glaringly notable for the virulence of his attacks on women, homosexuals, Blacks, Hispanics,

Asians, the physically disabled, and a wide range of other victims. He became the center of a storm of controversy when various other artists refused to appear with him and publicly attacked his bigotry. The furor began in May 1990, when Nora Dunn, a member of the regular "Saturday Night Live" cast, refused to appear with him, as did guest singer Sinead O'Connor. Their reaction was shared by others, on other shows, and at the same time, such prominent comedians as Robin Williams publicly attacked Clay. He also starred in the film *The Adventures of Ford Fairlane* (1990).

Clay was an obscure stand-up comedian during the 1980s, and also appeared, billed as Andrew Clay, as a continuing character in the television series "Crime Story" (1986–88). He was formerly married.

FURTHER READING

"Critics load the dice. . . ." DANIEL WATTENBERG. *Insight*, Sept. 10, 1990.
"Andrew Dice Clay. . . ." ANDREW ABRAHAMS. *People*, May 28, 1990.
"20 questions. . . ." DAVID RENSIN. *Playboy*, Jan. 1990.
"The comedy of hate." GERRI HIRSHEY. *GQ—Gentlemen's Quarterly*, Aug. 1989.

Clifton, Nat "Sweetwater" (1925–90) Basketball player Clifton was one of the first Blacks in the National Basketball Association (NBA). Chicago-born Clifton—nicknamed for his early love of soda pop—played basketball at New Orleans's Xavier University before joining the Harlem Globetrotters. Then, from 1950 to 1957 he was a popular forward and center on the New York Knicks, being named to the NBA All-Star team for the 1956–57 season and reaching the NBA finals three times. Later a cabdriver, he was inducted into the Black Athletes Hall of Fame in 1978. (d. Chicago; August 31, 1990.)

FURTHER READING

"Nat 'Sweetwater' Clifton. . . ." *Jet,* Sept. 24, 1990.
Obituary. *New York Times*, Sep 2, 1990.
"Famous Black athletes. . . ." NORMAN O. UNGER. *Jet*, Oct. 7, 1985.

Close, Glenn (1947–) For Close, this was a year of variety. In the fall of 1990, she opened in *Reversal of Fortune*, playing the comatose Sunny von Bulow, the film's narrator, opposite Jeremy Irons as her husband Claus. In filming during the summer, she played the prairie woman of the title in the Hallmark Hall of Fame television movie *Sarah, Plain and Tall* (1991); Gertrude to Mel Gibson's title role in Franco Zeffirelli's *Hamlet* (1990); and an opera diva in Istvan Szabo's *Meeting Venus*, shooting in Budapest and Paris. In the first overseas Oscar presentations in March 1990, Close and Gibson presented the London awards. She herself was honored by the Dartmouth Film Society and Harvard University's Hasty Pudding Theatricals group, and was runner-up to Meryl Streep in *American Film* magazine's critics' poll for best actress of the 1980s. Close was also heavily involved in discussions about a sequel to her *Jagged Edge* (1985), but reportedly bowed out in the end.

Connecticut-born Close, on stage from the early 1970s, emerged as a stage and screen star in the 1980s, winning a Tony for her Broadway role in *The Real Thing* (1984), and playing leads in such films as *The World According to Garp* (1982), *The Big Chill* (1983), *The Natural* (1984), *Fatal Attraction* (1987), and *Dangerous Liaisons* (1988). She was previously married to Cabot Wade, is married to James Marlas, and has one child. Her B.A. was from the College of William and Mary, in 1974.

FURTHER READING

"Glenn gets close." CLIFF JAHR. *Ladies Home Journal*, Jan. 1991.
"She's not Meryl. . . ." CHARLES MICHENER. *Esquire*, Nov. 1989.
"Glenn Close. . . ." BONNIE ALLEN. *Ms. Magazine*, Nov. 1989.
"Glenn Close." JUDY ELLIS. *Life*, Feb. 1989.

Collins, Judy (1939–) Singer-composer Collins made a notable comeback this year. Dropped by her former recording company, Elektra, in 1984, she recorded for the small Gold Castle label, but went six years without a major studio recording contract, before releasing her new album from Columbia, *Fires of Eden*, to both high acclaim and commercial success. Unlike many of her earlier albums, *Fires of Eden* had more of Collins's own songs. Singled out for special praise was "The Blizzard," the long, narrative ballad that opens the album, about a woman in a diner waiting out a blizzard, singing about the relationship just ended and her final recognition of her own strength. In keeping with the general affirmative tone of the album, Collins established the Garden of Eden Planet Foundation, which will use part of her profits from her album and its accompanying nationwide concert tour to plant trees in deforested parts of Colorado. Collins's hit version of "Amazing Grace" (1970) was recalled in fall 1990, when the Public Broadcasting System (PBS) showed a film focusing on the history and impact of the song she helped bring to a wider audience.

Seattle-born Collins was trained as a classical pianist before turning to the guitar and folk music. Much of her work of the 1960s and 1970s, when she was most popular, reflected her civil rights and peace movement concerns of the period, although a good deal of her most highly regarded work is far more personal and nostalgic. Her first album was *A Maid of Constant Sorrow* (1961). She went on to record over 20 more albums. Among the best-known are *In My Life* (1966), *Who Knows Where the Time Goes* (1968), *Wildflowers* (1968), *Recollections* (1970), *Both Sides Now* (1971), *Judith* (1975), *Bread and Roses* (1976), *Hard Times for Lovers* (1983), *Home Again* (1984), and *Trust Your Heart* (1987). In 1987, she published *Trust Your Heart: An Autobiography*. She was formerly married, and has one child.

FURTHER READING

"Switching from singer to scribe. . . ." MICHAEL SMALL. *People*, Dec. 7, 1987.
Artists of American Folk Music: The Legends of Traditional Folk, the Stars of the Sixties, the Virtuosi of New Acoustic Music. PHIL HOOD, ed. Morrow, 1986.

Collins, Phil (1951–) In February 1990, British drummer, singer, and songwriter Collins was named best British male vocalist of the year. His recent work includes the album *. . . But Seriously* (1989), which became a major hit, and won a November 1990 Billboard award, as did Collins, as best adult contemporary artist, and for best adult contemporary single, with "Do You Remember." In November 1990, his live album *Serious Hits . . . Live!* became another hit.

London-born Collins joined the rock band Genesis in 1971, as the group's drummer, and became lead singer in 1975, recording such albums as *And Then There Were Three* (1978), *Abacab* (1981), and *Genesis* (1983). He emerged as a major rock soloist in the 1980s, starting with the album *Face Value* (1981), and going on to the album *No Jacket Required* (1985), with its Grammy-winning "Against All Odds." He starred in the film *Buster* (1988), co-writing the Grammy-winning "Two Hearts." He has been married twice, last to Jill Collins in 1984, and has three children.

FURTHER READING

Phil Collins. TOBY GOLDSTEIN. Ballantine, 1987.
"Collins, Phil." *Current Biography*, Nov. 1986.
"Phil Collins." DAVID SHEFF. *Playboy*, Oct. 1986.
The Phil Collins Story. JOHNNY WALLER. H. Leonard, 1986.
"Short, pudgy and bald. . . ." ROGER WOLMUTH. *People*, July 8, 1985.
"The different drummer." CATHLEEN MCGUIGAN. *Newsweek*, May 27, 1985.
"Phil Collins beats the odds." ROB HOERBURGER. *Rolling Stone*, May 23, 1985.
Phil Collins. PHILIP KAMIN. H. Leonard, 1985.

Collor de Mello, Fernando (1949–) Collor de Mello founded Brazil's Reconstruction Party in 1989. He was elected to the presidency as his party's candidate in December 1989, with a program that stressed the importance of encouraging private enterprise, paying Brazil's huge international debts, and cutting social welfare programs. He took office in March 1990, succeeding José Sarney Costa, and immediately set in motion a series of massive changes, including substantial new taxes, large federal job cuts and the elimination of many federal agencies, wage and partial savings accounts freezes, and the privatization of some state-owned companies. He also took some steps to try to bar prospectors from the Amazon rain forest, as part of an attempt to slow down or stop the forest's destruction. By late 1990, his economic program had developed serious problems, with continuing inflation, huge foreign debts, a slowdown in the world economy, and internal opposition all in play against him.

Collor de Mello spent the early part of his career in his family's communications companies, becoming their president in 1978. He moved into politics in 1979, as the military government-appointed mayor of Maceió, in the state of Alagoas. He was elected to the federal legislature from Alagoas in 1982, and became governor of the state in 1986. He was formerly married to Lilibeth Monteiro de Carvalho, is married to Rosane Malta, and has two children. He attended the University of Brasilia.

FURTHER READING

"Collor de Mello, Fernando Affonso." *Current Biography*, Mar. 1990.
"Putting his best foot forward. . . ." MICHAEL S. SERRILL. *Time*, Jan. 1, 1990.

Connery, Sean (Thomas Connery, 1930–) Scottish actor Connery, named 1989's "sexiest man alive" (to his evident surprise) by *People* magazine, turned 60 in 1990. He has taken to playing some fathers, as in *Indiana Jones and the Last Crusade* (1989), and even grandfathers, as in *Family Business* (1989), with "son" Dustin Hoffman and "grandson" Matthew Broderick. (Connery's own son, Jason, in a notable casting twist, starred in a 1990 TNT telefilm *The Secret Life of Ian Fleming*, as the author of the James Bond novels.)

But for the most part, Sean Connery continues his career as an ageless international star, a status honored in 1990 with the British Academy of Film and Television Arts's prestigious Silver Mask Tribute Award (the BAFTA-Shell Tribute) for his "outstanding contribution for world cinema." Connery had two major new films in 1990. In *The Hunt for Red October*, based on Tom Clancy's bestselling novel, he plays a maverick Soviet submarine commander; despite the easing of the Cold War, it was a number one box office hit for some weeks. Then, in an adaptation of the John le Carré bestseller, *The Russia House*, he plays London publisher Barley Blair, who acts as go-between for a Soviet scientist and British intelligence, with Michelle Pfeiffer as love interest. He had been scheduled to star in Tom Stoppard's film version of his *Rosencrantz and Guildenstern Are Dead*, but was forced to withdraw because of a throat condition, which turned out to be nonmalignant polyps, and since operated on; a dispute with Stoppard over the withdrawal was settled out of court. In late 1990, Connery and Christopher Lambert were in Argentina shooting *Highlander II*, a sequel to their 1986 time-traveling adventure. Connery's next project, scheduled for shooting in early 1991, is *The Stand*. In this movie, he plays a research scientist who finds a cure for cancer while working in the Amazon.

Edinburgh-born Connery was on stage and screen in small roles during the 1950s and early 1960s; he became an instant star as sex-symbol James Bond in *Dr. No* (1962), and went on to become a worldwide celebrity in six more James Bond films: *From Russia With Love*

(1963), *Goldfinger* (1964), *Thunderball* (1965), *You Only Live Twice* (1967), *Diamonds are Forever* (1971), and *Never Say Never Again* (1983). But he soon became far more than a sex symbol, showing himself to be a strong and flexible dramatic actor in such films as *A Fine Madness* (1966), *The Molly Maguires* (1970), *The Wind and the Lion* (1975), *The Man Who Would Be King* (1975), *Robin and Marian* (1976), *Cuba* (1979), *The Untouchables* (1986, winning a Best Supporting Actor Oscar), and *The Name of the Rose* (1987). He has been married twice, and has one child.

FURTHER READING

"Back in the USSR." Robert Scheer. *Premiere*, Apr. 1990.
"A man called Connery." Susan Schindehette. *People*, Dec. 18, 1989.
"Sean Connery. . . ." John Culhane. *Reader's Digest*, Aug. 1989.
"Connery. . . ." Ben Fong-Torres. *American Film*, May 1989.
Sean Connery. Michael F. Callan. Scarborough House, 1985.
Sean Connery: A Biography. Kenneth Passingham. St. Martin's, 1983.
The Films of Sean Connery. Emma Andrews. Beaufort, 1982.

Connick, Harry, Jr. (1967–) New Orleans-born jazz and pop singer, songwriter, and pianist Connick studied with James Booker, 3rd, and Ellis Marsalis (head of the Marsalis clan) in his hometown while still in high school, and at the same time received much of his practical training playing the piano in French Quarter jazz clubs. When he was eighteen, he moved to New York City, attended the Manhattan School of Music, and, with the door-opening help of Wynton Marsalis, cut his first jazz record *Harry Connick, Jr.* (1987). A year later, now 20 years old, he cut his second record *20* (1988), notably featuring the classic jazz that was to make him famous. The next year, 1989, saw his breakthrough soundtrack contributions to the film *When Harry Met Sally . . .* (1989), which brought him to large popular audiences and won a Best Male Jazz Vocal Performance Grammy in 1990. In the summer of 1990, two of his albums were released at the same time: *Lofty's Roach*

Sean Connery (below) and Harrison Ford.

Souffle and *We Are in Love*. To many in the music world, he seems like a young Sinatra, ready for the same kind of extraordinary career. Connick also made his film debut in *Memphis Belle* (1990); forthcoming is a role opposite Jodie Foster in *Little Man Tate*.

FURTHER READING

"We're just wild. . . ." Jane Marion. *TV Guide*, Nov. 17, 1990.
"Connick, Harry, Jr." *Current Biography*, Nov. 1990.
"Harry's double take." Becca Pulliam. *Down Beat*, Oct. 1990.
"When Harry met. . . ." Michael Bourne. *Down Beat*, Mar. 1990.
"The entertainer. . . ." Rob Tannenbaum. *Rolling Stone*, Mar. 23, 1989.
"Harry Connick, Jr." Leslie Gourse. *Down Beat*, Apr. 1988.
"No longer first baby. . . ." Toby Kahn. *People*, Mar. 28, 1988.

Copland, Aaron (1900–90) Best-known as the creator of the enormously popular folk ballets *Billy the Kid* (1940), *Rodeo* (1942), and *Appalachian Spring* (1944), composer and conductor Copland worked most notably with American folk, jazz, country-and-western, and popular music themes to create classical music, in these and such other works as *Fanfare for the Common Man* and the very popular *Lincoln Portrait* (both in 1942), and the *Clarinet Concerto* (written with Benny Goodman in mind, in 1948). In the 1950s, he turned toward 12-tone composition, and away from the major line of his work. Copland also wrote the scores of several films, including *Of Mice and Men* (1939), *Our Town* (1940), and his Oscar-winning score for *The Heiress* (1948). He won a 1945 Pulitzer Prize. Among his autobiographical writings are *Copland: 1900 Through 1942* (1987) and *Copland: Since 1943* (1989), both with Vivian Perlis. (d. North Tarrytown, New York; December 2, 1990)

FURTHER READING

"Aaron Copland. . . ." Katrine Ames. *Newsweek*, Dec. 17, 1990.
"'It sounded so glorious to me' . . ." Michael Walsh. *Time*, Dec. 17, 1990.
Obituary. *Variety*, Dec. 10, 1990.
"America in music." *Economist*, Dec. 8, 1990.
Obituary. *The Times* (of London), Dec. 4, 1990.
Obituary. *New York Times*, Dec. 3, 1990.
"Aaron Copland. . . ." Philip Kennicott. *Dance Magazine*, Nov. 1990.

Coppola, Francis Ford (1939–) For filmmaker Coppola, this was another year of trying to recover the greatness of the past—in this case literally, as he was making *The Godfather Part III*, the sequel to his great films of the mid-1970s. Originally scheduled for Thanksgiving release, it was postponed to Christmas, as Coppola reassembled his cast—led by Al Pacino and Diane Keaton—in Sicily and New York for two weeks of additional shooting in September, on top of the six months and $55 million already spent on the film.

Coppola, personally, and his film production company, Zoetrope, have been in financial trouble since the failure of *One from the Heart* (1982)—only in 1990 did he finally settle a $3 million lawsuit over a loan for the film—and most reviews for his portion of the three-part, three-director *New York Stories* (1989) were dreadful. But film audiences who honor Coppola at his best continued to wait impatiently for his return to form. Reaction to *The Godfather Part III* ranged from mixed to raves. Coppola also became a founding member of the Beverly Hills-based Film Foundation, dedicated to preserving films of the past.

Detroit-born Coppola is best-known by far for two films: the Oscar-winning *The Godfather* (1972; he directed and co-wrote the screenplay) and the Oscar-winning *The Godfather Part II* (1974; he directed, produced, and wrote the screenplay), for which he also won Best Director and Best Screenplay Oscars. Together, these Sicilian-American Mafia stories are one of the greatest achievements of the American cinema. Although he created many other films, including the notable *Apocalypse Now* (1979), *Peggy Sue Got Married* (1986), and *Tucker: The Man and His Dream* (1988), nothing else even came close to duplicating his massive Godfather films. He was married to Eleanor Neil, and has had three children, one of whom died in a boating accident in 1986. His B.A. was from Hofstra University, in 1958; his M.A. in cinema was from the University of California at Los Angeles, in 1968.

FURTHER READING

"Godfather III." BARBARA GRIZZUTI HARRISON. *Life*, Nov. 1990.
Coppola. PETER COWIE. Macmillan, 1990.
On the Edge: The Life and Times of Francis Coppola. MICHAEL GOODWIN and NAOMI WISE. Morrow, 1989.
"Francis Ford Coppola. . . ." JILL KEARNEY. *Mother Jones*, Sept. 1988.
"Promises to keep. . . ." ROBERT LINDSEY. *New York Times Magazine*, July 24, 1988.
Francis Ford Coppola. JEAN-PAUL CHAILLET and ELIZABETH VINCENT. St. Martin's, 1985.

Cosby, Bill (1937–) Cosby faced some challenges at the top this year. During the 1989–90 season his "The Cosby Show" was constantly battling (primarily with "Roseanne" and "Cheers") for the number one spot on the rating charts. Then as the 1990–91 season began, the upstart Fox network pitted their animated hit, "The Simpsons," directly against Cosby; its popularity and the general loss of network viewers to cable and video rentals caused Cosby's show to fall sometimes out of the top ten. All was not easy in other quarters, either. Cosby's summer movie *Ghost Dad* was both a critical and commercial failure; his new book, *Love and Marriage,* published in mid-1989, came nowhere near the success of his previous blockbusters; and his record,

Where You Lay Your Head, by "Bill Cosby and Friends," was greeted with warmth, though the praise was less for the music than for Cosby's enthusiasm for jazz.

But in the fall of 1990, *Forbes* magazine reported, Cosby regained his ranking as the top-earning entertainer in the world (over Michael Jackson), earning approximately $4 million a month, largely from "Cosby Show" reruns. And he remains one of America's most popular entertainers, seen everywhere from a television *Bill Cosby Salutes Alvin Ailey* in December 1989, to extemporaneous stints on the cowbells in a summertime Playboy Jazz Festival.

Philadelphia-born Cosby became a television star and pioneering Black performing artist in the series "I Spy" (1965–68), and went on to star in his own *The Bill Cosby Show* (1969–71), which had a second life from 1972 to 1973. He also became a leading solo comedy performer and recording artist, as well as starring in several films, including *Uptown Saturday Night* (1974), *Let's Do It Again* (1975), and *Mother, Jugs and Speed* (1976). In 1984, with his long-running family situation comedy "The Cosby Show," he became one of the leading performers in American television, and with that also a leading celebrity. He married Camille Hanks in 1964; they have five children. He attended Temple University; his M.A. and Ed.D. were from the University of Massachusetts, in 1972 and 1977.

FURTHER READING

"Cosby swings. . . ." MICHAEL BOURNE. *Down Beat*, Apr. 1990.
"Bill Cosby." BRAD DARRACH. *People*, Fall 1989.
"Bill Cosby." *People*, Summer 1989.
"Bill Cosby loves jazz! . . ." MICHAEL BOURNE. *Down Beat*, July 1988.
"'I do believe in control'. . . ." DAN GOODGAME. *Time*, Sept. 28, 1987.
"Cosby, Inc. . . ." RICHARD ZOGLIN. *Time*, Sept. 28, 1987.
"Bill Cosby. . . ." MILTON BERLE. *Redbook*, June 1987.
Cosby. RONALD L. SMITH. St. Martin's, 1987.
Bill Cosby: Family Funny Man. LARRY KETTELKAMP. Messner, 1987.
Bill Cosby: Superstar. PATRICIA S. MARTIN. Rourke, 1987.
"Cosby, Bill." *Current Biography*, Oct. 1986.
Cosby. RONALD L. SMITH. St. Martin's, 1986.
The Picture Life of Bill Cosby. BARBARA JOHNSTON ADAMS. Watts, 1986.

Costakis, George (1912–90) Costakis, a Moscow-born Greek citizen, collected and rescued thousands of early 20th-century modern art works. At first, he collected Russian antiques from the 1930s, but in 1946, he was introduced to Russian abstract art, banned by Stalin. Entranced, he sold his antiques to pay for thousands of such works, making his Moscow apartment a world-famous illegal gallery. After problems with Soviet authorities, Costakis emigrated to Greece in 1977. He was allowed to take only 20 percent of his collection; the rest went to Moscow's Tretyakov Gallery. He had worked for the Canadian Embassy from 1943 to 1977. (d. Athens, Greece; March 9, 1990.)

FURTHER READING

Obituary. *The Times* (of London), Mar. 17, 1990.
Obituary. *New York Times*, Mar. 13, 1990.
"The lost art . . ." PHILIP MONK. *Maclean's*, July 19, 1982.

Costner, Kevin (1955–) Kevin Costner's career took a dramatic turning in 1990. He not only starred in, but also directed and coproduced, a major new film, *Dances With Wolves*, an epic set in the post-Civil War West about the relationship between Costner's Lt. John Dunbar and the Sioux tribes near where he is stationed, the title being his Sioux name. Honoring the sensitivity of his portrayal, the Sioux Nation formally adopted Costner into their tribe. Despite the fact that the film is a Western (far from box office magic these days), has subtitles (30 percent of the film is in Lakota, the Sioux language, in which Costner and his crew took a crash course), and runs three hours, *Dances With Wolves* not only got strong reviews but also surprisingly large audiences, winning several Oscars, notably for Best Director and Best Picture.

In early 1990, the highly popular fantasy-drama *Field of Dreams* (1989), in which Costner played a farmer summoning up baseball greats from the past, arrived in the video rental market, immediately jumping into the top ten. Later in 1990, Costner was executive-producing a new movie, *China Moon*, starring Ed Harris, and acting in the title role in *Robin Hood: Prince of Thieves*, scheduled for summer 1991 release. He also appeared opposite Anthony Quinn in *Revenge*.

California-born Costner emerged as a film star in the mid-1980s, in *Silverado* (1985), *The Untouchables* (1987), *No Way Out* (1987), and *Bull Durham* (1988). He attended California State University. He is married to Cindy Silva; they have three children.

FURTHER READING

"Kevin Costner." FRED SCHRUERS. Rolling *Stone*, Nov. 29, 1990.
"Pack leader. . . ." MARJORIE ROSEN. *People*, Nov. 19, 1990.
"Dancing with the wolves." FRED SCHRUERS. *Premiere*, Oct. 1990.
"Costner, Kevin." *Current Biography*, June 1990.
Dances with Wolves: The Illustrated Movie Tie-In. KEVIN COSTNER and MICHAEL BLAKE. Newmarket, 1990.
"Kevin Costner. . . ." NANCY ANDERSON. *Good Housekeeping*, Aug. 1989.
"Pursuing the dream. . . ." RICHARD CORLISS. *Time*, June 26, 1989.
"Hollywood's maverick hero." JENNIFER FOOTE. *Newsweek*, Apr. 24, 1989.
"The new Gary Cooper? Yup." PETER RAINER. *New York Times Magazine*, Apr. 23, 1989.

Cousins, Norman (1915–90) Joining the *Saturday Review of Literature* in 1940, editor and writer Cousins became its chief editor in 1942, and during the next 29 years turned the magazine into a major American cultural influence, and himself into a major cultural and political figure on the American scene. After the atomic bombing of Hiroshima and Nagasaki, Cousins became deeply involved in disarmament and world government issues. He left the magazine in 1971, returned from 1973 to 1977, and then took up a second, related career, as teacher and writer, most notably on health matters, as in his last work, the bestseller *Head First: the Biology of Hope* (1989). (d. Los Angeles; November 30, 1990.)

FURTHER READING

Obituary. *New York Times*, Dec. 2, 1990.
"Norman Cousins." SARA PACHER. *New Realities*, Jan.–Feb. 1985.
Human Options: An Autobiographical Notebook. NORMAN COUSINS. Norton, 1981.

Cousteau, Jacques-Yves (1910–) The celebrated French underwater explorer, inventor, photographer, filmmaker, and writer Cousteau in the late 1980s committed himself to a long, worldwide fight against the Wellington Convention. This was an international agreement signed at Wellington, New Zealand, in June 1988, that would allow oil drilling and mining in Antarctica, barred until then by the 37-nation, 1961 Antarctic Treaty. Cousteau, who favors treating Antarctica as an international nature reserve, helped France to reverse its earlier approval of the agreement. He gained the support of Australian prime minister Bob Hawke, and in July 1990, he met with American lawmakers in Washington to urge rejection of the agreement. At 79, Cousteau still continues to explore and create, as in 1989, when he and his son, Jean-Michel, filmed a nature film series in Papua, New Guinea. Cousteau has been one of the leading marine explorers and environmentalists of the 20th century. In 1943, he was one of the inventors of the Aqualung, now called scuba gear, and from the late 1940s he tested and further developed the bathysphere, now the chief vehicle for underwater exploration. He coauthored such very influential books as *The Silent World* (1952), and *The Living Sea* (1962); the former book was the basis of his 1956 Oscar-winning documentary film. He has also made many films for television, including the tremendously popular *The World of Jacques Cousteau* (1966–68), and *The Underwater World of Jacques Cousteau* (1968–76). In 1937, he married Simone Melchior, who accompanied him on his expeditions for four decades; she died on December 2, 1990. The couple had two children. Cousteau attended the Best Naval Academy.

FURTHER READING

Jacques Cousteau: A Biography. MARGARET DAVIDSON. Scholastic, 1991.
"Cousteau. . . ." ROBERT H. BOYLE. *Sports Illustrated*, Apr. 30, 1990.
Cousteau: An Unauthorized Biography. AXEL MADSEN. Beaufort, 1987.
"Around the world. . . ." HILLARY HAUSER. *Skin Diver*, Sept. 1986.
"On assignment." *National Geographic*, Dec. 1981.

Cranston, Alan (1914–) A four-time Democratic California senator, Cranston's recent career has been dominated by charges that in 1987 he and four other senators unethically intervened with federal bank regulators on behalf of the Lincoln Savings and Loan Association of Irvine, California, controlled by Charles H. Keating, Jr. The other four senators were Dennis DeConcini, John Glenn, John McCain, and Donald W. Riegle, Jr. The group came to be known as the "Keating Five." The bank was taken over in 1989 by federal banking authorities, in a bailout carrying an estimated cost of at least $2 billion. In late November 1990, Senate Ethics Committee hearings began on the "Keating Five."

Senator Cranston, with Senators Glenn, DeConcini, and McCain met with Edwin J. Gray, then chairman of the Federal Home Loan Bank Board, in DeConcini's Washington office, on April 2, 1987. Gray charged that the senators improperly put pressure on him on behalf of Lincoln, a charge they all denied. The same senators, and also Senator Riegle, met with Gray and members of the San Francisco Federal Home Bank in DeConcini's office on April 9, 1987. Cranston received $39,000 in

direct campaign contributions from Keating and his associates; Keating also gave $850,000 to political groups founded or controlled by Cranston.

Palo Alto-born Cranston was a foreign correspondent in the late 1930s, and a real estate executive after World War II. He was California state controller from 1959 to 1967, and made his first successful run for the Senate in 1968. He was Senate Democratic whip from 1977 to 1989, is chairman of the veterans affairs committee, and is a member of the banking and foreign relations committees. In November 1990, he announced that he had prostate cancer and would therefore not seek re-election as Senate Democratic whip or 1992 re-election. Cranston attended Pomona College and the University of Mexico, receiving his B.A. from Stanford University, in 1936. He has had two children.

FURTHER READING

"Cranston wiggling." WESTON KOSOVA. *New Republic*, Mar. 19, 1990.

"Seven sorry senators. . . ." MARGARET CARLSON. *Time*, Jan. 8, 1990.

"The snit brothers. . . ." FRED BARNES. *New Republic*, Nov. 10, 1986.

Cristiani Burchard, Alfredo (1948–) Cristiani, elected president of El Salvador in March 1989, and inaugurated in June 1989, continued to pursue his country's decade-long civil war, but with little success. National Liberation Front (FMLN) guerrillas continued to control much of the countryside and selectively attack in urban areas. He began peace talks with the rebels in May 1990; these continued through early autumn, breaking down in August and bringing the threat of renewed civil war. At the same time, Cristiani tried to soften international condemnation of such acts as the military death squad murders of six Jesuit priests and two women bystanders in November 1989, with prosecutions of some of the soldiers involved. However, critics accused him of whitewashing the murderers. In another widely reported case, American religious worker Jennifer Jean Casolo was arrested in November 1989, and charged with having a rebel arsenal buried in her backyard. She was released in December, after an international campaign for her freedom.

Cristiani was an executive in his family's companies before going into politics in the early 1980s. In 1985, he became leader of the right-wing Nationalist Republican Alliance Party (ARENA), succeeding Roberto D'Aubuisson, under whose leadership ARENA had been widely accused of being implicated in the mass killings by Salvadoran death squads. Cristiani was seen as a more moderate business-interests leader, and won a clear majority of those voting in the 1989 presidential elections. The elections were boycotted by FMLN and other armed revolutionary organizations. He is married to Margarita Cristiani, and attended Georgetown University.

FURTHER READING

"At home with President Cristiani." *America*, Dec. 8, 1990.
"Cristiani, Alfredo." *Current Biography*, Jan. 1990.

Cronyn, Hume (Hume Blake, 1911–)

Canadian actor and director Cronyn won his first Emmy in 1990, as best actor in a miniseries or special, in HBO's *Age-Old Friends* (1989). Cronyn as John Cooper, and Vincent Gardenia as his friend Michael Aylott, played relatively affluent residents in a home for the elderly, showing their fear not so much of death as of lifeless life, with mental acuity slipping away. In the drama, Cooper's daughter was played by his real-life daughter, actress Tandy Cronyn.

Privately, Cronyn and his wife, actress Jessica Tandy, also had to face the questions of physical decline. In seeking to get a zoning waiver to build an apartment above the detached three-car garage at their Easton, Connecticut, home, Cronyn said his eyesight was failing and Jessica Tandy was ailing, so they needed to have live-in help. Jessica Tandy and Hume Cronyn were among 12 people to receive the National Medal of the Arts in a White House ceremony in September 1990.

Ontario-born Cronyn has been on stage professionally for 60 years, from character roles in the 1930s to leading roles from the 1950s. His long, celebrated partnership with Jessica Tandy began with their marriage in 1942. Some of their co-starring roles were in *The Fourposter* (1951), *A Delicate Balance* (1966), *The Gin Game* (1977), and *Foxfire* (1982). He won a Tony for his Polonius in *Hamlet* (1964). Cronyn made his screen debut in *Shadow of a Doubt* (1943), and went on to play strong character roles in such films as *The Seventh Cross* (1944), *Lifeboat* (1944), *Sunrise at Campobello* (1960), *The World According to Garp* (1982), and *Cocoon* (1985). He attended Ridley University, McGill University, and the New York School of Drama. He and Jessica Tandy have three children.

FURTHER READING

"Two lives, one ambition. . . ." Gerald Clarke. Time, Apr. 2, 1990.
"Happily ever after." Jeanne Marie Laskas. *Life*, Apr. 1990.
"Cronyn, Hume." *Current Biography*, June 1988.
"Jessica Tandy and. . . ." Andrea Chambers. *People*, June 2, 1986.

Cruise, Tom (Thomas Cruise Mapother IV, 1962–)

Cruise was among the top five box-office stars of the 1980s, according to *Orbit Video* magazine's end-of-the-decade survey, behind Harrison Ford, Dan Aykroyd, Eddie Murphy, and Bill Murray. Cruise's latest entry in the box-office sweepstakes was *Days of Thunder* (1990), in which he played Cole Trickle, a rookie stock car driver out to prove himself and bury his past, opposite Robert Duvall's crusty veteran. It was a new version of an old story, which received mixed reviews and came up short in audience appeal. But Cruise did work of a far more serious, wide-ranging kind in Oliver Stone's *Born on the Fourth of July* (1989), based on the autobiography of disabled Vietnam War veteran Ron Kovic. Abandoning his sex-symbol image and taking Kovic from innocent, unthinking patriotism to wheelchair-bound anti-war activism, Cruise won wide praise on all sides, including an Oscar nomination.

Born in Syracuse, New York, Cruise became very popular in the early 1980s, in such films as *Endless Love* (1981), *All the Right Moves* (1983), *Legend* (1984), *The Color of Money* (1986), and *Rain Men* (1988). He married Mimi Rogers in 1987; they separated in 1990.

FURTHER READING

"Burn a little rubber. . . ." Jeannie Park. *People*, July 23, 1990.
"What's driving. . . ." Jeanne Marie Laskas. *Life*, June 1990.
"Cruise at the crossroads." Trip Gabriel. *Rolling Stone*, Jan. 11, 1990.
"Playboy interview. . . ." Robert Scheer. *Playboy*, Jan. 1990.
Top Gun: The Films of Tom Cruise. Ed Gross. Pioneer, 1990.
"Tom terrific." Richard Corliss. Time, Dec. 25, 1989.
"A conversation with. . . ." Lynn Hirschenberg. *Rolling Stone*, Aug. 11, 1988.
Tom Cruise. Jolene Anthony. St. Martin's, 1988.

Cruzan, Nancy Beth (1957–90) On January 11, 1983, Nancy Cruzan was severely injured in an automobile accident, and from then on was hospitalized, unable to care for herself or recognize the members of her family, and from February 1983, she was fed through a tube inserted into her stomach. In 1987, her parents took legal action to have the tube removed, so that she might die, as they said she would have wished, beginning a case that became a large part of the continuing national right-to-die controversy and finally went to the Supreme Court, after the state of Missouri refused their request. In June 1990, the Supreme Court ruled for the state, also making the point that a patient who clearly indicated a request to die had the right to have life-sustaining systems turned off, although there was not enough evidence to prove that Nancy Cruzan wanted to die. The point made, the state of Missouri dropped its opposition to the Cruzans' request, although right-to-life advocates unsuccessfully took court action to force maintenance of Nancy Cruzan's life support system. The Cruzans then tried again, and on December 14, 1990, a Missouri county judge ruled that there was enough evidence to prove that Nancy Cruzan would have wanted to die. Her feeding tube was removed that day. She died with her family at her bedside. (d. Mount Vernon, Missouri; December 26, 1990.)

FURTHER READING

Obituary. *New York Times*, Dec. 27, 1990.
"Private agony. . . ." DEBORAH BEROSET DIAMOND. *Ladies Home Journal*, June 1990.
"The right to die. . . ." *America*, Jan. 27, 1990.

Crystal, Billy (1947–) Comedian, actor, and producer Crystal played to an audience of an estimated one billion plus, as host of the televised 1990 Academy Award ceremonies. He was in practice for the assignment, having hosted three annual Grammy Award shows, most recently the 1989 Grammys. In May, he co-hosted the fourth annual *Comic Relief* benefit show for the homeless. At the 1990 Academy Awards event, he did make some remarks others considered offensive, most notably his comment that the MGM/UA film studio symbol Leo the Lion will no longer roar, but will take the Fifth Amendment, now that it is owned

by an Italian company. Many responded, including 52 members of the U.S. House of Representatives, 36 of them Italian-Americans, who protested to the Academy and demanded an apology.

And Crystal won at an award ceremony, as well, winning a shared 1990 Emmy for Best Variety or Musical Show. He also won an award for funniest film actor of 1989 at the fourth annual American Comedy Awards, as did co-star Meg Ryan in the film *When Harry Met Sally . . .* (1989). Crystal also produced and starred with Bruno Kirby and Daniel Stern in the forthcoming film *City Slickers*. Crystal repeated as Academy Awards host in 1991.

New York-born Crystal worked as a comedian in cabaret in the mid-1970s, and moved into television in the long-running "Soap" (1977–81), which was followed by the short-lived "The Billy Crystal Hour" (1982). He was well-received as a continuing character in the 1984–85 season of "Saturday Night Live," and has also appeared in several telefilms. He began playing film leads in the late 1980s, in *Running Scared* (1986), *Throw Momma From the Train* (1987), and *Memories of Me* (1988). Crystal attended Nassau Community College and New York University. He is married to Janice Crystal; they have two children.

FURTHER READING

"Billy Crystal. . . ." LARKIN WARREN. *Esquire*, Dec. 1989.
"Men, women. . . ." DAVID DENICOLO. *Glamour*, Sept. 1989.
"Crystal bawls. . . ." BRUCE BUSCHEL. *GQ—Gentlemen's Quarterly*, Aug. 1989.
"Billy Crystal." MILES BELLER. *Life*, July 1989.
"Pals." ROBERT LLOYD. *American Film*, July-Aug. 1989.
"The serious side of. . . ." IRA ROBBINS. *Video Magazine*, June 1989.
"Playboy interview. . . ." DAVID RENSIN. *Playboy*, Mar. 1988.
"Crystal, Billy." *Current Biography*, Feb. 1987.
Absolutely Mahvelous. BILLY CRYSTAL and DICK SCHAAP. Putnam, 1986.

Cugat, Xavier (1900–90) From the first appearances of his band at Hollywood's Cocoanut Grove nightclub, in 1928, Barcelona-born Cuban bandleader Cugat played a major role in introducing Latin American dance music to North American audiences. He and his band became fixtures at the Cocoanut Grove and at New York's Waldorf Astoria hotel, and also appeared on records and in such films as *You Were Never Lovelier* (1942), *Stage Door Canteen* (1943), and *Weekend at the Waldorf* (1945). The young Cugat was a cartoonist before becoming a bandleader. In 1985, he published the book *Rumba Is My Life*. (d. Barcelona, Spain; October 27, 1990)

FURTHER READING

Obituary. *Variety*, Nov. 5, 1990.
Obituary. *New York Times*, Oct. 26, 1990.
"At 80. . . ." David Sheff. *People*, July 28, 1980.
"Cugat still cooking. . . ." WILL TUSHER. *Variety*, Jan. 23, 1980.

Cullen, Bill (William Lawrence Cullen, 1920–90) Veteran game show host Cullen began his long career in radio as an announcer at WWSW, Pittsburgh. He was an announcer at CBS before hosting his first radio game show, *Winner Take All,* in 1946. He began his television career as a panelist with *I've Got a Secret*, in 1952, and stayed on as host until 1967. He was host of *The Price Is Right* from 1956 to 1965. He also hosted such shows as *Name that Tune, The $25,000 Pyramid,* and *Winner Take All,* and he was a panelist on several other shows, including *To Tell the Truth.* (d. Los Angeles; July 8, 1990)

FURTHER READING

Obituary. *Current Biography*, Sept. 1990.
Obituary. Variety, July 11, 1990.
"I've got a secret!" STEWART WEINER. *Los Angeles Magazine*, May 1983.

Cummings, Robert (Charles Clarence Robert Orville Cummings, 1908–90) Although best known for his comedic work in television, in the long-running "The Bob Cummings Show" (1955–59) and "The New Bob Cummings Show" (1961–62), Cummings was also a versatile film player, who appeared in scores of Hollywood films, from the mid-1930s through the mid-1950s, as in *Three Smart Girls Grow Up* (1939), *King's Row* (1941), *The Devil and Miss Jones* (1941), and *Dial M for Murder* (1954). He won an Emmy for his television role as the key juror in *Twelve Angry Men* (1954). (d. Los Angeles; December 2, 1990.)

FURTHER READING

Obituary. *The Times* (of London), Dec. 5, 1990.
Obituary. *New York Times*, Dec. 4, 1990.

Cunliffe, Marcus Falkner (1922–90) British writer and teacher Cunliffe emerged as a major British analyst of American literature with his *The Literature of the United States* (1952), which continued on through several editions. He taught American history and a more general range of American studies at Manchester University from 1949 to 1965, and then taught at the University of Sussex before relocating to the United States. (d. Washington, D. C.; September 2, 1990.)

FURTHER READING

Obituary. *New Republic*, Oct. 1, 1990.
Obituary. *New York Times*, Sept. 5, 1990.
Obituary. *The Times* (of London), Sept. 4, 1990.

Cuomo, Mario Matthew (1932–) New York's Governor Cuomo is a leading possibility for the Democratic presidential nomination. He was re-elected governor by a substantial margin in 1990, in a race against poorly showing Republican and Conservative candidates. However, Cuomo's 53 percent of the vote was less than expected, and his strongly supported environmental bond issue was rejected by the voters, partly reflecting great concern about the state's worsening financial condition, with rising deficits and lowered state bond ratings.

A leading liberal, Cuomo has refused to modify his pro-choice views, although he is also a Catholic, who was strongly attacked throughout 1990 by some Catholic Church figures. In January, auxiliary bishop Austin Vaughan said that Cuomo "was in serious risk of going to hell" because of his pro-choice stand. On June 14, Cardinal O'Connor raised the threat of excommunication of Catholic political leaders who were pro-choice, though on June 17, O'Connor denied that he had intended the threat. Cuomo has also refused to modify his anti-death-penalty position.

New York-born Cuomo moved into politics after two decades as a practicing lawyer and law teacher. He was New York's secretary of State from 1975 to 1979, lieutenant governor from 1979 to 1982, and he became his party's candidate and then governor in 1983, after defeating New York City Mayor Ed Koch in a hotly contested primary campaign. He wrote of the gubernatorial contest in his 1984 *Diaries of Mario M. Cuomo: The Campaign for Governor*. As governor, he became a powerful Democratic Party leader. Since his keynote address to the 1984 Democratic national convention, he has been a leading contender for the American presidency, although he declined to run in 1988. Cuomo is one of the leading liberal Democrats of his time, who may one day become the first Italian-American president. He is married to the former Matilda Raffa; they have five children. His B.A. was from St. John's College, in 1953; his LL.B. was from St. John's University.

FURTHER READING

"The prose (and poetry) of. . . ." CHARLES C. MANN. *Atlantic*, Dec. 1990.

"Wanted. . . ." DOUGLAS HARBRECHT. *Business Week*, Nov. 19, 1990.

"Mario the fire god." RICHARD BROOKHISER. *National Review*, May 28, 1990.

"Message for Mario. . . ." MAGIE MAHAR. *Barron's*, Mar. 12, 1990.

"Mario the magician. . . ." JOE KLEIN. *New York*, Feb. 5, 1990.

"Can Mario run?" MARTIN SCHRAM. *Washingtonian*, Jan. 1990.

"New York's new power brokers. . . ." *Manhattan, inc*, Sept. 1989.

"The mystery of. . . ." JEFFREY SCHMALZ. *New York Times Magazine*, May 15, 1988.

Mario Cuomo: A Biography. ROBERT S. MCELVAINE. Macmillan, 1988.

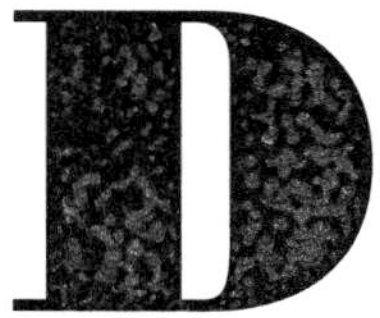

Daché, Lilly (1893–1990) French milliner Daché was probably best-known for her turbans, sometimes draped directly on the customers' heads. Emigrating to America at 16, Daché got a job with a New York City milliner, eventually buying the shop. When hats were still high-style, she became one of the country's most influential milliners, with many Hollywood stars among her customers. She retired in 1968, living alternately in Florida and France. (d. Louvecienne, France; December 31, 1989.)

FURTHER READING

Obituary. *Current Biography*, Mar. 1990.
Obituary. *New York Times*, Jan. 2, 1990.
"The legacy of. . . ." CAROLINE RENNOLDS MILBANK. *Interview*, May 1987.

Dahl, Roald (1916–90) British writer Dahl became a bestselling author with the adult short story collections *Someone Like You* (1953), and *Kiss Kiss* (1961), and an international figure with such children's books as *James and the Giant Peach* (1961), and his best-known book, *Charlie and the Chocolate Factory* (1964), which he adapted into the film *Willy Wonka and the Chocolate Factory* (1971). His many other works included the screenplays of *You Only Live Twice* (1967), and *Chitty Chitty Bang Bang* (1968). Although quite popular, his work was often criticized as much too concerned with cruelty and as attacking women, and these were especially matters of deep concern regarding his books for young children. But his most controversial moment came with his letter to *The Times* of London, attacking Salman Rushdie as the villain of the Satanic Verses affair. (d. Oxford; November 23, 1990.)

FURTHER READING

Obituary. *Variety*, Dec. 3, 1990.
Obituary. *The Times* (of London), Nov. 24, 1990.
Obituary. *New York Times*, Nov. 24, 1990.
Boy. ROALD DAHL. Viking Penguin, 1988.
Going Solo. ROALD DAHL. Farrar, Straus & Giroux, 1986; Viking Penguin, 1988.

Daly, Tyne (1947–) The star of television's "Cagney and Lacey" turned to the theater in 1989, starring on Broadway as Rose, the stage mother who successfully pushes her daughter to stardom as stripper Gypsy Rose Lee in the hit revival of the Stephen Sondheim-Jule Styne musical *Gypsy*, based on Lee's autobiography. Daly won a 1990 Tony as Best Actress in a Musical for her Rose, as had Angela Lansbury in the 1973 Broadway revival. The show also won a Tony, as best revival of a play or musical. Daly also starred in the hit 1990 cast album of the show.

Daly appeared in supporting stage and screen roles throughout the 1970s; she emerged as a television star as Mary Beth Lacey opposite Sharon Gless in the long-running "Cagney and

Lacey" (1982–88; she won Emmys in 1983, 1984, and 1988). In 1987, she starred in the film *Kids Like These*, directed by her husband, George Stanford Brown. Daughter of actor James Daly, she attended Brandeis University and the American Music and Drama Academy. Daly and Brown have three children.

FURTHER READING

"Tyne Daly. . . ." LESLIE BENNETTS. *McCall's*, Apr. 1990.

Danson, Ted (1947–) Danson, since 1982 a star of the long-running television series "Cheers," won a major award for his Sam Malone in 1990—an Emmy as Best Actor in a Comedy Series. He also played Jack Lemmon's son in the 1989 film *Dad*. In December 1990, he was on film again, this time with Tom Selleck and Steve Guttenberg as co-star of the sequel to their 1987 film comedy *Three Men and a Baby*, titled *Three Men and a Little Lady*, with Robin Weisman as five-year-old Mary.

Danson worked in the New York theater and in television in the early 1970s, beginning his film career with *The Onion Field* (1979), followed by such films as *Body Heat* (1981), *Creepshow* (1983), *Just Between Friends* (1986), *Three Men and a Baby* (1987), and *Cousins* (1989). His large body of television work includes the Emmy-winning *Something About Amelia* (1984), and the telefilm *When the Bough Breaks* (1986). Danson attended Stanford University and Carnegie-Mellon University. He has been married twice, and has two children.

FURTHER READING

"Three men and. . . ." JEFF ROVIN. *Ladies Home Journal*, Dec. 1990.
"Danson, Ted." *Current Biography*, Oct. 1990.
"Ted Danson." MERRILL SHINDLER. *Los Angeles Magazine*, Aug. 1988.
"Meet the new 'Mr. Moms.'" KATHY HENDERSON. *Redbook*, Nov. 1987.
"Ted Danson. . . ." LEAH ROZEN. *People Weekly*, May 11 1987.
"The cheers and. . . ." JUDY MARKEY. *Cosmopolitan*, Dec. 1985.

Darman, Richard Gordon (1943–) White House budget director Darman played a major role in the long budget fights that dominated relations between the Bush administration and Congress during 1989 and 1990, helping to develop such Bush proposals as the capital gains tax cut and the balanced budget amendment, and supporting a series of domestic spending cuts. After the June 26, 1990, Bush decision to raise taxes, Darman planned much of the new administration tax, deficit reduction, and budget programs, and was, with John Sununu, chief negotiator for the administration in the following talks with congressional leaders, all the way through the October conclusion of the annual crisis talks.

North Carolina-born Darman is a long-term Washington "insider," who emerged as a key figure in the 1980s, as a Reagan White House assistant from 1981 to 1985, and was deputy Treasury secretary from 1985 to 1987. He left Washington to become managing director of the Shearson Lehman Hutton investment banking firm from 1987 to 1988, and returned as Bush administration director of office management and the budget in 1989. He married Kathleen Emmet in 1967; they have two children. His B.A. and M.B.A. were from Harvard University.

FURTHER READING

"Beasts of the beltway. . . ." FRED BARNES. *New Republic*, Dec. 24, 1990.
"The newly charming budget chief." CHARLOTTE HAYS. *Insight*, June 12, 1989.

"Darman, Richard Gordon." *Current Biography*, May 1989.
"Driven to beat the budget." LAURENCE I. BARRETT. *Time*, Feb. 27, 1989.
"White House wonk. . . ." FRED BARNES. *New Republic*, Jan. 2, 1989.
"Richard Darman. . . ." LEE WALCZAK. *Business Week*, Apr. 13, 1987.

Davis, Ossie (1917–) In the fall of 1990, Davis premiered on CBS's prime-time comedy series "Evening Shade," continuing an association with Burt Reynolds that had begun in the 1989–90 season, when Davis joined the cast of "B.L. Stryker," one of four rotating private eye series on the "ABC Mystery Movie." Many observers were surprised when Davis was passed over for an Oscar nomination as best supporting actor for his role as a worldly wise observer in Spike Lee's *Do the Right Thing* (1989), which arrived on the video shelves in 1990. Privately, Davis joined the board of Kidwaves, a radio network aiming to combat illiteracy.

Georgia-born Davis has been on stage for over 50 years, as actor, writer, director, and producer, and he is one of the leading Black theater figures of his time. He is best-known for his portrayal of the Walter Lee Younger role in *A Raisin in the Sun* (1959), and for his play *Purlie Victorious* (1961), in which he also created the title role. He has also been a film director, and has acted in scores of films and telefilms, including his notable *The Emperor Jones* (1955), and *Harry and Son* (1983). He married the actress Ruby Dee in 1948. He and his wife have worked together in the theater and as social activists ever since. They have three children. Davis attended Howard University from 1935 to 1938.

FURTHER READING

"Ossie Davis and. . . ." JOYCE WANSLEY. *People Weekly*, Mar. 23, 1981.
"We've won some of the battles." ROBERT WARD. *TV Guide*, Mar. 22, 1980.

Davis, Sammy, Jr. (1925–90) The celebrated entertainer Sammy Davis, Jr., was on stage professionally with his father in the Will Mastin Troupe from the age of three, and from 1945 emerged as a star in variety with his father and Mastin in the Will Mastin Trio. On Broadway he starred in *Mr. Wonderful* (1956) and *Golden Boy* (1964), while on screen he

Ossie Davis and Ruby Dee.

appeared in such films as *Anna Lucasta* (1958), as Sportin' Life in *Porgy and Bess* (1959), and with his longtime friend Frank Sinatra in *Oceans Eleven* (1960).

He was a fully equal, Black major figure in American show business throughout his career, and in that sense a trailblazer. He also married White actress Mai Britt in 1960, in a pioneering interracial show business marriage that took much courage for both of them in those times. He was also a convert to Judaism, an entertainer whose work never reflected the 1954 loss of one eye in an automobile accident, and in sum, a man of enormous resource and vitality who ultimately was brought down by his alcohol and drug abuse addictions, and by several long illnesses. He wrote about his life and work in *Hollywood in a Suitcase* (1981), and *Why Me?: The Sammy Davis, Jr. Story* (1989), written with Jane Boyar and Burt Boyar. (d. Los Angeles; December 16, 1990.)

FURTHER READING

Obituary. *Dance Magazine*, Nov. 1990.
Obituary. *Down Beat*, Aug. 1990.
Obituary. *Current Biography*, July 1990.
"Sammy Davis Jr. . . ." Lerone Bennett, Jr. *Ebony*, July 1990.
"Sammy Davis Jr." Quincy Jones. *Rolling Stone*, June 28, 1990.
"The last vaudevillian." *New Republic*, June 11, 1990.
"A legend bows out." Victor Dwyer. *Maclean's*, May 28, 1990.
"The entertainer." Marjorie Rosen. *People Weekly*, May 28, 1990.
"Sammy Davis Jr. . . ." John Schwartz. *Newsweek*, May 28, 1990.
Obituary. Paul Gray. *Time*, May 28, 1990.
"The special ebullience. . . ." Miriam Horn. *U.S. News & World Report*, May 28, 1990.
"'Mr. Entertainment'. . . ." *Variety*, May 23, 1990.
Obituary. *The Times* (of London), May 17, 1990.
Obituary. *New York Times*, May 17, 1990.

Davison, Wild Bill (William Edward Davison, 1906–89) Cornetist Davison began his career in the early 1920s; almost seven decades later, he was still working, about to take his band on yet another European tour. After working in Chicago and Milwaukee, Davison came to New York in 1941, formed his own band, and began to record, most notably with Sidney Bechet. He worked with Eddie Condon in the mid-1940s, then in Europe, and then for many years led his own bands in California, Denmark, and back in California from the late 1970s, while always continuing to tour the world in concert and cabaret. (d. Santa Barbara, California; November 14, 1989.)

FURTHER READING

Obituary. *Down Beat*, Feb. 1990.
Obituary. *Variety*, Nov. 29, 1989.
Obituary. *The Times* (of London), Nov. 17, 1990.
Obituary. *New York Times*, Nov. 16, 1990.

Day-Lewis, Daniel (1958–) Since he burst on the screen in 1985 in *My Beautiful Laundrette,* Day-Lewis had been marked by critics and cinema lovers as an actor to watch, for both the variety and excellence of his portrayals. But in 1990, he was brought to the attention of far wider audiences when he won the Best Actor Oscar for his performance in *My Left Foot.* His character was the late Christy Brown, an Irish writer and painter so severely afflicted by cerebral palsy that he had sure control over only his left foot, with other movements, including speech, grossly difficult and uncertain. Unwilling to be a figure of pity, Brown was abrasive, corrosive, and

altogether difficult to live with, constantly fighting to be treated as a normal human being. Brown's efforts were well-conveyed by Day-Lewis, who was also named best actor by the British Academy, the National Society of Film Critics, and the New York and Los Angeles critics' circles.

Sensitized by discussions and preparatory work among people with cerebral palsy, Day-Lewis went to Washington, D.C., along with other film members and Brown's family, to support legislation to stop discrimination against people with disabilities; the film, itself, was shown to members of Congress. In 1989, Day-Lewis had starred in Richard Eyre's production of *Hamlet* at Britain's National Theatre; reviews were mixed. Day-Lewis left the production before the run ended due to illness, being replaced by Ian Charleson, in his last stage role.

Day-Lewis emerged as a leading dramatic actor in several late 1980s films, including *A Room With a View* (1985), and *The Unbearable Lightness of Being* (1988). He attended the Old Vic Theatre School. He is the son of writer Cecil Day-Lewis and actress Jill Bolcom.

FURTHER READING

"Day-Lewis, Daniel." *Current Biography*, July 1990.
"Risk taker supreme. . . ." MATTHEW GUREWITSCH. *Connoisseur*, Dec. 1989.
"Getting the skinny'. . . ." CHRISTINA DE LIAGRE. *Interview*, Apr. 1988.
Daniel Day-Lewis. . . ." DAVID HUTCHINGS. *People Weekly*, Feb. 22, 1988.
"'I bring you. . . .'" HARLAN KENNEDY. *Film Comment*, Jan.–Feb. 1988.
"Day-Lewis' brood. . . ." STEPHEN SCHAEFER. *Harper's Bazaar*, Jan. 1988.

DeConcini, Dennis (1937–) A three-time, U.S. Democratic Arizona senator, DeConcini's recent career has been dominated by charges that in 1987 he and four other senators unethically intervened with federal bank regulators on behalf of the Lincoln Savings and Loan Association of Irvine, California, controlled by Charles H. Keating, Jr. The other four senators were Alan Cranston, John Glenn, John McCain, and Donald W. Riegle, Jr.; the group came to be known as the "Keating Five." The bank was taken over in 1989 by federal banking authorities, in a bailout carrying an estimated cost of at least $2 billion.

In late November 1990, Senate Ethics Committee hearings began on the "Keating Five." Senator DeConcini, with senators Glenn, Cranston, and McCain met with Edwin J. Gray, then chairman of the Federal Home Loan Bank Board, in DeConcini's Washington office, on April 2, 1987. Gray charged that the senators improperly put pressure on him on behalf of Lincoln, a charge they all denied. The same senators, and also Senator Riegle, met with Gray and members of the San Francisco Federal Home Bank in DeConcini's office on April 9, 1987. DeConcini received $48,100 in campaign contributions from Keating and his associates; in September 1990, he said that he would return the contributions.

Tucson-born DeConcini practiced law in Tucson before going into local politics. He was a county attorney before his first election to the Senate, in 1976. He serves on several Senate committees, including the influential Appropriations and Judiciary committees. His B.A. and LL.B were from the University of Arizona, in 1959 and 1963. He married Susan Margaret Hurley in 1959; they have three children.

FURTHER READING

"Seven sorry senators. . . ." MARGARET CARLSON. *Time*, Jan. 8, 1990.

Dedijer, Vladimir (1914–90) Yugoslav political leader Dedijer, a Serb, began his career as a journalist in Belgrade in the mid-1930s, and soon moved to the left, becoming active as a Communist sympathizer. From 1936 to 1937, his family hid from the police Josef Broz, better known as Marshal Tito, who became prime minister and president of post-war Yugoslavia. Dedijer married Olga Popovic in 1937; together, he as a commissar and she as a battlefield surgeon, they fought the Germans with Tito's partisans during World War II. She died in battle; he buried her in Montenegro in 1943. After the war, he became an official in Tito's new Communist government, but defended Milovan Djilas when he was jailed for opposing Tito's dictatorship, and was then, himself, given a suspended sentence and denied a teaching post. He went into exile, teaching abroad from 1957 to 1965, and was then able to go home to teach. In the 1960s, he was chairman of the Russell Tribunal, which accused the United States of committing war crimes in Vietnam. Of Dedijer's several books, the best-known in English is *The Road to Sarajevo* (1967). His *The War Diaries of Vladimir Dedijer: From Apr. 8, 1941 to November 7, 1944* was published in 1989. (d. Rhinebeck, New York; December 1, 1990.)

FURTHER READING

Obituary. *New York Times*, Dec. 4, 1990.
Obituary. *The Times* (of London), Dec. 4, 1990.

Dee, Ruby (Ruby Ann Wallace, 1924–) Dee continued to be a major interpreter of the American Black experience, as she has been for the past five decades. Recently, she appeared on screen and television in some notable roles. In 1989, she and her husband, Ossie Davis, were the wise observers in Spike Lee's controversial 1989 film *Do the Right Thing*. In February 1990, Dee scored in a very notable tour de force, writing, narrating, and starring as Zora Neale Hurston on television's American Playhouse, in a cast that included Louis Gossett, Jr., Lynn Whitfield, and Flip Wilson. And in December 1990, she appeared in television's *Decoration Day*, creating the role of James Garner's rough-edged, co-equal housekeeper. She also won a 1990 Emmy nomination as best guest actress in a drama for an episode of "China Beach."

Cleveland-born Dee began her five-decades-long career in 1941, with the American Negro Theatre. Some of her most notable stage roles were in *Anna Lucasta* (1946); opposite Ossie Davis, whom she later married, in *Jeb* (1946); as Ruth Younger, again opposite Davis, in *Raisin in the Sun* (1959; both also appeared in the 1961 screen version); and again opposite Davis in *Purlie Victorious* (1961; both appeared in the 1963 film); and in *Boesman and Lena* (1970), *Wedding Band* (1972), and in several classic roles at the Stratford American Shakespeare Festival. Among her other films are *The Balcony* (1963), and *Buck and the Preacher* (1972). Dee has also often appeared on radio and television, perhaps most notably in the long-running radio series, the "Ossie Davis and Ruby Dee Story Hour" (1974–78), which she also coproduced. She has written a volume of poetry (*Glowchild*; 1972), and a wide range of short stories and essays. Dee's B.A. was from New York's Hunter College, in 1945. She married Davis in 1948; they have three children. (For photo, see Ossie Davis.)

FURTHER READING

"Ossie Davis and. . . ." JOYCE WANSLEY. *People Weekly*, Mar. 23, 1981.
"We've won some of the battles." ROBERT WARD. *TV Guide*, Mar. 22, 1980.

De Klerk, Frederik Willem (1936–) De Klerk became president of South Africa in September 1990. He brought with him a new spirit of reconciliation between the races, and moved to bring the long guerrilla war with the African National Congress (ANC) to an end. In October, de Klerk released eight long-term political prisoners, including Walter Sisulu of the ANC, six other ANC leaders, and Jafta Masemola of the Pan Africanist Congress. On February 2, 1990, he legalized the ANC and several other outlawed organizations, and on February 11 he freed ANC leader Nelson Mandela, opening a new chapter in South African history.

De Klerk then entered a very difficult period, with right-wing White South Africans sharply critical of his new policies, including his freeing of 48 more prominent political prisoners on June 9, while the ANC demanded further concessions as he refused to move toward majority rule. The situation was greatly complicated by the escalating civil war between the mostly Zulu Inkatha movement, led by Gatsha Buthelezi, and the ANC, which spread from Natal to other parts of the country in August. De Klerk scored a major personal victory on August 7, when the ANC agreed to a full ceasefire, bringing 30 years of guerrilla war between the South African government and the ANC to at least a temporary end. The government, in turn, agreed to free many more political prisoners, to allow many exiles to freely return home, and to relax several repressive laws. Both sides then began serious negotiations aimed at ending the system of apartheid and bringing a new kind of peaceful, multiracial order to South Africa.

De Klerk practiced law in the 1960s and early 1970s, and was elected to the national assembly in 1972. He became Transvaal leader of the ruling National Party in 1982. He held several cabinet posts from the mid-1970s, was education minister in the government of Pieter Willem Botha, and succeeded Botha as head of the National Party in February 1989. Botha resigned as president in August; De Klerk became acting president, and was named to a full five-year presidential term in September. He married Marike Willemse in 1959; they have three children. He attended Potchefstroom University.

FURTHER READING

"After apartheid. . . ." COLIN VALE and R.W. JOHNSON. *National Review,* Oct. 15, 1990.
"The authoritarian center. . . ." SANFORD J. UNGAR. *New Republic,* Oct. 1, 1990.
"The mandate for. . . ." ARNAUD DE BORCHGRAVE. *Insight,* July 2, 1990.
"A bold move. . . ." HOLGER JENSEN. *Maclean's,* Feb. 12, 1990.
"de Klerk, Frederik Willem." *Current Biography,* Feb. 1990.
"'We're committed to reform'. . . ." SPENCER REISS. *Newsweek,* Dec. 4, 1989.
"Brother against brother. . . ." SCOTT MACLEOD. *Time,* Oct. 9, 1989.
"A change of style. . . ." ANDREW BILSKI. *Maclean's,* Sept. 18, 1989.

Demy, Jacques (1931–90) French filmmaker Demy was best-known as the director of *The Umbrellas of Cherbourg* (1964), a romantic, nostalgic opera-like film musical, in which the entire dialogue was sung, rather than spoken. His work also included such films as his well-received, first feature film *Lola* (1961), *Bay of Angels* (1963), *The Young Girls of Rochefort* (1967), *The Model Shop* (1969), *Donkey Skin* (1971), *The Pied Piper* (1972), *A Slightly Pregnant Man* (1973), and *Lady Oscar* (1978). (d. Paris; October 27, 1990.)

FURTHER READING

Obituary. *Variety,* Nov. 5, 1990.
Obituary. *New York Times,* Oct. 30, 1990.
Obituary. *The Times* (of London), Oct. 30, 1990.

Deng Xiaoping (T'eng Hsiao-ping, 1904–) On November 9, 1989, Deng formally left his last major position, head of the Central Military Commission of the Chinese Communist Party. Yet he remained the real head of the Chinese government and Communist Party, as he had been since 1980. He had been known as a political and economic moderate during much of the previous 40 years of Communist power in China. Now, he was equally well-known as the political conservative who at first resisted the use of force during the student demonstrations of 1989, but then agreed to what became the Tienanmen Square massacre of June 4, 1989.

Although reportedly seriously ill, Deng made public appearances on several occasions during late 1989 and early 1990. He supported the demotion of former premier Zhao Ziyang after the 1989 student demonstrations, and the emergence of the hardline leadership of Li Peng. During 1990, he supported efforts to restore China's very badly damaged relations with the Western world, as the government freed some political prisoners, attempted to foster trade links abroad, and cultivated a moderate image in such international matters as the Persian Gulf Crisis.

Deng joined the Communist Party of China in the 1920s, while a student in France. He fought through the whole length of the Chinese Civil War, from 1927 to 1949, and is a survivor of the 1934 Long March. During Communist ascendancy, he became a major moderate leader, was purged twice, in 1973 and 1976, and survived to become the primary leader of Chinese communism. He married Cho Lin; they had five children. Deng attended the French School in Chongqing, studied in France during the 1920s, and attended Moscow's Far Eastern University.

FURTHER READING

"Rise of a perfect apparatchik. . . ." WILLIAM R. DOERNER. *Time*, July 10, 1989.
"An unlikely 'emperor.'" MARY NEMETH and LOUISE DODER. *Maclean's*, May 29, 1989.
Deng Xiaoping. ULI FRANZ. Harcourt Brace, 1988.
"Deng's policy. . . ." JOSH MARTIN. *Scholastic Update*, Sept. 18, 1987.
"Key leaders. . . ." TAMAR ROTHENBERG. *Scholastic Update*, Sept. 22, 1986.
"Beyond economic reform. . . ." MARIE GOTTSCHALK. *Nation*, Feb. 1, 1986.
"The comeback comrade." WILLIAM R. DOERNER. *Time*, Jan. 6, 1986.
"China; Deng Xiaoping leads. . . ." GEORGE J. CHURCH. *Time*, Jan. 6, 1986.
"The little man. . . ." HARRISON E. SALISBURY. *Time*, Sept. 30, 1985.

De Niro, Robert (1945–) In late 1990, De Niro added two more classic film roles to his extraordinary set of achievements. The first was his creation of Jimmy Conway in Martin Scorsese's *GoodFellas,* which was inevitably and immediately compared to his Jake La Motta role in Scorsese's *Raging Bull,* done ten years earlier. The second was his lead opposite Robin Williams in *Awakenings,* directed by Penny Marshall. By early January 1991, De Niro and Williams had already shared a National Board of Review best actor award, and De Niro had won the best actor award of the New York Film Critics Circle; later he was also nominated for a Best Actor Oscar, but lost. De Niro, whose films in the 1980s had been somewhat uneven, was once again very much on top of the cinema world. Meanwhile, he was also playing a McCarthy-era film director in *Guilty by Suspicion*, a movie released early in 1991.

New York-born De Niro became one of the leading actors of the American cinema in the mid-1970s, beginning with his strong supporting roles in *Bang the Drum Slowly* (1973), *Mean Streets* (1973), and as the young Vito

Corleone in *The Godfather Part II* (1974), for which he won a Best Supporting Actor Oscar. He went on to star in *Taxi Driver* (1976), *The Deer Hunter* (1978), and *Raging Bull* (1980), for which he won a Best Actor Oscar. His 1980s roles were in such strong, but less classic works as *Midnight Run* (1988), *We're No Angels* (1989), and *Stanley and Iris* (1989). He was previously married and has two children.

FURTHER READING

"Awake and sing." FRED SCHRUERS. *Premiere*, Jan. 1991.
"De Niro: man of few words." *Video Review*, Mar. 1989.
"Playboy interview. . . ." LAWRENCE GROBEL. *Playboy*, Jan. 1989.
"De Niro." FRED SCHRUERS. *Rolling Stone*, Aug. 25, 1988.
Robert De Niro: The Hero Behind the Mask. KEITH MCKAY. St. Martin's, 1986.

DeVito, Danny (Danny Michael DeVito, 1944–) Actor DeVito emerged as a substantial director and film star in the late 1980s. In 1989 he directed *The War of the Roses* starring Kathleen Turner and Michael Douglas as the maritally warring Barbara and Oliver Rose, with DeVito as the divorce lawyer who sets up the war. He then turned to the Norman Jewison film *Other People's Money*. Devito stars as corporate takeover financier Larry the Liquidator, opposite Penelope Ann Miller as the lawyer who opposes him.

New Jersey-born DeVito was a New York stage actor before making his main career in Hollywood. He appeared in such off-Broadway productions as *The Man With a Flower in His Mouth* (1969), and *One Flew Over the Cuckoo's Nest* (1971), re-creating his role in the 1975 film version, and went on to such films as *Car Wash* (1976), and *Goin' South* (1978). Then came his role as Louie in the long-running television series "Taxi Driver" (1978–83), for which he won a 1981 Emmy, and a move to such films as *Terms of Endearment* (1983), *Romancing the Stone* (1984), *Jewel of the Nile* (1985), and *Ruthless People* (1986). He had starring roles in *Tin Men* (1987), *Throw Momma from the Train* (1987; he also directed), and *Twins* (1988). (For photo, see Kathleen Turner.)

FURTHER READING

"Danny DeVito. . . ." MICHAEL J. BANDLER. *Ladies Home Journal*, Jan. 1990.
"Funny as hell." ROBERT SEIDENBERG. *American Film*, Sept. 1989.
"DeVito, Danny." *Current Biography*, Feb. 1988.
"DeLightful. . . ." JUDY MARKEY. *Cosmopolitan*, Jan. 1988.
"An all-round. . . ." MICHAEL REESE and LINDA BUCKLEY. *Newsweek*, Apr. 27, 1987.
"Those hips. . . ." JOHN STARK, LOIS ARMSTRONG, and JIM CALIO. *People Weekly*, July 28, 1986.
"Tinseltown's tiny terror. . . ." RICHARD CORLISS. *Time*, July 21, 1986.

Dexter, John (1925–90) British theater and opera director Dexter was the son of a Derby plumber and was, himself, a factory worker from the age 14, who discovered his dramatic talents during army service. From 1957, he worked with the Royal Court Theatre (he was reputedly the model for Webster in *Look Back in Anger,* by John Osborne, who introduced him there), becoming a key director of new British playwrights, notably Arnold Wesker and Peter Shaffer. Dexter was later associate director of Britain's National Theatre (1963–1971), and director of productions at New York's Metropolitan Opera (1974–81). Among his most acclaimed productions were *The Royal Hunt of the Sun* (1963), *Laurence Olivier's Othello* (1964), *Equus* (1973), and *M. Butterfly* (1988). The last two were Tony-winners. (d. London; March 23, 1990.)

FURTHER READING

Obituary. *Current Biography*, May 1990.
"Working radical. . . ." ROBERT MARX. *Opera News*, May 1990.
Obituary. *Variety*, Mar. 28, 1990.
Obituary. *The Times* (of London), Mar. 27, 1990.
Obituary. *New York Times*, Mar. 26, 1990.

Diana, Princess of Wales (Diana Frances Spencer, 1961–) Diana Frances Spencer married Charles, Prince of Wales, heir to the British throne, in July 1981, in a ceremony watched worldwide by hundreds of millions of viewers. Opera star and New Zealander Kiri Te Kanawa sang at their

wedding. The couple continue to be great celebrities, followed everywhere by the media, who chronicle and photograph every public and some private moves. In 1990, for example, the media gave equal, completely indiscriminate coverage to Charles's broken arm (in a polo match); ceremonial visits to Hungary, southeast Asia, and West Africa; unauthorized photos of Prince William urinating in a public park; and Diana in a modest bathing suit. Diana and Charles have two children: William Arthur Philip, born June 21, 1982; and Henry Charles Albert David, born September 15, 1984.

FURTHER READING

"Princess with a purpose." MARY H.J. FARRELL. *People Weekly*, July 16, 1990.
"Diana's double life." SUSIE PEARSON. *Ladies Home Journal*, Aug. 1989.
Princess Diana: A Book of Questions & Answers for Children. VICTORIA G. NESNICK. M. Evans, 1989.
"All in the family." *People Weekly*, Spring 1988.
"The lady who would be queen." *People Weekly*, Spring 1988.
Diana: An Intimate Portrait. INGRID SEWARD. Contemporary, 1988.
The Picture Life of Charles & Diana. HENRY RASOF. Watts, 1988.
Charles & Diana. RALPH G. MARTIN. Ivy, 1987.
Princess Diana. MARY V. FOX. Enslow, 1986.
Princess of Wales. JOSEPHINE ROSS. Trafalgar Square, 1986.

Dillon, Matt (1964–) Late in 1989, Dillon began to make the transition from teen idol to adult movie star, with his role as leader of a bunch of junkie drugstore thiefs in the black comedy *Drugstore Cowboy*. The Independent Feature Project/West Spirit Awards named Dillon best actor for his work in the film. Also released late in 1989, then shown on American Playhouse in 1990, was *Bloodhounds of Broadway*, a troubled project that had sat for years on the shelves. Based on four Damon Runyon stories, it focuses on a New Year's Eve bash in the Roaring 20s. During 1990, Dillon was filming a remake of *A Kiss Before Dying*, adapted from Ira Levin's novel; in the role originated by Robert Wagner in the 1956 version, he plays a man who marries a woman after murdering her sister.

Born in New Rochelle, New York, Dillon began his movie career as a teenager, in *Over the Edge* (1979), quickly followed by *Little Darlings* (1980), which established him as a leading teenage Hollywood star. During the 1980s, he starred in such films as *My Bodyguard* (1980), *Liar's Moon* (1982), *Tex* (1982), *The Outsiders* (1983), *Rumblefish* (1983), *The Flamingo Kid* (1984), *Native Son* (1986), and *Kansas* (1988). His younger brother is the actor Kevin Dillon.

FURTHER READING

"Mighty Matt." CARL WAYNE ARRINGTON. *Rolling Stone*, Nov. 30, 1989.
"Magnetic Matt Dillon. . . ." JEFF SILVERMAN. *Cosmopolitan*, Nov. 1985.
"Dillon, Matt." *Current Biography*, May 1985.
The Matt Dillon Scrap Book. CHERYL MEAD. St. Martin's, 1984.

Dinkins, David Norman (1927–), David Dinkins became the historic first Black mayor of New York City in 1989, after defeating incumbent Mayor Edward Koch in the 1989 Democratic mayoral primary, and defeating Republican Rudolph Giuliani in the general election. Dinkins drew votes from many ethnic groups with his soft-spoken call for racial and ethnic conciliation.

As have all of New York City's recent mayors, Dinkins found himself focusing on scores of very difficult matters during his administration, all the way from such basic

services as water supply and asbestos pollution in the schools to epidemic-sized AIDS and drug problems. As tensions between ethnic and racial groups continued to rise, he tried to be a peacemaker, without conspicuous success, in a time that included the Bensonhurst racial killing of August 1989 and the trials that followed, the April 1989 rape of the Central Park Jogger and the trials that followed, and a wave of demonstrations, boycotts, and highly publicized criminal actions that inflamed ethnic and racial relations in his city. He also faced the city's worsening economic situation, with lower tax receipts and increasing costs bringing the large tax increases and spending cuts of the May 1990 Dinkins budget and the further large tax increase projections of late 1990.

New Jersey-born Dinkins practiced law and politics in New York City from the mid-1950s. He was elected to the State Assembly in 1965 and served in several appointive posts, withdrawing from a deputy's mayor's position in 1973, at least partly because he had failed to file tax returns for several years. He was City Clerk from 1975 to 1985, and was the elected borough president of Manhattan from 1985 to 1988. He married Joyce Burrows in 1953; they have two children. He attended Howard University and Brooklyn Law School.

FURTHER READING

"Is he up to it?" Joe Klein. *New York*, Nov. 5, 1990.
"Inside Gracie Mansion. . . ." Laura B. Randolph. *Ebony*, Sept. 1990.
"Dinkins, David Norman." *Current Biography*, Mar. 1990.
"Mayor of 'The Big Apple'. . . ." D. Michael Cheers. *Ebony*, Feb. 1990.
"David Dinkins. . . ." Donald Baer. *U.S. News & World Report*, Nov. 20, 1989.
"Jackie Mason's racial remarks about Dinkins. . . ." *Jet*, Oct. 16, 1989.
"New Yorkers put faith in healer." *Insight*, Oct. 2, 1989.
"Can Dinkins do it?" *New York*, July 31, 1989.

Dixon, Sharon Pratt (1944–) Dixon appeared out of nowhere to became the first Black woman ever elected mayor of a major city. Her slogan helped—that shovels were needed to clean up city hall; mere brooms couldn't do it. So did her business experience, her no-nonsense style, and her Washington, D.C. birth, all unlike her predecessors. In the end, Sharon Pratt Dixon won 86 percent of the vote to take over the formidable job of running Washington, D.C.

As her main priorities, she stressed developing a model progressive educational system; use of government to spark rather than support, aiming to give more economic power to Blacks and Hispanics; and better integration of the local, federal, and international aspects of Washington political life. The problems she faces are formidable; the deficit is estimated at $300 million, but she is pledged neither to raise taxes nor to cut vital services; she has also vowed to cut the bloated government staff.

A third-generation Washingtonian, Dixon graduated from Howard University Law School in 1968. Three years later, after bearing two children, she joined her father's general practice law firm, handling divorce, child custody, estate cases, and incorporations. In 1972 she began teaching public interest law at the innovative Antioch Law School in Washington. From 1976, she worked at the Potomac Electric Power company as a corporate lawyer, becoming vice-president for consumer affairs. While remaining at PEPCO, she was elected D.C.'s delegate to the Democratic National Committee in 1977, and in 1984, she became the first Black and first woman to be treasurer of the Democratic National Committee. She was formerly married to Arrington L. Dixon, who served as chairman of the D.C. Council under ex-Mayor Marion Barry. They had two daughters.

FURTHER READING

"Sharon Dixon. . . ." GLORIA BORGER. *U.S. News & World Report*, Dec. 31, 1990.
"A clean sweep. . . ." WILLIAM LOWTHER. *Maclean's*, Nov. 19, 1990.
"Mayoral nominee fought against odds to win." *Jet*, Oct. 1, 1990.
"Who can beat Barry?" BARBARA MATUSOW and JOHN SANSING. *Washingtonian*, June 1990.

Doctorow, E. L. (Edgar Lawrence Doctorow, 1931–) Doctorow's Prohibition-era novel, *Billy Bathgate* (1989), was in the news as shooting for the film began in Saratoga Springs, New York, in October 1990, with Dustin Hoffman playing the central role of gangster Dutch Schultz. During the spring 1990 awards season, just as the paperback version was hitting the stands, the bestseller won the National Book Critics' Circle Award and the PEN/Faulkner Award, but just missed out on the Pulitzer Prize.

New York-born Doctorow worked in publishing in the 1960s, during the early stages of his writing career, and later held several university teaching positions. He became recognized as a major author in the 1970s, with his novels *The Book of Daniel* (1971) and *Ragtime* (1975), basis for the 1981 film. In the 1980s, he published *Loon Lake* (1980), *Lives of the Poets* (1984), and the American Book Award-winning *World's Fair* (1985). He married Helen Setzer in 1954; they have three children. His B.A. was from Kenyon College, in 1952.

FURTHER READING

"The audacious lure. . . ." ALVIN SANOFF. *U.S. News & World Report*, Mar. 6, 1989.
Writers at Work: The Paris Review Interviews. GEORGE PLIMPTON, ed. Viking Penguin, 1988.
"The myth maker." BRUCE WEBER. *New York Times Magazine*, Oct. 20, 1985.

Doe, Samuel Kanyon (1950–90) Former Liberian dictator Doe died on September 10, 1990, at the hands of the troops of Prince Johnson, during the three-way Liberian civil war that had convulsed the country since early spring. The civil war began with a small-scale National Patriotic Front insurrection led by Charles Taylor, whose force entered Liberia from the Ivory Coast in late 1989. The rebels gained strength throughout the spring and summer; by June, two rebel factions, one led by Taylor and the other by Prince Johnson, were advancing on Monrovia, the capital city. All three factions committed atrocities aimed at the tribal groups supporting the others. From August 5th to the 8th, a small U.S. Marine force evacuated an estimated 125 to 150 Western civilians, most of them Americans, after Prince Johnson had threatened to take Western hostages. Later in August, the Marines airlifted out over 1,000 more civilians from many nations. A multinational, African peacekeeping force entered Liberia on August 25, soon taking much of Monrovia; but the civil war continued. Doe was offered safe passage out of Liberia by the American military, but refused, vowing to fight to the death.

Doe had spent his entire adult life in the Liberian army, enlisting as a private in 1969 and working his way up through the ranks as far as master sergeant by 1979. He led a coup that overthrew William Tolbert in 1980; Tolbert was murdered in the presidential residence during the course of the coup. As dictator of Liberia until he was himself overthrown, Doe ran a regime quite notable for its abuses of human rights, beginning with the public executions of 13 former officials of the Tolbert government ten days after Doe took power. He ruled as military dictator from 1980 to 1985, and after the rigged presidential election of 1985, as president. He was married to Nancy B. Doe, and had four children.

FURTHER READING

"The civil war in hell." DENIS JOHNSON. *Esquire*, Dec. 1990.
"Death of a president. . . ." GUY D. GARCIA. *Time*, Sept. 24, 1990.
"Doe our dear. . . ." BILL BERKELEY. *New Republic*, Mar. 19, 1990.

Dole, Elizabeth Hanford (1936–) The new head of the American Red Cross was U.S. Secretary of Labor until October 1990. In that position, she had been one of the least visible members of the Bush cabinet, although she has for many years been one of the highest placed and best-known women in public life. She was the first Bush appointee to leave the cabinet.

North Carolina-born Dole is a long-term Washington "insider," who came to the capital as a Democrat in the late 1960s, and stayed to serve in the administrations of four Republican presidents. She was Ronald Reagan's Secretary of Transportation from 1983 to 1987, and campaigned for her husband, Senator Robert Dole, in his unsuccessful run for the 1988 Republican presidential nomination. Afterward, she was seriously discussed as a possible vice-presidential running mate for George Bush. In December 1988, she was named Secretary of Labor in the incoming Bush administration. Her B.A. was from Duke University, in 1958, her M.A. from Harvard University in 1960, and her J.D. from Harvard University, in 1965. Elizabeth Hanford married Robert Dole in 1975; together they published *Doles: Unlimited Partners* (1988).

FURTHER READING

"Labor's Elizabeth Dole." DIANE BARTLEY. *Saturday Evening Post*, May–June 1990.
"A nation at work." *American Legion Magazine*, May 1990.
"Elizabeth Dole. . . ." MAUREEN ORTH. *Glamour*, June 1988.
"Elizabeth Dole. . . ." KATIE LEISHMAN. *McCall's*, Apr. 1988.
"The ace in the Dole campaign." LESLIE PHILLIPS. *Savvy*, Jan. 1988.

Dole, Robert Joseph (1923–) Senior senator from Kansas and Republican Senate minority leader, Dole supported his party and president, after losing the notably bitter 1988 primary campaign to George Bush. But he also continued to pursue an independent course, voicing some cautions about such matters as the December 1989 Panamanian invasion and possibly premature United States military action during the Persian Gulf Crisis of late 1990; sharply criticizing Israel on several occasions; and meeting with Mikhail Gorbachev in June and September. Dole was a key figure during the long negotiations that led to the 1990 federal budget compromise.

Kansas-born Dole has spent three decades in Washington, starting with his four Congressional terms, from 1961 to 1969. A leading Republican, he has served in the Senate since 1969, and as Senate Republican leader since 1985. He was chairman of the Republican National Committee from 1971 to 1973, and he was his party's unsuccessful vice-presidential candidate in 1976. He made unsuccessful runs for the Republican presidential nomination in 1980 and 1988. His B.A. and LL.B were from Washburn Municipal University, at Topeka. Robert Dole married Elizabeth Hanford in 1975; together they published *Doles: Unlimited Partners* (1988).

FURTHER READING

"10 things. . . ." JAMES TRAUB. *Mother Jones*, June 1988.
"Dole's charm." HENDRIK HERTZBERG. *New Republic*, Mar. 7, 1988.
"Bush vs. Dole. . . ." ANN REILLY DOWD. *Fortune*, Feb. 15, 1988.
"Battling for the big prize. . . ." MICHAEL KRAMER and DONALD BAER. *U.S. News & World Report*, Jan. 25, 1988.
"'My whole life. . . .'" DAVID FROST. *U.S. News & World Report*, Jan. 11, 1988.
Bob Dole: American Political Phoenix. STANLEY G. HILTON. Contemporary, 1988.

Dos Santos, José Eduardo (1942–) As the chairman of the Popular Movement for the Liberation of Angola (MPLA) and head of the one-party Angolan government, Dos Santos continued to fight a civil war during 1989 and 1990. At the same time, he kept his country's economy barely afloat with a combination of oil revenues and continuing, though diminished, Soviet aid. The National Union for the Total Independence of Angola (UNITA), led by Jonas Savimbi and supported by United States aid, continued to fight government forces throughout the southern regions of Angola, as the brief ceasefire of June–August 1989 failed to hold. As the 1990s began, Angola had been at war—a revolution followed by a civil war—for 29 years.

Dos Santos has been an activist in the MPLA since he joined it in 1961. He went into exile that year and became president of the MPLA youth organization. From 1963 to 1970, he was educated in the Soviet Union, as a petroleum engineer and telecommunications specialist, the latter skills being used when he returned to the Angolan war of independence from the Portuguese in 1970. He became a member of the MPLA central committee in 1974, was foreign minister of the new Soviet-backed MPLA Angolan government in 1975, and held several cabinet-level posts during the next four years, as the civil war continued. After the death of President Augustinho Neto, Dos Santos became Angolan president, commander in chief, and head of the MPLA, and pursued the long civil war through the peace agreement of August 1988, which resulted in less Cuban and South African involvement, but did not end the civil war.

FURTHER READING

"Angola to pursue. . . ." *Washington Post*, June 30, 1987.

Douglas, James "Buster" (1961–) Heavyweight boxer Douglas stunned the fight world in February 1990, when he knocked out previously undefeated "Iron Mike" Tyson in the tenth round, in Tokyo. Suddenly, the unknown became the undisputed heavyweight champion of the world, with a record of 30–4–1. The media flocked to his door, hometown Columbus gave him a parade, and Buster Douglas was an instant celebrity. Hindsight indicates that it may have been too much too fast.

By autumn, Douglas was out of training, arguing with his manager, and troubled about being entangled with promoter Don King, whom he eventually paid $4 million to steer clear of him for his next fight. In October, out of condition and overweight, 246-pound Douglas went into his first title defense against the 208-pound Evander Holyfield in Las Vegas, and was knocked out in the third round. Many fight fans expressed anger that Douglas had not "bothered" to get into shape for the fight, or to put up a "proper" fight in the ring. Afterward, Douglas said he would fight again if the price was right. Don King, who still represents Tyson, ruled out a Tyson-Douglas rematch.

Ohio-born Douglas started fighting at age ten, becoming a Golden Gloves champion at the state fair. He made his professional debut in 1981, winning five straight fights before his first loss. Purses were small and he sometimes worked at other jobs. In 1987, he had a shot at the International Boxing Federation title, but gave out in the tenth round against Tony Tucker. His father and early trainer was Billy "Dynamite" Douglas, himself a former middleweight and light-heavyweight boxer; his grandfather, William, was an amateur boxer. He is married to Bertha Douglas and has one son. He attended Coffeyville Junior College, Sinclair Community College, and Mercyhurst College, on basketball scholarships.

FURTHER READING

"The fight of his life." Gary Smith. *Sports Illustrated*, Oct. 22, 1990.
"In this corner. . . ." Tony Fitzpatrick. *Playboy*, Oct. 1990.
"'I ain't no Rocky. . . .'" Davis Miller. *Sport*, July 1990.
"After a Rocky climb. . . ." Jack Friedman. *People*, Feb. 26, 1990.
"Adversity's adversary. . . ." Steve Wulf. *Sports Illustrated*, Feb. 19, 1990.

Douglas, Kirk (Issur Danielovich Demsky, 1916–) In October 1990, the American Film Institute announced that it would award its prestigious 1991 Life Achievement Award to Kirk Douglas. The 74-year-old Douglas heard the good news (from AFI trustee Steven Spielberg) while on location in southern France, filming *Welcome to Veraz* with Gerard Depardieu. Coincidentally, the date was the thirtieth anniversary of the Los Angeles premiere of *Spartacus,* directed by Stanley Kubrick, but produced by and starring Douglas. The film was in 1990 being restored—with five minutes of censored material replaced—for theatrical release in 1991. Earlier in the year, Douglas was busy giving interviews on, and signing copies of, his first novel, *Dance with the Devil,* which was published to mixed reviews.

Born "a ragman's son" in Amsterdam, New York, Douglas, the father of actor-producer Michael Douglas, has been a Hollywood star for over four decades, ever since his role in *Champion* (1949). In the peak years of his film career, he starred in *The Glass Menagerie* (1950), as van Gogh in *Lust For Life* (1956), and in such diverse films as *Gunfight at the O.K. Corral* (1957), *Paths of Glory* (1959), and *Seven Days in May* (1964). He also wrote the bestselling autobiography *The Ragman's Son* (1988). He was formerly married to Diana Dill, was married to Anne Buydens in 1954, and has four children. His B.A. was from St. Lawrence University, in 1938. He studied at the American Academy of Dramatic Arts, from 1939 to 1941.

FURTHER READING

"Douglas honored. . . ." *Variety*. Dec. 14, 1988.
"Kirk Douglas." Brad Darrach. *People*, Oct. 3, 1988.

Douglas, Michael (Michael Kirk Douglas, 1944–) New Jersey-born Douglas continued to pursue two major film careers simultaneously. As producer, he shepherded a new Columbia Pictures film, *Flatliners,* to its premiere in mid-August 1990. As an actor, he was by late 1990 filming *Shining Through,* a World War II romantic thriller with Melanie Griffith, shooting in Berlin and London. He also received the third annual Spencer Tracy award for his "instinctive, natural" acting style. The latest of the popular Michael Douglas-Kathleen Turner pairings, *The War of the Roses* (1989), a black comedy about marital strife, proved a hit in the theaters and reached the top of the video rental charts; Douglas's Japan-set *Black Rain* (1989) was also a video hit.

Son of actor Kirk Douglas, Michael Douglas first became a star in the television series "The Streets of San Francisco" (1972–75), paired with Karl Malden. Moving into films, he produced the Oscar-winning *One Flew Over the Cuckoo's Nest* (1975), and the notable nuclear-accident film *The China Syndrome* (1979); and he produced and starred in such films as *Romancing the Stone* (1984), and *Jewel of the Nile* (1985), both with Turner, and also *Fatal Attraction* (1987), and *Wall Street* (1987), winning a Best Actor Oscar and Golden Globe Award for the latter. He also acted in other films, such as *A Chorus Line* (1985). He married Diandra Mornell Luker in 1977; they have one son. His B.A. was from the University of California, in 1967.

FURTHER READING

"Business as usual." DAVID THOMSON. *Film Comment*, Jan.–Feb. 1990.
"A prince. . . ." LINDA BLANDFORD. *New York Times Magazine*, Dec. 3, 1989.
"Michael Douglas. . . ." ROSEMARIE ROBOTHAM. *Life*, Feb. 1988.
"Michael Douglas." ROBERT WALLACE. *Rolling Stone*, Nov. 5, 1987.
"The fatally attractive. . . ." TOM BURKE. *Cosmopolitan*, Oct. 1987.
"Douglas, Michael." *Current Biography*, Apr. 1987.

Drake, Fabia (Ethel McGlinchy, 1904–90) British actress Drake was probably best-known as Mabel Layton in television's "Jewel in the Crown" (1984). A stage debut at nine and professional work at ten began a 77-year-long acting career, especially notable for early Shakespearean roles (including *Twelfth Night's* Toby Belch at 13, role-reversing opposite ten-year-old Laurence Olivier's *Maria*). She retired briefly after marriage in 1938, but returned to the theater in 1946. Her widest popular success came late in television and movies, playing a series of strong-minded elderly women. (d. London; February 28, 1990.)

FURTHER READING

Obituary. *Variety*, Mar. 7, 1990.
Obituary. *The Times* (of London), Mar. 2, 1990.
Obituary. *New York Times*, Mar. 2, 1990.

Dreyfuss, Richard (Richard Stephan Dreyfuss, 1947–) Dreyfuss was as active as usual in 1990. First he made the romantic comedy, *Once Around*, in Texas; then he journeyed to Yugoslavia to take over the role of the Player King in Tom Stoppard's *Rosencrantz and Guildenstern Are Dead*, replacing Sean Connery. In late 1990 he opened in *Postcards From the Edge*, headlined by Meryl Streep and Shirley MacLaine. The film *Always* (1989), Steven Spielberg's romantic drama with Holly Hunter, overcame generally poor reviews in theatrical release to become a popular video rental. Privately, Dreyfuss continued active in social causes, and with his wife (who has lupus) was honored for work on behalf of the Lupus Foundation of America.

New York-born Dreyfuss became a leading film star of the 1970s, with his roles in *American Graffiti* (1973), *The Apprenticeship of Duddy Kravitz*, (1974), *Jaws* (1975), *Close Encounters of the Third Kind* (1977), and *The Goodbye Girl* (1977), for which he won a Best Actor Oscar. He went on to star in such films as *Whose Life Is It Anyway?* (1981), *Down and Out in Beverly Hills* (1986), and *Tin Men* (1987). He is married to Jeramie Rain (née Susan Davis); they have three children. He attended San Fernando Valley State College, from 1965 to 1967.

FURTHER READING

"Richard Dreyfuss. . . ." DIGBY DIEHL. *Cosmopolitan*, Nov. 1990.
"The Dreyfuss affair." JAMES KAPLAN. *Esquire*, Nov. 1987.
"A wise guy's resurrection. . . ." DAVID ANSEN. *Newsweek*, Aug. 10, 1987.

Duarte Fuentes, José Napoleón (1925–90) Duarte was President of El Salvador during his country's return to civilian-run democracy. Son of a San Salvador tailor, Duarte trained as a civil engineer, attending the University of Notre Dame. In 1960, he helped form a centrist political party, between the Communists and long-time military dictators. Apparently robbed of victory in a 1972 election, Duarte supported an unsuccessful military revolt and was exiled in Venezuela. In 1980, he returned by invitation to lead a joint civilian-military junta, and—though by then tainted by association with the military—won the 1984 election, serving until 1989, when he was constitutionally barred from running again. In 1986, he published *Duarte: My Story*, written with Diana Page. (d. San Salvador; February 23, 1990.)

FURTHER READING

Jose Duarte. Chelsea House, 1991.
Obituary. *Current Biography*, Apr. 1990.
"The hapless peacemaker. . . ." JILL SMOLOWE. *Time*. Mar. 5, 1990.
Obituary. *New York Times*, Feb. 24, 1990.
"Duarte's failed dream." DAVID GOLLOB. *Maclean's*, June 27, 1988.
"Duarte. . . ." DENNIS M. HANS. *National Catholic Reporter*, Mar. 7, 1986.

Dubcek, Alexander (1921–) After 20 years out in the cold, reformist Czechoslovak political leader Dubcek, head of government during the short-lived Prague Spring of 1968, emerged as one of the leaders of the new reform movement that swept away the Communist government. He began to speak out again in the spring of 1989, much to the dismay of the then-hardline Czech government, and on November 23 and 24, at massive Bratislava and Prague rallies, put his enormous prestige behind the new democratic movement. He announced his presidential candidacy on December 10, but a week later withdrew in favor of Vaclav Havel, and on December 28, 1989, the new Czech parliament unanimously elected him its chairman. On June 27, 1990, he was re-elected to the post.

Dubcek was a highly respected old-style Communist leader for much of his career. He fought in the anti-Nazi resistance during World War II, rose to head the Slovak Communist Party from 1962 to 1968, and in January 1968 became first secretary of the Czech Communist Party. From January–August 1968, he initiated a series of major democratic reforms, all abolished after the Soviet invasion of his country. He was expelled from his party in 1970. Dubcek attended Communist Party schools and Comenius University. He is married and has three children.

FURTHER READING

"'After a long darkness.'" RENEE KRAUSOVA. *World Press Review*, May 1990.
"Metamorphosis in Prague. . . ." LEONID SHINKAREV. *World Press Review*, May 1990.
Alexander Dubcek. INA NAVAZELSKIS. Chelsea House, 1989.
"Czech former prime minister. . . ." PETER HEBBLETHWAITE. *National Catholic Reporter*, Nov. 18, 1988.

Duff, Howard (1913–90) Actor Duff was widely known in his later years as the villain, Titus Semple, on television's "Flamingo Road" (from 1981). Born in Bremerton, Washington, he worked in local repertory and in the Armed Forces Radio Service, moving to Los Angeles after World War II. Early movie roles, in *Brute Force* (1947), and *The Naked City* (1948), were followed by numerous film and television leads, including several with his then-wife Ida Lupino, such as "Mr. Adams and Eve" (1957–58). Starring roles gave way to supporting roles and guest spots, until his career revived on television in the 1980s. (d. Santa Barbara, California; July 8, 1990.)

FURTHER READING

Obituary. *Variety*, July 11, 1990.
Obituary. *The Times* (of London), Jan. 11, 1990.
Obituary. *New York Times*, Jan. 10, 1990.

Dukakis, Michael Stanley (1933–) Having become a national figure as the unsuccessful 1988 Democratic candidate for the presidency, Dukakis returned to his post as governor of Massachusetts, and immediately declared that he would not seek a fourth term as governor, although leaving open the question of another run for the presidency. During his last two years as governor, he and his state ran into tremendous economic problems, as the real estate market collapsed, the banking industry suffered huge losses, the high technology companies that had provided so much of the state's prosperity encountered very hard times, the state's deficit rose, and the state's bond ratings dropped, forcing it to pay higher interest on its borrowings. His wife, Katherine "Kitty" Dukakis, also encountered serious problems, these personal, as a longstanding alcohol problem caused her to be hospitalized in November 1989.

Massachusetts-born Dukakis began his long political career while still in his 20s. He was a Massachusetts state legislator from 1962 to 1970, and governor from 1975 to 1979 and again from 1983 to 1991. He married Katherine Dukakis in 1963; they have two children. His B.A. was from Swarthmore College, in 1955; his LL.B. was from Harvard University, in 1960.

FURTHER READING

"An interview with Michael Dukakis." *Time*, Nov. 7, 1988.
"The men who would be president." ROBERT SCHEER. *Playboy*, Nov. 1988.
"The other Duke." FRED BARNES. *New Republic*, Oct. 31, 1988.
"Dukakis. . . ." STEVEN MANNING. *Scholastic Update*, Oct. 7, 1988.
"'He's pretty much a blank slate'. . . ." *Time*, Aug. 22, 1988.
"Up from Olympus. . . ." ALAN RICHMAN. *People*, July 25, 1988.
"Dukakis. . . ." LARRY MARTZ. *Newsweek*, July 25, 1988.
"A tale of two childhoods. . . ." MARGARET CARLSON. *Time*, June 20, 1988.
"Michael Dukakis up close." MARCI MCDONALD. *Maclean's*, June 6, 1988.
"The spartan. . . ." WILLIAM A. HENRY III. *Life*, June 1988.
"Michael Dukakis. . . ." *World Press Review*, May 1988.
"The tortoise. . . ." HENDRIK HERTZBERG. *New Republic*, May 16, 1988.
"Dukakis. . . ." FOX BUTTERFIELD. *New York Times Magazine*, May 8, 1988.
"A doer's. . . ." HARRISON RAINIE. *U.S. News & World Report*, Apr. 18, 1988.

Duke, David (1951–) Duke is a Louisiana politician, and a former leader of the Ku Klux Klan. Running on a White supremacist platform, he was elected as a Republican to the Louisiana legislature in 1989, although he had been denounced by the Republican Party. In 1990, he was defeated in a bid for the United States Senate by three-time, Democratic Senator J. Bennett Johnston. However, Duke received 44 percent of the total vote, and a majority of the statewide White vote, proving himself a considerable force in Louisiana politics; whether in spite of or because of his racism was a matter of dispute in Louisiana and throughout the country. Republican Party leaders, who had once again denounced Duke, were dismayed by his showing and attempted to distance themselves from his racist politics.

Duke was associated with the Ku Klux Klan from his youth. He joined the Klan while still in high school, and was active throughout the late 1960s and 1970s, becoming Grand Wizard of the Louisiana Knights of the Ku Klux Klan after the 1975 murder of his Klan leader,

James Lindsay. In the late 1970s, he moved from the raw, open bigotry that had characterized his career until then toward the more sanitized racism that marked his later political development, in an attempt to appeal to the White middle class. He continued that approach after he had officially left the Klan in 1980, then formed the National Association for the Advancement of White People. He was once married, and has two children. He attended Louisiana State University.

FURTHER READING

"Duke's duds." SIDNEY BLUMENTHAL. *New Republic*, Oct. 15, 1990.
"Read my liposuction. . . ." LAWRENCE N. POWELL. *New Republic*, Oct. 15, 1990.
"The hazards of. . . ." TOM BETHELL. *National Review*, Aug. 20, 1990.
David Duke: Evolution of a Klansman. MICHAEL ZATARAIN. Pelican, 1990.
"Hate gets a haircut. . . ." LUCIAN K. TRUSCOTT IV. *Esquire*, Nov. 1989.
"Republican racist. . . ." LARRY COHLER. *New Republic*, Sept. 18, 1989.
"Ex-KKK wizard. . . ." JASON BERRY. *National Catholic Reporter*, Feb. 17, 1989.

Dunaway, Faye (Dorothy Faye Dunaway, 1941–) Dunaway was seen in various guises in 1990. Taking greater control over her career, she produced and starred in the cable telefilms *Cold Sassy Tree,* playing Love Simpson opposite Richard Widmark in the turn-of-the-century Georgia tale, and *Silhouette,* in which she witnesses a murder and may be the next victim. For theatrical release, she also starred in the film *The Handmaid's Tale* (1990), playing an infertile wife in the anti-utopian futuristic tale based on Margaret Atwood's novel, and in Lina Wertmuller's 1991-scheduled film, *Crystal or Ash, Fire or Wind, as Long as It's Love,* vying with Nastasia Kinski for Rutger Hauer, unaware that he has AIDS. Dunaway's notable performance in *Chinatown* (1974) got wide new airing on television, with the release of Jack Nicholson's sequel, *The Two Jakes* (1990).

Florida-born, theater-trained Dunaway became a film star in 1967, with her portrayal of 1930s Midwestern outlaw Bonnie Parker in *Bonnie and Clyde*. She went on to become a leading Hollywood star, in such films as *The Thomas Crown Affair* (1968); *Network* (1976), for which she won a Best Actress Oscar; as Joan Crawford in *Mommie Dearest* (1981), a role she describes as "career suicide;" and *Barfly* (1987). On television, she appeared as revivalist preacher Aimée Semple McPherson in *The Disappearance of Aimée* (1976), and in the title role of *Evita Peron* (1982). She attended Boston University. She was formerly married to Peter Wolf, is married to Terrence O'Neill, and has one child.

FURTHER READING

"'I've been through . . .'. . . ." FRANKLIN ASHLEY. *TV Guide*, Oct. 14, 1989.
"Faye Dunaway." TINA JOHNSON. *Harper's Bazaar*, Sept. 1989.
Faye Dunaway. ALLAN HUNTER. St. Martin's, 1986.

Dunne, Irene (Irene Mary Dunne 1901–90)

One of the stars of Hollywood's Golden Age, Irene Dunne played in musical theater in the 1920s, most notably on tour in the title role in *Irene* and as Magnolia in *Show Boat.* On screen, her second film, *Cimarron* (1931), made her the star she would be throughout the 1930s and 1940s, in a wide range of musical and dramatic roles. Some of her most notable film roles were in *Back Street* (1932); in *Roberta* (1935; she sang "Smoke Gets in Your Eyes"); as Magnolia again in the classic *Show Boat* (1935), with Paul Robeson; in *Magnificent Obsession* (1935); opposite Cary Grant in *The Awful Truth* (1937), in *My Favorite Wife* (1940), and in *Penny Serenade* (1941); in the war films *A Guy Named Joe* (1943), and *The White Cliffs of Dover* (1944); in *Life With Father* (1944); and as Mama in *I Remember Mama* (1948). (d. Los Angeles; September 4, 1990.)

FURTHER READING

Obituary. *Current Biography*, Nov. 1990.
"Good night, Irene Dunne. . . ." *People*, Sept. 17, 1990.
Obituary. *Time*, Sept. 17, 1990.
"Irene Dunne. . . ." *Variety*, Sept. 10, 1990.
Obituary. *The Times* (of London), Sept. 6, 1990.
Obituary. *New York Times*, Sept. 6, 1990.
"Irene Dunne. . . ." RICHARD SCHICKEL. *Architectural Digest*, Apr. 1990.

Durenberger, David Ferdinand

(1934–) On July 25, 1990, after a year-long investigation, Minnesota Republican Senator Durenberger was denounced by the Senate for unethically taking a total of $95,000 more in speaking fees than Senate rules allowed, and for improperly accepting over $29,000 in travel expenses from the Senate. Durenberger, who had previously apologized and promised repayment, was ordered to repay $120,000 by the Senate. Several other charges were either dropped or not further pursued. Durenberger was not expelled from the Senate, however; his term runs to 1994.

Minnesota-born Durenberger became an active Republican in the early 1960s, while a practicing lawyer, and was elected to the U.S. Senate in 1978, beginning his second term in 1985. He married Gilda Beth Baran in 1971; he has 4 children. His B.A. was from St. Johns University, in 1955; his J.D. was from the University of Minnesota, in 1959.

FURTHER READING

"A senator's double life." GLORIA BORGER. *U.S. News & World Report*, June 25, 1990.
"Seven sorry senators. . . ." MARGARET CARLSON. *Time*, Jan. 8, 1990.
"Durenberger, David Ferdinand." *Current Biography*, Oct. 1988.

Durning, Charles (1923–)

Actor Durning was a powerful presence on Broadway in 1990, playing Big Daddy in the notable revival of

Tennessee Williams's *Cat on a Hot Tin Roof,* a performance that won him a Tony as Best Featured Actor in a Play. In late 1989, he created a quite different image, as Santa Claus in the telefilm *It Nearly Wasn't Christmas.* He also appeared in a cameo role in Warren Beatty's blockbusting feature takeoff on Chester Gould's comic strip, *Dick Tracy* (1990). Then in fall 1990, Durning joined Burt Reynolds in the cast of CBS's prime-time comedy series, "Evening Shade," as Doc Harlan Elldridge, family physician in the small Arkansas town.

Durning has been a strong character actor for over 30 years, creating a wide range of notable roles on stage, on television, and on screen. In the theater he memorably played the governor in *Best Little Whorehouse in Texas,* and on film he was unforgettable as Jessica Lange's father and Dustin Hoffman's would-be suitor in *Tootsie* (1982). Among his other films are *The Sting* (1973), *Mass Appeal* (1984), *The Rosary Murders* (1987), and *Far North* (1988). He married Mary Ann Amelio in 1974. He was born in Highland Falls, New York, and attended New York University and Columbia University.

FURTHER READING

"Playing a fiery big daddy. . . ." TOBY KAHN. *People,* June 4, 1990.

Durrell, Lawrence (Lawrence George Durrell, 1912–90) India-born, British writer Durrell was a novelist, poet, playwright, and essayist, but is best-known by far for his major work, the four novels of *The Alexandria Quartet: Justine* (1957), *Balthazar* (1958), *Mountolive* (1958), and *Clea* (1960). Earlier, he had written several novels; one of them, the *The Black Book* (1938), was sexually frank for its time, and was therefore seen as sophisticated, helping his career. He also wrote several books set in the Mediterranean, including *Prospero's Cell* (1945), *Reflections on a Marine Venus* (1953), and *Bitter Lemons* (1957). His later novels included *Tunc* (1968), and *Livia* (1978). His *Collected Poems* were published in 1980. (d. Sommières, France; November 7, 1990.)

FURTHER READING

Obituary. *New York Times*, Nov. 9, 1990.
Obituary. *The Times* (of London), Nov. 9, 1990.
Lawrence Durrell. JOHN A. WEIGEL. G. K. Hall, 1989.
"Laurence Durrell." ANDREW HARVEY and MARK MATOUSEK. *Interview*, Mar. 1988.
Lawrence Durrell. ALAN W. FRIEDMAN, ed. G. K. Hall, 1987.

Dürrenmatt, Friedrich (1921–90) The Swiss writer Dürrenmatt, who wrote in German, was best-known to English-language audiences for his play *The Visit* (1956), which was a major success on Broadway, with Alfred Lunt and Lynne Fontanne in the leading roles. His works also include the plays *Fools Are Passing Through* (1952), and *The Physicists* (1964); the screenplay for *End of the Game* (1970); and several detective novels. He also wrote for radio, and did several adaptations of classic plays. (d. Neuchâtel, Switzerland; December 14, 1990.)

FURTHER READING

Obituary. *New York Times*, Dec. 15, 1990.
Obituary. *The Times* (of London), Dec. 15, 1990.

Duvall, Robert (1931–) In mid-1990, Duvall premiered playing the crusty crew chief to Tom Cruise's rookie stock car racer in *Days of Thunder.* He also appeared in *The Handmaid's Tale,* playing the high-powered husband of an infertile wife (Faye Dunaway), in the anti-utopian tale adapted from Margaret Atwood's novel. But he declined to reprise his Oscar-nominated role as Tom Hagen, the consigliere, in Francis Ford Coppola's *The Godfather Part III,* charging that the producers were too "cheap," and that "two or three actors" were paid more than he was offered. By contrast, he noted Cruise's Christmas gift to him of a $25,000 jumping horse.

San Diego-born Duvall was recognized as a powerful supporting actor in such films as *To Kill a Mockingbird* (1963), *True Grit* (1969), *M*A*S*H* (1970), the first two *Godfather* films (1972, 1974), *Network* (1976), and *Apocalypse Now* (1979). He went on to win a Best Actor

Oscar for his lead in *Tender Mercies* (1983), while continuing to play strong supporting roles. On television, he played Dwight D. Eisenhower in the miniseries "Ike" (1979). He is married to Gail Youngs, and is a graduate of Principia College.

FURTHER READING

Robert Duvall: Hollywood Maverick. Judith Slawson. St. Martin's, 1985.
"Robert Duvall. . . ." Robert F. Jones. *People*, Apr. 23, 1984.
"The secret stardom. . . ." William Wolf. *New York*, Oct. 12, 1981.
"Robert Duvall. . . ." Lynde McCormick. *American Film*, Sept. 1981.

Dylan, Bob (Robert Alan Zimmerman, 1941–) For many music-lovers this year, the watchword was "Dylan's back." Following release of his critically acclaimed new album, *Oh Mercy,* in late 1989, Dylan kicked off an international tour at New Haven, Connecticut in January; moved on to Paris, where he was named a Commander of the Order of Arts and Letters; later was featured at a huge Brazilian rock festival; and by mid-summer was back in the United States, giving some small-scale concerts in the upper Midwest. Late in 1990, he unveiled a new album, *Under the Red Sky,* to even more praise. Dylan also continued active in the Traveling Wilburys, a group hailed in the 1989 American Music Awards as the Best New Artist, even though formed of several "grey eminences" of rock, including George Harrison, Tom Petty, Jeff Lynne, and Roy Orbison. After Orbison's death, the durability and resonance of Dylan's early songs was proved once again at the Orbison tribute in February 1990, televised to aid the homeless, when numerous luminaries—including Dylan himself—broke into an impromptu version of his "Hey! Mr. Tambourine Man." In late 1990, the remaining four issued a new record, *Traveling Wilburys, Volume 3* (actually their second volume). Less successful was Dylan's portrait of a washed-up rock star in the film *Hearts of Fire* (1989).

Duluth-born Dylan was one of the leading countercultural figures of the early 1960s, an enormously popular folk-rock singer and composer known to millions for many of his own songs, such as "The Times They Are A-Changin" (1963), and "Blowin' in the Wind." (1963). Later in the 1960s, and through the 1970s and 1980s, he was much more a rock than a folk-rock musician. Although he continued to be a very popular figure in concert and on records, his impact was greatest in the early years, when he burst upon the scene as a 1960s emblem of protest. He attended the University of Minnesota, in 1960.

FURTHER READING

"Bob Dylan. . . ." *Life*, Fall 1990.
Dylan: A Biography. Bob Spitz. McGraw-Hill, 1989.
Death of a Rebel. Marc Eliot. Watts, 1989.
"The house of the rising son. . . ." Joanne Kaufman. *People*, Oct. 17, 1988.
"Bob Dylan." Kurt Loder. *Rolling Stone*, Nov. 5, 1987.
"Positively Dylan." Mikal Gilmore. *Rolling Stone*, July 17, 1986.
No Direction Home: The Life & Music of Bob Dylan. Robert Shelton. Morrow, 1986.
Written in My Soul: Rock's Great Songwriters. . . Talk about Creating Their Music. Bill Flanagan. Contemporary, 1986.

E

Eastwood, Clint (1930–) In 1990, Eastwood gained considerable attention as director and star of a new movie, *White Hunter, Black Heart,* a tale roughly based on the making of *The African Queen* (1990), centering on an obsessive John Huston-like director, played by Eastwood, himself. The film premiered at Cannes, before going into general release. He also directed and starred in the police drama *The Rookie*, which opened in late 1990. As a change of pace, Eastwood joined country music star Randy Travis on a new record. The former mayor of Carmel, California (1986–88) also continued his involvement in his community. Late in 1989, he helped raise over $300,000 for Monterey-area victims of the recent earthquake. Privately, Eastwood filed a $20-million lawsuit, charging a supermarket tabloid, *The Globe*, with fabricating stories about extremists threatening to kill him. He had earlier won a libel lawsuit against a British tabloid.

San Francisco-born Eastwood was a star in television as the lead in the western series "Rawhide" (1958–65). He pursued the same western themes in the Italian-made Sergio Leone "spaghetti westerns" that made him a worldwide star, beginning with *A Fistful of Dollars* (1967). He then went on to become one of the most durable of all international action film stars, and beginning with *Play Misty For Me* (1971), he also directed and produced many of his films, such as *Honkytonk Man* (1982), and *Bird* (1988), about jazz great Charlie Parker. He attended Los Angeles City College. He is divorced and has one son, Kyle, who appeared in *Honkytonk Man*.

FURTHER READING

"The man who would be Huston." GRAHAM FULLER. *Interview*, Oct. 1990.
"Clint Eastwood. . . ." *Film Quarterly*, Spring, 1989.
"Eastwood, Clint." *Current Biography*, Mar. 1989.
"Bird land. . . ." STANLEY CROUCH. *New Republic*, Feb. 27, 1989.
"Flight of fancy. . . ." NAT HENTOFF. *American Film*, Sept. 1988.
The Films of Clint Eastwood. BORIS ZMIJEWSKY and LEE PFEIFFER. Carol, 1988.
Clint Eastwood. JEFFREY RYDER. Dell, 1987.
Clint Eastwood. FRANCOIS GUERIF. St. Martin's, 1986.
Screen Greats: Clint Eastwood. ALAN FRANK. Bookthrift, 1982.
The Man with No Name: A Biography of Clint Eastwood. IAIN JOHNSTONE. Morrow, 1981.

Edwards, Douglas (1917–90) Broadcaster Edwards was network television's first anchorman. Oklahoma-born, he moved to Alabama in his teens, debuting as "junior" announcer for a makeshift radio station in 1932. He attended universities in the South and worked at several radio stations, before joining the Columbia Broadcasting System (CBS) in 1942. Edwards worked on radio with Edward R. Murrow in London late in World War II, and again covering the 1948 presidential election, before CBS made him anchor on television's first evening news program. One of the earliest television reporters to work on location, Edwards helped establish television as a key source of news. He continued with CBS until 1988. (d. Sarasota, Florida; October 13, 1990.)

FURTHER READING

Obituary. *Variety*, Oct. 22, 1990.
Obituary. *New York Times*, Oct. 14, 1990.
"Edwards, Douglas." *Current Biography*, Aug. 1988.

Elizabeth II (Elizabeth Alexandra Mary, 1926–) Queen of the United Kingdom of Great Britain and Northern Ireland, and a constitutional monarch with little direct political power, she and the monarchy remain a massive symbol of continuity for her country. Still officially the Canadian Queen, she agreed—in a rare exercise of political intervention—to a request from Prime Minister Mulroney, and added eight new appointive seats to the Canadian Senate on September 27, 1990, so that Mulroney's government would have the votes to pass a highly controversial national sales tax. In an almost equally rare airing of domestic discord, the separation of her daughter, Princess Anne, and her husband, Mark Phillips, was announced in late 1989.

Elizabeth II was the daughter of George VI and Elizabeth Angela Marguerite, the Queen Mother. She succeeded her father to the throne in 1952. She married Philip Mountbatten in 1947, and is the mother of Prince Charles (1948–), Princess Anne (1956–), Prince Andrew (1960–), and Prince Edward (1964–). In 1952, she became head of the British Commonwealth.

FURTHER READING

Royal Sisters. ANNE EDWARDS. Morrow, 1990.
"Europe's reigning queens." PETER DRAGADZE and CATHERINE CALVERT. *Town & Country Monthly*, Apr. 1988.
"The world's ten most important women." *Ladies Home Journal*, Nov. 1987.
"Shrewd managers of regal riches." TERENCE PARE. *Fortune*, Oct. 12, 1987.
The Queen: The Life of Elizabeth II. ELIZABETH LONGFORD. Ballantine, 1984

Endara, Guillermo (1936–) Endara, the candidate of the Authentic Liberal Party, won the Panamanian presidential elections of May 7, 1989, by a wide margin, a fact verified by an international observers' team led by former United States President Jimmy Carter, who accused the Panamanian government of election fraud. Endara's margin was so wide that on May 10th Panamanian dictator Manuel Noriega annulled the election. That day, government thugs beat and hospitalized Endara and his running mates, Ricardo Arias Calderon and Guillermo (Billy) Ford. On November 20, 1989, the day that U.S. forces invaded Panama, Endara was installed as the U.S.-backed president of Panama. Widespread problems continued, and to dramatize his concern over the country's poor economic conditions and his call for more American aid, Endara even took the unusual step of conducting a 13-day public fast.

Endara, a lawyer, was an aide to former Panamanian president Arnulfo Arias Madrid. He practiced law in Panama from 1963 to 1988, and was not directly involved in Panamanian politics until he became the opposition candidate in 1988. He attended the University of Panama and New York University.

FURTHER READING

"After Noriega. . . ." MARK A. UHLIG. *New York Times*, Nov. 3, 1990
"Fat man's burden. . . ." CHRISTOPHER DICKEY. *New Republic*, Aug. 20, 1990.
"To many in Panama. . . ." DAVID E. PITT. *New York Times*, Jan. 28, 1990.
"Panama's new chief. . . ." DAVID E. PITT. *New York Times*, Jan. 18, 1990.
"Panama opposition chief. . . ." JOSEPH B. TREASTER. *New York Times*, Oct. 7, 1989.

Enriquez, Rene (1932–90) Nicaraguan-American actor Enriquez was best-known for his portrayal of Lt. Ray Calletano, second-in-command on television's "Hill Street Blues" (1981–87). Born in Granada, Nicaragua, nephew of a former president, Emiliano Chamorro, Enriquez attended college in San Francisco and served in the U.S. Air Force during the Korean War. He came to acting only in 1958, working in New York's Lincoln Center

Repertory Company, and then playing guest spots on television and supporting roles in several films, notably *Harry and Tonto* (1974), and *Under Fire* (1983), as President Somoza of Nicaragua. (d. Tarzana, California; March 23, 1990.)

FURTHER READING

Obituary. *Variety*, Apr. 4, 1990.
Obituary. *The Times* (of London), Mar. 31, 1990.
Obituary. *New York Times*, Mar. 28, 1990.
"There's discrimination, but. . . . "' RICHARD TURNER. *TV Guide*, Mar. 16, 1985.

Erté (Romain de Tirtoff, 1892–1990) St. Petersburg-born Erté emigrated to Paris in 1912, became a fashion and costume designer before World War I, and during the interwar period was one of the world's leading stage and costume designers, doing sets and costumes most notably for the Folies Bergère, Casino de Paris, Bal Tabarin, several British theaters, George White's *Scandals*, and the *Ziegfeld Follies*. From 1915 to 1937, he also designed hundreds of covers for *Harper's Bazaar* and other fashionable magazines. He also designed for the opera and ballet. He was "rediscovered" in the mid-1960s, and enjoyed great celebrity and reception as a major artist for the balance of his long life and career, continuing to work well into the 1980s. (d. Paris; April 21, 1990.)

FURTHER READING

"Romain de Tirtoff." *Dance Magazine*, Oct. 1990.
"Grand designs." JOHN MCLAUGHLIN. *Harper's Bazaar*, July 1990.
Obituary. *Current Biography*, June 1990.
Obituary. *Variety*, Apr. 25, 1990.
Obituary. *The Times* (of London), Apr. 23, 1990.
Obituary. *New York Times*, Apr. 22, 1990.
Erté: My Life—My Art. ERTÉ. New American Library-Dutton, 1989.

Ewing, Patrick (1962–) Ewing is one of the leading centers in modern basketball,

which became apparent while he was still a college player at Georgetown University. After his 1985 graduation from Georgetown, Jamaica-born Ewing joined the New York Knicks, beginning a career that would in the next five years take him to five all-star games (1986, 1987, 1988, 1989, and 1990; he was a starting center in the 1990 all-star game), and international celebrity, although a national championship for his team has not yet come—and that has in 1990 and 1991 been a matter of considerable, sometimes public distress on his part. The Knicks came from behind to defeat the Boston Celtics in the 1989–90 season playoffs, but were defeated in the second round by the Detroit Pistons, who went on to win the championship. Ewing has one child.

FURTHER READING

"Patrick Ewing." SPIKE LEE. *Interview*, May 1990.
Patrick Ewing. MATTHEW NEWMAN. Crestwood House, 1989.
"Jordan, Ewing. . . ." MARK VANCIL. *Sporting News*, Dec. 8, 1986.
"Patrick Ewing. . . ." WALTER LEAVY. *Ebony*, Feb. 1986.
"Patrick Ewing says. . . ." BOB PHILLIPS. *Scholastic Choices*, Jan. 1986.

Fabrizi, Aldo (1905–90) Rome-born Italian actor Fabrizi was best-known as Don Pietro, the Fascist-defying priest tortured and executed in Roberto Rossellini's *Open City* (1945). He started in music hall comedy in the 1930s, playing character roles in films from the 1940s. From 1949 through the 1950s, he also worked as a director and sometime screenwriter, but later mostly played character roles. A gourmet, Fabrizi wrote several cookbooks, with recipes in verse. (d. Rome; April 2, 1990)

FURTHER READING

Obituary. *Variety*, Apr. 11, 1990.
Obituary. *The Times* (of London), Apr. 4, 1990.
Obituary. *New York Times*, Apr. 3, 1990.

Fahd, Ibn Abdul al-Aziz (1923–) As the background to what was to become the Persian Gulf Crisis developed, and as Saddam Hussein flexed his muscles and toughened his public statements after coming out ahead in the long Iran-Iraq War, the Saudi Arabian king attempted to seek peaceful solutions to the growing conflicts in the area. In March 1990, he warmly greeted Saddam Hussein's visit to Saudi Arabia, and in the spring he moved toward more normal relations with Iran. In July, as Iraq's demands on Kuwait grew more urgent, he joined Egyptian President Mubarak in trying to mediate, encouraging Iraqi-Kuwaiti peace talks at Jiddah, in Saudi Arabia. But after Iraq's August 2 invasion of Kuwait, and facing Iraqi armed forces on the Saudi-Kuwait border, he reacted sharply, inviting American troops into Saudi Arabia on August 6, and from then on opening his country to and joining in the huge military buildup that followed, and actively participating in the Gulf War.

Riyadh-born Fahd is the son of King Abdul al-Aziz Ibn Saud. He succeeded to the throne in 1982, after the death of his half-brother Khalid. He had previously been a member of the Saudi delegation to the San Francisco founding meeting of the United Nations in 1945, education minister in 1953, interior minister from 1962 to 1975, and a deputy prime minister from 1962 to 1982. He became prime minister as well as king in 1982. He had been named Crown Prince in 1975, after the assassination of King Faisal.

FURTHER READING

"Lifting the veil. . . ." LISA BEYER. *Time*, Sept. 24, 1990.
"An exquisite balancing act. . . ." GEORGE J. CHURCH. *Time*, Sept. 24, 1990.
"All this and harems too. . . ." ALAN FARNHAM. *Fortune*, Oct. 12, 1987.
King Fahd and Saudi Arabia's Great Evolution. NASSER I. RASHID and ESBER I. SHAHEEN. International Institute of Technology, 1987.

Fain, Sammy (Samuel Feinberg, 1902–89) New York City-born Fain worked as a pianist early in his career and moved into songwriting in the mid-1920s. His first hit was "Nobody Knows What a Red-Headed Mama Can Do" (1925; with long-time collaborator Irving Kahal). Although he wrote such songs as "I'll Be Seeing You" (1938), and "I Can Dream, Can't I" (1938), for the Broadway musical theater, he became best-known for his work in film, which included such songs as his two Oscar-winners, "Secret Love" (from *Calamity Jane*, 1953), and "Love Is a Many-Splendored Thing" (the title song of the 1955 film). (d. Los Angeles; December 6, 1989)

FURTHER READING

Obituary. *Variety*, Dec. 13, 1989.
Obituary. *The Times* (of London), Dec. 8, 1989.
Obituary. *New York Times*, Dec. 7, 1989.

Faldo, Nick (1957–) After over a decade as a professional, the British golfer gained recognition as one of the world's leading golfers in the late 1980s, his wins including the 1987 British Open, the 1988 French Open, the 1989 Masters, the French Open again in 1989, and a second British Open in 1990. He had been somewhat underrated in the earlier years, as he had come from behind to win several of his major tournaments; but his July 1990 British Open set all doubts about him aside, for the win was by five strokes, and with a record-setting eighteen strokes under par.

Faldo became a leading junior British golfer in the mid-1970s, and turned professional in 1976. He was voted best new British golfer of the year in 1977, and went on to build a solid, unspectacular career, as he developed his game, to emerge as a major figure a decade later. He attended the University of Houston. He is married, and has two children.

FURTHER READING

"Britannia rules again. . . ." SARAH BALLARD. *Sports Illustrated*, July 10, 1989.
Golf: Tours & Detours. LAWRENCE LEVY and BRIAN MORGAN. Salem House, 1988.

Falk, Peter (1927–) Actor Falk was on screen in 1990 in yet another of his quirky roles, as a flamboyant 1950s soap opera writer hired to revive the flagging fortunes of a New Orleans radio station, in *Tune In Tomorrow*. The film, based on the Mario Vargas Llosa novel *Aunt Julia and the Scriptwriter*, was the favorite of audiences at the annual American film festival in Deauville, France. On television, Falk continued to appear periodically in the role for which he is best-known by far: the rumpled, raincoat-wearing, cigar-smoking, seemingly naive, actually crafty, and enormously popular detective, Columbo. In September 1990, his portrayal won him an Emmy for Best Actor in a Drama Series—28 years after his first Emmy for his performance in the "Price of Tomatoes" episode (replayed on late night television this year) on the old "Dick Powell Show." Falk's 1989 film, *Cookie,* found some modest success in the video rental market in 1990.

New York-born Falk won a Tony for his role in *The Prisoner of Second Avenue* (1971), and has appeared in many other plays and films, including the films *A Woman Under the Influence* (1976), *Murder by Death* (1976), *The Brink's Job* (1978), and *The In-Laws* (1979). But in public acclaim, no other role matches that of the detective series "Columbo" (1971–78), which was revived as part of "ABC Mystery Movies" series in 1988. Falk lost his right eye during surgery for a malignant tumor at the age of three. He was formerly married to Alyce Mayo, with whom he had two daughters, and later married Shera Danese. His B.A. was from the New School of Social Research, in 1951; his M.P.A. from Syracuse University, in 1953.

FURTHER READING

The Columbo Phile: A Casebook. MARK DAWIDZIAK. Mysterious Press, 1989.

Farrell, Charles (1901–90) A long-time movie and television star, Massachusetts-born Farrell was a struggling film actor until cast opposite Janet Gaynor in the silent film *Seventh Heaven* (1927). A popular cinema pair, Farrell and Gaynor moved into talkies together, making 11 more pictures by 1934. Farrell's career then waned and, after Navy service in World War II, he focused on running a resort hotel in Palm Springs, California, of which he was mayor from 1947 to 1955. His career revived in the 1950s with his television roles as the father on "My Little Margie" and as himself in "The Charlie Farrell Show." (d. Palm Springs, California; May 6, 1990)

FURTHER READING

Obituary. *New York Times*, May 12, 1990.

Farrow, Mia (Mia Villiers Farrow, 1945–) For nearly a year rumors flew—as they always do—about Woody Allen's new movie. As usual, the normally reclusive writer-director would say nothing about his work in progress, though it was known that Mia Farrow was among those in the cast. Then in late 1990, photos began to appear in the newspapers of a quirky, rather mischievous Farrow, head topped by a prim little hat; only later were words added to announce the new film, *Alice*, with Farrow in the title role, as the upper Manhattanite who learns there's a whole new world she doesn't know. The film and Farrow's performance in particular, among the usual large ensemble, were widely praised as among the best work ever done by Farrow—or Allen.

Los Angeles-born Farrow became a star in television in the mid-1960s, from 1964 to 1966 as Alison Mackenzie in "Peyton Place." On screen, she became a star in *Rosemary's Baby* (1968), went on to such films as *John and Mary* (1969), *The Great Gatsby* (1973), *Death on the Nile* (1978), *Zelig* (1983), *Broadway Danny Rose* (1984), *Hannah and Her Sisters* (1986), *Radio Days* (1987), and *Crimes and Misdemeanors* (1989). She also appeared in several leading stage roles in Britain during the mid-1970s, as a member of the Royal Shakespeare Company. The daughter of actress Maureen O'Sullivan and director John Farrow, she has been married twice, to Frank Sinatra and André Previn. Woody Allen is her longtime companion. She has nine children, five of them adopted Vietnamese.

FURTHER READING

Mia Farrow: Flower Child, Madonna, Muse. SAM RUBIN and RICHARD TAYLOR. St. Martin's, 1989.

Fauci, Anthony Stephen (1940–) For his work on AIDS, and his role in furthering public understanding and worldwide concentration on combatting the epidemic, Dr. Fauci is widely regarded as one of the world's great doctors and public health figures. One of his most recent accomplishments has been to lead in the establishment of the AIDS Clinical Trials Group, a group of federally-funded drug testing centers aiming to test new AIDS-fighting drugs. Dr. Fauci was one of the first to fully recognize and enter the fight against AIDS. He continues to lead that fight.

Brooklyn-born Fauci joined the National Institutes of Health in 1968, and in the following two decades rose to become deputy clinical director of the National Institute of Allergy and Infectious Diseases (1977–80), chief of that institute's immunoregulation laboratory from 1980, director of that institute from 1984, and director of the National Institutes of Health office of AIDS research in 1988. He is married to Christine Grady; they have two children. His B.A. was from Holy Cross, in 1962; his M.D. was from Cornell in 1966.

FURTHER READING

"Fauci, Anthony Stephen." *Current Biography*, Aug. 1988.

Faulk, John Henry (1914–90) Texas-born Faulk was an American humorist, who made a notable fight against blacklisting in the McCarthy era. He was a Will-Rogers-style country storyteller, discovered at a party in 1949 by CBS executives. With his own network radio show, "Johnny's Front Porch," and frequent television appearances, he had a promising career going, but was abruptly fired in 1957, after openly opposing the blacklist in 1955 and subsequently being listed in a pamphlet of Aware Inc., a self-appointed group purporting to identify Communist-oriented entertainment figures. With attorney Louis Nizer, Faulk sued Aware and won a landmark $3.5 million judgment in 1962 (collecting only $75,000), but his career never fully revived. He described his ordeal in his book *Fear on Trial* (revised edition, 1983), dramatized on CBS in 1975. (d. Austin, Texas; April 9, 1990)

FURTHER READING

"Johnny's fight." MOLLY IVINS. *Mother Jones*, July–Aug. 1990.
"Friend of freedom." ERWIN KNOLL. *Progressive*, June 1990.
Obituary. *Variety*, Apr. 18, 1990.
Obituary. *The Times* (of London), Apr. 12, 1990.
Obituary. *New York Times*, Apr. 11, 1990.
The Uncensored John Henry Faulk. Pacesetter Press, 1985.

Feinstein, Dianne (1933–) Former San Francisco mayor Feinstein emerged as a national political figure in 1990, with an unsuccessful gubernatorial run against Republican Senator Pete Wilson. In June, she won the Democratic nomination, defeating State Attorney General John Van de Kamp and nine other minor contenders, running as a centrist and feminist who supported the death penalty, favored abortion rights, and favored what many California Democrats saw as only modest environmental goals. In winning, she became an historic figure in her state, as the first woman to win a major party nomination for governor. In the autumn general election, running on the same platform, she appealed to moderate and independent voters, but not enough to defeat Wilson. Although defeated, she remained a major figure in California politics, and in national Democratic politics, as well; some spoke of her as a potential vice-presidential nominee in 1992.

San Francisco-born Feinstein was a long-term member of her city's Board of Supervisors (1970–79). She was president of the Board of Supervisors on November 27, 1978, when Dan White murdered San Francisco Mayor George Moscone and supervisor Harvey Milk, succeeded Moscone as acting mayor, and was then elected mayor (1979–88). As mayor, she became one of the most influential and highly visible women in American politics. She has been married three times, most recently to Richard Blum in 1980, and has one child. Her B.S. was from Stanford University, in 1955.

FURTHER READING

"Coastal dumping." MORTON KONDRACKE. *New Republic*, Nov. 12, 1990.
"Dianne Feinstein." J.D. REED. *People Weekly*, Oct. 8, 1990.
"A woman of. . . ." SIDNEY BLUMENTHAL. *New Republic*, Aug. 13, 1990.
"Charm is only. . . ." JORDAN BONFANTE. *Time*, June 18, 1990.
"Snow White's. . . ." DONALD BAER. *U.S. News & World Report*, June 18, 1990.
Careers for Women in Politics. RICHARD S. LEE and MARY P. LEE. Rosen, 1989.
"Feinstein's lost horizons." *Savvy*, Apr. 1988.

Fellini, Federico (1920–) A new film by Italian director and screenwriter Fellini is an event in the world of film: His *The Voice of the Moon* premiered on May 18, 1990, at the Cannes Film Festival. It was, almost predictably, a fantasy, this one a gentle, eccentric fable involving a man who hears voices and follows his heart, and about a silver slipper. The film was shown out of competition, and did not seek prizes. Fellini, however, was awarded a special prize for lifetime achievement. On June 21, he was also one of those who received a $100,000 Japanese-funded Praemium Imperiale award.

Fellini, one of the greatest film directors of the century, began his long career as co-screenwriter of Roberto Rossellini's two post-World War II classics, *Open City* (1945), and *Paisan* (1946). He moved into directing, though continuing to write all his screenplays, with *Variety Lights* (1950), which starred his wife Giulietta Masina; she also starred in his Oscar-winning classics *La Strada* (1954), and *The Nights of Cabiria* (1957), and the equally classic *Juliet of the Spirits* (1965). A few of his other major works are *La Dolce Vita* (1960), *8½* (1963), *Amarcord* (1974), *City of Women* (1979), and *And the Ship Sails On* (1984). Fellini and Masina married in 1943.

FURTHER READING

"Fellini talks about his latest opus." DEBORAH YOUNG. *Variety*, May 1989.
Comments on Film. FEDERICO FELLINI. CSU Press, Fresno, 1988.
The Films of Federico Fellini. CLAUDIO G. FAVA and ALDO VIGANO. Carol, 1988.
Fellini: A Life. HOLLIS ALPERT. Paragon House, 1987.
"Fellini's nostalgic antidote." PETER NICHOLS. *World Press Review*, Feb. 1986.
"And his ship sails on." GIDEON BACHMANN. *Film Comment*, May–June 1985.

Figueres Ferrer, José (1906–90) Spanish-born Figueres was one of the leading Costa Rican and Caribbean political leaders of the century. A democratic socialist, he went into opposition to President Rafael Calderón in 1942, and in 1948 led a successful Costa Rican revolution, serving as interim president until 1949. He then founded the National Liberation Party, and was twice the elected president of Costa Rica (1953–58 and 1970–74). His party, also the party of Oscar Arias Sanchez, continues to be a major force in Costa Rican and Caribbean politics. (d. June 8, 1990.)

FURTHER READING

Obituary. *The Times* (of London), June 12, 1990.
Nobel Costa Rica. SETH ROLBEIN. St. Martin's, 1988.
War and Peace in Central America: Reality & Illusion. FRANK MCNEIL. Macmillan, 1988.
Don Pepe: A Political Biography of Jose Figueres of Costa Rica. CHARLES D. AMERINGER. University of New Mexico Press, 1979.

Finley, Karen (1956–) In August 1990, American performance artist Finley became the center of a national storm and debate. Accused of "obscenity," she, Holly Hughes, John Fleck and Tim Miller were denied National Endowment for the Arts (NEA) grants. In canceling the grants, NEA chairman John Frohnmayer overruled the recommendations of an NEA panel. Some pointed out that at the time the NEA was under conservative attack in Congress, led by Senator Jesse Helms, and was in danger of being terminated. The majority of those in the arts, however, were outraged, and mounted a determined attack on what they saw as Frohnmayer's censorship.

Finley and Hughes had previously received NEA grants, Finley twice. The four artists took legal action and lost, as the storm mounted, as other grants were denied on similar grounds, and as the NEA instituted what amounted to a "non-obscenity oath," which caused Joseph

Papp and others to refuse offered NEA grants. On November 5, 1990, after NEA funding had been approved by Congress, without "anti-obscenity" provisions, the national council of the NEA overwhelmingly approved grants for Finley and Hughes; Frohnmayer did not oppose the grants.

As has often been so, the publicity and the anti-censorship cause greatly helped Finley's public recognition and career. Previously, she had been a well-regarded, rather moral figure, a feminist best-known for developing shocking stage images to portray what she sees as the appalling abuse of women. She deals by choice with such matters as incest, rape, other forms of sexual abuse directed at women and children, alcoholism, and the social effects of the AIDS epidemic, usually presented in strongly sexual and violent images and words. Now, Finley had become a national figure, who was interviewed everywhere as a serious artist. In the autumn of 1990, she went on a very well-attended, national tour with her controversial "We Keep Our Victims Ready" program, in which, among other things, she strips to the waist, smears chocolate on her breasts, and does a monologue about the experience of rape. She has also published her first book, *Shock Treatment* (1990).

Finley, who grew up in Chicago and Evanston, Illinois, attended the Art Institute of Chicago and the San Francisco Art Institute. She was formerly married.

FURTHER READING

"Blood and chocolate. . . ." LUC SANTE. *New Republic*, Oct. 15, 1990.
"Karen Finley. . . ." RICHARD SCHECHNER. *Drama Review*, Spring 1988.

Finney, Albert (1936–) Finney arrived on screen in 1990 in *Miller's Crossing*, produced by the Coen Brothers, the film that opened the 1990 New York Film Festival. Finney plays the Irish-born boss of the deeply corrupt Big Town, U.S.A., with Gabriel Byrne as his adviser and Jon Polito as his rival, in cheeky, not-always-successful homage to the 1920s gangster movies. On television, Finney was seen as a British M16 agent opposite George Segal as his CIA counterpart, in Showtime's labyrinthine spy movie *The Endless Game* (1990).

On the London stage, Finney in 1990 appeared with Janet Suzman, Sara Kestelman, and others in *Another Time*, by Ronald Harwood, author of *The Dresser* (Finney had starred in the 1983 film). In the unusually constructed play, set in South Africa and then in London 35 years later, the stage revolves, showing the same scene from different adjoining rooms, with events in each only momentarily audible in the other. Finney, himself, played a father, and later his own son, in a highly acclaimed performance, commended for

Karen Finley.

being part of a high-level ensemble performance, not a star turn. In July 1990, he was one of a large group of players performing Roger Waters's *The Wall* in the shadow of the Berlin Wall at Potsdamerplatz.

Born in Lancashire, Finney has been a major figure in the British theater for 30 years, from his appearance as *Billy Liar* (1960). He went on to star in such plays as *Luther* (1961), *A Day in the Death of Joe Egg* (1967), *Krapp's Last Tape* (1973), and in a wide range of classic works, including his National Theater *Macbeth* (1978). At the same time, he became a film star, as *Tom Jones* (1963), as Hercule Poiret in *Murder on the Orient Express* (1974), and in such films as *Gumshoe* (1972), *Annie* (1982), *Under the Volcano* (1984), and *Orphans* (1987). He has been married to Jane Wenham and Anouk Aimée, and has one child. He attended the Royal Academy of Dramatic Art.

FURTHER READING

"'The opportunity. . . .'" ALVIN SANOFF. *U.S. News & World Report*, Dec. 14, 1987.

Fisher, Carrie (Carrie Frances Fisher, 1956–) Actress and writer Fisher, the daughter of stars Debbie Reynolds and Eddie Fisher, adapted her semi-autobiographical 1987 novel, *Postcards From the Edge,* into the hit 1990 film, with Shirley MacLaine and Meryl Streep playing Hollywood mother and daughter. In 1990, she also had another best-selling novel, *Surrender the Pink*, which she was adapting for film. Fisher is also a leading actress, who added a starring role opposite John Sessions in television's *Sweet Revenge* (1990) to her earlier screen credits.

Los Angeles-born Fisher played her first starring role as Princess Leia in *Star Wars* (1977), and its sequels, *The Empire Strikes Back* (1980), and *Return of the Jedi* (1983). Her films also include *Hannah and Her Sisters* (1986), and *When Harry Met Sally. . .* (1989). She attended London's Central School of Speech and Drama. Fisher was briefly married to singer and songwriter Paul Simon (1983–84).

FURTHER READING

"A spy in her own house. . . ." CARL WAYNE ARRINGTON. *Time*, Oct. 15, 1990.
"Postcards from the top." JOANNE KAUFMAN. *Ladies Home Journal,* Sept. 1990.
"Straight up with a twist." TIM APPELO. *Savvy Woman*, Sept. 1990.
"Carrie Fisher." LISA LIEBMANN. *Interview*, Sept. 1990.
"A bookworm blossoms." STACY TITLE. *Premiere*, Aug. 1989.
"Foxy, fast-talking Carrie Fisher." MICHAEL SEGELL. *Cosmopolitan*, Apr. 1989.

Fitzwater, Marlin (Max Marlin Fitzwater, 1942–) White House press secretary Fitzwater has become a very familiar face on the television screen, informing, explaining, and discussing Bush administration viewpoints on the full range of national concerns. Kansas-born Fitzwater is a long-term Washington "insider," a writer and public relations professional who worked for the Department of Transportation, the Environmental Protection Administration, and the Treasury before becoming deputy press secretary to the president in the mid-1980s. He was press secretary to Vice-President George Bush from 1985 to 1987, became President Ronald Reagan's press secretary in 1987, and stayed on in the White House as press secretary to President Bush. He has four children. His B.S. is from Kansas State University, in 1965.

FURTHER READING

"Fitzwater, Max Marlin." *Current Biography*, May 1988.

Flexner, Stuart Berg (1928–90) Lexicographer and writer Flexner created several major works on American English. Early in his career, he coauthored the classic *Dictionary of American Slang* (1960; with Harold Wentworth). He wrote the very well-received works *I Hear America Talking* (1976), and *Listening to America* (1982), and collaborated on *The Oxford American Dictionary* (1980). As a leading editor in his field, he was a senior editor of the first unabridged *Random House Dictionary of the English Language* (1966), and editor-in-chief of the second edition of that work, published in 1987. (d. Greenwich, Connecticut; December 3, 1990.)

FURTHER READING

Obituary. *New York Times*, Dec. 5, 1990.
"From 'gadzooks' to 'nice'. . . ." *U.S. News & World Report*, Feb. 18, 1985.

Foley, Thomas Stephen (1929–) Democratic majority leader of the House of Representatives, Foley was elected 49th Speaker of the House on June 6, 1989, replacing James C. Wright, who had resigned while facing charges of ethics violations. As Speaker, he has been a major spokesperson for his party, opposing such domestic measures as proposed Social Security and social welfare budget cuts and playing a major role in defeating the anti-flag-burning constitutional amendment proposal, while urging new taxes and an attack on the huge budget deficit. At the same time, he has taken a generally middle-of-the-road position in international affairs, as in supporting the December 1989 Panamanian invasion, calling in the spring of 1990 for only moderate defense budget cuts, and generally supporting the early portion of the U.S. buildup in the Persian Gulf Crisis, while opposing the resolution authorizing President Bush to take the United States into the Gulf War.

Spokane-born Foley practiced law and was Washington State assistant attorney-general before going to Washington, D.C., as a lawyer in 1961. A liberal Democrat, he entered the House in 1965, and in 25 uninterrupted years, he rose to become chairman of the House Democratic Caucus in 1976, majority whip in 1981, and majority leader in 1987. He married Heather Strachan in 1968. His B.A. and LL.B. were from the University of Washington, in 1951 and 1957.

FURTHER READING

"Foley's law." MICHAEL ORESKES. *New York Times Magazine*, Nov. 11, 1990.
"Foley, Thomas Stephen." *Current Biography*, Sept. 1989.
"The rise of the accidental Speaker. . . ." GLORIA BORGER. *U.S. News & World Report*, June 5, 1989.
"Foley is taking his time. . . ." BILL WHALEN. *Insight*, May 1, 1989.

Fonda, Jane (1937–) Fonda starred, and was deeply involved, in two recent movies of good intentions but failed execution. In what turned out to be Martin Ritt's last movie, Fonda starred with Robert De Niro in *Stanley & Iris* (1990), a blue-collar love story in which she learns he is illiterate and sets out to change that. For *Old Gringo* (1989), Gregory Peck (playing author Ambrose Bierce) joined her and Jimmy Smits in a tale of Americans in the Mexican Revolution. Both films were criticized for being too muddled and focused on political and social aims to be artistically successful; neither had much commercial success either, in the theaters or in the video rental market. Still, Fonda is a formidable star. In the 1990 People's Choice Awards, she was one of the top vote-getters for World Favorite Motion Picture Actress. Not all agree, however; the anti-Oscar Annual Raspberry Awards put Fonda near the top of the list for worst actress in a movie.

Fonda's political views continued to make news in 1990. She was given the Golda Meir Fellowship Award for her work to free Soviet Jews. She worked for "green" causes, visiting some of East Germany's most polluted cities to support local environmentalists, and she helped raise funds for people and groups like Nelson Mandela and Czechoslovakia's Civic Forum. But her wartime visit to North Vietnam still rankles for many people. Even as late as 1990, Republican candidates in several states, including Texas, Colorado, and Indiana, were attacked for accepting donations from the Hollywood Women's Political Committee, of which Fonda is a member; and one was "accused" of having visited "Jane Fonda's home."

Recently divorced, Fonda formed a new relationship, with cable television mogul Ted Turner; they announced in late 1990 that they would marry, probably privately, in 1991. The two went to Moscow for the Soviet Union's first showing of *Gone With the Wind* (rights now owned by Turner); while there she made a television program about herself and her aerobics work, and also led some hundreds of Soviet women on a jog around Red Square, in her continuing campaign for physical fitness.

New York City-born Fonda appeared on the New York stage and in supporting film roles in the early 1960s, in the mid-1960s starring in such film comedies as *Cat Ballou* (1965), *Any Wednesday* (1966), and *Barefoot in the Park* (1967), and also in the science fiction film *Barbarella* (1968), directed by her first husband, Roger Vadim. She then emerged as a major film player, in drama and comedy, with such films as *They Shoot Horses, Don't They* (1969), her Oscar-winning role in *Klute*, (1970), *A Doll's House* (1973), *Fun With Dick and Jane* (1976), *Julia* (1977), her second Oscar-winning role in *Coming Home* (1978), *California Suite* (1978), *The China Syndrome* (1979), *The Electric Horseman* (1979), *Nine to Five* (1980), *On Golden Pond* (1981), *Agnes of God* (1985), and *The Morning After* (1986). She also wrote several widely circulated exercise books, starting with *Jane Fonda's Workout Book* (1981). She attended Vassar College. She has been married twice, to Vadim and to social activist Tom Hayden, and has two children. She is the daughter of actor Henry Fonda and the sister of actor Peter Fonda.

FURTHER READING

Jane Fonda: An Intimate Biography. Bill Davidson. NAL-Dutton, 1990.
Citizen Jane: The Turbulent Life of Jane Fonda. Christopher Andersen. Holt, 1990.
The Post-Feminist Hollywood Actress: Biographies and Filmographies of Stars Born After 1939. Kerry Segrave and Linda Martin. McFarland, 1990.
"Jane Fonda and Tom Hayden." David Sheff. *Rolling Stone*, Nov. 5, 1987.
"Fonda, Jane." *Current Biography*, June 1986.
Fonda: Her Life in Pictures. James Spada. Doubleday, 1985.
Jane Fonda: More Than a Movie Star. Ellen Erlanger. Lerner, 1984.
Jane Fonda: Heroine for Our Time. Thomas Kiernan. Berkley, 1983.

Forbes, Malcolm (1919–90) Forbes was the multimillionaire publisher of *Forbes Magazine*, which he marketed as "The Capitalist Tool." Third son of a Scottish immigrant, New Jersey-born Forbes graduated from Princeton and briefly ran two Ohio newspapers, before serving as a World War II machine gun sergeant in Europe, wounded and decorated. After the war, except for a 1950s sojourn into politics, he joined his father's publishing interests, taking them over in 1954 and much expanding and diversifying them. Forbes was well-known for the flamboyant style of his private activities, including ballooning, motorcycling, yachting, bridge-playing, book-writing, and even party-giving, as in his highly publicized 70th-birthday bash, for which he flew nearly 1,000 guests to Morocco. (d. Far Hills, New Jersey; February 24, 1990.)

FURTHER READING

"Malcolm Forbes. . . ." Rand V. Araskog. *Forbes*, Apr. 30, 1990.
Obituary. *Current Biography*, Apr. 1990.
Obituary. William F. Buckley, Jr. *National Review*, Mar. 19, 1990.
"A paladin of publicity. . . ." Charles E. Cohen. *People*, Mar. 19, 1990.
Obituary. Mortimer B. Zuckerman. *U.S. News & World Report*, Mar. 12, 1990.

"American original. . . ." JONATHAN ALTER. *Newsweek*, Mar. 5, 1990.
Obituary. *New York Times*, Feb. 26, 1990.
Obituary. *The Times* (of London), Feb. 26, 1990.
Malcolm Forbes: The Man Who Had Everything. CHRISTOPHER WINANS. St. Martin's, 1990.

Ford, Gerald Rudolph Jr. (1913–) Like the other living ex-presidents, Gerald Ford in the late 1980s and early 1990s continued to function as a symbol of continuity and stability, for his party and country. Long effectively retired, he briefly rejoined the political wars during the 1988 presidential campaign, speaking at the Republican National Convention and campaigning with George Bush. His other appearances are largely ceremonial, as in his attendance at the July 1990 opening of the Nixon Library, in Yorba Linda, California.

Omaha-born Ford, then vice-president, became the 38th President of the United States in August 1974, with the resignation of Richard Nixon, who faced impeachment because of his complicity in the Watergate affair. A month later, Ford pardoned Nixon. A year earlier, Ford had been appointed by Nixon to replace Vice-President Spiro Agnew, who had resigned under fire.

The Ford presidency was relatively uneventful, seeming especially so after the turbulence of the 1960s, the Vietnam War, and the shock of Watergate. That shock did enable him to curb the excesses of the Central Intelligence Agency (CIA) and other national security organizations, however; beyond that, he began little new legislation, attempted with little success to mediate continuing Middle East crises, and furthered American relations with China. He defeated Ronald Reagan's bid for the Republican presidential nomination, but was, himself, defeated by Jimmy Carter in the 1976 presidential election. He wrote of his life and experiences in *A Time to Heal: The Autobiography of Gerald R. Ford* (1979).

Earlier, Ford had been an All-American college football player, a naval officer in World War II, and was from 1941 to 1949 a lawyer in Grand Rapids, Michigan. He went to Washington as a congressman in 1949, and was minority leader of the House from 1965 to 1973. He married Elizabeth Bloomer in 1948; they have four children. His B.A. was from the University of Michigan, in 1935; his LL.B was from Yale University in 1941.

FURTHER READING

Farewell to the Chief: Former Presidents in American Public Life. RICHARD N. SMITH and TIMOTHY WALCH, EDS. High Plains, 1990.
Gerald R. Ford's Date with Destiny: A Political Biography. EDWARD L. SCHAPSMEIER and FREDERICK H. SCHAPSMEIER. Peter Lang, 1989.
"Former presidents reflect. . . ." MICHAEL DELON. *USA Today*, Nov. 1988.
"Often, momentum. . . ." DAVID FROST. *U.S. News & World Report*, Dec. 7, 1987.
"Gerald R. Ford. . . ." ALAN M. WEBBER. *Harvard Business Review*, Sept–Oct. 1987.
Gerald R. Ford: President. SALLIE RANDOLPH. Walker, 1987.

Ford, Harrison (1942–) At least two surveys of the 1980s (from the American Video Association and *Orbit Video* magazine) found Harrison Ford the decade's top box-office actor, largely due to his roles in enormously popular fantasy-adventure films. But Ford has steadfastly resisted stereotyping, and in 1990 he opened in a very different role, as the beleaguered prosecuting attorney accused of murder in *Presumed Innocent*, a tour de force that gained him much critical praise.

Privately, Ford won a lawsuit against a British newspaper that made charges against him in connection with the filming of the 1988 Indiana Jones film; Ford accepted damages (amount undisclosed) in settlement of the suit. Credited with popularizing archeology, Ford also donated his Indiana Jones bullwhip to London's Institute of Archaeology, for their building fund-raising drive.

Chicago-born Ford played mostly in supporting roles, working part-time as a carpenter, for a decade before breaking through as Han Solo in *Star Wars* (1977), to become a leading movie actor. He completed the Star Wars trilogy with *The Empire Strikes Back* (1980), and *Return of the Jedi* (1983), meanwhile doing the blockbuster Indiana Jones trilogy: *Raiders of the Lost Ark* (1981), *Indiana Jones and the Temple of Doom* (1984), and *Indiana Jones and the Last Crusade* (1989). Among his other films are *Witness* (1985), *The Mosquito Coast* (1986), and *Working Girl* (1988). He has been married twice and has two children. He attended Ripon College. (For photo, see Sean Connery.)

FURTHER READING

The Films of Harrison Ford. Ed Gross. Pioneer Books, 1990.
"Harrison Ford. . . ." Steve Oney. *Cosmopolitan*, June 1988.
"Harrison Ford. . . ." *Playboy*, Apr. 1988.
Harrison Ford. Minty Clinch. Trafalgar Square, 1988.
Harrison Ford. Toledo Vare. St. Martin's, 1988.
"Harrison Ford. . . ." Guy Martin. *Esquire*, Oct. 1986.

Foreman, David (1947–) Environmentalist Foreman continued to pursue the radical environmental activism espoused by the Earth First! organization that he helped found. He faced legal charges filed in May 1989 as one of four people who allegedly conspired to sabotage the Palo Verde Nuclear Generating Station in western Arizona, simultaneously with similar actions against nuclear facilities in California and Colorado. According to the FBI, damage was directed not at the power plants themselves, but at transmission towers, by the other two men and a woman. Foreman himself was alleged to have financed and conspired to carry out the operation; he denied the charges. He was released on bond in June 1989 (the other three co-defendants were held without bail). The charges carry penalties of five to ten years in prison and fines of $10,000 to 50,000.

Among Earth First!'s main targets have been logging firms, meat-packing and ranching complexes, nuclear plants, skiing and off-road vehicle areas, mining operations, and related government and private offices. The group's actions, which they call "monkeywrenching," range from civil disobedience and noisy demonstrations to vandalism and sabotage. They have been accused—but not convicted—of committing arson and bombings, and of such bizarre operations as stringing a lethal wire at neck level, to prevent a cross-country motor race, and canvassing for terminally ill activists to carry out kamikaze-like bombing operations against mountain dams. One of Earth First!'s best-known "eco-guerrilla" tactics has been driving long spikes into old trees, to make them useless for logging and so to save them from cutting. The hazard is that loggers can be seriously injured or even killed if they unknowingly attempt to cut down a spiked tree. Earth First! had reportedly renounced the policy and no spiking had been reported for about two years. But in August 1990, seven ten-inch spikes were found in some Douglas fir logs being readied for sawing in northern California, though no one was injured. In 1990, Foreman suggested that he had largely withdrawn from active monkeywrenching, to devote more time to developing the group's strategy. He also published the autobiographical *Confessions of an Eco-Warrior* (1991).

Foreman moved from political conservatism to radical activism early in his career. He chaired the Young Americans for Freedom chapter and campaigned for Barry Goldwater in college, but then in the early 1970s, he became a lobbyist for the Wilderness Society. In 1978, losing faith in the democratic political process, he and three friends, Mike Roselle, Bart Koehler, and Howie Wolke, founded Earth First!, an activist, environmentalist organization that urged sabotage and other acts of guerrilla violence in what they saw as the unending battle to save the environment. His book *Ecodefense: A Field Guide to Monkeywrenching* (1985; 2nd ed., 1987) is the "bible" of the Earth First! movement. Foreman has been married twice, since 1986 to Nancy Morton. He attended the University of New Mexico.

FURTHER READING

"Earth First! What next?" STEPHEN TALBOT. *Mother Jones*, Nov.–Dec. 1990.
"Eco-warrior Dave Foreman. . . ." SUSAN REED. *People*, Apr. 16, 1990.
"Dave Foreman!. . . ." CHARLES BOWDEN. *BUZZWORM: The Environmental Journal*, Mar.–Apr. 1990.
"Dave Foreman. . . ." *Mother Earth News*, Jan.–Feb. 1985.

Forman, Milos (1932–) Forman was showered with honors this year. In December 1989, the Public Braodcasting System (PBS) produced an hour-long profile of him as part of their *American Masters* series. Early in 1990, American Cinematheque gave him a weekend salute, for which the Directors Guild arranged a special showing of seven Forman films. One was his five-time-Oscar-winning movie *One Flew Over the Cuckoo's Nest*, after which he and several cast members, including Jack Nicholson, Louise Fletcher, and Danny DeVito, participated in a question-and-answer session. Late in the year, Forman was awarded the 1990 Eastman Second Century Award for his work in developing young talent in the entertainment industry.

Unfortunately, Forman's main new film, *Valmont*, which opened in late 1989, suffered from the previous year's success of Stephen Frears's *Dangerous Liaisons*, based on the same 18th-century novel, Choderlos de Laclos's *Les Liaisons Dangereuses*. *Valmont* won some critical praise, and Forman's version had a very different feel to it, with its characters younger, more insidiously intriguing, and less obviously poisonous. But many people apparently felt that two versions were, as one reviewer put it, "one too many." In the wake of the 1989 peaceful revolution in his homeland, Czechoslovakia, Forman also participated in various events, raising funds for the needy there and honoring the country's new president, Vaclav Havel. One tribute was televised on PBS.

Forman was one of Czechoslovakia's leading film directors in the mid-1960s, with such films as *Black Peter* (1964), *The Knave of Spades* (1965), *A Blonde in Love* (1965), and *A Fireman's Ball* (1968). He fled to the West after the 1968 invasion of Czechoslovakia and settled in the United States. Here he won Oscars for *One Flew Over the Cuckoo's Nest* (1975), and *Amadeus* (1983), also directing such films as *Taking Off* (1971), *Hair* (1979), and *Ragtime* (1981).

FURTHER READING

"Hollywood continues. . . ." LAWRENCE COHN. *Variety*, Oct. 25, 1989.
Milos Forman: A Bio-Bibliography. THOMAS J. SLATER. Greenwood, 1987.
"Magic shadows. . . ." RICHARD CORLISS. *Time*, July 8, 1985.

Foster, Jodie (Alicia Christian Foster, 1962–) American actress Foster moved to take more control over her professional life, signing a two-year agreement to star in, direct, and/or produce films for Orion Pictures, starting with *Little Man Tate*, which she directs and stars in, playing the mother of a boy genius in the scientific research world. She was also shooting a new film, released early in 1991, *The Silence of the Lambs*, playing an FBI recruit attempting to use one serial killer to catch another. Privately, Foster remained shadowed by memories of Foster-obsessed John Hinckley, Jr., who, in 1981, attempted to assassinate President Ronald Reagan, apparently to gain her attention. In late 1989, a judge made public the documents in which Hinckley thanked a man for sending him a semi-nude caricature of Foster, while also praising Charles Manson as a "cool dude."

Los Angeles-born Foster was a leading child actor in television, beginning with "Mayberry, R.F.D." in 1969. In her early teens, she very successfully played major roles in such films as *Alice Doesn't Live Here Any More* (1975) and *Taxi Driver* (1976). She then made the often extremely difficult transition to adult roles, in such films as *The Hotel New Hampshire* (1984), *Five Corners* (1986), and most notably *The Accused* (1988), for which she won a Best Actress Oscar. Her B.A. was from Yale University, in 1985.

FURTHER READING

"Child of the movies." JONATHAN VAN METER. *New York Times Magazine*, Jan. 6, 1991.
"American original." MICHAEL A. LERNER. *Interview*, Sept. 1989.
"Jodie Foster." TODD GOLD. *Harper's Bazaar*, Sept. 1989.
"Jodie Foster. . . ." LINDA R. MILLER. *Cosmopolitan*, Feb. 1989.
"Victor of circumstances." LINDA R. MILLER. *American Film*, Oct. 1988.
"The prime of Miss Jodie Foster." DIANA MAYCHICK. *Mademoiselle*, Sept. 1987.
"Educating Jodie. . . ." *Life*, Sept. 1987.

Fox, Michael J. (1961–) The third film in Fox's Marty McFly series debuted in mid-1990, with the time-traveling hero this time winding up in the Old West. *Back to the Future Part III* was more widely praised than its predecessor (which broke box office records on its opening in late 1989) and was a strong commercial success, in some cities playing briefly as part of a marathon, triple-feature program. In *The Hard Way*, which opened in late 1990, Fox had a chance to spoof the cop-buddy genre, playing an actor who researches a role by shadowing a homicide detective (James Woods).

Personally, Fox faced problems of fame, being forced to go to court after receiving over 5,000 threatening letters from a California shipping clerk. The woman, Tina Marie Ledbetter, pleaded guilty to making terrorist threats and was ordered to receive psychiatric therapy, sentenced to three years probation, and warned to stay away from Fox and his family.

Vancouver-born Fox became a popular television player as the conservative young son in the series "Family Ties" (1982–89), and a film star in the teenage fantasy-comedies *Back to the Future* (1985), and *Back to the Future II* (1989). He also starred in the highly regarded *Casualties of War* (1989). He married Tracy Pollan in 1988; they have one child.

FURTHER READING

Secret of Michael J. Fox's Success. EDWARD GROSS. Movie Publications Services, 1990.
"Getting back to his future." MICHAEL ALEXANDER. *People*, Dec. 4, 1989 .
"Michael J. Fox. . . ." KEVIN SESSUMS and PHILLIP DIXON. *Interview*, Jan. 1988.
"Fox, Michael J." *Current Biography*, Nov. 1987.
"Michael J. Fox." *Playboy*, June 1987.
"Little big man. . . ." ALAN RICHMAN. *People*, Apr. 20, 1987.
"The star has risen." BRIAN D. JOHNSON. *Maclean's*, Feb. 9, 1987.
Michael J. Fox Scrapbook. MIMI KASBAH. Ballantine, 1987.
Michael J. Fox. KEITH E. GREENBERG. Lerner, 1986.

Frank, Barney (1940–) Massachusetts Democratic Congressman Frank, openly a homosexual, became involved in a headline-getting situation in August 1989, when a newspaper story charged that he had put a male prostitute on his payroll in 1985 and that the man, Steven L. Gobie, had then run a house of prostitution out of Frank's Washington apartment. On July 25, 1990, after a long investigation, the House of Representatives reprimanded Frank for using his office to improperly help Gobie; at the same time, the House rejected the original charges. Frank was re-elected to the House in November 1990.

Frank was a Massachusetts state legislator from 1972 to 1980, after teaching at Harvard University and working as a political assistant in Boston and Washington. He began his Congressional career in 1981. His B.A. and J.D. were from Harvard, in 1962 and 1977.

FURTHER READING

"Sodom and begorra." *Boston Magazine*, Nov. 1989.

"In defense of Barney. . . ." MORTON KONDRACKE. *New Republic*, Oct. 9, 1989.
"'I was emotionally vulnerable'. . . ." ELEANOR CLIFT. *Newsweek*, Sept. 25, 1989.

Franz, Josef II (1906–89) Nephew of Austrian Archduke Franz Ferdinand, whose assassination sparked World War I, Franz Josef was the Prince of Liechtenstein, 12th ruler of Liechtenstein, a 61-square-mile remainder of the Holy Roman Empire, located between Switzerland and Austria. He was the first to live there full-time, rather than in Vienna. At his death, he was the world's longest-reigning monarch. Taking office as constitutional monarch in 1938, he maintained neutrality during World War II, afterward protecting from extradition some 500 Russians, including the heir to the Russian throne. Under Franz Josef, Liechtenstein was modernized and liberalized, coming to have one of the highest per capita incomes in the world. In 1984, he gave executive power to his son and heir, Hans Adam. (d. Vaduz, Liechtenstein; November 13, 1990)

FURTHER READING

Obituary. *New York Times*, Nov. 15, 1989.
Obituary. *The Times* (of London), Nov. 15, 1989.
"Liechtenstein:. . . ." RICHARD Z. CHESNOFF. *U.S. News & World Report*, June 22, 1987.

Freeman, Morgan (1938–) Freeman emerged as a leading screen and stage player late in his career, beginning with his lead off-Broadway as Hoke Colburn, the Black chauffeur in *Driving Miss Daisy* (1987), and in strong supporting roles in such films as *Street Smart* (1987) and *Clean and Sober* (1988). His major breakthrough came in 1989, with his film re-creation of the *Driving Miss Daisy* role, for which he won a 1990 Oscar nomination. In the same year, he appeared in *Glory*, and created the Joe Clark role in *Lean On Me*. In 1990, he appeared as Petruchio opposite Tracey Ullman in the New York production of *The Taming of the Shrew*.

Freeman has spent most of his long career in the theater, winning a 1978 Tony nomination

for his role in *The Mighty Gents*, and appearing in a wide range of Shakespearean and other classical roles. He has also appeared as a regular on two television series: public television's children's show "The Electric Company" (1971–76) and for a time in the early 1980s, "Another World," a daytime soap opera.

FURTHER READING

"In the driver's seat. . . ." JANICE C. SIMPSON. *Time*, Jan. 8, 1990.
"Two for the road." HENRY ALFORD and PAULA BULLWINKEL. *Interview*, Nov. 1989.
"Johnny Handsome. . . ." ROBERT SEIDENBERG. *American Film*, Oct. 1989.
"Oscar hopeful. . . ." SUSAN TOEPFER. *People*, Apr. 4, 1988.
"Morgan Freeman. . . ." ROSS WETZSTEON. *New York*, Mar. 14, 1988.

Friedkin, William (1939–) Director Friedkin continued his work in the supernatural-horror-thriller genre with *The Guardian* in April 1990, and *The Exorcist III* in August. Neither won much critical acclaim, with many reviewers finding *The Guardian*'s homicidal trees silly, rather than shocking, and box office results were far from overwhelming. Personally, Friedkin supported his wife, Kelly Lange, anchorwoman for Los Angeles's KNBC-TV, in her successful court case against an obsessed fan, Warren Hudson, who in numerous letters threatened to "blow her head off."

Chicago-born Friedkin is best known for such films as *The Night They Raided Minsky's* (1968), his Oscar-winning *The French Connection* (1971), *The Exorcist* (1973), *Sorcerer* (1977), *Cruising* (1980), and *To Live and Die in L.A.* (1985). He was formerly married to Lesley-Anne Down, and has one child.

FURTHER READING

Hurricane Billy: The Stormy Life & Films of William Friedkin. Nat Segaloff. Morrow, 1990.
William Friedkin: Films of Aberration, Obsession & Reality. Thomas D. Clagett. McFarland, 1990.
"William Friedkin. . . ." Frank Spotnitz. *American Film*, Dec. 1990.
"Friedkin, William." *Current Biography*, June 1987.

Frohnmayer, John Edward (1942–) Frohnmayer, a lawyer, was appointed chairman of the National Endowment for the Arts (NEA) by President George Bush in July 1989, and very quickly emerged as a highly controversial figure. In November 1989, he canceled a $10,000 grant to a New York gallery to fund an AIDS exhibit, calling the show too "political." The massive anti-censorship campaign that resulted caused him to change his mind, and to reinstate the grant a week later. But that campaign was only a rehearsal for the tremendous national campaign set off in August 1990, when Frohnmayer refused already-recommended grants to four artists, all accused of "obscenity." These were Karen Finley, Holly Hughes, John Fleck, and Tim Miller, from then on known as the "NEA Four." Frohnmayer went on to deny several more grants, and to institute an "anti-obscenity oath," a pledge by those receiving federal grants through the NEA that they would not use the money to create "obscene" art. Joseph Papp of the New York Shakespeare Festival, among others, refused to take offered NEA grants as long as the oath was in effect.

Throughout the period, the existence of the NEA was threatened by congressional conservatives, led by Senator Jesse Helms, who tried to cut off NEA funding. Some people thought Frohnmayer's actions were largely an attempt to soften conservative opposition to the NEA, as implied by Frohnmayer on several occasions; most did not reach for his motives, seeing the attempted censorship as inexcusable. In November, after Congress had approved NEA funding, Finley and Hughes received NEA grants, without opposition from Frohnmayer, and in December he declared himself unwilling to enforce "decency" restrictions on grants.

Oregon-born Frohnmayer practiced law in Oregon from 1972 to 1989. He was also a member of the Oregon Arts Commission from 1978 to 1985, has been a singer, and has been active in the development of regional musical groups. His 1964 B.A. was from Stanford University, his 1969 M.A. was from the University of Chicago, and his 1972 J.D. was from the University of Oregon. He married Leah Thorpe in 1967; they have two children.

FURTHER READING

"Frohnmayer, John Edward." *Current Biography*, Apr. 1990.

Fugard, Athol (1932–) South African writer-actor Fugard spent much of the past year in southern California. In February, he opened his latest play, *My Children! My Africa!*, at the La Jolla Playhouse; this West Coast premiere was something of a surprise, since many of his previous plays had opened at Los Angeles's Mark Taper Forum. The production was also directed by Fugard, with the cast including Brock Peters, as a teacher whose students are debating apartheid, and John Kani, a South African actor long associated with Fugard's work. The production was later moved on to Hollywood, there produced by hair-styling tycoon Vidal Sassoon. Like his characters, Fugard was involved in numerous public discussions about South African questions. In 1990, he also published his *Notebooks: 1960–1977*. Fugard is South Africa's leading playwright, and far more—he is one of the leading playwrights of the modern world theater, who takes many of his themes from the tragic conflicts in his homeland, and sees those conflicts as deeply affecting his own White community, as well as the Black, Colored, and Asian communities of South Africa. He became a world figure with his Port Elizabeth trilogy: *Blood Knot* (1961), *Hello and Goodbye* (1965), and *Boesman and Lena* (1969). He went on to write such plays as *Sizwe Bansi Is Dead* (1973), *A Lesson from Aloes* (1979), *Master Harold and the Boys* (1981), and *The Road to Mecca* (1984). He married Sheila Fugard in 1956; they have one child.

FURTHER READING

"Interview with. . . ." PAUL ALLEN. *New Statesman & Society*, Sept. 7, 1990.

"Athol Fugard." JAMAICA KINCAID. *Interview*, Aug. 1990.

"Athol Fugard's South Africa." ANDRE BRINK. *World Press Review*, July 1990.

Athol Fugard. DENNIS WALDER. St. Martin's, 1990; Grove-Weidenfeld, 1985.

Truths the Hand Can Touch: The Theater of Athol Fugard. RUSSELL VANDENBROUCKE. Theater Communications, 1985.

Fujimori, Alberto (1938–) Peruvian agricultural engineer Fujimori, in his first entry into politics, was the candidate of the Cambio '90 Party (Change '90) in the 1990 Peruvian presidential elections. On June 10, he was surprise winner of the Peruvian presidency in a runoff against novelist Mario Vargas Llosa, candidate of the ruling Aprista (American Popular Revolutionary Alliance) Party. Although a Catholic, Fujimori had been opposed by the Catholic Church and strongly supported by the Peruvian evangelical Christian movement throughout his successful campaign, and was greatly aided by poor voters' perception of Vargas Llosa as rich, White, and sophisticated, rather than attuned

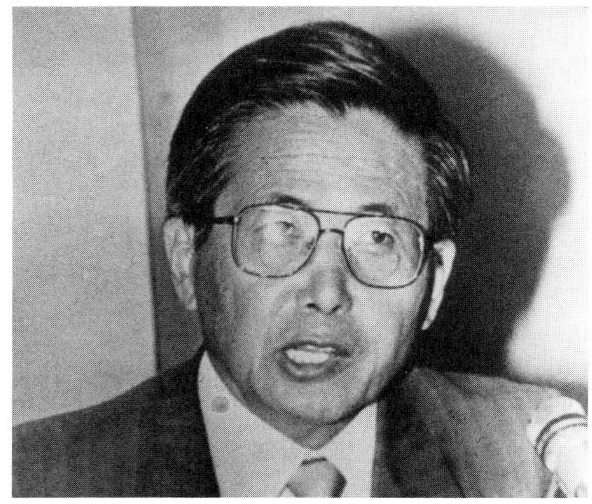

to the needs of Peru's poor, mestizo, and Indian majority.

Although Fujimori's campaign had stressed that economic changes proposed by Vargas Llosa would greatly damage Peru's poor, the chief feature of his own economic program, once in office, was a severe austerity program, begun in August 1990, which caused huge price rises, deeply affecting the poor, and resulted in rioting in many cities. The program was a condition set by the International Monetary Fund, as part of an agreement to resume international loans to Peru.

Fujimori also made a series of major moves to consolidate power and restore the power of his allies in the army. Sworn in as president on July 28, on that day he removed the heads of the air force and navy. On August 2 he made major changes at the top of the national police force, bringing it more under army control and forcing out some leaders of the anti-drug force. In September, he also refused U.S. anti-drug military assistance funds. Going further, and on other matters, Fujimori in November 1990, sharply criticized the Catholic Church's position on birth control, calling it "medieval." Throughout the period, Peru's Shining Path revolutionary movement continued to gain strength in the Andean provinces, and extended its control of the countryside to include other sections of the country, as the long Peruvian civil war continued and expanded.

Peruvian-born Fujimori, the son of Japanese-Peruvian immigrants, attended "La Molina," the National Agrarian University, graduating in 1961, and then taught at the university. His

1969 Master's degree was in mathematics, from the University of Wisconsin. He became dean of the science faculty at La Molina in 1984, was principal of the university from 1984 to 1989, and was president of the Peruvian National Council of Principals from 1987 to 1989. He married civil engineer Susana Higuchi in 1974; they have four children.

FURTHER READING

"The 'Karate Kid' meets. . . ." TOM VOGEL, JR. *Commonweal*, Jan. 11, 1991.

"Fujimori, Alberto." *Current Biography,* Nov. 1990.

"Fujimori. . . ." JEFFREY KLAIBER. *America,* Sept. 8, 1990.

"The outsiders. . . ." *Economist,* July 7, 1990.

"Who is Fujimori anyway?" LINDA ROBINSON. *U.S. News & World Report,* Apr. 23, 1990.

"Engulfed by 'the Tsunami'. . . ." FREDERICK UNGEHEUER. *Time,* Apr. 23, 1990.

"Peru. . . ." JOSEPH CONTRERAS. *Newsweek,* Apr. 23, 1990.

"The man from nowhere." *Economist,* Apr. 14, 1990.

G

Gandhi, Rajiv (1944–) Former prime minister Gandhi's five years in office (1984–89) were dominated by India's continuing ethnic and religious problems, as a virtual civil war continued in the Punjab and Kashmir, periodic Hindu-Muslim fighting flared in the North, and serious unrest continued among the Gurkhas of the Northeast and the Tamils in the South. In the summer of 1987, Gandhi directly intervened in the Sri Lankan civil war, sending Indian troops who remained in Sri Lanka through 1989.

Ultimately, in late November 1989, the mounting level of violence forced Gandhi's Congress Party out of power, for only the second time since independence was achieved in 1947. He resigned on November 29th; he was succeeded by National Front coalition leader Vishwanath Pratap Singh. Gandhi, as president of the Congress Party, became leader of the opposition, as the intractable problems that had forced him out of office continued to plague his successors. Singh resigned on November 7, 1990; he was succeeded by Chandra Shekhar, after Gandhi had rejected the prime minister's post, as a matter of political strategy.

Gandhi is the son of assassinated Indian prime minister Indira Gandhi, and the grandson of Indian founding father Jawaharlal Nehru; but he did not originally head for a political career. Instead, he became an engineer and airline pilot, and entered politics only in 1981, taking the congressional seat of his brother Sanjay, who had died in a 1980 airplane crash. Rajiv Gandhi was his mother's political successor. He became head of the Congress Party in 1983, and took office as prime minister after the October 1984 assassination of Indira Gandhi by two of her Sikh bodyguards. He married Sonia Maino in 1968; they have two children. He attended Trinity College, Cambridge.

FURTHER READING

"Pilot error. . . ." JULIAN CRANDALL HOLLICK. *New Republic*, Dec. 4, 1989.

India under Indira & Rajiv Gandhi. JAMES HASKINS. Enslow, 1989.

"Gandhi under the gun." DARRYL D'MONTE. *New Leader*, June 29, 1987.

"'We don't have the bomb'." PRANAY B. GUPTE. *Forbes*, May 18, 1987.

"Rajiv Gandhi stumbles. . . ." HARRY ANDERSON. *Newsweek*, Feb. 23, 1987.

Portrait of Rajiv Gandhi. SHRIKANT VERMA. Arnold-Heinemann, 1986.

"Gandhi, Rajiv (Ratna)." *Current Biography*, Apr. 1985.

Garbo, Greta (Greta Louise Gustafsson, 1905–90) From 1926, when she starred in Hollywood in the silent film *Torrent,* until her 1941 retirement into five decades of public silence, the Swedish actress Garbo (she became an American citizen in 1951) was one of the greatest of all film stars. She began her career in Swedish films, as the 17-year-old protégé of director Maurice Stiller, in *The Legend of Gösta Bjerling* (1922), and went with him to Hollywood, where they soon parted. Garbo went on to star opposite John Gilbert in *Flesh and the Devil* (1927), and in such silent film classics as *Love* (1927) and *The Kiss* (1929), before starring in such classic sound films of Hollywood's Golden Age as *Anna Christie* (1930), *Mata Hari* (1931), *Queen Christina* (1933), *Anna Karenina* (1935), *Camille* (1937), and *Ninotchka* (1939). Before her death, she strongly protested the accuracy of Antoni Gronowicz's biography *Garbo* (1990). (d. New York City; April 15, 1990)

FURTHER READING

"The mysterious lady." ROBERT HORTON. *Film Comment*, July–Aug. 1990.
Obituary. *Current Biography*, June 1990.
"Garbo's last days." *New York*, May 21, 1990.
"Greta Garbo." STANLEY KAUFFMANN. *New Republic*, May 21, 1990.
Obituary. *National Review*, May 14, 1990.
Obituary. *New Republic*, May 7, 1990.
"The last mysterious lady. . . ." RICHARD CORLISS. *Time*, Apr. 30, 1990.
"The great Garbo." SUSAN SCHINDEHETTE. *People*, Apr. 30, 1990.
"Great Garbo. . . ." DAVID ANSEN. *Newsweek*, Apr. 30, 1990.
"Garbo, screen's classiest siren. . . ." LAWRENCE COHN. *Variety*, Apr. 18, 1990.
Obituary. *New York Times*, Apr. 16, 1990.

Garcia Marquez, Gabriel (1928–)

Colombian writer Garcia Marquez is a leading Latin American novelist and a world literary figure. His most recent major work is the novel *The General in His Labyrinth* (1989), published in the United States in September 1990. The book is a fictional exploration of the last days of Simon Bolivar, a re-examination of the hero and of his frailties, which caused great controversy in Latin America. Garcia Marquez is politically independent, critical of socialism and capitalism, though he was greatly influenced by Marxism through the early 1960s, and is very close to Cuban leader Fidel Castro, a personal friend.

Garcia Marquez won the Nobel Prize for literature in 1982, in recognition of a body of novels and short stories that by then had made him a world figure, and included the novels *One Hundred Years of Solitude* (1967), *Death of a Patriarch* (1975), and *Love in the Time of Cholera* (1984). He attended the National University at Bogotá. He is married to Mercedes Garcia Marquez; they have two children.

FURTHER READING

Garcia Marquez: The Man & His Work. GENE H. BELL-VILLADA. University of North Carolina Press, 1990.
"Love and. . . ." TIM MCCARTHY. *National Catholic Reporter*, May 12, 1989.
"The best years. . . ." MARLISLE SIMONS. *New York Times Book Review*, Apr. 10, 1988.
"A wizard of words. . . ." Edwin MCDOWELL. *Americas*, July–Aug. 1986.
"Mutiny and love. . . ." WILSON RUIZ. *Maclean's*, July 28, 1986.
Gabriel Garcia Marquez. RAYMOND WILLIAMS. G.K. Hall, 1985.

Gardiner, Gerald Austin (1900–90)

Gardiner was a British barrister, a leading defense lawyer of the interwar period, who became a key initiator of major social and legal reforms. Educated at Harrow and Oxford, Gardiner served in both world wars (in the first as an officer, the second in a Friends' Ambulance Unit). He joined the Labour Party in the late 1930s. From 1925, he built up a successful practice, appearing in many key cases, as in defense of the book *Lady Chatterley's Lover*. After the war, he focused on legal reform, especially on abolishing the death penalty, liberalizing laws regarding abortion and homosexuality, instituting family courts and ombudsmen, and generally overhauling his country's legal machinery. In 1963, he was created a Life Peer, serving as Britain's Lord Chancellor from 1964 to 1970. (d. January 7, 1990)

FURTHER READING

Obituary. *The Times* (of London), Jan. 9, 1990.
"Rebel Advocate." MARK BENNEY. *New Statesman*, May 20, 1983.

Gardner, Ava (1922–90) South Carolina-born Gardner became a Hollywood starlet at the age of 18, and played in minor roles before emerging as a star in such films as *The Killers* (1946), *The Hucksters* (1947), *One Touch of Venus* (1948), and as Julie in *Show Boat* (1948), which began to show her acting talents, as well as displaying her sexual presence. She went on to appear in such films as *Mogambo* (1953), *The Barefoot Contessa* (1954), *Bhowani Junction* (1956), and *The Sun Also Rises* (1957). She lived and worked mainly in Europe from the late 1950s, in Spain until 1968, and from then on in Britain, and appeared in such films as *On the Beach* (1959), *Seven Days in May* (1964), *The Night of the Iguana* (1964), and *Mayerling* (1969). Before her death she had completed her autobiography, *Ava: My Story* (1990). (d. London; January 25, 1990)

FURTHER READING

"Ave Ava." Reid Buckley. *National Review*, Apr. 16, 1990.
Obituary. *Current Biography*, Mar. 1990.
"Many passions, no regrets." Michelle Green. *People*, Feb. 12, 1990.
"Amorous Ava." Walter Thomas. *Harper's Bazaar*, Feb. 1990.
"Screen beauty. . . ." Joseph McBride. *Variety*, Jan. 31, 1990.
Obituary. *New York Times*, Jan. 26, 1990.
Obituary. *The Times* (of London), Jan. 26, 1990.
Ava's Men: The Private Life of Ava Gardner. Jane E. Wayne. St. Martin's, 1990.
Ava Gardner: A Bio-Bibliography. Karin J. Fowler. Greenwood, 1990.
Ava Gardner. John Daniell. St. Martin's, 1983.

Garner, James (James Baumgarner, 1928–) Still a maverick, James Garner in 1989 settled his running, eight-year battle with Universal Studios, over his share of the profits in his former NBC hit series "The Rockford Files," the second time he had fought such a battle and won. Garner left both "Rockford" and his earlier ABC hit series, "Maverick," in protest over unfair treatment, and he has little good to say about television studios. Yet his most recent projects have been for television. In late 1990, he starred in the Hallmark Hall of Fame production *Decoration Day*, in a Golden-Globe-winning performance as a crusty widower and retired judge who reluctantly acts on behalf of an old but estranged friend, a Black man (played by Bill Cobbs) who wants to refuse a belatedly offered Congressional Medal of Honor. Garner had previously worked on other Hallmark productions, including *Promise* (1986), which won five Emmys, including best drama, and *My Name Is Bill W* (1989), as one of the cofounders of Alcoholics Anonymous. At the end of 1990, he was again working for television, this time producing an ABC television movie, *Mittleman's Hardware,* starring George C. Scott.

Oklahoma-born Garner began his long career in the mid-1950s, in a small, nonspeaking role in *The Caine Mutiny Court Martial* (1954), and in bit parts in television. He quickly emerged as a major television series star, in the title role of the western "Maverick" (1957–61), and later as private investigator Jim Rockford in "The Rockford Files" (1974–80). His wide range of films included *Sayonara* (1957), *The Great Escape* (1963), *The Americanization of Emily* (1964), *Marlowe* (1969), *They Only Kill Their Masters* (1972), *Victor/Victoria* (1982), and *Sunset* (1987). Garner attended the University of Oklahoma. He married Lois Clarke in 1956; they have three children.

FURTHER READING

"Meet a James Garner. . . ." MARY MURPHY. *TV Guide*, Dec. 13, 1986.
"The man is back." JANE HALL. *People*, Apr. 22, 1985.
James Garner: A Biography. RAYMOND STRAIT. St. Martin's, 1985.

Gathers, Hank (1966-90) The star center of the Loyola Marymount college basketball team collapsed and died on March 4, 1990, during a game against Portland. He was one of the leading college players of his time, in the 1988–89 season becoming only the second in National Collegiate Athletic Association history to lead the country in both scoring and rebounding. He also had a serious heart condition. He had collapsed during a December 9, 1989 game, only three months earlier, and tests had shown an irregular heartbeat. The doctors for his team then purchased a defibrillation machine, used in emergencies to restore a normal heartbeat; but he continued to play, allegedly at his own insistence, while taking medication. Whether or not he should have been allowed to play at all with a serious heart problem became a national controversy. It also became a court case; in April, his family began a lawsuit against the college, charging negligence. (d. Los Angeles; March 4, 1990)

FURTHER READING

"Not what the doctor. . . ." SHELLEY SMITH. *Sports Illustrated*, June 11, 1990.
"College star Hank Gathers dies. . . ." LORENZO BENET. *People*, Mar. 19, 1990.
"The death of a dream." SHELLEY SMITH. *Sports Illustrated*, Mar. 19, 1990.
"Death on the basketball court. . . ." PHILIP ELMER-DEWITT. *Time*, Mar. 19, 1990.
"Basketball was his life." CHARLES LEERHSEN. *Newsweek*, Mar. 19, 1990.
"Death on the court." SHELLEY SMITH. *Sports Illustrated*, Mar. 12, 1990.
Obituary. *New York Times*, Mar. 6, 1990

Gavin, James Maurice (1907–90) Gavin was a dissenting U.S. general, who resigned from the Army in 1958, in protest over the Army's loss of primary control over missile development. An orphan raised in Pennsylvania, Gavin was a school dropout who entered the Army at 17, studying independently to enter West Point. During World War II, he rose rapidly from captain to major general, serving in the invasions of Sicily and Normandy, winning numerous decorations, and was noted for talking with soldiers face-to-face. Post-war, as Army's chief of research and development, he developed helicopter-borne forces later used in Vietnam, but resigned in 1958 after various disagreements, especially on neglect of conventional forces and overreliance on nuclear weapons. He remained a critic of the armed forces, writing several books, later served as President John F. Kennedy's ambassador to France, and was in 1968 suggested for the presidential nomination, which he declined to pursue. (d. Baltimore, Maryland; February 23, 1990)

FURTHER READING

Obituary. *Current Biography*, Apr. 1990.
Obituary. *New York Times*, Feb. 25, 1990.
On to Berlin. JAMES M. GAVIN. Bantam, 1985.

Gaviria Trujillo, César (1947–) Gaviria Trujillo was elected president of Colombia on May 27, 1990, succeeding Virgilio Barco Vargas, who, during 1989, had greatly expanded the Colombian internal war against the drug cartels; the cartels had then stepped up the terrorist war they had been conducting against the government from the mid-1980s. Inaugurated on August 7th, Gaviria pledged to continue the anti-cartel war. At the same time, he sought a peaceful resolution of Colombia's long, low-level civil war, including opposition M-19 leader Antonio Navarro Wolf in his new cabinet. In early September, Gaviria offered the drug cartels a series of incentives to surrender and give up drugdealing, including lighter sentences and trial in Colombia, rather than extradition to the United States.

Gaviria, an economist, entered politics at the age of 27, as mayor of his home town of Pereira. He later served several terms in the national assembly, and in 1986, he became finance minister in the Barco Vargas government, later serving in other cabinet-level posts. He became campaign manager for Liberal

Party presidential candidate Luis Carlos Galan Sarmiento in 1989. After Galan's August assassination, Gaviria became a candidate, and was nominated by his party in March 1990. He attended the University of the Andes.

FURTHER READING

"Colombia's next president. . . ." LINDA ROBINSON. *U.S. News & World Report*, July 30, 1990.
"Colombia's elections." C. DOMINIQUE VAN DE STADT. *World Press Review*, July 1990.
"President of last resort." *Time*, June 11, 1990.
"Cartel killer?" *U.S. News & World Report*, June 11, 1990.

Gelbart, Larry (1925–) Writer-producer Gelbart won acclaim on Broadway for his work on the new hard-boiled private-eye musical, *City of Angels*, set in the film noir world of 1940s Los Angeles. The show won him Tony awards as writer of the best book for a musical (based on his 1982 play of the same title) and as coproducer (with Cy Coleman) of the year's best musical. Meanwhile, the Tony-winning musical, *A Funny Thing Happened on the Way to the Forum* (1961), which Gelbart co-wrote with Burt Shevelove, was revived to high praise at the La Jolla Playhouse. Chicago-born Gelbart began his long career in 1945, as a comedy writer for radio's "Duffy's Tavern", and since then has written an enormous amount of material for television, films, and theater. He was a leading comedy writer in early television, and on such films as *The Wrong Box* (1966), and *Tootsie* (1982). He was also the writer and producer of the long-running television series "M*A*S*H*" (1972–76). He married Pat Marshall in 1956; they have five children.

FURTHER READING

"Producers defend Oscar show. . . ." RAY LOYND. *Variety*, Apr. 3, 1985.

Gendron, Maurice (1920–90) French cellist, conductor, and teacher Gendron began his career in Paris, in the late 1930s, and emerged as a major artist during the postwar period, making his London debut in 1945, with the western European premiere of Prokofiev's Cello Concerto. Gendron often appeared at the Bath Festival, with Yehudi Menuhin conducting. He also taught at the Menuhin School, and was conducted by Pablo Casals. Gendron was a leading teacher of master classes, and taught at the Paris Conservatoire. He was also for over three decades a very highly regarded recording artist. (d. August 21, 1990)

FURTHER READING

Obituary. *New York Times*, Aug. 22, 1990.

Gephardt, Richard Andrew (1941–) Gephardt is a seven-term Missouri Democratic congressman, who, after his unsuccessful bid for the 1988 Democratic presidential nomination, was widely expected to spend much of the next four years preparing to run again. But with the forced 1989 resignations of House of Representative Speaker Jim Wright and Democratic Party whip Tony Coelho, Gephardt shifted his sights somewhat, winning election as House Majority Leader. From that position, he became a leading Democratic spokesperson, sharply criticizing the Bush administration and putting forward for his party, sometimes on his own, such proposals as a tax cut, defense cuts, and a toughened attitude toward unequal Japanese-American trading rules. As the Persian Gulf Crisis deepened in late 1990, he stressed more sharply the need for an American energy policy aimed at reducing dependence on foreign oil.

St. Louis-born Gephardt began his political career as a St. Louis alderman (1971–76) and his congressional career in 1979. He emerged as a front-running Democratic presidential candidate for a time during the run-up to the 1988 elections, but dropped out during the long primary campaign. He married Jane Ann Byrnes in 1966; they have three children. His B.S. was from Northwestern University, in 1962; his J.D. was from the University of Michigan, in 1965.

FURTHER READING

"Wanted. . . ." DOUGLAS HARBRECHT. *Business Week*, Nov. 19, 1990.
"Gephardt speaks for the majority." BILL WHALEN. *Insight*, July 3, 1989.
"Man for all seasons. . . ." MORTON M. KONDRACKE. *New Republic*, July 3, 1989.

"The man to beat." FRED BARNES. *New Republic*, Mar. 7, 1988.
"The men who would be president." *Black Enterprise*, Mar. 1988.
"Those wacky Democrats." RICHARD BROOKHISER. *National Review*, Jan. 22, 1988.
"'Give people. . . .'" DAVID FROST. *U.S. News & World Report*, Jan. 11, 1988.
"Gephardt, Richard (Andrew)." *Current Biography*, Oct. 1987.

Gere, Richard (1949–) After several years in the doldrums, Gere's career received an enormous boost in 1990 from the unexpected popularity of *Pretty Woman,* the Pygmalion-like romantic comedy in which he co-starred with Julia Roberts. The film reached number one at the box office and, when released on video in late 1990, quickly jumped into the top spot. *Internal Affairs* (1989), in which Gere played an unscrupulous cop, shared in the success, jumping into the top five video rentals by mid-1990. Long interested in Buddhism and Eastern philosophy, Gere was cast as a Japanese-American for Akira Kurosawa's next movie, *Rhapsody in August,* due in mid-1991, a selection that drew protests from some Asian-Americans.

Philadelphia-born Gere began his theater career in the early 1970s, and became a star in such films as *Report to the Commissioner* (1975), *Looking for Mr. Goodbar* (1977), *Yanks* (1979), and *An Officer and a Gentleman* (1982). He attended the University of Massachusetts.

FURTHER READING

"Richard Gere." MAURA MOYNIHAN and ANDY WARHOL. *Interview*, Oct. 1983.
"Richard Gere. . . ." LINDA E. WATSON. *Teen*, Apr. 1983.
Richard Gere: An Unauthorized Biography. JUDITH DAVIS. NAL-Dutton, 1983.
"Mister Richard Gere. . . ." RICHARD PRICE. *Rolling Stone*, Sept. 30, 1982.
"Gere, Richard." *Current Biography*, Aug. 1980.

Gibbons, Stella (1902–89) British novelist Gibbons was best-known for her *Cold Comfort Farm* (1932), a parody of English "country-fied" novels, notably those of Mary Webb. London born and educated, Gibbons worked as a journalist early in her career. Her first book was a volume of poems, published in 1930. She then turned to her chronicles of the Starkadder clan, dramatized as a BBC miniseries in 1968. Over 30 more volumes appeared in the next four decades, mostly novels, though none had the same popular success. (d. December 19, 1989)

FURTHER READING

Obituary. *The Times* (of London), Dec. 20, 1989.

Gibson, Mel (1956–) Gibson was one of the busiest actors in Hollywood in 1990. In late spring, he opened opposite Goldie Hawn in John Badham's action-comedy *Bird on a Wire,* which did not do quite as well as expected at the box office, but quickly arrived in the video rental market, where it had stronger appeal. The summer saw the opening of *Air America,* set during the Vietnam War, in which Gibson plays a pilot working for the Central Intelligence Agency out of Laos (shot in Thailand), opposite Robert Downey, Jr. Though panned by the critics, it drew fairly large audiences. Then in December, he opened in the title role in Franco Zeffirelli's version of *Hamlet,* shot in Scotland with Glenn

Close as Gertrude, in a cast that also included Alan Bates and Paul Scofield. Gibson's performance drew somewhat surprised praise from critics, especially for its raw power and intensity. At the first intercontinental Academy Awards, in March 1990, Gibson and Close were the Oscar-presenters from London.

Gibson is certainly among the most popular actors. A survey by *Spy* magazine for a television program *How to Be Famous* named him as the nation's most-liked celebrity, *Vanity Fair* dubbed him "the very model of a modern motion-picture star," and *People* named him as one of the world's 50 most beautiful people. But after making four movies without a break, Gibson announced that he was exhausted and would go home to his Australian cattle ranch and "lead my own life instead of someone else's" for ten months to a year.

Born in Peekskill, New York, Gibson emigrated to Australia with his family in 1968. He appeared on stage and screen in Australia from 1977, in the classics in South Australian regional theater, in several television series, and most notably in the film *Tim* (1979). He soon became a popular worldwide film star, in such action films as *Mad Max* (1979), and its two sequels: *The Road Warrior* (1982), and *Mad Max Beyond Thunderdome* (1985); the dramas *Gallipoli* (1981), and *The Year of Living Dangerously* (1983); and the two extraordinarily popular *Lethal Weapon* films (1987, 1989). He married Robyn Moore in 1979; they have six children. He attended the Australian National Institute of Dramatic Arts.

FURTHER READING

"Mel Gibson. . . ." John Lahr. *Cosmopolitan*, Dec. 1990.
"Road worrier. . . ." *Harper's Magazine*, Aug. 1990.
"Talking with Mel Gibson. . . ." Carson Jones. *Redbook*, Aug. 1990.
"Mel Gibson." Lynn Hirschberg. *Rolling Stone*, Jan. 12, 1989.
"What's hot in hunks. . . ." Eric Sherman. *Ladies Home Journal*, Aug. 1987.
Mel Gibson: Australia's Restless Superstar. Keith McKay. Doubleday, 1986.
Mel Gibson. David Ragan. Dell, 1985.

Gilford, Jack (Jacob Gellman, 1907–90) An actor and comedian, Gilford began his career in the late 1930s, touring with Milton Berle, and continued to be a leading comic in cabaret for 50 years. He made his Broadway debut in 1940, appearing in such plays as *The World of Sholom Aleichem* (1953), *Diary of Anne Frank* (1955), *A Funny Thing Happened on the Way to the Forum* (1962; and in the 1965 film), *Cabaret* (1966), *The Sunshine Boys* (1972), and *Sly Fox* (1976). His films also included *Catch-22* (1969), *Save the Tiger* (1972; he received a best supporting actor Oscar nomination), and *Harry and Walter Go to New York* (1976). He was blacklisted by the film industry from 1956 to 1965, after being an "unfriendly" witness before the House Committee on Un-American Activities. He also appeared in radio and television, and in 1950 appeared as the drunken jailer, Frosch, at the Metropolitan Opera in *Die Fledermaus,* a role he often repeated with the company. (d. New York City; June 4, 1990)

FURTHER READING

Obituary. *Variety*, June 6, 1990.
Obituary. *New York Times*, June 5, 1990.

Gillespie, Dizzy (John Birks Gillespie, 1917–) In his mid-70s, and one of the most celebrated figures in the history of jazz, Gillespie is also a very active musician right now. In March 1990, he was invited by President-elect Sam Nujoma of Namibia to play at Nujoma's inauguration, before an audience that included many African and other world leaders; the inauguration marked the end of the long Namibian war of independence. Gillespie, his band, and Secretary of State James Baker flew to Windhoeck aboard Air Force 2. It was the beginning of a world tour that also took Gillespie to Berlin's Brandenburg Gate, Prague, and Moscow.

Gillespie's 1990 also included a starring role in the forthcoming film *Winter in Lisbon*, about a jazz musician who leaves the United States for Europe because of racial discrimination, leaves music, and then returns. Also on screen, his feature-length documentary, *A Night in Havana,* went into worldwide release. And there were more awards: On June 10, he received the first Duke Ellington Award, at Washington's Kennedy Center. On December 4, he received a National Medal of the Arts from President George Bush at the White House.

South Carolina-born Gillespie, a trumpeter, composer, arranger, bandleader, and recording artist, became a leading jazz figure in the mid-1940s; in that period, with Charlie Parker and others, he is credited with having originated "bop," also often called "be-bop." Gillespie became a trumpeter in the early 1930s, and played with Teddy Hill, Cab Calloway, Benny Carter, Duke Ellington, and others until he formed his first successful band, in 1946. Gillespie composed such jazz and popular standards as "Night in Tunisia" (1942), "Salt Peanuts" (1945), and "Manteca" (1947), and has toured widely and recorded for the past five decades. In 1955, he published *To Be or Not to Bop: Memoirs of Dizzy Gillespie*, written with Al Fraser. He married Lorraine Wills in 1940.

FURTHER READING

Dizzy Gillespie. Tony Gentry. Chelsea House, 1991.
"Dizzy." Whitney Balliett. *New Yorker*, Sept. 17, 1990.
"Dizzy Gillespie. . . ." James Jones, IV. *Down Beat*, Aug. 1990.
"Bebop's joyful pop. . . ." Tim Powis. *Maclean's*, Mar. 20, 1989.
Dizzy Gillespie. Barry McRae. Phaidon Universe, 1989.
"Dizzy Gillespie." Marilyn Marshall. *Ebony*, Sept. 1986.
"Let us now praise Diz." (two parts) Bill Milkowski. *Down Beat*, Dec. 1985 and Jan. 1986.
Dizzy Gillespie. Raymond Horricks. Hippocrene, 1984.

Gingrich, Newt (Newton Leroy Gingrich, 1943–) House Republican whip Gingrich drew national attention in 1987 and 1988, as chief accuser of Democratic House Speaker Jim Wright, who ultimately resigned from the House. In August 1989, he urged ethics probes of seventeen other congressional Democrats, as well. Gingrich, himself, was accused of earlier ethics violations in April 1989, soon after his March 1989 selection as House Republican whip, and faced further ethics charges in October; but all charges against him were dropped in March 1990. A Republican conservative and hardline tax opponent, Gingrich sharply criticized Republican President George Bush for agreeing to tax increases as part of the late 1990 set of federal budget compromises.

Pennsylvania-born Gingrich taught at West Georgia College before his election to the House of Representatives in 1979. He has been married twice, and has two children. In 1984, with David Drake and Marianne Gingrich, he published *Window of Opportunity: A Blueprint for the Future*. He attended Emory and Tulane Universities.

FURTHER READING

"A party's Newt testament. . . ." Daniel Wattenberg. *Insight*, Nov. 12, 1990.
"Having read George Bush's lips. . . ." Bill Hewitt. *People*, Nov. 12, 1990.
"New Newt news." David Beers. *Mother Jones*, Feb–Mar. 1990.
"Master of disaster. . . ." David Beers. *Mother Jones*, Oct. 1989.
"Gingrich, Newton Leroy." *Current Biography*, July 1989.
"Stars of the 99th Congress." Sandra McElwaine. *Cosmopolitan*, Sept. 1985.

Girodias, Maurice (1919–90) Girodias was owner-publisher of Paris's Olympia Press, which first published Vladimir Nabokov's *Lolita* in 1955, when American publishing firms shied away from the controversial novel. The book made the fortune of the two-year-old firm, though Nabokov disliked Girodias's use of it in an anti-censorship crusade. At odds with French government censors, Girodias went to

America in 1964 and became a citizen, returning to France ten years later, where he continued to publish controversial, often erotic, works. (d. Paris; July 3, 1990)

FURTHER READING

Obituary. *The Times*, July 5, 1990.
"Checking in: Maurice Girodias." *Boston Magazine*, Mar. 1981.
"Pioneer in print." HERBERT MITGANG. *New York Times Book Review*, Dec. 7, 1980.

Glass, Philip (1937–) Composer and musician Glass introduced a major new opera, *The Hydrogen Jukebox,* which premiered in a concert version at Philadelphia's American Music Theater Festival in April 1990, and in a full production the next month at the Festival of Two Worlds: the Spoleto Festivals in Charleston, South Carolina, and then in Spoleto, Italy. The work was produced in collaboration with poet Allen Ginsberg and visual artist Jerome Sirlin, starting from a cantata based on Ginsberg's anti-war poem, "Wichita Vortex Sutra," which now forms the climax of the opera's first act.

In a different vein, Godfrey Reggio's non-narrative, experimental film *Koyaanisqatsi* (1983), was released on video this year, bringing to new audiences Glass's haunting score, reflecting the serenity of nature disrupted by human activities; the title is Hopi for "life out of balance." Glass's music was used to score other works as well, such as Errol Morris's *The Thin Blue Line* (1988) and ABC's Peter Jennings special, *Guns* (1990).

In his developing body of work, Baltimore-born Glass has wiped out any "line" that might still be said to exist between modern classical and popular music. He emerged as a leading modern composer in the late 1960s, after a Paris period in which he worked with Ravi Shankar and studied with Nadia Boulanger, then weaving modernist and Indian themes and techniques into his music. He founded the Philip Glass Ensemble in 1968, and became a well-known figure on tour and a popular recording artist in the early 1970s, with such works as *Music in 12 Parts* (1971–74), and *Glassworks* (1982). He also began a major career as a classical composer in the 1970s, with *Einstein On the Beach* (1976), still his best-known classical work, and the other two parts of his celebrated "portrait opera" trilogy: *Akhnaten* (1980), and *Satyagraha* (1985). Among his other operas are *The Civil Wars* (1982–84), *The Making of the Representative for Planet 8* (1988), *One Thousand Airplanes on the Roof* (1988), and *Mattogrosso* (1989). In 1987, he published the memoir, *Music by Philip Glass*. Glass attended the University of Chicago and The Juilliard School of Music. He was formerly married, and has two children.

FURTHER READING

American Music Makers. JANET NICHOLS. Walker, 1990.
"Glass." TIM PAGE. *Opera News*, June 1988.
"Philip Glass." HOWARD MANDEL. *Down Beat*, Apr. 1986.

Glenn, John Herschel, Jr. (1921–) Glenn is a leading American pilot, pioneering astronaut, and three-term Ohio Democratic senator, but his recent career has been dominated by charges that in 1987, he and four other senators unethically intervened with federal bank regulators on behalf of the Lincoln Savings and Loan Association of Irvine, California, controlled by Charles H. Keating, Jr.

The other four senators were Alan Cranston, Dennis DeConcini, John McCain, and Donald W. Riegle, Jr. The group came to be known as the "Keating Five." The bank was taken over in 1989 by federal banking authorities, in a bailout carrying an estimated cost of at least $2 billion.

In late November 1990, Senate Ethics Committee hearings began on the "Keating Five." Senator Glenn, with Senators DeConcini, Cranston, and McCain met with Edwin J. Gray, then chairman of the Federal Home Loan Bank Board, in DeConcini's Washington office, on April 2, 1987. Gray charged that the senators improperly put pressure on him on behalf of Lincoln, a charge they all denied. The same senators, and also Senator Riegle, met with Gray and members of the San Francisco Federal Home Bank in DeConcini's office on April 9, 1987. Glenn, a Democratic presidential nomination candidate in 1984, received $34,000 in direct political contributions from Keating and his associates, and a Glenn-associated political action committee received $200,000.

Ohio-born Glenn became a Marine pilot in 1943, and saw service in the Pacific during World War II and the Korean War, winning a long series of decorations. He became a leading test pilot, as well, and on July 16, 1957, was the first transcontinental pilot to fly at supersonic speeds. In 1959, he became a Project Mercury astronaut, and on February 20, 1962, piloting *Friendship 7*, he became a historic figure, as the first American to orbit Earth in a spacecraft. In 1974, he was elected to his first term as Ohio Democratic senator. Glenn's 1962 B.Sc. was from Muskingum College; he had been a student at the college from 1939 to 1942. He also attended naval flight schools. He married Anna Margaret Castor in 1943; the couple had two children.

FURTHER READING

"Seven sorry senators. . . ." Margaret Carlson. *Time*, Jan. 8, 1990.

Presidential Odyssey of John Glenn. Richard F. Fenno, Jr. Congressional Quarterly, 1990.

John Glenn: Space Pioneer. Ann Angel. Fawcett, 1989.

Famous in America: Jane Fonda, George Wallace, Phyllis Schafly, John Glenn. Peter N. Carroll. NAL-Dutton, 1986.

John Glenn: Around the World in Ninety Minutes. Paul Westman. Dillon, 1980.

Goddard, Paulette (Marion Levy, 1911–90) In the 1920s, still a teenager, Goddard appeared on Broadway in the Ziegfeld Follies. In the early 1930s, she was a Hollywood starlet, met and married Charles Chaplin, and played her first, unforgettable major role as the barefoot young girl in his classic *Modern Times* (1936). She appeared with him again in *The Great Dictator* (1940). She also starred in such films as *The Cat and the Canary* (1939), *The Ghost Breakers* (1940), *Reap the Wild Wind* (1942), *Kitty* (1946), *The Diary of a Chambermaid* (1946), and *Unconquered* (1947). In 1958, she married writer Erich Maria Remarque, and then lived with him in Switzerland, appearing only occasionally in films and television. (d. Switzerland; April 23, 1990)

FURTHER READING

Obituary. *Current Biography*, June, 1990.

"'40s star. . . ." Lawrence Cohn. Variety, Apr. 25, 1990.

Obituary. *New York Times*, Apr. 24, 1990.

Paulette: The Adventurous Life of Paulette Goddard. Joe Morella and Edward Z. Epstein. St. Martin's, 1985.

Goldberg, Arthur Joseph (1908–90) American lawyer and public servant, Goldberg was born poor and educated in Chicago, with experience in the Army and Office of Strategic Services (OSS) during World War II. In 1948, he became general counsel to the United Steelworkers of America and the Council of Industrial Organizations (CIO), negotiating labor-management contracts and the formation of the AFL-CIO. President John F. Kennedy appointed him secretary of labor in 1961 and associate justice of the Supreme Court the next year. That is normally a lifelong position; but, at Lyndon Johnson's urging, Goldberg resigned in 1965 to become ambassador to the United Nations, leaving the UN in 1968, largely over his opposition to the Vietnam War. He then resumed his law practice, often working for human rights, and was an ambassador-at-large during the Carter administration. In the 1970 New York gubernatorial race, he lost to Nelson Rockefeller. (d. Washington, D.C.; January 19, 1990)

FURTHER READING

Obituary. *Current Biography*, Mar. 1990.
"The liberal who could." *U.S. News & World Report*, Jan. 29, 1990.
Obituary. *The Times* (of London), Jan. 23, 1990.
Obituary. *New York Times*, Jan. 20, 1990.

Goldberg, Whoopi (Caryn Johnson, 1950–) Actress and comedian Goldberg scored a major success as the Harlem-based Black psychic in 1990's surprise top-grossing film, *Ghost,* winning the 1991 Best Supporting Actress Oscar. Largely because of her role in *Ghost,* Goldberg was named entertainer of the year at the 23rd annual Image Awards ceremony. She also received the annual award for excellence of the Sixth Annual Women in Film Festival. Goldberg signed a long-term feature film contract with Paramount. On screen, she also starred opposite Sissy Spacek in *The Long Walk Home,* set in the 1950s South during the civil rights struggle years. The television series "Bagdad Cafe," starring Goldberg and Jean Stapleton, began airing in April and stopped production in November. She also appeared in cabaret.

New York City-born Goldberg, who had previously worked as a popular cabaret and stage entertainer, emerged as a film star in *The Color Purple* (1985; she received an Oscar nomination), and went on to such films as *Jumpin' Jack Flash* (1986), *Fatal Beauty* (1987), and *Burglar* (1988). She had a one-woman show on Broadway in 1984, and toured in a second one-woman show in 1988. Goldberg was previously married and has one child.

FURTHER READING

"Whoopi unveils act. . . ." *Variety*, Feb. 10, 1988.
"Whoopi sounds off. . . ." *Jet*, June 15, 1987.
"Whoopi Goldberg." David Rensin. *Playboy*, June, 1987.
"Whoopi Goldberg talks. . . ." *Jet,* Nov. 3, 1986.
"Whoopi Goldberg." *People*, Dec. 23, 1985.
"Whoopi Goldberg. . . ." Jill Kearney. *American Film*, Dec. 1985.
"Goldberg, Whoopi." *Current Biography*, Mar. 1985.

Goldblum, Jeff (1952–) Goldblum's recent work continues to demonstrate his range. It includes a starring role opposite his wife, Geena Davis, in the film comedy *Earth Girls Are Easy* (1989); *Twisted Obsession* (1990), a psychological drama set in Paris; the film comedy *The Tall Guy* (1990), in which he plays an American actor in London; the fantasy *Mr. Frost* (1990), in which he plays opposite Alan Bates and Kathy Baker; and the television movie *Framed* (1990), a crime drama in which he plays opposite Kristin Scott-Thomas as a painter framed for forgery by his lover.

Pittsburgh-born Goldblum played in the New York theater in the early 1970s, most notably in *Two Gentlemen of Verona* (1971). His wide range of films includes *Invasion of the Body Snatchers* (1978), *The Big Chill* (1983), *The Right Stuff* (1983), *Silverado* (1985), *The Fly* (1986), and *Beyond Therapy* (1987). He also appeared in the television series "Tenspeed and Brownshoe" (1980) and in the notable 1987 telefilm *The Race for the Double Helix*, as James Watson. Goldblum attended the Neighborhood Playhouse.

FURTHER READING

"Married. . . . with chicken." Johanna Schneller. *GQ—Gentlemen's Quarterly*, June 1989.
"The new Jeff Goldblum. . . ." Jack Curry. *Cosmopolitan*, May 1987.
"Lord of the flies. . . ." David Ansen. *Newsweek*, Sept. 15, 1986.

Goldfarb, David (1918–90) Soviet-Jewish geneticist Goldfarb's fight to leave the Soviet Union received worldwide publicity. Born in the Ukraine, Goldfarb lost his left leg at Stalingrad during World War II. Later, he helped shape modern genetics in the Soviet Union, but in 1978, he resigned his top post and sought to join his son in the United States. Denial of his right to emigrate became an international issue, more poignant because he was seriously ill with diabetes and heart disease. Helped by international businessman Armand Hammer, Goldfarb and his wife were allowed to emigrate in 1986; he became a visiting scholar at the National Institutes of Health. (d. Washington, DC; February 24, 1990)

FURTHER READING

Obituary. *The Times* (of London), Mar. 3, 1990.
Obituary. *New York Times*, Feb. 26, 1990.

"Ex-refusenik dies." CONSTANCE HOLDEN. *Science*, Mar. 9, 1990.
"Mission from Moscow." *Time*, Oct. 27, 1986.

Gonzalez Márquez, Felipe (1942–) The leader of the Spanish Socialist Workers Party (PSOE) and democratic socialist prime minister of Spain won a third term in the October 1989 elections, though only by one parliamentary seat; and on review, that seat was lost by his party, leaving him without a clear parliamentary majority. Yet, he continued in office, surviving a one-day general strike in December 1989, winning a vote of confidence in April 1990 in spite of a cabinet-level scandal, and further integrating Spain into the new Europe that emerged after the end of the Cold War.

A growing problem during 1989 and 1990 was the emergence of a new round of inflation and the growth of foreign trade imbalances, although the Spanish economy continued to grow strongly. Another problem was the continuance of U.S. military activity in Spain, although Gonzalez Márquez pursued negotiations aimed at limiting that American military presence, with increasing success as the Cold War wound down. He supported early American action in the Persian Gulf Crisis, triggering considerable domestic opposition in historically neutralist Spain.

Gonzalez Márquez became a member of the then-illegal Spanish Socialist Workers Party in 1964, having been a socialist youth group member since 1962. He rose to become his party's leader, and succeeded Adolfo Suarez González as prime minister with his party's victory in the 1982 elections. He was the first socialist prime minister of Spain since the Spanish Civil War; his election signaled the full emergence of a new Spain after the long night of the Franco period. In 1986, he took Spain into the European common market. He is married to Carmen Romero; they have three children. He attended the Catholic University of Louvaine.

FURTHER READING

"For Spain and 'Felipe'. . . ." JOHN DARNTON. *New York Times*, June 26, 1984.
"Parliament in Spain. . . ." JAMES A. MARKHAM. *New York Times*, Dec. 2, 1982.

Goodman, John (1952–) Actor-comedian Goodman enjoyed continuing success as Roseanne Barr's husband on television's "Roseanne," a role for which he was named the funniest male in a series at the 1990 American Comedy Awards. His film career also continued to develop: Late in 1989 he opened in Steven Spielberg's *Always,* with Richard Dreyfuss and Holly Hunter. Early in 1990, he opened in *Stella,* a campy remake of *Stella Dallas,* opposite Bette Midler. Both films did poorly at the box office, but did well when they arrived in the video rental market later in the year. Late in 1990, Goodman also appeared in *Tom & Jerry's 50th Birthday Bash,* a Turner Broadcasting Company (TBS) salute to the Hanna-Barbera cartoon characters. For 1991, he was set to appear as a screenwriter in the Coen Brothers' 1940s Hollywood mystery *Barton Fink* and in *King Ralph,* as a Las Vegas lounge pianist who becomes King of England.

Privately, Goodman and three New Orleans police officers were sued by a free-lance photographer who alleged that he was "roughed up" after trying to take pictures of Goodman and his new bride after their 1989 wedding reception. Goodman was grand marshal in the New Orleans Mardi Gras parade, and also the city's first celebrity Santa Claus in the annual Canal Street Christmas parade.

Before his "Roseanne" role catapulted him to stardom, Missouri-born Goodman had played in strong character roles in the theater and in films, on Broadway in such plays as *Loose Ends* (1979), and *Big River* (1985), and in such films as *Eddie Macon's Run* (1983), *True Stories* (1986), *Raising Arizona* (1987), and *Sea of Love* (1989). He married Anna Elizabeth (Annabeth) Hartzog in 1989; they have one daughter. Goodman attended Southwest Missouri State College.

FURTHER READING

"John Goodman. . . ." FRED ROBBINS. *Woman's Day*, May 1, 1990.
"Everybody's all American. . . ." RICHARD ZOGLIN. *Time*, Feb. 19, 1990.
"New-age sex symbol. . . ." TOM GREEN. *Cosmopolitan*, Sept. 1989.
"'Getting married. . . .'" VICKI JO RADOVSKY. *Redbook*, Sept. 1989.
"Playing second fiddle. . . ." KIM HUBBARD. *People*, Nov. 28, 1988.

Gorbachev, Mikhail Sergeyevich

(1931–) Soviet leader Mikhail Gorbachev has become a centrally important figure in recent world history, who has made an enormous contribution to world peace and the end of the Cold War, and has brought massive and welcome changes to his own country and the European world. Yet he faces tremendous economic and political problems and charges of a return to dictatorial rule at home.

In 1985, Gorbachev became general secretary of the Soviet Communist Party Central Committee and, effectively, leader of the Soviet Union. In power, he immediately began the processes of internal change. His two main slogans were *perestroika*, meaning a massive restructuring of the Soviet economy, away from central planning, bureaucracy, and full state ownership and toward a market economy, private enterprise, and even private ownership of land; and *glasnost*, or "openness," meaning a move toward basic democratic freedoms. As of this writing, both processes were continuing, although often erratically, unevenly, and with great difficulty, and have so far resulted in bringing about an end to the central role of the Communist Party, the reorganization of the Soviet government, and the development of a

democratic parliament, while also triggering enormous economic problems and ethnic and national unrest in his country, all of which is proving very hard to handle. In early 1991, with internal security forces attacks on nationalist and separatist groups in the Baltic Republics, at least a partial return to authoritarian rule was greatly feared by Soviet reformers.

Abroad, Gorbachev also moved very quickly once in power. In a series of meetings with Presidents Ronald Reagan and George Bush, he initiated what became the end of the 45-year-long Cold War, beginning with the 1987 Intermediate-range Nuclear Forces (INF) Treaty, and helped to negotiate the end of a series of regional conflicts, as in Central America and southern Africa. At the same time, he normalized relations with China, bringing that 30-year-old conflict to an end. And, during the late 1980s, he essentially agreed to set the peoples of Eastern Europe free, encouraging the development of what became independent, noncommunist governments in Poland, Czechoslovakia, Hungary, Bulgaria, Romania, and East Germany. The developments in East Germany led directly to the tearing down of the Berlin Wall and the 1990 unification of Germany. He drew the line, however, at least as of this writing, on the independence of the Baltic Republics, Moldavia Georgia, the Ukraine, and several other Soviet republics, maintaining that, once started, the process would lead to the dismemberment of the Soviet Union, and instead proposed a looser federation of Soviet republics. In 1990, he was awarded the Nobel Peace Prize. Among his recent works explaining himself and his philosophy to the West are *Perestroika and Soviet-American Relations* (1990), *At the Summit: A New Start in U.S.-Soviet Relations* (1988), and *Toward a Better World* and *Perestroika: New Thinking for Our Country and the World* (both 1987).

Gorbachev's early career proceeded in orthodox Soviet fashion: He joined the Communist Party of the Soviet Union in 1952, and for the next 33 years moved up through the party and government. He became a member of his party's central committee in 1971, and was minister of agriculture from 1978 to 1985. Mikhail Gorbachev and Raisa Maximova Titorenko married in 1956; they have one child. He attended Moscow State University and the Stavropol Agricultural Institute.

FURTHER READING

"What Gorbachev wants. . . ." JASON McMANUS and MARSHALL LOEB. *Fortune*, Dec. 31, 1990.
"No peace for Gorbachev." STEVEN MANNING. *Scholastic Update*, Dec. 7, 1990.
"Gorbachev's home remedy. . . ." JOHN KOHAN. *Time*, Sept. 17, 1990.
"Shared goals." *Newsweek*, Sept. 17, 1990.
"'I am an optimist'. . . ." *Time*, June 4, 1990.
"Mikhail Gorbachev: the first Soviet President." *Soviet Life*, June 1990.
"Survival mode. . . ." ANNIE KRIEGEL. *New Republic*, May 14, 1990.
"Gorbachev's intellectual odyssey. . . ." JOSHUA MURAVCHIK. *New Republic*, Mar. 5, 1990.
"The year of the people. . . ." BRUCE W. NELAN. *Time*, Jan. 1, 1990.
"Russian revolution—the sequel." ROBIN BLACKBURN. *Progressive*, Jan. 1990.
Gorbachev: Heretic in the Kremlin. DUSKO DODER and LOUISE BRANSON. Viking Penguin, 1990.
Mikhail Gorbachev: A Leader for Soviet Change. WALTER OLEKSY. Childrens, 1989.
Mikhail Gorbachev: The Soviet Innovator. STEVEN OTFINOSKI. Fawcett, 1989.
Mikhail S. Gorbachev: An Intimate Biography. DONALD MORRISON. New American Library-Dutton, 1988.
Gorbachev! Has the Real Antichrist Come?. ROBERT W. FAID. Victory House, 1988.
Gorbachev: A Biography. THOMAS G. BUTSON. Scarborough House, 1986.
The Picture Life of Mikhail Gorbachev. JANET CAULKINS. Watts, 1985.
"Gorbachev, Mikhail (Sergeyevich)." *Current Biography*, Aug. 1985.

Gorbachev, Raisa Maksimova Titorenko (1934–) The wife of Soviet leader Mikhail Gorbachev, Raisa Gorbachev, a former teacher, has had considerable impact in her own right, speaking out for reform on many of the difficult questions facing the Soviet Union during the Gorbachev era. Although not herself a political leader, she has served in some ways as model for many Soviet women, her popularity and status being very different from that of previous women in her position, who were seldom seen and never spoke out. Even her clothes and shopping trips while abroad made news in her country, as Soviet women reached out for lifestyles already common in most other industrial countries, although some Soviet conservatives criticized her for what they saw as extravagance. She made a particularly notable impression in the United States during the June 1990 Washington summit, making highly publicized visits to several American cities and joining Barbara Bush as a commencement speaker at Wellesley College.

Raisa Gorbachev was born in Stavropol, attended Moscow University and the Stavropol Teachers Training College, and was a teacher in Stavropol when she married Mikhail Gorbachev in 1956. From 1957 to 1961, she was on the staff of the Stavropol Teachers Training Institute. She and Mikhail Gorbachev have one child.

FURTHER READING

Raisa Gorbachev. Chelsea House, 1991.
"'My wife is. . . . '" HOWARD G. CHUA-EOAN. Time, June 6, 1988.

"Gorbachev, Raisa." *Current Biography*, May 1988.
"Washington welcomes Raisa." TRUDE B. FELDMAN. *McCall's*, Mar. 1988.
"The rise and rise of Raisa. . . ." GEORGE J. CHURCH. *Time*, Jan. 4, 1988.
"Gorbo's other woman. . . . " FREIDIN GREGORY. *New Republic*, Dec. 28, 1987.
"The world's ten most important women." *Ladies Home Journal*, Nov. 1987.
"A new style first lady." MYRNA BLYTH. *Ladies Home Journal*, Sept. 1987.

Gordimer, Nadine (1923–) South African writer Gordimer saw her latest novel off the presses in late 1990, and marked the occasion by visiting the United States. *My Son's Story,* set as usual in her home country, spins the tale of a son who discovers that his father, a "Colored" activist, has a relationship with a White woman. Amazed and pleased at the recent changes in South Africa—she had thought she would never live to see the African National Congress (ANC) a legal political organization and Nelson Mandela freed—the woman sometimes called the "conscience of South Africa" is still very much aware of how much more needs to be done. As soon as the ban on the ANC was removed, she joined, and says proudly, "I'm happy to be a card-carrying member of the ANC."

At one point in 1990, rumors circulated that Gordimer was being asked to write Mandela's autobiography; but Gordimer says she and Mandela met only because he wanted her advice about the workings of the publishing industry. They also talked about banning; three of Gordimer's books were banned for years, most notably *Burger's Daughter*. Gordimer was a logical person for such discussions, because she is a founder and active member of the Congress of South African Writers, consisting mostly of Black writers and often allied with the ANC.

Gordimer is often described as a White South African writer whose work illuminates the multiple corruptions and injustices at the heart of a racist society; and so it does, but through the personal lives and concerns of the people in her work, rather than as a set of direct political statements. Her novels include *The Lying Days* (1953), *A World of Strangers* (1958), *Occasion for Loving* (1963), *The Late Bourgeois World* (1966), *A Guest of Honour* (1970), *The Conservationist* (1974; for which she shared a Booker Prize), *Burger's Daughter* (1979), *July's People* (1981), and *A Sport of Nature* (1987). She has also published many volumes of short stories, from *The Soft Voice of the Serpent* (1953), to *Six Feet of Country* (1986), and several volumes of essays. She has been married twice, and has three children.

FURTHER READING

"Ordinary loves. . . ." LAUREL GRAEBER. *New York Times Book Review*, Oct. 21, 1990.
Nadine Gordimer. JUDIE NEWMAN. Routledge Chapman & Hall, 1988.
"Nadine Gordimer. . . ." CAROL STERNHELL. *Ms.*, Sept. 1987.
"A land where. . . ." ALVIN P. SANOFF. *U.S. News & World Report,* May 25, 1987.
"Shocked by. . . ." MARK A. UHLIG. *New York Times Book Review*, May 3, 1987.

Gordon, Dexter (1923–90) While still in his late teens, in 1940, Los Angeles-born jazz saxophonist Gordon joined Lionel Hampton's band, and also played with Louis Armstrong, Fletcher Henderson, and Billy Eckstine during World War II, becoming a soloist in 1945. He went back to Los Angeles in 1946, and from then into the early 1950s, with Wardell Gray, emerged as a leading be-bop saxophonist. He encountered serious problems in the 1950s, spending 1952 to 1954 and 1956 to 1960 in jail on drug convictions. He relocated to Copenhagen in 1962, and was a major jazz figure in Europe into the late 1970s. Gordon came out of retirement to star in Bernard Tavernier's film *'Round Midnight* (1986), as a Paris-based jazz musician much like himself, and won an Oscar nomination for the role. (d. Philadelphia; April 25, 1990)

FURTHER READING

Obituary. ART LANGE. *Down Beat*, July 1990.
"Dexter Gordon. . . ." LEE JESKE. *Rolling Stone*, June 14, 1990.
"Jazz legend. . . ." *Jet*, May 14, 1990.
Obituary. *Variety*, May 2, 1990.
Obituary. *The Times* (of London), Apr. 27, 1990.

Obituary. *New York Times*, Apr. 26, 1990.
"Dexter Gordon. . . ." CHUCK BERG. *Down Beat*, Sept. 1989.
Dexter Gordon: A Musical Biography. STAN BRITT. Da Capo, 1989.

Gorney, Jay (1897–1990) Gorney was the composer of the Depression-era standard, "Brother, Can You Spare a Dime?" (1932; lyrics, E.Y. Harburg). Immigrating from Russia as a child, Gorney began songwriting in New York in the 1920s, moved to Hollywood in 1933, and collaborated with many lyricists. Among his other well-known songs are "Baby, Take a Bow," "You're My Thrill," and "Ah, But Is It Love?" (d. New York; June 14, 1990)

FURTHER READING

"Last laugh. . . ." *New York*, June 25, 1990.
Obituary. *Variety*, June 20, 1990.
Obituary. *New York Times*, June 15, 1990.

Gossett, Louis, Jr. (1936–) Gossett was seen in several guises on television in 1990. In February he starred with Ruby Dee in an American Playhouse production, *Zora Is My Name!;* in July he was an aging gunslinger in HBO's comedy-western *El Diablo;* and in September he faced racism in a small 1943 Georgia town in Lifetime's *Sudie and Simpson.* His film work included *Toy Soldiers,* a movie scheduled for 1991 release, about terrorists taking over a boys' prep school. He was one of several actors honored by the Black American Cinema Society. Privately, he continued working for social causes, notably against homelessness and inner-city poverty.

After over two decades as a highly regarded character actor in theater, films, and television, Brooklyn-born Gossett won an Emmy for his role as Fiddler in television's *Roots* (1977). He then went on to win a Best Supporting Actor Oscar in *An Officer and a Gentleman* (1982), and to appear in such films as *Iron Eagle* (1985), and *The Principal* (1987), and in such telefilms as *Sadat* (1983), and *A Gathering of Old Men* (1987). His B.A. was from New York University, in 1959.

FURTHER READING

"Gossett, Louis, Jr." *Current Biography*, Nov. 1990.
"Minority view. . . ." ROBERT HOFLER. *Life*, Mar. 1989.

Goulding, Raymond Walter (1922–90) Massachusetts-born Goulding was the "Ray" of the comic duo "Bob and Ray." He entered radio after high school in 1939, returning after war service to become a newscaster in Boston, where his future partner, Bob Elliott, was a disk jockey. Their banter, much of it spoofing radio shows, developed into a partnership and their own show. They soon moved to network radio and television popularity, especially in the 1950s. In 1970, they appeared on Broadway as *The Two and Only* and they later published *From Approximately Coast to Coast . . . It's the Bob & Ray Show* (1983), and *The New! Improved! Bob & Ray Book* (1985). Bob Elliott and Ray Goulding were most comfortable on radio, however, and they worked together until 1988 when Goulding retired with ill health. (d. Manhasset, New York; March 24, 1990)

FURTHER READING

Obituary. *Current Biography*, May 1990.
"Of many things." GEORGE W. HUNT. *America*, Apr. 7, 1990.
Obituary. *Variety*, Mar. 28, 1990.
Obituary. *New York Times*, Mar. 26, 1990.
"Bob & Ray. . . ." EDIE CLARK. *Yankee*, Sept. 1987.

Graf, Steffi (Stephanie Maria Graf, 1969–) German tennis player Graf encountered problems in 1990. The world's dominant tennis player since 1987, with a string of 66 consecutive victories, she lost four big matches in mid-year: the German Open, the French Open, Wimbledon, and the U.S. Open. Her problems were both physical and psychological. In February, while fleeing pressing photographers, she fell on a ski slope, fracturing her thumb and knocking her out of competition for over two months. Then in July, she had a sinus problem that required a minor operation, with more time lost.

More debilitating, Peter Graf, her father and mentor, was involved in a scandal that filled the German papers. Early in the year he told her that he was being harassed by a woman named Nicole Meissner, a former Playboy model. By mid-year, the newspapers had picked up the story of the extramarital affair and attempts by Meissner and her boyfriend to extort money from Peter Graf, reportedly $430,000. By November the scandal had reached the courts, with Peter Graf required to submit to a blood test in a paternity suit. All of this led to the uncharacteristic letdown in Steffi Graf's powerful game, reportedly causing some re-evaluations of her life and relationship to her father. Gradually, she seemed to regather her strength and return to her winning ways, starting with the Leipzig tournament in late September.

Graf emerged as a leading under-14 tennis player in the early 1980s, and a world-class star in the late 1980s, winning the German Open in 1986, the French Open in 1987, and becoming World Champion in 1988, the year she won the U.S., Wimbledon, Australian, and French Opens, along with the Olympic championship. She won the U.S., Wimbledon, and German Opens again in 1989. From her earliest years, she was coached by her father, Peter Graf.

FURTHER READING

Steffi Graf. Little, Brown, 1990.
"Serving her country." Curry Kirkpatrick. *Sports Illustrated*, June 26, 1989.
"Graf, Steffi." *Current Biography*, Feb. 1989.
"Bringing up baby. . . ." Peter Graf and Cindy Shmerler. *World Tennis*, May 1988.
Steffi Graf. Judy Monroe. Crestwood House, 1988.
"Germany shows a pair of aces. . . ." Tom Callahan. *Time*, June 29, 1987.
"One step to stardom." Joan Ryan. *Women's Sports and Fitness*, June 1987.

Graziano, Rocky (Thomas Rocco Barbella, 1922–90) The hard-punching, American boxer Graziano, portrayed in the 1956 movie *Somebody Up There Likes Me* (based on his autobiography), was the inspiration for *Rocky* (1976). Raised on Manhattan's Lower East Side, he was in and out of reform schools, becoming a powerful street fighter. While AWOL from the Army (after a fight with an officer, leading to a dishonorable discharge), he fought as Rocky Graziano (his sister's boyfriend's name), winning New York's amateur welterweight championship in 1941. Turning professional, Graziano built a record of 67 wins, 10 losses, and 6 draws. He won the world middleweight championship in 1947 in the second of three brutal fights with Tony Zale, but failed in a title comeback against Sugar Ray Robinson in 1952. He later worked as an actor. He published a second autobiographical work, *Somebody Down Here Likes Me, Too,* in 1981. (d. New York; May 22, 1990)

FURTHER READING

"Graziano's death. . . ." Ben Henkey. *Sporting News*, June 4, 1990.
"Not to be forgotten." *Sports Illustrated*, June 4, 1990.
Obituary. *New York Times*, May 24, 1990.
Obituary. *The Times* (of London), May 24, 1990.

Greenspan, Alan (1926–) Greenspan moved into the center of national economic activity when he was appointed head of the Federal Reserve System by President Ronald Reagan in 1987, and continued to exert a powerful deflationary effect on the American economy through the late 1980s and into the early years of the Bush administration, refusing to significantly lower interest rates

and loosen money supplies, despite much pressure from both parties and the president. Throughout 1989 and 1990, he continued to stress the twin threats of inflation and skyrocketing, uncontrolled deficits. He insisted that a recession had not yet arrived, no matter how adverse the current economic news was, and that deficit control was necessary before he would authorize lower interest rates.

As the recession deepened, however, and the banking and credit crisis became more acute, he did slightly loosen money policy in July, and in October, after the federal budget compromise agreement, slightly lowered interest rates. As the Persian Gulf Crisis developed, he strongly resisted further action, while waiting to see how oil prices and the cost of the American commitment might affect economic growth, inflation, and recession. In January and February 1991, he did move to cut interest rates.

Greenspan, a leading free-market economic conservative, was a key economic consultant to Presidents Nixon and Ford, and was chairman of the Council of Economic Advisers from 1974 to 1976. A New Yorker, Greenspan received his B.S. in 1948, his M.A. in 1950, and his Ph.D in 1977, all from New York University.

FURTHER READING

"Is Alan Greenspan impotent?" Robin Wright. *New Republic*, Apr. 9, 1990.
"Greenspan, Alan." *Current Biography*, Jan. 1989.
"Greenspan isn't a Volcker clone." Lee Smith. *Fortune*, July 6, 1987.
"A conservative who. . . ." Barbara Rudolph. *Time*, June 15, 1987.
"The new Mr. Dollar. . . ." George Russell. *Time*, June 15, 1987.
"A celebrity economist. . . ." Mickey Kaus. *Newsweek*, June 15, 1987.
Reagan's man at the Fed. . . ." Bill Powell. *Newsweek*, June 15, 1987.
"The wisdom of Salomon. . . ." John Liscio. *Barron's*, June 8, 1987.

Gretzky, Wayne (1961–) On October 26, 1990, Gretzky reached a milestone in hockey history, when he scored his 2,000th point in regular season play, in a game against the Winnipeg Jets at Winnipeg Arena. It was a plateau once thought unreachable—Gretzky, himself, had years earlier said reaching 2,000 points was out of the question. But he reached it and was still counting, with a long career still ahead of him. At age 29, he says he plans to play for another six seasons. By the time he reached the 2,000 point mark, Gretzky also held numerous other National Hockey League records, including most regular season assists (1,316), most assists including playoffs (1,511), most points including playoffs (2,284), and most games with three or more goals (46).

In 1990 he also published *Gretzky: An Autobiography*, written with Rick Reilly, a follow-up to his *Gretzky: From the Backyard Rink to the Stanley Rink* (1985), written with Jim Taylor. Gretzky had some excitement in a different quarter, too, as part owner of Saumarez, a racehorse that won the Continent's biggest race, the Prix de l'Arc de Triomphe, though not—or not yet—having the same success in North America.

Ontario-born Gretzky was by far the leading player in professional hockey during the 1980s, as Edmonton Oiler center (1979 to 1988) and Los Angeles Kings center (from 1988). He was rookie of the year in 1979, the Most Valuable Player in the National Hockey League for nine of the ten years of the 1980s (1980 to 1987, 1989), and the leading point scorer in the league from 1981 to 1987. He married Janet Jones in 1988; they have one child.

FURTHER READING

Wayne Gretzky: Hockey Great. Tom Raber. Lerner, 1991.
"The charmed life of Wayne & Janet." *Chatelaine*, Nov. 1990.

Wayne Gretzky. Steve Hanks. St. Martin's, 1990.
"Regrets?. . . ." GORDON EDES. *Sporting News*, Oct. 3, 1988.
"Relax, Canada. . . ." JOHANNA SCHNELLER. *Chatelaine*, May, 1988.
"A national celebration." HAL QUINN. *Maclean's*, Jan. 25, 1988.
"The best in the world." PETER GZOWSKI. *Maclean's*, Jan. 25, 1988.
Record Breakers of Pro Sports. NATHAN AASENG. Lerner, 1987.
Wayne Gretzky. JANE M. LEDER. Crestwood House, 1985.

Griffith, Melanie (1957–) Griffith's 1988 hit film *Working Girl* continued to bring her great attention, winning her a 1989 Oscar nomination, and in April 1990 generating a situation comedy of that name, starring Sandra Bullock in Griffith's Tess McGill role. Griffith, a promising new face in the late 1970s, had emerged as a mature star opposite Harrison Ford in *Working Girl*. Once achieved, she kept up the momentum: In 1990, she starred opposite Matthew Modine and Michael Keaton in John Schlesinger's film thriller *Pacific Heights*, set in San Francisco, and opposite Tom Hanks and Bruce Willis in the Brian De Palma film version of the Tom Wolfe bestseller *The Bonfire of the Vanities*. She will star as an anti-Nazi American working in 1941 Germany in the forthcoming film *Shining Through,* opposite Michael Douglas, in a cast that also includes John Gielgud.

New York City-born Griffith got off to a quick start, playing strong, young supporting roles in three 1975 films: *Night Moves*, *The Drowning Pool*, and *Smile*, but then she encountered personal and professional problems. She re-emerged as a leading dramatic actress in the mid-1980s, in such films as *Something Wild* (1986), *The Milagro Beanfield War* (1988), and *Stormy Monday* (1988).

FURTHER READING

"Griffith, Melanie." *Current Biography*, Oct. 1990.
"Melanie mellows out." BONNIE SIEGLER. *Ladies Home Journal*, Oct. 1990.
"Melanie Griffith." JEANNINE STEIN. *Harper's Bazaar*, Sept. 1989.
"Melanie Griffith. . . ." JESSE KORNBLUTH. *Cosmopolitan*, July 1989.
"Then and now. . . ." *Teen*, May 1989.
"Melanie Griffith." MERRILL SHINDLER. *Los Angeles Magazine*, May 1989.
"It's Miami Nice. . . ." *TV Guide*, Jan. 28, 1989.
"Working her way. . . ." CATHLEEN MCGUIGAN. *Newsweek*, Jan. 2, 1989.
The New Breed: Actors Coming of Age. KAREN HARDY and KEVIN J. KOFFLER. Holt, 1988.

Grishchenko, Anatoly (1937–90) Grishchenko was a hero of Chernobyl, a Soviet pilot who in April 1986 repeatedly flew his helicopter into the radioactive gases over the burning nuclear plant, dumping sand and cement to cap the reactor. With totally inadequate attempts at protective shielding, he contracted radiation sickness and then leukemia, for which he was given a bone marrow transplant in the United States in April 1990. (d. Seattle, Washington; July 13, 1990)

FURTHER READING

Obituary. *New York Times*, July 14, 1990.

Groening, Matt (Matthew Akbar Groening, 1954–) Writer and cartoonist Groening shook up the family sitcom world with his ornery, eccentric, outrageous, dysfunctional, anti-traditional, and anti-sweetness-and-light animated family, "The Simpsons," including groveling father Homer, mother Marge (noted for her blue beehive hairstyle), and their bratty children, Bart, Lisa, and Maggie. First seen as spots on "The Tracey Ullman Show," the Simpsons became a phenomenon from the show's first regular airing in early 1990, a ratings hit, even though it appears on the upstart Fox Network, which is not available to all homes—and even though in fall 1990, it was scheduled opposite NBC's high-rated "The Cosby Show." The Simpsons even appeared on the cover of *TV Guide,* offering inside their own peculiar brand of television commentary.

As creator and executive producer of the show some people label "Father Knows Worst," Groening has overall responsibility for the main drawing and scripts, though others further develop the scripts and animation for the screen form. Groening also collects royalties on the wide range of merchandise and advertisements that feature the bug-eyed Simpson characters. In 1990, Groening also published his latest set of cartoons, *The Big Book of Hell*. On the side, he designed the cover art for Harry Shearer's spoofing rap single "(If U Want Free Speech) Go to Russia." In the works was a record album *The Simpsons Sing the Blues*.

Son of a cartoonist and advertising filmmaker (coincidentally named Homer), Oregon-born Groening began cartooning in college and later for alternative newspapers in Los Angeles from 1977, then emerged as a leading cartoonist in the 1980s, with his comic strip *Life in Hell* (1980–) and such books as *Love Is Hell* and *Work Is Hell* (both 1986), *Childhood Is Hell* (1987), and *School Is Hell* and *Akbar and Jeff's Guide to Life* (both 1988). His B.A. was from Evergreen State College in 1977. He married Deborah Lee Caplan in 1986, the year she published his first book, which was the foundation of their Life in Hell Company, which she now runs. They have one son, named Homer.

FURTHER READING

"Groening, Matt." *Current Biography*, Sept. 1990.
"20 questions. . . ." NEIL TESSER. *Playboy*, July 1990.
"Is TV the coolest invention. . . ." SEAN ELDER. *Mother Jones*, Dec. 1989.
"Cartoon from hell." ROBERT LLOYD. *American Film*, Oct. 1989.
"Hell can wait." DANIEL WEIZMAN. *California*. Oct. 1989.

Guare, John (1938–)

The playwright scored a huge success with the Broadway production of his new play *Six Degrees of Separation,* set in an upper-class, East Side, New York apartment and based on the real-life 1983 story of a Black con man who successfully posed as "David Poitier," Sidney Poitier's "son," and ultimately stayed with, borrowed money from, and then robbed his victims. Guare's play raised many continuing questions of New York's racial and class relations, homelessness, Black despair, and liberal guilt; it was extremely well-received, becoming the hit drama of the season. In Guare's play, directed by Jerry Zaks, the Black con man is named Paul Poitier, and played by James McDaniel; he successfully makes his pitch to Ouisa and Fran Kittredge (Stockard Channing and John Cunningham).

New York City-born Guare wrote the plays *Muzeeka* (1968), and *Cop-out* (1969) before emerging as a major modern playwright with his celebrated *House of Blue Leaves* (1971). His later plays included *Landscape of the Body* (1977), *Bosoms and Neglect* (1979), *Lydie Breeze* (1982), and *Moon Over Miami* (1988). He received an Oscar nomination for his 1981 *Atlantic City* screenplay. His 1961 B.A. was from Georgetown University, and his M.A. was from Yale University. He is married to Adele Chatfield-Taylor.

FURTHER READING

"Guare, John." *Current Biography*, Aug. 1982.
"Malle's American connection." SCOT HALLER. *Saturday Review*, June 1982.
"The coming of age. . . ." ROSS WETZSTEON. *New York*, Feb. 22, 1982.

Gumble, Bryant Charles (1948–)

NBC "Today" show anchor Gumbel was the man in the middle in 1989 and 1990. When Deborah Norville came to "Today" as news reader in August 1989, the media immediately portrayed her as a schemer out to oust Jane Pauley, breaking up her long and successful anchoring partnership with Gumbel. When Pauley decided to move out to do her own prime-time news show and Norville took her place in January 1990, the show took a ratings slump of about 17 percent. As the easy, longstanding relationship between Gumbel and Pauley was replaced by the cooler, more businesslike Gumble-Norville pairing, the show floundered. Former co-anchor Joe Garagiola was brought back to try to stabilize the show, and Faith Daniels was added to the mix. In May 1990, Gumbel and the rest of the "Today" staff even took off to go "camping" in Pennsylvania's Pocono Mountains. Ratings did revive strongly in August, when Gumbel went to Saudi Arabia to report on the Gulf Crisis.

Even before the Pauley-Norville affair, Gumbel had sparked controversy over "Today", when a supposedly confidential memo was leaked to the press. In suggesting various format changes, Gumbel had criticized most of his colleagues (except Pauley), notably popular weatherman Willard Scott. When that was publicized, Gumbel's image was damaged, and Gumbel and Scott had to work hard to re-establish an easy, on-screen relationship.

A former sports commentator and avid golfer, Gumbel was in 1990 named host for most of NBC's golf tournaments. In 1989, he had hosted the first Bryant Gumbel/Walt Disney World Pro-Am Golf Tournament in Florida, raising money for the United Negro College Fund. Always an interviewer, rarely an interviewee, he made a rare appearance on ABC, talking with Barbara Walters on *20/20* in March 1990.

New Orleans-born Gumbel began his career as a writer and then editor (1971–72) of the magazine *Black Sports*. He moved into broadcasting as a California sportscaster (KNBC, Burbank, 1972–81), and from 1975 to 1982 was also a widely known NBC network sportscaster, receiving 1976 and 1977 Emmy awards. He became a national figure as co-host of the "Today Show" (1982–), a trailblazer as the first Black star of a television morning show. His B.A. was from Bates College, in 1973. He married June Baranco in 1973; they have three children. Sportscaster Greg Gumbel is his brother.

FURTHER READING

"It's brother vs. brother. . . ." JANE MARION. *TV Guide*, July 14, 1990.
"The mourning anchor." RICK REILLY. *Sports Illustrated*, Sept. 26, 1988.
"Gumbel does little to dispel rumors. . . ." *Variety*, Apr. 20, 1988.
"Today's man. . . ." SHEILA WELLER. *McCall's*, June 1987.
"Bryant Gumbel." DAVID RENSIN. *Playboy*, Dec. 1986.
"Today's man. . . ." DAVID BLUM. *New York*, Aug. 4, 1986.
"Gumbel, Bryant." *Current Biography*, July 1986.
"Bryant Gumbel. . . ." CHRIS CHASE. *Cosmopolitan*, Feb. 1986.

Guttenberg, Steve (1958–) Having appeared in four of the six *Police Academy* and both of the *Cocoon* films, Guttenberg continued on in sequels, starring with Ted Danson and Tom Selleck in the sequel to their 1987 comedy *Three Men and a Baby*, this one titled *Three Men and a Little Lady* (1990); Robin Weisman was five-year-old Mary. He also played the cartoonist-biker in *Don't Tell Her It's Me*, with Shelley Long and Jami Gertz. He and Long star in the forthcoming film comedy *The Boyfriend School*, as a brother and sister who run a charm school.

Brooklyn-born Guttenberg emerged as a leading young film star in the early 1980s, with his role in *Diner* (1982). He went on to appear in the first four of the *Police Academy* films (1984, 1985, 1986, and 1987), the two *Cocoon* films (1985, 1988), and in such films as *The Bedroom Window* (1987), *Three Men and a Baby* (1987), and *High Spirits* (1988), and he also appeared in several telefilms, including *The Day After* (1984). He attended the State University at Albany.

FURTHER READING

"Three men and. . . ." JEFF ROVIN. *Ladies Home Journal*, Dec. 1990.
"Steve Guttenberg. . . ." STU SCHREIBERG. *Cosmopolitan*, July 1988.
"Meet the new 'Mr. Moms'." KATHY HENDERSON. *Redbook*, Nov. 1987.

H

Habash, George (1925–) As general secretary of the Popular Front for the Liberation of Palestine (PFLP), Habash has consistently urged armed action against Israel, and only very reluctantly went along with the nonterrorist position taken by Yasir Arafat in the late 1980s, though he and his group opposed that policy. But by early 1990, he was once again urging guerrilla warfare, and attacking the Arafat policy. After the August Iraqi invasion of Kuwait, Habash moved his headquarters from Syria, which opposed the invasion, to Iraq, and strongly supported Saddam Hussein.

A Christian Palestinian doctor, Habash practiced medicine in the 1950s, and was a founder of the Heroes of the Return Organization, which in 1967 merged with two other groups to form the PFLP, a left socialist faction in the Palestinian movement. He graduated as a doctor from the American University of Beirut.

FURTHER READING

"Habash, George." *Current Biography,* Apr. 1988.
"Beirut's Dr. death." *Newsweek*, Jan. 1, 1979.

Hackman, Gene (1930–) In 1990, Hackman played an outstanding cameo role as a tough moviemaker in the critically acclaimed *Postcards from the Edge*. His *Narrow Margin*, with Anne Archer, was a more traditional action-thriller, as was *Loose Cannons*, a cop-buddy movie with Dan Aykroyd; another of his action pictures, *The Package* (1989), did well when released in the video market. Among the films Hackman was shooting in 1990 were *Class Action*, as a rumpled lawyer taking on a car company, and *Indian Runner*, Sean Penn's writing-directing debut about a returning Vietnam veteran. Privately, Hackman underwent surgery to clear a much-narrowed heart artery.

California-born Hackman became a star in his Best Actor Oscar-winning role as Popeye Doyle in *The French Connection* (1971), a role he repeated in *The French Connection II* (1975). Among his other films are *The Poseidon Adventure* (1972), *The Conversation* (1974),

Night Moves (1975), and the notable *Mississippi Burning* (1988). He was previously married to Faye Maltese, and has three children.

FURTHER READING

"Hollywood's uncommon man." MICHAEL NORMAN. *New York Times Magazine*, Mar. 19, 1989.
"Fire this time. . . ." ELIZABETH L. BLAND, JACK E. WHITE, and RICHARD CORLISS. *Time*, Jan. 9, 1989.
"The last honest man. . . ." BEVERLY WALKER. *Film Comment*, Nov.–Dec. 1988.
Gene Hackman. ALLAN HUNTER. St. Martin's, 1988.

Hale, Alan, Jr. (1918–90) American actor Hale was the jovial Skipper on television's "Gilligan's Island" (1964–67). Son of actor Alan Hale, he played in various films, including *The West Point Story* (1950), but had his greatest success in television, with many guest appearances and several comedy series before becoming a "Gilligan's" regular. Three reunion specials (1978–1981), and widespread reruns kept fresh the Skipper image, which he also adopted at his Hollywood lobster restaurant. (d. Los Angeles; January 2, 1990)

FURTHER READING

Obituary. Variety, Jan. 10, 1990.
Obituary. New York Times, Jan. 4, 1990.

Hall, Arsenio (1955–) Comedian and actor Hall became a leading talk-show host in 1989 and 1990—quite apart from being the first Black talk-show host in television history. Syndicated by Paramount, his show appears nationwide on well over 150 stations, partly overlapping and sometimes directly competing with Hall's early inspiration and idol, Johnny Carson. Carson seems not to be threatened, since his audiences tend to be older, more conservative, and less urban than Hall's; and Hall's approach is more hip and gossipy, less political and topical, focusing very much on show business people, often quite controversial ones, such as Andrew Dice Clay and Madonna. But other shows in Hall's time slot have felt a real pinch, notably "The Pat Sajak Show," which was canceled partway through the 1989–90 season; "Late Night with David Letterman," which slipped in ratings after the arrival of Hall; and "Nightline," which was bumped from its time slot in favor of Hall in some cities. Through his production company, Hall also developed a new music-and-dance show, "The Party Machine With Nia Peeples," to follow his own, starting in early 1991, and has an agreement with Paramount to become a film producer.

Hall became famous enough to be signed to do commercials, notably for Sprite soft drinks. He also hosted the 1990 MTV Video Music Awards show. Noted for his Italian designer suits (supplied by Sam Dinar of Los Angeles), he was even named the best-dressed man in television by the Tailors Council of America, in late 1989. Hall also uses his celebrity for social causes; in 1990, he was named first national ambassador for DARE (Drug Abuse Resistance Education).

Celebrity often breeds lawsuits, and Hall was recently involved in three. The most serious is a 1989 $10-million slander and libel suit against him by Willis Edwards, head of the Beverly Hills-Hollywood chapter of the NAACP. According to a newspaper interview in November 1988, Edwards charged that Hall refused to hire Blacks in responsible positions, saying that no qualified Blacks were available. Replying on a radio talk show, Hall denied the charges and allegedly labeled Edwards an extortionist, demanding $40,000 for not publicly charging Hall with failure to hire Blacks. In early 1990, a judge dismissed one of two parts of Edwards's suit; the other was pending. Also, writer-columnist Art Buchwald claimed that the script for the 1987 film *Coming to America* had been plagiarized from a story of his; he named Hall, Eddie Murphy, and Paramount in a suit claiming a share of the film's profits. Hall and Murphy both denied the charges, affirming that they had written the concept together, but lost the suit. At year's end, the court was examining Paramount's books, since they had claimed that the movie—which grossed $300 million—had made no profits. In addition, Hall is the target of a breach-of-contract suit filed by Robert Wachs, his manager from 1987 to mid-1990, claiming half of the profits from Hall's show.

Cleveland-born Hall began his career as a stand-up comedian in the late 1970s, and moved to Los Angeles in the early 1980s. His first sustained talk-show exposure was on the late-night "Thicke of the Night" (1983); he was also host of "Solid Gold," a rock and roll series. He was a guest host on Fox's "The Late Show" in 1987, and appeared in *Coming to America*, before breaking through with his "The Arsenio Hall Show" in 1989. His B.A. was from Kent State University.

FURTHER READING

"Arsenio Hall talks. . . ." Laura B. Randolph. *Ebony*, Dec. 1990.
"TV person of the year. . . ." Mary Murphy. *TV Guide*, June 23, 1990.
"The rise and rise. . . ." Digby Diehl. *Cosmopolitan*, Mar. 1990.
"'Let's get busy!'. . . ." Richard Zoglin. *Time*, Nov. 13, 1989.
"Alone at the top." Patrick Goldstein. *Rolling Stone*, Nov. 2, 1989.
"Late-night cool." Michael Norman. *New York Times Magazine*, Oct. 1, 1989.
"Arsenio Hall. . . ." Michael Leahy. *TV Guide*, Sept. 30, 1989.
"Hall, Arsenio." *Current Biography*, Sept. 1989.

Hall, Peter (Peter Reginald Frederick Hall, 1930–) British director and producer Hall scored two notable trans-Atlantic successes in 1989 and 1990, directing Vanessa Redgrave in Tennessee Williams's *Orpheus Descending*, and Dustin Hoffman and Geraldine James in Shakespeare's *The Merchant of Venice*. Both productions opened to great acclaim in London in 1989, then came to Broadway in 1990, being commercial hits in both cities. Both also appeared in television adaptations. Hall's "semi-operatic" version of *Orpheus* was hailed not only for Redgrave's acting but also as a complete work, rescuing from unwarranted obscurity a Williams play properly seen as a major work. Hall's version of *Merchant* was lauded for its crackle and drive, presented not as a "problem play," but as a fresh and entertaining story for modern audiences.

Like several other modern directors, Hall has also worked in opera. He had been artistic director of the Glyndebourne Festival Opera in England since 1984, though his association with it dates back 20 years. However, in mid-1990, Hall resigned bitterly from Glyndebourne, after a long struggle over future directions; in particular, he said he had not been consulted about Peter Sellars's radically modern production of Mozart's *Magic Flute*, set on a Los Angeles Freeway.

Hall has been one of the leading directors of the British theater since the mid-1950s. He directed the very notable first English-language production of Samuel Beckett's *Waiting For Godot* in London in 1955, and went on to direct scores of productions of the traditional classics, and to introduce such other modern classics as *The Homecoming* (1965; and the 1973 film version), *No Man's Land* (1975), and *Amadeus* (1979, and New York, 1980). He won directing Tonys for *The Homecoming* and *Amadeus*. He was managing director of the Royal Shakespeare Company (1960–68), and co-director of the National Theatre with Laurence Olivier (1973–88). He has also directed many operas, most of them at Covent Garden and the Glyndebourne Festival, and also at the Metropolitan Opera andother American houses. He published *Peter Hall's Diaries* in 1984. Hall attended St. Catherine's College, Cambridge. He has been married three times, and has five children.

FURTHER READING

Peter Hall Directs Anthony & Cleopatra. Tirzah Lowen. Limelight, 1991.
"Weldon-Minskoff-Hall heat up. . . ." Richard Hummler. *Variety*, Oct. 4, 1989.
"London uproar. . . ." Jack Pitman. *Variety*, July 2, 1986.

Halston (Roy Halston Frowick, 1932–90) Midwesterner Halston, who became a key fashion designer of the 1970s, opened his first millinery shop at Chicago's Ambassador Hotel in the 1950s, serving celebrities from the start. In 1957, he moved to New York, working with Lilly Daché and then Bergdorf Goodman, for whom he traveled to Paris fashion shows. As hats declined, Halston moved to clothes designing, introducing his first collection at Bergdorf's in 1966 and founding his own company in 1968. He specialized in clothes more tailored than traditional high-fashion clothes, and later, he branched out to accessories, including perfumes, and theatrical design. After signing with J. C. Penney in 1982 to design lower-priced clothes, he lost much of his fashionable clientele. Halston died of complications from AIDS. (d. San Francisco; March 26, 1990)

FURTHER READING

"American original." Jon Etra. *Harper's Bazaar*, July 1990.
Obituary. *Current Biography*, May 1990.
"The great Halston." Elizabeth Sporkin. *People*, Apr. 9, 1990.
"Death of a trendsetter. . . ." Nina Darnton. *Newsweek*, Apr. 9, 1990.
"Hat man." *U.S. News & World Report*, Apr. 9, 1990.
Obituary. *New York Times*, Mar. 28, 1990.
"The inimitable Halston. . . ." Nina Darnton. *Newsweek*, Aug. 7, 1989.

Hammer, Armand (1898–1990) As a leading financier and industrialist, whose holdings included control of Occidental Petroleum and Cities Service, Hammer was a major figure. He was also a notable art collector, whose collection of Old Masters and other works toured the world during the 1980s. And he was an internationally minded philanthropist, who gave tens of millions of dollars to cancer and other medical research, and to a wide range of charities and educational projects. But it was his extraordinary relationship of trust with recent generations of Soviet leaders, stemming back to his friendship with Lenin in the early 1920s, that made him unique among world business leaders. Hammer was active in Soviet medical relief and in many business activities in the Soviet Union in the 1920s. He backed away considerably during the Stalin period, and actively promoted Soviet-American trade and investment from the mid-1950s through 1990. In 1987, he published his autobiographical *Hammer: A Witness to History,* written with Neil Lyndon. (d. Westwood, California, December 10, 1990)

FURTHER READING

"An American life." Ann E. Andrews. *U.S. News & World Report*, Dec. 24, 1990.
Obituary. *New York Times*, Dec. 12, 1990.
Armand Hammer: The Untold Story. Steve Weinberg. Little, Brown, 1989.
"Hammer hits 90!. . . ." Anthony Ramirez. *Fortune*, Nov. 7, 1988.
"Doctor Hammer is 90 . . ." Stewart Toy, et al. *Business Week*, May 30, 1988.
"Armand Hammer. . . ." Brian O'Reilly. *Fortune*, Aug. 3, 1987.
"Armand Hammer's. . . ." Steve Weinberg. *Bulletin of the Atomic Scientists*, Aug.–Sept. 1986.
The World of Armand Hammer. John Bryson. Abrams, 1985.

Hammer, M. C. (Stanley Kirk Burrell, 1962–) Rap singer and dancer Hammer scored an enormous hit in 1990, with his second album, *Please Hammer Don't Hurt 'Em,* which sold over eight million copies, and had several hit singles, including "U Can't Touch This." He is the first major rap artist to make a fully successful crossover to popular music, his shows on tour going far beyond what had been rap's hard, stark, purposely shocking presentation to a far more conventional big-stage-show treatment, with words and music not at all threatening to large, interracial pop audiences.

Oakland-born Hammer became the Oakland Athletic's batboy in the mid-1970s, and often traveled with the team, after he caught the attention of club owner Charles Finley, who saw him doing dance routines in the stadium parking lot. His start as a recording artist came with his own production of some of his songs, with the help of A's players Mike Davis and Dwayne Murphy (with whom he had later had financial disagreements). His first professional album was *Let's Get It Started*. Hammer also runs his own studio and record company, Bust It Productions. He is married, and has one child.

FURTHER READING

"'It's Hammer time!'. . . ." *Ebony*, Dec. 1990.
"M.C. Hammer says. . . ." CLARENCE WALDRON. *Jet*, Sept. 17, 1990.
"Hammer time. . . ." JEFFREY RESSNER. *Rolling Stone*, Sept. 6, 1990.
"M.C. Hammer. . . ." LISA RUSSELL. *People*, Aug. 6, 1990.

Hanks, Tom (1956–) Actor Hanks continues to have strong audience appeal, even without critical support for his films; certainly American college students, in their 1990 poll, named him as one of the top half-dozen movie actors. Though Hanks has won critical praise, notably for his performance in *Big,* his most recent movies have been tepidly received by film critics. In the romantic comedy *Joe Versus the Volcano* (1990), opposite Meg Ryan in a triple role (fresh off her hit with *When Harry Met Sally . . .*), Hanks as Joe was trying to pack a lifetime into what he thinks are his last days. The film had a reasonable box-office success, which translated into video rental success later in the year. The future of *The Bonfire of the Vanities* remains to be seen. After a somewhat troubled production, the Brian De Palma film, with Hanks as the cocky investment banker whose life is changed by a hit-and-run accident in which a young Black man is killed, opened to mixed reviews late in 1990. Many critics focused on crucial changes made in the movie from the Tom Wolfe novel. Meanwhile, Hanks's *Turner and Hooch* (1989), with Hanks as a cop with a hound for a partner, was topping the video rental charts in early 1990. Among future projects planned for Hanks is *Night and the City,* a remake of the 1950 Jules Dassin film, with Hanks as a boxing promoter.

California-born Hanks appeared in the television series "Bosom Buddies" (1980–82), emerged as a film star in the mid-1980s, with *Splash* (1984), and went on to star in such films as *Bachelor Party* (1984), *Volunteers* (1985), *The Man with One Red Shoe,* (1985), *The Money Pit* (1986), *Every Time We Say Goodbye* (1986), *Big* (1988), and *Punchline* (1988). He attended California State University at Sacramento. He has been married twice, and has two children.

FURTHER READING

"'It's a cool gig'. . . ." CAROL TROY. *American Film*, Apr. 1990.
"Tom Hanks." NANCY ANDERSON. *Good Housekeeping*, May 1989.
"Tom Hanks, seriously." CHRISTOPHER CONNELLY. *Premiere*, Apr. 1989.
"Hanks, Tom." *Current Biography*, Apr. 1989.
"Hanks to you." BEVERLY WALKER. *Film Comment*, Mar.–Apr. 1989.
"Playboy interview. . . ." DAVID SHEFF. *Playboy*, Mar. 1989.
"Tom Hanks." *People*, Dec. 26, 1988.
"A stand-up guy. . . ." DAVID ANSEN. *Newsweek*, Sept. 26, 1988.
"Mr. Big." BILL ZEHME. *Rolling Stone*, June 30, 1988.
"The eternal cutup at work." GERALD CLARKE. *Time*, June 6, 1988.

Hare, David (1947–) British writer and director Hare brought his play *The Secret Rapture* (1988) to the United States during 1989 and 1990. Originally directed by Howard Davies, the play won raves in London; it then moved to New York, with Hare, himself, directing, first at the Public Theater and then on Broadway, starring Blair Brown, for whom Hare had originally written the part. When the production was blasted by powerful *New York Times* critic Frank Rich—who had loved the London production but hated Hare's New York direction—Hare protested vociferously and publicly. The show-business publication *Variety* summed up the altercation this way: "Ruffled Hare Airs Rich Bitch."

Though it quickly closed on Broadway, the play survived in the regional theaters, including Chicago's Steppenwolf and Costa Mesa's South Coast Repertory, which both had 1990 productions. Inspired, Hare says, by Arthur Miller's writings, the modern morality play is set in Margaret Thatcher's Britain and follows the events that entangle the surviving daughters and widow after the death of a father. The title, as Hare explained it, refers to "the moment before a dying nun is reunited with Christ."

Hare emerged as a leading British playwright of social protest in the 1970s, with such plays as *Slag* (1970) and *Fanshen* (1975), and went on to write such well-received works as *Plenty* (1978; also the 1985 film adaptation), *A Map of the World* (1982), *Pravda* (1985), *The Secret Rapture* (1988), *Plays and Player* (1988), and *Racing Demon* (1990). He wrote and directed the film *Wetherby* (1984). He also wrote the filmscripts for *Paris By Night* (1988), and *Strapless* (1989), and has written several telefilms. Hare attended Jesus College, Cambridge. He was formerly married, and has three children.

FURTHER READING

David Hare. JOAN F. DEAN. G. K. Hall, 1990.
David Hare: Theatricalizing Politics. JUDY L. OLIVA. UMI Research Press, 1990.
"Ruffled Hare airs Rich bitch. . . ." RICHARD HUMMLER. *Variety*, Nov. 15, 1989.
"Dramatically speaking." DAVID BAILEY and KATHLEEN TYNAN. *Interview*, Apr. 1989.
"Hare apparent. . . ." STEVE LAWSON. *Film Comment*, Sept.–Oct. 1985.

Harmon, Tom (1919–90) The greatest college football player of his day, Harmon was an All-American in his junior and senior years (1939, 1940) at the University of Michigan, and won the Heisman Trophy in his senior year. He was then what is no longer possible in the game—a "triple-threat" runner, passer, and kicker. His professional career did not develop because of World War II; he played one game in 1941, enlisted in December 1941, and became a much-decorated fighter pilot, winning a Silver Star and a Purple Heart. He did play for two seasons after the war with the Los Angeles Rams, but without his former strength and speed, probably due to wartime injuries. He spent much of the rest of his career as a sports broadcaster. (d. Los Angeles; March 15, 1990)

FURTHER READING

Obituary. *Sporting News*, Mar. 26, 1990.
Obituary. *New York Times*, Mar. 17, 1990.
"Old 98 a contrast. . . ." JOE FALLS. *Sporting News*, Feb. 21, 1981.

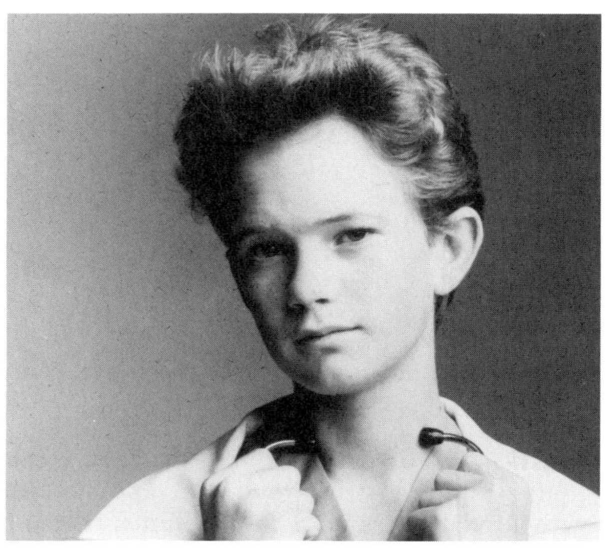

Harris, Neil Patrick (1973–) Since the show's September 19, 1989 premiere, 16-year-old Harris has been the star of the popular television series "Doogie Howser, M.D.," in the imaginative role of a teenage doctor who graduated from medical school at the age of 14. Harris grew up in the little town of Ruidoso, New Mexico, acted in school productions, and was discovered by playwright Mark Medoff at a summer drama camp. He then went into his first film, *Clara's Heart* (1988), and into such telefilms as *Cold Sassy Tree* (1989), and *Leave Her to Heaven* (1989). He has also appeared in guest roles in several television series.

FURTHER READING

"Neil Patrick Harris. . . ." Joanne Kaufman. *People*, Mar. 19, 1990.
"New teens on the tube." *Teen*, Jan. 1990.
"Would you let. . . ." Bill O'Hallaren and Dawn Hudson. *TV Guide*, Dec. 16, 1989.

Harrison, George (1943–) The British songwriter and performer became a historic figure as a member of the Beatles. He scored a substantial comeback in 1987, with the album *Cloud Nine*, and in 1988, he was the prime mover in the organization of the extraordinary "new" group *The Traveling Wilburys,* consisting of Harrison, Bob Dylan, Roy Orbison, Tom Petty, and Jeff Lynne, all long-time stars. On tour, and with their first two albums, *Volume 1* (1988), and *Volume 3* (1990; actually their second volume, recorded after Orbison's death), they were a great hit. Harrison also coproduced the film *Checking Out* (1989). In 1990,

Harrison also recorded on the album *Nobody's Child*, on behalf of the Romanian Angel Appeal, created by Olivia Harrison, Barbara Bach (Starkey), Linda McCartney, Yoko Ono, and Elton John.

Liverpool-born Harrison, then a guitarist, joined The Quarrymen in 1958, and in 1960, with Paul McCartney, John Lennon, and Pete Best (replaced by Ringo Starr in 1962) formed the Beatles; he was lead guitarist and sometimes a singer. As a member of the group, he helped trigger a revolution in popular music, and in the early 1960s emerged as a worldwide celebrity. He also played a special role, studying with Indian musician Ravi Shankar, learning the sitar and several other Indian instruments, and introducing Indian strains into the work of the Beatles. He therefore helped to bring Indian music into the Western popular music of his time. His main work as a songwriter developed after the Beatles years. He also formed his own film production and rock management companies. Harrison was active in organizing Bangladesh relief concerts in 1971. He has been married twice, and has one child.

FURTHER READING

Dark Horse: The Private Life of George Harrison. Geoffrey Giuliano. NAL-Dutton, 1990.
"Harrison, George." *Current Biography*, Jan. 1989.
"The rise of a craftsman." Nicholas Jennings. *Maclean's*, Oct. 17, 1988.
"Handmade man." Elaine Dutka. *Film Comment*, May–June 1988.
"George Harrison." Anthony DeCurtis. *Rolling Stone*, Nov. 5, 1987.
"The jungle music. . . ." Dan Forte. *Guitar Player*, Nov. 1987.
"George Harrison gets back." Anthony DeCurtis. *Rolling Stone*, Oct. 22, 1987.
It Was Twenty Years Ago Today. Derek Taylor. Simon & Schuster, 1987.
Yesterday—the Beatles 1963–1965. Robert Freeman. Holt, 1983.
The Beatles A-Z: John Lennon, Paul McCartney, George Harrison & Ringo Starr. Goldie Friede, Sue Weiner, and Robin Titone. Routledge Chapman & Hall, 1981.

Harrison, Michael (1946–) Pediatric surgeon Harrison and the other members of his surgical team made medical history in 1989 and 1990. On April 17, 1990, operating on a fetus, the trailblazing team was able to successfully remove a malformed lung from the unborn child of pregnant mother Beth Schultz, correcting a condition called congenital cystic adenomatoid malformation (CCAM). The procedure included partially removing the fetus from the uterus of the mother, operating to remove the lung from the chest of the fetus, returning the fetus to the womb, and closing up the incision to let the pregnancy continue normally.

Harrison was a founder of the fetal treatment program at the University of California in 1978. After a period of experimentation and trial, and several early failures with human babies, the team began to be successful, developing life-saving fetal surgery techniques to treat a blocked urethra and diaphragmatic hernia. The work has been widely hailed as opening a new chapter in the treatment of many life-threatening problems facing unborn children. Harrison is a graduate of Harvard Medical School.

FURTHER READING

"Saving lives not yet begun." Montgomery Brower. *People*, June 18, 1990.

Harrison, Rex (Reginald Carey Harrison, 1908–90) Harrison, for many, was inseparable from his role as Henry Higgins in *My Fair Lady,* which he played—talking, rather than singing, the songs—first in New York (1956), then in London, in the film (1964), and in the 1981 Broadway revival. Born near Liverpool, England, Harrison had no formal training, but began working in the theater at age 16, making his London debut in *The Admirable Crichton* (1930). He continued to work on stage until May 11, 1989, when he was forced by illness to leave a Broadway production of William Somerset Maugham's *The Circle*. Harrison also had a strong film career, starring in such classics as *Major Barbara* (1941), *Blithe Spirit* (1945), *Anna and the King of Siam* (1946), *The Ghost and Mrs. Muir* (1947), *Cleopatra* (1963), and *Doctor Doolittle* (1967). He wrote two autobiographical works: *Rex: An Autobiography* (1975) and the posthumously published *A Damned Serious Business* (1991). (d. New York; June 2, 1990)

FURTHER READING

Obituary. *Current Biography*, July 1990.
Obituary. *National Review*, June 25, 1990.
"After a six-decade reign. . . ." *People*, June 18, 1990.
"We grew accustomed to his face." JACK KROLL. *Newsweek*, June 11, 1990.
"Dapper star. . . ." LAWRENCE COHN. *Variety*, June 6, 1990.
Obituary. *The Times* (of London), June 4, 1990.
Obituary. *New York Times*, June 3, 1990.
Rex Harrison: A Biography. ROY MOSELEY, PHILIP MASHETER, and MARTIN MASHETER. St. Martin's, 1987.
"Harrison, Rex." *Current Biography*, Feb. 1986.
Rex Harrison. ALLEN EYLES. Carol, 1986.

Hart, Marion Rice (1892–90) Woman aviator Hart made her first trans-Atlantic flight in 1953; she was 61 years old at the time. She made headlines with her first solo trans-Atlantic flight in 1966, at the age of 74. Altogether, she made seven solo flights across the Atlantic, the last when she was 83, and she continued flying until she was 87. Hart was educated as a chemical engineer, graduating from the Massachusetts Institute of Technology in 1936. She practiced engineering only briefly, and from 1936 to 1939, she sailed around the world with a crew of four. Her books were *Who Called That Lady a Skipper?* (1938), *How to Navigate Today* (1940), and *I Fly as I Please* (1953). (d. Berkeley, California; July 2, 1990)

FURTHER READING

Obituary. *New York Times*, July 4, 1990.

Hartung, Hans (Heinrich Ernst Hartung, 1904–89) Dresden-born Hartung, a leading European abstract painter, began his career in Germany in the late 1920s, and lived and worked on Minorca and in France during the 1930s. An anti-Nazi, he fled Germany after briefly returning in 1935. He fought with the French Foreign Legion during World War II, lost a leg in battle in 1944, and became a French citizen after the war, in 1946. From the mid-1930s, he emerged as as a leading abstractionist, working in an action painting style that paralleled that of the American abstract expressionists, and stemmed directly from Kandinsky and the main line of European abstractionism. (d. Antibes, France; December 7, 1989)

FURTHER READING

Obituary. *Current Biography*, Feb. 1990.
Obituary. *New York Times*, Dec. 11, 1989.
Obituary. *The Times* (of London), Dec. 11, 1989.
"A universe of storms and stars." MICHAEL PEPPIATT. *Architectural Digest*, Oct. 1986.

Havel, Vaclav (1936–) In November and December 1989, democracy triumphed in Czechoslovakia; on December 29, 1989, Czech writer and dissenter Vaclav Havel became the first noncommunist president of his country since 1948. He also immediately became a worldwide symbol of the triumph of the former dissenters of Eastern Europe. His first move as president, which he announced in his New Year's Day speech, was to free an estimated 20,000 prisoners, in an amnesty that released all political prisoners and many others imprisoned for minor offenses by the former hardline communist government. Havel then visited many countries, including the United States, Great Britain, and the Soviet Union, seeking help for his newly democratic and needy small country; everywhere, he was treated as a world figure.

Havel's first brief presidential term was as interim president. On July 5, 1990, he was re-elected to the presidency for a full two-year term. And his plays, so long banned in his country, were once again produced on the Czech stage: *Audience* opened in Prague on January 10, 1990. With events moving faster than publishing schedules, an interview-by-mail with the then-proscribed Havel was published in 1990, as *Long Distance Interrogation*.

Havel has been a leading Czech playwright since the early 1960s. Such plays as *The Garden Party* (1963), and *The Memorandum* helped bring about the "Prague Spring" of 1968, and were repressed after the Soviet invasion that destroyed the new Czech government. Havel's plays were banned from the Czech stage for two decades, while he continued to be a leading dissenter. He was a leader of the Charter 77 organization in 1977, was under house arrest from 1977 to 1979, in prison from 1979 to 1983, and was imprisoned again in early 1989; he emerged as leader of his country later in the year. In 1964, Havel married Olga Splíchalová, to whom he wrote *Letters to Olga* (1989), from prison. Among his other non-dramatic works was *Vaclav Havel; Or, Living in Truth* (1987).

FURTHER READING

"All the president's plays. . . ." STANISLAW BARANCZAK. *New Republic*, July 23, 1990.
"Metamorphosis in Prague. . . ." LEONID SHINKAREV. *World Press Review*, May 1990.
"The prisoner who. . . ." RICHARD Z. CHESNOFF. *U.S. News & World Report*, Feb. 26, 1990.
"A life like a work of art. . . ." MILAN KUNDERA. *New Republic*, Jan. 29, 1990.
"Life turns upside down. . . ." ANDREA CHAMBERS. *People*, Jan. 22, 1990.
"Prague's choice takes office." MARY NEMETH. *Maclean's*, Jan. 8, 1990.
"Dissident to president. . . ." WILLIAM A. HENRY III. *Time*, Jan. 8, 1990.
"Vaclav Havel. . . ." WILLIAM ECHIKSON. *Reader's Digest* (Canadian), Dec. 1989.
"The Czechs' defiant playwright." MARIE WINN. *New York Times Magazine*, Oct. 25, 1987.
"Havel, Vaclav." *Current Biography*, Mar. 1985.

Hawke, Bob (Robert James Lee Hawke, 1929–) At the head of the Australian Labor Party, Prime Minister Hawke won his record-setting fourth term in the elections of March

1990, though with a somewhat thinner parliamentary majority than in the 1987 elections. He continued to capture much of the Australian "middle," coming forward as a moderate socialist with strongly environmentalist and anti-nuclear testing positions. However, further left elements in his own party criticized those positions as not being as strong as they would desire. In early August 1990, Hawke was one of the earliest world leaders to commit armed forces to Saudi Arabia in the Persian Gulf Crisis. Hawke had publicly confessed adultery and heavy drinking during a television broadcast interview in March 1989; the admissions apparently did him no political damage.

Hawke began his long career as a trade unionist in 1958, as an economist with the Australian Council of Trade Unions, acting as ACTU's president from 1970 to 1980. At the same time, he moved into Labour Party politics, moving up to become president of his party in 1978, and leader in 1983; in that year, with party victory, he became prime minister, succeeding John Malcolm Fraser. He married Hazel Masterson in 1956; they have three children. He attended the University of Western Australia and Oxford University.

FURTHER READING

"Hawke, Bob." *Current Biography*, Aug. 1983.
"Robert J.L. Hawke." *Town and Country*, Nov. 1982.

Hawking, Stephen William (1942–) British physicist and mathematician Hawking created a surprise bestseller with his *A Brief History of Time: From the Big Bang to Black Holes* (1988), a clearly written work on the nature of reality and the origins of the universe, which has been translated into over 20 languages. Hawking, long a leading scientist, has also become a worldwide celebrity because he is a symbol of human ability to triumph over terribly adverse personal problems. He has been progressively disabled by amytrophic lateral sclerosis (Lou Gehrig's disease) from the age of 20; by 1990, he was confined to a wheelchair and had only the use of two fingers, which he uses to successfully run a computer and motorized wheelchair, while he continues to teach and write.

Tokens of Hawking's celebrity abound; he is a much-appreciated world figure. In addition to many profiles, PBS produced an hour-long program, *Hawking's Universe*; Steven Spielberg filmed a television feature documentary on Hawking's life and his book; Britain's Queen Elizabeth II named him a Companion of Honor in 1989; and two Chicago bar owners even started a Stephen Hawking fan club, and quickly sold over 7,500 Hawking T-shirts.

Oxford-born Hawking has made key contributions to modern scientific theory, most notably as to the nature of black holes, gravitational theory, and the "big bang" theory of the origin of the universe. He was educated at University College, Oxford, and Trinity Hall, Cambridge, and has been associated with Cambridge in a series of research and teaching positions since 1965. He has been married twice.

FURTHER READING

Unlocking the Universe: A Biography of Stephen Hawking. Sheridan Simon. Dillon, 1991.
"Stephen Hawking and. . . ." Chet Raymo. *Commonweal*, Apr. 6, 1990.
"Playboy interview. . . ." Morgan Strong. *Playboy*, Apr. 1990.
"Glimpses of God." Ric Dolphin. *Maclean's*, Sept. 19, 1988.
"Reading God's mind. . . ." Jerry Adler. *Newsweek*, June 13, 1988.
"Roaming the cosmos. . . ." Leon Jaroff. *Time*, Feb. 8, 1988.

Hawn, Goldie (1945–) In the summer of 1990, Hawn starred in a "big" summer film, opposite Mel Gibson in John Badham's *Bird on a Wire*. The action-comedy was criticized for overdoing the action, which got in the way of both the comedy and the star chemistry. Audiences still came out for the stars; though the $100 million+ film took in "only" $68.8 million in the theaters, it quickly shot to the top ten in the video rental market. In mid-1990, Hawn was in Key West shooting a new film, *Crisscross*, starring as a stripper who finds that her son is a drug pusher. Meanwhile, Hawn continued to diversify her career, working as co-executive producer on the Herbert Ross film *My Blue Heaven*, which also opened in 1990, starring Steve Martin. In late 1989, Hawn was honored with a special tribute in the Hollywood Palladium by the Big Sisters Guild.

Hawn began her career as a dancer in the mid-1960s, and became a star comedian in television, in the "dumb blonde" role she created for Rowan and Martin's "Laugh-In" (1968–73). Her film career includes a Best Supporting Actress Oscar in *Cactus Flower* (1969), and starring roles in several popular film comedies, including *There's A Girl in My Soup* (1970), *Butterflies Are Free* (1972), *The Sugarland Express* (1973), *Shampoo* (1975), *The Duchess and the Dirtwater Fox* (1976),

Private Benjamin (1980), *Best Friends* (1982), *Swing Shift* (1984), *Overboard* (1987), and *Last Wish* (1988). She attended American University. She has been married twice, and has four children.

FURTHER READING

"Goldie Hawn. . . ." STEPHEN FARBER. *Cosmopolitan*, Aug. 1990.
"Pure Goldie." KRISTINE MCKENNA. *Harper's Bazaar*, July. 1990.
"24-karat Goldie!" JIM JEROME. *People*, June 11, 1990.
Sweethearts of Sixties TV. RONALD L. SMITH. St. Martin's, 1989.
"Goldie Hawn starting over. . . . again." *McCall's*, Mar. 1988.
"Goldie Hawn's new life." JEFF ROVIN. *Ladies Home Journal*, Sept, 1986.
Solid Goldie: An Illustrated Biography of Goldie Hawn. CONNIE BERMAN. Simon & Schuster, 1981.

Helm, Buck (1931–89) Traveling to visit his family in northern California, longshoreman Helm was caught in the California earthquake of October 17, 1989; he was trapped when Oakland's Nimitz Freeway collapsed, and he was pulled out of the wreckage of the freeway 90 hours after the earthquake. Spotted by an engineering inspector, after rescue workers had given up hope of more survivors, Helm was finally rescued, but had suffered fractures of the skull and ribs, dehydration, and much other damage. His dramatic October 21st rescue and then his powerful fight for life caught international attention, bringing thousands of cards and letters. (d. Oakland; November 18, 1989)

FURTHER READING

Obituary. *New York Times*, Nov. 20, 1989.
"Digging out from under." BILL HEWITT. *People*, Nov. 6, 1989.

Helms, Jesse (1921–) North Carolina Republican Senator Helms scored a significant victory in September 1989, as Congress restricted the National Endowment for the Arts (NEA) as to federal grants for allegedly obscene artworks, creating the climate within which the NEA then required a "non-obscenity pledge" as a condition for grants. Helms continued to express an ultra-conservative point of view in the Senate, voting against the nomination of Health and Human Resources Secretary Louis Sullivan, opposing new legislation on such matters as AIDS relief and civil rights, and opposing Republican President Bush on a wide range of domestic and international matters. Helms was re-elected in 1990, weathering a powerful challenge by former Charlotte Mayor Harvey B. Gantt, a challenge made even more notable because Gantt was a Black candidate facing a highly visible anti-civil-rights conservative.

North Carolina-born Helms began his senatorial career in 1973, after a career in broadcasting, and has, since 1987, been the most senior Republican in the Senate, with memberships on several key committees. He married Dorothy Jane Coble in 1942; they have three children. He attended Wingate College and Wake Forest College.

FURTHER READING

"Race-baiting wins again. . . ." LAURENCE I. BARRETT. *Time*, Nov. 19, 1990.
"Republican of fear." SIDNEY BLUMENTHAL. *New Republic*, Nov. 12, 1990.
"Gantt versus. . . ." DOROTHY VIDULICH. *National Catholic Reporter*, Oct. 26, 1990.
"Jesse Helms. . . ." DONALD BAER. *U.S. News & World Report*, May 14, 1990.
"Our most effective. . . ." PAUL WEYRICH. *Conservative Digest*, Jan.–Feb. 1989.
"Scourge of the senate." TED GUP. *Time*, May 30, 1988.

"Same ol' Jesse." ERNEST B. FURGURSON. *Washingtonian*, Oct. 1986.
"Helmstactics." FERREL GUILLORY. *America*, Sept. 13, 1986.
Hard Right: The Rise of Jesse Helms. ERNEST B. FURGURSON. Norton, 1986.

Helmsley, Leona (Leona Mindy Helmsley, 1920–) Embattled hotelier Helmsley spent considerable time and effort trying to rehabilitate her enormously negative public image, after her August 1989 conviction on 33 of 41 counts of tax fraud. It was an uphill battle. People all over the country had read, watched, and heard reports from the New York City trial about her harsh methods of dealing with subordinates and her arrogant comments, notably that "only the little people pay taxes." In September 1990, she was even the subject of a made-for television movie, *The Queen of Mean,* starring Suzanne Pleshette, based on Ransdell Pierson's "unauthorized biography" (1989).

In autumn 1990, though, Helmsley was presenting herself as a patriot and humanitarian, taking a full-page ad in the *New York Times*, at a cost of about $40,000, to tell Saddam Hussein to let his hostages leave, and objecting to his calling them "guests," noting "I know something about how one is supposed to treat guests, Mr. Hussein." This was a reference to the image of herself, carefully cultivated in a long series of advertisements only just ended, as the "Queen" of the Helmsley Palace, taking special care of her guests. By December 1989, New York newspapers were reporting on a new "humble" Helmsley, appearing at the employees' Christmas party. In April 1990, she even went before the television cameras on "A Current Affair," to sign a check for $42,065,000 to the Internal Revenue Service (IRS), the balance of her taxes for 1989, unrelated to the earlier disputed taxes.

Facing a possible $8.9 million in fines and 127 years in prison from her August conviction for failing to pay over a million dollars in taxes on personal items charged as business expenses, Helmsley had, in December 1989, been sentenced to four years in prison and $7.1 million in fines, and was ordered to pay $1.2 million in back federal taxes and nearly $500,000 in state taxes. The judge, who harshly criticized her "naked greed," also ordered her to serve 750 hours in a facility that treats drug-addicted or AIDS-afflicted babies. Remaining free, she promptly hired Harvard law professor Alan Dershowitz to handle her appeal. Helmsley also faced state tax fraud charges, though most of those were dropped, as constituting double jeopardy; she refused to accept a plea-bargained deal offering concurrent sentence for state tax fraud, insisting on her innocence.

New Yorker Helmsley married real estate multi-billionaire Harry Helmsley in 1972, after a career that had included several responsible positions in real estate firms. She became senior vice president of the Helmsley-Spear division just six months later, and the highly visible president of Helmsley Hotels in 1980. Although originally indicted with his wife, 80-year-old Harry Helmsley was not tried, since a judge ruled that he had suffered such a severe memory loss from a stroke that he could not assist in his own defense. Leona Helmsley had been married twice before and had one son.

FURTHER READING

"Playboy interview. . . ." GLENN PLASKIN. *Playboy*, Nov. 1990.
"Trying to save Leona. . . ." DINITIA SMITH. *New York*, Mar. 12, 1990.
Unreal Estate: The Rise and Fall of Harry and Leona Helmsley. RICHARD HAMMER. New American Library-Dutton, 1990.
"Queen, pawns, checkmate." JAMES S. KUNEN. *People*, Sept. 11, 1989.
"Revenge of the little people. . . ." MARGARET CARLSON. *Time*, Sept. 11, 1989.

"Leona and Harry. . . ." JEANIE KASINDORF. *New York*, Oct. 3, 1988.
"For the love of money." JOYCE WADLER. *People*, May 2, 1988.

Henson, Jim (James Maury Henson, 1937–90) Mississippi-born Henson was the puppeteer who created the internationally famous Muppets. He studied puppetry at the University of Maryland, where he developed Kermit the Frog in 1956 and, with his partner and later wife, Jane Nebel, did his first television show. Commercials and network appearances followed, as on "The Ed Sullivan Show," but his major breakthrough came with the popularity of the children's show "Sesame Street" from 1969. He brought Kermit, Miss Piggy, and friends back into all-ages television with "The Muppet Show" (1976–81), and subsequent movies. Winner of numerous awards, Henson died of pneumonia shortly after arranging to sell his firm to Walt Disney, a sale that fell through after his death. (d. New York; May 16, 1990)

FURTHER READING

Obituary. *Current Biography*, July 1990.
"Legacy of a gentle genius." SUSAN SCHINDEHETTE. *People*, June 18, 1990.
"The muppet magician." VICTOR DWYER. *Maclean's*, May 28, 1990.
Obituary. JEAN SELIGMANN. *Newsweek*, May 28, 1990.
Obituary. J.D. REED. *Time*, May 28, 1990.
"Now, who. . . ." HARRISON RAINIE. *U.S. News & World Report*, May 28, 1990.
"Muppet maker. . . ." JOSEPH MCBRIDE. *Variety*, May 23, 1990.
Obituary. *New York Times*, May 17, 1990.
Obituary. *The Times* (of London), May 17, 1990.
Jim Henson: Muppet Master. NATHAN AASENG. Lerner, 1988.
Jim Henson: From Puppets to Muppets. GERALDINE WOODS. Dillon, 1987.

Hepburn, Katharine (1907–) For Hepburn, this was a year of reflecting on the past. Though she has in previous years declined to publicly accept such awards—she did not even claim any of her Oscars—she this year accepted Kennedy Center honors for lifetime cultural achievements by Americans. Other honorees were jazz great Dizzy Gillespie, opera star Rise Stevens, composer Jule Styne, and film director Billy Wilder, but by all accounts Hepburn stole the show. When the lights came up after the audience had watched clips from her movies, she leaned forward from the honorees' box, and said "They were all remarkable actors. . . . I was very lucky."

In 1990 Hepburn also announced that she was ready to write her autobiography, noting "It's later than you think." World rights were quickly snapped up jointly by publishers Knopf and Ballantine, with publication scheduled for 1991; rumors circulated that Knopf had paid her $4.25 million, which the publisher neither confirmed nor denied. In 1987, she had published, also with Knopf, *The Making of "The African Queen": Or How I Went to Africa with Bogart, Bacall and Huston and Almost Lost My Life.*

Hepburn was (along with Betty Ford) also honored at Planned Parenthood's 25th anniversary gala in Los Angeles; her support of the organization continues a family tradition, since her parents had aided early birth-control pioneer Margaret Sanger. She also this year donated to the North American Wildlife Association's benefit auction one of her paintings, a Pacific Ocean scene painted at John Barrymore's house in the 1960s; though she had once said, "I wouldn't give you a nickel for it," it sold for $5,000.

Hepburn's career spans over six decades; it began on stage in 1928, but it is her work as a leading film actress that has made her a world figure. She has won four Best Actress Oscars—more than any other performer—and starred opposite Spencer Tracy in nine classic films. Her first film role was the lead opposite John Barrymore in *Bill of Divorcement* (1934). She went on to win Oscars for *Morning Glory* (1936), opposite Tracy in their last film together, *Guess Who's Coming to Dinner* (1967), *The Lion in Winter* (1968), and *On Golden Pond* (1981). Some of her other most notable films were *The Philadelphia Story* (1940; also the 1939 Broadway play), *Little Women* (1933), *Stage Door* (1937), *Holiday* (1938), *Woman of the Year* (1942), *Keeper of the Flame* (1942), *The Sea of Grass* (1947), *State of the Union* (1948), *Adam's Rib* (1949), *The African Queen* (1951), *Pat and Mike* (1952), *Summertime* (1955), *Desk Set* (1957), *Suddenly Last Summer* (1959), *Long Day's Journey Into Night*

(1962), *A Delicate Balance* (1973), and *Rooster Cogburn* (1976). On Broadway, she played the lead in *Coco* (1969). Hepburn attended Bryn Mawr College. She was formerly married to Ludlow Ogden Smith. Her long personal relationship with Spencer Tracy ended with his death, in 1967.

FURTHER READING

"Katharine Hepburn." Pope Brock. *People*, Nov. 5, 1990.
"Katharine Hepburn. . . ." Susan Ware. *History Today*, Apr. 1990.
"Katharine Hepburn. . . ." A. Scott Berg and John Bryson. *Architectural Digest*, Apr. 1990.
The Private World of Katharine Hepburn. John Bryson, Photographer. Little, Brown, 1990.
The Films of Katharine Hepburn, rev. ed. Homer Dickens. Carol, 1990.
"Katharine Hepburn at 80." Barbara Lovenheim. *McCall's*, Nov. 1989.
Katharine Hepburn. Caroline Latham. Chelsea House, 1989.
Young Kate: The Remarkable Hepburns and the Childhood That Shaped an American Legend. Christopher Andersen. Holt, 1988.
Tracy and Hepburn. Garson Kanin. Donald I. Fine, 1988.
A Remarkable Woman: A Biography of Katharine Hepburn. Anne Edwards. Morrow, 1985.
Katharine Hepburn. Sheridan Morley. Little, Brown, 1984; Viking Penguin 1990.
Katharine Hepburn: A Hollywood Yankee. Gary K. Carey. Dell, 1984.
Katharine Hepburn. Michael Freedland. Salem House, 1984.
Kate: The Life of Katharine Hepburn. Charles Higham. New American Library-Dutton, 1981.

Heston, Charlton (Charles Carter, 1923–) Heston saw the past revived this year. One of his biggest hits, William Wyler's *Ben-Hur* (1959), was re-released into theaters in all its newly restored chariot-racing splendor with six-channel stereo; in his Oscar-winning role, Heston as Judah Ben-Hur once again battled Stephen Boyd's Messala. A restored version of Cecil B. DeMille's epic *The Ten Commandments* (1956), with Heston as Moses, also had a limited run in some theaters. During 1990, he was also writing a new, as-yet-untitled book on the theater.

Heston appeared in two new television movies, *The Little Kidnappers*, as embittered patriarch of Nova Scotia's MacKenzie clan, and a remake of *Treasure Island*, as Long John Silver. The latter is a bow to the future, since the film was written, directed, and produced by Heston's son, Fraser C. Heston. For the screen, Heston was also shooting a new feature film, *Solar Crisis*, about a mission to the sun in 2050. In the theater, Heston and Jean Simmons formed one of various occasional pairs doing A. R. Gurney's *Love Letters* in Los Angeles in summer 1990. In the first international Oscars-by-satellite, Heston was in Buenos Aires with Argentine actress Norma Aleandro to present the awards for documentary films. Working in audio as well, Heston released a well-reviewed new reading of Ernest Hemingway's *The Old Man and the Sea*. Such work is not new; in late 1989, the U.S. Department of Energy acknowledged that Heston has for six years had the highest nuclear weapons security clearance, allowing him to narrate films and videotapes containing classified information.

Formerly a president of the Screen Actors Guild (1965–71), Heston in 1990 resigned his membership in Actors Equity, in protest over the union's barring of British actor Jonathan Pryce from playing on Broadway the Eurasian character he had originated in London. Actors Equity wanted the part to go to an actor of Asian descent, which Heston charged was an "obscenely racist" position, from which the union later backed down.

Illinois-born Heston began his long stage and screen career in the late 1940s; on stage, his work has included three appearances as *Macbeth* (1954, 1959, 1976), and leads in *A Man For All Seasons* (1965 and 1987), and *The Caine Mutiny Court Martial* (1985; he directed and starred in the 1988 film version). On screen, he has been a star since the early 1950s, in such films as *Julius Caesar* (1950 and 1970), *The Greatest Show on Earth* (1952), *The Far Horizons* (1955), *The Wreck of the Mary Deare* (1959), *El Cid* (1961), *Diamond Head* (1962), *55 Days at Peking* (1962), *The Greatest Story Ever Told* (1965), *Khartoum* (1966), *Planet of the Apes* (1967; and the 1969 sequel), *Soylent Green* (1973), and *Midway* (1975). He married Lydia Clark in 1944; the couple have one child. He attended Northwestern University.

FURTHER READING

"Charlton Heston." Ivor Davis. *Los Angeles Magazine*, Apr. 1988.
"Hollywood biggies note dismay. . . ." David Robb. *Variety*, Dec. 31, 1986.
"Heston, Charlton." *Current Biography*, July 1986.
"Charlton Heston's life story." Vernon Scott. *Good Housekeeping*, May 1986.
Charlton Heston: A Biography. Michael Munn. St. Martin's, 1986.
"Charlton Heston." Ina Ginsburg. *Interview*, Sept. 1985.

Heyerdahl, Thor (1914–) Norwegian ethnologist, explorer, and author Heyerdahl developed a new enthusiasm in the late 1980s, beginning a new series of archeological excavations at Tecumbe, in northern Peru. There, 30 miles from the Pacific, he is working at a site said to contain 26 untouched Mochica burial sites, pyramids therefore thought to date back approximately 1,500 years. He is reported as believing they will cast light on the settlement of Easter Island. In 1989, he published a new book: *Easter Island: The Mystery Solved.*

Heyerdahl, born in Larvik, Norway, has been one of the world's leading explorer-authors since the appearance of his book *Kon-Tiki* (1948). That was the story of his balsa-wood raft crossing of the Pacific in an attempt to prove his thesis that early settlers of South America could very well have come from Asia across the Pacific, and that the world's cultures tended to diffuse from common centers, rather than developing independently. He pursued the same theory in his 1969 to 1970 journey across the Atlantic in *Ra-II,* an Egyptian reed boat, which he related in *The Ra Expeditions* (1972). He has also led several other expeditions, to Easter Island, the Maldives, and the Galapagos Islands, among others, and has written extensively in his field. He has been married twice, and has three children. He attended Larvik College.

FURTHER READING

"Thor Heyerdahl. . . ." Thomas Moore. U.S. News & World Report, Apr. 2, 1990.
"Thor Heyerdahl." Pope Brock. *People*, Dec. 11, 1989.
"Profiles. . . ." Daniel H. Minassian. *Architectural Digest*, Feb. 1987.
Thor Heyerdahl: Across the Seas of Time. Paul Westman. Dillon, 1982.

Hines, Gregory (Gregory Oliver Hines 1946–) A leader of the tap revival of the 1980s, Hines is a multitalented tapdancer, actor, and variety entertainer. In 1990, he moved for the first time into film direction, with the independently produced *Gotta Dance*. On screen, he starred in *Eve of Destruction*, a futuristic action-thriller set in the present, about a sharpshooter and a berserk android. He continued to appear in cabaret and dance recitals, as with the Jazz Tap Ensemble at Harlem's Apollo Theatre in July 1990.

New York City-born Hines was on stage professionally at the age of five, touring with his brother Maurice as the "Hines Kids" (1949–55), the "Hines Brothers" (1955–63), and then with their father, Maurice, as "Hines, Hines, and Dad" (1963–73). On stage, he won Tony nominations in *Eubie* (1978), *Comin' Uptown* (1980), and *Sophisticated Ladies* (1981), and emerged as a film star in the 1980s, in such movies as *Wolfen* (1981), *The Cotton Club* (1984), *White Nights* (1985), *Running Scared* (1986), and *Off Limits* (1988). He has been married twice, last to Pamela Koslow in 1981, and has three children.

FURTHER READING

Black Dance in America: A History Through Its People. James Haskins. Harper, 1990.
"Hines on tap." Sally Sommer. *Dance Magazine*, Dec. 1988.
"Gregory Hines. . . ." Lynn Norment. *Ebony*, Oct, 1986.
"Far from running scared. . . ." Mary Vespa. *People*, Aug. 11, 1986.
"Gregory Hines." *Playboy*, Sept. 1986.
"Gregory Hines stars. . . ." *Jet*, Dec. 9, 1985.
"Hines, Gregory." *Current Biography*, July 1985.

Hoffman, Dustin (Dustin Lee Hoffman, 1937–) Hoffman made Shakespeare a commercial hit when he brought his Tony-nominated Shylock from London to Broadway in Peter Hall's production of *The Merchant of*

Venice (1990). He also played a notable cameo as Mumbles in Warren Beatty's film *Dick Tracy* (1990). At year's end, Hoffman was playing Dutch Schultz in the film *Billy Bathgate*, scheduled for 1991 release, and was set to play Captain Hook in Steven Spielberg's Peter Pan film. His *Family Business* (1989), with Sean Connery and Matthew Broderick, was a box-office flop, but a 1990 video rental hit. In the People's Choice awards, Hoffman was among the top vote-getters in the category of World Favorite Motion Picture Actor.

Los Angeles-born Hoffman has been a major film star since his breakthrough role as *The Graduate* (1967), which he followed with such films as *Midnight Cowboy* (1969), *Little Big Man* (1971), *Lenny* (1974), *All the President's Men* (1976), *Marathon Man* (1976), *Kramer vs. Kramer* (1979), winning a Best Actor Oscar, *Tootsie* (1982), and *Rain Man*, for a second Best Actor Oscar. On stage, he was a notable Willy Loman in the 1984 revival of *Death of a Salesman* (televised in 1985). He was formerly married to Anne Byrne, married Lisa Gottsegen in 1980, and has five children. He attended Santa Monica City College.

FURTHER READING

"Acting his age. . . ." MARK ROWLAND. *American Film*, Dec. 1988.
"Rebirth of a salesman." MARIE BRENNER. *New York*, Mar. 26, 1984.
Dustin Hoffman. IAIN JOHNSTONE. Hippocrene, 1984.
Making Tootsie: A Film Study With Dustin Hoffman and Sydney Pollack. SUSAN DWORKIN. Newmarket, 1983.
The Films of Dustin Hoffman. DOUGLAS BRODE. Carol, 1983.
Dustin Hoffman: Hollywood's Anti-Hero. JEFF LENBURG. St. Martin's, 1982.

Hofstadter, Robert (1915–90) For his basic research on the exact size and shape of the proton and neutron, Hofstadter won a 1961 Nobel Prize in Physics. That research was only one of several major contributions he made to modern science, including his work with sodium iodide as a tool for exploring subatomic particles, and his later work with coronary angiography. During World War II, as a physicist with the National Bureau of Standards, he developed the antiaircraft proximity fuse. Hofstadter taught at Princeton, City College, and from 1950 to 1985 at Stanford, and was from 1967 to 1974, director of the Stanford high energy physics laboratory. (d. Palo Alto, California; November 17, 1990)

FURTHER READING

Obituary. *The Times* (of London), Nov. 26, 1989.
Obituary. *New York Times*, Nov. 19, 1989.
"President awards. . . ." *Physics Today*, July 1986.

Holmes à Court, Robert (Michael Robert Hamilton Holmes à Court, 1939–90) The Australian financier and maverick corporate raider Holmes à Court was for a time one of Australia's richest men. Born and educated in South Africa, he first studied agricultural science in New Zealand, then law in Australia, becoming a successful commercial lawyer. Starting in 1970, with a nearly insolvent textiles company, he began amassing the huge corporate conglomeration he called the Bell Group, at its height worth 1.3 million Australian dollars. He lost control of Bell after the 1987 worldwide stock crash, but was rebuilding his empire at his death. (d. Western Australia; September 2, 1990)

FURTHER READING

Obituary. *Variety*, Sept. 10, 1990.
Obituary. *The Times* (of London), Sept. 3, 1990.
Obituary. *New York Times*, Sept. 3, 1990.
"Holmes à Court sells control. . . ." BLAKE MURDOCH. *Variety*, May 4, 1988.
"Holmes à Court's fortunes. . . ." CHERYL DEBES. *Business Week*, Dec. 7, 1987.
"Jaws: the Australian. . . ." JANICE CASTRO. *Time*, July 27, 1987.

Holyfield, Evander (1962–) In an extraordinary upset, professional boxer Evander Holyfield, fighting at a weight of 208 pounds, knocked out 246-pound, world heavyweight champion James "Buster" Douglas in the third round of their Las Vegas, Nevada, title match in November 1990. Douglas, far overweight and in poor condition for a title fight, at no point threatened to defeat Holyfield, landing very few blows and remaining on the defensive for most of the brief match. The ex-champion's share of

the fight's proceeds was a reported $24 million. As the new, undisputed world heavyweight champion, Holyfield scheduled a fight with George Foreman, and was required by the world boxing groups to meet challenger and ex-champion Mike Tyson within a year of his victory of Douglas.

Alabama-born Holyfield won a bronze medal in the 1984 Olympics, and turned professional in 1986. For most of his career, he has been a light-heavyweight, rather than a heavyweight, and he became World Boxing Association light-heavyweight world champion in 1986; many observers thought he would have great difficulty in beating the heavier and probably stronger Douglas. Going into the title fight, Holyfield was undefeated as a professional, having won 24 straight fights. He is married, and has four children.

FURTHER READING

"Evander Holyfield makes hard work pay off. . . ." *Jet*, Nov. 19, 1990.

"At last!" DAVID MILLER. *Sport*, Nov. 1990.

Honecker, Erich (1912–) The former leader of East Germany experienced a very sharp reversal of fortune in late 1989, as East Germans toppled his regime and then moved toward German reunification. Honecker held his government's hardline position until quite late in the process of Eastern European liberation; but when change began, it came quickly. In July 1989, hundreds of East Germans took refuge in foreign embassies in Budapest and West Berlin. In September, hundreds of thousands of demonstrators in Leipzig and other East German cities called for Honecker's resignation and a new political system, while tens of thousands of East Germans fled to the West. On October 18, 1989, the Honecker government fell, and he resigned all official positions. Afterward, he was briefly held under house arrest, while corruption charges were being investigated, but was freed in early January 1990; shortly after that, he underwent an operation for cancer. He was also investigated for possible treason, rearrested in late January, and again freed, as possible treason charges were not pursued.

Before his sudden fall from power, Honecker had been the hardline leader of East German communism for 18 years, succeeding Walter Ulbricht as head of the ruling Socialist Unity Party in 1971. An anti-fascist leader in the early 1930s, he was captured by the Nazis and imprisoned from 1935 to 1945; after Allied victory, he rose quickly in Soviet-dominated East Germany. He was formerly married to Edith Baumann, married Margot Feist in 1953, and has two children.

FURTHER READING

"'Ample opportunities'. . . ." ROBIN KNIGHT. *U.S. News & World Report*, Jan. 12, 1987.

"Key leaders. . . ." TAMAR ROTHENBERG. *Scholastic Update*, Sept. 22, 1986.

Honecker's Germany. DAVID CHILDS, ED. Unwin Hyman, 1985.

From My Life. ERICH HONECKER. Pergamon, 1981.

Hooker, John Lee (1917–) Singer-songwriter-guitarist Hooker was named to the Rock Hall of Fame in a Los Angeles ceremony in October 1990. The legendary blues performer was not resting on his laurels, however. He and jazz great Miles Davis, among others, were recording the sound track for a new Dennis Hopper movie, *The Hot Spot,* starring Don Johnson and Virginia Madsen. In late 1989, Hooker had released a new record, *The Healer,* in which he was paired with numerous other musicians, most notably in a cut with Bonnie Raitt, "I'm in the Mood," which won the 1990 Grammy for best traditional blues recording. Hooker also continued to play around the country, in late 1989 appearing as a guest with the Rolling Stones in the last leg of their U.S. tour, in a performance recorded for showing on cable television.

Mississippi-born Hooker became a leading blues musician in the late 1940s, with such songs as "Boogie Chillun" (1948), and "I'm in the Mood" (1951), and became a popular figure during the folk and blues revival of the 1960s, appearing often at the Newport and other jazz festivals, and recording scores of albums, such as *The Folklore of John Lee Hooker* (1962), and *The Big Soul of John Lee Hooker* (1964). He enjoyed yet another revival in the late 1980s, on tour again and with such albums as *Jealous* (1986).

FURTHER READING

"John Lee Hooker. . . ." STEVE DOUGHERTY. *People*, Oct. 29, 1990.
"John Lee Hooker. . . ." JOSEF WOODARD. *Down Beat*, Feb. 1990.
"John Lee Hooker. . . ." JAS OBRECHT. *Guitar Player*, Nov. 1989.

Horowitz, Vladimir (1904–89) Russian-born Horowitz was a pianist whose virtuosity and verve won legions of music-lovers, and influenced a whole generation of musicians, though some critics found his style too eccentric. After study in Kiev, young Horowitz made his debut in Kharkov in 1921, soon playing in the major cities of the Western world, including New York (1928), where his racing ahead of the conductor to the finish of Tchaikovsky's First Piano Concerto early fueled Horowitz legends. His health was often uncertain and he periodically "retired," making notable returns, such as his 1965 Carnegie Hall recital. His 1986 concert in the Soviet Union, after years of opposition to the communist government, was a major event. His last public concert was in 1987, though he continued to record. (d. New York; November 5, 1990)

FURTHER READING

Obituary. *Current Biography*, Jan. 1990.
Obituary. S. CHAPIN. *National Review*, Dec. 8, 1989.
"A life of rhapsody." GENE HAYDEN. *Maclean's*, Nov. 20, 1989.
"Lord of all he surveyed. . . ." MICHAEL WALSH. *Time*, Nov. 20, 1989 .
"Music's last romantic. . . ." LAURA SHAPIRO. *Newsweek*, Nov. 20, 1989.
"For purity and pyrotechnics. . . ." *People*, Nov. 20, 1989.
Obituary. *Variety*, Nov. 8, 1989.
Obituary. *The Times* (of London), Nov. 7, 1989.
Obituary. *New York Times*, Nov. 6, 1989.
Horowitz: A Biography of Vladimir Horowitz. GLENN PLASKIN. Morrow, 1983.

Houghton, Arthur Amory (1906–90) An industrialist and rare book collector, Houghton was also a very active fundraiser and leader in the arts. A great-grandson of Amory Houghton, founder of Corning Glass, he became president of Steuben Glass in 1933, and in the next four decades developed it into a major company. He also developed the Corning Glass Center in 1951, a forerunner of the Corning Museum of Glass. He was curator of rare books at the Library of Congress from 1940 to 1942, and an air corps officer from 1942 to 1945. Houghton was a board member of the Metropolitan Museum of Art from 1952 to 1974, president from 1964 to 1969, and board chairman from 1969 to 1972. He was also board chairman of the New York Philharmonic Society from 1958 to 1963, and was active in scores of other educational and philanthropic organizations. He personally funded the Houghton Library at Harvard University, and later donated his Keats collection to the library. (d. Venice, Florida; April 3, 1990)

FURTHER READING

Obituary. *New York Times*, Apr. 4, 1990.

Houston, Whitney (1963–) Singer Houston found it more crowded than usual at the top this year, when she brought out her first new album in three years, late in 1990, one with a harder-pounding rhythm-and-blues feel than the lighter touch of previous albums. Her single "I'm Your Baby Tonight" quickly hit number one, but the album of the same title did not immediately take the top spot—unusual, since she previously had had two consecutive number one albums. Certainly with her extraordinary voice, Houston remains a major star and musical force, as the Songwriters Hall of Fame recognized when they honored her with their 1990 Hitmaker Award. Meanwhile, Houston is branching out. Even though she has never acted in a feature film, she signed a multi-picture agreement with 20th-Century Fox to star in and produce projects through her Nippy Productions, headed by her father, John Houston.

New Jersey-born Houston suddenly became known as a leading popular singer in the mid-1980s, with her first album, the Grammy-winning *Whitney Houston* (1985), followed by *Whitney* (1986), and with such songs as "Didn't We Almost Have it All," "The Greatest Love of All," and "How Will I Know." She is the daughter of singer Cissy Houston, and the cousin of singer Aretha Franklin.

FURTHER READING

"Singer Whitney Houston. . . ." *Jet*, July 16, 1990.
"Whitney Houston." David Van Biema. *Life*, Oct. 1990.
"Whitney Houston." *Harper's Bazaar*, Sept. 1989.
The Picture Life of Whitney Houston. Gene Busnar. Watts, 1988.
Whitney Houston. Keith E. Greenberg. Lerner, 1988.
"The prom queen of soul. . . ." Richard Corliss. *Time*, July 13, 1987.
"Whitney Houston top AMA star. . . ." *Variety*, Jan. 28, 1987.
"Whitney's greatest love." Kendra Silverman. *Teen*, Dec. 1986.
"Houston, Whitney." *Current Biography*, Nov. 1986.
"Top families." *People*, Oct. 27, 1986.
"Pop music. . . ." Nicholas Jennings. *Maclean's*, Aug. 25, 1986.
"Whitney Houston. . . ." Susan Korones. *Cosmopolitan*, May 1986.

Howard, Ron (1954–) Actor-director-producer Howard had a huge success with his comedy about modern family life, *Parenthood* (1989), starring Steve Martin and Mary Steenburgen. Theater audiences flocked to it, and so did video renters; it was also chosen to open the 33rd London Film Festival. In keeping with the family theme, when Howard (himself the father of five) was honored at the annual Moving Picture Ball with the prestigious American Cinematheque Award for his ongoing contributions to the film industry in March 1990, he was joined not only by his actual parents but also by his television parents from "Happy Days," Tom Bosley and Marion Ross. Howard was also (with Brian Grazer) executive producer and writer of the NBC series spun off from *Parenthood*. In late 1990, Howard was in Chicago directing *Arson*, a film drama about an arson investigation as seen through the eyes of a rookie firefighter, with a cast including Donald Sutherland and Robert De Niro.

Oklahoma-born Howard was a child star in television, as Opie in "The Andy Griffith Show" (1960–68), and later in "The Smith Family" (1971–72), and "Happy Days" (1974-80). He also appeared in such films as *The Music Man* (1962), *American Graffiti* (1973), and *The Shootist* (1976). As an adult, he directed, and in several instances co-wrote and produced, such films as *Splash* (1984), *Cocoon* (1985), *No Man's Land* (1987), *Clean and Sober* (1988), and *Willow* (1988). He attended the University of Southern California. He married Cheryl Alley in 1975; they have five children.

FURTHER READING

"A night of vice with Mr. Nice." *Esquire*, Dec. 1986.
"The metamorphosis of Ron Howard." Samir Hachem. *Horizon*, June 1985.

Howell, Wilson Nathaniel (1939–) A career U.S. diplomat, Howell was ambassador to Kuwait at the time of the August 2, 1990, Iraqi invasion. In the following 132 days at the Kuwait City embassy, he, deputy chief of mission, Barbara Bodine, and the remaining six members of the embassy staff, along with 19 others who had taken refuge in the embassy, refused Iraqi demands that the embassy be vacated, at least until all American hostages were freed by the Iraqis. During the long, tense standoff that resulted, they lived on short rations and dug a well to supplement their limited water supply, as Iraqi troops surrounded the embassy, but did not enter to force them out. The Iraqi government in that period was trying to avoid a provocation that would lead to immediate war. After the hostages had been freed, the embassy was closed, as Howell and the others were evacuated from Kuwait.

Virginia-born Howell became a diplomat in the late 1960s, and spent the next two decades in a series of increasingly responsible posts, most of them either in the Near East (Abu Dhabi, Lebanon, Algeria, and then Kuwait) or as a Near Eastern specialist in the United States. He became U.S. ambassador to Kuwait in 1987. His 1961 B.A. and 1965 Ph.D. were from the University of Virginia. He married Margie Anne Saunders in 1961; they have two children.

FURTHER READING

"Envoy to Kuwait. . . ." CLIFFORD KRAUSS. *New York Times*, Dec. 15, 1990.
"U.S. diplomat. . . ." JENNIFER TOTH. *Los Angeles Times*, Dec. 15, 1990.
"Linguist with. . . ." DAVID LAMB. *Los Angeles Times*, Aug. 25, 1990.
"Two U.S. envoys. . . ." *Washington Post*, Aug. 25, 1990.

Hurt, William (1950–) Hurt spent much of 1990 under wraps, working with normally secretive Woody Allen on Allen's new film. The film *Alice,* opened during the 1990 Christmas season, with Hurt as Doug opposite Mia Farrow in the title role; the film and its players premiered to critical praise. Privately, Hurt prevailed in the lawsuit brought by ex-lover Sandra Jennings, when an appeals court failed to overturn a ruling in his favor on the 1989 palimony case; Jennings had claimed that they had a common-law marriage and asked for a substantial settlement.

Born in Washington, D.C., Hurt became a leading dramatic actor in the late 1970s, starring in such films as *Body Heat* (1978), *The Big Chill* (1983), *Gorky Park* (1983), *Kiss of the Spider Woman* (1985), for which he won a Best Actor Oscar, *Children of a Lesser God* (1986), *Broadcast News* (1987), and *The Accidental Tourist* (1988). He married Heidi Henderson in 1989; they have one son. He attended Tufts University and The Juilliard School.

FURTHER READING

"The news about. . . ." JANE HALL and BRAD DARRACH. *People*, Feb. 1, 1988.
William Hurt: The Actor and His Work. TOBY GOLDSTEIN. St. Martin's, 1987.
"William Hurt. . . ." JACK KROLL. *Esquire*, Oct. 1986.
"Hurt, William." *Current Biography*, May 1986.
"A proud day for the bozos. . . ." JACK KROLL. *Newsweek*, Apr. 7, 1986.

Hussein I (Hussein ibn Talal, 1935–) The Jordanian king, caught between his far more powerful Iraqi and Israeli neighbors, and sheltering a large pro-Iraqi Palestinian population, found himself in a nearly impossible situation as the August 1990 Persian Gulf Crisis developed into the Gulf War. He responded by trying to walk a tightrope between the huge, worldwide anti-Iraqi alliance and Iraq, embarking upon a series of visits to Arab and Western countries in an attempt to begin some kind of peace dialogue between the opposing sides, though with very little apparent success. On August 13, he met with Saddam Hussein, and three days later met with George Bush; in late August, he began a fruitless series of visits to Arab leaders. Though often appearing to support the Iraqi side, he was, in practice, viewed as a neutral by the Arab nations and the West, with economic and refugee aid coming from many nations in the months that followed. As the war developed, he attempted to remain a neutral, vowing to resist any violations of his country's land or air space, though clearly with inadequate strength to do so.

Hussein became the king of Jordan in 1953, succeeding his father, Abdullah Ibn Hussein, himself the son of Hussein Ibn Ali, head of the 1916 Arab revolt against the Turks during World War I, the revolt assisted by British officer T. E. Lawrence ("Lawrence of Arabia"). For almost four decades, Hussein survived as a moderate in the turbulent politics of the Middle East, although he was drawn into the 1967 Third Arab-Israeli War, and lost control over the West Bank and Jerusalem, which Israel has occupied ever since. He gave up all territorial claims to these in 1988, during the Palestinian Intifada, to pave the way for a Palestinian declaration of independence. In 1970, he fought and won a war against the Palestine Liberation Organization (PLO), then headquartered in his country, although by 1990, the relatively large Palestinian population of Jordan strongly influenced his position on the Iraqi invasion of Kuwait, which was supported by most Palestinians. He has been married four times, and has eleven children. He attended Victoria College and Sandhurst.

FURTHER READING

"Divided loyalties." JOEL BRINKLEY. *New York Times Magazine*, Dec. 16, 1990.
"Facing a no-win. . . ." DEAN FISCHER and JAMES WILDE. *Time*, Nov. 5, 1990.
"Dangerous crossroads. . . ." *Maclean's*, July 9, 1990.
Hussein of Jordan: From Survivor to Statesman. JAMES LUNT. Morrow, 1989.
King Hussein and the Challenge of Arab Radicalism: Jordan, 1955–1967. URIEL DANN. Oxford University Press, 1989.
"Hussein, King of Jordan." *Current Biography*, Apr. 1986.
"Hussein's predicament. . . ." HIRSH GOODMAN. *New Republic*, Aug. 26, 1985.

Hussein, Saddam (1937–) With the end of the long Iran-Iraq war, Iraqi president Saddam Hussein emerged as a Middle Eastern strongman. His reportedly million-man, Soviet-supplied army was led by over 5,000 tanks, covered by over 600 aircraft, and possessed short- and medium-range ballistic missiles. He possessed chemical weapons, which he had used repeatedly against Iran and then against his own people, and which he quickly threatened to use against Israel, in an attempt to mobilize Arab nations in a new crusade against Israel,

with himself as leader. His real target, as it turned out on August 2, 1990, was oil-rich Kuwait, which his armies quickly took. He then turned toward far richer Saudi Arabia, whether to invade or to intimidate, and was met by the U.S.-led multinational response, coupled with United Nations action, which resulted in the sanctions, blockade, and ultimately, the Persian Gulf War.

Takrit-born Hussein joined the Ba'ath socialist party in 1957, and went into Egyptian exile in 1958, after he took part in the failed attempt to assassinate general Karim Kassem, premier of the Iraqi republic. He returned to Iraq in 1963, after the army coup in which Kassem was killed. Hussein was a leader of the Ba'ath coup of 1968, and took full power in 1971, then surrounding himself with followers from his home village, instituting a reign of terror in his country, and becoming the dictator of Iraq. He also then began to develop a massive "cult of personality" around himself.

In 1980, Hussein's forces attacked Iran, beginning the 1980 to 1988 Iran-Iraq war. His forces used large amounts of poison gas against the Iranians, although such chemical warfare has been outlawed throughout the world. In the late 1980s, after the 1988 ceasefire with Iran, his forces continued to use poison gas, this time against Iraq's own rebellious Kurdish population, killing thousands of civilians, and forcing hundreds of thousands to flee into exile. Hussein married Sajidal Khairalla in 1963, and has four children. He attended Cairo University and Baghdad's al-Mujstanseriya University.

FURTHER READING

"Saddam. . . ." LISA BEYER. *Time*, Jan. 7, 1991.
Instant Empire: Saddam Hussein's Ambition for Iraq. SIMON HENDERSON. Mercury House, 1991.
"Blood Baath. . . ." DAVID A. KORN. *New Republic*, Oct. 29, 1990.
"Iraq's strongman. . . ." LAUREN TARSHIS. *Scholastic Update*, Oct. 5, 1990.
"Saddam's shadow. . . ." JAMES HOGGARD. *Texas Monthly*, Oct. 1990.
"'What makes. . . .'" BRIAN DUFFY. *U.S. News & World Report*, Sept. 10, 1990.
"Saddam Hussein's. . . ." LOUISE LIEF. *U.S. News & World Report*, Sept. 10, 1990.
"Like a wolf. . . ." J.B. KELLY and BRIAN CROZIER. *National Review*, Sept. 3, 1990.
"Thief of Baghdad. . . ." FOUAD AJAMI. *New Republic*, Sept. 3, 1990.
"The pan-Arab fantasy. . . ." MARTIN PERETZ. *New Republic*, Sept. 3, 1990.
"Portrait of power. . . ." BRIAN BERGMAN. *Maclean's*, Aug. 20, 1990.
"Behind Saddam Hussein's smile. . . ." *People*, Aug. 20, 1990.
"Tyrant of the Gulf." JOHN BIERMAN. *Maclean's*, Aug. 13, 1990.
"Master of his universe." OTTO FRIEDRICH. *Time*, Aug. 13, 1990.
"Resourceful aggressor. . . ." MAGGIE MAHAR. *Barron's*, Aug. 13, 1990.
Saddam Hussein and the Crisis in the Gulf. JUDITH MILLER and LAURIE MYLORIE. Random, 1990.

Huston, Anjelica (1952–) Huston, who continues to emerge as one of the leading screen actresses of the modern period, appeared in several striking new roles during 1989 and 1990. In Paul Mazursky's black comedy, *Enemies, A Love Story* (1989), she played Tamara, an unexpected survivor of the Holocaust; the role won her the National Society of Film Critics' award as best supporting actress. In Woody Allen's *Crimes and Misdemeanors* (1989), she was a mistress discarded, then killed. Then in Stephen Frears's *The Grifters* (1990), this time surprisingly as a blond, she was a toughened victim-victimizer in the racing world, in an Oscar-nominated performance. Also in 1990, she opened in the late Jim Henson's last film, *The Witches,* playing the Grand High Witch of the World, out to turn all England's children into mice. Late in the year, she was shooting in yet another quirky role, this time as Morticia in a feature film of *The Addams Family,* with Raul Julia and Christopher Lloyd.

Born in Los Angeles but raised in Ireland, Huston took a critical pounding when her father, actor-director John Huston, cast the 15-year-old in his film *A Walk With Love and Death* (1967). She retreated from film to the stage, but became known as a leading dramatic film actress in the mid-1980s, winning a Best Supporting Actress Oscar as Maerose Prizzi in John Huston's *Prizzi's Honor* (1985), and starring also in *Gardens of Stone* (1987), *The Dead,* John Huston's last film (1987; with screenplay by brother Tony Huston), *Mr. North* (1988; directed by half-brother Danny Huston), and *A Handful of Dust* (1988). She is the granddaughter of actor Walter Huston. She recently ended a 17-year relationship with Jack Nicholson. She worked with acting coach Peggy Feury.

FURTHER READING

"A bit of a coyote. . . ." DAVID THOMSON. *American Film*, Nov. 1990.
"Anjelica Huston. . . ." VICKI WOODS. *Vogue*, Nov. 1990.
"Huston, Anjelica." *Current Biography*, July 1990.
"Anjelica Huston." YONA ZELDIS MCDONOUGH. *Harper's Bazaar*, Sept. 1989.
"Anjelica rising. . . ." JAMES KAPLAN. *New York Times Magazine*, Feb. 12, 1989.
Anjelica Huston: The Lady and the Legacy. MARTHA HARRIS. St. Martin's, 1989.
The Hustons. LAWRENCE GROBEL. Macmillan, 1989.

I

Iacocca, Lee (Lido Anthony Iacocca, 1924–) During the mid-1980s, Chrysler chairman Iacocca was the prime mover in the restoration of the Statue of Liberty and the reclamation of Ellis Island. The former immigration station opened as a museum of American immigration and a national shrine, on September 9, 1990. Iacocca was an honored guest, although he had been by then partially pushed aside for political reasons by the Bush administration.

During 1989 and 1990, Iacocca and Chrysler faced very hard times, as the auto industry continued to withstand Japanese and other foreign competition, and as the U.S. economy moved into recession. In 1990, Chrysler reported a $250 million third quarter loss, wiping out the profits of its first two quarters; and more losses were expected.

Iacocca began his long career with the Ford Motor Company in 1946; he rose to the presidency of the Ford division in 1970, leaving in 1978 to become the highly visible president and chief operating officer of Chrysler. He saved near-bankrupt Chrysler from looming bankruptcy with the help of a massive federal "bail-out," and went on to become a leading figure in American industry. He published two best-selling autobiographical works, *Iacocca: An Autobiography* (1986; with William Novak), and *Talking Straight* (1989). Pennsylvania-born Iacocca married Mary McCleary in 1956; they had two children. His B.S. was from Lehigh University, in 1945; his M.E. was from Princeton, in 1946.

FURTHER READING

"Playboy interview. . . ." PETER ROSS RANGE. *Playboy*, Jan. 1991.

"Iacocca talks. . . ." ALEX TAYLOR III. *Fortune*, Feb. 12, 1990.

"Iacocca, Lee Anthony." *Current Biography*, Oct. 1988.

"Iacocca; in his own words. . . ." ALEX TAYLOR III. *Fortune*, Aug. 29, 1988.

"Lee Iacocca looks ahead." D'ARCY JENISH. *Maclean's*, Aug. 1, 1988.

Standing up for America: A Biography of Lee Iacocca. PATRICIA HADDOCK. Dillon, 1987.

The Unknown Iacocca. PETER WYDEN. Morrow, 1987.

Ibarruri, Dolores ("La Pasionaria," or Passion Flower; 1895–1989) La Pasionaria was a legendary Spanish Civil War heroine and president of the Spanish Communist Party. Eighth of the 11 children in a miner's family, Ibarruri was in school until age 15, then worked as a dressmaker and maid before marrying a miner and bearing six children (four of whom died in infancy). Exchanging her Roman Catholicism for Marxism, she wrote for a miner's newspaper from 1918, under her well-known pseudonym. Always dressed in black, she became an increasingly important Party spokesperson, based in Madrid from 1931. Her famous slogan "No pasarán!" ("They shall not pass"; earlier used as the French slogan at Verdun, in World War I) was from 1936 a Republican rallying cry. When the Republicans lost the Civil War, she moved to Moscow, returning only in 1977, after her old enemy, Francisco Franco, had died. In 1976 she published *They Shall Not Pass: The Autobiography of La Pasionaria.* (d. Madrid; November 12, 1989)

FURTHER READING

Obituary. *Current Biography*, Jan. 1990.
Obituary. *National Review*, Dec. 8, 1989.
Obituary. *New York Times*, Nov. 13, 1989.
"Notebook." *New Republic*, Aug. 8, 1983.

Iliescu, Ion (1930–) At the beginning of the Romanian Revolution, on December 22, 1989, Iliescu emerged as a member of the revolutionary council, the National Salvation Front. On December 23, as president of the Front, he announced the arrest of former dictator Nicolae Ceausescu and his wife, Elena, who were executed on December 25. On December 26 Iliescu was named provisional president of Romania. In the months that followed, he continued to lead the country, withstanding a strong attack on the government by those who felt that it was being run by high officials, like Iliescu, in the former communist government. Iliescu became the first freely elected president of post-Ceausescu Romania in May formally taking office as president on June 20.

Iliescu has been associated with the Romanian Communist Party ever since joining its youth organization in 1944. He rose swiftly in the party hierarchy until the early 1970s, becoming a member of his party's central committee in 1967, and was youth minister from 1967 to 1972. But then he fell into disfavor with dictator Nicolae Ceausescu, and was sidetracked and demoted. He was head of a state-run publishing house in 1989, when Ceausescu fell. In that fall, Iliescu rose. He is married to Elena Iliescu, and attended the Bucharest Polytechnical Institute and Moscow University.

FURTHER READING

"Iliescu, Ion." *Current Biography*, June 1990.
"Between revolutions. . . ." VLADIMIR TISMANEANU. *New Republic*, Apr. 23, 1990.

Ireland, Jill (1936–90) British-born film actress Ireland was often co-starred in action-adventure pictures with her second husband, Charles Bronson. Trained early in ballet, Ireland debuted in films in 1955, playing numerous roles before moving to Hollywood in 1962, where she made guest appearances on television and, after her 1967 marriage to Bronson, moved back into films. Breast cancer changed her life, and she used her experiences, described in her books *Life Wish* (1987), and *Life Lines* (1990), to help other women recognize and deal with breast cancer in its early stages. She also worked with the American Cancer Society and testified before Congress, seeking improved cancer diagnosis and treatment. (d. Malibu, California; May 18, 1990)

FURTHER READING

"Jill Ireland. . . ." SUSAN SCHINDEHETTE. *People*, June 4, 1990.
Obituary. *Variety*, May 23, 1990.
Obituary. *The Times* (of London), May 21, 1990.
Obituary. *New York Times*, May 19, 1990.
"Shattered for. . . ." BARBARA KANTROWITZ. *Newsweek*, May 8, 1989.
"'I will live. . . .'" VERNON SCOTT. *Good Housekeeping*, May 1989.

Irons, Jeremy (1948–) British actor Irons scored in another stunning role as the icy aristocrat Claus von Bulow, accused of attempting to murder his wealthy wife, Sunny

(Glenn Close), in *Reversal of Fortune* (1990). Audiences at film festivals and in general theaters were struck by the film's balance between courtroom suspense and comedy of manners, with Irons singled out for high praise and in early 1991 the Academy Award for Best Actor. In late 1989, he had appeared to less general praise—for himself and the film—in the movie version of Alan Ayckbourn's *A Chorus of Disapproval,* playing muddled Guy Jones acting in a Scarborough production of *The Beggar's Opera.* In 1989 he also played in a new Roger Corman film, *Frankenstein Unbound,* as a 21st-century scientist who travels back in time to explore the Frankenstein story. Meanwhile, Irons's chilling portrayal of twin gynecologists in disintegration, *Dead Ringers* (1989), was widely seen on the television screens.

Irons became known as a screen and stage star in the early 1980s. In 1981, he created the Charles Ryder role in "Brideshead Revisited," the celebrated television miniseries adaptation of the Evelyn Waugh novel. In the same year, he played opposite Meryl Streep in *The French Lieutenant's Woman.* He went on to star in such films as *Moonlighting* (1982), *Betrayal* (1983), *The Wild Duck* (1983), *Swann in Love* (1984), and *The Mission* (1986). He won a Best Actor Tony for *The Real Thing* (1984). He is married to actress Sinéad Cusack; they have two children.

FURTHER READING

"Claus encounters." Ellen Stern. *GQ—Gentlemen's Quarterly*, Nov. 1990.
"Irons." David DeNicolo. *Interview*, June 1990.
"Visit to the doctor." Karen Jaehne. *Film Comment*, Sept.–Oct. 1988.
Actors: A Celebration. Rita Gam. St. Martin's, 1988.

Ivory, James (James Francis Ivory, 1928–) Ivory, a leading film director, turned in a new direction with his most recent films. In a sharp departure from his earlier films, mostly collaborations with producer Ismail Merchant and writer Ruth Prawer Jhabvala, he focused on ultra-hip, ultimately desperate New York yuppies in *Slaves of New York* (1989), based on Tama Janowitz's script from her own stories. The film, starring Bernadette Peters, was not generally well-received. Far more successful was *Mr. and Mrs. Bridge,* based on two Evan S. Connell novels, starring Paul Newman and Joanne Woodward in the title roles as Walter and India Bridge, a Kansas City lawyer and his wife reflecting on their staid, upper-middle-class, mid-20th-century life. Seen as a "quality" film in the Ivory-Merchant-Jhabvala tradition, it was highly praised for its acting, especially by Woodward, but some felt it was too decorous and superficial.

California-born Ivory began his long, fruitful collaboration with Merchant and Jhabvala in the early 1960s, with such films as *Shakespeare Wallah* (1965), *Bombay Talkie* (1970), and *Autobiography of a Princess* (1975), all of them largely set in India. His later films included *The Europeans* (1979), *Heat and Dust* (1983), *A Room With a View* (1986), and *Maurice* (1987). His B.F.A. was from the University of Oregon, in 1951; his M.A. was from the University of Southern California.

FURTHER READING

"Mr. and Mrs. Bridge." Graham Fuller. *Interview*, Nov. 1990.
"'Rarely is. . . .'" Pamela Sherrid. *U.S. News & World Report*, Dec. 21, 1987.
"The Raj duet. . . ." Dinitia Smith. *New York*, Oct. 5, 1987.
"Producer with a view." Richard C. Morais. *Forbes*, Mar. 23, 1987.
"View from Prospero's island. . . ." Gerald Clarke. *Time*, Jan. 12, 1987.
"Merchant and Ivory." *American Film*, Jan.–Feb. 1987.

J

Jackson, Glenda (1936–) Theater and film lovers all over the world were hoping this year that at least one seat in the north of London would not go to the Labour Party in the next parliamentary election, to be held sometime before mid-1992. That is because British actress Glenda Jackson, in March 1990, beat out three other contenders for the right to run as the Labour Party candidate for that seat, and says that if she wins she will give up acting. She has not done so yet, however, and despite her political activities continued to appear on stage and screen, as in Los Angeles in late 1989 in a notable production of *Who's Afraid of Virginia Woolf,* opposite John Lithgow, directed by the playwright himself, Edward Albee. In 1989, she also appeared in the Ken Russell film version of D. H. Lawrence's *The Rainbow.*

Jackson made her stage debut in 1957. She joined the Royal Shakespeare Company in 1964, and that year emerged as a powerful dramatic actress, as Charlotte Corday in *Marat/Sade*, a role she re-created on Broadway in 1965, and in the 1966 film. She went on to become a very notable stage and screen star, on stage as Ophelia in *Hamlet* (1965), Masha in *The Three Sisters* (1967), as *Hedda Gabler* (1975), and as poet Stevie Smith in *Stevie* (1977; and in the 1977 film), and in such plays as *Rose* (1980), *Strange Interlude* (1984), and *Macbeth* (1988). On screen, she played Elizabeth I in the television miniseries "Elizabeth R" (1971), won Best Actress Oscars for *Women in Love* (1969), and *A Touch of Class* (1973), and also starred in such films as *Sunday Bloody Sunday* (1971), *The Abbess of Crewe* (1976), *The Return of the Soldier* (1982), and *Turtle Diary* (1985). She attended the Royal Academy of Dramatic Art. She was formerly married, and has one child.

FURTHER READING

"With more than a touch. . . ." ANDREA CHAMBERS. *People*, Mar. 18, 1985.
Glenda Jackson: A Study in Fire & Ice. IAN WOODWARD. St. Martin's, 1985.
"Applause! Applause!" *America*, Sept. 1, 1984.
Glenda Jackson. DAVID NATHAN. Hippocrene, 1984.

Jackson, Gordon (1923–90) Scottish actor Jackson was best-known for his television roles, especially as the butler, Hudson, in "Upstairs, Downstairs" (1970–75) and the lawyer in "A Town Like Alice" (1980). Glasgow-born Jackson was a Rolls-Royce draftsman when the British Broadcasting Company (BBC), recalling his childhood radio broadcasts, tapped him for a film role in 1941. Numerous movie roles followed, notably in *Whisky Galore* (1948), *Tunes of Glory* (1960), *The Great Escape* (1962), *The Prime of Miss Jean Brodie* (1968), and *The Shooting Party* (1984). Jackson also worked in repertory theater, making his London stage debut in 1951, and playing key supporting roles and occasionally leads, in Shakespeare as well as contemporary plays, before moving to the wide, popular success of television. (d. London; January 14, 1990)

FURTHER READING

Obituary. *Variety*, Jan. 17, 1990.
Obituary. *New York Times*, Jan. 16, 1990.
Obituary. *The Times* (of London), Jan. 16, 1990.

Jackson, Janet (1966–) The popularity of the youngest member of the Jackson family soared with appearance of her 1989 hit album *Rhythm Nation: 1814*, which quickly sold over 4 million copies and generated several hit singles; by March 1990, her "Escapade" was the top popular single. Singer and dancer Jackson began her first concert tour on March 1, in Miami, and from there went on to tour the United States, Japan, and Europe. The American portion of her tour included a benefit for the United Negro College Fund at New York's Madison Square Garden. On May 18, she opened at the Tokyo Dome, to an audience of over 50,000. But the "road" also took its toll: She collapsed on stage in St. Louis on August 5, with what was diagnosed as a viral infection, and this postponed two Detroit appearances. In late November, Jackson won eight awards at the Santa Monica annual Billboard Music Awards, among them, top rhythm and blues artist; *Rhythm Nation: 1814* was named best pop and best rhythm and blues album.

Jackson, the sister of singer Michael Jackson, appeared as a child with her brothers, then the Jackson Five. She made three albums in the early 1980s: *Janet Jackson* (1982), *Dream Street* (1984), and *Control* (1986); the latter introduced several hit singles, and suggested the major career that would blossom a few years later. She was formerly married.

FURTHER READING

"Janet Jackson and Paula Abdul. . . ." *Jet*, May 7, 1990.
"Rock's leading ladies. . . ." TIMOTHY CARLSON. *TV Guide*, Sept. 1, 1990.
"Free at last." ANTHONY DECURTIS. *Rolling Stone*, Feb. 22, 1990.
"Janet Jackson. . . ." ROBERT E. JOHNSON. *Ebony*, Feb. 1990.
My Family, The Jacksons. KATHERINE JACKSON. St. Martin's, 1990.
"Janet Jackson turns serious. . . ." ROBERT E. JOHNSON. *Jet*, Nov. 6, 1989.
Janet Jackson. D.L. MABERY. Lerner, 1988.
"Janet Jackson." LISA ROBINSON. *Interview*, Feb. 1987.
Janet Jackson: In Control. NANCY ROBISON. Dillon, 1987.

Jackson, Jesse (Jesse Louis Jackson, 1941–) During the 1988 presidential campaign, Jackson made a great deal of news; since then, he has often been in the news, but made far less of it. He also often traveled abroad, most notably to South Africa and Namibia in February and March 1990, after having addressed the United Nations General Assembly on Namibia in October 1989. He went to Iraq as a journalist, in late August, after the development of the Persian Gulf Crisis; there he interviewed Saddam Hussein, and on September 2 he brought out a small group of American hostages.

At home, Jackson was seen as a possible candidate for the Washington mayoralty, especially after Mayor Marion Barry decided not to run, following his drug-related conviction; but Jackson decided not to run for the office, instead winning election to the new post of District of Columbia "statehood senator." Jackson also worked as a journalist and host of his own syndicated television interview show during the 1990–1991 season.

Long active in the civil rights movement, Jackson directed the Southern Christian

Leadership Operation Breadbasket from 1967 to 1971, and in 1971, he founded Operation PUSH (People United to Save Humanity), and later founded the Rainbow Coalition. He made an unsuccessful bid for the Democratic presidential nomination in 1984, but emerged as a major figure. He ran again in 1988, becoming the leading Black political figure of that time, perhaps most notably for his address to the 1988 Democratic convention. In that year, he also published *A Time to Speak: The Autobiography of the Reverend Jesse Jackson*.

South Carolina-born Jackson married Jacqueline Brown in 1964; they have five children. His B.A. was from North Carolina Agricultural and Technical University, in 1964. After postgraduate work at the Chicago Theological Seminary, he became a Baptist minister, in 1968.

FURTHER READING

Jesse Jackson. ROBERT JAKOUBEK. Chelsea House, 1991.

Jesse Jackson: A Biography. PATRICIA C. MCKISSACK. Scholastic, 1991.

Jesse Jackson: Still Fighting for the Dream. BRENDA WILKINSON. Silver Burdett, 1990.

"Jesse Jackson for mayor?. . . ." *Business Week*, May 22, 1989.

The Jackson Phenomenon: The Man, the Power, & the Message. ELIZABETH O. COULTON. Doubleday, 1989.

Jesse Jackson: A Voice for Change. STEVE OFFINOSKI. Fawcett, 1989.

"What makes Jesse run?" AMIRI BARAKA. *Playboy*, July 1988.

"Man in the mirror. . . ." JULIUS LESTER. *New Republic*, May 23, 1988.

"The private Jackson. . . ." GEORGE HACKETT. *Newsweek*, Apr. 25, 1988.

"The men who would be president." *Black Enterprise*, Mar, 1988.

"Jesse meets Rolling Stone." *Rolling Stone*, May 19, 1988.

Jesse Jackson. ANNA KOSOF. Watts, 1987.

"Jackson, Jesse (Louis)." *Current Biography*, Jan. 1986.

Up with Hope: A Biography of Jesse Jackson. DOROTHY CHAPLIK. Dillon, 1986.

Jackson, Michael (Michael Joseph Jackson, 1958–) To many people, the 1980s were the Michael Jackson decade. *Vanity Fair,* for example, named him celebrity of the decade, and *Billboard*'s review of the 1980s placed him at or near the top in various areas, including

pop, Black, and dance, noting that his *Thriller* (1982) was the best-selling album of all time, with some 40 million copies. His dominance was not so obvious in 1990—indeed, his sister, Janet Jackson, was riding the top of the record charts, not Michael—but he is still an undoubted star of the highest magnitude, with an electrifying stage presence.

For Michael Jackson, 1990 was certainly a year of transition, rebounding from the events of the previous year. In early 1989, Jackson stunned the record industry by abruptly firing Frank Dileo, his manager and close confidant, at least partly because his album *Bad* (1988) did not come anywhere near the success of *Thriller*. His 94-minute, 1988 film, *Moonwalker* was rejected for distribution by American theaters (though it was in theatrical release elsewhere). Critics charged that it was mostly strung-together promotional clips for *Bad*. And the video *Michael Jackson . . . The Legend Continues*, released in mid-1989, struck some critics as overly ego-ridden.

Indiana-born Jackson began his extraordinary career in 1969, as the 11-year-old lead singer of his family singing group, the Jackson Five. He became a leading popular soloist in the late 1970s, with such albums as *Off the Wall* (1979), and *Thriller* (1982), and such singles as "I Can't Stop Loving You." He starred opposite Diana Ross in the film version of *The Wiz* (1978).

FURTHER READING

Michael Jackson: A Life in Music. HAL SCHUSTER. Movie Publications, 1990.
My Family, The Jacksons. KATHERINE JACKSON. St. Martin's, 1990.
Sequins & Shades: The Michael Jackson Reference Guide. CAROL TERRY. Popular Culture, 1989.
Moonwalk. MICHAEL JACKSON. Doubleday, 1988; Writers Digest, 1989.
"Michael Jackson turns 30!" *Jet*, Aug. 29, 1988.
"Michael turns 30!" QUINCY TROUPE. *Essence*, July 1988.
Michael Jackson Electrifying. GREG QUILL. Barron, 1988.
The Michael Jackson Story. NELSON GEORGE. Dell, 1987.
Trapped: Michael Jackson & the Crossover Dream. DAVE MARSH. Bantam, 1985.
About Michael Jackson. JAMES HASKINS. Enslow, 1985.
The Magic of Michael Jackson. STARBOOK STAFF. NAL-Dutton, 1984.
Michael Jackson. GORDON MATTHEWS. Messner, 1984.
Michael Jackson, Superstar. PATRICIA MCKISSACK. Childrens, 1984.
Michael Jackson: Thrill. CAROLINE LATHAM. Zebra, 1984.
This Is Michael Jackson. D.L. MABERY. Lerner, 1984.
The Thrill of Michael Jackson. PAUL HONEYFORD. Morrow, 1984.
Picture Life of Michael Jackson. WARREN J. HALLIBURTON. Watts, 1984.

Jagger, Mick (Michael Philip Jagger, 1941–) British singer-songwriter Jagger and his Rolling Stones rolled on around America and the world in 1989 and 1990, showing that the 28-year-old rock group still had enormous vitality and drawing power. Starting in late August 1989, they stormed across North America in a four-month, 60-show tour that coincided with their new album *Steel Wheels* (1989), their first in four years. They generally played before sellout crowds, with a live Atlantic City concert televised on a pay-per-view basis, even making the cover of *Time* magazine. On the way, they toured sites of recent earthquake damage in northern California, and pledged $500,000 to aid victims of the quake and Hurricane Hugo.

Then they went international, on what was dubbed their "Urban Jungle" tour, for their set exemplifying inner-city decay. Celebrating, with much of the world, the opening of Eastern Europe, where they had not performed since the late 1960s, they wrapped up their tour in August 1990, by playing before some 50,000 East and West Germans in East Berlin, then traveling on to Czechoslovakia to celebrate that country's democratic revolution, with new president—and Stones fan—Vaclav Havel, donating concert proceeds to a charity for disabled children.

Privately, Jagger and his long time companion, model Jerry Hall, married with great secrecy in November 1990, attended by their two young children, in a traditional Indonesian ceremony on the island of Bali. At the same time, the couple reportedly signed a document stating their commitment to the Hindu faith.

Jagger was, in 1962, the chief organizer of the enormously popular rock group The Rolling Stones. He and Keith Richards were the group's main songwriters, and Jagger was its leading performer, playing the role of an angry, deeply alienated, uncontrollably violent, mythic sexual figure, as a model for the scores of other such rock and popular music figures that would follow in the next three decades. Such albums as *The Rolling Stones* (1964; and two 1965 sequels), *Aftermath* (1966), and *Their Satanic Majesties Request* (1967), coupled with their worldwide tours, established them as one of the leading popular musical groups of the century. In 1969, after a murder by their Hell's Angels security guards at an Altamont, California Stones concert, the group toned down their image somewhat. Although they continued to tour and record throughout the 1980s, their popularity lessened after the mid-1970s. Jagger also appeared in such films as *Ned Kelly* (1969), and in the film of the Altamont concert, *Gimme Shelter* (1972). He has also done some solo recordings. Jagger attended the London School of Economics. He was married to Bianca Jagger (Bianca Pérez Morena de Macîas) from 1971 to 1979, and has four children.

FURTHER READING

"The third guitarist. . . ." CHRIS JAGGER. *Guitar Player*, Oct. 1989.
"Roll them bones." JAY COCKS. *Time*, Sept. 4, 1989.
The Rolling Stone Interviews: The 1980s. St. Martin's, 1989.
"Mick Jagger." MIKAL GILMORE. *Rolling Stone*, Nov. 5, 1987.

Written in My Soul: Rock's Great Songwriters . . . Talk about Creating Their Music. BILL FLANAGAN. Contemporary, 1986.
"Mick Jagger." ALLAN SONNENSCHEIN. *Penthouse*, Mar. 1985.
The Rolling Stones: The Early Years. DEZO HOFFMAN. McGraw-Hill, 1985.
The Rolling Stones. TIM DOWLEY. Hippocrene, 1984.

Jamison, Judith (1944–) Late in 1989, dancer-choreographer Jamison was leading her fledgling company, the Jamison Project, in a series of programs marked by intense energy, lyricism, and technical prowess. But when her old mentor, Alvin Ailey, died on December 1, 1989, she returned home to take his place as artistic director of the Alvin Ailey American Dance Theater. While continuing with her own company's commitments over the next few months, she quickly moved to take some of her dancers and her repertory and merge them into the Ailey, so the future of the company would "reflect his vision and mine." In its first Jamison year, the company's performance focused on honoring Ailey by performing his classic works, and Jamison was widely praised for reinvigorating the Ailey.

Philadelphia-born Jamison made her debut in 1965, with the American Ballet Theater. She danced with the Alvin Ailey company in 1965, and rejoined it as the company's leading dancer from 1967 to 1980, in that period becoming one of the world's first-rank dancers, with special emphasis on her work on African-American themes. In 1980, she left the company, starred on Broadway in *Sophisticated Ladies* (1980), and spent most of the 1980s as guest dancer and choreographer with several American ballet companies. She founded the Jamison Project in 1988.

FURTHER READING

"Judith Jamison. . . ." *Ebony*, Dec. 1990.
"Judith Jamison." STEPHEN FRIED. *Philadelphia Magazine*, July 1988.
Black Dance in America: A History Through Its People. JAMES HASKINS. Harper, 1990.
Judith Jamison: Aspects of a Dancer. OLGA MAYNARD. Doubleday, 1982.

Janis, Sidney (1896–1989) A leading, New York City art dealer, Janis shared major responsibility for promoting the work of Jackson Pollock, Mark Rothko, and other leading abstract expressionists of the postwar period. Janis was a successful shirt manufacturer, who became an art collector during the interwar period, and developed strong interests in American folk and primitive art, and in Surrealism. He opened his first gallery in 1948, and quickly became a leading figure in the New York art world. Janis also moved with the times and trends, becoming a key promoter of Pop Art in the 1960s. (d. New York City; November 23, 1989)

FURTHER READING

Obituary. *Current Biography*, Jan. 1990.
Obituary. *The Times* (of London), Dec. 5, 1989.
Obituary. *New York Times*, Nov. 24, 1989.
"Sidney Janis. . . ." JAMIE JAMES. *ARTnews*, Dec. 1987.
"Powers in the art mart." JUDITH GOLDMAN. *Vogue*, Aug. 1979.

Jennings, Peter Charles (1938–) As the 1980s ended, American Broadcasting Company (ABC) news anchor Peter Jennings was being hailed as the Walter Cronkite of the 1990s. With the rise of 24-hour cable news and 2-hour local news programs, perhaps no anchor will ever again have Cronkite's dominance, but some observers think Jennings might be headed in that direction. In late 1989, his "World News Tonight" took over the top spot from the formerly top-rated Columbia

Broadcasting System (CBS) and, with occasional lead changes, generally held it—partly because of Jennings's attractive, straightforward style and partly because his experience as foreign correspondent gives him special authority when international news is at the forefront, as in 1989 and 1990. Jennings capitalized on that experience by traveling around the world, reporting on the major international stories from the democratization of Prague, to the Bush-Gorbachev summit at Malta, to the tearing down of the Berlin Wall, though when others were off to the Middle East, he chose to stay in New York to coordinate reporting on the Persian Gulf Crisis.

In addition to the nightly news, Jennings has an occasional series, "Peter Jennings Reporting," taking on a variety of subjects, premiering with "Guns" in January 1990, and including "From the Killing Fields," on Cambodia. He also hosted a much-praised end-of-the-decade report, *Images of the '80s*. As the Gulf War grew, he also hosted a Saturday show for children with questions about the war. Apart from ABC, Jennings also anchors the acclaimed "AIDS Quarterly," a magazine-format report on current developments, for the Public Broadcasting Service (PBS); he even appeared as a guest on the National Braodcasting Company's (NBC) "The Tonight Show With Johnny Carson."

Toronto-born Jennings worked in Canadian broadcasting before joining ABC News in 1964. During the next two decades, much of that time spent abroad, he rose to become chief London correspondent for ABC, became the anchor of "World News Tonight" in 1983, and with his colleagues at CBS and NBC is one of the three key American interpreters of the world news. Twice divorced, he is married to writer Kati Marton; he has two children. He attended Carleton University, and his LL.D. is from Rider College.

FURTHER READING

Anchors: Brokaw, Jennings, Rather & the Evening News. Robert Goldberg and Gerald J. Goldberg. Carol, 1990.

"The kiss of the anchor man." E. Jean Carroll. *Playboy*, Dec. 1990.

"Peter Jennings gets no self-respect." Elizabeth Kaye. *Esquire*, Sept. 1989.

"The A-B-Cs of Peter Jennings." Norman Atkins. *Rolling Stone*, May 4, 1989.

"Up from 'Club Thirteen'. . . ." David Blum. *New York*, Nov. 30, 1987.

"The most trusted men in America." Carol Kramer. *McCall's*, July 1987.

"Cosmo talks to Peter Jennings. . . ." Janet Spencer King. *Cosmopolitan*, Apr. 1987.

"'I don't think he will ever. . . .'" Joanmarie Kalter. *TV Guide*, Jan. 3, 1987.

Joel, Billy (William Martin Joel, 1949–) Singer, songwriter, and pianist Joel was dubbed "King of the Road," as his "Storm Front" tour, to promote his new album of the same name, proved to be the top pop concert attraction of the first half of 1990. The most notable of his new hits was "We Didn't Start the Fire," which condenses 40 years of history and requires a rapid-fire delivery particularly difficult in a live concert setting. Though some critics labeled Joel's work as shallow and commercial, the single and the full *Storm Front* album both hit the top of the Billboard pop charts. Another recent single, "That's Not Her Style," sparked charges of sexism because of advertisements showing Joel hiding behind a backward-facing, naked woman. Joel also performed on the early 1990 Grammy Awards show, and later in 1990 was one of several musical stars honored in a televised *Grammy Legends Show*. In early 1991, Joel was to be found in the Philippines, on a U.S.O. tour of the troops stationed there.

Privately, Joel was involved in a $90 million lawsuit against his former manager (and ex-brother-in-law), charging fraud and breach of contract and fiduciary duties, reportedly the

largest such suit ever filed in the pop world. In fact, Joel reported that he had embarked on his 15-month Storm Front tour to "get himself out of a sea of red ink."

New York City-born Joel became a leading popular recording artist in the mid-1970s, with such albums as *Piano Man* (1974), *Streetlight Serenade* (1974), *The Stranger* (1976), *52nd Street* (1978), *Glass Houses* (1980), *An Innocent Man* (1983), *The Bridge* (1986), and *A Matter of Trust* (1988). His 1987 Soviet tour generated the album *Live in the U.S.S.R.* (1987). His voice was featured in the animated film *Oliver and Company* (1988). He has been married twice, last to model Christie Brinkley in 1985, and has one child.

FURTHER READING

"Billy Joel. . . ." DAVID WILD. *Rolling Stone*, Jan. 25, 1990.
"Billy Joel." *Life*, Sept. 1987.
"Billy Joel." PAUL NATKIN. *Penthouse*, Dec. 1985.
"A dreamboat wedding." *People*, Apr. 8, 1985.
Billy Joel. DEBBIE GELLER and TOM HIBBERT. McGraw-Hill, 1985.
Billy Joel. MICHAEL MCKENSIE. Ballantine, 1984.

John Paul II, Pope (Karol Wojtyla, 1920–) As political change swept Eastern Europe and the Soviet Union, the pope led in the re-establishment of a strong Catholic presence in several countries from which his church had been effectively barred, including the Soviet Union. He continued to focus on the less-developed countries of the world, visiting Africa in January 1990 and Mexico in May. At the same time, the conservative pope continued to resist attempts to liberalize the Catholic Church, in late June declaring that Catholic theologians had no right to dissent from present church teachings; the church had previously penalized some liberals for dissenting on such matters as abortion and several issues involving social action.

John Paul II is the first pope of Polish origin, and the first non-Italian pope in the last four centuries. He was ordained as a Catholic priest in 1946, and then moved steadily upward in the Polish Catholic Church, becoming a professor of theology in the 1950s, and ultimately, archbishop of Cracow from 1963 to 1978. He

became a cardinal in 1967, and then pope in 1978. He has been largely a very conservative pope, strongly opposing abortion and strongly discouraging liberal social action on the part of the priesthood. He attended Cracow's Jagellonian University and Rome's Angelicum.

FURTHER READING

Portrait of John Paul II. ANDRE FROSSARD. Ignatius, 1990.
"The triumph of John Paul II. . . ." STEFAN KANFER. *Life*, Dec. 1989.
"John Paul's first decade. . . ." PETER HEBBLETHWAITE. *National Catholic Reporter*, Oct. 14, 1988.
"Television: the Papal medium." MICHAEL A. RUSSO. *America*, July 23, 1988.
"The post-modern Pope." NATHAN GARDELS. *New Perspectives Quarterly (NPQ)*, Fall 1988.
Pope John Paul II: Pilgrim of Peace. POPE JOHN PAUL II, Crown, 1987.
Pope John Paul II: The People's Pope. GEORGE SULLIVAN. Walker, 1984.
Pope John Paul II. MIECZYSLAW MALINSKI. Doubleday, 1982.
Pope John Paul II: An Authorized Biography. LORD LONGFORD. Morrow, 1982.

Johnson, Earvin "Magic," Jr. (1959–)

During the 1989–90 season, Johnson was once again, for the third time, named the National Basketball League's Most Valuable Player (MVP), was also the top vote-getter in the balloting for the National Basketball Association (NBA) All-Star Game, and was for the first time selected MVP in the All-Star Game. It was a difficult time, though. Johnson's longtime teammate, Kareem Abdul Jabbar, retired; even so, Johnson led his Los Angeles Lakers to the best regular season in the league, only to lose in the playoffs, being knocked out in the Western Conference semifinals by the Phoenix Suns. Partly as a result of that loss, the longtime Laker coach, Pat Riley, resigned, making the 1990–91 season a rebuilding season, under the new coach, Mike Dunleavy. Johnson continued to do his part, on the court and off, not only continuing MVP-calibre play, but also giving up part of his salary so that his team could acquire a new player, Terry Teagle, that management thought could help the team.

But Johnson recognizes that his basketball-playing days are numbered, and he is planning his transition to a non-basketball future. In the summer of 1990, Johnson and a partner bought a Pepsi-Cola franchise in the Washington, D.C., area, the largest minority-owned Pepsi franchise in the country. Meanwhile, he continued his philanthropic work. The all-star classic—Midsummer's Night Magic—that was started and continued by Johnson raised over a million dollars for the United Negro College Fund in 1990 (and in 1989), and has inspired similar fundraisers by other Black athletes and celebrities.

Michigan-born Johnson is one of the leading players in basketball history, and with Larry Bird was one of the two dominant players in the game during the 1980s. He attended Michigan State University from 1976 to 1978, leading his team to a National Collegiate Athletic Association (NCAA) championship in 1979. He led the Los Angeles Lakers to five National Basketball Association titles in the 1980s—1980, 1982, 1985, 1987, and 1988. He published two autobiographical works, *Magic* (1983; with Richard Levin), and *Magic's Touch* (1989; with Roy S. Johnson).

FURTHER READING

"Magic's kingdom. . . ." RICHARD HOFFER. *Sports Illustrated*, Dec. 3, 1990.
"The Sport athlete of the decade. . . ." *Sport*, Oct. 1989.
The Sports Great Magic Johnson. JAMES HASKINS. Enslow, 1989.
Magic Johnson. MICHAEL E. GOODMAN. Crestwood, 1988.
"The magic touch." ALEX WARD. *New York Times Magazine*, Dec. 6, 1987.
Magic Johnson Larry Bird. BRUCE WEBER. Avon, 1986.

Jones, James Earl (1931–) Jones stunned the theatrical community in July by announcing his retirement from the stage, but later said he was simply concentrating more on less taxing film and television work, especially his new television series "Gabriel's Fire" (1990–), in which he plays an ex-cop/ex-convict turned investigator. On film during 1990, Jones was seen in *The Hunt for Red October*, the NBC movie *Last Flight Out*, TNT and the National Audubon Society's *The Last Elephant*, and HBO's *By Dawn's Early Light*. He was also widely seen and heard in television commercials and as a narrator on documentaries.

Mississippi-born Jones has been a leading figure in the American theater since his starring role as Black heavyweight champion Jack Jefferson (inspired by the real-life Jack Johnson) in *The Great White Hope* (1958, on film 1970). A classical actor of enormous range, he is highly regarded for such roles as *Macbeth* (1962), *King Lear* (1973), Hickey in *The Iceman Cometh* (1973), *Othello* (1982), and his starring role in *Fences* (1988), for which he won a Tony. He was the voice of Darth Vader in *Star Wars* (1977), Alex Haley in television's *Roots II* (1979), and he played major roles in such films as *Gardens of Stone* (1987), and *Field of Dreams* (1989). He married Cecilia Hart in 1982. His B.A. was from the University of Michigan, in 1957.

FURTHER READING

"The struggle to be. . . ." MICHELLE GREEN. *Saturday Review*, Feb. 1982.

Jones, Quincy (Quincy Delight Jones, Jr., 1933–) A leading jazz musician, Jones is a celebrated producer, arranger, composer, trumpeter, and bandleader. In December 1989, he released his new album *Back on the Block,* with songs ranging across three generations of jazz artists, from Ella Fitzgerald, Ray Charles, and Sarah Vaughan, to young rap artists. The album quickly sold over a million copies. In June 1990, he sold half of his Quincy Jones Entertainment and Quincy Jones Broadcasting companies to Time Warner for an estimated $30 million, and in October issued his heavily promoted documentary *Listen Up: The Lives of Quincy Jones.* Jones also continued to work in social causes, as well: in July he gave $100,000 to the Nelson Mandela Freedom Fund, and in late 1990 his company produced the syndicated series hosted by Jesse Jackson.

Chicago-born Jones has had a long and varied career, which in four decades has included arranging and working as a trumpeter with Lionel Hampton and Dizzy Gillespie in the mid-1950s; working as an arranger for many of the leading singers of the 1950s and 1960s; working in the 1960s as music director and producer for Mercury Records; and composing and conducting many film scores. From 1969, he was a prolific recording artist, with such albums as *Walking in Space* (1969), *Smackwater Jack* (1971), and *Mellow Madness* (1975). He was, most notably, producer of the Michael Jackson records *Off the Wall* (1980), and *Thriller* (1982). Jones attended the Berkelee College of Music and the Boston Conservatory. He was formerly married, and has five children.

FURTHER READING

"On Q." DIANE K. SHAH. *New York Times Magazine*, Nov. 18, 1990.
"Quincy Jones." STEVE DOUGHERTY. *People*, Oct. 15, 1990.
"Story of Q." BRENDAN LEMON. *Interview*, Sept. 1990.
"Playboy interview. . . ." ALEX HALEY. *Playboy*, July 1990.
"Quincy Jones." ELIOT TIEGEL. *Stereo Review*, June 1990.
"After 40 years. . . ." ALDORE COLLIER. *Ebony*, Apr. 1990.
"Back on the block. . . ." ROBERT L. DOERSCHUK. *Interview*, Jan. 1990.
"Herbie & Quincy. . . ." JOSEF WOODARD. *Down Beat*, Jan. 1990.
Quincy Jones. RAYMOND HORRICKS. Hippocrene, 1986.

Jordan, Michael (1963–) Jordan is one of the leading basketball players of the late 1980s and early 1990s. An extraordinarily versatile, high-scoring guard, he has also throughout his career been a leading defensive player. He led his team, the Chicago Bulls, to victory over Milwaukee and Philadelphia in the first two rounds of the 1990 playoffs, before being defeated by Detroit in the third round. Jordan has become a major celebrity, and is also seen endorsing a wide range of products, from Coca Cola to Wheaties to Air Jordan sneakers. He is also an eager, very talented amateur golfer.

Jordan starred at the University of North Carolina in the early 1980s, was an Olympic gold medalist before turning professional in 1984, and immediately emerged as a star player for the Chicago Bulls. He was rookie of the year in the 1984–85 season, and National Basketball Association Most Valuable Player (MVP) and best defensive player in the 1987–88 season. He is married to Juanita Jordan; they have one child.

FURTHER READING

"Michael Jordan, king of style." BRUCE SHLAIN. *Sport*, Jan. 1991.

"Michael Jordan leaps. . . ." JOHN EDGAR WIDEMAN. *Esquire*, Nov. 1990.

Michael Jordan. Little, Brown, 1990.

"Michael Jordan. . . ." LARKIN WARREN. *Esquire*, Dec. 1989.

"An air of superstardom." CHARLES LEERHSEN. *Newsweek*, May 29, 1989.

"Great leapin' lizards!" SALLY B. DONNELLY. *Time*, Jan. 9, 1989.

Michael Jordan: Gentleman Superstar. GENE L. MARTIN. Tudor, 1988.

Michael Jordan, Basketball's Soaring Star. PAUL J. DEEGAN. Lerner, 1988.

Michael Jordan. MITCHELL KRUGEL. St. Martin's, 1988.

Michael Jordan. DAN MCCUNE. Crestwood, 1988.

"Jordan, Michael." *Current Biography*, Sept. 1987.

Michael Jordan: The Bull's Air Power. MICHAEL HERBERT. Childrens, 1987.

Kahane, Meir (Martin Kahane, also known as Michael King, 1932–90) When New York City-born Kahane was a Brooklyn teenager, he was active in Betar, a right-wing Jewish paramilitary organization. He became a rabbi in the mid-1950s, and founded the terrorist Jewish Defense League (JDL) in 1968, popularizing the slogan "Never Again." After a prison sentence for bomb-making, Kahane emigrated to Israel in 1971, there founding the ultra-rightist Kach Party in 1971, through which he advocated a series of racist positions, including expulsion of all Arabs from Israel, prohibition of sexual relations between Arabs and Jews, and a system of separate ghettos for Arabs, all much like the Nazi Nuremberg Laws. His views generated some popular support, and in 1984 he was elected to the Israeli parliament, the Knesset, but his party was banned in 1988 for its racism. Among his written works were *They Must Go* (1981). On November 5, 1990, at a Zionist conference in New York's Marriott East Side hotel, he was assassinated, allegedly by El Sayyid a Nassair.

FURTHER READING

"After a career of preaching hatred. . . ." Bill Hewitt. *People*, Nov. 19, 1990.
Obituary. David Makovsky. *U.S. News & World Report*, Nov. 19, 1990.
"Where hatred begets hatred. . . ." *Time*, Nov. 19, 1990.
Obituary. *New York Times*, Nov. 7, 1990.
Obituary. *The Times* (of London), Nov. 7, 1990.
The False Prophet: Rabbi Meir Kahane—from FBI Informant to Knesset Member. Robert I. Friedman. L. Hill, 1990.
Israel's Ayatollahs: Meir Kahane & the Far Right in Israel. Raphael Mergui and Philippe Simonnot. Interlink, 1990.
"The sayings. . . ." Robert I. Friedman. *New York Review of Books*, Feb. 13, 1986.
Meir Kahane, Ideologue, Hero, Thinker. S. Daniel Breslauer. E. Mellen, 1986.
Heil Kahane. Yair Kotler. Adama, 1986.

Kaifu, Toshiki (1931–) After the Recruit stock scandal of 1988, which implicated many key aides of former Japanese Prime Minister Nakasone and ultimately forced the resignation of Prime Minister Takeshita, the ruling Liberal Democratic Party named Sosuke Uno to the post. He lasted two months, before being forced to resign due to a sex scandal. Kaifu, one of the

few high-ranking Liberal Democrats still viewed as "clean," was then named president of the party on August 8 and prime minister on August 9, 1989.

Kaifu, at first, was widely viewed as merely a caretaker and figurehead, to serve until some of the heat generated by the multiple scandals died down. However, he developed far more popularity than had been expected, and led his party to a major recovery in the February 1990 elections. His position then strengthened greatly, and even more so when he named a largely "clean" cabinet that also included the trailblazing appointment of the first two women to ever achieve cabinet rank in Japan.

In office, Kaifu continued to negotiate the difficult issue of Japanese-U.S. trade imbalances, to the continuing great advantage of Japan; his promise of action on these issues, made during the March visit to Washington for talks with President George Bush, brought April removal of the U.S. "unfair trader" classification. At home, Kaifu faced growing economic problems, as the Japanese stock market fell sharply, Japanese banks curtailed loans abroad, and the Japanese real estate market faltered, mirroring a worldwide trend. With the sudden August explosion of the Persian Gulf Crisis, oil-dependent Japan joined the United States and its allies in bringing international pressure on Iraq to withdraw from Kuwait, though the post-World War II Japanese constitution barred the use of Japanese troops abroad.

Kaifu is a career politician, who entered the Japanese parliament in 1960, after working in political staff jobs. He held several cabinet-level positions before becoming prime minister. He is married to Sachiyo Kaifu and has two children. Kaifu graduated from Tokyo's Waseta University.

FURTHER READING

"Kaifu, Toshiki." *Current Biography*, June 1990.
"Cleaning house. . . ." HOLGER JENSEN. *Maclean's*, Aug. 21, 1989.

Kasparov, Gary (Gary Kimovich Kasparov, 1963–) On October 8, 1990, in New York City, Kasparov began another defense of his world chess championship against Soviet challenger Anatoly Karpov, with a maximum of 24 games to be played, 12 in New York City and 12 in Lyon, France. On December 22, leading 12 games to 10, he and Karpov played to a draw in Lyon, assuring that Kasparov would keep his title. On December 29, in Lyon, Kasparov won a final 23rd game in 29 minutes, the shortest game of the series, settling the players' shares of the $1.5 million in prize money. Soviet anti-communist Kasparov, a founder and the deputy chairman of the Democratic Party, insisted on playing his matches under the flag of the Russian Republic, rather than under the Soviet flag, although officially sponsored by the Soviet Chess Federation, which displayed the Soviet flag for both players. This was the fifth Kasparov-Karpov match; after the first, in 1984, was discontinued because both players were ill, Kasparov won the second, in 1985, becoming the world's youngest chess champion. He successfully defended his title against Karpov in 1986 and 1987.

Kasparov has been a leading chess player since the mid-1970s. He won the Azerbaijan championship and the Soviet junior championship in 1975, was world junior champion in 1980, and Soviet champion in 1981. He won the 1989 World Chess Cup, the year his world life chess rating reached a recordbreaking 2795, passing Bobby Fischer's rating of 2780. Kasparov married Maria Kasparova in 1989.

FURTHER READING

"King Kasparov." FRED WAITZKIN. *New York Times Magazine*, Oct. 7, 1990.
"Playboy interview. . . . " RUDOLPH CHELMINSKI. *Playboy*, Nov. 1989.

"Hello, is that Garry Kasparov?" *Soviet Life*, May 1987.
"Kasparov, Gary." *Current Biography*, Apr. 1986.
Fighting Chess: My Games & Career. GARRI KASPAROV. State Mutual, 1985.

Keating, Charles Humphrey, III

(1923–) Accused financier Keating bought control of the Lincoln Savings Bank, in Irvine, California, in 1984, for $51 million and began the process of building it into a $6 billion bank, heavily invested in junk bonds and heavily committed to what turned out to be very weak real estate loans, many of them the projects of the Phoenix-based American Continental Corporation, which Keating owned. Faced with opposition from the Federal Home Loan Bank Board, Keating engaged in a long-running battle with regulators, which included substantial contributions to many key Washington and state politicians, and set the stage for the investigations of senators Alan Cranston, Dennis DeConcini, John Glenn, John McCain, and Donald W. Riegle, Jr., who came to be known as the "Keating Five." Lincoln was taken over by federal bank regulators on April 14, 1990, as the national savings and loan crisis developed; the cost of the government bailout was estimated to be at least $2 billion.

A very long series of federal and state investigations followed, which began to generate indictments and public hearings late in 1990. In September 1990, Keating was indicted by a California state grand jury on 42 counts of fraud; three of his business associates were also indicted. Keating was jailed after failing to raise $5 million in bail and was set free a month later when bail was reduced to $300,000. The federal government has filed a $1.1 billion fraud and racketeering suit against Keating. Keating maintains that he is innocent of all wrongdoing. In late November 1990, Senate Ethics Committee hearings began on the "Keating Five;" Keating refused to testify, as the savings and loan crisis and what may prove to be a set of major related scandals continued to unfold.

Keating emerged as a corporate takeover figure in the late 1970s, as executive vice-president of the Cincinnati-based American Financial Corporation. In 1979, he and Carl H. Lindner were accused of personal use of substantial company funds; both men agreed to a consent order agreeing not to violate securities laws, without admitting or denying the truth of the charges against them. Keating has, from the early 1970s, also been a substantial Cincinnati-based anti-pornography contributor; he founded an anti-pornography organization in the 1950s, and was a member of the 1969–70 Presidential Commission on Obscenity and Pornography. He attended the University of Cincinnati and was a star swimmer, becoming 1946 national collegiate breast stroke champion. He married Mary Elaine Fette in 1941; they have six children.

FURTHER READING

"The great banks robbery. . . ." JAMES K. GLASSMAN. *New Republic*, Oct. 8, 1990.
"Money talks. . . ." MARGARET CARLSON. *Time*, Apr. 9, 1990.
"Dirty bookkeeping. . . ." DAVID CORN. *New Republic*, Apr. 2, 1990.
"The man who shot Lincoln Savings." PHIL GARLINGTON. *California*, Mar. 1990.
"Seven sorry senators . . . . " MARGARET CARLSON. *Time*, Jan. 8, 1990.
The Greatest-Ever Bank Robbery: The Collapse of the Savings & Loan Industry. MARTIN MAYER. Macmillan, 1990.

Keaton, Diane

(1946–) Keaton spent much of the year reprising her role as Kay Corleone in Francis Ford Coppola's sequel, *The Godfather Part III,* which opened in December 1990 to much critical praise. Her comedy, *The Lemon Sisters,* about three White women who emulate the Supremes, originally Keaton's idea, opened to much less attention, and quickly faded from view. Keaton has also been moving to the other side of the camera, for television directing an episode of "China Beach" and a Schoolbreak Special, *The Girl with the Crazy Brother.*

California-born Keaton made the transition from the New York theater to Hollywood in Woody Allen's *Play It Again, Sam*, starring opposite Allen on Broadway in 1971, and again in the 1972 film version. She was Michael Corleone's wife in the classic *Godfather* films (1972, 1974), won a Best Actress Oscar for Allen's *Annie Hall* (1977), and also starred in his *Interiors* (1978), and *Manhattan* (1979). She went on to star in such films as *Reds* (1981), *The Little Drummer Girl* (1984), *Crimes of the Heart* (1986), and *Radio Days* (1987). She was a student at New York's Neighborhood Playhouse in 1968.

FURTHER READING

Diane Keaton. JONATHAN MOOR. St. Martin's, 1989.
"Hotel 'Heaven'. . . ." MARLAINE GLICKSMAN. *Film Comment*, Mar.–Apr. 1987.
"Knockin' on heaven's door. . . ." DAVID EDELSTEIN. *Rolling Stone*, May 7, 1987.
"Diane Keaton." GERALD L'ECUYER. *Interview*, Jan. 1987.
"Heaven? Can't wait!" SUSAN LINFIELD. *American Film*, Jan.–Feb. 1986.

Keaton, Michael (Michael Douglas, 1951–) Previously a well-regarded but newly arriving film star, Keaton became a major Hollywood star in 1989, in the title role of *Batman* (1989), though Jack Nicholson's Joker to some extent "stole" the film. The same year saw his starring role in the film comedy *The Dream Team.* In late 1990, he created the Carter Hayes role, as the psychotic renter in John Schlesinger's *Pacific Heights,* opposite Melanie Griffith and Matthew Modine as the prosperous young couple who have bought and renovated their turn-of-the-century San Francisco home. He stars as a police officer in the forthcoming *One Good Cop.*

Pittsburgh-born Keaton began his career as a comedian with the Los Angeles Second City group, appeared in television from the mid-1970s, and played in such films as *Night Shift* (1982), *Mr. Mom* (1983), and *Touch and Go* (1987). He emerged as a dramatic star in the film Clean *and Sober* (1988). Keaton attended Kent State University. He married Caroline McWilliams in 1982; they have one child.

FURTHER READING

"Batguy." TERRI MINSKY. *Premiere*, July 1989.
"Michael Keaton. . . ." STEPHEN SCHAEFER. *Cosmopolitan*, Apr. 1986.

Kemp, Jack (Jack French Kemp, 1935–) Secretary of Housing and Urban Development Kemp spent much of his first year in office attempting to clean up his department, as the real size and scope of the massive HUD scandal began to emerge. During the spring and summer of 1989, he suspended several scandal-ridden HUD programs and developed a reform package for HUD, some of which was passed by Congress in November 1989. During 1990, he participated in developing the omnibus housing bill passed by Congress in June, which provided some funds for affordable housing and some emergency funds for the poor and homeless.

California-born Kemp is a former star football player, who moved into politics after a 13-year professional football career, and was from 1971 to 1989 a Republican Congressman from western New York. He made an unsuccessful run for his party's 1988 presidential nomination and became a member of the Bush cabinet in 1989. He is married to the former Joanne Main; they have four children. His B.A. was from Occidental College, in 1957.

FURTHER READING

"Party politics." GLORIA BORGER. *U.S. News & World Report*, Dec. 24, 1990.
"Bleeding-heart conservative. . . ." ROBERT KUTTNER. *New Republic*, June 11, 1990.
"Sure, he'd rather be president. . . ." JAMES S. KUNEN. *People*, June 18, 1990.
"Prince of poverty." FRED BARNES. *New Republic*, Oct. 8, 1990.
"The men who would be president." *Black Enterprise*, Mar. 1988.
"Kemp at. . . ." RICHARD BROOKHISER. *National Review*, Feb. 19, 1988.

Kennedy, Anthony McLeod (1936–) Justice Kennedy in most instances voted with the conservative majority of the Supreme Court during the 1989–90 session, as in the landmark *Cruzan* v. *Missouri* "right to die" case, which denied Nancy Cruzan's family the right to remove her from her life support system; in *Spallone* v. *U.S.,* which upset court-imposed fines on Yonkers elected officials in a housing discrimination case; and in many of the cases involving police powers, law enforcement, and defendant's rights ruled on by the Court's conservative majority. He wrote the majority opinion in *Ohio* v. *Akron Center for Reproductive Health,* which upheld an Ohio law requiring either notification of one parent or a court hearing, before an abortion could be performed on a minor, and in *Saffle* v. *Parks* denying prisoners convicted in state courts the right to appeal their convictions as unconstitutional in federal courts, by means of a writ of habeas corpus.

But it is oversimple to describe most Supreme Court justices as liberal or conservative: he joined most of the Court's liberals in *U. S.* v. *Eichman*, striking down the federal anti-flag desecration law. Kennedy was on the losing side on such cases as *Rutan* v. *Republican Party of Illinois*, cutting the power of politicians in power to name party sympathizers to most low-level government jobs; and *Metro Broadcasting* v. *FCC,* supporting an affirmative action program in the broadcasting industry.

California-born Kennedy was appointed to the Sacramento-based 9th Circuit U.S. Court of Appeals in 1975; he had been recommended for the post by then-California Governor Ronald Reagan. Thirteen years later, in 1988, President Reagan appointed him to the Supreme Court, after his nomination of Robert Bork was rejected by the Senate. He is married to Mary Davis; they have three children. His B.A. was from Stanford, in 1958; his LL.B. was from Harvard University, in 1961.

FURTHER READING

Reshaping the Supreme Court: New Justices, New Directions. ANNE B. RIERDEN. Watts, 1988.
Packing the Courts: The Conservatives' Campaign to Rewrite the Constitution. HERMAN SCHWARTZ. Macmillan, 1988.
"Kennedy, Anthony McLeod." *Current Biography*, July 1988.
"Far more judicious." GEORGE J. CHURCH and AMY WILENTZ. *Time*, Nov. 23, 1987.
"A conservative's conservative?" *U.S. News & World Report*, Nov. 23, 1987.

Kennedy, Arthur (John Arthur Kennedy, 1914–90) A highly regarded character actor, Kennedy created roles in several Arthur Miller plays, most notably Biff in *Death of a Salesman* (1949). Son of a Massachusetts dentist, Kennedy was on stage from the mid-1930s and on screen from 1940, playing key supporting roles in such films as *High Sierra* (1941), *Elmer Gantry* (1960), and *Lawrence of Arabia* (1962, as the correspondent), and playing innumerable villains and heroes in westerns. (d. Branford, Connecticut; January 5, 1990)

FURTHER READING

Obituary. *The Times* (of London), Jan. 10, 1990.
Obituary. *New York Times*, Jan. 7, 1990.

Kennedy, Edward (Edward Moore Kennedy, 1932–) Ted Kennedy, the senior senator from Massachusetts, is chairman of the Senate Labor and Human Resources Committee and a key member of the Judiciary Committee. He is a leading liberal and social reformer who is a centrally important figure in the Democratic Party and always a possible Democratic presidential candidate. He was a leader of the liberal opposition during the first two years of the Bush administration, on such issues as the increased minimum wage, aid to El Salvador and the Nicaraguan Contras, nuclear plant licensing, and the scope of needed environmental action, and was the only member of the Judiciary Committee to vote against the nomination of David H. Souter to the Supreme Court.

Boston-born Kennedy is the fourth son of Joseph and Rose Fitzgerald Kennedy and the brother of President John Fitzgerald Kennedy, assassinated in 1963, and Senator Robert Francis Kennedy, assassinated while a presidential candidate in 1968. He has represented Massachusetts in the Senate since 1963. He probably would have been his party's presidential candidate in 1972, and in later elections as well, but for the Chappaquiddick incident of 1969, in which he left the scene of a fatal accident. Kennedy married Virginia Joan Bennett in 1958, and has three children. His B.A. was from Harvard in 1956, his LL.B. from the University of Virginia in 1959.

FURTHER READING

"Ted Kennedy. . . ." MICHAEL KELLY. *GQ—Gentlemen's Quarterly*, Feb. 1990.
Chappaquiddick Revealed. KENNETH R. KAPPEL and JOHN H. DAVIS. Shapolsky, 1989.
"What happened at. . . ." LEO DAMORE. *Washingtonian*, June 1988.
"The king of. . . ." HARRISON RAINIE. *U.S. News & World Report*, Apr. 4, 1988.
Senatorial Privilege: The Chappaquiddick Coverup. LEO DAMORE. Regnery, 1988; Dell, 1989.
"Edward Kennedy." WILLIAM GREIDER. *Rolling Stone*, Nov. 5, 1987.

Kennedy, John F., Jr. (1960–) The son of assassinated American president John F. Kennedy and Jacqueline Bouvier Kennedy (later Onassis) continued to be the focus of an inordinate amount of attention. The world watches his every move, and unfairly so; his failure to pass the New York State bar examination on his first two tries was not unusual. In fact, thousands of other lawyers have had the same bar exam experience and gone on to long and successful careers in the law and politics; the Manhattan District Attorney's office, Kennedy's employer, routinely allows law school graduates three tries at the bar exam.

But Kennedy's failures were the subject of enormous media attention, with two New York newspapers trumpeting in their headlines "The Hunk Flunks," a reference to *People* magazine's labeling him the 1988 "Hunk of the Year." After passing the exam on his third try, Kennedy was confirmed in his position as an assistant district attorney for Manhattan, at a salary of $34,000 a year, and in November 1990, after formal admittance to the bar, he argued his first case before the state appellate court. The Manhattan District Attorney for whom he works is Robert M. Morgenthau, named U.S. District Attorney in New York by President John F. Kennedy in 1961. Also in 1990, Kennedy passed the Connecticut bar exam.

Kennedy's B.A. was from Brown University in 1983 and his J.D. from New York University in 1989. Between college and law school, from

1984–86, he worked for the New York City Office of Business Development. He became a New York assistant district attorney in 1989.

FURTHER READING

"Favorite son. . . ." Michael Gross. *New York*, Mar. 20, 1989.
"Then & now." Jean Libman Block. *Good Housekeeping*, Nov. 1988.
"John F. Kennedy, Jr." Lester David. *McCall's*, Nov. 1988.
"The sexiest Kennedy." Joyce Wadler. *People*, Sept. 12, 1988.

Khamenei, Hojatolislam Ali (1940–) Ayatollah Khamenei became supreme Iranian Shiite Muslim religious leader after the 1989 death of Ayatollah Ruhollah Khomeini. A hard-line fundamentalist, Khamenei throughout the 1980s took a leading role in denouncing Western nations, especially the United States, and in opposing any Iranian government moves to normalize relations with the West. He restated those views sharply during the spring and summer of 1989, and in February and again in June 1990 also rebuffed attempts to soften the Iranian death sentence against *The Satanic Verses* author Salman Rushdie.

Khamenei was a disciple and political ally of Ayatollah Ruhollah Khomenei; he was imprisoned in Iran on several occasions during the 1960s and 1970s, and exiled in 1978, returning to Iran when Khomeini came to power in 1979. He was president of Iran from 1981–89, and continued to be Iran's hard-line fundamentalist religious leader and a competitor in the internal struggle for state power after Khomeini's death in 1989. He is married and has five children.

FURTHER READING

"Iran without Khomeini." Michael Ledeen. *American Spectator*, Aug. 1989.
"Change in Teheran. . . ." *National Review*, June 30, 1989.
"Burying the passions. . . ." Bill Hewitt. *Newsweek*, June 19, 1989.
"The end of. . . ." Harry Anderson. *Newsweek*, June 12, 1989.
"Khamenei, Hojatolislam (Sayed) Ali." *Current Biography*, Nov. 1987.

King, Betsy (1955–) In 1990, King consolidated her position as the leading player in women's professional golf. In April, she won the Nabisco Dinah Shore tournament, and followed it with a second consecutive U.S. Open victory in July, a September win of the Rail Charity Classic, and a December World Match Play championship. She was women's golf Player of the Year for a second time in 1989, with six major championship wins.

King joined the women's golf professional tour in 1977, and for several years did fairly, but not very well. She hit her stride in 1984, making major changes in her style of play, largely through the influence of Ed Oldfield, who became her coach in 1980. She was a star golfer at Furman University. The strongly religious King is active in Christian causes.

FURTHER READING

"In a world of her own." JOHN GARRITY. *Sports Illustrated*, Feb. 12, 1990.
"Rolex player of the year. . . ." CHRIS YURKO. *Golf Magazine*, Feb. 1990.
"Golf queen King. . . ." RICHARD SOWERS. *Sporting News*, Oct. 30, 1989.
"A King is crowned queen." JOHN GARRITY. *Sports Illustrated*, July 24, 1989.
"Betsy King; player of the year." *Golf Magazine*, Dec. 1987.

Kinnock, Neil (Neil Gordon Kinnock, 1942–) The leader of the British Labour Party and of the parliamentary opposition made substantial gains during 1989 and 1990; by the autumn of 1990, Kinnock was consistently running 15–20 percent ahead of Margaret Thatcher in public opinion polls, a fact that had a great deal to do with Thatcher's November removal from the leadership of her party and the prime minister's post. Kinnock had by then captured much of the left center from the other parties of the left, and many of the moderate voters as well, through a combination of Labour Party changes of position and Conservative Party misfires. On May 8, 1989, Labour reversed its longstanding unilateral nuclear disarmament stand, calling for mutual nuclear disarmament. On May 23, Labour softened its longstanding opposition to many aspects of British integration into the European Community. Throughout 1989 and 1990, Labour attacked Margaret Thatcher's extremely unpopular poll taxes, though Kinnock also continued to hold the center by deploring the riots that accompanied some of the March 1990 poll tax protests.

Kinnock began his political career in the mid-1960s, in Labour Party educational work, became a Labour Member of Parliament in 1970, and has remained in Parliament for two decades while steadily moving up in his party. He became party leader and leader of the parliamentary opposition in 1983. He married Glenys Elizabeth Parry in 1967; they have two children. He attended the University College of Cardiff.

FURTHER READING

"A coal miner's son." MARY NEMETH. *Maclean's*, May 14, 1990.
Making Our Way: Investing in Britain's Future. NEIL KINNOCK. Basil Blackwell, 1987.
"Coal miner's son. . . ." CLAUDIA DREIFUS. *Mother Jones*, Jan. 1985.
"Kinnock, Neil (Gordon)." *Current Biography*, Apr. 1984.
Neil Kinnock: The Path to Leadership. G.M. DROWER. Weidenfeld & Nicolson, 1984.

Kirk, Lisa (1928–90) Singer, dancer, and actress, Kirk became a star singing "The Gentleman Is a Dope" on Broadway in the Rodgers and Hammerstein hit *Allegro* (1947). A year later she was on Broadway again, singing "Always True to You in My Fashion" in Cole Porter's *Kiss Me, Kate*. She went on to build a long career in musical theater and cabaret, surviving a serious late 1960s automobile accident and coming back to resume her career fully in the early 1970s. (d. New York City; November 11, 1990)

FURTHER READING

Obituary. *New York Times*, Nov. 13, 1990.

Kliban, B. (Bernard Kliban, 1935–90) Cartoonist Kliban was best known for his striped, goggle-eyed, eccentrically dressed cats. Connecticut-born Kliban dropped out of New York City art schools and roamed the country, coming to rest in California in 1959. There he began doing advertising drawings and cartoons, publishing his first book, *Cat*, in 1975. Ten other highly successful books followed, starting with *Never Eat Anything Bigger Than Your Head* (1976), spawning a multimillion-dollar industry, as Kliban's cats were used on everything from greeting cards to umbrellas. (d. San Francisco; August 12, 1990)

FURTHER READING

Obituary. *New York Times*, Aug. 14, 1990.

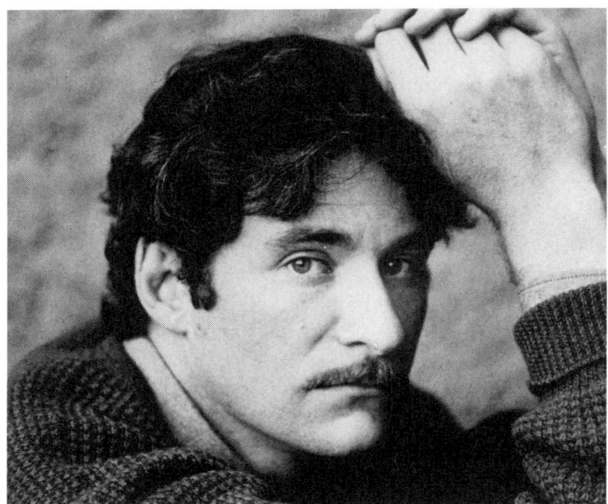

Kline, Kevin (Kevin Delaney Kline, 1947–) Kline starred in and directed *Hamlet* for PBS's Great Performances series, a 1990 production lauded somewhat more for its good intentions than its execution. *I Love You to Death* (1990), a black comedy with Kline co-starring as Tracey Ullman's philandering husband, also failed to work as intended. A year after winning a Best Supporting Oscar for his role in *A Fish Called Wanda* (1988), Kline wrote an apology to the National Stuttering Project for any inadvertent pain he might have caused by his mocking imitations of Michael Palin's stutter in the film, though he previously said he thought they had missed the humor in the role. ABC said they would edit out some of the mock stammering when it runs the film.

St. Louis-born Kline became a star on Broadway in the late 1970s, winning a Tony for *On the Twentieth Century* (1978), starring in *Loose Ends* (1979), and winning a second Tony for *Pirates of Penzance* (1980), a role he repeated in the 1983 film version. He also appeared off-Broadway in the early 1970s, and as *Richard III* (1983), *Henry V* (1984), and *Hamlet* (1986). On screen, he also played in such films as *Sophie's Choice* (1982), *The Big Chill* (1983), and *Silverado* (1985). He married Phoebe Cates in 1989. His B.A. was from Indiana University, and he also attended the Juilliard School.

FURTHER READING

"Kline, Kevin." *Current Biography*, July 1986.

"Kevin Kline's. . . ." William A. Henry III and Cathy Booth. *Time*, Mar. 24, 1986.

Kohl, Helmut (1930–) As the Cold War faded and then ended, West German prime minister Kohl seized the opportunity offered by the outbreak of peace between the Soviet Union and the United States and quickly and successfully pushed for and achieved a united Germany, long before anyone considering the matter before 1989 might have thought possible. In the process, his popularity and political standing, which had been sagging, became enormous in Germany, and he emerged as a leading figure in the developing European Community.

Once the unification process began, it moved very quickly. It started in July 1989, with hundreds of East Germans taking refuge in foreign embassies in Budapest and West Berlin. By September, the hard-line Honecker government was crumbling, as hundreds of thousands demonstrated in Leipzig and other East German cities and tens of thousands fled to the West. The Honecker government fell on October 18, and on November 9, 1989, came the historic opening of the Berlin Wall; the whole world watched as East Germans began to tear it down. On November 28, Kohl put forward his first reunification plan. In March 1990, the four occupying powers started talks on unification and East Germans elected a government favoring swift union of the two Germanys. In July, German monetary union began, and the Soviet Union dropped its opposition to German membership in NATO; on August 31, the two

Germanys agreed to join, effective October 3, 1990, with an all-German election set for early December. On September 12, the historic Final Settlement was signed by the two Germanys and the World War II allies.

Kohl began his political career in the Rhineland, becoming Christian Democratic Party chairman there from 1966–73 and deputy national chairman of his party in 1969; he has been national chairman since 1973. He was opposition leader in the West German parliament from 1976–82, and then succeeded chancellor Helmut Schmidt. He has throughout his career been a rather careful centrist, much concerned with the development of the European Community and pursuing a Western-oriented but also independent course. He married Hannelore Renner in 1960; the couple have two children. He attended the University of Frankfurt and the University of Heidelberg.

FURTHER READING

"Kohl. . . ." Bruce W. Nelan. *Time*, Jan. 7, 1991.
"Herr Klutz. . . ." Anne McElvoy. *New Republic*, Dec. 10, 1990.
"Kohl power." Edward M. Steen. *Inc.*, Nov. 1990.
"Helmut Kohl. . . . "David Gow. *World Press Review*, Oct. 1990.
"Driving toward. . . ." Henry Muller and Karsten Prager. *Time*, June 25, 1990.
"Immoral equivalence. . . ." Charles S. Maier. *New Republic*, Dec. 1, 1986.

Koppel, Ted (1940–) Broadcast journalist Koppel continues to be television's interviewer par excellence. His "Nightline" program, originally born out of international crisis, continued to be at its best when dealing with actors in major world events. Koppel scored a notable coup in 1990, when he was the first Western reporter allowed into Baghdad after Iraq's invasion of Kuwait and weighed in with the first interview with Iraq's foreign minister, Tariq Aziz, although CBS's Dan Rather followed a day later and was first to interview Saddam Hussein. Not all interviews were necessarily approved of; in late August, *Newsweek* reported that President George Bush was irritated that American hostages were moved from their hotel because Koppel and his staff were so eager in seeking interviews, and that Bush was pleased that the

newscasters were shortly forced to leave Iraq, a report Koppel characterized as "nonsense."

In addition to interviews, Koppel also hosted on "Nightline" various town meeting–style discussions, such as that on December 7 (date of the Japanese attack on Pearl Harbor) about whether the United States should or should not go to war against Iraq. Another town-meeting program featured Nelson Mandela, who gave Koppel his first formal American interview. Koppel was not alone in late-night news; from September 1990 he faced formidable competition from Lesley Stahl and Charles Kuralt on CBS's nightly series "America Tonight." He also did occasional news specials under the title, "The Koppel Report," and for PBS hosted a three-part series, "World Without Walls," about the massive political, social, and economic changes sweeping Eastern Europe.

British-born Koppel emigrated to the United States with his German refugee family in 1953. He began his broadcasting career at New York's WMCA in 1963, in that year moving to ABC, where he was to spend his entire career. He went to Vietnam as an ABC correspondent, worked in Hong Kong and Miami as an ABC bureau chief, and anchored the "ABC Saturday Night News" in the late 1970s. In March 1980, he emerged as a leading figure in American broadcast journalism as ABC turned its nightly reports on the Iran hostage crisis into the Koppel-anchored Monday-to-Friday "Nightline," identified with him ever since. His 11:30 P.M. broadcasts, featuring interviews with many of the world's leading people, have made a good deal of news, as well as reporting it. He is married to Grace Anne Dorney; the couple have four children, one of whom—Andrea—is also a television journalist. His B.A. in journalism was from Syracuse University, his M.A. in journalism from Stanford. He has also anchored and co-authored several television specials.

FURTHER READING

"50/50: happy birthday. . . ." JOANNA ELM. *TV Guide*, Feb. 3, 1990.
"Ted Koppel." RICHARD M. COHEN. *Life*, Oct. 1988.
"Ted Koppel's edge." MARSHALL BLONSKY. *New York Times Magazine*, Aug. 14, 1988.
"America's Q&A man. . . ." JONATHAN ALTER. *Newsweek*, June 15, 1987.
"Koppel: on values & ideas. . . ." *Variety*, Oct. 23, 1985.
"Koppel, Ted." *Current Biography*, July 1984.

Kreisky, Bruno (1911–90) The former chancellor of Austria was one of Europe's key post-World War II leaders. Born into a Jewish industrial family in Vienna, Kreisky was an agnostic and a Socialist, arrested and imprisoned in 1935–36 for his activities in the Social Democratic Party and again by the Nazis in 1938. After escaping and spending the war years as a correspondent and diplomatic adviser in Sweden, Kreisky began his political rise, becoming state secretary for foreign affairs in 1953, negotiating restoration of Austria's independence as a neutral country, and becoming the first Socialist foreign minister in 1959 and chairman of the Socialist Party in 1967. During his 1970–83 tenure as Austria's longest-serving chancellor, Kreisky restored much of his country's prestige abroad and prosperity at home. (d. Vienna; July 29, 1990)

FURTHER READING

Obituary. *Current Biography*, Sept. 1990.
Obituary. *The Times* (of London), July 30, 1990.
Obituary. *New York Times*, July 30, 1990.

Kristofferson, Kris (1936–) Actor-singer-songwriter Kristofferson went on the road again in 1990, making a ten-city concert tour with his friends Johnny Cash, Waylon Jennings, and Willie Nelson as the Highwaymen, although they had to win a court battle with CBS to use the name. Kristofferson and Nelson were earlier paired in the CBS television movie, "Pair of Aces." On film, Kristofferson appeared in late 1989 in *Welcome Home,* about a Vietnam veteran who was thought dead but returned home after 17 years, and in mid-1990 was shooting a new film, *Tipperary,* playing a detective to Drew Barrymore's potential victim. Privately, he also did benefits on behalf of the homeless, hard-pressed farmers, and others.

Texas-born Kristofferson has appeared in such films as *Cisco Pike* (1972), *Alice Doesn't Live Here Anymore* (1974), *The Sailor Who Fell From Grace with the Sea* (1976), *Heaven's Gate*, (1981), and *Rollover* (1981), and such telefilms as *Stagecoach* (1986) and *Amerika* (1987). He is also a well-known country and western singer and songwriter. He has been married three times and has three children. He attended Pomona College and Oxford University.

FURTHER READING

"Kris Kristofferson. . . ." PATRICK CARR. *Country Music*, Jan.–Feb. 1988.
"Prime-time patriotism. . . ." JEFF GOTTLIEB. *Mother Jones*, Jan. 1987.
"The incredible thinking man. . . ." MOLLY HASKELL. *Vogue*, Feb. 1986.
Written in My Soul: Rock's Great Songwriters. . . . Talk About Creating Their Music. BILL FLANAGAN. Contemporary, 1986.

Kurosawa, Akira (1910–) Japanese film director Kurosawa was specially honored in 1990. At the March Academy Award ceremonies, he was awarded a special Oscar for lifetime achievement. It was, coincidentally, his 80th birthday and, in the first Academy Awards satellite hookup, film luminaries from several continents joined in singing "Happy Birthday" to the man many regard as the world's greatest living film director. Kurosawa also received the 1990 Japan Society Award for "increasing appreciation and understanding of Japanese society and culture."

He did not, however, simply rest on his laurels, but presented a new film, *Akira Kurosawa's Dreams*, to open the 1990 Cannes Film Festival. Based on eight of the director's actual dreams, with beautifully haunting images often involving antiwar (including antinuclear) and pro-environment concerns, the episodic movie was regarded—even by those who had reservations about some portions—as a major film event. In one especially notable sequence, the actor playing the young Kurosawa enters one of Van Gogh's paintings and meets the artist, played by Martin Scorsese, himself a celebrated film director.

Meanwhile, Kurosawa was actively planning his 30th film, *Rhapsody in August*, about the reconciliation between a Japanese family and their relatives who had emigrated to the United States before World War II. The casting of Richard Gere to play the son of a Japanese man and a Caucasian woman in the film caused some controversy, being criticized as "far-fetched" by the Association of Asian Pacific American Artists.

Kurosawa was an assistant director from 1936–43; his first film as a director was *Sugata Sanshiro* (1943). He emerged as a major figure during the postwar period, bringing Japanese films to a world audience in the 1950s with such films as *Rashomon* (1950), which won a Best Foreign Film Oscar; *The Seven Samurai* (1954); and *Throne of Blood* (1957), his adaptation of *Macbeth*. His later films included such classics as *Yojimbo* (1961), *Redbeard* (1964), *Derzu Uzala* (1976), *Kagemusha* (1980), and *Ran* (1984), his adaptation of *King Lear*. In 1982 he published *Something Like an Autobiography*.

FURTHER READING

The Warrior's Camera: The Cinema of Akira Kurosawa. Stephen Prince. Princeton University Press, 1991.
"A. Kurosawa." Ralph Rugoff. *Interview*, Sept. 1990.
"Akira Kurosawa." John Clark. *Premiere*, Aug. 1990.
"Japan's emperor. . . ." Ian Buruma. *New York Times Magazine*, Oct. 29, 1989.
"DGA Pays Tribute. . . ." *Variety*, Apr. 2, 1986.
"Akira Kurosawa." Gerald Peary. *American Film*, Apr. 1989.
"Akira Kurosawa." *People*, Dec. 23, 1985.
"Samurai Lear. . . ." Dave Kehr. *American Film*, Sept. 1985.

L

Lancaster, Burt (Burton Stephen Lancaster, 1913–) Lancaster headed an international cast on television in 1990 in the new role of father to the *Phantom of the Opera* in NBC's elaborate miniseries. *Rocket Gibraltar* (1989), in which he played the patriarch at a family reunion, became available for video rental while continuing to play on cable. In 1989, he had also appeared as baseball old-timer Archie Graham in the popular movie *Field of Dreams*. Late in 1990, Lancaster was hospitalized with a stroke.

New York–born Lancaster was an acrobat from 1932-39, half of the team of Lang and Cravat. Following World War II, he very quickly became a leading film star, after his extraordinary debut in *The Killers* (1946). A few of his many notable films were *All My Sons* (1948); *From Here to Eternity* (1953); *The Rose Tattoo*, (1955); *Gunfight at the O.K. Corral* (1957); *Separate Tables* (1958); *The Devil's Disciple* (1959); *Elmer Gantry* (1960), for which he won a Best Actor Oscar; *Judgment at Nuremberg* (1961); *Bird Man of Alcatraz* (1962); *The Leopard* (1963); *Seven Days in May* (1964); *The Swimmer* (1968); and *Atlantic City*, (1980). He was married for the third time to Susan Scherer in 1990 and has five children. He attended New York University.

FURTHER READING

The Cinema History of Burt Lancaster. David Fury. Artists Press, 1989.

Shooting Stars: Heroes & Heroines of Western Film. Archie P. McDonald. Indiana University Press, 1987.

"Lancaster, Burt." *Current Biography,* April 1986.

Burt Lancaster. Minty Clinch. Scarborough House, 1985.

Burt Lancaster. Robert Windeler. St. Martin's, 1984; Jove, 1985.

Burt Lancaster: The Man & His Movies. Allan Hunter. St. Martin's, 1984.

Landsbergis, Vytautas (1932–) Landsbergis, a music professor, began to emerge as a major Lithuanian and Soviet political figure in 1989, at the head of Sajudis, the leading noncommunist Lithuanian nationalist organization. In May 1989, he was a highly visible Lithuanian nationalist delegate to the first session of the Soviet Congress of People's Deputies. On March 11, 1990, the Lithuanian parliament passed a declaration of secession from the Soviet Union and elected Landsbergis the first president of independent Lithuania.

The Lithuanian declaration of independence was an historic "first," and for a few months Landsbergis became a world figure as speculation grew as to the possible breakup of the Soviet Union. Landsbergis and other Baltic leaders sought support from other world leaders, but found none who were willing to try to seriously intervene beyond verbal expressions of support. In June, after dialogue with Soviet president Gorbachev had begun,

Landsbergis supported the Lithuanian parliamentary vote to temporarily suspend the declaration of independence while talks with the central government continued, but the situation worsened, with renewed repression occurring late in the year.

Landsbergis became a politician only recently. He has spent most of his working life as a distinguished Soviet musicologist, teaching at the Vilnius Conservatory. Divorced, then remarried, he has three children.

FURTHER READING

"Landsbergis talks tough. . . ." *U.S. News & World Report,* Dec. 17, 1990.
"Landsbergis, Vytautas." *Current Biography,* July 1990.
"The meddlesome musicologist. . . ." JEFF TRIMBLE. *U.S. News & World Report,* May 14, 1990.

Lange, Jessica (1949–) Lange won critical praise, though small audiences, for her role as a stunned widow with two sons in *Men Don't Leave,* released on video in 1990. Also made available on video, and gaining wider audiences than in theatrical release, was the Constantin Costa-Gavras film *Music Box* (1989), in which she played a lawyer defending her father, accused of Nazi war crimes; the film was co-winner of the Golden Bear, top award at the 1990 Berlin Film Festival. In mid-1990 Lange made the film *Blue Sky,* set on a 1960s southern Army base.

Minnesota-born Lange became one of the leading movie stars of the late 1970s and 1980s with such films as *All That Jazz* (1979), *The Postman Always Rings Twice* (1981), *Frances* (1982), *Tootsie* (1982), and *Crimes of the Heart* (1986). She was formerly married to director Paco Grande and has three children. She attended the University of Minnesota.

FURTHER READING

"Jessica Lange." *American Film,* Aug. 1990.
"The enigmatic allure. . . ." LINDA BIRD FRANCKE. *Cosmopolitan,* Feb. 1990.
"Jessica Lange." *American Film,* June 1987.
Jessica Lange. J. T. JEFFRIES. St. Martin's, 1986.
"Jessica Lange speaks. . . ." BOB GREENE. *Esquire,* Dec. 1985.
"Lange, Jessica." *Current Biography,* May 1983.

Lansbury, Angela (Angela Brigid Lansbury, 1925–) In 1990, Lansbury continued easing her way out of her role as Jessica Fletcher, mystery writer/sleuth on the series "Murder, She Wrote," which won her the 1990 Golden Globe award as best television actress. For 1989-91, she starred in only 13 episodes a season, introducing and closing the rest, which star other characters. She plans to do more television movies, such as the Hallmark Hall of Fame production *The Shell Seekers* in December 1989 and *The Love She Sought* in October 1990, opposite Denholm Elliott, and has contracted with a Disney division to star in feature films. In 1990, Lansbury was honored by the Academy of Television Arts and Sciences and the Hollywood Women's Press Club, and she also received her first college degree, an

honorary doctorate of humane letters from Boston University.

British-born Lansbury began her long film and theater career with a supporting role in *Gaslight* (1944), and played competently in over a score of substantial film roles during the following 25 years. But it was on Broadway and in television, both much later, that she became a major star. She won four Tony awards on Broadway—for *Mame* (1966), *Dear World* (1969), *Gypsy* (1973), and *Sweeney Todd* (1979). Then, quite late in her career, she became a major television star with "Murder, She Wrote" (1984–). She married Peter Shaw in 1949; they have two children.

FURTHER READING

"Angela Lansbury has. . . ." SUZANNE ADELSON. *People,* Nov. 7, 1988.
"'I had to save my family.'" PATRICIA NOLAN. *50 Plus,* Oct. 1988.
"Solving the case of. . . ." PHYLLIS BATTELLE. *Woman's Day,* Sept. 13, 1988.
"Angela Lansbury. . . ." JOHN CULHANE. *Reader's Digest,* June 1987; Canadian version, Aug. 1987.
"The Angela Lansbury story." BOB THOMAS. *Good Housekeeping,* Mar. 1987.
Angela Lansbury: A Biography. MARGARET W. BONNANO. St. Martin's, 1987.

Larsen, Leif (1906–90) During World War II, Larsen was captain of one of a group of Norwegian fishing boats known collectively as the "Shetland bus," operating out of the Shetland Islands and ferrying Allied agents, arms, and supplies across the North Sea into Nazi-occupied Norway, and Norwegians, refugees from many countries, and escaped prisoners to freedom. Larsen made over 50 voyages, survived shipwreck twice, and lived to become one of Norway's most celebrated resistance heroes. (d. Bergen, Norway; October 12, 1990)

FURTHER READING

Obituary. *The Times* (of London), Oct. 17, 1990.

Lausche, Frank (1905–1990) A lawyer, judge, and conservative Democratic politician, Lausche practiced law in Ohio from 1920 to 1931, and then was an appointed municipal judge. A decade later, in 1941, he was elected mayor of Cleveland, serving two terms before his first election as Ohio's governor (1945–46). He was elected again in 1948, served four more terms (1949–56), and then served two terms in the U.S. Senate, where he supported John F. Kennedy, for the presidency and then became a very conservative critic of the Kennedy social welfare and civil rights programs. He was defeated in the 1968 senatorial primary. (d. Cleveland; April 21, 1990)

FURTHER READING

Obituary. *Current Biography,* June 1990.
Obituary. *New York Times,* Apr. 22, 1990.

Lee, Spike (Shelton Jackson Lee; 1957–) Writer and director Lee became one of the world's most notable young filmmakers in 1989 with release of his film *Do the Right Thing,* a fictional story that sharply explored racial tensions in his home area of Bedford-Stuyvesant, in Brooklyn, from one Black point of view. The film—one of the most controversial of the 1980s—featured Danny Aiello as the Italian pizza restaurant owner, Lee himself, and such players as Ossie Davis, Ruby Dee, and John Savage. Aiello received an Oscar nomination, although many expressed surprise and dismay that Lee and the film did not. Denzel Washington starred in Lee's equally controversial 1990 film, *Mo' Better Blues,* attacked by many as anti-Semitic for its depiction of two Jewish club owners in a story of the exploitation of Black artists.

Atlanta-born Lee is a very recent professional filmmaker, with such early films as *She's Gotta Have It* (1986) and *School Daze* (1988); with Lisa Jones, he wrote books about the making of both films. His 1979 B.A. was from Morehouse College, and his 1983 M.A. in filmmaking from New York University.

FURTHER READING

"Spike Lee does. . . ." MARK LANDLER. *Business Week,* Aug. 6, 1990.
"Mo' better Spike." JILL NELSON. *Essence,* Aug. 1990.
"The declaration of Independents." JIM JARMUSCH. *Interview,* Aug. 1990.
"Spike Lee." *People,* Dec. 25, 1989.
"Spike Lee: filmmaker." LARKIN WARREN. *Esquire,* Dec. 1989.
"Spike Lee. . . ." LYNN NORMENT. *Ebony,* Oct. 1989.
"He's got to have it his way. . . ." JEANNE MCDOWELL. *Time,* July 17, 1989.
"Spike Lee's. . . ." MARLAINE GLICKSMAN. *Film Comment,* July–Aug. 1989.
"Local hero. . . ." THULANI DAVIS. *American Film,* July–Aug. 1989.
"Lee, Spike." *Current Biography,* Mar. 1989.

Lehmann, Rosamond (Rosamond Nina Lehmann, 1901-90) British novelist Lehmann wrote with lyrical sensitivity about human feelings, perceptions, and misperceptions. Born near London and educated at Girton College, Cambridge, she came to fame in 1927 with her first work, *Dusty Answer*, the story of a girl's maturation. Other novels and shorter works followed over the decades, most notably *Invitation to the Waltz* (1932) and *The Ballad and the Source* (1944), many of which were given new life by republication in recent decades. (d. London; March 12, 1990)

FURTHER READING

Obituary. *New York Times,* Mar. 15, 1990.
Obituary. *The Times* (of London), Mar. 14, 1990.
Rosamond Lehmann: A Thirties Writer. RUTH SIEGEL. Peter Lang, 1989.

LeMay, Curtis (Curtis Emerson Lemay, 1906–90) The former head of the U.S. Air Force was a key architect of strategic air bombing. Son of a French-Canadian-American ironworker, LeMay entered the military through the reserves, being commissioned as a navigator-pilot in 1930. During World War II, he pioneered transatlantic plane-ferrying routes, led numerous bombing raids over Germany, and as Strategic Air Forces chief of staff from 1945 oversaw the bombing of mainland Japan, including the atomic bomb; and in 1947 he returned to Germany to direct the Berlin airlift. LeMay helped build the Strategic Air Command's massive B-52 fleets during the crucial Cold War years, as leader of SAC from 1948–57 and of the Air Force from 1961–64. During the Vietnam War, and while running for vice president with George Wallace in 1968, he advocated using "all available means," including nuclear weapons. In 1989, he published (with Bill Yenne) *Superfortress: The Story of the B-29 and American Air Power in World War II.* (d. March Air Force Base, California; October 1, 1990)

FURTHER READING

Obituary. *Current Biography,* Nov. 1990.
Obituary. MEL ELFIN. *U.S. News & World Report,* Oct. 15, 1990.
Obituary. *The Times* (of London), Oct. 3, 1990.
Obituary. *New York Times,* Oct. 2, 1990.
Strategic Air Warfare: An Interview with Generals. . . . RICHARD H. KOHN and JOSEPH P. HARAHAN, eds. U.S. Government Printing Office, 1989.
Iron Eagle: The Turbulent Life of General Curtis LeMay. THOMAS M. COFFEY. Crown, 1986; Avon, 1988.

Lemmon, Jack (John Lemmon III, 1925–) In December 1989, the Screen Actors Guild awarded Jack Lemmon its highest honor, the Annual Achievement Award, which recognizes both professional work and contributions to social causes. Lemmon's special talents were on display in *Dad* (1989), in which he played considerably older than his age as a 75-year-old retiree slipping into senility. In an Academy Award first, Lemmon presented the 1990 Oscar for the best foreign-language film by satellite from Moscow; other international presenters were in London and Buenos Aires.

Boston-born Lemmon, who acted in early television, began his long film career by winning a Best Supporting Actor Oscar for his

Ensign Pulver in *Mister Roberts* (1954). Nineteen years later, he won a Best Actor Oscar for *Save the Tiger* (1973). Among his other films, a few of the most notable were *Bell, Book, and Candle* (1958), *Some Like It Hot* (1959), *The Apartment* (1960), *Days of Wine and Roses* (1962), *Irma La Douce* (1963), *The Odd Couple* (1968), *The Prisoner of Second Avenue* (1975), *The China Syndrome* (1978), *Missing* (1981), and *Mass Appeal* (1984). Formerly married to Cynthia Boyd Stone, he married Felicia Farr in 1962 and has two children. His B.A. and B.S. are from Harvard.

FURTHER READING

"Lemmon, Jack." *Current Biography,* Aug. 1988.
"Jack of all trades." BURT PRELUTSKI. *American Film,* Mar. 1988.
Actors: A Celebration. RITA GAM. St. Martin's, 1988.
The Films of Jack Lemmon. JOE BALTAKE. State Mutual, 1987.
"Jack's journey. . . ." JACK KROLL. *Newsweek,* May 5, 1986.
Jack Lemmon. MICHAEL FREEDLAND. St. Martin's, 1985.

LeMond, Greg (1961–) After a 1987 hunting accident that disabled him, top U.S. cyclist LeMond was entirely out of racing for two years. After a tremendous effort to heal and retrain himself, he was able to return to competitive racing in 1989, but only on a very limited basis. Yet in July 1989, he made an extraordinary comeback, winning his second Tour de France, and then went on to win a third Tour de France in 1990. Late in 1990, he encountered some health problems and was forced to cancel several races.

California-born LeMond became a leading amateur cyclist in the early 1980s and turned professional in 1983, then quickly began to win the series of races that established him as one of the world's top cyclists. In 1986, he first won cycling's most important race, the Tour de France. Greg and Kathy LeMond married in 1981; they have two children.

FURTHER READING

Greg LeMond: Premier Cyclist. A.P. PORTER. Lerner, 1990.
"Greg LeMond. . . ." HAL HIGDON. *Boys' Life,* June 1990.
LeMond: The Incredible Comeback of an American Hero. SAMUEL ABT. Random House, 1990.
"Struggling back." SAMUEL ABT. *New York Times Magazine,* June 5, 1988.
"No more Mr. Nice Guy. . . ." DAVID WALSH. *Bicycling,* April 1988.

Lendl, Ivan (1960–) At the end of 1989, Lendl was the world's top-ranked tennis player, although in early December he had lost to Stefan Edberg in the semifinals of the Masters. In February 1990, still ranked first and top seeded in the tournament, he beat Tim Mayotte in straight sets to win the Milan indoor tournament title. But in the summer of 1990, he faltered; although top seeded at Wimbledon, the only major tournament he had never won, he was eliminated by unseeded Goran Ivanisevic. In August, he lost to MalaVai Washington at New Haven, in the Volvo International ATP Championships. He reached the quarterfinals of the U.S. Open but lost to eventual winner Pete Sampras. In October, he lost to Stefan Edberg in the semifinals of the Australian Indoor Championships but came back to beat Michael Chang and win the Hong Kong Marlboro tournament. In the November Paris Open he was defeated by Jonas Svensson.

Czech-born Lendl became a leading junior player in the late 1970s, turned professional in 1979, and was one of the world's leading male tennis players in the mid-1980s. He was ranked World Champion in 1985 and 1986; in 1985, he won the U.S. Open and the Masters, and in 1986 he won the U.S. Open, the French Open, and the Italian Open. He continued to win major tournaments throughout the 1980s, although a 1988 operation limited his play that year. He married Samantha Frankel in 1989.

FURTHER READING

"Getting Ivan. . . ." CINDY SHMERLER. *World Tennis,* Feb. 1990.
"Ivan Lendl. . . ." PETER BODO. *Tennis,* Sept. 1989.
"Obsession. . . ." TONY SCHWARTZ. *New York,* June 26, 1989.
"12 questions. . . ." ANDELA GAUDIOSO. *Tennis,* Sept. 1988.
Ivan Lendl. CHIP ELIOT. Crestwood House, 1988.
"On guard. . . ." GARY SMITH. *Sports Illustrated,* Apr. 28, 1986.
"Lendl, Ivan." *Current Biography,* Sept. 1984.

Leonard, "Sugar" Ray (Ray Charles Leonard, 1956–) Most people thought Leonard would have hung up his gloves long before now; back in 1976, having won the Olympic gold medal at Montreal, he had said, "I've fought my last fight. My journey is ended. My dream is fulfilled." But Leonard continued to be in the ring and in the news. After fighting Thomas Hearns to a draw in June 1989, Leonard buckled down and in December 1989 decisively beat Roberto Duran in Las Vegas, though it took 60 stitches to close up his cuts.

For his work, Leonard is paid handsomely. In August 1990, *Forbes* magazine listed Leonard as the third-highest-paid sports figure, including salary, winnings, and endorsements, with an estimated income of $13 million in 1990. Some of that money went to Leonard's ex-wife Juanita; the two were for a time locked in public divorce proceedings but finally agreed on an out-of-court settlement. Among Leonard's other activities were continuing sponsorship of the Sugar Ray Leonard summer basketball league and participation in a group seeking a baseball expansion franchise, both in the Washington, D.C., area where he lives. Leonard has also served as a sometime boxing commentator on HBO.

After his 1976 Olympic gold, North Carolina-born Leonard turned professional in 1977 and won the World Boxing Council welterweight title in 1979, the World Boxing Association middleweight title in 1981, and the combined welterweight title in 1981. He then retired, after eye surgery, but returned to win the World Boxing Council middleweight title in 1987 and the World Boxing Council light-heavyweight title in 1988. He married Juanita Wilkinson in 1980; they have two children. Ray Leonard, Jr., at age 8, became a Junior Golden Gloves champion.

FURTHER READING

"The world according to Ray." GARY SMITH. *Sports Illustrated,* Dec. 4, 1989.
"Leonard bashing." DAVID MILLER. *Sport,* Dec. 1989.
"Sugar Ray Leonard." ED KIERSH. *Interview,* Mar. 1987.
Sugar Ray Leonard: And Other Noble Warriors. SAM TOPEROFF. McGraw-Hill, 1987.
Sugar Ray Leonard. CAROLYN GLOECKNER. Crestwood House, 1985.
Sports Star: Sugar Ray Leonard. S. H. BURCHARD. Harcourt Brace, Jovanovich, 1983.
Sugar Ray Leonard. JAMES HASKINS. Lothrop, 1982.
Sugar Ray Leonard: The Baby-faced Boxer. BERT ROSENTHAL. Childrens, 1982.
"Leonard, 'Sugar' Ray." *Current Biography,* Feb. 1981.
A Fistful of Sugar: The Sugar Ray Leonard Story. ALAN GOLDSTEIN. Putnam, 1981.

Lin, Maya (Maya Ying Lin, 1960–) Architect-sculptor Lin, best known for her Vietnam Veterans Memorial, created a striking new memorial, commissioned by the Southern Poverty Law Center in Montgomery, Alabama, to honor the civil rights movement. Dedicated

in November 1989, the new structure consists of a curved black wall facing a black granite disk; flowing over both is a stream of running water. Written on the tablelike disk in gold letters are the key events of the civil rights movement and the names of people who died in it, while on the wall is printed a quotation from Martin Luther King, Jr.'s "I have a dream" speech, tying in with the flowing water: "We will not be satisfied until 'justice rolls down like waters and righteousness like a mighty stream.'" Like the Vietnam memorial, it is meant for people to touch.

Among Lin's other projects are a sculpture for New York City's Penn Station, a commemorative piece commissioned by the Gleitsman Foundation to be given (along with $100,000) to the recipient of their annual award, various noncommissioned sculptures, and such architectural projects as renovating a 19th-century Connecticut house with a fellow architect.

Brought to America as a child by her Chinese immigrant parents, Lin was only 21 years old and still a student at Yale in 1981 when she won the competition to design the Vietnam Veterans Memorial in Washington, D.C. Her simple black granite wall, inscribed with the names of those Americans who died in Vietnam, was at first seen by many as far too plain and even stark, but the memorial has, since its unveiling in 1982, become one of the most revered and visited of American national monuments. After graduating from Yale, she studied architecture at Harvard. She began the civil rights memorial, her second major historic project, in 1988.

FURTHER READING

"Maya Lin is young. . . ." CHARLES GANDEE. *House & Garden,* Mar. 1990.
"Civil Rights Memorial Dedicated." *Art in America,* Dec. 1989.
"Maya Lin. . . ." DAVID GROGAN. *People,* Nov. 20, 1989.
"First she looks inward. . . ." JONATHAN COLEMAN. *Time,* Nov. 6, 1989.
"Monumental Talent." *U.S. News & World Report,* Nov. 6, 1989.
"The wall. . . ." CAROL KRAMER. *McCall's,* June 1988.
Always to Remember: The Story of the Vietnam Veterans Memorial. BRENT ASHABRANNER. Putnam, 1988.
The Vietnam Veterans Memorial. MICHAEL KATAKIS. Crown, 1988.

Li Peng (1928–) The prime minister of the People's Republic of China became leader of his party's conservative faction in the late 1980s, although he was always second to Deng Xiaoping in the party and government. He became acting prime minister in 1987 and prime minister in 1988, and was the central figure in the triumph of the conservative faction in 1989, with its accompanying Tiananmen Square massacre of student demonstrators on June 4, 1989.

Li maintained his hard-line internal position during the balance of 1989 and 1990, forcing the demotion of former moderate premier Zhao Ziyang after the 1989 student demonstrations, prosecuting dissidents, and strengthening the organs of state control of Chinese society. At the same time, he attempted to restore China's very badly damaged image and prestige abroad, lifting martial law in Beijing in early January and freeing some dissidents in May, just before seeking the renewal of China's "favored nation" trading status with the United States.

Li Peng began his long, steady rise in the Chinese Communist bureaucracy as a young protegé of premier Zhou En-lai. Li emerged as a major figure in the 1980s, as minister of power in 1981, and as a Politburo member in 1985. In the late 1980s, as great tension developed between the liberal and conservative wings of the Chinese leadership, he became a conservative faction leader. He married Zhu Lin in 1958; they have three children. He attended the Moscow Power Institute.

FURTHER READING

Tiananmen Square. Scott Simmie and Bob Nixon. University of Washington Press, 1989.
"Li Peng." *Current Biography,* Nov. 1988.
"What a way to welcome. . . ." *U.S. News & World Report.* Apr. 18, 1988.

List, John E. (1926–) On November 9, 1971, at his home in Westfield, New Jersey, John List murdered his wife, his mother, and their three children. He then disappeared, taking up a new identity as Robert P. Clark in the Denver area, where he went back to work as an accountant and later remarried. He and his second wife moved to Richmond, Virginia, in 1988. He was identified and arrested in 1989, after the television program "America's Most Wanted" featured the story of the 18-year-old multiple murders. List's lawyer defended him on grounds of mental illness, but the jury in the case rejected that defense, finding List guilty of premeditated murder in the first degree. On May 1, 1990, he was sentenced to five consecutive life terms, the maximum sentence possible, ensuring that he would remain in jail for the rest of his life.

FURTHER READING

"The mystery of. . . ." Marianne Jacobbi. *Good Housekeeping,* Jan. 1990.
Death Sentence: The Murderous Odyssey of John List. Joe Sharkey. NAL-Dutton, 1990.
"In hiding for18 years. . . ." Ken Gross. *People,* June 19, 1989.
"Murder, they broadcast." Tamar Jacoby. *Newsweek,* June 12, 1989.
"After 18 years, a bust." *Time,* June 12, 1989.
"The three faces of John List." *U.S. News & World Report,* June 12, 1989.

Lithgow, John (John Arthur Lithgow, 1945–) The versatile dramatic actor worked in Britain in the summer of 1989, filming David Puttnam's *Memphis Belle.* He made a very notable theater appearance in Los Angeles that fall, starring opposite Glenda Jackson in *Who's Afraid of Virginia Woolf?,* with playwright Edward Albee directing. He also appeared in a National Audobon Society–sponsored fiction film—the society's first—starring with James Earl Jones and Isabella Rossellini in *The Last Elephant*, about the killing of endangered East African elephants for their ivory. In addition, he starred as Leslie Huben, an American Christian evangelist working in Brazil's Amazon region, in the film *At Play in the Fields of the Lord,* based on the 1965 Peter Matthiessen novel. Forthcoming is the television film *The Boys,* in which he costars with James Woods.

Rochester-born Lithgow began playing substantial roles on the New York stage in the early 1970s in such plays as *The Changing Room* (1972), *Beyond Therapy* (1982), *Requiem for a Heavyweight* (1985), and *M. Butterfly* (1988). His most notable earlier films include *The World According to Garp* (1982;

he received an Oscar nomination), *Terms of Endearment* (1983; and a second Oscar nomination), and *The Manhattan Project* (1986). He has also appeared in several television films, including *The Day After* (1983) and *Amazing Stories* (1987; he won an Emmy). Lithgow is a 1967 Harvard graduate, and also attended the London Academy of Music and Dramatic Art. He has been married twice, last to Mary Yeager in 1981, and has two children.

FURTHER READING

"John Lithgow. . . ." MEGAN ROSENFELD. *American Baby,* Aug. 1988.
"Fatherhood is the favorite role. . . ." GAIL BUCHALTER. *People,* July 4, 1983.

Lleras Camargo, Alberto (1906-90) Born and educated in Bogotá, Lleras Camargo was long active politically, with the Liberal Party and the Liberal-minded newspaper *El Tiempo,* holding ministerial posts in several reform governments. He was appointed to fill out a presidential term (1945–46), and served again as president (1958–1963), helping to form a coalition government that was able to stop Colombia's murderous civil war *(La Violencia)* and pass land reform legislation. A strong supporter of international cooperation, Lleras Camargo served as the first secretary-general of the Organization of American States (1948–54). (d. Bogotá; January 4, 1990)

FURTHER READING

Obituary. *Current Biography,* Mar. 1990.
Obituary. *The Times* (of London), Jan. 6, 1990.
Obituary. *New York Times,* Jan. 5, 1990.

Lloyd Webber, Andrew (1948–) British composer Lloyd Webber continued his enormous success in the theater, branching out in new directions as well. Major productions of his previous musical hits—most notably *Cats* (1981), *Starlight Express* (1984), *The Phantom of the Opera* (1988), and *Aspects of Love* (1989)—were still playing in New York, London, Los Angeles, and elsewhere. *Aspects of Love* opened in New York in spring 1990 to mixed critical

response, did well initially at the box office, but closed in February 1991 with a record Broadway loss of $8 million. At the end of 1990 Lloyd Webber opened a new musical, *Freudiana,* in the psychologist's hometown, Vienna, to record-breaking advance ticket sales. His theatrical corporation, the Really Useful Group, was so profitable that it interested major investors, hindering his attempts to buy back all of the company's stock.

Lloyd Webber moved into other areas as well, announcing his intention to write a movie musical and agreeing with Disney to produce a major new nighttime water spectacular, *Noah's Ark,* for Disney World, in Orlando, Florida, writing an original symphonic score for the pageant. Disney was also attempting to buy from its current owners the film rights to his *Evita* (1978), reportedly as a vehicle for the hot rock star Madonna. Lloyd Webber and Steven Spielberg agreed to do a full-length animated feature-film version of *Cats.*

On the personal side, Lloyd Webber made a much-publicized break with his wife, Sarah Brightman, in 1990 and later married British fashion entrepreneur Madeleine Gurdon. Brightman and Lloyd Webber continued their professional relationship, however; she went ahead on schedule to join the Broadway production of *Aspects of Love* as the rising French actress Rose, although production of the film of *The Phantom of the Opera,* in which she was scheduled to star, was postponed until at least summer 1991.

Lloyd Webber emerged as a leading musical theater composer in 1968, with *Joseph and the*

Amazing Technicolor Dreamcoat, lyrics by Tim Rice; he then wrote the trailblazing rock opera *Jesus Christ Superstar* (1970), with lyrics again by Rice. He won Tonys for the musicals *Evita* and *Cats*. His compositions also include *Requiem Mass* (1975) and *Variations on a Theme by Paganini* (1977), as well as the film scores for *Jesus Christ Superstar*, *Gumshoe* (1971), and *The Odessa File* (1974). Lloyd Webber attended Oxford University and the Royal Academy of Music. He has been married three times, and has two children. He is the brother of cellist Julian Lloyd Webber.

FURTHER READING

"Andrew Lloyd Webber leaves. . . ." TOM GLIATTO. *People,* July 23, 1990.
Andrew Lloyd Webber: His Life & Works. MICHAEL WALSH. Abrams, 1989.
"Broadway's age. . . ." MIRIAM HORN. *U.S. News & World Report,* Feb. 1, 1988.
"The changing face of Broadway. . . ." MARILYN STASIO. *Life,* Feb. 1988.
"Magician of the musical. . . ." MICHAEL WALSH. *Time,* Jan. 18, 1988.
"Andrew Lloyd Webber. . . ." JOHN ROCKWELL. *New York Times Magazine,* Dec. 20, 1987.

Lockwood, Margaret (Margaret Mary Lockwood, 1916–90) British actress Lockwood became an international star in Hitchcock's *The Lady Vanishes* (1938). Born in Pakistan of British parents but largely raised in England, Lockwood made her stage debut at 15 and played on film from 1935. Briefly in Hollywood, her main work was in Britain, as in Carol Reed's *The Stars Look Down* (1939), *The Man in Grey* (1943), *The Wicked Lady* (1945), and *Jassy* (1947), becoming Britain's leading box-office star in the 1940s, specializing in villainesses. After her film popularity's abrupt decline in the mid-1950s, she returned to the stage and also played on television. (d. London; July 15, 1990)

FURTHER READING

Obituary. *Current Biography,* Sept. 1990.
Obituary. *Variety,* July 18, 1990.
Obituary. *The Times* (of London), July 17, 1990.
Obituary. *New York Times,* July 17, 1990.

London, Ephraim (1912–90) London was one of the most successful American civil liberties lawyers of the century, most notably in two landmark New York cases involving film censorship. The first involved the Roberto Rossellini film *The Miracle*; in 1950, it was banned in New York after protests by Roman Catholic clergy that it was sacrilegious. The U.S. Supreme Court agreed with London that the First Amendment protected films as well as written works. The second was the film *Lady Chatterley's Lover,* banned in New York in 1959; again the Court agreed with London that the film could not be banned constitutionally. London also won the Lenny Bruce case, and several other censorship and Fifth Amendment cases, most of them while swimming against the political tide of the times in defense of the Bill of Rights. Brooklyn-born London graduated from New York University Law School in 1934. He was a leading member of the American Civil Liberties Union. (d. New York City; June 12, 1990)

FURTHER READING

Obituary. *New York Times,* June 14, 1990.

Lumet, Sidney (1924–) Film director Lumet did not have immediate success with *Family Business* (1989). Despite Lumet's vaunted direction and the attraction of its stars—Sean Connery, Dustin Hoffman, and Matthew Broderick—the three-generational caper did not attract many viewers to movie theaters. Only when it came onto the video rental market in 1990 did the film seem to find its audience. Much the same seemed to be happening with his next movie, *Q&A*, starring Nick Nolte as a bloated, corrupt cop and Timothy Hutton as the rookie D.A. who investigates him. Excellent reviews did not seem to translate into box office pull; how Lumet's latest urban morality tale will fare in the long run remains to be seen. With several other film and theater luminaries, Lumet was honored in 1990 at NBC's *Night of 100 Stars* at Radio City Music Hall.

Philadelphia-born Lumet, the son of actor Baruch Lumet, appeared on stage from the age of four and played on the Broadway stage in the 1930s, including a role in *Dead End* (1935). He was a leading director in television during the 1950s; moved into films with *12 Angry Men* (1957), which he had first directed for television; and for over three decades, has been a leading Hollywood director of such films as *Stage Struck* (1958), *The Fugitive Kind* (1960), *Long Day's Journey into Night* (1962), *Fail Safe* (1964), *The Pawnbroker* (1965), *The Anderson Tapes* (1971), *Murder on the Orient Express* (1974), *Dog Day Afternoon* (1975), *Network* (1976), *Equus* (1977), *The Wiz* (1978), *The Verdict* (1982), *The Morning After* (1987), and *Running on Empty* (1988). Lumet attended Columbia University. He has been married four times, and has two children; one of his children is the actress Jenny Lumet.

FURTHER READING

"The blunder years. . . ." TODD GITLIN. *American Film,* Sept. 1988.
"Road worriers. . . ." GAVIN SMITH. *Film Comment,* July–Aug. 1988.
Sidney Lumet: A Guide to References and Resources. STEPHEN BOWLES. G. K. Hall, 1979.

Lynch, David (1946–) With the April 1990 premiere of his television series "Twin Peaks," a nighttime soap opera that was hailed by many as a new, surreal, entirely offbeat approach to the seamy side of American small town life, Lynch suddenly emerged as a major director and also as a highly publicized media figure. The series, set in a Pacific Northwest town, received 14 Emmy nominations and a great deal of critical acclaim, although by the end of its second season it had slipped so far in the ratings as to make a third season questionable. Lynch's next large work was the film *Wild at Heart* (1990), which starred Nicholas Cage and Laura Dern and explored similar themes; the film won the grand prize at the Cannes Film Festival, although it was not as well received in the United States.

Montana-born Lynch directed four films before 1990: *Eraserhead* (1977); *The Elephant Man* (1980), adapted from the stage play; the science fiction *Dune* (1984); and *Blue Velvet* (1986), a film about American small town life that is widely regarded as an earlier approach to the themes of his recent works. He attended the Corcoran School of Art, the Boston Museum School of Fine Arts, and the Pennsylvania Academy of Fine Arts. He has been married twice and has two children.

FURTHER READING

"The Rolling Stone interview. . . ." DAVID BRESKIN. *Rolling Stone,* Sept. 6, 1990.
"David Lynch." JIM JEROME. *People,* Sept. 3, 1990.
"David Lynch." JOHN CLARK. *Premiere,* Sept. 1990.
"Weird America." JOSEPH SOBRAN. *National Review,* Oct. 1, 1990.
"Czar of bizarre. . . ." RICHARD CORLISS. *Time,* Oct. 1, 1990.
"Lynch-time." BART BULL. *Vogue,* Feb. 1990.
"Lynch, David." *Current Biography,* May 1987.
"David Lynch." GERALD L'ECUYER. *Interview,* Mar. 1987.
"Out to Lynch." DAVID CHUTE. *Film Comment,* Oct. 1986.

Lynn, Loretta (Loretta Lynn Webb, 1935–) Once illiterate herself, country singer-songwriter Lynn has recorded two songs to help fund a literacy program, with First Lady Barbara Bush. Lynn appeared at numerous concerts and country fairs and was a main attraction at the June 1990 International Country Music Fan Fair. She was also one of many to appear with Randy Travis in a series of duets on the record *Heroes and Friends (1990).*

Born in Butcher Hollow, Kentucky, Lynn came up the hard way to become one of the leading country music figures of her time, from her first appearance on Grand Ole Opry in 1960 through her songs and albums of the late 1980s. She is perhaps best known for such songs as "Success" (1962) and "Coal Miner's Daughter" (1970), also the title of her 1976 autobiography and the 1980 film based on it, for which Sissy Spacek won a Best Actress Oscar as Lynn. Lynn has also expressed herself powerfully on women's rights matters. Bearing in mind that she married Oliver Lynn, Jr., in 1948, when she was only 14 years old and quickly had four of their six children, she wrote and strongly supported the pro–birth control song "The Pill" in 1975. Country singer Crystal Gayle, with whom she sometimes performs, is Lynn's sister.

FURTHER READING

"The importance of. . . ." BOB ALLEN. *Country Music,* Sept.–Oct. 1988.

Behind Closed Doors: Talking with the Legends of Country Music. ALANNA NASH. Knopf, 1988.

"In Colorado. . . ." GREGORY JAYNES. *Time,* Mar. 24, 1986.

"Loretta Lynn. . . ." BOB ALLEN. *Country Music,* Nov–Dec, 1985.

"'How I found. . . .'" NANCY ANDERSON. *Good Housekeeping,* Apr. 1985.

Loretta Lynn's World of Music. LAURENCE J. ZWISOHN. Palm Tree, 1980.

M

McCain, John Sidney III (1936–)

The recent career of the Arizona Republican senator has been dominated by charges that in 1987 he and four other senators unethically intervened with federal bank regulators on behalf of the Lincoln Savings and Loan Association of Irvine, California, controlled by Charles H. Keating, Jr. The four other senators were Dennis DeConcini, John Glenn, Alan Cranston, and Donald W. Riegle, Jr.; the group came to be known as the "Keating Five." In 1989, the bank was taken over by federal banking authorities in a bailout carrying an estimated cost of at least $2 billion. In late November 1990, Senate Ethics Committee hearings began on the Keating Five.

Senator McCain, with Senators Glenn, DeConcini, and Cranston, met with Edwin J. Gray, then chairman of the Federal Home Loan Bank Board, in DeConcini's Washington office on April 2, 1987; Gray charged that the senators improperly put pressure on him on behalf of Lincoln, which they all deny. The same senators, and also Senator Riegle, met with Gray and members of the San Francisco Federal Home Bank in DeConcini's office on April 9, 1987. McCain received $112,000 in campaign contributions from Keating and his associates, and further contributions in form of travel expenses; in 1990, McCain announced his intention to repay over $13,000 in such gifts.

McCain is a much-decorated career naval officer who fought in Vietnam and was a North Vietnamese prisoner of war from 1967 to 1973. He was Washington-based from 1977–81, leaving the navy as a captain. Turning to politics, he became a two-term Arizona Republican congressman (1982–86), and began his senatorial term in 1987. He graduated from the Naval Academy in 1958 and attended the National War College in 1973–74. He married Cindy Hensley in 1980; they have six children.

FURTHER READING

"Seven sorry senators. . . ." Margaret Carlson. *Time*, Jan. 8, 1990.

"McCain, John Sidney 3d." *Current Biography*, Feb. 1989.

"New faces in the Senate." *Time*, Nov. 17, 1986.

"John McCain." Vera Glaser. *Washingtonian*, Apr. 1986.

McCartney, Paul (1942–) Ex-Beatle McCartney was on the road for the first time in 13 years with a world tour that started in Norway in September 1989, reached Los Angeles in November 1989, and ended the following July in Chicago. In those 11 months, he played to an estimated 2.8 million people in 102 concerts, performing in Liverpool for the first time since 1979 and in Rio de Janeiro (his only South American stop) in April, before a crowd of 184,000, noted in the *Guinness Book of World Records* as the largest ever paid attendance at a public event. McCartney found the live performances so stimulating that he immediately began plans for another international tour starting in late 1991.

A one-hour "rockumentary" was filmed of McCartney and his band's preparations for the tour and their recording of their new album, *Flowers in the Dirt*. Songs from the new album were mixed with oldies from the 1960s in the tour concerts, which produced a live album, *Tripping the Live Fantastic*, released in November 1990. Included on it was a version of the Beatles' "Birthday," which McCartney released as a single on October 9, which would have been the 50th birthday of his late partner John Lennon. In September 1990, the performing-rights organization BMI noted that the Lennon-McCartney song "Yesterday" was tied with "Never My Love" as the most performed song in those 50 years; each tallied over 5 million performances, with "Yesterday" reaching that plateau first, in May 1990.

At the Grammys in February 1990, McCartney was honored with the Lifetime Achievement Award, with a special tribute that included Stevie Wonder's performance of the Beatles' song "We Can Work It Out." He was also honored by Britain's Performing Rights Society, who presented him with a gold miniature of the Hofner bass guitar long associated with him. In November 1989 McCartney suggested the possibility of a reunion of the three surviving Beatles, but George Harrison quickly squelched that idea.

In his concerts, McCartney spoke out on environmental issues, notably on the activities of Friends of the Earth, and while in Brazil made a special trip to the Amazonian rain forest to film a segment of *The Hard Rock Cafe Save the Planet Special* for CBS. McCartney's vegetarian views caused some brief consternation in cattle-raising Iowa, but the concerts went on without a significant hitch—and without meat being banned from stadium concession stands. McCartney also participated in the long-standing rock charity concert, Knebworth '90, shown in America on MTV; gave a concert for the Bay Area homeless in February; and made large contributions to organizations such as the New York City's Memorial Sloan-Kettering Cancer Center. He was also seen in quite a different guise, in a widely viewed commercial for the VISA credit card, which sponsored his U.S. concerts.

Liverpool native McCartney is a major figure in popular music; from 1960–70, with John Lennon, George Harrison, and Ringo Starr, he was a member of the Beatles, as rhythm guitarist and then bass guitarist. He and John Lennon wrote a great many of the Beatles' songs, and he was often the group's lead singer. In 1970, he went on his own, and in 1971 he formed Wings; for the next two decades he continued to compose, perform, and record for worldwide audiences. In 1984 he published *Give My Regards to Broad Street*. He married Linda Eastman in 1969; they have four children.

FURTHER READING

Strange Days: The Music of John, Paul, George & Ringo Twenty Years On. WALTER PODRAZIK. Popular Culture, 1991.
"Paul McCartney." TOM MULHERN. *Guitar Player*, July 1990.
Yesterday: The Biography of a Beatle. CHET FLIPPO. Doubleday, 1988.
"Paul McCartney." ANTHONY DECURTIS. *Rolling Stone*, Nov. 5, 1987.
It Was Twenty Years Ago Today. DEREK TAYLOR. Simon & Schuster, 1987.
"McCartney, Paul." *Current Biography*, Jan. 1986.
McCartney: The Definitive Biography. CHRIS SALEWICZ. St. Martin's, 1986.
The Beatles, 2nd ed. HUNTER DAVIES. McGraw-Hill, 1985.
Yesterday. . . . Came Suddenly: The Definitive History of the Beatles. BOB CEPICAN, and WALEED ALI. Morrow, 1984.
Paul McCartney: In His Own Words. PAUL GAMBACCINI. Putnam, 1983.
Paul McCartney. ALAN HAMILTON. Trafalgar Square, 1983.

McCrea, Joel (1905–90) U.S. movie actor McCrea was strongly identified with westerns, especially from the mid-1940's. Grandson of a California stagecoach driver and a forty-niner, McCrea entered films as an extra in the 1920s and, after his first significant role in *The Jazz Age* (1929), became an all-purpose leading man. His best-known films include *These Three* (1936), *Wells Fargo* (1937; his first Western), *Dead End* (1937), *Union Pacific* (1939), *Foreign Correspondent* (1940), *Sullivan's Travels* (1941), *The Palm Beach Story* (1942), and, after years of retirement as a millionaire rancher, *Ride the High Country* (1962). (d. Woodland Hill, California; October 20, 1990)

FURTHER READING

"Amiable comedy, western. . . ." JOSEPH MCBRIDE. *Variety*, Oct. 29, 1990.
Obituary. *The Times* (of London), Oct. 22, 1990.
Obituary. *New York Times*, Oct. 21, 1990.

MacDonald, Peter, Sr. (1928–) Navajo political leader MacDonald was the center of a series of dramatic events in the late 1980s and early 1990s. Long at odds with the federal

government over alleged financial irregularities, in 1987 MacDonald was engaged in a series of transactions involving the Big Boquillas Ranch, near Flagstaff, Arizona, and a series of events began that led to his downfall. In February 1989, Senate committee hearings uncovered substantial fraud in the sale of the ranch, with payments to MacDonald of $500,000 or more and a series of other, smaller frauds involving tribal monies. On February 17, the Navajo Tribal Council removed MacDonald from office, placing him on leave. He refused to leave office, and his faction occupied the tribal offices at Window Rock, Arizona, until removed on May 24 by Navajo police. On July 24, his supporters once again attempted to occupy tribal offices; a fight broke out, and two of his supporters were killed by tribal police gunfire.

In November 1989, MacDonald was indicted on 107 criminal counts and pleaded not guilty to all of them; his son, Peter MacDonald, Jr., was also indicted. In October 1990, both were convicted by a Navajo tribal court; he was sentenced to a jail term of almost six years and fined $11,000; his son was sentenced to one and a half years and fined $2,500. They both appealed their convictions, maintaining their innocence. They were convicted on many further criminal counts in a second trial; a third trial on more counts was to follow.

MacDonald told his side of the story in *The Last Warrior: Peter MacDonald and the Navajo Nation*, scheduled for 1991 publication.

MacDonald, born on Navajo tribal land in Arizona, served in World War II as an underage marine; after the war, he attended the University of Oklahoma and trained as an electrical engineer. He returned home in 1963, as director of the Office of Navajo Economic Opportunity. In 1970, he was elected chairman of the Navajo Tribal Council. He quickly became an enormously popular leader. However, by mid-1970s he was involved in the long series of charges and disputes that would embitter his relationship with the federal government; although a 1977 indictment for financial irregularities resulted in his acquittal, he was ultimately defeated.

FURTHER READING

"Chief offender." *Time*, Oct. 29, 1990.
"Showdown at. . . ." SANDY TOLAN. *New York Times Magazine*, Nov. 26, 1989.
"A Navajo horse trader. . . ." *U.S. News & World Report*, Feb. 20, 1989.
"Casting a long shadow. . . ." JAMES N. BAKER. *Newsweek*, Jan. 2, 1989.
"Free enterprise, Navajo style." ALYSSA A. LAPPEN. *Forbes*, July 11, 1988.
"Up by the bootstraps. . . ." JOSEPH P. SHAPIRO. *U.S. News & World Report*, Feb. 22, 1988.
"Chairman of the tribe." JAMES COOK. *Forbes*, May 18, 1987.

MacLaine, Shirley (Shirley MacLean Beaty, 1934–) MacLaine won wide praise for her Hollywood mother to Meryl Streep's actress daughter in the 1990 film *Postcards from the Edge*. Her role as a sexy small-town grandma in the film *Waiting for the Light* was somewhat less successful. But audiences raved about her return to live theater with a musical revue, *Out There Tonight*, especially astonishing because her "national comeback tour" was postponed four months when she tore a cartilage in her right knee, in what might have been a career-ending accident. She was honored in 1990 by the National Academy of Dance. Meanwhile, MacLaine was also seen in the strong ensemble film *Steel Magnolias* (1989), which arrived in the video rental stores in summer. On the writing side of her career, MacLaine learned in April 1990 that the Supreme Court would not review a lower court's ruling that her 1983 best-seller *Out on a Limb* did not infringe the copyright of a 1977 book, *Date with the Gods*, by Charles Silva.

Virginia-born MacLaine, the sister of actor Warren Beatty, became a Hollywood star in the 1960s with such light films as *The Apartment* (1960), *Two for the Seesaw* (1962), *Irma La Douce* (1963), and *Sweet Charity* (1969). Later in her career, she became a leading dramatic actress in such films as *The Turning Point* (1977); *Being There* (1979); *Terms of Endearment* (1983), for which she won a Best Actress Oscar; and *Madame Sousatzka* (1988). She also produced, co-directed, and appeared in the documentary film *The Other Half of the Sky: A China Memoir* (1975), and has written several very popular books, notably on spiritual questions and reincarnation, including *Many Happy Returns* (1984), *Dancing in the Light* (1985), and *Don't Fall off the Mountain* (1987). She was previously married and has one child.

FURTHER READING

"Shirley MacLaine lives." PAT DOWELL. *Washingtonian*, Oct. 1988.
Shirley MacLaine and the New Age Movement. JAMES W. SIRE. Inter-Varsity, 1988.
"Good heavens, Shirley!" KIM GARFIELD. *Ladies Home Journal*, Oct. 1987.
"Isness is. . . ." MARTIN GARDNER. *New York Review of Books*, Apr. 9, 1987.
"Star in the New Age." MICHAEL D. TRUE. *Christianity Today*, May 16, 1986.
Shirley MacLaine. MICHAEL FREEDLAND. Salem House, 1986.
Shirley Maclaine. ROY PICKARD. Hippocrene, 1985.
The Films of Shirley Maclaine. CHRISTOPHER DENIS. Carol, 1982.

MacLennan, Hugh (1907–90) In modern Canadian literature, MacLennan's early novels occupy a place of honor, for they are among the first to celebrate being Canadian, looking at the world through Canadian eyes, bringing forward the idea of Canadian identity. These were *Barometer Rising* (1941), set in his native Nova Scotia, and *Two Solitudes* (1945), which explored often-bitter French-English relationships; these two books established him as a major novelist. Among his other novels are *The Precipice*

(1948), *Each Man's Son* (1951), and *The Watch that Ends the Night* (1959). His other work includes *The Rivers of Canada* (1962), *The Colour of Canada* (1967), and *The Scotchman Returns and Other Essays* (1960). (d. Montreal; November 7, 1990)

FURTHER READING

Obituary. *The Times* (of London), Nov. 26, 1990.
"A passion for Canada. . . ." PETER C. NEWMAN. *Maclean's*, Nov. 19, 1990.
Obituary. *New York Times,* Nov. 10, 1990.
Hugh MacLennan. T. D. MACLULICH. G. K. Hall, 1983.
Hugh MacLennan: A Writer's Life. ELSPETH CAMERON. University of Toronto Press, 1981.
Annotated Bibliography of Canada's Major Authors, Vol. I. . . . ROBERT LECKER and JACK DAVID, eds. G. K. Hall, 1980.

Madonna (Madonna Louise Ciccone, 1958–) Madonna made big news as both singer and actress in 1990. Back to being blonde, she played the sexy Breathless Mahoney in one of the most widely publicized movies of the year, Warren Beatty's *Dick Tracy*. When the film opened in June, Madonna took to the road in the United States, Canada, Japan, and Europe with her "Blond Ambition" concert tour, an elaborately designed production that wound up two months later in Nice, France. The final concert, televised on tape delay, won HBO one of its largest audiences ever. Madonna's concert was also released on videodisc.

Late in 1990 she also released a new album of her greatest hits, *The Immaculate Collection,* and a Tracy tie-in album, *I'm Breathless*, both of which spawned best-selling singles. As she pushed sexual titillation to the edge in her videos, Madonna found herself at the center of controversy. Her video of "Justify My Love" was judged so steamy that MTV refused to air it; naturally the single became an immediate best-seller. In 1989, Pepsi had cancelled a sponsorship deal with her over some scenes in her "Like a Prayer" video.

Michigan-born Madonna is one of the most highly visible entertainers and celebrities of the 1980s and early 1990s, in concert and with such albums as *Madonna* (1983), *Like a Virgin* (1983), *True Blue* (1986), *You Can Dance* (1987), and *Like a Prayer* (1989). She is also a competent actress, as demonstrated in such films as *Desperately Seeking Susan* (1985) and *Who's That Girl?* (1987) and her Broadway stage debut in *Speed-the-Plow* (1988). She married actor Sean Penn in 1985; they filed for divorce in 1989. She attended the University of Michigan from 1976–78.

FURTHER READING

"Madonna Flexes. . . ." RICHARD PRICE. *Ladies Home Journal*, Nov. 1990.
"A brain for. . . ." MATTHEW SCHIFRIN and PETER NEWCOMB. *Forbes*, Oct. 1, 1990.
"Unlike a virgin. . . ." LUC SANTE. *New Republic*, Aug. 20, 1990.
"Spanking new Madonna. . . ." BRIAN D. JOHNSON. *Maclean's*, June 18, 1990.
"Madonna." GLENN O'BRIEN. *Interview*, June 1990.
"TV's in-vogue Video Vamp." ANNE AYERS. *TV Guide*, May 19, 1990.
"Madonna. . . . " DAVID ANSEN. *Cosmopolitan*, May 1990.
"Confession of. . . ." KOTO BOLOFO and BECKY JOHNSTON. *Interview*, May 1989.
"Madonna." BILL ZEHME. *Rolling Stone*, March 23, 1989.
Icons: Intimate Portraits. DENISE WORRELL. Atlantic Monthly, 1989.
"Madonna. . . ." WILL SLATTERY. *McCall's*, Sept. 1988.
Madonna, Spirit & Flesh. SHARON STARBOOKS. NAL-Dutton, 1985.
Madonna: Lucky Star. MICHAEL MCKENZIE. Contemporary, 1985.
Madonna. PHILIP KAMIN. H. Leonard, 1985.
Madonna. GORDON MATTHEWS. Messner, 1985.

Major, John (1943–) Major succeeded Margaret Thatcher as prime minister on November 27, 1990, after Thatcher had failed to withstand a challenge to her leadership by former cabinet minister Michael Heseltine and resigned. In the leadership struggle that followed, front-runner Heseltine and foreign secretary Douglas Hurd both fell short of the necessary Conservative parliamentary votes; Major, who was favored by Thatcher, came within two votes of winning on a first ballot, and Heseltine and Hurd then both withdrew in his favor.

Major, a little-known and only recently important member of Thatcher's cabinet, was at the age of 47 also the youngest British prime minister of the 20th century. Immediately after his election, he moved to show continuity with the Thatcher government and its main policies, renaming Hurd foreign secretary and bringing Heseltine into the cabinet. At the same time, he signaled a somewhat more flexible approach to some of the most controversial elements of the Thatcher program, including most notably the very unpopular poll tax and several health care, welfare, and educational programs.

London-born Major's first career was with Standard Chartered Bank (1965–79). He joined the Conservative Party in 1960, was a Lambeth borough councillor from 1968–71, and became a member of Parliament in 1979 after two unsuccessful tries. His rise in the Thatcher government was very rapid; by 1985, he was a junior minister at the department of health, and in 1986 he was social security minister. He became treasury chief secretary in 1987, foreign secretary in July 1989, and chancellor of the exchequer in October 1989. He married Norma Johnson in 1970; they have two children.

FURTHER READING

"A quiet dropout. . . ." Bill Hewitt. *People*, Dec. 10, 1990.
"Thatcher's favorite." Andrew Bilski. *Maclean's*, Dec. 3, 1990.
"John Major." *Economist*, Nov. 24, 1990.
"Major, John." *Current Biography*, Oct. 1990.

Malkovich, John (1953–) Malkovich took his highly praised stage performance in Lanford Wilson's *Burn This* from New York to London late in 1990, making his British stage debut. Like their American counterparts, British critics lauded Malkovich's portrayal of Pale, smoldering brother of a just-deceased gay dancer, with one paper citing his "wall-blasting intensity."

Also late in 1990, Malkovich opened in a new Bernardo Bertolucci film, *The Sheltering Sky*, based on a Paul Bowles novel. The post–World War II romance was filmed in the Sahara, with a cast including Debra Winger and Campbell Scott (son of George C. Scott and Colleen Dewhurst). Earlier in the year, Malkovich had been in London to shoot another film, *The Object of Beauty*, opposite Andie MacDowell.

Before becoming a New York stage actor, Illinois-born Malkovich was a leading member of Chicago's Steppenwolf theater company beginning in 1976. He won an Obie off-Broadway for his role in *True West* (1982), and appeared as Biff to Dustin Hoffman's Willy Loman in the 1984 Broadway revival of *Death of a Salesman*. He began his film career that year, in *Places in the Heart*, and went on to strong dramatic roles in such films as *The Killing Fields* (1984), *Eleni* (1985), *The Glass Menagerie* (1987), *Empire of the Sun* (1987), and *Dangerous Liaisons* (1988). He has also appeared and directed in regional theater, and appeared on television. He is married to actress Glen Headly.

FURTHER READING

"Life, art and Malkovich." Joe Morgenstern. *Playboy*, May 1990.

"Wild card." BECKY JOHNSTON and BRIGITTE LACOMBE. *Interview*, Mar. 1989.
"Malkovich, John." *Current Biography*, May 1988.
"Acting's burning talent." *Harper's Bazaar*, Nov. 1987.
"Mind over Malkovich." MARGY ROCHLIN. *Interview*, Oct. 1987.
"True mid west." DON SHEWEY. *American Film*, Oct. 1985.
"The Malkovich. . . ." DENA KLEIMAN. *New York Times Magazine*, Sept. 15, 1985.

Malle, Louis (1932–) French director Louis Malle turned to his own and his country's past again in 1990. This time he turned not to occupied France in World War II, the setting for his classic *Au Revoir Les Enfants* (1987), but to the spring of 1968, a time of student revolt and workers' strikes that crippled the land. These events form only a relatively distant backdrop, however, as *May Fools* focuses on family members returning to their wine-country home on the death of the matriarch. Focusing less on human iniquity than on human foibles, *May Fools* starred Michel Piccoli as Milou, head of the family and the vineyard; Miou-Miou, as Camille, his money-minded bourgeois daughter; Michel Duchaussoy as Georges, his younger brother; Harriet Walter as Georges' English wife, an actress; and Dominique Blanc as Claire, Milou's orphaned granddaughter. Admirers of Malle were thankful to have a new film from the highly regarded director, although *May Fools* was seen as a lesser work than his earlier classics.

Malle entered the film world as assistant to Jacques Cousteau; they co-directed and Malle shot part of *The Silent World* (1956), the classic documentary of life in the sea. His first fiction film was *Frantic* (1958), followed by such films as *The Lovers* (1958), *Zazie in the Underground* (1960), *The Fire Within* (1963), *The Thief of Paris* (1967), *Lacombe, Lucien* (1973), *Pretty Baby* (1978), *Atlantic City* (1980), *My Dinner with Andre* (1981), and the classic *Au Revoir Les Enfants* (1987), based on an incident in his childhood, in which a Jewish boy hidden in his boarding school was later captured and killed by the Nazis. Malle attended the Sorbonne and the Cinematography Institute. He has been married twice, last in 1980 to actress Candice Bergen, and has three children.

FURTHER READING

"My dejeuner with Louis. . . ." KATHY BISHOP. *American Film*, July 1990.
"Louis Malle." CANDICE BERGEN. *Interview*, June 1990.
"Louis Malle." *American Film*, Apr. 1989.
"Malle adroit. . . ." Donald Chase. *Horizon*, Jan.–Feb. 1988.
"Louis Malle's. . . ." DANIELE HEYMANN. *World Press Review*, Jan. 1988.
"Louis Malle. . . ." JOHN CULHANE. *New York Times Magazine*, Apr. 7, 1985.

Mandela, Nelson (Nelson Rolihiahia Mandela, 1918–) Mandela became a worldwide symbol of the long fight against South African racism while under sentence of life imprisonment for sabotage. On February 11, 1990, his release by prime minister Frederik Willem De Klerk's new South African government ushered in a new period in South African history.

Mandela then led the African National Congress (ANC) and its allies in a long, complex series of negotiations with the De Klerk government. Ultimately, these talks brought the ANC-government agreements of August 7, 1990, and a full cease-fire after 30 years of guerrilla warfare, in return for several important government concessions, including the freeing of a large number of political prisoners, the free return of many exiles, and changes in several harsh and repressive laws.

Mandela and De Klerk then began negotiations toward bringing permanent peace and ending the apartheid system. Mandela also spent much of 1990 touring the world on behalf of the South African freedom movement, finding a particularly warm reception during his June 20–28 U.S. visit. On the negative side, he and the ANC faced an escalating civil war with the largely Zulu Inkatha movement, led by Gatsha Buthelezi. In January 1991, Mandela and Buthelezi met and announced an agreement to stop the fighting, although many had reservations as to how long their truce would last.

Mandela was a leading advocate of nonviolence from 1944–60, but both he and the previously nonviolent ANC began to use violence after the Sharpeville Massacre of 1960. He was imprisoned in 1962 and held for 28 years, emerging in 1990 as leader of the South African freedom movement. Among his autobiographical writings are *No Easy Walk to Freedom* (1986) and *Nelson Mandela: The Struggle Is My Life* (rev. ed., 1986). He attended the University College of Fort Hare and the University of the Witwatersrand, and practiced law in Johannesburg in the early 1950s. He married Winnie Mandela, his second wife, in 1958.

FURTHER READING

Nelson Mandela: "No Easy Walk to Freedom." BARRY DENENBERG. Scholastic, 1991.
Nelson Mandela. BRIAN FEINBERG. Chelsea House, 1991.
Nelson Mandela. RICHARD TAMES. Watts, 1991.
"Mandela in America." JOSHUA MURAVCHIK. *Commentary*, Oct. 1990.
"An interview with. . . ." SCOTT MACLEOD. *Time*, June 25, 1990.
"Nelson Mandela. . . ." D. MICHAEL CHEERS. *Ebony*, May 1990.
"Nelson Mandela, Freed." LINDA BRIDGES. *National Review*, Apr. 30, 1990.
"No easy walk. . . ." DAVID OLIVER RELIN. *Scholastic Update*, Mar. 23, 1990.
"Nelson Mandela." BILL HEWITT. *People*, Feb. 26, 1990.
"The leader no one knows. . . ." TOM MATHEWS. *Newsweek*, Feb. 19, 1990.
"A symbol of freedom." RAE CORELLI. *Maclean's*, Feb. 12, 1990.
"Who Is Nelson Mandela?" *U.S. News & World Report*, Jan. 22, 1990.
Nelson Mandela: A Voice Set Free. REBECCA STEFFOF. Fawcett, 1990.
Mandela: Echoes of Era. ALF KUMALO and MPHAHLELE ES'KIA. Viking Penguin, 1990.
The Struggle: A History of the African National Congress. HEIDI HOLLAND. Braziller, 1990.
Higher Than Hope: The Authorized Biography of Nelson Mandela. FATIMA MEER. HarperCollins, 1989.
Nelson Mandela: South Africa's Silent Voice of Protest. J. HARGROVE. Childrens, 1989.

Mandela, Winnie (Winnie Nomzano, 1934–) As the wife of imprisoned South African leader Nelson Mandela and as a leader in her own right, Winnie Mandela long held a unique place in the South African freedom movement. But during the late 1980s she encountered a good deal of criticism from other leaders of that movement, which peaked in early 1989, when her bodyguards were charged with the beating and murder of a young boy in Soweto and she was said to have been involved in the initial beating. In February 1989, she was publicly censured by the leadership of the African National Congress (ANC) and other leaders. In May 1990 two of her bodyguards were convicted of murder; she was not charged, but the judge in the case accused her of involvement. In September 1990, she was formally charged with kidnapping and assault and trial was set for February 1991.

All this happened while major events were occurring in South Africa: On February 11, 1990, 28 years after his imprisonment, Nelson Mandela was freed and immediately assumed leadership of the South African freedom movement, beginning a long set of negotiations aimed at changing the future of his country. He defended his wife throughout the balance of the year, claiming that the charges and eventual prosecution aimed at her were in reality an attempt to embarrass him and the freedom movement. During the balance of 1990, Winnie Mandela spent much of her time touring the world with her husband in support of the ANC.

Winnie Mandela was a social worker before becoming active in the ANC in 1956. She married Nelson Mandela in 1958; the couple then joined their work in the South African freedom movement. She, too, became a worldwide symbol of resistance to racism as she pressed for his release during his 28 years in prison and at the same time continued her antiapartheid work. She was forced into silence for long periods by the South African government and internally exiled in 1977, but from 1985 she was able to defy the government, due to growing worldwide condemnation of apartheid and of the imprisonment of Nelson Mandela. Among her writings is *A Part of My Soul Went with Him* (1985).

FURTHER READING

"The ordeal and. . . ." D. MICHAEL CHEERS and JESSE JACKSON. *Ebony*, May 1990.
"Decline and fall. . . ." BRUCE W. NELAN. *Time*, Feb. 27, 1989.
"'Mother of the Nation.'" ANDREW BILSKI. *Maclean's*, Feb. 12, 1990.
"Winnie the shrew. . . ." STEVEN MUFSON. *New Republic*, Mar. 13, 1989.
Nelson and Winnie Mandela. JOHN VAIL. Chelsea House, 1989.
Winnie Mandela: Life of Struggle. JAMES HASKINS. Putnam, 1988.
"Winnie Mandela." AMINA FRENSE. *Ms*, Jan. 1987.
Nelson and Winnie Mandela. DOROTHY HOOBLER and THOMAS HOOBLER. Watts, 1987.
"Mandela, (Nomzamo) Winnie." *Current Biography*, Jan. 1986.
Winnie Mandela. NANCY HARRISON, Braziller, 1986.
Winnie Mandela: The Soul of South Africa. MILTON MELTZER. Viking Child, 1986.

Mangano, Silvana (1930–89) The Italian movie actress burst on the international scene as the sensuous fieldworker in *Bitter Rice* (1949). Born in Rome of an Italian father and English mother, Mangano studied dancing and came to acting by way of modeling and beauty contests. Spurning Hollywood offers, she married *Bitter Rice*'s producer, Dino De Laurentiis, in 1949 and remained in Italy, working in films such as *Gold of Naples* (1954), *Ulysses* (1954), *Barabbas* (1962), *Oedipus Rex* (1967), *Death in Venice* (1971), and *Conversation Piece* (1975), later often in aristocratic character roles. (d. Madrid, Spain; December 16, 1990)

FURTHER READING

Obituary. *Variety*, Dec. 20, 1989.
Obituary. *The Times* (of London), Dec. 18, 1990.
Obituary. *New York Times*, Dec. 17, 1990.
"Splitsville." *People*, Sept. 5, 1988.

Mannes, Marya (1904–90) New York City–born Mannes was a journalist and author, probably best remembered for her social criticism during her years as a staff writer for the magazine *The Reporter* (1952–63). She also wrote for a wide range of other magazines, including the *New Yorker* and *The New York Times*. Her best-known books were *More in Anger* (1958), a collection of essays, and *Out of My Time* (1971), her autobiography. She was the daughter of David Mannes and Clara Damrosch, founders of the Mannes Music School. (d. San Francisco; September 13, 1990)

FURTHER READING

Obituary. *New York Times,* Sept. 15, 1990.
The Best of Marya Mannes. Robert Mottley, ed. Eagle, 1986.

Maradona, Diego (Diego Armando Maradona, 1961–) The Argentinian soccer star is the best-known, highest paid, and by far most controversial player in the world. Since his extraordinary performance in leading the Argentine national team to victory in the 1986 World Cup contest in Mexico City, he is probably also the world's leading player. He has played for Naples since 1984, on a multiyear contract, and led the club to Italian league titles in 1987 and 1990 and to a European Soccer Cup win in 1989. Playing for Argentina in the Rome World Cup contest in July 1990, he led his team to beat the Italian national team

on the way to a 1–0 loss to West Germany in the finals; Maradona was quoted as blaming the loss on Mafia intervention. Maradona made news of a different sort in November 1989 in Buenos Aires, his hometown, when he married his longtime companion, Claudia Villafanes, in a strikingly lavish ceremony attended by 1,200 guests, including Argentine President Carlos Menem and a planeload of Maradona's Naples teammates.

Maradona turned professional in 1976, at the age of 15, with the Buenos Aires Argentinos Juniors team, and a year later joined the national team. He did not make the 1978 World Cup national team, although he did play in 1982, when his team did not make the finals. His contract was sold to Barcelona in 1982 and to Naples in 1984. The Maradonas have two children.

FURTHER READING

"Maradona, Diego." *Current Biography*, Nov. 1990.
"The biggest little athlete alive. . . ." RON ARIAS. *People*, June 18, 1990.
"Soccer's little. . . ." GEORGE VECSEY. *New York Times Magazine*, May 27, 1990.
"Prima Dona." RICK TELANDER. *Sports Illustrated*, May 14, 1990.

Marble, Alice (1913–90) By far the leading women's tennis player of her time, Marble was four-time U.S. singles champion (1936, 1938, 1939, and 1940), all after a comeback from a severe case of tuberculosis. She was also the player who transformed the game of women's tennis by introducing the serve-and-volley style, until then played only in the men's game and since then the normal way to play tennis for both sexes. Marble, who turned professional in 1940, was also the most popular tennis star of her day and one of the first to experience the great celebrity that would come to women tennis stars later in the century. (d. Palm Springs, California; December 13, 1990)

FURTHER READING

Obituary. *New York Times*, Dec. 15, 1990.

Marcos, Imelda Romualdez (1930–) The highly publicized trial of Imelda Marcos, widow of former Philippines dictator Ferdinand Marcos, opened in New York on March 20, 1990. She was charged with illegal financial dealings in connection with her ownership of several U.S. real estate properties, allegedly bought with money stolen from the Philippine Republic. Saudi Arabian billionaire Adnan Khashoggi was charged with helping her to conceal her ownership of the properties. On July 2, after a long trial and five days of deliberation, the jury acquitted Marcos and Khashoggi on all counts.

As the wife of Ferdinand Marcos, Imelda Marcos drew a great deal of media attention, which especially focused on her exceedingly rich life style. She fled her country with Marcos after he was deposed in 1986.

FURTHER READING

"Shopping a plea. . . ." JOSEPH TREEN. *New Republic*, May 28, 1990.
Imelda: Steel Butterfly of the Philippines. KATHERINE ELLISON. McGraw-Hill, 1989.
"Imelda and. . . ." KEN KELLEY and PHIL BRONSTEIN. *Playboy*, Aug. 1987.
Imelda Marcos: The Rise & Fall of One of the World's Most Powerful Women. CARMEN N. PEDROSA. St. Martin's, 1987.
Inside the Palace: The Rise & Fall of Ferdinand & Imelda Marcos. BETH D. ROMULO. Putnam, 1987.
The Marcos Dynasty: The Incredible Inside Story Behind the Rise of Imelda and Ferdinand Marcos. . . . STERLING SEAGRAVE. Harper, 1987.

Marsalis, Wynton (1961–) Jazz musician Marsalis issued a critically praised third album in his *Standard Time* series, called *The Resolution of Romance*, playing trumpet to his father's piano. He also delighted audiences with numerous live performances, most notably a rendition of "The Battle Hymn of the Republic" with Pearl Bailey at New York's summer jazz festival; a solo re-creation of Satchmo's "Dear Old Southland" in a Los Angeles tribute to Louis Armstrong; and appearances at the Mt. Fuji Jazz Festival.

New Orleans–born Marsalis is the son of pianist and teacher Ellis Marsalis, younger brother of saxophonist Branford Marsalis, and older brother of trombonist Delfeayo Marsalis. After briefly playing with Art Blakey's Jazz Messengers, Wynton Marsalis emerged as one of the leading trumpet soloists of his time, functioning equally well in the classics and in jazz, although he focused on jazz in the late 1980s and early 1990s. A few of his many notable albums were *Fathers and Sons* (1982), *Wynton Marsalis* (1982), *Trumpet Concertos* (1983), *Black Codes from the Underground* (1985), and *Majesty of the Blues* (1989). He was a student at the Juilliard School of Music from 1979–81.

FURTHER READING

"Horns of plenty. . . ." Thomas Sancton. *Time*, Oct. 22, 1990.

"Wynton. . . ." Dave Helland. *Down Beat*, Sept. 1990.

Outcats: Jazz Composers, Instrumentalists, and Singers. Francis Davis. Oxford University Press, 1990.

"Wynton and Branford Marsalis. . . ." A. James Liska. *Down Beat*, Sept. 1989.

"Wynton Marsalis: 1987." Stanley Crouch. *Down Beat*, Nov. 1987.

"Wynton Marsalis." Pamela Johnson. *Essence*, Oct. 1987.

"Marsalis, Wynton." *Current Biography*, Oct. 1984.

Marshall, Thurgood (1908–) Justice Marshall is an historic figure, the most celebrated civil rights lawyer of his time and the first Black member of the U.S. Supreme Court. During the 1989–90 Court term, he continued to be a leading Court liberal, as in *U.S.* v. *Eichman*, striking down the federal law against flag burning; in *Rutan* v. *Republican Party of Illinois*, cutting the power of politicians in power to name party sympathizers to most low-level government jobs; and in *Metro Broadcasting* v. *FCC*, supporting an affirmative action program in the broadcasting industry.

He was on the losing side in the larger number of cases, however, as in the landmark *Cruzan* v. *Missouri* "right to die" case, which denied Nancy Cruzan's family the right to remove her from her life-support system; in a group of abortion-related cases, upholding the right of states to pass laws requiring notification of parents or a court hearing before an abortion is performed; and in a series of cases involving law

enforcement and defendant's rights. He wrote the majority opinion in *Chauffeurs* v. *Terry*, giving union members suing their union the right to a jury trial.

As top lawyer for the National Association for the Advancement of Colored People (NAACP) from 1940 to 1962, Baltimore-born Marshall was at the center of the long struggle for civil rights. His most important case was *Brown* v. *Board of Education of Topeka, Kansas* (1954), which destroyed the basis of school segregation and paved the way for the civil rights revolution that soon came. President John F. Kennedy appointed him to the second circuit court of appeals in 1962. Three years later, in 1965, President Lyndon B. Johnson appointed him U.S. Solicitor-General and then in 1967 to the Supreme Court, where he became a leading liberal. He was formerly married to Vivian Burey; married Cecilia Suyat in 1955 and has two children. He attended Lincoln University and Howard University Law School.

FURTHER READING

"Ebony interview with. . . ." *Ebony*, Nov. 1990.
"The Thurgood Marshall. . . ." JUAN WILLIAMS. *Ebony*, May 1990.
Thurgood Marshall: The Fight for Equal Justice. DEBRA HESS. Silver Burdett, 1990.
Thurgood Marshall. LISA ALDRED. Chelsea House, 1990.
Eight Men and a Lady. HERMAN SCHWARTZ, ANDREA NEAL, and DAVID SAVAGE. National Press, 1990.
"Marshall, Thurgood." *Current Biography*, Sept. 1989.
"What they say it is. . . ." *Time*, July 6, 1987.
"Nine who decide. . . ." ELIZABETH WARD. *Scholastic Update*, Sept. 8, 1986.
Marshall: Hero for Our Times. LEONARD MOSLEY. Hearst, 1982.

Martin, Billy (1928–89) A colorful and highly regarded second baseman for the New York Yankees in the 1950s who played on five Yankee World Series–winning teams, Martin was also a fighter, on and off the field. Two of his most highly publicized fights were a 1957 barroom brawl at New York's Copacabana nightclub and a 1960 fight in which he broke pitcher Jim Brewer's jaw. Although he was a very successful manager later in his career, it was his brawling that brought him the most public attention, including the broken arm he received in a 1988 fight with Yankee pitcher Ed Whitson. His stormy relationship with Yankee owner George Steinbrenner also received much public attention: between 1975 and 1988, Martin was hired and fired five times as Yankee manager. Martin was named American League manager of the year in 1974, and managed the 1976 pennant-winning Yankee team. With Peter Golenbock, he wrote the autobiographical *Number One* (1980). (d. Binghamton, New York; December 25, 1989)

FURTHER READING

Obituary. *Current Biography*, Feb. 1990.
"A violent death. . . ." BARBARA WICKENS. *Maclean's*, Jan. 8, 1990.
"Pickup crash kills. . . ." *Sporting News*, Jan. 8, 1990.
"A great writer. . . ." *People*, Jan. 8, 1990.
"A pair of battlers." CRAIG NEFF. *Sports Illustrated*, Jan. 8, 1990.
"Billy's last inning." *U.S. News & World Report*, Jan. 8, 1990.
Obituary. *New York Times*, Dec. 26, 1990.
Damn Yankee: The Billy Martin Story. *Maury Allen*. Times, 1980.
Billy Martin. GENE SCHOOR. Doubleday, 1980.

Martin, Kiel (1944–90) Actor Martin was best known by far for his long-running role as detective John (J.D.) Larue in television's "Hill Street Blues" (1981–87), partnered with Taurean Blacque as detective Neal Washington. He went on to a starring role in the television series "Second Chance" (1987–88). Before his "Hill Street Blues" role, he had appeared as a cast regular in the daytime soap opera "The Edge of Night". He had also appeared in supporting roles in several films, and as a comedian in cabaret. (d. Rancho Mirage, California; December 28, 1990)

FURTHER READING

Obituary. *New York Times*, Jan. 2, 1991.

Martin, Mary (Mary Virginia Martin, 1913–90) The vivacious singer and dancer was a leading figure in the American musical theater. A self-taught dancer, Texas-born Martin ran a dancing school, bore a son—actor

Larry Hagman—and tried Hollywood, radio, and nightclubs before her big break on Broadway singing "My Heart Belongs to Daddy" in *Leave It to Me* (1938). Several undistinguished Hollywood years followed before a return to the theater in 1943, including a tour in *Annie Get Your Gun*. Her greatest Broadway successes were in *South Pacific* (1949) as Nellie Forbush; *Peter Pan* (1954); *The Sound of Music* (1959) as Maria von Trapp; and *I Do, I Do* (1966) She later revived these roles, including a notable Peter Pan on television, although others were given the film roles. Her autobiography is *My Heart Belongs* (rev. ed., 1984). (d. Rancho Mirage, California; November 3, 1990)

FURTHER READING

"After giving Broadway. . . ." *People*, Nov. 19, 1990.
Obituary. *Variety*, Nov. 12, 1990.
Obituary. *The Times* (of London), Nov. 16, 1990.
Obituary. *New York Times,* Nov. 15, 1990.
"The unsinkable Mary Martin." FRED ROBBINS. *50 Plus*, Jan. 1988.
"My son, Larry Hagman." ELLIOTT SIRKIN. *Good Housekeeping*, July 1987.

Martin, Steve (1945–) In October 1990, writer-director-actor Martin, along with his wife, actress Victoria Tennant, were the first entertainers brought to Saudi Arabia by the USO to visit GIs stationed there during the Persian Gulf Crisis. No shows were presented because of a Saudi Arabian ban on public entertainment; all they could do, Martin said, was "grip and grin. We grip your hand and grin at you."

In late 1989, Martin appeared in an enormously successful film, Ron Howard's *Parenthood*, a comic view of modern family life with a large cast that included Mary Steenburgen. In early 1990, he opened in Herbert Ross's film *My Blue Heaven*, starring as gangster Vinnie Antonelli, an important witness-in-hiding who gets into trouble with his FBI chaperon (Rick Moranis). Poorly reviewed, the movie also did not fare well at the box office. As 1990 ended, Martin starred opposite Tennant in a new comedy, *L.A. Story*, which he also wrote; the film, about a weatherman who wants to roller-skate through the world's greatest museums, was released in 1991.

Martin also had a notable success on stage in 1989, when he and Robin Williams played in a well-received New York revival of *Waiting for Godot*. Martin the writer arranged to donate original scripts of his work to the University of Texas library. Martin and Chevy Chase also took time out to help singer Paul Simon make a video to accompany his new album, *Rhythm of the Saints*; the pair's job was holding down a giant Casper the Friendly Ghost balloon.

Texas-born Martin was a television comedy writer and comedian in cabaret before emerging as a leading comedian on television, on records, and and in films in the late 1970s, most notably as a prominent guest and sometimes host on "Saturday Night Live" and with his Grammy-winning albums *Let's Get Small* (1977) and *A Wild and Crazy Guy* (1978). He became a leading comedy film star with *The Jerk* (1979) and went on to such films as *Pennies from Heaven* (1981), *Dead Men Don't Wear Plaid* (1982), *The Man with Two Brains* (1983), *The Lonely Guy* (1984), *All of Me* (1984), *Three Amigos* (1986), *Little Shop of Horrors* (1986), *Planes, Trains and Automobiles* (1987), *Roxanne* (1987; he also wrote and produced), and *Dirty Rotten Scoundrels* (1988). Martin attended the University of California. He married Tennant in 1986.

FURTHER READING

"The king of. . . ." ELVIS MITCHELL. *GQ—Gentlemen's Quarterly*, July 1990.
"Steve Martin. . . ." CORK MILLNER. *Saturday Evening Post*, Nov.–Dec. 1989.
Icons: Intimate Portraits. DENISE WORRELL. Atlantic Monthly, 1989.
"I'm just a White guy. . . . " ELVIS MITCHELL. *American Film*, Nov. 1988.
"The private eye of. . . .." ROBERT HUGHES. *House & Garden*, April 1988.
"Sensational Steve. . . ." RICHARD CORLISS. *Time*, Aug. 24, 1987.
Steve Martin—A Wild & Crazy Guy: An Unauthorized Biography—Well Excuuuse Us! MARSHA DALY. NAL-Dutton, 1980.
Steve Martin: The Unauthorized Biography. GREG LENBURG, RANDY SKREVEDT, and JEFF LENBURG. St. Martin's, 1980.

Mason, Jackie (Yacov Moshe Maza, 1930–) Stand-up comedian Mason, whose act focuses to a considerable extent on his Jewishness, ran into quite a different kind of ethnic question in 1989. At an August 31, 1989,

luncheon with *Newsweek* magazine reporters, with Mason-supported New York mayoral candidate Rudolf Giuliani present, Mason called mayoral candidate David Dinkins a "schvartzer," a Yiddish word always used in a racially insulting way to denote a Black person. In September, the *Village Voice* ran an article accusing Mason of several other racial insults, triggering a major reaction. Mason denied having made the remarks but was quickly asked to leave the Giuliani campaign; Mason then apologized for his insensitivity. The completely documented *Newsweek* remark surfaced later.

In a possibly related incident, although it was denied by ABC, in early November 1989 the network canceled the new and rather popular series "Chicken Soup", starring Mason and Lynn Redgrave, after only seven episodes. Mason continued to play club dates. In October 1990, Mason opened a new one-man show on Broadway: *Jackie Mason: Brand New*. He also published *How to Talk Jewish* (1991), written with Ira Berkow.

Mason, the child of a rabbinical family, became an ordained rabbi at 24, but in the mid-1950s he moved into show business, playing Catskill resorts and soon changing his stage name to Jackie Mason. The comic became a popular guest on television and in cabaret in the early 1960s, but his career went steeply downhill from the mid-1960s through the mid-1980s, although he continued to appear in cabaret and on television. He scored a comeback in his one-man Broadway show *The World According to Me!* (1986–87) and in 1987 released a book with the same title; together with Ken Gross, he wrote of his resurrection in *Jackie, Oy!: The Birth and Rebirth of Jackie Mason* (1988). He has also appeared in several films.

FURTHER READING

"Enough with the. . . ." MARK JACOBSON. *Esquire*, Sept. 1990.
"Jackie Mason's racial remarks. . . ." *Jet*, Oct. 16, 1989.
"The world according to Mason." HAP ERSTEIN. *Insight*, July 10, 1989.
"The Yiddish. . . ." JOHN MCCOLLISTER. *Saturday Evening Post*, Mar. 1989.
"The casualness of it." WHITNEY BALLIETT. *New Yorker*, Sept. 19, 1988.
"Rabbi's son makes good. . . ." STANLEY KANFER. *Time*, Nov. 23, 1987.
"Mason, Jackie." *Current Biography*, July 1987.
Jackie Mason's America. JACKIE MASON. Carol, 1983.

Mastroianni, Marcello (1923–) Italian actor Mastroianni continued his career as a major international star in 1990, appearing in a wide variety of roles. At the 1990 Cannes Film Festival, he was lauded for his work in Giuseppe Tornatore's *Everything's Fine*, playing a retired widower who tours Italy visiting his grown children and old friends, some of whom barely remember him. He also played an aging man in Ettore Scola's *What Time Is It?*, for which he and co-star Massimo Troisi shared the best actor award at the 1989 Venice Film Festival.

By contrast, in mid-1990 Mastroianni was in Paris playing a dashing Italian architect opposite Julie Andrews' prim-and-proper Englishwoman in the romantic comedy *Tchin Tchin*: the two learn that their spouses are having an affair. Later, he was in Greece shooting a new film called *The Suspended of the Stork*, directed by Theodore Angelopoulos. The filmmakers ran afoul of the local Greek Orthodox bishop, who charged that the film contained erotic scenes and unpatriotically proposed abolition of national borders. Local clerics threatened to burn the film set and excommunicate any local inhabitants who helped make the film, but the national government openly supported the film. Mastroianni had appeared in an earlier Angelopoulos film, *The Beekeeper* (1988), another "road movie" shown at the 1990 American Film Institute International Film Festival (AFIFEST) in Los Angeles.

Mastroianni began his film career in 1947 and emerged to world prominence in the late 1950s in such films as *White Nights* (1957), *La Dolce Vita* (1960), *The Night* (1961), *Divorce Italian Style* (1961), *8½* (1963), *Yesterday, Today, and Tomorrow* (1963), and *Marriage Italian Style* (1964). His later work includes such films as *Down the Ancient Stairs* (1974), *City of Women* (1980), *La Nuit de Varennes* (1983), *Dark Eyes* (1987), and *Splendor* (1989). Mastroianni attended the University of Rome. He was formerly married and has one child.

FURTHER READING

"Marcello Mastroianni." BRAD DARRACH. *People*, Dec. 7, 1987.
"Maestro Mastroianni." GREGORY SPECK. *Interview*, Nov. 1987.
"Cary Grant, Italian style. . . ." RICHARD CORLISS. *Time*, Oct. 12, 1987.
"Still Mastroianni." CURTIS BILL PEPPER. *New York Times Magazine*, Sept. 20, 1987.

Masur, Kurt (1927–) In April 1990, German conductor Masur was named to succeed Zubin Mehta as music director of the New York Philharmonic, one of the most prestigious posts in the world of classical music, beginning with the 1992–93 season. He was also a major figure in the events that led up to the peaceful East German revolution of 1990. In June he acted as a mediator on behalf of young Leipzig street musicians who were being harassed by the government; in October, faced with the massive Leipzig demonstrations that brought East Germany close to civil war, he intervened again, bringing government and revolutionaries together in the first of a long series of talks that ultimately led to the peaceful German revolution. Afterward, his prestige was so great that there was talk of making him head of the new government, much like the writer Vaclav Havel in Czechoslovakia—but Masur chose to stay with his musical career and accepted the Philharmonic post.

Masur is one of Germany's leading conductors, developing the bulk of his career in

East Germany before unification. He was an opera company director in Erfurt and Leipzig, conductor of the Dresden Philharmonic (1955–58), director of the Mecklenburg State Opera (1958–60), music director of Berlin's Komische Opera (1960–64), again music director of the Dresden Philharmonic (1967–72), and director of the Leipzig Gewandhaus from 1972 to 1990. He has also toured widely, and is principal guest conductor of the London Philharmonic. Masur attended the National Musical School at Breslau and the Leipzig Conservatory. Twice divorced, he is married to singer Tomoko Sakurai and has five children.

FURTHER READING

"Masur, Kurt." *Current Biography*, Sept. 1990.

Maxwell, Robert (Ian Robert Maxwell, 1923–) British publisher Maxwell is a major figure in the world communications industry. In light of clouded 1990 economic conditions, he cautiously continued to expand his publishing interests in Europe and the United States. A few of his most notable moves were the mid-May launch of the English-language continental newspaper *The European*, which began as a weekly; his mid-May bid to purchase the U. S. tabloids the *Globe*, the *Sun*, and the *National Examiner*, with a combined weekly circulation of 2.5 million; his investment in *Berliner Verlag*, East Germany's largest publisher; and his late September development of the Maxwell

Central and East European Partnership L.P., aimed at enhancing Western investment in the newly freed countries of Eastern Europe.

Czech-born Maxwell emerged as a major figure during the post–World War II period. He founded Pergamon Press in 1949, and during the next four decades expanded his areas of control to include such companies as Great Britain's Mirror Group of newspapers, New York's Macmillan, Inc., and a wide range of other publishing, printing, broadcast media, and related companies. Maxwell was a Labour Member of Parliament from 1964–70. He married Elisabeth Meynard in 1945; they have nine children.

FURTHER READING

"New worlds to conquer." WILLIAM KAY. *Barron's*, Sept. 3, 1990.
"Media wars. . . ." D'ARCY JENISH. *Maclean's*, July 17, 1989.
"Conquering hearts and minds. . . ." BEN H. BAGDIKIAN. *Nation*, June 12, 1989.
"The year's 25 most fascinating business people." *Fortune*, Jan. 2, 1989.
"Larger than life." MARTHA SMILGIS. *Time*, Nov. 28, 1988.
"Maxwell, Ian Robert." *Current Biography*, Sept. 1988.
"Jealous of Rupert." CLAIRE POOLE. *Forbes*, July 25, 1988.
"Britain's maverick. . . ." STEVE LOHR. *New York Times Magazine*, May 1, 1988.
"Money and happiness." MARY MCIVER. *Maclean's*, Mar. 21, 1988.
Maxwell. JOE HAINES. Houghton Mifflin, 1988.

Mazowiecki, Tadeusz (1927–) On August 4, 1989, Polish Catholic human rights activist and Solidarity leader Mazowiecki became a historic figure as the first noncommunist head of a Soviet-bloc country, as the first democratically elected noncommunist to replace a communist leadership, and as Poland's first democratically elected premier since 1948.

During the year that followed, he made major contributions to the development of Polish democracy, while at the same time trying to rebuild Poland's shattered economy, partly by seeking foreign aid and investment. He visited Germany, Italy, and the Soviet Union in the months after taking office, and the United States in March 1990. But the Polish economy remained sluggish, and in some ways worsened, and many in Solidarity criticized the pace of reform. In June Lech Walesa decided to make a presidential run; in September, so did Mazowiecki. He was badly defeated in the 1990 Polish presidential elections and resigned his office, though remaining in Polish political life.

Mazowiecki, a lawyer and journalist, worked as a journalist for the Catholic association PAX in the early postwar period. Fired in 1955, in 1958 he founded the reformist Catholic monthly *Wiez* (Bond), which he edited until 1981. He was elected to the Polish parliament in 1961, and was a member until being barred in 1972, having gone over to even sharper opposition to the government in the late 1960s. He became a key Solidarity adviser and ally in 1980, and in 1981 organized and was first chief editor of the Solidarity newspaper. He was imprisoned during 1981–82, then continued to be a Solidarity leader and close co-worker of Lech Walesa throughout the 1980s. He participated in the 1989 Solidarity-government talks that led to the establishment of Polish democracy. Mazowiecki has been married and widowed twice and has three sons.

FURTHER READING

"What's left. . . ." ALMA GUILLERMOPRIETO. *Mother Jones*, Sept.–Oct. 1990.
"Mazowiecki, Tadeusz." *Current Biography*, Feb. 1990.
"'The transition to. . . .'" SYLVIE KAUFFMANN. *World Press Review*, Oct. 1989.
"'People are impatient'. . . ." JOHN BORRELL and TADEUSZ KUCHARSKI. *Time*, Sept. 11, 1989
"The new man at the top." HOLGER JENSEN. *Maclean's*, Aug. 28, 1989.
"An epochal shift. . . ." MARGUERITE JOHNSON. *Time*, Aug. 28, 1989.

Mazurki, Mike (Michael Mazurkiewicz, 1909–90) Ukrainian-American actor Mazurki was a professional wrestler before making his film debut in the first of many character roles in *The Shanghai Gesture* (1941). His most memorable role by far was as Moose Malloy in the classic *Farewell, My Lovely* (1944) to Dick Powell's Philip Marlowe. He also appeared in such films as *Some Like it Hot* (1959) and

Cheyenne Autumn (1964), and on television in the comedy series *The Chicago Teddy Bears* (1971). (d. Los Angeles; December 26, 1990)

FURTHER READING

Obituary. *The Times* (of London), Dec. 28, 1990.
Obituary. *Variety*, Dec. 17, 1990.
Obituary. *Los Angeles Times,* Dec. 11, 1990.

Mazursky, Paul (1930–) Mazursky played four roles—director, producer, co-writer, and actor—when he opened his new film *Enemies, A Love Story* in late 1989. The black comedy about the intertwined loves, hates, and passions of a group of Holocaust survivors—a man and his three wives—was based on a story by Isaac Bashevis Singer and starred Ron Silver and Anjelica Huston. Mazursky himself played a small but juicy villainous role, decked out in 1949-era oversized suit and fedora. Critics applauded the new movie, some hailing it as the best of Mazursky's career. The New York Film Critics Circle named Mazursky as best director of the year, and *American Film* magazine's poll of 80 film critics showed him in second place, behind Spike Lee; both, however, were ignored in the Oscar nominations. In midyear, Mazursky began shooting a new comedy *Scenes from a Mall* (1991), for which he also co-wrote the screenplay; it starred Woody Allen and Bette Midler as a lawyer and his psychologist wife spending the day of their 16th anniversary at a mall.

Brooklyn-born Mazursky worked as a New York–based actor and comedian during the 1950s, moving to Los Angeles in 1959. He became a writer for television in the 1960s, most notably with the "Danny Kaye Show" from 1963 to 1967, and wrote his first film, *I Love You, Alice B. Toklas* (1968), with Larry Tucker. His breakthrough film was *Bob & Carol & Ted & Alice* (1970), which he wrote and directed, setting the pattern of his work of the next two decades. Some of his most notable films were *Blume in Love* (1973), *Harry and Tonto* (1974), *An Unmarried Woman* (1978), and *Moscow on the Hudson* (1985), all of which he wrote and directed; and *Down and Out in Beverly Hills* (1985) and *Moon Over Parador* (1988), which he also produced. He married Betsy Purdy in 1953; the couple have two children. His B.A. was from Brooklyn College.

FURTHER READING

"Paul Mazursky." *American Film*, Jan. 1990.
"Paul Mazursky. . . ." Digby Diehl. *People*, June 16, 1986.
"Bourgeois blues. . . ." Joel E. Siegel. *American Film*, May 1984.
"Mazursky, Paul." *Current Biography*, May 1980.

Mem, Aleksandr (1935–90) A Russian Orthodox priest from a Jewish and Christian family, Father Mem was ordained in 1961 and became an archpriest in 1970. He was a church leader whose published works and preachings contributed to developing Soviet dissidence, even during the Brezhnev era. During the Gorbachev era, beginning in the mid-1980s, he became a well-known national liberal Christian voice, as a founder of the Russian Bible Society, on television, and as a leading Christian voice against resurgent Soviet anti-Semitism. He was murdered at Zagorsk, near Moscow, on September 9, 1990.

FURTHER READING

Obituary. *The Times* (of London), Sept. 15, 1990.

Menem, Carlos Saul (1935–) Menem was elected president of Argentina in May 1989 and succeeded president Raul Foulkes Alfonsin on July 8, four months before his scheduled December inauguration, because of Argentina's economic problems. He took office after food riots and the declaration of a state of siege. His early popularity waned as the economic crisis continued, accompanied by rapid inflation, loss of savings and earnings, and the national austerity program announced in early March 1990. In October 1989, Menem pardoned hundreds of those accused of crimes during the "dirty war" of 1976 to 1982, in which tens of thousands of Argentinians were murdered by the military government. On the personal side, Menem and his wife, Zulema Menem, suffered a highly publicized breakup of their marriage, which ultimately resulted in her June 1990 eviction from the presidential mansion by an army contingent.

Menem has spent almost all of his long career in law and politics in his home province of Rioja, beginning with his Peronist youth group activities of the mid-1950s and association with the provincial labor confederation. He became president of the Rioja Justicialist party in 1963 and was three times elected provincial governor (1973, 1983, 1987). His presidency is his first national office. He married Zulema Fatima Yoma in 1966, and has two children. He attended Cordoba University.

FURTHER READING

"A talk with. . . ." LINDA ROBINSON. U.S. News & World Report, May 7, 1990.
"Menem, Carlos Saul." *Current Biography*, Nov. 1989.
"Madcap nation's maddening crisis." GLENN EMERY. *Insight*, June 26, 1989.

Mengistu, Haile Mariam (1937–)

During 1989–90, the position of Ethiopian dictator Mengistu declined rapidly, as a combination of battlefield defeat, war-weariness at home, and Soviet aid withdrawal weakened his hold on Ethiopia. By May 1990, facing the loss of all of Tigre province and a good deal of adjoining territory, and with the Ethiopian army suffering tens of thousands of new casualties in the long, unsuccessful war against Eritrean nationalist forces, Mengistu attempted to improve relations with the United States, as he began to talk about a possible multiparty system and allowed relief supplies to flow through the Eritrean-held port of Massawa to hundreds of thousands and perhaps millions starving in northern Ethiopia and Eritrea. At the same time, he replaced some of the lost Soviet aid with Israeli weaponry, but only to a limited extent. By November, he was close to suing for peace with Eritrea, as strongly suggested by his former Soviet patrons. Meanwhile, starvation and disease continued to claim tens of thousands of lives as the long war continued.

Until emerging as one of the leaders of the military coup that deposed emperor Haile Selassie in 1974, Mengistu was an army major. He became dictator of the one-party Ethiopian state in 1977. In 1984, he established the Worker's Party and in 1987 the Democratic Republic of Ethiopia, both of which he leads. His period of rule has been dominated by war and characterized by widespread famine and disease. With a great deal of material help from the Soviet Union and with Cuban troops fighting on the Ethiopan side in the field, he has continued and deepened the long Eritrean-Ethiopian civil war (1962–). Neither side has been able to win, and new insurgency has developed in Tigre province, which by late 1988 was largely in rebel hands. His forces in the Ogaden region of Ethiopia also fought and drove back the Somalis in 1977–78 but have been unable to conquer rebel forces in that area. The period of his rule has seen an estimated 1–2 million civilian deaths, mostly from disease and famine, and many of them because one or both sides stopped the shipment of emergency relief supplies. Mengistu is married to Wubanchi Bishaw and attended the Holeta Military Academy.

FURTHER READING

Ethiopia. DENNIS B. FRADIN. Childrens, 1988.
"The famine next time." *New Republic*, Dec. 15, 1986.
"Political change. . . ." PETER SCHWAB. *Current History*, May 1985.
"Communism, African-style. . . ." *Time*, July 4, 1983.

Menninger, Karl (Karl Augustus Menninger, 1893–1990)

A leading American psychiatrist, Menninger graduated from Harvard Medical School and, after military service, studied and taught psychopathology before returning to Topeka in 1925 to found the Menninger Clinic with his father and brother. Though an early Freudian psychoanalyst, he was flexible in his approaches to therapy, believing that no patient was untreatable and that a supportive, humane total environment was vital to therapy. These ideas were widely adopted by other psychiatric institutions and spread by many psychiatrists who studied at the center and by Menninger's own writings, including best-selling works such as *Love Against Hate* (1959) and *Crime of Punishment* (1988). (d. Topeka, Kansas; July 18, 1990)

FURTHER READING

Obituary. *Current Biography*, Sept. 1990.
"Karl Menninger. . . ." *Life*, Fall 1990.
"A Kansas pioneer. . . ." *U.S. News & World Report*, July 30, 1990.

Obituary. *New York Times,* July 19, 1990.
Menninger: The Family and the Clinic. Lawrence J. Freidman. Knopf, 1990.
The Selected Correspondence of Dr. Karl A. Menninger, 1919–1945. Howard J. Faulkner and Virginia D. Pruitt, eds. Yale University Press, 1989.
"Menninger. . . ." Erica E. Goode. *U.S. News & World Report,* Dec. 12, 1988.

Merrill, Gary (Gary Franklin Merrill, 1915–90) Actor Merrill was best known as Bette Davis's director and fiancé in *All About Eve* (1950). A New Englander, Merrill started in regional theater and reached Broadway in 1939, during World War II acting in Army radio and films such as Irving Berlin's *This Is the Army* and creating the reporter's role in Broadway's *Born Yesterday* (1946). The postwar years brought leading film roles, and a ten-year marriage to Bette Davis and a relationship with Rita Hayworth—both stormy—as he described in *Bette, Rita & the Rest of My Life* (1988; with John Cole). Much of his later work was in less-notable plays, films, television, documentaries, and commercials. (d. Falmouth, Maine; March 5, 1990)

FURTHER READING

Obituary. *Variety,* Mar. 14, 1990.
Obituary. *The Times* (of London), Mar. 8, 1990.
Obituary. *New York Times,* Mar. 7, 1990.

Michener, James (James Albert Michener, 1907–) In 1989–90, Michener published two works, *Caribbean* (1989), a multigenerational historical work in the traditional Michener style, and the more personal *Pilgrimage: A Memoir of Poland and Rome* (1990). He announced in 1990 that he would be writing no more "big books," but clearly had no intention of fading away, noting that "a mere quiescent retirement is quite often fatal." Rather, he planned to continue writing five hours a day and to do some teaching during the winters. He and his wife spent considerable time scouting retirement locations, one main requisite being the availability of a college library for research. They finally settled on Brunswick, Maine, for their summer home and St. Petersburg, Florida, for the winter.

Michener continued his longtime support for young writers and for freedom of speech, in November 1989 establishing a $400,000 fund for young Polish writers to support publication of books and other writings outside the commercial publishing mainstream. The announcement was made at a breakfast attended by Lech Walesa; the country had in 1988 given Michener, author of *Poland* (1983), its highest award. He also became involved in a 1990 controversy over various resignations at his longtime publisher, Random House, publicly threatening to leave them if he did not receive assurances (which were given) that the house would abide by "the old traditions" of publishing.

Michener was a teacher and editor during the late 1930s and the 1940s. He emerged as a major U.S. popular author in 1947, with his Pultizer Prize–winning first novel, *Tales of the South Pacific*; the book was adapted into the musical *South Pacific* in 1949. He went on to write many best-sellers, several of them historical novels and several adapted into hit movies. Some of his best known novels are *The Bridges at Toko-ri* (1953), *Sayonara* (1954), *The Bridge at Andau* (1957), *Hawaii* (1959), *The Source* (1965), *Iberia* (1968), *Centennial* (1974), *Chesapeake* (1978), *The Covenant* (1980), *Space* (1982), *Texas* (1985), and *Alaska* (1988). He has also written several volumes of essays and edited several art books. Michener attended Swarthmore College. He has been married three times, since 1955 to Mari Yoriko Sabusawa.

FURTHER READING

“The continuing sagas of. . . .” JIM SHAHIN. *Saturday Evening Post*, Mar. 1990.
“What makes love last. . . .” SUSAN ARNOUT. *McCall's*, Feb. 1987.
“The Michener phenomenon.” CARYN JAMES. *New York Times Magazine*, Sept. 8, 1985.
“At home with. . . .” JENNY ANDREWS HARWELL. *Saturday Evening Post*, Sept. 1985.
“James Michener. . . .” WILLIAM ECENBARGER. *Modern Maturity*, Aug.–Sept. 1985.
James A. Michener: A Biography. JOHN P. HAYES. Macmillan, 1984.

Middleton, Drew (1913–90) New York–born Middleton was a long-time foreign correspondent for the *New York Times*. He worked for the Associated Press in London from 1939, at first covering sports but soon as war correspondent, beginning his long association with the *New York Times* in 1942. He provided a key view of Allied activities from North Africa and Italy, and on to Normandy and the reconquest of Europe. He then reported on the new Europe from Germany (1947–53), London (1953–63), and elsewhere before returning home as military correspondent (1970–84). He also wrote several books and numerous articles. (d. New York City; January 1, 1990)

FURTHER READING

Obituary. *Current Biography*, Mar. 1990.
Obituary. *The Times* (of London), Jan. 13, 1990.
Obituary. *New York Times,* Jan. 12, 1990.

Midler, Bette (1945–) Actress-entertainer Midler's “Wind Beneath My Wings” was named best song at the 1990 Grammy Awards, and her recording of it was named Record of the Year; Midler herself had also been nominated for best female vocal performance and her album for best album of the year. In the wake of the award, her single rose sharply on the record charts once again. Then, late in 1990, she had probably the biggest album of her career with *Some People's Lives*. Though some reviewers criticized its overload of “sentimental, uplifting songs,” the record-buying public clearly loved it and the album broke into the top 10 on the *Billboard* record charts in November 1990. On screen Midler appeared in *Stella*, a remake of the 1937 Barbara Stanwyck tearjerker *Stella Dallas*, opposite John Goodman; although the film did not do as well as expected in theatrical release, it did very well later in the year in the video rental market. For ABC's *Earth Day Special,* on April 15, 1990, Midler played Mother Earth, dressed in garbage to portray the fouling of the environment.

Hawaii-born Midler, on stage and screen from 1965, was in the early 1970s the long-running lead singer at New York's Continental Baths, a gay men's health club. She began her recording career with the album *The Divine Miss M* (1973), also recording such albums as *Bette Midler* (1973), *Thighs and Whispers* (1979), and *Divine Madness* (1980), as well the soundtrack album from *The Rose* (1980), her first starring film role. She went on to play in such films as *Jinxed* (1982), *Down and Out in Beverly Hills* (1986), *Ruthless People* (1986), *Outrageous Fortune* (1987), and *Beaches* (1989), and also appeared on television. In print, she published *A View from a Broad* (1980). Midler married Martin von Haselberg in 1984; they have one child. She attended the University of Hawaii.

FURTHER READING

“The best Bette yet.” CLIFF JAHR. *Ladies Home Journal*, Jan. 1990.
Bette Midler. ACE COLLINS. St. Martin's, 1989.
“Talking with Bette Midler. . . .” PETER RICHARDS. *Redbook*, July 1988.
“Appeals Court sez. . . .” AMY DAWES. *Variety*, June 29, 1988.
“The jokers are wild.” GREGG KILDAY. *Savvy*, July 1988.
“Bette Midler.” GLORIA STEINEM. *Ms.*, Jan. 1988.
Bette Midler: Outrageously Divine. MARK BEGO. NAL-Dutton, 1987.

Milken, Michael (1946–) Milken was the chief figure in the massive Drexel, Burnham, Lambert stock scandals of the late 1980s. These began with several low-level insider trading cases in 1986, one of them that of Drexel employee Dennis Levine, and resulted in multiple indictments of the Drexel firm in 1988 after a two-year investigation that was aided by convicted stock market manipulator Ivan

Boesky. Drexel pleaded guilty to six felony counts in 1988 and agreed to pay $650 million. In March 1989, Milken was indicted on 98 counts; in June 1989, he resigned from Drexel; and in April 1990 he pleaded guilty to six felony counts and agreed to pay $600 million. On November 21, 1990, he was sentenced to ten years in prison, three years on probation, and 1,800 hours of community service. Milken still faced many large pending civil lawsuits.

Milken's entire career was with Drexel, Burnham, Lambert. He worked part-time with the firm while in college and joined its bond department in 1970. During the 1970s, he began his long career as a high-yield bond trader, developing the "junk bond" concept. He moved the firm's bond department to Beverly Hills, California, in 1978 and vastly expanded junk bond operations throughout the 1980s, using it as a financing technique to raise tens of billions of dollars and billions in fees for the firm. He personally earned over $1 billion. But in the mid-1980s, allegations of insider trading and other securities frauds began to surface, and a long series of federal investigations and prosecutions began. Milken's B.B.A. was from the University of California, and his M.B.A. from the Wharton School of the University of Pennsylvania. He is married to Lori Anne Hackett.

FURTHER READING

"Junk bonding." Joe M. Domanick. *Inc.*, Oct. 1990.
"History is bunk. . . ." Stanley Sheinbaum, et al. *New Perspectives Quarterly (NPQ)*, Fall 1989.
"Michael Milken." Brad Darrach. *People*, Fall 1989.
"The man with. . . ." Christopher Elias. *Insight*, June 12, 1989.
New Crowd: The Changing of the Jewish Guard on Wall Street. Judith R. Ehrlich and Barry J. Rehfeld. Little, Brown, 1989.
"Mike's Midas touch." Brian O'Reilly. *Fortune*, Oct. 10, 1988.
"A chat with Michael Milken." Allan Sloan. *Forbes*, July 13, 1987.

Miller, Arthur (1915–) Writer Miller has become increasingly disenchanted with the climate for the arts in America. At the Illinois Humanities Council Expressions of Freedom festival in November 1990, he warned that American artists are censoring their own works to get government grants, allowing freedom to be "killed without a trace." Unhappy with conditions on Broadway, Miller is planning to open his next play in London in 1991, where in recent years several of Miller's plays have been revived in major productions and hailed as masterworks, most notably *A View from the Bridge*. In early 1990, Miller was in London for a revival of *The Price* at the Old Vic.

In Hollywood, Miller wrote his first screenplay since *The Misfits*, for Karel Reisz's *Everybody Wins*, starring Nick Nolte and Debra Winger; however, it received poor-to-mixed critical reviews and similarly tepid audience response when it appeared in early 1990. American regional theaters continue to present Miller's major plays around the country, as in 1990 with *Death of a Salesman* in Los Angeles and *The Crucible* in New Haven. Miller's recent work also includes an Americanized adaptation of Ibsen's *An Enemy of the People*, done in a televised production for PBS's *American Playhouse,* and a televised play, *Clara* (1991).

Miller has been a leading American playwright since the 1947 production of *All My Sons*, which won a New York Drama Critics Award. He became a world figure with his Pulitzer Prize–winning *Death of a Salesman* (1949), in which Lee J. Cobb created the memorable Willy Loman. His most notable further work included the Tony-winning *The Crucible* (1953), the Pulitzer-winning *A View from the Bridge* (1955), *After the Fall* (1963), *Incident at Vichy* (1965), *The Price* (1968), and *The American Clock* (1979). He wrote the screenplay for *The Misfits* (1961), which starred his second wife, Marilyn Monroe, who committed suicide in 1962. In 1987, he published *Timebends: A Life*. Miller attended the University of Michigan. He has been married three times, since 1962 to photographer Inge Morath, with whom he has collaborated on two travel books, and he has two children.

FURTHER READING

"'The theater. . . .'" ALVIN P. SANOFF. *U.S. News & World Report*, Jan. 11, 1988.
Miller the Playwright. DENNIS WELLAND. Heinemann, 1988.
"Arthur Miller." WENDY SMITH. *Publishers Weekly*, Nov. 6, 1987.
"On the shuttle. . . ." JEREMY GERARD. *New York Times Book Review*, Nov. 8, 1987.
Conversations with Arthur Miller. MATTHEW C. ROUDANE, ed. University Press of Mississippi, 1987.

Minnelli, Liza (1946–) Actress-entertainer Minnelli tried on a new, somewhat hipper image with her new album *But I Am Hip*, produced by the Pet Shop Boys in late 1989. The album was a notable success in Europe, although less so in America. Minnelli was also on the road in early 1990, touring with Frank Sinatra and Sammy Davis, Jr., until Davis was forced to drop out because of the throat cancer that later killed him. In Toronto in 1990 she filmed her new comedy film *Stepping Out*, about a tap-dance teacher's professional and extracurricular relationships with her students. She also honored her father in 1990, giving a special Father's Day concert of songs from Vincente Minnelli film musicals, which kicked off an eight-week retrospective of his films in Los Angeles.

Minnelli, the daughter of Judy Garland and Vincente Minnelli, began her stage and recording career in 1963. In 1964, she appeared at the London Palladium with Garland, and went on to become one of the leading popular entertainers of her time. She won a Best Actress Oscar for *Cabaret* (1972), and also appeared in such films as *Charlie Bubbles* (1967), *The Sterile Cuckoo* (1969), *Tell Me That You Love Me, Junie Moon* (1970), *Lucky Lady* (1975), *Silent Movie* (1976), *New York, New York* (1977), *Arthur* (1981), and *Sam Found Out* (1988). On stage, she has appeared in such musicals as *Flora, the Red Menace* (1965), *The Act* (1977), and *The Rink* (1984), and has also often appeared on television. Minnelli has been married three times.

FURTHER READING

"Minnelli, Liza." *Current Biography*, July 1988.
"Liza battles back. . . ." ERIC SHERMAN. *Ladies Home Journal*, July 1987.
Liza! Liza!: An Unauthorized Biography of Liza Minnelli. ALAN W. PETRUCELLI. Karz-Cohl, 1983.

Minotis, Alexis (Alexander Minotakis, 1900–90) Minotis was the leading Greek tragic actor of his time and also a leading Greek theater director and producer. He and actress Katina Paxinou worked together in the late 1920s, and in the 1930s in the Greek National Theater; they married in 1940, and their careers continued together until her death in 1973. They fled to America during World War II, returning in 1951 to rejoin the national theater and to help develop a classical revival. Minotis directed and starred as Oedipus in their classic *Oedipus Rex* at Delphi, with Paxinou as Jocasta, which was seen in New York and Western Europe in 1952. Both starred yearly in the great classic roles at the Epidaurus Festival. Minotis, a leading Shakespearean actor as well, played in and directed the classics and modern classics of many countries, translated and adapted into Greek. He was the artistic director of the national theater from 1964–67 and its director-general from 1974–81. (d. Athens; November 11, 1990)

FURTHER READING

Obituary. *The Times* (of London), Nov. 17, 1990.
Obituary. *New York Times*, Nov. 13, 1990.

Mitchell, George (George John Mitchell, 1933–) The senator from Maine is a highly visible possible future Democratic presidential candidate, and as Senate majority leader a spokesperson for his party on the whole range of matters at issue between the two major parties, many of them emerging as disagreements over proposed administration social welfare program cuts in the crisis-ridden 1990 and 1991 budgets; he has also called for stronger federal environmental legislation. Mitchell has also attacked administration foreign policy, calling for support for Lithuanian independence and criticizing administration China policy moves after the Tienanmen Square massacres of 1988 as too timid. He was a leader in the unsuccessful fight against the congressional resolutions that authorized the Persian Gulf War, urging further time for sanctions and diplomatic efforts to end the crisis.

Maine-born Mitchell began his career in Washington as a Justice Department attorney from 1960–62 and as an assistant to Maine Democratic senator Edmund Muskie from 1962–65. He went home to practice law and politics in Maine, became a U.S. attorney and then U.S. district judge in the late 1970s and a Maine Democratic senator in 1981, succeeding Muskie. Mitchell rose quickly in the Senate and in his party; he became majority leader of the Senate in 1988. His B.A. was from Bowdoin College, in 1954, his LL.B. from Georgetown University, in 1960. He has one child.

FURTHER READING

"Mitchell, George John." *Current Biography*, April 1989.
"A hardball player. . . ." HAYS GOREY. *Time*, Dec. 12, 1988.
Men of Zeal: A Candid Story of the Iran-Contra Hearings. WILLIAM S. COHEN and GEORGE J. MITCHELL. Viking Penguin, 1988.

Mitchum, Robert (1917–) Quintessentially American actor Mitchum appeared in an unusual setting in 1990 as star of his first television series, "A Family for Joe." In the NBC family comedy, Mitchum played a rather crusty homeless man drafted by four orphaned children to play the part of their grandfather to prevent their being split up into different foster homes. The pilot was shown in February 1990; though critics were not overwhelmed, the pilot was among the top 30 shows. The series later began a six-part trial run but did not draw sufficient audience response to be picked up for additional shows.

Mitchum has been on screen for over four decades, from his very promising Oscar-nominated debut in *The Story of G.I. Joe* (1945) through his massive Pug Henry role in television's "The Winds of War" (1983) and its sequel, "War and Remembrance" (1987). He has played leads and strong character roles in dozens of films, such as *Out of the Past* (1947), *The Night of the Hunter* (1955), *The Wonderful Country* (1959), *The Sundowners* (1960), *El Dorado* (1967), *Ryan's Daughter* (1971), *Farewell, My Lovely* (1975), *The Big Sleep* (1977), and *The Ambassador* (1984), as well as in many television roles. He married Dorothy Spencer in 1940; the couple have two children.

FURTHER READING

Them Ornery Mitchum Boys: The Adventures of Robert and John Mitchum. JOHN MITCHUM. Creatures at Large, 1989.
Robert Mitchum: A Biography. GEORGE EELLS. Watts, 1984; Jove, 1985.
Robert Mitchum. DEREK MALCOLM. Hippocrene, 1984.

Mitterrand, François (François Maurice Marie Mitterrand 1916–) President of France Mitterrand has played a major role in the development of the European Community and in encouraging the integration of the newly democratic nations of Eastern Europe into the new European financial and political system. In January 1990, he supported the principle of all-European confederation, and in late April he and German chancellor Helmut Kohl led in developing the principle of European Community (EC) political union. All of this was in the most general terms; the 12-nation EC meeting in Dublin in April agreed only to study and develop unity proposals. But in view of German reunification and the very specific steps being taken toward EC monetary and other aspects of economic union, the principle of earlier-than-expected political unity began to be taken very seriously.

At home, Mitterrand's position was considerably weaker as Socialist Party premier Michel Rocard continued to lead a minority government that depended on alliances with other parties to stay in office. One especially difficult problem Mitterrand faced at home was that of racism, as violence against Muslims and Jews flared in the spring of 1990, encouraged by such right-wing politicians as Jean-Marie Le Pen, head of the National Front Party. In

mid-May, after several Jewish graves had been desecrated, Mitterrand once again stated his deep opposition to racism and anti-Semitism, and on May 14 he marched with an estimated 80,000–100,000 Parisians to protest the resurgence of fascism and racism in France; he was joined by the leaders of the other major French political parties.

Mitterrand, a soldier during World War II, escaped from the Germans after having been captured early in the war and became an active Resistance fighter. He entered politics after the war and was a Socialist deputy in the national assembly from 1946 to 1958 and 1962 to 1981, holding many Cabinet positions in the early years, when his party held power. At the same time, he rose within the Socialist Party and was its First Secretary from 1971 to 1981, while also becoming a vice president of the Socialist International from 1972 to 1981. In 1981, he was elected President of France; in 1988, he was reelected. He married Danielle Gouze in 1944; they have two children. He attended the University of Paris. His brother is General Jacques Mitterrand.

FURTHER READING

Seven Years in France: François Mitterrand & Unintended Revolution, 1981–1988. JULIUS W. FRIEND. Westview, 1988.

The Black and the Red: François Mitterrand and the Story of an Ambition. CATHERINE NAY. Harcourt Brace Jovanovich, 1987.

Mitterrand's France. SONIA MAZEY and MICHAEL NEWMAN, eds. Routledge Chapman & Hall, 1987.

Francois Mitterrand: A Political Odyssey. DENIS MACSHANE. Phaidon, 1983.

Montana, Joe (Joseph C. Montana, Jr., 1956–) He just might be the greatest quarterback ever to play the game of football. That thought was on the minds of many who watched Montana throughout 1989 and 1990. Certainly, by the National Football League's statistical ranking system he is the highest-rated quarterback in history. As recently as 1986, when he had back surgery, it seemed as if his career might be over. But in January 1990, he led his San Francisco 49ers to their second straight Super Bowl win in the most lopsided Super Bowl win in history, 55–10 over the Denver Broncos. Even though Montana left the game with 11 minutes to go, he completed 22 of 29 passes for 297 yards and threw for a Super Bowl record of five touchdowns with no interceptions, becoming the only 3-time winner of the Super Bowl's most valuable player award. Among other Super Bowl records he set were consecutive completions (13), career passes (122), career passing yardage (1142), career completions (83), and pass attempts without an interception (122).

No end was in sight. In summer 1990, Montana agreed to a reported four-year, $14 million contract, making him the highest-paid player in team sports. The 49ers under Montana opened the 1990–91 season with a 12-game winning streak and by year's end seemed a good bet to end up in the 1991 Super Bowl, but they were defeated for the National Football Conference championship by the New York Giants. In December 1990, *Sports Illustrated* named Montana their sportsman of the year, the first time a football player has received the award unshared. In 1989, he had been named the Associated Press's male athlete of the year, as well as most valuable player in the National Football League. He wrote about his experiences in *Cool Under Fire: Reflections on the San Francisco 49ers—How We Came of Age in the 1980's* (1989, with Alan Steinberg).

After a notable career as quarterback at the University of Notre Dame, Pennsylvania-born Montana became a leading player in professional football during the 1980s. As quarterback of the San Francisco 49ers from 1979, he led his team to three Super Bowl championships (1982, 1985, 1989) and was most valuable player in the Super Bowl in 1982 and 1985. In 1986, he published *Audibles: My Life in Football*, written with Bob Raissman. Montana was formerly married to Kim Monses and then Cass Castillo, and married Jennifer Wallace in 1984; they have two children. His B.B.A. was from Notre Dame in 1978.

FURTHER READING

"An American dream. . . ." LEIGH MONTVILLE. *Sports Illustrated*, Dec. 24, 1990.
"Joe Montana." J. DAVID MILLER. *Sport*, Nov. 1990.
"Joe Montana. . . ." WALTER ROESSING. *Boys' Life*, Oct. 1990.
"Born to be a quarterback," Pt. 1; "The Ultimate Winner." Pt. 2. PAUL ZIMMERMAN. *Sports Illustrated*. Aug. 6 and 13, 1990.
The Quarterbacks: The Uncensored Truth about the Men in the Pocket. MICKEY HERSKOWITZ. Morrow, 1990.
"Joe Montana. . . ." IRVIN MUCHNICK. *New York Times Magazine*, Dec. 17, 1989.
Joe Montana: Comeback Quarterback. THOMAS R. RABER. Lerner, 1989.
"Montana, Joe." *Current Biography*, Sept. 1983.

Moore, Mary Tyler (1936–) Longtime television star Mary Tyler Moore tried to make a series comeback in the 1988–89 season with "Annie McGuire." When that failed, she sold her production company, MTM Productions, formed with ex-husband (later NBC head) Grant Tinker, and disappeared into a country life, openly expressing frustration over the shortage of good roles for women over 50. Roles may still be hard to come by, but in November 1990 Moore reappeared in two television movies. She played a key role in the ensemble family cast of the black comedy "Thanksgiving Day," a production battered by the critics as tasteless, witless, and juiceless. She had far better fortune with her other film, *The Last Best Year*, in which she played a psychologist who helps a single career woman (Bernadette Peters) deal with her impending death from liver cancer and the simultaneous loss of her married lover; both stars won praise for their work.

Cable viewers can expect to see more of Moore, since the new Ha! The TV Comedy Network has bought rights to the old "Mary Tyler Moore Show," along with other classic comedy series—eight of them from MTM Productions—for reruns. Privately, Moore also continued her long-term active work on behalf of the Juvenile Diabetes Foundation, co-hosting their annual fund-raising program televised on the USA Network.

Brooklyn-born Moore began her long television career in the 1950s and emerged as a leading player on "The Dick Van Dyke Show" (1961–66). She became a major star as career woman Mary Richards in "The Mary Tyler Moore Show" (1970–77) and also starred in her own shows in 1978 and 1979, as well as in many telefilms. Her movies include *Thoroughly Modern Millie* (1967), *Ordinary People* (1980; she was nominated for a Best Actress Oscar), *Six Weeks* (1982), and *Just Between Friends* (1986). On stage, she appeared on Broadway in *Whose Life Is It Anyway?* (1980) and *Sweet Sue* (1987). She has been married three times, since 1984 to Dr. Robert Levine, and had one child.

FURTHER READING

"Mary Tyler Moore." *People*, Summer 1989.
Sweethearts of Sixties TV. RONALD L. SMITH. St. Martin's, 1989.
Love Is All Around: The Making of the Mary Tyler Moore Show. ROBERT S. ALLEY and IRBY B. BROWN. Delacorte, 1989.
"Mary Tyler Moore. . . ." MARGO JEFFERSON. *Vogue*, Mar. 1986.
"The triumphant second act. . . ." CHRIS CHASE. *Cosmopolitan*, Mar. 1986.
"Growing up with Mary." BRIAN D. JOHNSON. *Maclean's*, Jan. 13, 1986.
Mary Tyler Moore: The Woman Behind the Smile. REBECCA STEFOFF. NAL-Dutton, 1986.
Mary Tyler Moore: A Biography. JASON BONDEROFF. St. Martin's, 1985.

Moravia, Alberto (Alberto Pincherle, 1907–90) Moravia was a leading Italian novelist and essayist whose work often focused on alienation, corruption, and sexuality. Son of a Jewish architect and a Slavic countess, Roman-born Moravia was taught by governesses and read widely during his youth, mostly bedridden until age 18 with tuberculosis of the leg bones. By age 20, he was writing for various literary reviews and self-published his first novel, *Gli indifferenti (Time of Indifference)*, which was praised by critics but censured by the Fascists, who forbade reviews of his works and later barred him from writing newspaper articles. He continued to write under a pseudonym, sometimes traveling abroad, but fled to the mountains with his wife, novelist Elsa Morante, during 1943–44. His finest works are from the postwar years, including *The Woman of Rome* (1949), *The Conformist* (1951), *Conjugal Love* (1951), *Roman Tales* (1957), *Two Women* (1958), and *The Empty Canvas* (1961). For a time, the Vatican also proscribed his works. He was elected a left-wing member of the European Parliament in 1983. (d. Rome; September 26, 1990.)

FURTHER READING

Obituary. *Current Biography*, Nov. 1990.
"The silence of re-reading." *Economist*, Oct. 6, 1990.
Obituary. *Variety*, Oct. 1, 1990.
Obituary. *The Times* (of London), Sept. 27, 1990.
Obituary. *New York Times*, Sept. 27, 1990.
"A visit with Italy's man of letters." CHARLOTTE AILLAUD. *Architectural Digest*, March 1988.

Morgan, Dr. Elizabeth (1948–), **Foretich, Dr. Eric A.** (1943–), and **Foretich, Hilary** (1983–) Elizabeth Morgan and Eric Foretich are the parents of Hilary Foretich; the three are the principal figures in a child-custody fight that stirred worldwide interest. In late November 1990, a New Zealand family court awarded temporary custody of Hilary to Morgan, then residing in New Zealand, beginning what may be the final chapter in a five-year-long battle, while Foretich was barred from visiting Hilary "in the immediate future."

In August 1987, Morgan was jailed for civil contempt by District of Columbia Superior Court judge Herbert B. Dixon, Jr., for refusing to tell him the whereabouts of her daughter Hilary, then five years old; Morgan charged that the child had been sexually abused by her father. Morgan remained in jail for 25 months until Congress, which has jurisdiction over the district, passed a law limiting jail terms for contempt in child-custody cases in the district to one year. After President Bush signed the bill into law, Morgan was released. Hilary Foretich remained in hiding in the custody of her grandparents, Antonia and William Morgan, who hid her for 31 months, on a set of journeys that took them to the Bahamas, Canada, Great

Elizabeth Morgan and Eric Foretich with Ted Koppel (left).

Britain, and New Zealand until she was finally discovered in Auckland. Eric Foretich still sought custody; litigation continued in New Zealand during 1991. Morgan was taking her case to the public with her book *Custody: A True Story*, although New Zealand courts have barred its publication there.

Elizabeth Morgan and Eric Foretich are both physicians, he an oral surgeon, she a plastic surgeon who wrote *Solo Practice: A Woman Surgeon's Story* (1980). They were divorced in 1982, before Hilary's birth. In 1990, Morgan remarried, to U.S. Federal Court of Appeals judge Paul R. Michel, whom she met while in jail.

Foretich has another daughter, Heather (1981–), from a previous marriage; according to court documents, she reportedly claimed that he had molested her, although a judge reviewing the case noted that she seemed to have been coached by her mother. Foretich vehemently denies the charges but has been barred from exercising visitation rights.

FURTHER READING

"Little girl lost. . . ." BARBARA KANTROWITZ. *Newsweek*, Mar. 12, 1990.
"A child's odyssey. . . ." NORA UNDERWOOD. *Maclean's*, Mar. 12, 1990.
"The little girl. . . ." BILL HEWITT. *People*, Mar. 12, 1990.
"As far away. . . ." *Time*, Mar. 5, 1990.
"The Morgan case. . . ." *Newsweek*, Mar. 5, 1990.
"Elizabeth Morgan." *People*, Dec. 25, 1989.
"Elizabeth Morgan's powerful allies." DON KOWET. *Insight*, Nov. 20, 1989.
"A courageous. . . ." PAULA CHIN and JANE SIMS PODESTA. *People*, Oct. 16, 1989.
"Vowing to protect. . . ." PAULA CHIN. *People*, June 12, 1989.
"Stalemate for. . . ." PAULA CHIN and JANE SIMS PODESTA. *People*, Jan. 23, 1989.

Morse, Robert (Robert Alan Morse, 1931–) A stage and screen star in the 1960s, by the 1980s Morse was making his living playing in dinner theater. Yet in 1989, it all came round again; he had his first real opportunity since the mid-1970s; the chance to play author Truman Capote in the one-man show *Tru*, written and directed by Jay Presson Allen. The rest is the working out of the kind of theater legend that hardly ever comes true; the show tried out in Los Angeles, moved to Broadway's Booth Theatre in December, was a hit, and Morse was once again a star on Broadway. He capped it all by winning a Best Actor Tony for the role.

Massachusetts-born Morse scored his greatest stage and screen successes in the 1960s, most notably as the Tony-winning comic lead in *How to Succeed in Business Without Really Trying* (1960), a role he re-created on-screen in the 1967 film version. He also appeared in such plays as *Take Me Along* (1959) and *Sugar* (1972); such films as *The Loved One* (1965), and *Oh Dad, Poor Dad, Where Were You When the Lights Went Out* (1968); and the television series "That's Life" (1968–69). He was formerly married, and has three children.

FURTHER READING

"How to succeed. . . ." JACK KROLL. *Newsweek*, June 18, 1990.
"'Tru' grit." AIMEE LEE BALL. *New York*, Feb. 5, 1990.
"His boyishness. . . ." DAVID HUTCHINGS. *People*, Jan. 15, 1990.

Mothopeng, Zephania Lekoane (1913–90) President of the Pan-Africanist Congress (PAC), Mothopeng was a longtime foe of South Africa's system of apartheid. He was a teacher and principal, dismissed for criticizing inferior education for Blacks in 1952. A member of the African National Congress from 1940, he helped form the more hard-line PAC in 1959, seeking return of not just South Africa but all Africa to its native inhabitants. Jailed for militant political activities in 1960–61, 1964–67, and 1976–88, and elected PAC president in 1986, Mothopeng rejected negotiations and compromise with the South African government. (d. Johannesburg; October 23, 1990.)

FURTHER READING

Obituary. *The Times* (of London), Oct. 25, 1990.
Obituary. *New York Times*, Oct. 24, 1990.

Moynihan, Daniel Patrick (1927–) Three-time New York Democratic Senator Moynihan, long a leading Democratic liberal, is chairman of the Senate Finance Committee's subcommittee on Social Security. During 1990, he mounted a year-long attack aimed at reducing Social Security taxes, arguing that mounting Social Security surpluses were being used to mask mounting deficits and that the surpluses were an unnecessary drain on those least able to pay. In March, the Democratic National Committee backed his proposal to reduce taxes by an estimated $55 billion in 1991 and considerably more in later years. In mid-October, the Senate shelved his proposal in light of the recurrent federal budget crisis then being negotiated by Congress and the President; but Moynihan and others will be back with the same proposal in 1991. Moynihan also led Senate liberals on such issues as repeal of the McCarran-Walter Immigration Act of 1952 and in opposing the proposed flag-burning amendment as an attack on the Bill of Rights.

Oklahoma-born Moynihan, a Democrat, served in appointive positions in New York State government in the early 1960s, in that period also co-authoring the influential and controversial *Beyond the Melting Pot* (1963). He was Harvard-based from 1966 to 1977, while also holding a series of appointive federal positions, notably as ambassador to India (1973–75) and American UN representative (1975–76). Moving into electoral politics, he began the first of his three senatorial terms in 1977. In the Senate he has been a member of the influential rules, taxation, foreign relations, and finance committees, in finance becoming head of the highly visible Social Security subcommittee. Among his more recent written works are *Counting Our Blessings: Reflections on the Future of America* (1980), *Loyalties* (1984), *Family and Nation* (1986), and *Came the Revolution: Argument in the Reagan Era* (1988). His B.A. was from New York's City College, in 1943, and his M.A. and Ph.D. from Tufts University in 1948 and 1949; he also attended the London School of Economics. He married Elizabeth Brennan in 1955; the couple have four children.

FURTHER READING

"Liberal? Conservative?. . . ." JAMES TRAUB. *New York Times Magazine*, Sept. 16, 1990.

"'A true capacity for governance'." MAURA MOYNIHAN. *American Heritage*, Oct.–Nov. 1986.

"Moynihan, Daniel Patrick." *Current Biography*, Feb. 1986.

Mubarak, Mohammed Hosni (1928–)
During the late 1980s and early 1990s, Egyptian President Mubarak faced mounting problems at home as Islamic fundamentalist unrest seriously threatened Egyptian democracy while difficult economic conditions caused widespread unemployment and poverty in an already poor nation. At the same time, the World Bank, the United States, and other sources of economic aid pressed him to make economic reforms as a condition of receiving further aid, although he expressed great concern over the impact of such reforms on unemployment and social unrest and did not make many of the changes demanded.

On the international side, Mubarak continued to be a considerable force in the search for Middle East and Arab-Israeli peace, while as president of the Organization of African Unity from July 1989 he tried to help settle such regional conflicts as those in Ethiopia, Chad, and Namibia. After the August 1990 Iraqi attack on Kuwait, he led moderate Arab response, convening an Arab summit meeting on August 8 and attempting to convince Saddam Hussein to withdraw. When the Iraqis refused, Mubarak led in the formation of the multinational Arab army sent to Saudi Arabia.

Mubarak was a career air force officer who moved up to direct the air academy from 1967–1969, was air force chief of staff from 1969 to 1972, and was commander-in-chief from 1972 to 1975. He became Anwar Sadat's vice president in 1975 and moved into the presidency in 1981, after Sadat's assassination. He won a second term in the 1987 elections. In 1988, the Mubarak government again moved against the fundamentalists, beginning a period of widespread arrests under emergency decrees in effect since the Sadat assassination. Mubarak has been a moderate within the Arab world throughout his presidency, continuing peaceful relations with Israel and attempting to foster a full-scale Arab-Israeli peace, although with little success. He attended the Egyptian military and air academies.

FURTHER READING

"A call to negotiate. . . ." DEAN FISHER. *Time*, Sept. 10, 1990.
"The view from Cairo." MORTIMER B. ZUCKERMAN. *U.S. News & World Report*, Apr. 16, 1990.
Egypt After Nasser: Sadat, Peace & the Mirage of Prosperity. THOMAS W. LIPPMAN. Paragon, 1989.
"Egypt's cautious man. . . ." *U.S. News & World Report*, Mar. 18, 1985.
"Mubarak, Hosni." *Current Biography*, Apr. 1982.

Muggeridge, Malcolm (1903–90) Child of a socialist family, journalist Muggeridge experimented with and then fell away from organized religion in the 1920s and then became disillusioned with Soviet communism after a 1932–33 assignment in Moscow as a reporter for the *Manchester Guardian*. He worked in British intelligence during World War II, was a writer and editor with the *Daily Telegraph* from 1945 to 1952, and was editor of *Punch* from 1952 to 1957. During the 1960s, he became a well-known and often controversial writer, lecturer, and television figure, and also made several documentary films, in the late 1960s once again embracing Christianity; he became a Catholic in the early 1980s. The first two volumes of his unfinished autobiography were *Chronicles of Wasted Time: The Green Stick* (1972) and *The Infernal Grove* (1973). His other autobiographical works included *Like It Was: The Diaries of Malcolm Muggeridge* (1982), *A Third Testament* (1983), and *My Life in Pictures* (1987). (d. Sussex; November 13, 1990.)

FURTHER READING

"Beneath the carapace." CHRISTOPHER BOOKER and RICHARD NEUHAUS. *National Review*, Dec. 31, 1990.
Obituary. WILLIAM F. BUCKLEY, JR. *National Review*, Dec. 17, 1990.
Obituary. *Christianity Today*, Dec. 17, 1990.
Obituary. *Variety*, Nov. 26, 1990.
Obituary. *The Times* (of London), Nov. 15, 1990.
Obituary. *New York Times*, Nov. 15, 1990.

Mulroney, Brian (Martin Brian Mulroney, 1939–) During 1989–90, the Canadian prime minister continued to focus on the troubled Canadian economy. But it was the issue of Quebec that convulsed his country, threatening its continued existence as had no other issue in recent Canadian history. Mulroney was the prime mover in negotiating the Meech Lake Accords of June 1987, which had guaranteed Quebec a new status beyond its identity as part of Canada and were widely seen as opening the way to the eventual separation of Quebec from Canada. In June 1990, after an extraordinarily bitter national debate, the accords died, unratified by the rest of Canada. The issue of Quebec was still unresolved, many Canadians felt that their country faced a very uncertain future, and the Canadian prime minister had lost much of his support.

Mulroney practiced law in Montreal from 1965 to 1976, and then moved into industry, as executive vice president and then president of the Iron Ore Company of Canada from 1976 to 1983. He became Progressive Party leader and a Member of Parliament in 1983, and Prime Minister in 1984. He was returned to power in the general election of November 1988, after having made the election a virtual referendum on the recently concluded 1988 Canada-U.S.

trade pact. He married Mila Pivnicki in 1973; the couple have four children. He attended St. Francis Xavier and Laval universities.

FURTHER READING

"Under the gun. . . ." BRUCE WALLACE. *Maclean's*, Sept. 24, 1990.
"'Off to the races'." KEVIN DOYLE and ANTHONY WILSON-SMITH. *Maclean's*, June 25, 1990.
"An interview with. . . ." *Reader's Digest* (Canadian), Oct. 1988.
"A commonality of values." *Maclean's*, June 20, 1988.
"Mulroney on his record." *Maclean's*, Dec. 21, 1987.
Sacred Trust: Brian Mulroney & the Conservative Party in Power. DAVID BERCUSON. Doubleday, 1987.

Mumford, Lewis (1895–1990) Mumford was for five decades a leading U.S. social critic whose work ranged over philosophy, literary criticism, history, culture, and politics, with special emphasis on planning and architecture. Born and educated in New York, Mumford began working as an editor and writer for various magazines just after World War I. In 1922 he published his first book, *The Story of Utopias*, and the next year he co-founded the Regional Planning Association of America. Numerous books followed over the decades, most notably *Technics and Civilization* (1934), *The Culture of Cities* (1938), and *The City in History* (1961), along with a stream of articles and columns such as his "Sky Line" column for *The New Yorker*. In 1982 he published *Sketches from Life: The Autobiography of Lewis Mumford—The Early Years*. (d. Amenia, New York; January 26, 1990.)

FURTHER READING

"Remembering a prince. . . ." RUSSELL LYNES. *Architectural Digest*, Nov. 1990.
"Homage to Mumford." BRENDAN GILL. *New Yorker*, Apr. 2, 1990.
"Memories of Mumford." SELDEN RODMAN. *National Review*, Mar. 5, 1990.
Obituary. *Current Biography*, Mar. 1990.
Obituary. KIRKPATRICK SALE. *Nation*. Feb. 19, 1990.
Obituary. *The Times* (of London), Jan. 29, 1990.
Obituary. *New York Times*, Jan. 28, 1990.
Lewis Mumford: A Life. DONALD L. MILLER. Grove-Weidenfeld, 1989.
Lewis Mumford-David Liebovitz Letters. BETTINA L. KNAPP, ed. Whitston, 1983.

Murdoch, Rupert (Keith Rupert Murdoch, 1931–) Australian-American publisher Murdoch started with a small Australian family newspaper in 1952 and by 1990 had built a large worldwide communications company, controlling such publications and companies as Fox Television, 20th Century-Fox Films, *The Times* of London, HarperCollins Publishers, Sky Television, *The Australian* and many other publications in Australia, *New York* magazine, and Triangle Publications, purchased for $3 billion in 1988 and until then the largest acquisition in publishing history

In the 1980s, Murdoch financed his acquisitions with borrowings from easy-lending bankers and with the sale of other assets that had grown in value since he originally purchased them, as when he financed half of the Triangle purchase with the sale of Reuters stock, real estate, and other assets. Although he sold over $1.5 billion in assets in 1989–90, his total debts continued to grow, partly due to investments in printing plants and in his new Sky Television operation; in mid-1990 he was able to reduce substantially his Sky Television cash ouflow. Meanwhile, worldwide advertising revenues fell in a growing recession, existing assets realized less money on sale, and interest rates continued high, even increasing. His debts were an estimated $6–7 billion by late 1990, and in the changed atmosphere of the early 1990s he quickly ran into major problems, as it became very difficult to meet debt and interest payments. In early 1991, he was involved in negotiations with his bank creditors in an attempt to restructure and stretch out loan repayment. Murdoch married Anna Maria Torv in 1967; the couple have two children. He attended Oxford University.

FURTHER READING

Outfoxed: Marvin Davis, Barry Diller, Rupert Murdoch and the Inside Story of America's Fourth Television Network. ALEX B. BLOCK. St. Martin's, 1990.

"'I can think of. . . .'" WOLFGANG J. KOSCHNICK. *Forbes*, Nov. 27, 1989.

"New York's new power brokers. . . ." *Manhattan, inc.*, Sept. 1989.

"Media wars. . . ." D'ARCY JENISH. *Maclean's*, July 17, 1989.

"Conquering hearts and minds. . . ." BEN H. BAGDIKIAN. *Nation*, June 12, 1989.

Rupert Murdoch. JEROME TUCCILLE. Donald I. Fine, 1989.

Citizen Murdoch: The Unexpurgated Story of Rupert Murdoch—The World's Most Powerful & Controversial Media Lord. THOMAS KIERNAN. Dodd, Mead, 1986.

Arrogant Aussie: The Rupert Murdoch Story. MICHAEL LEAPMAN. Carol, 1985.

Murphy, Eddie (1961–) Comedian-actor Murphy continued to ride a crest of popularity in the early 1990s. In reviewing the 1980s, *Orbit Video* magazine found Murphy was the third biggest box-office star (after Harrison Ford and Dan Aykroyd); another report, by Baseline, Inc., noted that of all the enormously successful "Saturday Night Live" alumni, Murphy led the list with earnings through 1989 of over $825 million.

In 1990, Murphy and Nick Nolte released the long-awaited sequel to their 1982 pairing, *Another 48 Hours*. Widely criticized as a formula film with excessive violence and a crude rehashing of the original, the film did well at the box office, though not as well as expected, earning "only" $80 million; released in the video market later in the year, it quickly topped the charts. Murphy's *Harlem Nights* (1989), also released into the video rental market, did not do as well but reached the top five.

Success was not unalloyed. During the year, Murphy, his co-writer Arsenio Hall, and Paramount Pictures were sued by columnist Art Buchwald, who charged that their highly

successful film *Coming to America* (1988) had been based on Buchwald's story *King for a Day*. Murphy, Hall, and Paramount denied the charges but lost the case. As 1990 ended, the participants in the suit were still waiting for the court to rule on the nature of damages to be paid to Buchwald, which involved disentangling various questions about the way profits are calculated under the film contract. Although the movie grossed over $350 million, the plaintiffs had claimed that it had made no net profits, necessitating an audit of the kinds of expenses charged to the film.

Meanwhile, Murphy faced another plagiarism suit from Oman Oba Adele Mouftaou, the self-proclaimed Prince Johnny Osseni-Bello of Nigeria, who claimed that *Coming to America* was actually based on his 1983 screenplay (co-written with Shelby M. Gregory), *Toto, the African Prince*, and that he had discussed the idea with Murphy in 1982. And a further suit, by Long Island screenwriter Michael Greene, charged that *Harlem Nights* was based on a script he wrote for Murphy in 1988.

Despite such difficulties, Murphy continued to work closely with Paramount. In July 1990, the first Paramount Pictures/Eddie Murphy Fellowships were awarded, giving film students a year's experience at the studio, and Eddie Murphy Television Enterprises is producing films with Paramount.

Brooklyn-born Murphy was one of the leading entertainment celebrities of the 1980s, beginning with his regular featured role on television's "Saturday Night Live" (1980–84). His recording career began with the album *Eddie Murphy* (1982) and included *Eddie Murphy Comedian* (1983) and *So Happy* (1989). He began a spectacular film career with *48 Hours* (1982) and went on to such other films as *Trading Places* (1983) and *Beverly Hills Cop* (1983; *II*, 1986; *III*, 1989).

FURTHER READING

"Eddie Murphy. . . ." WALTER LEAVY. *Ebony*, Jan. 1990.
Films of Eddie Murphy. EDWARD GROSS. Movie Publications, 1990.
"Eddie Murphy. . . ." BILL ZEHME. *Rolling Stone*, Aug. 24, 1989.
"Eddie Murphy. . . ." BONNIE ALLEN. *Essence*, Dec. 1988.
"Eddie Murphy comes clean. . . ." JAMES MCBRIDE. *People*, Aug. 8, 1988.
"The prince of Paramount. . . ." ELVIS MITCHELL. *Interview*, Sept. 1987.
"Free Eddie Murphy. . . ." DAVID HANDELMAN. *Rolling Stone*, July 2, 1987.
Eddie Murphy. TERESA KOENIG and RIVIAN BELL. Lerner, 1985.
Eddie: Eddie Murphy from A to Z. MARIANNE RUTH. Holloway, 1985.
The Unofficial Eddie Murphy Scrapbook. JUDITH DAVIS. NAL-Dutton, 1984.

Murray, Bill (1950–) Actor-comedian Murray took his career in some new directions in 1990, co-directing and co-producing as well as starring in his new comedy, *Quick Change*, about a trio (including Geena Davis and Randy Quaid) who successfully execute a $1 million bank holdup—and then have to try to get out of New York City unscathed. The film won some critical praise, although it was not a box-office blockbuster. The blockbuster was *Ghostbusters II*, Murray's big 1989 hit, which continued its success in the video rental market in 1990. Largely because of the *Ghostbuster* films, Murray emerged as the fourth biggest box-office star of the 1980s, according to a survey by *Orbit Video* magazine.

Illinois-born Murray began his career with Chicago's Second City Troupe; he emerged as a television star in the late 1970s as a regular on "Saturday Night Live." He has appeared in such films as *Meatballs* (1977), *Caddyshack* (1980), *Stripes* (1981), *Ghostbusters* (1984), *Little Shop of Horrors* (1986), and *Scrooged* (1988). Murray attended Regis College. He married Margaret Kelly in 1980; the couple have two children.

FURTHER READING

The Rolling Stone Interviews: The 1980s. St. Martin's, 1989.
"The rumpled anarchy. . . ." TIMOTHY WHITE. *New York Times Magazine*, Nov. 20, 1988.
The Second City. DONNA MCCROHAN. Putnam, 1987.
"Murray, Bill." *Current Biography*, Jan. 1985.
"Bill Murray. . . ." ROY BLOUNT, JR. *People*, Dec. 24, 1984.
"Bill Murray. . . ." CHRIS CHASE. *Cosmopolitan*, Dec. 1984.
"Bill Murray. . . ." KARIN STABINER. *McCall's*, Oct. 1984.

Nagurski, "Bronko" (Bronislau Nagurski, 1908–90) Nagurski was a powerful football player, both running back and defensive tackle. Born to Ukrainian immigrants in Rainy River, Ontario, Nagurski grew up in nearby International Falls, Minnesota, becoming an All-American at the University of Minnesota from 1927 to 1929. Turning professional in 1930, he joined the Chicago Bears, helping to win the 1932 and 1933 championships and being voted All-Pro three times. A wrestler from 1938 to 1960, ineligible for military service due to injuries, he returned to the Bears for another championship year in 1943. (d. International Falls; January 7, 1990)

FURTHER READING

"Bustin' Bronko. . . ." FRED CRAFTS. *Boys' Life*, Oct. 1990.
"Bronko was a shy blockbuster." *Sporting News*, Jan. 22, 1990.
Obituary. *New York Times*, Jan. 9, 1990.
"The Bronk and. . . ." PAUL ZIMMERMAN. *Sports Illustrated*, Sept. 11, 1989.

Nakashima, George (1905–90) Furniture maker, designer, and wood sculptor Nakashima was trained as an architect and moved into carpentry while working as an architect in Japan during the late 1930s. Interned as a Japanese-American during World War II, he began his furniture-making career at New Hope in 1945 and in the following decades emerged as a leading American artist in wood. His work appears in many museums and other public institutions. In 1981, he published *The Soul of a Tree: A Woodworker's Reflections*. (d. New Hope, Pennsylvania; June 15, 1990)

FURTHER READING

Obituary. SAM MALOOF. *American Craft*, Oct.–Nov. 1990.
Obituary. *New York Times*, June 17, 1990.
"Something of a Druid. . . ." J. D. REED. *Time*, June 26, 1989.
"Nakashima. . . ." DONNA SAPOLIN. *Metropolitan Home*, June 1989.
George Nakashima: Full Circle. DEREK OSTERGARD. Grove-Weidenfeld, 1989.

Navratilova, Martina (1956–) Czech-American Navratilova is one of the greatest players in the history of tennis. Her career waned somewhat in the late 1980s and, after a series of losses, including one to Steffi Graf in the 1989 U.S. Open, she seriously thought of retirement. But she continued, coming back to defeat Zina Garrison to win her record-breaking ninth Wimbledon singles championship in July 1990. At the August–September U.S. Open, Navratilova was upset in the fourth round by Manuela Maleeva-Fragniere; but she and Gigi Fernandez won the doubles championship, sweeping the main doubles championships for the year.

On the personal side, Navratilova was criticized by some for being openly gay; but her detractors were few, and she was defended as a fine role model for younger players by such tennis greats as her former competitor, champion Chris Evert. In May, she made her first trip home to a free Czechoslovakia, there to be welcomed by President Vaclav Havel.

Prague-born Navratilova emerged as a leading Czech tennis player while still in her early teens and was Czech national champion from 1972–75. She was a very notable defector to the West in 1975, and then went on to become the top-ranked woman tennis player in the world for four years in a row (1982–85), as well as 1983–84 Grand Slam winner. She continued to win major tournaments throughout the later 1980s as well, winning for the eighth time at Wimbledon in 1987 and also winning the U.S. Open that year. In 1985 she published *Martina: Autobiography*, written with George Vecsey.

FURTHER READING

"'Not obsessed about. . . .'" JIM MARTZ. *Sporting News*, July 2, 1990.
"Postscript to. . . ." ANN SMITH and LEWIS ROTHLEIN. *Women's Sports and Fitness*, Mar. 1990.
"Martina on the Brink." SKIP BAYLESS. *Sport*, Oct. 1988.
"Navratilova." KEN RAPPOPORT. *Saturday Evening Post*, Mar. 1988.
"Ms. conversation." MICHELE KORT. *Ms.*, Feb. 1988.
"Leading ladies." CINDY SHMERLER. *World Tennis*, Jan. 1988.
"Martina Navratilova." MICHELE KORT. *Ms.*, Jan. 1988.
Martina Navratilova: Tennis Power. R. R. KNUDSON. Viking, 1986; Puffin, 1987.
Martina Navratilova. JANE M. LEDER. Crestwood House, 1985.

Nelson, Willie (1933–) Singer-guitarist-songwriter Nelson was on the road again with his friends Johnny Cash, Waylon Jennings, and Kris Kristofferson in 1990. In April, they won a legal battle with CBS to use the name The Highwaymen in performances and recordings. Nelson and Kristofferson also appeared together in a CBS television movie, *Pair of Aces*, about a country con man (Nelson) and Texas Ranger (Kristofferson) hunting a serial killer of high-school cheerleaders. In 1989, Nelson had a hit song on the country-and-western record charts, "Nothing I Can Do About It Now." Late in the year he was honored, with several other performing artists, at the Grammy Living Legends Awards.

In April 1990, Nelson organized and headlined at the Farm Aid IV concert at the Hoosier Dome in Indianapolis. Nelson, Neil Young, and John Cougar Mellencamp had founded the Farm Aid organization in 1985; the three earlier Farm Aid concerts—in 1985, 1986, and 1987—had raised about $12 million to aid poor and minority farmers. The Federation of Southern Cooperatives honored Nelson in 1989 for his "color-blind" efforts to help farmers; the group of mostly Black farmers had received $700,000. The Farm Aid organization itself was in some financial difficulty, but president Nelson expressed hope that they could forge a coalition between family farmers and environmentalists.

Nelson had his own financial difficulties. His longtime tax troubles reached a crisis in 1990 as the IRS—claiming that Nelson owed $16.7 million in back taxes—first placed liens on his real estate and personal property in six states (Texas, Alabama, California, Colorado, Hawaii, and Washington), including his golf course and recording studio, then padlocked them and later auctioned them off. Meanwhile, Nelson filed a $45 million suit against his former accounting firm, Price Waterhouse, alleging a persistent pattern of fraud from 1979 as well as poor investments that lost substantial amounts of money.

Nelson also retained his close ties with his home state, Texas. After a three-year hiatus, Nelson again held his famous Fourth of July "picnic" in Austin. He was also partner in a new Houston nightclub, Willie Nelson's Night Life, modeled on the famous Gilley's, and served as chairman of the board for a new Cowboy Channel seeking cable outlets.

Nelson began composing and recording in the early 1960s, emerging as a country music star in the mid-1970s, then crossing over to become a major popular music star as well, on records, in concert, and on the screen. His first national hit was the song "Blue Eyes Cryin' in the Rain," from his *Redheaded Stranger* album (1975). He went on to become one of the most popular musicians of the 1970s and 1980s, with such songs as "Georgia on My Mind," "Stardust," "On the Road Again," and "Blue Skies" and such albums as *Waylon and Willie* (1978), *Stardust* (1978), and *Honeysuckle Rose*, the sound-track album of his 1980 film of that name. He has also appeared in such films as *Barbarossa* (1982) and *Red-Headed Stranger* (1986). In 1988, he published his autobiography *Willie*. Nelson has been married three times and has five children. He attended Baylor University.

FURTHER READING

"Willie Nelson. . . ." TERESA TAYLOR VON-FREDERICK. *McCall's*, May 1988.

"With strings attached. . . ." JOE NICK PATOSKI. *Texas Monthly*, Feb. 1988.

"Catching up with. . . ." PATRICK CARR. *Country Music*, Jan.–Feb. 1987.

Country Musicians. . .Other Great American Artists—Their Music and How They Made It. JUDIE EREMO, ed. Grove-Weidenfeld, 1987.

Heart Worn Memories: A Daughter's Personal Biography of Willie Nelson. SUSIE NELSON. Eakin Press, 1987.

Willie: A Biography of Willie Nelson. MICHAEL BANE. Dell, 1984.

Willie Nelson: Country Outlaw. LOLA SCOBEY. Zebra, 1982.

Newman, Paul (1925–) In his 65th year, Newman gave a notable performance opposite his wife, Joanne Woodward, in *Mr. and Mrs. Bridge*, opening late in 1990. His work in *Blaze* (1990) was also well regarded, although the film did poorly at the box office; by summer 1990 it had moved into the top ten among video rentals. *Fat Man and Little Boy* (late 1989), in which Newman played General Leslie Groves, head of the atomic bomb–building Manhattan Project, also did poorly at the box office. Still Newman remains enormously popular; in the People's Choice Awards, he was one of the top vote-getters in the category of World's Favorite Motion Picture Actor.

He also continued his philanthropic work, most notably contributing all profits from his Newman's Own food line—over $7 million in 1989 alone—to various charitable causes and also sometimes making direct food donations, such as lemonade to troops in Saudi Arabia and spaghetti sauce to victims of the October 1989 San Francisco Bay Area earthquake. In 1989–90, he successfully fought off a claim by a Connecticut delicatessen owner to a share in the company's profits. He is also a founder of the Hole in the Wall Gang Camp Fund, a charity for seriously ill children and their families, and of the Scott Newman Center against substance abuse, named for Newman's son, whose 1980 death was drug-related.

Cleveland-born Newman has been a film star for 35 years, breaking through in *Somebody up There Likes Me* (1956) and *Cat on a Hot Tin Roof* (1958). A few of his many major films were *Exodus* (1960), *The Hustler* (1961), *Sweet Bird Of Youth* (1962; he had starred in the Broadway play in 1959), *Hud* (1963), *Harper* (1966), *Cool Hand Luke* (1967), *Butch Cassidy and the Sundance Kid* (1969), *The Sting* (1973), *Absence of Malice* (1981), *Harry and Son* (1984; he also wrote and directed), and *The Color of Money* (1986), for which he won a Best Actor Oscar. He was previously married to Jacqueline Witte; he married Joanne Woodward in 1958 and has had six children. His B.A. was from Kenyon College, in 1949; he also attended Yale Drama School. Newman has also been a racing-car driver.

FURTHER READING

"Paul Newman and. . . ." MAUREEN DOWD. *McCall's*, Jan. 1991.

"Mr. and Mrs. Bridge." GRAHAM FULLER. *Interview*, Nov. 1990.

"Joanne Woodward. . . ." BETH WEINHOUSE. *Redbook*, Jan. 1990.

"Paul Newman. . . ." LESTER DAVID and IRENE DAVID. *McCall's*, Mar. 1989.

Paul Newman. ELENA OUMANO. St. Martin's, 1989.
Icons: Intimate Portraits. DENISE WORRELL. *Atlantic Monthly*, 1989.
No Tricks in My Pocket: Paul Newman Directs. STEWART STERN. Grove-Weidenfeld, 1989.
Paul and Joanne: A Biography of Paul Newman and Joanne Woodward. JOE MORELLA and EDWARD Z. EPSTEIN. Delacorte, 1988.
"Testing himself. . . ." MAUREEN DOWD. *New York Times Magazine*, Sept. 28, 1986.
"Newman, Paul." *Current Biography*, May 1985.
Paul Newman: An Illustrated Biography. J. LANDRY. McGraw-Hill, 1983.
The Films of Paul Newman. LAWRENCE J. QUIRK. Carol, 1981.

Nichols, Mike (Michael Igor Pechowsky, 1931–) Director-actor Nichols came in at the top in 1990. When his latest film, *Postcards From the Edge*, opened in September, it immediately became the top box-office film. More to the point, it won high praise from a wide range of critics. The tale of a Hollywood mother-daughter relationship, starring Meryl Streep as a drug-dependent actress and Shirley MacLaine as her actress-mother, was based on Carrie Fisher's semiautobiograpical novel. Nichols's direction was praised for its finely honed comic tone, in what some hailed as his best directorial work since *Carnal Knowledge*.

In 1989, Nichols directed a notable revival of Samuel Beckett's *Waiting for Godot*, with Robin Williams and Steve Martin, lauded for making the usually obscure play understandable to audiences, although some charged the approach "vulgarized" the work. Elsewhere, Nichols was among those called in to advise on how the troubled *Annie 2* musical might be salvaged. He received an honorary doctorate in 1989 from New York's Juilliard School. Forthcoming is the film *Regarding Henry*, starring Harrison Ford, about a powerful trial lawyer injured by a bullet to the head.

Berlin-born Nichols appeared in cabaret during the late 1950s and was partnered with Elaine May on Broadway in 1960, in *An Evening with Mike Nichols and Elaine May*. He received a Best Director Tony for *The Odd Couple* (1965) and has directed five Tony-winning plays: *Barefoot in the Park* (1963), *Luv* (1964), *Plaza Suite* (1968), *The Prisoner of Second Avenue* (1971), and *The Real Thing* (1984). He has also directed such films as *Who's Afraid of Virginia Woolf* (1966), the Oscar-winning *The Graduate* (1967), *Carnal Knowledge* (1971), *Silkwood* (1983), *Biloxi Blues* (1987), and *Working Girl* (1988). In 1988, he published *Life, and Other Ways to Kill Time*. He was formerly married to Patricia Scott and Margot Callas, and married Diane Sawyer in 1988. He attended the University of Chicago, from 1950 to 1953.

FURTHER READING

"Mr. Success." ALICE ARLEN. *Interview*, Dec. 1988.
"The happiest couple. . . ." LISA GRUNWALD. *Esquire*, Dec. 1988.
"Genius of Broadway." RHODA KOENIG. *New York*, Dec. 24, 1984.

Nicholson, Jack (1937–) Actor Nicholson, this time doubling as director, went back to the scene of one of his finest portrayals as private eye Jake Gittes in *Chinatown* (1974). In the sequel, *Two Jakes* (1990), he investigated a murder involving Jake Berman, played by Harvey Keitel. Although Gittes is somewhat mellower, Los Angeles is not, and the movie is thick with complex plot lines involving oil rights, passion, and memories of the past—so strong that some critics noted that the movie was only fully appreciated (or perhaps even understandable) by people who had seen *Chinatown*.

The sequel's 16-year progress to the screen was much troubled; five years before, a version involving the original's producer and writer, Robert Evans and Robert Towne, stopped just short of shooting; Nicholson finally completed the project from a Towne screenplay. Despite Nicholson's stardom and considerable (though not unalloyed) critical praise, the film was not a commercial success in theatrical release; its long-range status, as a companion to the original, remains to be seen. Some see a further sequel in the offing.

In January 1990, Nicholson joined other cast members from *One Flew over the Cuckoo's Nest* in American Cinematheque's weekend salute to its director, Milos Forman. Also in 1990 Nicholson was awarded France's highest honor for artistic excellence, being named Commander of Arts and Letters.

New Jersey–born Nicholson played strong supporting roles from the late 1950s, most notably in *Easy Rider* (1969), and then moved into the powerful dramatic roles that made him a major figure for the next two decades in such films as *Five Easy Pieces* (1970), *Chinatown* (1974), *One Flew over the Cuckoo's Nest* (1975; he won a Best Actor Oscar), *The Postman Always Rings Twice* (1981), *Reds* (1981), *Terms of Endearment* (1983; he won a Best Supporting Actor Oscar), *Prizzi's Honor* (1985), *Heartburn* (1986), *Ironweed* (1987), and *Batman* (1989). He was formerly married to Sandra Knight, had a 17-year relationship with Anjelica Huston, and has one child.

FURTHER READING

"The myth that Jack built." STEVE ERICKSON. *Esquire*, Sept. 1990.
"Hollywood's wild card." BRIAN D. JOHNSON. *Maclean's*, Aug. 20, 1990.
"Jake Jake. . . ." JULIAN SCHNABEL. *Interview*, Aug. 1990.
"Forget it, Jack. . . ." JAMES GREENBERG. *American Film*, Feb. 1990.
The Films of Jack Nicholson. DOUGLAS BRODE. Carol, 1990.
"Jack Nicholson." LYNN HIRSCHBERG. *Rolling Stone*, Nov. 5, 1987.
"A devil of a fine actor." PATRICIA HLUCHY. *Maclean's*, July 28, 1986.
Jack Nicholson: A Biography. DAVID DOWNING. Scraborough House, 1984.

Nidal, Abu (Sabry Khalil al-Banna, 1937–) A Palestinian guerrilla leader and leading terrorist, Abu Nidal has long been associated with Libyan leader Muammar Qaddafi and Iraqi leader Saddam Hussein. In the early 1970s, before Nidal's split with Yasir Arafat and the Palestine Liberation Organization (PLO), he was PLO representative in Iraq, and was headquartered in Libya during the late 1980s. In October 1989, he began a factional war within his own Fatah Revolutionary Council, which spread throughout the organization and became a series of battles between rival militias in northern Lebanon. In May–June 1990, his forces in Lebanon were defeated with the help of PLO forces in the area. But later in the year, he renewed and strengthened the Iraqi tie as Saddam Hussein prepared the invasion of Kuwait. Nidal remains the leader of an experienced and well-organized terrorist force.

Sabry Khalil al-Banna was born in Jaffa, then located in British-ruled Palestine. He took the name Abu Nidal as his PLO work name and in the 1970s became a powerful dissident terrorist leader within the organization. When the PLO moved away from unrestrained terrorism in the mid-1970s, he broke with Yasir Arafat and the main body of the PLO, forming the Fatah Revolutionary Council, which then became a major terrorist group. Nidal was reported to have been sentenced to death in absentia by the PLO for plotting to kill Yasir Arafat. In the mid-1980s, he also went over to mass organization, forming militias that operated in southern Lebanon and were also involved in the long Lebanese civil war. Abu Nidal and Fatah are widely believed to have been responsible for many assassinations of PLO leaders and for such mass murders as the 1986 Istanbul synagogue shootings and the 1985 Rome and Berlin airport murders.

FURTHER READING

"Finis for the master terrorist?. . . ." DAVID BRAND. *Time*, Dec. 11, 1989.
Terrorism: Past, Present, Future. THOMAS P. RAYNOR. Watts, 1987; Avon, 1987.
"Master of mystery. . . ." GEORGE RUSSELL. *Time*, Jan. 13, 1986.
"The 'evil spirit'. . . ." ROD NORDLAND. *Newsweek*, Jan. 13, 1986.
"When terror. . . ." JAMES WALLACE. *U.S. News & World Report*, Jan. 13, 1986.
The Master Terrorist: The True Story Behind Abu Nidal. YOSSI MELMAN. Adama, 1986.

Nixon, Richard Milhous (1913–) Although the disgrace of Watergate was far from forgotten, former president Nixon found himself able to move and speak very freely in the late 1980s and early 1990s. In October 1989, he made an unofficial visit to China and met with top Chinese leaders, including Deng Xiaoping and Li Peng. He later dined with President George Bush in the White House and reported on his Chinese visit. In mid-1990, his autobiographical book *In the Arena: A Memoir of Victory, Defeat, and Renewal* made the bestseller lists. In 1988 he had published *1999: Victory Without War*. On July 19, 1990, the privately financed Richard Nixon Library, at Yorba Linda, California, was dedicated; the dedication was attended by President Bush and by former presidents Ford and Reagan. In 1990 (and previously in 1988), previously unpublished documents from Nixon's Watergate period files were published under the title *From the President*.

California-born Nixon became the 37th President of the United States in 1969 and resigned to avoid impeachment in 1974, after his complicity in the Watergate scandal was exposed. He had previously been a leading member of the House Un-American Activities Committee while a California congressman from 1947–51, senator from California in the early 1950s, and Dwight D. Eisenhower's vice president from 1953–61. He was defeated for the presidency by John F. Kennedy in 1960 and came back to defeat Hubert Humphrey in 1968 and George McGovern in 1972. He presided over the last stages of his country's defeat in Vietnam and played a key role in reestablishing U.S.-Chinese relations. However, in the long run he is chiefly notable for his multiple illegal attacks on domestic political opponents, which climaxed with the Watergate Democratic National Committee break-ins of his "plumbers," which ultimately destroyed his career and reputation.

Among his earlier autobiographical works are *RN: Memoirs of Richard Nixon* (1978) and *The Memoirs of Richard Nixon* (2 vols.; 1978–79). In 1940, Nixon married Thelma Patricia Ryan; as First Lady, she was known as "Pat" Nixon. The couple have two children. His B.A. was from Whittier College, in 1934; his LL.B. from Duke, in 1937.

FURTHER READING

The Biography of Richard Nixon. Laurie Nadel. Macmillan, 1991.
"Means of descent. . . ." Alan Brinkley. *New Republic*, Oct. 1, 1990.
"Paying the price. . . ." John Stacks and Strobe Talbott. *Time*, Apr. 2, 1990.
Richard Nixon and His America. Herbert S. Parmet. Little, Brown, 1990.
Nixon—Triumph of a Politician. Stephen E. Ambrose. Simon and Schuster, 1990.
Richard Nixon: One of Us. Tom Wicker. Random, 1990.
Richard M. Nixon, President. Sallie Randolph. Walker, 1989.
Richard Milhous Nixon: The Rise of an American Politician. Roger Morris. Holt, 1989.
Nixon: The Triumph of a Politician, 1962–1972. Stephen E. Ambrose. Simon & Schuster, 1989.
"Former presidents reflect. . . ." Michael Delon. *USA Today*, Nov. 1988.
Richard Nixon. Dee Lillegard. Childrens, 1988.
Richard M. Nixon: A Biographic Exploration. Dale E. Casper. Garland, 1988.
Nixon: The Education of a Politician, 1913–1962. Stephen E. Ambrose. Simion & Schuster, 1987.
The World & Richard Nixon. C. L. Sulzberger. Prentice-Hall, 1987.
Breach of Faith: The Fall of Richard Nixon. Theodore H. White. Dell, 1986.
Richard Nixon: The Shaping of His Character. Fawn M. Brodie. Harvard University Press, 1983.

Nolte, Nick (1942–) A new and larger Nick Nolte emerged this year. For his role as the alcoholic, bigoted, brutal New York City detective Mike Brennan in Sidney Lumet's *Q&A*, Nolte put on 40 pounds. In this urban morality tale, opposite Timothy Hutton as assistant district attorney who investigates his killing of a drug dealer, Nolte earned his full share of the critical praise showered on the movie.

Then he quickly had to lose the pounds gained for *Q&A*, to prepare for the long-awaited sequel to his classic 1981 pairing with Eddie Murphy. *Another 48 Hours*, which opened in June, was a disappointment to many, widely criticized for excess violence and for being a crude rehash of the original. The movie still did well at the box office, taking in $80 million but not reaching projections of over $100 million; when released in the video rental market in December, however, it surged to number one.

Earlier in 1990, Nolte had opened in Karel Reisz's *Everybody Wins*, playing private eye Tom O'Toole opposite the shady Debra Winger; although the screenplay was by Arthur Miller, only his second screenplay since *The Misfits* (1961), the film generally pleased neither critics nor general audiences. For his next project, Nolte is scheduled to play a South Carolina coach-teacher opposite Barbra Streisand's psychiatrist in *The Prince of Tides*, Streisand's movie based on the Pat Conroy novel.

Nebraska-born Nolte spent years in regional theater before emerging as a leading film player in the mid-1970s in *The Deep* (1977), and went on to play leads in such films as *Who'll*

Stop the Rain (1978), *North Dallas Forty* (1979), *Cannery Row* (1982), *48 Hours* (1982), *Under Fire* (1983), *Down and Out in Beverly Hills* (1986), and *Three Fugitives* (1989). He has also appeared on television, most notably in "Rich Man, Poor Man" (1976). He has been married three times and has one child. He attended Pasadena College.

FURTHER READING

"Nick Nolte. . . ." STEVE ONEY. *Cosmopolitan*, June 1989.
"The prime of. . . ." CATHLEEN MCGUIGAN. *Newsweek*, Feb. 27, 1989.
"The taming of. . . ." TOM BURKE. *Cosmopolitan*, Jan. 1988.
"He's no Teacher's pet. . . ." MICHELLE GREEN. *People*, Nov. 5, 1984.
"Nick Nolte untamed." LEO JANOS. *Cosmopolitan*, Oct. 1983.
"Nolte, Nick." *Current Biography*, Nov. 1980.

Nono, Luigi (1924–90) A leading post–World War II Italian composer, Nono was both a musical modernist and a Marxist. His early work was composed wholly in Schoenberg's twelve-tone scale, and from the mid-1950s he was widely recognized as a pioneer in electronic classical music. He became an international figure with the political choral work *Il Canto Sospeso* (1956), its words taken from the letters of World War II Resistance fighters, and went on to write many other political works, taking as his themes such matters as the atomic bomb, the Vietnam War, World War II concentration camps, and intolerance. (d. Venice; June 11, 1990)

FURTHER READING

Obituary. *New York Times*, May 11, 1990.
Obituary. *The Times* (of London), May 11, 1990.

Noriega, Manuel (Manuel Antonio Noriega Morena, 1938–) Former Panamanian dictator and U.S. ally Manuel Noriega withstood two major challenges during 1989. The first was the presidential election of May 7, in which his handpicked candidate lost by an estimated 3–1 margin to Guillermo Endara despite Noriega's attempt to rig the election, as attested by former U.S. president Jimmy Carter. On May 10, Noriega annulled the election; that day, Endara and his running mates were beaten by government thugs and hospitalized. The second challenge was the failed anti-Noriega coup of October 3, which the U.S. had encouraged but did not physically support.

But Noriega's rule did not survive the third challenge—the November 20, 1989, U.S. invasion of Panama. His armed forces were quickly defeated, and he went into hiding, surfacing to claim asylum in the Vatican diplomatic mission in Panama City on December 24. After a period of attempted negotiation, he surrendered to U.S. forces on January 3, 1990, and was flown to Miami and arraigned on drug trade–related charges, although he claimed the status of a political prisoner. He remained in prison throughout the balance of 1990. In November 1990, Cable News Network (CNN) broadcast tapes of Noriega's conversations with his lawyer, allegedly made illegally by his captors while he was in jail, prompting a lawsuit to bar further broadcasts.

Noriega was a career Panamanian military intelligence officer. As head of Panamanian intelligence from 1970 to 1982 and dictator from 1982 to 1989, he was deeply involved with U.S. military and intelligence activities in Latin America and was on the CIA payroll for many years. He was also even more profitably associated with one or more drug cartels in the same period. Both arrangements were upset by his February 1988 Florida drug indictment, the same charges for which he was jailed in

Miami in 1990. He is married to Felicidad Sieiro, and has three children. He attended Panama University.

FURTHER READING

"Our man in Panama. . . ." SEYMOUR M. HERSH. *Life*, Mar. 1990.
"Noriega on ice. . . ." RICHARD LACAYO. *Time*, Jan. 15, 1990.
"The Noriega files." FREDERICK KEMPE. *Newsweek*, Jan. 15, 1990.
"Lifestyle of a dictator." RAE CORELLI. *Maclean's*, Jan. 1, 1990.
Our Man in Panama: How General Noriega Used the United States—and Made Millions in Drugs and Arms. JOHN DINGES. Random, 1990.
Divorcing the Dictator: America's Bungled Affair with Noriega. FREDERICK KEMPE. Putnam, 1990.
In the Time of the Tyrants. BORBON G. SANCHEZ. Norton, 1990.
"Noriega Morena, Manuel Antonio." *Current Biography*, Mar. 1988.

Norris, Chuck (1940–) Actor Norris lives an action-filled life. The dominant features of his latest movie, *Delta Force 2: Operation Stranglehold* (1990), are the striking international locations and elaborate parachuting and helicopter stunts. The danger is real. In filming this tale, in which Norris and his special U.S. Army unit set out to get the world's biggest drug dealer, five stuntmen lost their lives and a sixth was seriously injured when their helicopter crashed in the Philippines; families of the six later filed suit against the filmmaker, Cannon Films, naming (among others) the star's brother, Aaron Norris, one of the film's directors. On its release, the resulting film was widely criticized for its cardboard characters, script clichés, and nonstop violence, although that did not deter Norris fans. Meanwhile, Norris was filming a new action adventure, *50/50*, about a team working to oust the dictator of a fictional country and restore the rightful democratic president.

Privately, in August Norris conducted his self-described "Assault on the Great Lakes," piloting his 46-foot boat *Drambuie Challenger* 605 miles from Chicago to Detroit in 12 hours, 8 minutes, 42 seconds, breaking the 1983 record previously held by Michael Reagan, son of the former president. In April he won the superboat class of the 1990 Queen Mary–to–Catalina Offshore Powerboat Races, speeding his 50-foot speedboat over the 140-mile course at an average of 81.2 miles per hour; fourth place was taken by a boat with fellow actors Don Johnson and Kurt Russell aboard. In the Offshore Professional Tour Superboat race off Miami Beach in May, he and Don Johnson (in separate boats) lost a photo-finish race to Pennsylvania speedboater John Gehert.

Oklahoma-born Norris was a karate expert before becoming an actor; he was world middleweight champion from 1968 to 1974, and later used his skills to great advantage in many of his films, beginning with *Return of the Dragon* (1972). He became a major action film star in the mid-1980s, in *Missing in Action* (1984), which was followed by the sequels *Missing in Action II—The Beginning* (1985) and *Braddock—Missing in Action III* (1987). His very popular later films also include *Code of Silence* (1985), *Invasion, U.S.A.* (1985), *Delta Force* (1986), *Firewalker* (1986), and *The Hero and the Terror* (1988). In 1988 he published *The Secret of Inner Strength*, written with Joe Hyams. He is married to Dianne Norris; the couple have two children.

FURTHER READING

"Norris, Chuck." *Current Biography*, Jan. 1989.
"Double trouble." PETER A. JANSSEN. *Motor Boating & Sailing*, July 1988.
"Chuck Norris. . . ." BARNEY COHEN. *Cosmopolitan*, Feb. 1986.
Chuck Norris. BYRON COLEY. St. Martin's, 1986.
"Want a kick?. . . ." SANDRA HINSON. *People*, June 3, 1985.

North, Edmund Hall (1911–90) Manhattan-born screenwriter North shared a 1970 Academy Award (with Francis Ford Coppola) for the script of *Patton*. He toured vaudeville with his parents as a child and began writing plays in school, his first screen credit being *One Night of Love* (1934). Best-known of his other scripts are *Young Man with a Horn* (1950), *The Day the Earth Stood Still* (1951), *Sink the Bismarck!* (1960), and *Damn the Defiant* (1962). He was long active in the Writers Guild of America. (d. Santa Monica, California; July 31, 1990)

FURTHER READING

Obituary. *The Times* (of London), Sept. 4, 1990.
Obituary. *New York Times*, Aug. 31, 1990.

North, Oliver (1943–) Marine officer and former White House aide North was indicted on Iran-Contra–related charges on March 14, 1988, after a long grand jury investigation directed by special prosecutor Lawrence E. Walsh. He resigned from the Marine Corps two days later, then went on tour to raise money for his defense. In May 1989, he was convicted on three felony counts and appealed the conviction. In May 1990, a three-judge federal appeals court set aside all three convictions, overturning one and returning the other two to the trial court. In September, Walsh asked the appeals court to reconsider its decisions; the case continued.

North, a career marine officer, was on active service in Vietnam in 1968 to 1969. From 1981 to 1986, he was deputy director of the military affairs bureau of the U.S. National Security Council, working directly out of the White House; he became a marine lieutenant colonel in 1983. North was involved in developing several covert operations during his White House years; one of them blew up in late 1986, becoming the Iran-Contra affair, a set of scandals that resulted in North's dismissal from his White House post, although not from the Marines, in November 1986. North then became an international figure as he testified on television before congressional committees. North is a graduate of the U. S. Naval Academy at Annapolis. He is married to Betsy (Frances Elizabeth) Stuart; they have three children.

FURTHER READING

Opening Arguments: A Young Lawyer's First Case: United States v. Oliver L. North. Jeffrey Toobin. Viking Penguin, 1991.
"True North." Asa Baber. *Playboy*, Mar. 1988.
Guts and Glory: The Oliver North Story. Ben Bradlee, Jr. Donald I. Fine, 1988.
The Secret Government. Bill Moyers. Seven Locks, 1988.
Men of Zeal: A Candid Story of the Iran-Contra Hearings. William S. Cohen and George J. Mitchell. Viking Penguin, 1988.
Defiant Patriot: The Life and Exploits of Lieutenant Colonel Oliver North. Peter Meyer. St. Martin's, 1987.
Taking the Stand: The Testimony of Lieutenant Colonel Oliver L. North. Daniel Schorr, ed. Pocket Books, 1987.

Norville, Deborah (1958–) Television journalist Norville was cast as the spoiler on NBC's "Today" show in 1989–90. News reporter on "NBC News at Sunrise," she was promoted to news reader on "Today," replacing John Palmer (actually, they switched jobs) in August 1989 as part of the new executive producer's bid to attract younger viewers. Although Jane Pauley, the show's regular co-host with Bryant Gumbel, had been informed of the change, Norville's promotion to the main desk in an upgraded role triggered enormous media discussion of a presumed feud between the two

women, with Norville seen as breaking up a happy and successful television "marriage." In the end, Pauley decided to move on to her own prime-time news program, announcing her decision on the air with an emotional hug and presentation of her alarm clock to Norville.

Although the two worked hard to dispel the media conception of a feud between them, the public felt strong sympathy for the popular Pauley. After her exit, the show's ratings dropped sharply, at one point by about 17 percent, although Norville urged, "Don't shoot me before I'm in the saddle—let me get up there and ride a bit." Charging sexism, she asserted that the media would not have portrayed her as a villainness if she had been a 31-year-old man with over 11 years of reporting experience. Other changes were made in the show to try to stop the ratings slide; the whole show even went "camping" in Pennsylvania's Pocono Mountains to drum up ratings. Norville left on maternity leave in early 1991, and in April was replaced permanently by Katherine Couric. Norville anchored her own NBC News special, "Sex, Buys & Advertising" in July 1990, and in April 1990 reported from Nicaragua on the transition of power.

After graduating summa cum laude from the University of Georgia's broadcasting journalism program, Georgia-born Norville broke into television in 1978 at Atlanta's WAGA and in 1981 moved on to Chicago's WMAQ (once also Pauley's professional home), where she won an Emmy for local news reporting. In early 1987 she came to New York with "NBC News at Sunrise." She is married to fine-arts-auction executive Karl Wellner and has one child.

FURTHER READING

"Norville, Deborah." *Current Biography*, Apr. 1990.
"Deborah Norville. . . ." Larry B. Dendy. *Saturday Evening Post*, Mar. 1990.
"TV's new golden girl." Jan Hoffman. *GQ—Gentlemen's Quarterly*, June 1989.
"Yes, she's more. . . ." Joanmarie Kalter. *TV Guide*, Aug. 1, 1987.
"NBC's crack (of dawn). . . ." Jane Hall. *People*, July 27, 1987.

Noyce, Robert (1927–90) Iowa-born Noyce was an inventor of the microchip that revolutionized computers. He became fascinated with solid-state electronics in college and, after earning a doctorate at the Massachusetts Institute of Technology, he began working with semiconductors. In 1957, he developed a method for interconnecting tiny transistors on a single chip (working independently of Jack Kilby, who also developed a microchip). These microchips allowed the miniaturization of modern electronics products. Noyce helped found several high-technology companies in California's Silicon Valley, including Intel Corporation in 1968, and became a major spokesman for the computer industry. (d. Austin, Texas; June 3, 1990)

FURTHER READING

"Death of an entrepreneur." *Economist*, June 9, 1990.
Obituary. *The Times* (of London), June 5, 1990.
Obituary. *New York Times*, June 4, 1990.
"The U.S. Business Hall of Fame." Walter Guzzardi. *Fortune*, Mar. 13, 1989.
"Bob Noyce created. . . ." Otis Port and Richard Brandt. *Business Week*, Aug. 15, 1988.
"Four financial genies." Charles P. Alexander. *Time*, Jan. 23, 1984.

Nujoma, Sam (Sam Daniel Nujoma, 1929–) On September 14, 1989, Sam Nujoma returned to Namibia, moving into legal politics after 30 years in exile, 22 of them in armed struggle as the guerrilla leader of the Southwest Africa People's Organization (SWAPO). He then led his country toward development of a constitution guaranteeing a multiparty democracy and on February 16 was elected the first president of Namibia by the new constituent assembly.

He was inaugurated on March 21, 1990, a little over six months after his return from exile; UN Secretary General Pérez de Cuéllar administered the oath of office; South African president F. W. De Klerk attended the ceremony. So ended 75 years of South African domination of the last European colony on the continent. Nujoma called for the full development of democracy in Namibia, the stimulation of the country's economy by public and private means, and racial and ethnic cooperation.

Nujoma was a co-founder of SWAPO in 1959. He was imprisoned in that year, went into exile in 1960, and from 1960 to 1966 led the campaign to gain independence by peaceful means. After being expelled by the occupying South Africans in 1966, he led the Namibian independence movement in the 22-year-long guerrilla war that ended with South African withdrawal from Namibia. He is married to Kowambo Theoplidine Katjimuina; they have four children.

FURTHER READING

"Nujoma, Samuel Daniel." *Current Biography*, Feb. 1990.

Namibia: Struggle for Independence. Y. GORBUNOV and S. NUJOMA. Imported Publications, 1988.

Nunn, Sam (Samuel Nunn, Jr., 1938–) During the late 1980s, Nunn emerged as a powerful, highly visible figure in American politics as chairman of the Senate Armed Services Committee. In 1989–90, as the Cold War wound down, he moved from general support of military spending plans toward a call for large cuts in spending, armaments, and force levels, and by April 1990 he was urging European forces cuts of two-thirds and the withdrawal of nuclear missiles and artillery from Europe. In late July, his committee reported the first large Senate defense-cuts bill in decades, beginning the 1991 defense budgeting process.

While supporting both the late-1989 invasion of Panama and the American commitment in the Persian Gulf Crisis, Nunn voiced concern about both, calling the Panama invasion the result of years of poor policy in the area and urging the United States to act with its allies in the Gulf and use force only as a last resort. His most recent of numerous publications on military matters was *Nunn Nineteen Ninety: A New Military Strategy* (1990).

Georgia-born Nunn was a Georgia state legislator from 1968 to 1972 and began his long career in the Senate in 1973. He became chairman of the Senate Armed Services Committee in 1986 and was regarded as a possible 1988 Democratic presidential and then vice presidential candidate during the run up to the Dukakis nomination, but refused the vice-presidential nomination when it was offered. He is clearly a possible candidate for the 1992 Democratic presidential nomination. He married Colleen O'Brien in 1964; the couple have two children. His B.A. and LL.B. were from Atlanta's Emory University.

FURTHER READING

"Wanted. . . ." DOUGLAS HARBRECHT. *Business Week*, Nov. 19, 1990.

"Born to be mild. . . ." TIMOTHY NOAH. *Washington Monthly*, Dec. 1989 .

"Smart, dull and very powerful." MICHAEL KRAMER. *Time*, Mar. 13, 1989.

"Bar Nunn." HENDRIK HERTZBERG. *New Republic*, May 23, 1988.

"Advice and consent. . . ." *U.S. News & World Report*, Feb. 8, 1988.

"Nunn too soon for President?" *U.S. News & World Report*, Jan. 19, 1987.

"Sam Nunn's rising star." PHIL GAILEY. *New York Times Magazine*, Jan. 4, 1987.

Nureyev, Rudolf (Rudolf Hametovich Nureyev, 1938–) Soviet-born dancer and choreographer Nureyev has for three decades been one of the world's most celebrated dancers, and during the 1980s he became a leading choreographer as well. He was artistic director of the Paris Opera Ballet from 1983 to 1989 and became its principal choreographer in 1989 while continuing to dance throughout the world. In the summer of 1989, he appeared in Flemming Flindt's new ballet, in a role based on Gogol's *The Overcoat* and created for him by Flindt. In 1989–90 he also starred on stage in musical theater for the first time, in a U.S. tour of *The King and I*. His heavy schedule took him away from the Paris Opera Ballet even more than before—and Pierre Bergé, director of the company, stepped up previous objections to the amount of time Nureyev spent in Paris.

The matter was settled by Nureyev's November 1989 resignation as dance director; he was named first choreographer in an attempt to keep him with the company on some basis. He was replaced by Patrick Dupond as dance director in February 1990; meanwhile, there began what promised to be a long legal fight over ownership of the ballets Nureyev had created during his period with the company.

Nureyev joined the Leningrad-based Kirov Ballet as a soloist in 1958 and quickly became a leading Soviet dancer. Three years later, in 1961, he defected to the West, and within a year he was a world figure in the ballet, very notably often as Margot Fonteyn's partner at London's Royal Ballet. During the next quarter century, he danced as a guest artist in many countries and became a leading choreographer, as well, of such works as *Tancredi* (1966), *Romeo and Juliet* (1977), and *Washington Square* (1985). He has also appeared in several films, including *Valentino* (1977) and *Exposed* (1982).

FURTHER READING

"Nureyev now!" PAUL H. LEMAY. *Dance*, May 1990.
"Nureyev resigns. . . ." ROBERT JOHNSON. *Dance*, Feb. 1990.
"The force still with us." JOHN GRUEN. *Dance*, July 1986.
"Rudolf Nureyev." MICHAEL PYE and DAVID HOCKNEY. *Geo*, Aug. 1983.

Oakeshott, Michael Joseph (1901–90) British political scientist, historian, and philosopher Oakeshott, child of a Fabian Socialist family, strongly influenced the development of conservative British political thinking during the post-World War II period, although he was not involved in Conservative Party politics. He was a lecturer in history at Cambridge from 1929 to 1949 and a professor of political science at the London School of Economics from 1950 to 1969, and wrote such works as *Experience and Its Modes* (1933), *Social and Political Doctrines of Contemporary Europe* (1937), *Rationalism and Politics* (1962), *On Human Conduct* (1975), *On History* (1983), *Essays on Learning and Teaching* (1989), and *The Voice of Liberal Learning* (1989). (d. Dorset; Dec. 18, 1990)

FURTHER READING

Obituary. *The Times* (of London), Dec. 22, 1990.
Obituary. *New York Times*, Dec. 22, 1990.
The Political Philosophy of Michael Oakeshott. Paul Franco. Yale University Press, 1990.

O'Brien, Lawrence Francis, Jr. (1917–90) Democratic Party strategist O'Brien orchestrated John F. Kennedy's senatorial and presidential campaigns and was the intended target of the 1972 Watergate burglaries. He learned practical politics from his Irish immigrant family in Springfield, Massachusetts. After law school, union work, and military service, he ran a 1946 political campaign, going to Washington as an assistant and from 1952 running Kennedy's campaigns. As congressional liaison under Kennedy and then Lyndon Johnson, he eased passage of such major legislation as the 1964 Civil Rights Act and Medicare. He later served as postmaster general (1965–68), twice Democratic Party national chairman (1968 and 1970–72), and commissioner of the National Basketball Association (1975–84). (d. New York; September 28, 1990)

FURTHER READING

Obituary. *Current Biography*, Nov. 1990.
Obituary. *Sporting News*, Oct. 8, 1990.
Obituary. *The Times* (of London), Oct. 2, 1990.
Obituary. *New York Times*, Sept. 29, 1990

O'Connor, Cardinal John J. (1920–) The Roman Catholic archbishop of New York, always notable for his frankly expressed conservative views, became a highly controversial figure in 1989 and 1990 as he spoke out on such matters as his opposition to abortion, homosexuality, the use of condoms to combat AIDS, and heavy-metal music, seen as aiding demonic possession. On June 14, 1990, he made an implied threat to excommunicate Catholic political leaders who favored abortion, a threat widely thought to be aimed at New York governor Mario Cuomo; O'Connor withdrew the threat three days later. His running battle with New York's gay community expressed itself in scores of demonstrations outside St. Patrick's Cathedral; the largest of these, on December 10, 1989, drew 4,000–5,000 demonstrators. O'Connor recently published two books involving encounters with others of often-differing views, *His Eminence and Hizzoner: A Candid Exchange* (1989), with former New York mayor Ed Koch, and *A Journey of Faith: A Dialogue Between Elie Wiesel and John Cardinal O'Connor* (1990).

Philadelphia-born O'Connor was ordained in 1945. He became a U.S. Navy chaplain in 1952 and ultimately chief navy chaplain, a rear admiral, and in 1979 an auxiliary bishop. He became bishop of Scranton, Pennsylvania, in 1983, archbishop of the New York archdiocese in 1984, and cardinal in 1985. His degrees include an M.A. from St. Charles College in 1949, an M.A. from Catholic University of America in 1954, a Ph.D. from Georgetown University in 1970, and a D.R.E. from Villanova University in 1976.

FURTHER READING

"Cardinal. . . ." JEFFERY L. SHELER. *U.S. News & World Report*, Dec. 31, 1990.

"New York's new power brokers. . . ." *Manhattan, inc.*, Sept. 1989.

"Quizzing the men. . . ." ARTHUR JONES. *National Catholic Reporter*, Feb. 26, 1988.

John Cardinal O'Connor: At the Storm Center of a Changing American Catholic Church. NAT HENTOFF. Macmillan/Scribner, 1988.

"Profiles. . . ." (two parts) NAT HENTOFF. *New Yorker*, Mar. 23 and 30, 1987.

"Meet Cardinal. . . ." ARTHUR JONES. *National Catholic Reporter*, May 3, 1985.

"O'Connor, John J(oseph)." *Current Biography*, June 1984.

O'Connor, Sandra Day (1930–) Justice O'Connor is a historic figure, the first woman to serve on the U.S. Supreme Court. During the 1989–90 term, she most often voted with the conservative majority of the Court, as in the landmark *Cruzan* v. *Missouri* "right to die" case, which denied Nancy Cruzan's family the right to remove her from her life support system, and *Spallone* v. *U.S.*, which upset court-imposed fines on elected officials in a housing discrimination case in Yonkers, New York.

O'Connor wrote the majority opinions in *Board of Education of Westside Community Schools* v. *Mergens*, which upheld the right of students to form a Bible club, and *Maryland* v. *Craig*, which established the right of children in some child abuse cases to testify indirectly, as by closed circuit television. She was on the losing side in several key cases won by the liberal minority, most notably including *U.S.* v. *Eichman*, striking down the federal law against flag burning; *Rutan* v. *Republican Party of Illinois*, cutting the power of politicians in power to name party sympathizers to most low-level government jobs; and *Metro Broadcasting* v. *FCC*, supporting an affirmative action program in the broadcasting industry.

El Paso–born O'Connor made history in 1981 when she became the first woman Supreme Court justice, the climax of long careers in law and politics. She had moved from private practice to become Arizona assistant attorney general from 1965 to 1969, into politics as an Arizona state senator from 1969 to 1975, and then back into a series of Arizona judicial posts, ultimately becoming a state court of appeals judge from 1979 to 1981. She married John Jay O'Connor in 1952; the couple have one child. Her B.A. and LL.B. were from Stanford, in 1950 and 1952.

FURTHER READING

Sandra Day O'Connor. BEVERLY GHERMAN. Viking Penguin, 1991.
"The politics of the family. . . . " MARILYN BERLIN SNELL. *New Perspectives Quarterly (NPQ)*, Winter 1990.
Sandra Day O'Connor. PETER HUBER. Chelsea House, 1990.
Eight Men and a Lady. HERMAN SCHWARTZ, ANDREA NEAL, and DAVID SAVAGE. National Press, 1990.
"America's most influential woman." MARJORIE WILLIAMS and AL KAMEN. *Reader's Digest*, Dec. 1989.
"Sandra Day O'Connor. . . ." MERRILL MCLOUGHLIN. *Ladies' Home Journal*, Nov. 1989.
"What they say it is. . . ." *Time*, July 6, 1987.
"Nine who decide. . . ." ELIZABETH WARD. *Scholastic Update*, Sept. 8, 1986.
"Establishing her independence. . . ." RICHARD LACAYO. *Time*, May 12, 1986.
Equal Justice: A Biography of Sandra Day O'Connor. HAROLD WOODS and GERALDINE WOODS. Dillon, 1985.
Justice Sandra Day O'Connor. JUDITH BENTLEY. Messner, 1985.
Justice Sandra Day O'Connor. MARY V. FOX. Enslow, 1983.
"Sandra Day O'Connor." *Current Biography*, Jan. 1982.
Sandra Day O'Connor: First Woman on the Supreme Court. CAROL GREENE. Childrens, 1982.

Oliver, Raymond (1909–90) Son and grandson of chefs, born in the Bordeaux region, acclaimed French chef Oliver learned cooking from his grandmother and was apprenticed to his father at 15. During World War II, while running an alpine hotel, he was active in the Resistance, hiding downed American pilots. In 1948 he bought Paris's historic Le Grand Véfour restaurant, creating the elegant classic cuisine that won the coveted third Michelin star in 1954 and brought him fame and an international clientele. Oliver also taught cooking, personally and through books, television shows, and records, retiring after a bomb of unknown origin exploded in his restaurant in 1983. (d. France; November 5, 1990)

FURTHER READING

Obituary. *The Times* (of London), Nov. 7, 1990.
Obituary. *New York Times*, Nov. 6, 1990.

Ortega, Daniel Saavedra (1945–) Ortega was the Marxist leader of Sandinista-ruled Nicaragua from 1981 to 1990, and president from 1985 to 1990. After the cease-fire of March 1988 effectively ended the eight-year-long Nicaraguan civil war, he negotiated a series of agreements with the Contras that paved the way for the transition to democracy. Ortega's then-surprising agreement to allow free elections was one of the notable features of the period. After the election of Violeta Chamorro to the presidency in February 1990, he remained leader of the Sandinista National Liberation Front (FSLN) and a substantial figure in Latin American politics.

Ortega became active in the movement to overthrow the Anastasio Somoza dictatorship while a teenager, became a Sandinista guerrilla fighter in 1963, and was a national leader of the Sandinista movement in 1966–67. He was imprisoned from 1967 to 1974 and in the late 1970s became a major leader of the successful rebellion against Somoza. In 1979, he and Violeta Chamorro were two of the five leaders of the coalition that ruled Nicaragua after Somoza fled. He is married to Rosario Murillo; they have seven children. He attended Managua's Centralamerican University.

FURTHER READING

"Crisis of the clans. . . . ARTURO CRUZ, JR., and CONSUELO CRUZ SEQUEIRA. *New Republic*, May 21, 1990.

Life Stories of the Nicaraguan Revolution. Denis L. Heyck. Routledge Chapman and Hall, 1990.
Daniel Ortega. John Stockwell. Chelsea House,1989.
"Daniel Ortega." Claudia Dreifus. *Playboy*, Nov. 1987.
"Ortega's version." *Maclean's*, Feb. 23, 1987.
Assault on Nicaragua: The Untold Story of the U. S. "Secret War". Daniel Ortega and Daniel Sheehan. Walnut, 1987.
Where Is Nicaragua? Peter Davis. Simon & Schuster, 1987.
"Key leaders. . . ." Tamar Rothenberg. *Scholastic Update*, Sept. 22, 1986.
"Ortega, Daniel." *Current Biography*, Oct. 1984.

O'Toole, Peter Seamus (1932–)
Irish actor O'Toole appeared in a diverse set of stage, film, and television works in 1989–90, continuing to make his career in several media and on both sides of the Atlantic. Late in 1989, he appeared in London in the Keith Waterhouse play *Jeffrey Bernard Is Unwell*, based on the life and work of a writer, with Ned Sherrin directing. In April 1990, he starred in the telefilm *Crossing to Freedom*, as an old Britisher in France who evades Hitler's invading armies and takes seven children to safety during World War II. In 1991 he appeared in the film comedy *King Ralph*, opposite John Goodman, written and directed by David Ward.

Galway-born O'Toole began his long theater career in the mid 1950s in repertory with the Bristol Old Vic Theatre, and went on to play in a wide range of stage roles for the next three decades with such companies as the Old Vic, the National Theatre, and Dublin's Abbey Theatre. He is best known by far for his films, quickly emerging as a major international star in the title role of *Lawrence of Arabia* (1960) and going on to such films as *Becket* (1964), *The Lion in Winter* (1968), *Man of La Mancha* (1972), *Zulu Dawn* (1978), *My Favorite Year* (1982), and *The Last Emperor* (1986). He attended the Royal Academy of Dramatic Art. He was formerly married to actress Sian Phillips and has three children.

FURTHER READING

Peter O'Toole: A Biography. Nicholas Wapshott. Beaufort, 1984.
Peter O'Toole. Michael Freedland. St. Martin's, 1983.
"The life and. . . ." Cathleen McGuigan. *Rolling Stone*, Nov. 25, 1982.
"The double life of. . . ." O'Connell Driscoll. *Playboy*, Aug. 1982.

P

Pacino, Al (Alfredo Pacino, 1940–) Pacino spent much of 1990 updating the past, shooting *The Godfather Part III*, the long-awaited sequel to Francis Ford Coppola's earlier Oscar-winning mob sagas. After six months of shooting in Italy and New York and two unexpected weeks of reshooting in September, the film originally scheduled for Thanksgiving opened on Christmas Day. For many reviewers, it was well worth the wait. Pacino, as the now-60ish Michael Corleone seeking finally to go "legitimate" by way of the Catholic hierarchy and also trying to reestablish ties with his ex-wife and children, won special praise from the critics.

Pacino also had a huge box-office success with the *Sea of Love* (1989), as a cop seeking a murderer linked to a singles ad who becomes involved with a suspect; the film's success continued when it reached the video rental market in 1990. He was also seen in an Oscar-nominated comic cameo role as Big Boy Caprice in Warren Beatty's big summer movie, *Dick Tracy* (1990), based on Chester Gould's comic strip.

New York–born Pacino is one of the leading alumni of the Actor's Studio, beginning his long association with the group in 1966 and becoming one of its artistic directors from 1982 to 1984. He worked in the theater through the 1960s and in the early 1970s emerged as a major film star, breaking through as Michael Corleone in *The Godfather* (1972). He went on to star in such films as *Serpico* (1973), *The Godfather Part II* (1974), *Dog Day Afternoon* (1975), *Cruising* (1980), and *Scarface* (1983). He also continued to work in the theater, in such plays as *Camino Real* (1973), *Richard III* (1973), and *American Buffalo* (1981).

FURTHER READING

"Al Pacino has. . . ." Larry Grobel. *Rolling Stone*, Feb. 2, 1984.

Paley, William S. (1901–90) Son of Ukrainian-Jewish immigrants, Paley became head of the Columbia Broadcasting System and a broadcasting giant. Chicago-born Paley joined his multimillionaire father's Philadelphia cigar company after graduation from the Wharton School, sponsoring his first radio show in Philadelphia in 1925. In 1928, with his father's backing, he bought the tiny CBS radio network and quickly developed the approach of providing free material to affiliates for carrying sponsored shows. With radio and later television and recordings, he became an impresario, discovering or bringing to wide audiences such stars as Bing Crosby, Lucille Ball, Ed Sullivan, Jack Benny, Jackie Gleason, Frank Sinatra, and George Burns; providing critically acclaimed cultural programming such as "Playhouse 90"; and developing a highly regarded news division headed by Walter Cronkite and Edward R. Murrow, whom he later forced out. As CBS's president and later chairman, Paley was a personally difficult autocrat, reluctant to pass on control, but he played a key role in shaping modern broadcasting, as he described in 1979 in his *As It Happened: A Memoir*. He was also longtime president and trustee of the Museum of Modern Art, to which he willed his substantial art collection. (d. New York; October 26, 1990)

FURTHER READING

Obituary. ANN E. ANDREWS. *U.S. News & World Report*, Nov. 12, 1990.
"TV's long-running tastemaker. . . ." STEPHEN KOEPP. *Time*, Nov. 5, 1990.
"Broadcast visionary. . . ." PATRICIA HLUCHY. *Maclean's*, Nov. 5, 1990.
Obituary. MORRIE GELMAN. *Variety*, Nov. 5, 1990.
Obituary. *The Times* (of London), Oct. 29, 1990.
Obituary. *New York Times*, Oct. 28, 1990.
"William Paley. . . ." *Life*, Fall 1990.
Paley. SALLY B. SMITH. Simon & Schuster, 1990.
Empire: The Life and Times of William Paley. LEWIS J. PAPER. St. Martin's, 1987.
The Media Moguls: From Joseph Pulitzer to William S. Paley: The Wheelings & Dealings of America's News Merchants. DANA L. THOMAS. Putnam, 1981.

Pan, Hermes (Hermes Panagiotopolous, 1910–90) Memphis-born dancer and choreographer Pan helped create many classic Fred Astaire-Ginger Rogers dances. He worked briefly on Broadway before meeting Astaire on the film *Flying Down to Rio* (1933). With Astaire, he choreographed nine of the ten Astaire-Rogers films, including *The Gay Divorcée* (1934), *Top Hat* (1935), and *Shall We Dance* (1937), as well as *Damsel in Distress* (1937), winning an Oscar for the last. His choreography of a 1961 television special won an Emmy. He also choreographed (and occasionally danced in) many other films and many stage musicals, including *Kiss Me Kate* (1953), *Porgy and Bess* (1959), *My Fair Lady* (1964), and *Finian's Rainbow* (1968). (d. Beverly Hills, California; September 19, 1990)

FURTHER READING

Obituary. ROBERT C. ROMAN. *Dance*, Jan. 1991.
Obituary. *Variety*, Sept. 24, 1990.
Obituary. *The Times* (of London), Sept. 23, 1990.
Obituary. *New York Times*, Sept. 22, 1990.
"Choreography. . . ." DIANA RICO. *Interview*, Sept. 1985.

Pandit, Vijaya Lakshmi (1900–90) The first woman president of the United Nations General Assembly (1953–54), Pandit was a leader of the long fight for Indian independence, side by side with her father Pandit Motilal Nehru and her brother Jawaharlal Nehru. She was imprisoned by the British several times during the interwar period, was in local government in the late 1930s, and with independence became one of India's leading diplomats as ambassador to the Soviet Union (1947–49), the United States (1949–51), and Great Britain (1954–61). She was active in Indian politics from 1962 to 1968. (d. Bombay; December 1, 1990)

FURTHER READING

Obituary. *The Times* (of London), Dec. 3, 1990.
Obituary. *New York Times*, Dec. 2, 1990.

Papp, Joseph (Joseph Papirovsky, 1921–) Producer-director Papp stood up and was counted in 1990. In April the head of the New York Shakespeare Festival turned down two grants totaling $450,000 from the National Endowment for the Arts (NEA). With his action, announced in a letter to NEA Chairman John E. Frohnmayer, Papp became the first major arts figure to turn down NEA funds in protest over antiobscenity provisions that conservative members of Congress had pressed on the NEA. Congress later softened the controls imposed on the agency in reponse to widespread protests. Although some artists reconsidered their rejections, Papp announced in November 1990 that he would still reject grants and a month later announced layoffs of 30 employees and closing of the sound, lighting, set, and prop departments. Also in April, Papp presided over a highly emotional event: the closing of *A Chorus Line*. Originally a Public Theatre production, it had moved to Broadway in 1975 and become the longest-running Broadway show in history, closing after 6,137 performances.

Brooklyn-born Papp has been a key figure in the American theater for three decades. He founded New York's Shakespeare Workshop in 1954, which he developed into the landmark New York Shakespeare Festival, housing it in the Public Theatre and Central Park's Delacorte Theatre; it became the leading

American theater company in the presentation of the classics and the introduction of new plays. Many new plays and productions of the classics went on to Broadway, as did *Hair* (1967) and *A Chorus Line*. From 1973 to 1977, the Shakespeare Festival was the theater portion of New York's Lincoln Center. Papp has also produced for films and television. He has been married four times and has five children. He attended the Los Angeles Actor's Lab.

FURTHER READING

"Joe Papp." VANCE MUSE. *Life*, Apr. 1989.
Joseph Papp. . . ." DONALD R. GALLO. *English Journal*, Nov. 1988.
Joseph Papp and the New York State Shakespeare Festival: An Annotated Bibliography. CHRISTINE E. KING and BRENDA COVEN. Garland, 1988.
"The public and private. . . ." MICHIKO KAKUTANI. *New York Times Magazine*, June 23, 1985.

Paradjanov, Sergei (Sarkis Paradjanian, 1924–90) Two early films were the main works of the Armenian Soviet filmmaker Paradjanov: *Shadows of Our Forgotten Ancestors* (1964), a story of mountain people set in the Carpathians, and *The Color of Pomegranates* (1969), set in 18th-century Armenia, both nonpolitical ethnic works that proved highly unacceptable to the conservative Soviet film authorities of the time. Paradjanov, a dissident, was attacked and charged with many fictional offenses, and in 1973 he was jailed for "homosexuality"; after international pressure, he was released in 1976. He was not jailed again, although he was arrested in 1982, and began making movies again in the early 1980s. (d. Yerevan, Armenia; July 20, 1990)

FURTHER READING

Obituary. *Variety*, July 25, 1990.
Obituary. *The Times* (of London), July 24, 1990.
"In the Soviet orbit. . . ." ANNE WILLIAMSON. *Film Comment*, May–June 1989.

Parkinson, Norman (Ronald William Parkinson Smith, 1913–90) One of Britain's leading fashion and portrait photographers, Parkinson published fashion pictures in such magazines as *Vogue*, *Life*, and *Look* during the interwar period and later emerged as a major figure in Britain for his photo portraits of many members of the British Royal Family. His portrait photo of the Queen Mother on her 80th birthday was used on commemorative stamps. He also published several books of his portrait photos. Among his written works were *Fifty Years of Style and Fashion* (1983) and *Would You Let Your Daughter?* (1985). (d. Singapore; February 5, 1990)

FURTHER READING

"'Parks'. . . ." *Town & Country Monthly*, May 1990.
Obituary. *New York Times*, Feb. 17, 1990.
Obituary. *The Times* (of London), Feb. 16, 1990.
Scenes from the Fashionable World. KENNEDY FRASER. Knopf, 1987.
"The light in the eye." KENNEDY FRASER. *New Yorker*, Dec. 10, 1984.
"Norman Parkinson." ROBERT HAYES and MARC BALET. *Interview*, June 1983.
"Royal shutterbug." *People*, Apr. 18, 1983.
"'Parks'. . . ." *Town and Country*, Apr. 1983.

Pauley, Jane (1950–) Broadcast journalist Pauley left home this year to strike out on her own. After 13 years with Bryant Gumbel as co-anchor on NBC's top-rated "Today" show, she departed to anchor her own prime-time news program for NBC, "Real Life with Jane Pauley," which focuses on daily problems and concerns with a leavening of celebrity interviews. The trigger for this action was the arrival of Deborah Norville to replace John Palmer as news announcer on "Today." Although informed of the change in advance, Pauley became increasingly unhappy about the media focus on a presumed battle between her and Norville, fed by Norville's upgraded role, and in the end opted to move on. She made it official on the air on October 28, 1989, when she handed her alarm clock to Norville with a hug; between then and her December 28 departure, she and Norville were at pains to show their warm feelings toward each other.

After Pauley's departure, the "Today" show's ratings dropped precipitously, at one point by about 17 percent. However, Pauley's new prime-time show, which debuted during the summer, attracted strong audiences and late in 1990 found a not-every-week place in NBC's evening schedule. For a time, rumors flew that she might be made co-anchor of "NBC Nightly News" with Tom Brokaw (her former "Today" partner); they proved unfounded, but she became a regular substitute for him. The two co-anchored a high-rated end-of-the-decade retrospective, *The Eighties*.

Pauley also anchored some news specials, such as the March 1990 *Changes: Conversations with Jane Pauley* and the May 1990 *The Secret Race: The East German Sports Machine*, after the Berlin Wall's demise. Outside of NBC, she appeared on the Fox network as co-host, with Candice Bergen and Jay Leno, of the 1990 Emmy Awards and on HBO from New York's Radio City Music Hall for the comedy marathon *Comic Relief*.

Indianapolis-born Pauley began her television career in 1972 as a reporter for WISH, Indianapolis, and moved to anchor Chicago's WMAQ. In 1976, she became a national figure as co-anchor of the "Today" show, also working as a reporter for "NBC Nightly News" in the early 1980s. She is married to cartoonist Gary Trudeau; they have three children. Her B.A. was from Indiana Univerisity in 1978.

FURTHER READING

"Surviving nicely, thanks. . . ." RICHARD ZOGLIN. *Time*, Aug. 20, 1990.
"Jane's search for tomorrow." JEFF ROVIN. *Ladies' Home Journal*, July 1990.
"The loved one." PHOEBE HOBAN. *New York*, July 23, 1990.
"Yesterday, today and tomorrow." GLENN PLASKIN. *American Health*, Mar. 1990.
The Imperfect Mirror: Inside Stories of Television Newscasters. DANIEL PAISNER. Morrow, 1989.
"Today's Jane Pauley. . . ." BARBARA COSTIKYAN. *Cosmopolitan*, Nov. 1984.
"Pauley, Jane." *Current Biography*, May 1980.

Payne, John (1912–89) Virginia-born film actor Payne is probably best remembered as Santa Claus's lawyer in *Miracle on 34th Street* (1947). He appeared briefly on Broadway before making his film debut in *Dodsworth* (1936). Numerous movies followed (with time out for service in the army air corps), in the 1940s mostly musicals such as *Tin Pan Alley* (1940), *Sun Valley Serenade* (1941), *Hello, Frisco, Hello* (1943), and *The Dolly Sisters* (1945). He later made primarily westerns and action films, as well as television programs, including "The Restless Gun" (1957–59), retiring after a 1961 car accident but returning to tour in a 1973 production of *Good News*. (d. Malibu, California; December 6, 1989)

FURTHER READING

Obituary. *Variety*, Dec. 13, 1989.
Obituary. *The Times* (of London), Dec. 8, 1989.
Obituary. *New York Times*, Dec. 8, 1989.

Payne, Melvin Monroe (1911–90) For 55 years, from 1932 to 1987, Payne was identified with the National Geographic Society. He worked for the organization as a secretary in 1932, and beginning in 1935 was involved as participant or sponsor of a long series of National Geographic explorations, from early high-altitude balloon flights in the mid-1930s to the underwater explorations of Jacques Cousteau. He was president of the society from 1967 to 1976, and board chairman from 1976 until his retirement in 1987. (d. Washington, D.C.; October 6, 1990)

FURTHER READING

Obituary. *New York Times*, Oct. 9, 1990.

Paz, Octavio (1914–) Mexican poet, essayist, editor, and critic Paz has been a leading Latin American literary figure for much of the past 60 years; in 1990, he was awarded the

Nobel Prize for literature. At the time the prize was awarded, Paz was in New York City, opening an exhibition of Mexican art at the Metropolitan Museum of Art.

Paz, who is a former diplomat and was a figure on the Latin American left for decades, now occupies an independent position, criticizing and being criticized by both right and left; he has been especially critical of Mexico's long-ruling Institutional Revolutionary Party governments. He continues his artistic production: In 1989, he published *Sor Juana: Or, The Traps of Faith* and also a new collection of poetry, *The Other Voice*.

Paz was a central figure in the development of modern Mexican literature, founding several key literary reviews in the 1930s and 1940s, starting with *Barandel* (1931) and most influentially with *Taller* (1939), after his return from the Spanish Civil War. In 1950, he published the celebrated long essay *The Labyrinth of Solitude*, an analysis of Mexican character and of modern Mexican society. Much of his poetic work celebrates Mexico's Indian heritage, as in *Sun Stone* (1957). His collected poetry was published in 1987. He was also a diplomat in the service of his country, most notably as Mexico's ambassador to India from 1962 to 1968; he resigned in protest after Mexican police fired on demonstrating students during the 1968 Olympics. Paz attended the University of Mexico. He is married to Marie Tramini; they have one child.

FURTHER READING

"The Mexican as laureate." Stephen Spender. *Economist*, Oct. 20, 1990.
"The house of glances." Marilyn Berlin Snell. *New Perspectives Quarterly (NPQ)*, Summer 1990.
Octavio Paz. Jason Wilson. G. K. Hall, 1986.

Peck, Gregory (Eldred Gregory Peck, 1916–) Peck's most visible activities in 1990 were ceremonial ones. In February he hosted the American Film Institute's tribute to movie director David Lean, winner of their Life Achievement Award; that same month, Peck was among the numerous stars paying tribute to Czechoslovakian president and playwright Vaclav Havel on his visit to New York, with the proceedings televised on PBS. In June, Peck acted as master of ceremonies at Los Angeles's tribute to Nelson Mandela, windup of the South African leader's American tour. Peck was honored by the American Society of Cinematographers with their first board of governors award, citing his activities on behalf of camera operators and cinematography in general.

Professionally, Peck worked as narrator for the documentary film *Super Chief—The Life and Legacy of Earl Warren*. Meanwhile, his most recent feature movie, *Old Gringo* (1989), a tale of the Mexican Revolution, with Peck in the Ambrose Bierce role opposite Jane Fonda and Jimmy Smits, appeared on the video rental market. Although the film was neither a commercial nor a critical success, many filmgoers were happy to see Peck on the screen again after a too-long hiatus.

California-born Peck is one of the leading American actors of the century; for the past 46 years, he has been a massive, incorruptible presence on the American film scene. He made his New York theater debut in 1942 and emerged as a Hollywood star in 1945 with *The Keys of the Kingdom*; he then went on to star in such films as *The Yearling* (1946), *Duel in the Sun* (1947), *Gentlemen's Agreement* (1947), *Twelve O'Clock High* (1949), *The Gunfighter* (1950), *Captain Horatio Hornblower* (1951), *The Snows of Kilimanjaro* (1952), *Roman Holiday* (1953), *Moby Dick* (1954), *The Man in the Grey Flannel Suit* (1956), *The Big Country* (1958), *Pork Chop Hill* (1959), *On the Beach* (1959), *The Guns of Navarone* (1961), *To Kill a Mockingbird* (1962; he won a best actor Oscar), *Cape Fear* (1962),

Behold a Pale Horse (1964), *Mirage* (1965), *Arabesque* (1966), *The Stalking Moon* (1968), *I Walk the Line* (1970), *The Omen* (1976), *MacArthur* (1977), and *The Boys from Brazil* (1978). Peck studied at the University of California and New York's Neighborhood Playhouse. He has been married twice, last in 1955 to Veronique Passani, and has had five children, two of whom—Anthony and Cecilia—pursue acting careers.

FURTHER READING

"Gregory Peck. . . ." RON HAVER. *American Film*, Mar. 1989.
"Impeccable. . . ." ROSEMARY HOLUSHA. *Saturday Evening Post*, Jan.–Feb. 1989.
"Gregory Peck. . . ." JENNY CULLEN. *Ladies' Home Journal*, Nov. 1988.
"Gregory Peck. . . ." BRAD DARRACH. *People*, June 15, 1987.
The Films of Gregory Peck. JOHN GRIGGS. Carol, 1987.
Gregory Peck. MICHAEL FREEDLAND. Morrow, 1980.

Penn, Sean (1960–) Actor Penn continued with his string of bad-boy roles, in fall 1990 opening in *State of Grace*, about an Irish mob in New York City's Hell's Kitchen. At the same time, his career was taking a new turn. Late in the year he was in Nebraska shooting *The Indian Runner*—not as an actor but as a first-time director and writer. The film, starring Gene Hackman and Sandy Dennis, is about a Vietnam veteran's troubled return to his farming family.

In late 1989, Penn and Robert De Niro opened in *We're No Angels*, a remake of the 1955 Humphrey Bogart film; although it drew small audiences in the theaters, it proved to be more popular when released in the video rental market in midyear. *Casualties of War* (1989), in which Penn starred with Michael J. Fox, also proved far more popular on video than in the theaters, jumping quickly into the top-ten rental favorites when released in spring 1990.

California-born Penn, son of director Leo Penn, emerged as one of the leading young film stars of the 1980s in such films as *Taps* (1981); *Fast Times at Ridgemont High* (1982); *Bad Boys* (1983); *Racing with the Moon* (1984); *The Falcon and the Snowman* (1985); *At Close Range* (1986); with his brother Christopher Penn; *Colors* (1988); and *Judgment in Berlin* (1988). Onstage, he has appeared in such plays as *Heartland* (1981) and *Hurlyburly* (1988). He was married to Madonna (Madonna Louise Ciccone) from 1985 to 1989. In the fall of 1990, he announced plans to marry actress Robin Wright.

FURTHER READING

"Sean Penn pulls. . . ." GRAYDON CARTER. *Vogue*, May 1988.
"Desperately seeking matrimony. . . ." CAROL WALLACE. *People*, July 8, 1985.
"Hollywood's Brat Pack." DAVID BLUM. *New York*, June 10, 1985.
"Sean and Chris Penn. . . ." *Teen*, Sept. 1984.

Percy, Walker (1916–90) Novelist Percy is best known for his first novel, *The Moviegoer*, which won the 1961 National Book Award. Born in Birmingham, Alabama, orphaned, and raised by a cousin in Mississippi, Percy became a doctor but contracted tuberculosis in 1942 and spent over two years in sanitariums, increasingly focusing on reading, writing, and philosophy, and becoming a Catholic in 1946. Abandoning medicine, he turned to fiction, often exploring themes of alienation and faith in works including *The Last Gentleman* (1966), *Love in the Ruins* (1971), *Lancelot* (1977), *The Second Coming* (1980), and *The Thanatos Syndrome* (1987). (d. Covington, Louisiana; May 10, 1990)

FURTHER READING

Obituary. *Current Biography*, July 1990.
Obituary. BEN C. TOLEDANO. *National Review*, June 11, 1990.
"Of many things." GEORGE W. HUNT. *America*, May 26, 1990.
"The leader of a search party." *U.S. News & World Report*, May 21, 1990.
Obituary. *The Times* (of London), May 12, 1990.
Obituary. *New York Times*, May 11, 1990.
Walker Percy: A Southern Wayfarer. WILLIAM R. ALLEN. University Press of Mississippi, 1986.
Conversations with Walker Percy. LEWIS A. LAWSON and VICTOR A. KRAMER, eds. University Press of Mississippi, 1985.
Walker Percy. JAC THARPE. G. K. Hall, 1983.

Peter, Laurence J. (1919–90) Peter was the social commentator who formulated the "Peter Principle" that "in a hierarchy every employee tends to rise to his level of incompetence." Vancouver-born Peter taught education in British Columbia and California but retired after publishing *The Peter Principle: Why Things Always Go Wrong* (1970; co-written with friend Raymond Hull), a best-seller previously rejected by 30 publishers. Several sequels followed. (d. Palos Verdes, California; January 14, 1990)

FURTHER READING

"The passing of Peter." *Economist*, Jan. 20, 1990.
Obituary. *The Times* (of London), Jan. 16, 1990.
Obituary. *New York Times*, Jan. 15, 1990.

Pérez de Cuéllar, Javier (1920–) As secretary-general of the United Nations, Pérez de Cuéllar has continued to play a substantial role as a mediator and troubleshooter, although he has seldom had an opportunity to deal seriously with matters affecting the great powers. During 1990, he and the UN made a contribution to the continuing negotiations aimed at ending several regional conflicts, including the civil wars in Cambodia, Nicaragua, and El Salvador, and in negotiating a cease-fire and then the freedom of Namibia; Pérez de Cuéllar administered the oath of office to Namibian president Sam Nujoma at the March 21 Windhoek independence day celebration. He met with far less success in his attempt to mediate the Persian Gulf Crisis of late 1990, although the UN did serve as a world forum during the crisis and took a series of increasingly serious collective actions against Iraq as the crisis developed.

Pérez de Cuéllar joined the UN after a long Peruvian diplomatic career, which included ambassadorships to Switzerland and the Soviet Union. He was Peruvian permanent representative to the UN from 1971 to 1975, a member of the Security Council in 1973–74, and UN president in 1974. He was UN mediator and troubleshooter in the late 1970s and early 1980s, and became its fifth secretary-general in 1982. He had little direct impact on the course of international events during the 1980s, a period in which the United States and the Soviet Union played a major role in ending the Cold War and with it many regional conflicts, but in 1988 he did play a substantial role in mediating the end of the long Iran-Iraq war. He married Marcela Temple; they have two children. He attended Lima's Catholic University.

FURTHER READING

"Javier of the U.N. . . ." MORTON KONDRACKE. *New Republic*, Aug. 13, 1990.
"Negotiating peace. . . ." HUGO SADA. *World Press Review*, May 1989.
"Three who fight. . . ." LEE KRAVITZ. *Scholastic Update*, May 4, 1987.
"Pérez de Cuéllar, Javier." *Current Biography*, Aug. 1982.

Pfeiffer, Michelle (1959–) A major Hollywood star of the late 1980s and early 1990s, in 1989 Pfeiffer won an Oscar nomination for her role as Susie Diamond in *The Fabulous Baker Boys*. In the summer of 1989, she appeared somewhat less successfully as Olivia in *Twelfth Night* at the New York Shakespeare Festival, outdoors in Central Park. In 1990, she starred opposite Sean Connery and Klaus Maria Brandauer in the film *The Russia House*, adapted by Tom Stoppard from the John le Carré novel and shot in Moscow. Forthcoming is the film *Love Field*, followed by a starring role opposite Al Pacino in the film *Frankie and Johnny at the Clair de Lune*.

California-born Pfeiffer quickly emerged as one of the leading film players of the 1980s, starring in such films as *Grease 2* (1982), *Scarface* (1983), *Into the Night* (1984), *Ladyhawke* (1985),

Sweet Liberty (1986), *The Witches of Eastwick* (1987), *Married to the Mob* (1988), *Tequila Sunrise* (1988), and *Dangerous Liaisons* (1989). She was formerly married to actor Peter Horton.

FURTHER READING

"The fabulous Pfeiffer girl." ROBERT SEIDENBERG. *American Film*, Jan. 1991.
"Michelle Pfeiffer as. . . ." HAL HINSON. *Esquire*, Dec. 1990.
"Pfeiffer, Michelle." *Current Biography*, Mar. 1990.
"Michelle Pfeiffer." *People*, Dec. 25, 1989.
"Michelle Pfeiffer. . . ." LARKIN WARREN. *Esquire*, Dec. 1989.
"Fabulous Pfeiffer." DAVID ANSEN. *Newsweek*, Nov. 6, 1989.
"Starface." GRAYDON CARTER. *Vogue*, Oct. 1989.
"Hit-woman Pfeiffer." *Video Review*, Mar. 1989.
"Fabulous, foxy. . . ." JAMES KAPLAN. *Cosmopolitan*, Jan. 1989.
"Blond Venus. . . ." PETER STONE and HERB RITTS. *Interview*, Aug. 1988.

Phillips, Lou Diamond (1962–) Clearly a rising star, Phillips plays in three substantial forthcoming films: as a Navajo tribal policeman in *Dark Wind*, adapted from the Tony Hillerman novel, directed by Erroll Morris, and produced by Robert Redford; as a novelist in the psychological thriller *Mind Game*, for which he wrote the script; and in the title role as the young Eskimo in the Jacques Dorfman film *Agaguk*, in a cast that includes Toshiro Mifune and Jennifer Tilly. The American Indian Registry for the Performing Arts originally criticized the casting of part-Cherokee Phillips as a Navajo in *Dark Wind*, but Phillips's involvement was supported by a Navajo organization.

After playing in cabaret as a comedian and in small roles in theater and television, Phillips suddenly emerged as one of the leading young film stars of the late 1980s, beginning with his role as Mexican-American rock star Richie Valens in the Luis Valdez film *La Bamba* (1987). He went on to appear in such films as *Stand and Deliver* (1987), *Young Guns* (1988; and the 1990 sequel *Young Guns II*), *Disorganized Crime* (1989), *Renegades* (1989), *First Power* (1989), and *Show of Force* (1989). Texas-born Phillips attended the University of Texas. He is married to actress Julie Cypher.

FURTHER READING

"Does Lou Diamond Phillips. . . ." ALICE LANE. *Mademoiselle*, Feb. 1990.
"Lou Diamond Phillips. . . ." *Teen*, Sept. 1989.
"A bright new diamond. . . ." JOHN STARK. *People*, Aug. 17, 1987.
"Arriba! . . ." *Texas Monthly*, July 1987.
"Lou Diamond Phillips. . . ." JIM SEALE. *Los Angeles Magazine*, July 1987.

Pickering, Thomas Reeve (1931–) The permanent United States representative to the United Nations is a career diplomat whose long experience in the Middle East and Africa dates back to the 1960s and whose period as U.S. ambassador to Israel in the late 1980s helped prepare him for the Persian Gulf Crisis that erupted in August 1990. Pickering was a key figure in developing the long series of Security Council resolutions that ultimately committed the United Nations to the use of force in the Persian Gulf, at the same time distancing the United States from Israel at the UN as the Israeli-Palestinian conflict worsened, increasing numbers of Palestinians were killed and injured by Israeli police and soldiers, and the Security Council reacted with censuring resolutions directed at Israel.

New Jersey–born Pickering joined the foreign service in 1959, after serving in the navy. His long career took him to posts in sub-Saharan

Africa in the late 1960s and to a series of very "hot spot" ambassador's posts: from the mid-1970s, in Jordan, Nigeria, and El Salvador; from 1985 to 1988 in Israel; and in 1989 to the United Nations in a non-cabinet-level position. He married Alice Stover in 1955; they have two children. His B.A. was from Bowdoin in 1953, his M.A. from the Fletcher School in 1954.

FURTHER READING

"Cosmo talks to. . . ." MICHELE WILLENS. *Cosmopolitan*, Sept. 1989.
"Targetting a U.S. ambassador." MARK STARR. *Newsweek*, July 2, 1984.

FURTHER READING

"The Pinter principle." DONALD CHASE. *American Film*, Oct. 1990.
Harold Pinter, 2nd ed. BERNARD F. DUKORE. St. Martin's, 1990.
Harold Pinter. LOIS GORDON, ed. Garland, 1990.
"Breaking the silence." DOUGLAS KENNEDY. *New Statesman & Society*, Oct. 28, 1988.
Pinter the Playwright, 4th ed. MARTIN ESSLIN. Heinemann, 1988.
Harold Pinter. HAROLD BLOOM, ed. Chelsea House, 1987.
Pinter: The Player's Playwright. DAVID T. THOMPSON. Schocken, 1985.
Harold Pinter. GUIDO ALMANSI and SIMON HENDERSON. Routledge Chapman & Hall, 1983.

Pinter, Harold (1930–) The British writer, actor, and director scored another success with his 1990 film adaptation of Margaret Atwood's novel *The Handmaid's Tale*, a cautionary tale set in a future United States after a right-wing religious coup and an assortment of other disasters. Volker Schlondorff directed a cast that included Faye Dunaway, Robert Duvall, and Natasha Richardson. Pinter's recent work also includes the television adaptation of the Elizabeth Bowen novel *The Heat of the Day*, set in World War II London and starring Michael York, Patricia Hodge, and Michael Gambon. Forthcoming is his film adaptation of a Rupert Everett novella, *The Comfort of Strangers*; Paul Schrader directs a cast that includes Christopher Walken, Helen Mirren, and Natasha Richardson.

London-born Pinter began his career as an actor, from 1949 working largely in repertory. He moved into playwriting in the late 1950s, scoring his first major success with *The Caretaker* (1960; he also adapted it into the 1964 film) and going on to such works as *The Homecoming* (1965; and the 1973 film), *Old Times* (1970), *No Man's Land* (1975), and *Family Voices* (1980). He has also directed such plays as *Exiles* (1970), *Butley* (1971; and the 1973 film), *Otherwise Engaged* (1975), and *The Common Pursuit* (1984), and has written many screenplays, including *The Servant* (1962), *The Quiller Memorandum* (1965), *The Go-Between* (1969), *The French Lieutenant's Woman* (1980), and *The Turtle Diary* (1984). He has been married twice, to the actress Vivien Merchant and since 1980 to the writer Antonia Fraser, and has one child.

Pippin, Nick (1955–90) Florida-born Pippin was an actor who went into the New York theater after his 1976 graduation from Pensacola Junior College. In the decade that followed, he appeared in several works on stage and screen, as well as in many commercials. He learned that he had AIDS in 1986. In 1987, he founded the People with AIDS Theater Workshop, working with other AIDS-stricken theater people to show the discrimination and prejudice met by people with AIDS, and by showing it to help stop it, thus doing something worthwhile with what was left of their lives. The workshop won an Obie Award for its 1989 New York production of *AIDS Alive*. (d. New York City; July 27, 1990)

FURTHER READING

Obituary. *New York Times*, July 29, 1990.

Poindexter, John Marlan (1936–) Naval officer and former National Security Adviser Poindexter was indicted on seven Iran-Contra–related charges on March 14, 1988, after a long grand jury investigation directed by special prosecutor Lawrence E. Walsh. On April 7, 1990, after six days of deliberation, a federal jury convicted him on five felony counts. On June 11, he received a six-month jail term, becoming the first Iran-Contra scandal figure to be sentenced to prison.

Rear Admiral Poindexter, a career naval officer, joined the White House–based national security staff in 1981. He became deputy national security adviser in 1983 and national security adviser in 1985, resigning on November 25, 1986, as the Iran-Contra scandal blew up; it was the most highly visible of the many covert operations developed during his White House years. Poindexter then refused to testify before congressional committees without a grant of immunity, and ultimately did testify with limited immunity. He retired from the navy in December 1987. Poindexter attended the U.S. Naval Academy at Annapolis and the California Institute of Technology. He is married and has four children.

FURTHER READING

Perilous Statecraft. MICHAEL LEDEEN. Macmillan, 1989.

Inside the National Security Council: The True Story of the Making and Unmaking of Reagan's Foreign Policy. CONSTANTINE C. MENGES. Simon & Schuster, 1988.

Men of Zeal: A Candid Story of the Iran-Contra Hearings. WILLIAM S. COHEN and GEORGE J. MITCHELL. Viking Penguin, 1988.

"Poindexter, John M(arlan)." *Current Biography,* Nov. 1987.

"Next, the most important. . . ." GEORGE J. CHURCH. *Time,* July 20, 1987.

"Calm in the eye. . . ." *Time,* Apr. 6, 1987.

"That shy fellow. . . ." ED MAGNUSON. *Time,* July 28, 1986.

Poitier, Sidney (1924–) While Poitier the actor continued his too-long absence from films, Poitier the director weighed in with a new film, *Ghost Dad,* in summer 1990. Starring his longtime colleague Bill Cosby, *Ghost Dad* is another of the spate of recent films in which the stars are invisible, watching events as they occur and trying to help shape them, in this case a father watching over his orphaned children. Unfortunately, this one did not seem to work, perhaps—some suggested—because the characters were too traditionally "homespun," without the hard edges that might give spark and life to the proceedings. In February 1990, Poitier was on hand to present the National Board of Review of Motion Pictures' D. W. Griffith Career Achievement Award to Richard Widmark; the two had starred together in *No Way Out* (1952)

Poitier's name (though not Poitier himself) was in the news in a very different connection in 1990. John Guare's acclaimed new play *Six Degrees of Separation* was based on a true incident of a young Black man who charmed his way into affluent New York homes, supposedly as a college friend of their children, saying he was David Poitier, son of Sidney, had been mugged, and needed a place to spend the night until his father arrived the next day. Invited to stay, he then robbed his hosts and departed.

Miami-born Poitier grew up in the Bahamas, retaining his West Indian accent in a 45-year-long stage and screen career that included appearances in such plays as *Anna Lucasta* (1948) and *A Raisin in the Sun* (1959). He became Hollywood's first major Black movie star in the late 1950s; his most notable films were *The Defiant Ones* (1958), *Porgy and Bess* (1959), the film version of *A Raisin in the Sun* (1961), *Lilies of the Field* (1963; he was the first Black actor to win a Best Actor Academy Award), *In the Heat of the Night* (1967), and *Guess Who's Coming to Dinner* (1967). He also became a director, of such films as *Buck and the Preacher* (1972; he also starred), *Uptown Saturday Night*

(1982), and *Hanky Panky* (1984). In 1980 he published the autobiographical *This Life*. He has been married twice and has six children.

FURTHER READING

"Poitier's stellar career. . . ." *Jet*, Mar. 20, 1989.
"Poitier thanks. . . ." RALPH TYLER. *Variety*, Mar. 8, 1989.
Sidney Poitier. CAROL BERGMAN. Chelsea House, 1989.
"Sidney Poitier is back." HERBERT NIPSON. *Ebony*, May 1988.
"Sidney Poitier returns. . . ." *Jet*, Mar. 14, 1988.
"A superstar returns. . . ." DAVID ANSEN. *Newsweek*, Feb. 22, 1988.
Long Journey: A Biography of Sidney Poitier. CAROLYN EWERS. NAL-Dutton, 1981.

Pol Pot (Tol Saut; Saloh Sar; 1928–) The Cambodian Khmer Rouge (Red Khmer) leader was the key figure in the organization of the 1975–78 Cambodian holocaust, in which an estimated two to three million of his own people died before the Vietnamese invasion of 1978. After the September 1989 Vietnamese withdrawal, Pol Pot's forces fought the Cambodian government, at first in coalition with U.S.-backed and Soviet-backed rebel forces and then as an increasingly powerful single organization, which by midsummer 1990 was threatening to take Phnom Penh, the capital city. With the Cambodian holocaust very much in mind, the United States stopped its aid to Cambodian rebel forces in July 1990 and the UN moved to develop peace plans—while Pol Pot continued to gain strength in Cambodia.

Pol Pot has spent his whole life as a Communist activist, beginning as a teenager in the Indochinese Communist Party in the 1940s. After World War II, he moved up in the Cambodian Communist Party and in 1963 emerged as party general secretary and organizer of the Khmer Rouge Army. He became prime minister of Cambodia, then renamed Kampuchea, in 1976, after the 1975 Khmer Rouge victory. He resumed his career as a guerrilla leader after the successful Vietnamese invasion of Cambodia in 1978, continuing to fight on through the Vietnamese occupation and 1989 withdrawal. He withdrew from direct command of the Khmer Rouge armed forces in 1985 but is generally thought to have continued on as the central figure in the Khmer Rouge leadership. His wife is Khieu Ponnary.

FURTHER READING

Pol Pot: A Political Biography. DAVID P. CHANDLER. Westview, 1991.
"Skeletons in the closet. . . ." STEPHEN J. MORRIS. *New Republic*, June 4, 1990.
Leftism: From de Sade and Marx to Hitler and Pol Pot. ERIK LEDDIHN. Regnery Gateway, 1990.
Pol Pot. REBECCA STEFOFF. Chelsea House, 1989.
Pol Pot Plans the Future: Confidential Leadership Documents from Democratic Kampuchea, 1976–1977. DAVID P. CHANDLER, ed. Yale University, Southeast Asia, 1989.
Beyond the Horizon: Five Years with the Khmer Rouge. LAURENCE PICQ. St. Martin's, 1989.
How Pol Pot Came to Power. BEN KIERNAN. Schocken, 1985.
"Pol Pot." *Current Biography*, Apr. 1980.

Porter, Eliot (Eliot Furness Porter, 1901–90) A photographer and conservationist, Porter and his work were long linked with the Sierra Club. Son of an Illinois architect, he learned photography from his father, notably on Canadian Rockies camping trips. He studied chemical engineering and medicine and taught biochemistry at Harvard and Radcliffe (1929–39), before becoming a full-time photographer, quickly establishing his reputation with Kodak's then-new color film. Porter donated many photographs to the Sierra Club and focused on nature in his published works, including *In Wilderness Is the Preservation of the World* (1962), *The Place No One Knew* (1963), *The Tree Where Man Was Born* (1972), and *Antarctica* (1973). (d. Santa Fe, New Mexico; November 2, 1990)

FURTHER READING

Obituary. *New York Times*, Nov. 3, 1990.
"Eliot Porter." MILTON ESTEROW. *ARTnews*, Apr. 1989.
"Eliot Porter. . . ." MARTHA A. SANDWEISS. *National Wildlife*, Feb.–Mar. 1989.
Eliot Porter. ELIOT PORTER. Bulfinch, 1987; Crown, 1988.

Powell, Colin (Colin Luther Powell, 1937–) Lieutenant General Powell was appointed chairman of the Joint Chiefs of Staff by President Bush on August 10, 1989; it was a historic "first," as he was the first Black to hold the post. One of his earliest major tasks was the organization of the December 1989 invasion of Panama. He has also sent American forces into El Salvador, Liberia, and the Philippines, and in August 1990 he began the huge American buildup in the Persian Gulf Crisis, then becoming a key figure in the war that followed.

New York–born Powell began his long military career in 1958; he has held a series of line and staff posts in Europe and the United States, including command posts in the 101st Airborne and 4th Infantry divisions. He was National Security Affairs assistant to President Ronald Reagan from 1987 to 1989. He married Alma Johnson in 1962; the couple have three children. His B.S. was from the City University of New York, in 1958, his M.B.A. from George Washington University in 1971. Most unusually for one who has gone so far in the U.S. Army, he is not a West Point graduate, instead becoming an officer through the Reserve Officer Training Corps.

FURTHER READING

"'You go in. . . . '" MORTIMER B. ZUCKERMAN and BRUCE B. AUSTER. *U.S. News & World Report*, Dec. 24, 1990.

Colin Powell (left) and Norman Schwarzkopf.

"Ready for action." BRUCE W. NELAN. *Time*, Nov. 12, 1990.
"Pulled to the top. . . ." RICHARD MACKENZIE. *Insight*, Oct. 8, 1990.
"Colin Powell. . . ." JAMES S. KUNEN. *People*, Sept. 10, 1990.
"Gen. Colin L. Powell. . . ." LAURA B. RANDOLPH. *Ebony*, Feb. 1990.
"A 'complete soldier'. . . ." BARRETT SEAMAN. *Time*, Aug. 21, 1989.
"Colin L. Powell. . . ." SIMEON BOOKER. *Ebony*, July 1988.
"Powell, Colin Luther." *Current Biography*, June 1988.

Powell, Michael (1905–90) Working in films from his 20s, the individualistic and influential British filmmaker Powell directed low-budget films from 1931 and first won notice with *The Edge of the World* (1937). But his best-known films were in collaboration with screenwriter Emeric Pressburger, including *The Forty-Ninth Parallel* (1942), *The Life and Death of Colonel Blimp* (1943), *I Know Where I'm Going* (1945), *A Matter of Life and Death* (*Stairway to Heaven*) (1946), *Black Narcissus* (1947), and *The Red Shoes* (1948). From 1957 working mostly without Pressburger, he directed other films, notably the controversial *Peeping Tom* (1960); he worked mainly abroad, often unable to fund productions. He also published *A Life in Movies: An Autobiography* (1986). (d. Avening; Gloucestershire; February 19, 1990)

FURTHER READING

"A modest magician." HARLAN KENNEDY. *American Film*, July 1990.
Obituary. DAVID THOMSON. *Film Comment*, May–June, 1990.
Obituary. *Current Biography*, Apr. 1990.
"British filmmaker. . . ." LAWRENCE COHN. *Variety*, Feb. 28, 1990.
"The last of the banned." *Economist*, Feb. 24, 1990.
Obituary. *The Times* (of London), Feb. 21, 1990.
Obituary. *New York Times*, Feb. 21, 1990.
"Powell, Michael." *Current Biography*, Aug. 1987.

Prego, Virginia (1958–) Dr. Prego was a health-care worker at Kings County Hospital in Brooklyn in January 1983; she claimed that she had contracted AIDS from a contaminated needle negligently left on a hospital bed and had previously received no orientation on AIDS or on the proper precautions to take when dealing with AIDS-related materials. She said that when she reported the pinprick to hospital authorities she received verbal reassurances and no treatment of any kind. She tested positive for the AIDS virus in 1984 and fell ill with the disease in 1987. The hospital denied negligence while offering settlement on terms unacceptable to Prego.

On March 8, 1990, after a 10-week trial, and only a few hours before closing arguments in the case were to be heard, a settlement was reached. The defendants admitted no guilt, while the New York City Health and Hospitals Corporation agreed to pay Dr. Prego an undisclosed sum, probably in excess of $1 million. Dr. Prego, who had been described by her doctor during the trial as having less than a year to live, said that she was satisfied with the outcome. The case was the first of its kind involving a big-city hospital, and was therefore closely watched. Although the settlement meant that no negligence was established, the size of the settlement made it clear that hospitals and other health care providers would be well advised to be extremely careful in handling AIDS, encouraging an already developing trend.

Prego had graduated from medical school in Argentina and became an "extern," an unpaid medical assistant, at Kings County Hospital in 1982. She did an internship at a Veterans Administration hospital, completed her internship and residency at Kings County, and had a fellowship there in gastroenterology. Although she had pricked her finger in 1983 and perhaps again in 1984, she did not learn she had AIDS until 1987.

FURTHER READING

"Settled. . . ." *Time*, Mar. 19, 1990.
"A dying doctor. . . ." *U.S. News & World Report*, Jan. 22, 1990.

Prestes, Luís Carlos (1898–1990) A Brazilian army engineer, Prestes joined in an unsuccessful revolt against the government of president Artur Bernardes in 1924. He then led a column of rebel troops, later dubbed the Prestes Column, on a two-year "Long March" through the Brazilian back country, a trek that became famous in Latin America. He finally went into exile in Bolivia and later in the Soviet Union, where he became a Communist. Prestes went home in the early 1930s, became leader of the Brazilian Communist Party, and was its leader for five decades; he was Latin America's leading Communist before Fidel Castro came to power in Cuba. He served in the Brazilian Senate from 1945 until his party was again banned in 1947. Prestes went into Soviet exile again in the mid-1960s, returning home freely in 1979. An old-line Communist who resisted the winds of change sweeping the world Communist movement, he lost his post as party leader in 1980 and was expelled from his party in 1984. (d. Rio de Janiero; March 7, 1990)

FURTHER READING

Obituary. *New York Times*, Mar. 9, 1990.
Obituary. *The Times* (of London), Mar. 8, 1990.
Olga. Fernando Morais. Grove-Weidenfeld, 1990.

Prophet, Elizabeth Clare (Elizabeth Clare Ytreberg, 1939–) Sometimes called "Guru Ma," Prophet is the head of the Church Universal and Triumphant, which has built an imminent-end-of-the-world retreat, complete with large fallout shelters and fortified emplacements, in Montana's otherwise peaceful Paradise Valley, north of Yellowstone Park. In 1990, approximately 3,000 of her well-armed followers

lived in the valley, ready to retire into their shelters and live in them for up to three years while defending themselves against possible invaders, much to the dismay of many others living in the valley, who claim environmental contamination and harm to the valley's wildlife and cattle; a large oil spill from underground tanks was discovered during the spring of 1990. Further dismay was caused by the arms held by Prophet's followers; her husband has served a brief jail term for trying to buy illegal semiautomatic weapons and armor-piercing ammunition.

Prophet, originally a Lutheran, grew up in Red Bank, New Jersey. She met her first husband, Mark Prophet, founder of her church, in 1958. The couple then moved the church and themselves to Colorado; after his death in 1973, she moved church headquarters to Malibu, California, and in 1986 to Paradise Valley. She has been married four times, most recently to Edward Francis, and has four children. She attended Boston University.

FURTHER READING

"The cloud over Paradise Valley. . . ." Bill Shaw. *People*, June 4, 1990.
"Trouble in paradise. . . ." Holger Jensen. *Maclean's*, May 7, 1990.

"Heading for the hills. . . ." RICHARD LACAYO. *Time*, Mar. 26, 1990.
"Shelters of the Lord." *Economist*, Mar. 24, 1990.
"Paradise under siege. . . ." MICHAEL HARRIS. *Time*, Aug. 28, 1989.

Puig, Manuel (1932–90) Argentine novelist Puig became internationally known for his *Kiss of the Spider Woman* (1976; filmed 1985). Born in an isolated country town, Puig knew the wider world largely through movies and later education in Buenos Aires. After five years abroad, studying film in Rome and working on special effects for *A Farewell to Arms*, he returned home to write his first, semiautobiographical novel, *Betrayed by Rita Hayworth* (1968). Several other works followed, including *Painted Little Mouths* (1969) and *The Buenos Aires Affair* (1973). He lived in self-imposed exile after Juan Perón's return to Argentina in 1973. (d. Cuernavaca, Mexico; July 22, 1990)

FURTHER READING

Obituary. *Current Biography*, Sept. 1990.
Obituary. *Variety*, July 25, 1990.
Obituary. *New York Times*, July 24, 1990.
"A novelist copes. . . ." ROSA MONTERO. *World Press Review*, Mar. 1989.
"Puig, Manuel." *Current Biography*, Jan. 1988.
Pop Culture into Art: The Novels of Manuel Puig. NORMAN LAVERS. University of Missouri Press, 1988.

Pynchon, Thomas (1937–) Perhaps the most secretive writer since B. Traven, Thomas Pynchon came to public attention in late 1989 with the publication of his first book in 16 years, *Vineland*. Pynchon himself was nowhere to be seen. In a world of self-promoters, he chooses to remain totally private, with only a few people—notably publishers and editors—knowing who he actually is or where he lives, and these being sworn to silence. Pynchon devotees and mystery-lovers avidly fill in the void with speculation and rumor, searching his work for clues to his identity. From the detailed knowledge shown in *Vineland*'s setting, many guess that Pynchon now lives in northern California; some have even suggested that he is J. D. Salinger, another recluse, writing under apseudonym. Most unusually, the publishers released *Vineland* without prior notice, not providing the usual advance galleys to reviewers and international publishers, so the book appeared to burst upon the scene.

All of which fuels publicity machines but has nothing to do with Pynchon's work, a complex tale of modern California culture revolving around a 60s-type central character, Zoyd Wheeler, with Pynchon's own special mixture of obscurities, ambiguities, and metaphors. Reviews of *Vineland* ranged from raves to mixed, with some hailing it as a great novel and others expressing disappointment, sometimes perhaps only because their expectations were so high. The Book-of-the-Month Club made it a main selection. How the work will be assessed in the long run is unclear.

In 1963, Pynchon erupted into the literary world with his highly regarded first novel, *V.* His next two novels were *The Crying of Lot 49* (1966) and *Gravity's Rainbow* (1973), which won a National Book Award. Then followed a long period in which he continued to write but produced no very substantial work until he published *Vineland*. Pynchon was born in Glen Cove, New York. His B.A. was from Cornell University; he later worked as a technical writer for Boeing.

FURTHER READING

"The mystery of. . . ." JAMIE DIAMOND. *People*, Jan. 29, 1990.
"Shadowy presence." PAUL GRAY. *Time*, Jan. 15, 1990.
"Pynchon, Thomas." *Current Biography*, Oct. 1987
Thomas Pynchon. HAROLD BLOOM, ed. Chelsea House, 1987.
Thomas Pynchon. TONY TANNER. Routledge Chapman & Hall, 1982.

Qaddafi, Muammar Muhammed al-

(1942-) In the late 1980s, facing increasing economic difficulties and a growing Islamic fundamentalist movement that had turned against him, Qaddafi began to present a somewhat different, considerably less-militant face to the world. In May 1989, Libya and Egypt reopened their borders; in October, Qaddafi and Egyptian president Mubarak met and made a series of agreements aimed at normalizing relations between the two countries.

Qaddafi, engaged in a serious attempt to attract Western capital and to break out of self-generated isolation, also cut back his support of terrorists; some groups then left to headquarter in Syria and Iraq. He also reportedly placed Palestinian terrorist Abu Nidal under house arrest, beginning in November 1989. Qaddafi also offered to send troops to Saudi Arabia early in the Persian Gulf Crisis, although he is generally regarded as sympathetic to the Iraqis.

Qaddafi is a career military officer; he led the 1969 military coup and quickly seized power for himself, holding it as a dictator from then on; he had himself named president in 1977. He has made repeated, largely unsuccessful attempts to establish himself as a major radical leader of the Arab world, fanning anti-Western Islamic fundamentalism, supporting terrorist activities, and supporting Iraq during the Persian Gulf Crisis. His long direct intervention in the civil war in Chad (1975–87) was no more successful; he was finally forced to sue for peace after battlefield defeat, the loss of large air bases, and Chadian invasion of southern Libya. His influence on the new revolutionary government of Chad may be considerable. He has stopped just short of going to war with Egypt on several occasions. There have also been several armed clashes with the United States; in the most serious of these, U.S. warplanes and ships bombarded Libya in April 1986. Qaddafi is married and has five children. He attended Libya University.

FURTHER READING

Qaddafi on the Edge. CAMELIA SADAT. HarperCollins, 1991.
Qaddafi, Terrorism, and the Origins of the U.S. Attack on Libya. BRIAN L. DAVIS. Greenwood, 1990.
Muammar El-Qaddafi. TED GOTTFRIED. Chelsea House, 1987.
Qaddafi and the Libyan Revolution. DAVID BLUNDY and ANDREW LYCETT. Little, Brown, 1987.
The Making of a Pariah State: The Adventurist Politics of Mummar Quaddafi, MARTIN SICKER. Greenwood, 1987.
Qaddafi: His Ideology in Theory and Practice. MOHAMED EL-KHAWAS. Gordon, 1987.
"'I am a mixture . . .'" *U.S. News & World Report, Nov. 10, 1986.*
"A jackal at bay." DAVID GROGAN. *People,* May 5, 1986.
"Gaddafi's world." KARL GUNTHER BARTH, et al. *World Press Review,* Mar. 1986.
Libya: Qadhafi's Revolution and the Modern State. LILLIAN C. HARRIS. Westview, 1986.

Quaid, Dennis (Dennis William Quaid, 1954–) A leading film actor throughout the 1980s, Quaid finished the decade as singer Jerry Lee Lewis in the film biography *Great Balls of Fire* (1989). He began the 1990s with two notable films, both released late in the year. He starred opposite Tamlyn Tomita in Alan Parker's *Come See the Paradise*, dealing with the internment of over 100,000 Japanese-Americans early in World War II. And in *Postcards from the Edge*, he played a third lead as wickedly glib movie producer Jack Falkner, opposite Shirley MacLaine and Meryl Streep.

Houston-born Quaid played a lead as one of the four young men in *Breaking Away* (1979) and went on to roles in such 1980s films as *The Long Riders* (1979; with his brother, actor Randy Quaid), *The Right Stuff* (1983), *Dreamscape* (1984), *Enemy Mine* (1985), and *The Big Easy* (1987). He attended the University of Houston. He is married to actress Meg Ryan.

FURTHER READING

"The devil and. . . ." JAN HOFFMAN. *Premiere,* Aug. 1989.
"Playing the killer." NICK TOSCHES. *Vogue,* July 1989.
"Simmer down, son." ROBERT PALMER. *American Film,* June 1989.
"Goodness gracious." JOHN ED BRADLEY. *Esquire,* Mar. 1989.
"Whole lotta shakin'." HERB RITTS and KEVIN SESSUMS. *Interview,* June 1989.
"Dennis Quaid. . . ." MICHAEL NORMAN. *New York Times Magazine, Nov. 6, 1988.*
Dennis Quaid. GAIL BIRNBAUM. St. Martin's, 1988.

Quayle, Dan (James Danforth Quayle, III, 1947–) Quayle's vice presidential career has been little different from that of other vice presidents, including George Bush, Lyndon Johnson, Richard Nixon, and Harry Truman. He has been "in" on Bush administration meetings without having any real impact on policies or actions; traveled widely, meeting the world's leaders without having any real power to work with them in any serious way; and attended large numbers of ceremonial functions, expressing the administration viewpoint on a wide range of matters.

Quayle has been a somewhat unusual vice president in a rather negative way. During the 1988 presidential campaign, and then during his early months in office, he drew a great deal of unfavorable media attention, which swelled into a kind of national and worldwide derision that has so far haunted him throughout his term in office, prompting the publication of works such as *The Dan Quayle Quiz Book: For People Who Think They Are Smarter than the Vice President* (Jeremy Solomon and Ken Brady; 1989). Quayle also demonstrated views considerably to the right of George Bush in some areas, as when in early December 1989 he questioned the sincerity of Soviet peaceful intentions just as Bush and Mikhail Gorbachev were in the process of negotiating the end of the Cold War and Gorbachev was dismantling the Soviet Eastern European empire. Although he withdrew the view a few days later, his comments did not improve his standing in the administration and in the media. During much of 1990, however, he seemed far more able to withstand and survive media attack, and played his administration role without public abrasion.

Indiana-born Quayle worked in his family's newspaper business for several years before becoming an Indiana state employee in 1971. He became a congressman in 1977, was a U.S. senator from Indiana from 1981 to 1989, and was chosen by George Bush to be his running mate in the 1988 presidential campaign. He married Marilyn Tucker in 1972; they have three children. His B.S. was from DePauw University in 1969, his J.D. from Indiana University in 1974.

FURTHER READING

"Roasting Quayle. . . ." Marci McDonald. *Maclean's*, Nov. 19, 1990.

"Quayle etches national profile. . . ." Bill Whalen. *Insight*, Nov. 5, 1990.

"Late bloomer." Garry Wills. *Time*, Apr. 23, 1990.

"Quayle, (James) Dan(forth)." *Current Biography*, June 1989.

"Talking to Dan Quayle. . . ." Lally Weymouth. *New York*, Mar. 13, 1989.

"Late bloomer." Timothy Noah. *New Republic*, Sept. 26, 1988.

"A profile of. . . ." Randy Arndt. *Nation's Cities Weekly*, Aug. 22, 1988.

"Who is Dan Quayle?. . . ." Jonathan Alter. *Newsweek*, Aug. 29, 1988.

"Family, golf and politics. . . ." Margaret B. Carlson. *Time*, Aug. 29, 1988.

Quayle Droppings: The Politics of J. Danforth Quayle. Arthur F. Ide. Liberal Press, 1988.

Quinn, Anthony (Anthony Rudolph Oaxaca Quinn, 1915–) In over five decades on screen, Quinn has played in a wide range of starring and strong supporting roles. His recent work includes the starring role in a 1990 television film based on Ernest Hemingway's *The Old Man and the Sea*, with a cast that included his daughter Valentina and his son Francesco. He also saw another son, Lorenzo, play Salvador Dali in a new film. Also in 1990, Quinn himself starred opposite Kevin Costner in *Revenge* and also appeared in *Ghosts Do It*. His recent televison work also included a starring role in *Onassis: The Richest Man in the World* (1988). Meanwhile, he continues to mount exhibitions of his artworks, most recently in Mexico City and Paris, both in 1990.

Chihuahua-born Quinn appeared in a wide range of supporting roles in action films early in his career, as in *The Plainsman* (1937), *Blood and Sand* (1941), and *Viva Zapata* (1952; he won a Best Supporting Actor Oscar), and then was able to broaden his work greatly, appearing as Zampanò opposite Giulietta Masina's Gelsomina in Federico Fellini's classic film *La Strada* (1954); in *Lust For Life* (1956), for which he won a second Best Supporting Actor Oscar; and in such further films as *The Guns of Navarone* (1961), *Lawrence of Arabia* (1962), *Zorba the Greek* (1964), *The Shoes of the Fisherman* (1968), and *Lion of the Desert* (1980). He starred on Broadway in the title role of *Zorba* (1983–86). Quinn has been married twice, most recently to Iolanda Addolori in 1966, and has eight children. He has published an autobiography, *The Original Sin: A Self-Portrait* (1972).

FURTHER READING

"'It's not very hard work . . .'" Joanna Elm. *TV Guide*, Mar. 24, 1990.

"As Zorba the Greek. . . ." Julie Greenwalt. *People*, May 2, 1983.

The Films of Anthony Quinn. Alvin H. Marill and Arthur Kennedy. Carol, 1975.

Rafsanjani, Hojatoleslam Hashemi (1934–) Rafsanjani became president of Iran in August 1989, after a period of maneuver following the death of Ayatollah Ruhollah Khomeini. In office, he somewhat moderated the level of Iranian offical anti-American and anti-Western rhetoric, and made a series of small moves to establish more normal international relations. At the same time, he has on many occasions responded to internal Islamic fundamentist pressures, as when he softened the Salman Rushdie death threat in January 1990 and a few months later strongly restated the threat.

As the Persian Gulf Crisis developed, Rafsanjani responded to Iraqi overtures, exchanging remaining Iran-Iraq war prisoners, negotiating Iraqi withdrawal from disputed terrritory, and in September reestablishing diplomatic relations with Iraq, all in return for promised assistance to Iraq, then in the process of being surrounded and blockaded by allied mideastern forces. In January 1991, his country provided refuge for a large portion of the Iraqi air force, in flight from the battle for Kuwait, and in February he offered to act as mediator between the combatants.

Rafsanjani was long associated with Ayatollah Khomeini under whom he studied at Qom Theological Seminary. He became a key figure in Iranian politics as speaker of the National Assembly during the 1980s. As speaker, he sometimes played the role of hard-line Iranian politician, as when he called for the assassination of the author Salman Rushdie for writing the book *The Satanic Verses* (1988); but he also sometimes functioned as a relative moderate, as when he made tentative overtures to the West in a bid to reestablish broken relations. Rafsanjani's personal life has been kept very private, but it is known that he is married and has several children.

FURTHER READING

"Rafsanjani, Ali Akbar Hashemi." *Current Biography*, Nov. 1989.

"'Rafsanjani would have. . .'" ALFRED BALK. *World Press Review*, Aug. 1989.

"Iran without Khomeini." MICHAEL LEDEEN. *American Spectator*, Aug. 1989.

"Burying the Passions. . . ." BILL HEWITT. *Newsweek*, June 19, 1989.

"Santa satan?. . . ." MAGGIE MAHAR. *Barron's*, Jan. 16, 1989.

Rahman Putra, Tunku Abdul (1903–90) Malayan Tunku (Prince) Abdul Rahman Putra spent the years 1919 to 1931 in Britain, served in the Malayan civil service from 1931 through the end of the Japanese occupation, and returned to Britain in 1945, becoming a lawyer in 1949. Back in Malaya in 1951, the Tunku, until then looked on by many as a playboy, became head of the United Malays National Organization and of the succeeding Malay-Chinese coalition that helped defeat the Communist insurgency. From 1957 to 1963 he was the first prime minister of independent Malaya, and from 1963 to 1969 was first president of the Federation of Malaya. (d. Kuala Lumpur, Malaysia; December 6, 1990)

FURTHER READING

Obituary. *New York Times*, Dec. 7, 1990.
Obituary. *The Times* (of London), Dec. 7, 1990.
Tunku Abdul Rahman. A. M. HEALY. University of Queensland Press, 1982.

Raitt, Bonnie (Bonnie Lynn Raitt, 1949–) Singer-musician-composer Raitt scored a phenomenal success in February 1990 with a sweep of the Grammy awards, winning best album, best female pop vocal, and best female rock vocal for her *Nick of Time* album and its title song, and best traditional blues recording for "I'm in the Mood," a duet with John Lee Hooker on Hooker's album *The Healer*. Within the next month *Nick of Time* sold half a million copies and soon jumped to number one on *Billboard* magazine's national album charts, a status she had never reached before. Her new record company, Capitol, quickly issued a retrospective album, *The Bonnie Raitt Collection*, while she gave concerts around the country, ending in September in Los Angeles. She continued her support of social causes, as in her performances in aid of abortion rights and in honor of Nelson Mandela.

California-born Raitt, the daughter of singer John Raitt, became a popular folk and blues figure in the early 1970s with such albums as *Bonnie Raitt* (1971), *Give It Up* (1972), *Streetlights* (1974), and *Sweet Forgiveness* (1977). She was far less popular in the late 1970s and throughout the 1980s, and was dropped by her old record company, Warner, reviving her career only with *Nick of Time*. She attended Radcliffe College.

FURTHER READING

"Raitt, Bonnie." *Current Biography*, Aug. 1990.
"Bonnie Raitt. . . ." JAMES HENKE. *Rolling Stone*, May 3, 1990.
"20 questions. . . ." PAUL ENGLEMAN and JOHN REZEK. *Playboy*, Nov. 1989.
"Veteran rocker. . . ." KIM HUBBARD. *People*, Apr. 24, 1989.

Rajneesh, Baghwan Shree (Chandra Mohan Jain or Osho Rajneesh, 1931–90) The Indian guru Rajneesh was deported from the United States in 1985 for activities at his controversial Oregon commune. Educated in philosophy, Rajneesh founded an ashram (religious community) in Poona, India, stressing free love and Eastern spirituality and attracting thousands of wealthy followers who paid substantial fees. After Indian tax authorities raised questions, Rajneesh transferred his ostentatious wealth and activities to the United States in 1981, but serious problems within the Rajneeshpuram community—including attempted murder, arson, and immigration fraud—led to his deportation and return to India. In 1980 he published *The Sound of Running Water*. (d. Poona; January 19, 1990)

FURTHER READING

Obituary. *The Times* (of London), Jan. 23, 1990.
Obituary. *New York Times*, Jan. 20, 1990.
"A reporter at large; Rajneeshpuram" (two parts). FRANCES FITZGERALD. *New Yorker*, Sept. 22 and 29, 1986.
The Awakened One: The Life & Work of Bhagwan Shree Rajneesh. VASANT JOSHI. Harper San Francisco, 1982.

Rappaport, David (1952–90) The British character actor Rappaport played Mighty Mouth on the television series "L.A. Law." Only 3 feet, 11 inches tall (the result of achondroplasia),

Rappaport studied psychology and taught school before becoming an actor. British theater, cabaret, and television work led to parts in *Time Bandits* (1981) and *The Bride* (1985), roles that brought him international attention. In Los Angeles from 1986, he starred in the television series "The Wizard" (1986–87). Apparently depressed at the show's failure and discrimination because of his height, he attempted suicide in March 1990, succeeding two months later. (d. Los Angeles; May 2, 1990)

FURTHER READING

Obituary. *New York Times*, May 5, 1990.
Obituary. *The Times* (of London), May 5, 1990.
"The first little person. . . ." DAVID VAN BIEMA and MARY ANN NORBOM. *People*, Oct. 6, 1986.

Rashid bin Said al Maktoum (1914–90) Sheikh Rashid succeeded his father to the throne of oil-rich Dubai in 1958, when the Trucial States of the Persian Gulf were still dependent upon British forces. In 1971, when those forces withdrew, he was a leading figure in organizing seven small states in the area, including Dubai, into the United Arab Emirates. He became federation prime minister in 1981 and attempted to steer a neutral course in the long Iran-Iraq war. He was succeeded by his eldest son, Sheikh Maktoum bin Rashid, a notable breeder of racehorses as were his other sons. (d. Dubai; October 9, 1990)

FURTHER READING

Obituary. *The Times* (of London), Oct. 9, 1990.

Rather, Dan (1931–) "CBS Evening News" anchor Dan Rather came under enormous pressure in 1989–90. The network's domination of the news, established under Walter Cronkite, had gradually slipped away and by late 1989, ABC's "World News Tonight" with Peter Jennings had taken over the top spot and, with occasional shifts in the lead (measured in tenths of a point), continued to hold it, with CBS sometimes falling to third. Part of the problem is that some people—with international news to the fore—turned to Jennings, a former foreign correspondent;

Rather's strength has traditionally been in domestic reporting. Rather's 1988 on-the-air confrontation with George Bush also reportedly cost him viewers. To many, Rather has never seemed as fully comfortable in the anchor role as he had been as a reporter; in 1990, he made some stylistic changes, standing up to deliver the news and using a new sign-off: "And that's part of our world tonight." He also took steps to link himself with international events for example, as by going to Iraq to interview Saddam Hussein in late August 1990.

Another problem Rather faced was a controversy over use of some faked film in an award-winning series of reports for the nightly news and a 1987 documentary special on Afghanistan. The film was provided by a freelance photographer, and only in 1989 was it found to have included faked and restaged sabotage and battle sequences. CBS was apparently unaware of the faking but was criticized for not checking more carefully on a story Rather was pushing within the news department. Although the simulation was not deliberate, and though the increased use of freelance and even amateur videotape makes all news stations vulnerable to the problem, the incident may also have damaged confidence in Rather and CBS News.

Texas-born Rather became CBS news anchor in 1981, climaxing a long career that began in Houston in the early 1950s. His breakthrough came when, as a young CBS correspondent in Dallas, he reported live to the nation on the November 22, 1963, assassination of President John F. Kennedy. After working as a CBS White House correspondent in 1964, and then abroad, he returned to Washington as CBS White House correspondent from 1966 to 1974, and played a substantial role as an investigative reporter during the unfolding Watergate affair and through the resignation of Richard Nixon. With his opposite numbers at ABC and NBC, he has for a decade been one of the three chief American reporters and interpreters of the news. His B.A. was from Sam Houston State College, in 1951. He is married to Jean Goebel; they have two children.

FURTHER READING

Anchors: Brokaw, Jennings, Rather & the Evening News. Robert Goldberg and Gerald J. Goldberg. Carol, 1990.
Happy Talk: Confessions of a TV Journalist. Fred Graham. Norton, 1990.
"Rather's influence. . . ." Verne Gay. *Variety*, Feb. 8, 1989.
"'Some things are . . .'" Merrill Brown and Peter Ainslie. *Channels*, Oct. 1988.
Prime Times, Bad Times. Ed Joyce. Doubleday, 1988.
"The most trusted men. . . ." Carol Kramer. *McCall's*, July 1987.
Dan Rather and Other Rough Drafts. Martha A. Turner. Eakin, 1987.
In the Storm of the Eye: A Lifetime at CBS. Bill Leonard. Putnam, 1987.

Ray, Johnnie (1927–90) Oregon-born singer Ray was best known for his double-sided 1951 hit record "Cry" and "The Little White Cloud That Cried." Partly deaf from a childhood accident, he worked in nightclubs as a singer and pianist before being signed by Okeh Records. Among his other 1950s hits were "Walkin' My Baby Back Home" and "Just Walking in the Rain." Later he sang internationally in nightclubs, also appearing in *There's No Business Like Show Business*. (1954). (d. Los Angeles; February 24, 1990)

FURTHER READING

Obituary. *Variety*, Mar. 14, 1990.
Obituary. *New York Times*, Feb. 26, 1990.

Reagan, Ronald Wilson (1911–) Reagan became the 40th President of the United States in 1981 and was succeeded by George Bush in 1989, after two terms in the presidency. In the spring of 1989, he was able to put the Iran-Contra affair behind him, successfully claiming executive privilege as to his diaries during the trial of Admiral John Poindexter, and limiting his involvement to videotape testimony at that trial. November 1990 saw publication of his best-selling autobiography *An American Life;* his wife had published her view in 1989 in *My Turn: The Memoirs of Nancy Reagan*. Highly speculative but very persistent rumors also hinted that he might also be considering acting once again. Late in 1989, Reagan came under considerable criticism for his moneymaking visit to Japan, where he received $2 million from the Fujisankei Communications Group for two 20-minute speeches and a few public appearances and where he solicited Japan's Sony Corporation for a $1 million donation to his presidential library.

For Illinois-born Ronald Reagan, the presidency was the culmination of his second major career; after briefly working as a sportscaster in the Midwest, he had become a film actor in the late 1930s and early 1940s, playing in such movies as *Knute Rockne—All American* (1940) and *King's Row* (1942). He headed the Screen Actors Guild from 1947 to 1952.

A liberal-turned-conservative, Reagan moved into Republican politics in the early 1960s, was governor of California from 1967 to 1975, and after two unsuccessful runs for the Republican presidential nomination was ultimately nominated; he defeated Jimmy Carter in the 1980 election. During his presidency, he most notably began with the hard-line anti-communism of his "evil empire" speech and ended with the series of treaties and Reagan-Gorbachev meetings that brought the long Cold War to a close. He also presided over the buildup of a national debt that had approached $2 trillion by the time he left office. He was married to Jane Wyman from 1940 to 1948; they had two children. He married Nancy Davis Reagan in 1952; they had two more children. His B.A. was from Eureka College in 1932.

FURTHER READING

Very Special Relationship, Reagan and Thatcher. Geoffrey Smith. Norton, 1991.

"What you saw. . . ." BARRETT SEAMAN. *Time*, Nov. 5, 1990.
Ronald Reagan. JOHN DEVANEY. Walker, 1990.
Reagan as President: Contemporary Views of the Man, His Politics, and His Policies. PAUL BOYER, ed. I. R. Dee, 1990.
"Misha and Ron. . . ." TODD BREWSTER. *Life*, Fall, 1989.
"The enigma. . . ." ROBERT J. SAMUELSON. *New Republic*, Jan. 9, 1989.
"Mr. Average. . . ." ANDREW SULLIVAN. *New Republic*, Jan. 9, 1989.
"Nap-Master Ronnie. . . ." FRED BARNES. *New Republic*, Jan. 9, 1989.
The Reagan Years. HODDING CARTER. Braziller, 1988.
Early Reagan: The Rise to Power. ANNE EDWARDS. Morrow, 1987.
Mister President: The Story of Ronald Reagan, rev. ed. MARY V. FOX. Enslow, 1986.
Make-Believe: The Story of Nancy & Ronald Reagan. LAURENCE LEAMER. Dell, 1984.
Hollywood on Ronald Reagan: Friends & Enemies Discuss Our President, the Actor. DOUG MCCLELLAND. Faber & Faber, 1983.

Redford, Robert (Charles Robert Redford, Jr., 1937–) In early 1990, Redford the actor was in the Dominican Republic shooting *Havana,* a romantic adventure story set in late-1950s Cuba; the film opened late in the year. By that time the multifaceted Redford was in the Southwest producing *The Dark Wind,* based on Tony Hillerman's novel, with Navajo policeman Jim Chee played by Lou Diamond Phillips. The casting of part-Cherokee Phillips was criticized by the American Indian Registry for the Performing Arts but supported by a Navajo organization. With seven other top filmmakers, Redford founded the Film Foundation to help preserve America's film heritage. He also continued his efforts to preserve the environment and was awarded the National Audubon Society's highest honor, the Audubon Medal.

California-born Redford began his spectacular film career in the late 1960s; his first starring role was in *Barefoot in the Park* (1967), a role he had played on Broadway in 1963. He went on to star in such classics as *Butch Cassidy and the Sundance Kid* (1969), *Jeremiah Johnson* (1972), *The Way We Were* (1973), *The Sting* (1973), and *All the President's Men* (1976). He later directed the Oscar-winning *Ordinary People* (1980), directed and starred in *The Natural* (1984), starred in *Out of Africa* (1985), and directed and produced *The Milagro Beanfield War* (1988). During the 1980s, his film institute at Sundance, Colorado, became a mecca for moviemakers from all over the world. He attended the University of Colorado, Pratt Institute, and the American Academy of Dramatic Arts.

FURTHER READING

"Redford talks. . . ." NEIL GABLER. *New York*, Dec. 10, 1990.
"Hollywood goes Havana. . . ." MERLE LINDA WOLIN. *New Republic*, Apr. 16, 1990.
"Robert Redford at 50. . . ." NATALIE GITTELSON. *McCall's*, Feb. 1988.
"Bored with his name." STEPHEN SCHAEFER. *Film Comment*, Jan.–Feb. 1988.
Robert Redford. BRUCE CROWTHER. Hippocrene, 1985.
Robert Redford. DAVID DOWNING. St. Martin's, 1983.
"Robert Redford." *Current Biography*, March 1982.

Redgrave, Lynn (1943–) The versatile Redgrave continued her long stage, screen, and television career; but from late 1990 with a significant difference. In December 1990, she and her sister, Vanessa Redgrave, acted together for the first time when they opened on the London stage in Chekhov's *The Three Sisters.* They were directed by their brother, Corin Redgrave, and the rest of the cast included their niece Jemma, Christopher Reeve, and Sigourney Weaver. Carrying the family enterprise one step further, Lynn and Vanessa appeared in February 1991 in the television drama *What Ever Happened to Baby Jane?,* with Vanessa as Blanche (the Joan Crawford role) and Lynn as Baby Jane (the Bette Davis role). In 1989, Lynn Redgrave played opposite Jackie Mason in the short-lived television series "Chicken Soup."

London-born Redgrave quickly emerged as a star in the film *Georgy Girl* (1966; she was nominated for an Oscar). She went on to a very diverse career in theater, films, and television, on both sides of the Atlantic, which included everything from *Tom Jones* (1963) to *The Happy Hooker* (1975) on screen; *St Joan* (1977) to *Sweet Sue* (1987) on stage; and "Centennial" (1978) to the series "House Calls" (1984) on television. Redgrave attended London's Central School of Speech and Drama. She married director John Clark in 1967; they have three children. She is the daughter of actress Rachel Kempson and actor Michael Redgrave, the sister of actress Vanessa Redgrave, and actor-director Corin Redgrave, and the aunt of actresses Jemma Redgrave and Joely and Natasha Richardson.

FURTHER READING

"Catching up with. . . ." LEE RANDALL. *Weight Watchers* magazine. Aug. 1990.
"Soup's on!" ISOBEL SILDEN. *Weight Watchers* magazine, Dec. 1989.
Life among the Redgraves. RACHEL KEMPSON. NAL-Dutton, 1988.
This Is Living: An Inspirational Guide to Freedom from the Fat Ogre. LYNN REDGRAVE. NAL-Dutton, 1988.
"Lynn Redgrave." TRISHA THOMPSON. *Weight Watchers magazine*, Jan. 1984.
"Lynn Redgrave fights. . . ." KATHY MACKAY. *People*, Aug. 17, 1981.

Lynn Redgrave (standing) and Vanessa Redgrave.

Redgrave, Vanessa (1937–) British actress Vanessa Redgrave scored a notable success on Broadway in 1990, bringing from London Peter Hall's acclaimed revival of Tennessee Williams's *Orpheus Descending*. It was her first visit to Broadway in 12 years, at least partly because of her controversial politics. The "semi-operatic" *Orpheus* production was also seen in a television version on the cable network TNT.

In July 1990, Redgrave filmed another Southern story, in Texas—*Ballad of the Sad Café*, an adaptation of Carson McCullers's novel, directed by Simon Callow, with Ismail Merchant (the usual partner of director James Ivory) producing. Redgrave then turned toward two projects with her sister, Lynn Redgrave, with whom she had never publicly performed. First they shot a remake of the former Bette Davis-Joan Crawford vehicle, *What Ever Happened to Baby Jane?*, which was shown on ABC-TV in February 1991. Then the sisters opened in London in a highly praised production of Chekhov's *The Three Sisters*, joined by their niece Jemma Redgrave (in a role originally planned for Vanessa's daughter Joely Richardson) and directed by their brother Corin Redgrave.

Vanessa Redgrave is one of the most celebrated stage and screen actresses of her time, emerging in the early 1960s in the classics and then in her very notable starring role in the stage version of Muriel Spark's *The Prime of Miss Jean Brodie* (1966). She reached world audiences on screen in such films as *Isadora* (1968), *Julia* (1977), *Agatha* (1978), television's *Playing For Time* (1979), *The Bostonians* (1983), and *Comrades* (1986). Active in far-left politics for many years, and notably a supporter of the Palestine Liberation Organization, she also produced and narrated *The Palestinians* (1977). She was formerly married to director Tony Richardson and has two daughters, actresses Natasha and Joely Richardson, and a son. She is the daughter of Michael Redgrave and Rachel Kempson. She attended the Central School of Speech and Drama.

FURTHER READING

"Vanessa ascending. . . ." WILLIAM A. HENRY, III. *Time*, Oct. 9, 1989.
Life Among the Redgraves. RACHEL KEMPSON. NAL-Dutton, 1988.
"Vanessa Redgrave protests." KATHLEEN FURY. *TV Guide*, May 25, 1985.

"Redgrave wins part. . . ." GUY LIVINGSTON. *Variety*, Nov. 14, 1984.
"Redgrave vs. BSO. . . ." *Variety*, Nov. 7, 1984.
"Redgrave's suit. . . ." GUY LIVINGSTON. *Variety*, Oct. 31, 1984.

Redmond, Liam (1913–89) Limerick-born Redmond made his acting debut at Dublin's Abbey Theatre in a 1935 revival of Sean O'Casey's *The Silver Tassie,* and continued as actor and director at the Abbey until after World War II. In the late 1940s, he appeared in substantial parts on the London stage in such plays as *The White Steed* (1947) and *The Playboy of the Western World* (1947), and during the decades that followed he became a veteran character actor in a wide range of plays in Britain and the United States, also appearing on television and in several films. (d. November, 1989)

FURTHER READING

Obituary. *The Times* (of London), Nov. 22, 1989.

Reeve, Christopher (1952–) Reeve became a worldwide film star in *Superman* (1978) and its three sequels (1980, 1983, and 1987). A fifth Superman film is forthcoming. Best known for his screen work, Reeve has spent much of his recent time working on stage. He played a starring role in a New York Shakespeare Festival production of Shakespeare's *The Winter's Tale* (1989) and late in 1990 he performed on the London stage, joining the Redgrave family—Lynn and Vanessa with their niece, Jemma Redgrave—in a production of Chekhov's *The Three Sisters,* directed by Corin Redgrave. Reeve also had a leading role in the forthcoming film *Midnight Spy,* set in Germany and Poland before World War II.

New York City–born Reeve has appeared on Broadway in *A Matter of Gravity* (1978) and *Fifth of July* (1980) and has played a wide range of roles in regional theater, as well as working in London opposite Vanessa Redgrave and Wendy Hiller in *The Aspern Papers* (1984). He has also appeared in such films as *Somewhere in Time* (1980), *Deathtrap* (1982), *Monsignor* (1982), *The Bostonians* (1984), and *Switching Channels* (1988), and in several television films, recently *The Great Escape* (1988). He attended the Juilliard School; his B.A. is from Cornell University. He has two children.

FURTHER READING

"Christopher Reeve. . . ." MICHAEL J. BANDLER. *McCall's*, Sept. 1987.
"Christopher Reeve." GREGORY SPECK. *Interview*, Mar. 1986.
Caught in the Act: New York Actors Face to Face. DON SHEWEY and SUSAN SHACTER. NAL-Dutton, 1986.
"A down-to-earth Actor . . . " LINDA E. WATSON. *Teen*, June 1983.
"Christopher Reeve. . . ." JOAN BARTHEL. *Cosmopolitan*, Mar. 1983.
"Reeve, Christopher." *Current Biography*, May 1982.
The Christopher Reeve Scrapbook. MARGERY STEINBERG. Putnam, 1981.

Rehnquist, William Hubbs (1924–) Chief Justice Rehnquist, the leading conservative in the modern history of the U.S. Supreme Court, wrote many of the conservative majority's decisions during the 1989–90 session of the Court, in such cases as the landmark *Cruzan* v. *Missouri* "right to die" case, which denied Nancy Cruzan's family the right to remove her from her life–support system; *Spallone* v. *U.S.*, which upset court-imposed fines on elected officials in a housing discrimination case in Yonkers, New York; and *Whitmore* v. *Arkansas*, which refused review of a death sentence. The last case was one of the many involving police powers, law enforcement, and defendant's rights decided by the Court's conservative majority.

Rehnquist was on the losing side in a smaller number of cases, most notably including *U.S.* v. *Eichman,* which struck down the federal law against flag burning; *Rutan* v. *Republican Party of Illinois,* which curtailed the power of politicians in power to name party sympathizers to most low-level government jobs; and *Metro Broadcasting* v. *FCC,* which supported an affirmative action program in the broadcasting industry.

Milwaukee-born Rehnquist clerked with Supreme Court Justice Robert Jackson in 1952–53 and then practiced law in Phoenix until 1969. He was a Washington-based assistant attorney general from 1969 to 1971, was named to the Supreme Court by then-president Richard Nixon in 1971, and was confirmed only after a sharp Senate battle over his allegedly extremely conservative views. President Ronald Reagan appointed him Chief Justice in 1986; he was confirmed after another Senate battle. He married Natalie Cornell in 1953; they have two children. His B.A. was from Stanford in 1958, his M.A. from Harvard in 1949, and his LL.B. from Stanford in 1952.

FURTHER READING

Eight Men and a Lady. HERMAN SCHWARTZ, ANDREA NEAL, and DAVID SAVAGE. National Press, 1990.
Packing the Courts: The Conservatives' Campaign to Rewrite the Constitution. HERMAN SCHWARTZ. Scribner/Macmillan, 1988.
"Coup at the court." RENATA ADLER. *New Republic*, Sept. 14, 1987.
"What they say it is. . . ." *Time*, July 6, 1987.
The Supreme Court: The Way It Was—the Way It Is. WILLIAM H. REHNQUIST. Morrow, 1987.
"Nine who decide. . . ." ELIZABETH WARD. *Scholastic Update*, Sept. 8, 1986.
"From 'lone dissenter' to chief." *U.S. News & World Report*, June 30, 1986.
"Reagan's Mr. Right. . . ." EVAN THOMAS and RICHARD LACAYO. *Time*, June 30, 1986.
"A pair for the court. . . ." LARRY MARTZ. *Newsweek*, June 30, 1986.

Reilly, William Kane (1940–) The head of the U.S. Environmental Protection Agency (EPA) was a leading environmentalist before joining the Bush administration in January 1989. In office, he took strong positions on a number of major environmental problems, pledging action on such issues as acid rain, a long-overdue revision of the clean air law, ozone, and the greenhouse effect, and was able to make significant contributions to the Clean Air Act signed into law in November 1990, and to international agreements aimed at stopping the damaging depletion of the ozone layer.

He was also able to take action on several major specific problems, such as the March 1989 *Exxon Valdez* Alaska oil spill and the controversial Two Forks Dam on the South Platte River, in Colorado. He ordered a review of the dam on March 24, 1989, the date of the *Exxon Valdez* spill; on November 23, 1990, after a national controversy, he stopped the project. On a number of other key issues, however, Reilly found himself at odds with others in the Bush administration, one of them John Sununu, and was therefore unable to go forward on many high-priority environmental issues.

Illinois-born Reilly has held a series of key environmental posts, including the presidency of the Conservation Fund from 1973, presidency of the World Wildlife Fund from 1985 to 1989, and several federal government positions. His B.A. was from Yale, in 1962; his J.D. was from Harvard in 1965, and his M.S. in urban planning was from Columbia in 1971.

FURTHER READING

"Preventing pollution won't hurt. . . ." *Design News*, Sept. 17, 1990.

"Reilly, William Kane." *Current Biography*, July 1989.
"RC-DC: Bush's Catholic appointments." *National Catholic Reporter*, Jan. 13, 1989.

Reiner, Rob (1945–) Actor, writer, director, and producer Reiner scored a substantial success in 1989 with the film comedy *When Harry Met Sally. . .* , directing a cast that included Billy Crystal, Meg Ryan, and Carrie Fisher; he also co-produced the work. His film drama *Misery* opened late in 1990; it starred James Caan as the disabled, victimized romance novelist held hostage by an insane fan, played by Kathy Bates in an Oscar-winning performance. Reiner directed from William Goldman's adaptation of the Stephen King novel.

New York City–born Reiner became a television scriptwriter in the late 1960s and emerged as a notable television actor as "Meathead" in the long-running television series "All in the Family" (1971–78), for which he won Emmys in 1974 and 1978. He moved into film direction in the mid-1980s, with the documentary *This Is Spinal Tap* (1984), and then directed several well-received feature films, including *The Sure Thing* (1985), *Stand by Me* (1986), and *The Princess Bride* (1987). Reiner attended the University of California at Los Angeles. He has been married twice, last to Michele Singer in 1989. He is the son of actor-writer-director Carl Reiner.

FURTHER READING

"Pals." Robert Lloyd. *American Film*, July–Aug. 1989.
"Reiner's reason." April Bernard and Michelle Singer. *Interview*, July 1989.
"Reiner, Rob." *Current Biography*, May 1988.
"Prince Rob." Harlan Jacobson. *Film Comment*, Sept.–Oct. 1987.
"Rob Reiner." Betsy Borns and Joe Gaffney. *Interview*, Oct. 1986.

Reischauer, Edwin (Edwin Oldfather Reischauer, 1910–90) Reischauer was a notable East Asian scholar and U.S. ambassador to Japan (1961–66). Born in Tokyo to American missionaries, he attended Tokyo's American School, completed college in America, then returned to Japan on a Harvard fellowship (1933–39), during this period helping to devise the phonetic system for transcribing Korean into Western letters. After war service in intelligence and the State Department, Reischauer taught at Harvard (1956–61), writing (with John Fairbank) a standard history text, the two-volume *East Asia*. As ambassador, he was popular and energetic in increasing American-Japanese understanding. In 1986 he published *My Life Between Japan and America*. (d. La Jolla, California; September 1, 1990)

FURTHER READING

Obituary. *Current Biography*, Nov. 1990.
Obituary. *The Times* (of London), Sept. 4, 1990.
Obituary. *New York Times*, Sept. 2, 1990.
"The Ambassadors." Elizabeth Shannon. *Boston Magazine*, Feb. 1986.

Revere, Anne (1903–90) As Elizabeth Taylor's mother in *National Velvet* (1945), Revere won a Best Supporting Actress Oscar. Fifteen years later, in 1960, she won a Tony for her role on Broadway in Lillian Hellman's *Toys in the Attic*. In between, in 1951, at the height of the McCarthy erea, she was blacklisted by the film industry for taking the protection of the Fifth Amendment and refusing to "name names" for the House Un-American Activities Committee. Revere's first hit role on Broadway came in an earlier Hellman play; *The Children's Hour* (1934). She went to Hollywood in 1940 and appeared in a wide range of films during the next 11 years, including *The Howards of Virginia* (1940), *The Song of Bernadette* (1943; she was nominated for an Oscar), *Gentlemen's Agreement* (1947; and another Oscar nomination), and *A Place in the Sun* (1951). Long after the McCarthy period, she returned to films, appearing in several small roles from 1970, and in one more substantial role, in *Birch Interval* (1976). (d. Locust Valley, Long Island; December 18, 1990)

FURTHER READING

Obituary. *The Times* (of London), Dec. 21, 1990.
Obituary. *New York Times*, Dec. 19, 1990.

Reynolds, Burt (1936–) During the 1989–90 television season, Reynolds was B. L. Stryker, one of four detectives rotating in the Saturday night "ABC Mystery Movie" slot. With the 1990–91 season, Reynolds had switched to CBS, starring in a much-praised situation comedy, "Evening Shade", playing an ex–football player returning with his family to coach football in Evening Shade, Arkansas. *Breaking In* (1989), a low-budget film in which Reynolds got rave reviews, did poorly in theatrical release but showed surprising strength in the video rental market. Late in 1990, he was set to direct his third film, the comedy *Alby's House of Bondage*. Reynolds was honored in 1990 by the Motion Picture and Television Fund.

Georgia-born Reynolds became a very popular film star in the 1970s with such films as *Deliverance* (1972), *The Man Who Loved Cat Dancing* (1973), *White Lightning* (1973), *The Longest Yard* (1974), *W.W. and the Dixie Dance Kings* (1975), *Nickelodeon* (1976), the two *Smokey and the Bandit* films (1977, 1980), *Hooper* (1978), *Sharkey's Machine* (1981), the two *Cannonball Run* films (1981, 1984), and *Physical Evidence* (1989). On television, he appeared in many episodes of "Gunsmoke" (1965) and starred in the series "Hawk" (1966) and "Dan August" (1970–71). He was formerly married to Judy Carne, married Loni Anderson in 1988, and has one child. He attended Florida State University and Palm Beach Junior College.

FURTHER READING

"Talking with Loni Anderson. . . ." LAWRENCE EISENBERG. *Redbook*, Dec. 1988.
"Loni Anderson. . . ." NATALIE GITTELSON. *McCall's*, May 1987.
Burt Reynolds: Superstar. CAROLINE LATHAM. Putnam, 1986.
"'Why I always leave . . .'" A. E. HOTCHNER. *McCall's*, Jan. 1984.
Burt!: The Unauthorized Biography. MARC ELIOT. Dell, 1982.
Burt Reynolds: An Unauthorized Biography. SYLVIA RESNICK. St. Martin's, 1982.
The Films of Burt Reynolds. NANCY STREEBECK. Carol, 1982.

Richards, Ann (Dorothy Ann Willis Richards, 1933–) On November 6, 1990, Democratic Texas State Treasurer Ann Richards became governor-elect of the state, winning by a very small margin (51 percent–49 percent) over first-time Republican candidate Clayton W. Williams, Jr., in an unusually dirty campaign marked by its negative advertising and name-calling. Many attributed the Richards win to errors by Williams occurring late in the campaign; in late September, several polls had indicated a clear-cut lead for Williams.

Richards had emerged victorious in a three-way Democratic campaign in April, coming out ahead but without a clear majority against state attorney general Jim Mattox and former governor Mark White and then defeating Mattox in a runoff. Those contests had been extremely dirty as well, with Mattox accusing Richards of earlier illegal drug use and later facing illegal drug use accusations himself, and White facing Richards's accusations of unethical actions while in office.

Waco-born Richards began her political career in 1972 as a campaign worker for and then administrative assistant to Austin state representative Sarah Weddington. Richards won election as a county commissioner in 1976, was elected state treasurer in 1982, and was re-elected in 1986. She drew national attention as keynote speaker at the 1988 Democratic National Convention in an address featured by sharp attacks, some of them rather personal, on Republican presidential candidate George Bush. She attended Baylor University. Divorced from lawyer David Richards, she has four children and is a recovered alcoholic.

FURTHER READING

"How to beat Bubba. . . ." CAROL UNGER. *New Republic*, Oct. 22, 1990.
"Ann Richards. . . ." MIMI SWARTZ. *Texas Monthly*, Oct. 1990.
"After a mudslinging primary. . . ." WILLIAM PLUMMER. *People*, April 30, 1990.
"Money, media and magic. . . ." PAUL BURKA. *Texas Monthly*, Feb. 1990.
Straight from the Heart—My Life. ANN RICHARDS. Simon & Schuster, 1990.
"The many lives of. . . ." LESLIE BENNETT. *Woman's Day*, Oct. 3, 1989.
"Ann Richards's success story." SARA SANBORN. *Ms*, June 1984.

Riegle, Donald Wayne Jr. (1938–) A four-term Democratic senator from Michigan, Riegle, together with four other senators, was charged in 1987 with unethically intervening with federal bank regulators on behalf of the Lincoln Savings and Loan Association of Irvine, California, controlled by Charles H. Keating, Jr. The four other senators were Dennis DeConcini, John Glenn, Alan Cranston, and John McCain; the group came to known as the "Keating Five." In 1989, the bank was taken over by federal banking authorities in a bailout carrying an estimated cost of at least $2 billion. In late November 1990, Senate Ethics Committee hearings began on the "Keating Five."

Senators McCain, Glenn, DeConcini, and Cranston met with Edwin J. Gray, then chairman of the Federal Home Loan Bank Board, in DeConcini's Washington office on April 2, 1987; Gray charges that the senators improperly pressured him on behalf of Lincoln, a charge they all deny. The same four senators, and also Senator Riegle, met with Gray and members of the San Francisco Federal Home Bank in DeConcini's office on April 9, 1987. Riegle received $76,100 in campaign contributions from Keating and his associates; he later declared that he would return the contributions.

Flint-born Riegle worked at IBM and was a college teacher in the early 1960s, then turned toward a political career. He was a four-term Michigan Democratic congressman before his 1977 entry into the Senate. In 1989, he became the very influential chairman of the Senate's Banking, Housing, and Urban Affairs Committee. His 1960 B.A. was from the University of Michigan, his 1961 M.B.A. from Michigan State, and his 1970 LL.D. from St. Benedict's College. He married Lori Hansen in 1978; the couple have four children.

FURTHER READING

"Seven sorry senators. . . ." MARGARET CARLSON. *Time*, Jan. 8, 1990.
"Riegle, Donald W(ayne), Jr." *Current Biography*, Oct. 1986.

Riley, Patrick James (1945–) In his nine years as head coach of the Los Angeles Lakers (1981–90), Riley and his teams won 533 regular season games and lost only 194 games, and won 102 playoff games, while losing only 47, on their way to four National Basketball Association (NBA) championships (1982, 1985, 1987, and 1988). In June 1990, after a winning season but an early elimination in the play-offs, he resigned, and was replaced by Mike Dunleavy, formerly an assistant coach with the Milwaukee Bucks. Earlier in the year, he had for the first time been named NBA Coach of the Year and also The Associated Press's Coach of the Decade. After his resignation, he became a basketball broadcaster with NBC.

Riley has spent his whole career in and around basketball. During his eight-year career as a professional basketball player, he was a guard with the San Diego Rockets (1967–70), the Los Angeles Lakers (1970–75), and the Phoenix Suns (1975–76). He was an assistant coach with the Lakers from 1979 to 1981, and in 1981 he began his extraordinarily successful nine-year run as Laker head coach. His team dominated professional basketball for much of the 1980s. He broadcast Laker games from 1977 to 1979 and returned to broadcasting after resigning his coaching job. In 1988 he published *Show Time: Inside the Laker's Breakthrough Season*. He is married to Chris Riley; they have two children.

FURTHER READING

"'Call me Mister Riley.'" AL STUMP. *Los Angeles Magazine*, Oct. 1989.
"The transformation. . ." DIANE K. SHAH. *GQ—Gentlemen's Quarterly*, Jan. 1989.
"Riley, Pat." *Current Biography*, Aug. 1988.
"With a special. . . ." NED GEESLIN. *People*, May 4, 1987.
"Pat Riley." JOHN CAPOUYA. *Sport*, June 1987.

Ritt, Martin (1919–90) New York City–born Ritt began his long career as an actor and director in the Group Theatre, making his stage debut in *Golden Boy* (1937) and appearing in *Winged Victory* (1943) while in the armed forces in World War II. After the war, he moved into television, largely as a director, until he was blacklisted in 1951 after being accused of communist affiliations. He then taught at the Actor's Studio and in 1955 directed Arthur Miller's *A View from the Bridge*. With the end of the McCarthy period, he began the major part of his career, as a film director, often dealing with social themes. His many credits include *Edge of the City* (1957), *The Long Hot Summer* (1958), *The Sound and the Fury* (1959), *Hud* (1960), *The Spy Who Came in from the Cold* (1965), *The Great White Hope* (1970), *Sounder* (1972), *The Front* (1976; his direct attack on blacklisting), *Norma Rae* (1979), and *Stanley and Iris* (1990). (d. Santa Monica, California; December 8, 1990)

FURTHER READING

Obituary. *Variety*, Dec. 17, 1990.
Obituary. *The Times* (of London), Dec. 11, 1990.
Obituary. *New York Times*, Dec. 10, 1990.
"Ritt large." PAT GILLIGAN. *Film Comment*, Jan.–Feb. 1986.

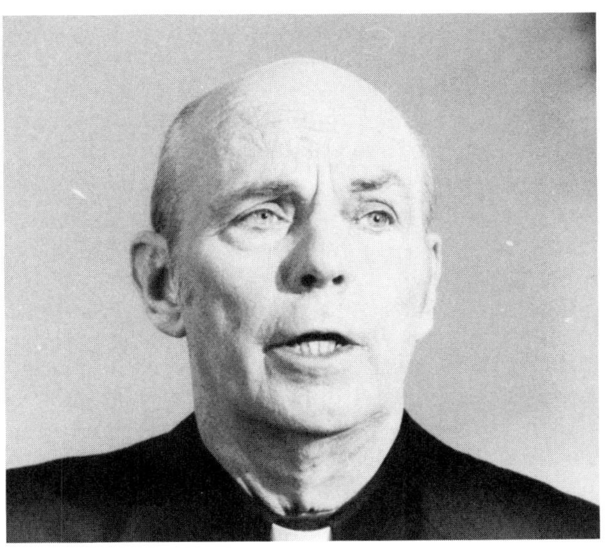

Ritter, Bruce (1927–) The year 1990 saw the apparent end of the public career of Rev. Bruce Ritter, the Catholic priest who was founder and president of Covenant House, the famous shelter for runaways. Late in 1989, a former male prostitute charged that he had been lured into a sexual relationship with Father Ritter and that Ritter had used organization funds to provide him with money, gifts, and a private apartment. Although Ritter strongly denied the charges, other young men later made similar allegations of sexual involvement, and in February he stepped aside as head of Covenant House, apparently before being removed.

The Manhattan district attorney brought no criminal charges of financial or sexual impropriety against Ritter, and an investigation by the Franciscan Order (to which Ritter belongs) was not made public, except that Ritter was ordered to live in a friary. However, a four-month investigation ordered by Covenant House, headed by ex–New York police commissioner Robert J. McGuire, reported that sexual misconduct, some of it with minors, dated back 20 years and that Covenant House and Franciscan staff had heard rumors of Ritter's sexual activities but had believed his denials.

The report also noted that Ritter had run Covenant House as his personal domain. In particular, unknown to his board or the Franciscans, Ritter received an annual salary of $96,000 and placed large amounts of it in a personally controlled fund called The

Franciscan Charitable Trust, which he handled loosely, making loans to his sister and former board members and residents and also buying land. Ritter refused to cooperate with the investigation and continued his denial of its findings.

New Jersey–born Father Ritter founded Covenant House in 1968, building it from a single site to a network of free shelters in five U.S. cities and four other countries. In the process, he became a widely known expert on runaways, including the sexually exploited. He has received many honorary degrees and other awards, and served on former attorney general Edwin Meese's Commission on Pornography. He was a professor of theology at Manhattan College from 1963 to 1968. He described his life's work in *Covenant House: Lifeline to the Street* (1987). He attended Immaculate Conception Seminary and Chestnut Hill College.

FURTHER READING

"New 51-page report. . . . Evan Gahr. *National Catholic Reporter*, Aug. 24, 1990.
"Ritter steps aside. . . . " Evan Gahr. *National Catholic Reporter*, Feb. 16, 1990.
"Sexual allegations. . . ." Joe Feuerherd. *National Catholic Reporter*, Jan. 26, 1990.
"Ritter, Bruce." *Current Biography*, June 1983.

Robards, Jason, Jr. (Jason Nelson Robards, Jr. 1922–) Robards was part of a major hit movie, *Parenthood* (1989), playing the crusty family patriarch opposite Steve Martin and Mary Steenburgen. The film was just as big a success in 1990 when it hit the video rental markets and cable television, since many more parents could emphathize with Robards as he growled, "The thing about being a parent is that it never, never ends." In 1990, Robards was also heard as the voice of General Ulysses S. Grant in the celebrated documentary television miniseries "The Civil War." The film *Black Rainbow,* in which Robards starred with Rosanna Arquette, was a hit at the March 1990 Santa Barbara Film Fest, although it did not immediately get general theatrical distribution. In late 1990, Robards made a new Disney telefilm, *Mark Twain and Me,* about the relationship between the author and an 11-year-old admirer, Dorothy Quick, whose autobiography sparked the movie. The movie was scheduled for 1991 release.

Chicago-born Robards became a leading player on the American stage in 1956, as Hickey in Eugene O'Neill's *The Iceman Cometh*, a role he repeated in 1976 and 1988. His work in O'Neill included *Long Day's Journey into Night* (1956, 1976, 1986), *A Moon for the Misbegotten* (1973), and *A Touch of the Poet* (1977). He won a Tony in *The Disenchanted* (1958) and also starred in such plays as *A Thousand Clowns* (1962; and the 1965 film), *After the Fall* (1964), and *The Country Girl* (1972). On screen, he appeared in many films, largely in strong supporting roles; his most notable films include *The Loves of Isadora* (1969), *All the President's Men* (1976; he won a Best Supporting Actor Oscar), *Julia* (1977; and a second Best Supporting Actor Oscar), and *Melvin and Howard* (1979), as well as many telefilms, most notably *The Iceman Cometh* (1961), *One Day in the Life of Ivan Denisovitch* (1963), *Haywire* (1980), *The Day After* (1983), *Sakharov* (1984), and *Inherit the Wind* (1988). Robards attended the American Academy of Dramatic Arts. He has been married four times and has seven children. He is the son of actor Jason Robards, Sr.

FURTHER READING

"Jason Robards Jr.. . . ." Eirik Knutzen. *Dynamic Years*, Sept.–Oct. 1982.
"The one great scorer. . . ." *People*, Dec. 28, 1981.

Rodale, Robert (1930–90) New York City–born Rodale, head of the environmentally oriented Rodale Press, became fascinated with organic farming in the late 1930s while an IRS auditor, and bought a farm in Emmaus, Pennsylvania, for agricultural experiments. This became the base for Rodale Press, founded by his father in 1949 but headed by Robert from then on. Early publications—*Organic Gardening* and *Farming and Prevention* magazines—were followed by a host of other magazines and books concerned with health and agriculture. In 1983 he wrote *The Best Health Ideas I Know: My Personal Plan for Living.* Active in cross-cultural exchanges, Rodale was killed in an auto accident abroad in the Soviet Union. (d. Moscow; September 20, 1990)

FURTHER READING

Obituary. *Prevention*, Nov. 1990.

Obituary. Stevie O. Daniels. *Organic Gardening*, Nov. 1990.
"Phenomena, comment. . . ." John P. Wiley, Jr. *Smithsonian*, Dec. 1990.
"Robert Rodale. . . ." Madalynne Reuter. *Publishers Weekly*, Oct. 5, 1990.
Obituary. *New York Times*, Sept. 21, 1990.
"Robert Rodale." *Whole Earth Review*, Winter 1988.

Roh Tae Woo (1932–) South Korean president Roh Tae Woo, originally elected in a three-candidate race and winning less than 40 percent of the vote, greatly strengthened his position in February 1990 with a merger of his and two other conservative parties. The resulting coalition had a clear parliamentary majority. However, he faced the continuing problem of dissension within the coalition and continuing unrest in the country as well, most notably in May with the massive Kwanju student demonstrations. He was also widely accused of human rights abuses, including the arrest and torture of dissidents. A January 1990 Amnesty International report verified many of the charges. During 1990, a slight softening of relations with North Korea began to seem possible, for the first time since the Korean War, as both sides made offers to symbolically open their borders to citizens of the other Korea for limited periods of time.

Roh was a career military officer who fought in the Korean War; in the late 1970s he rose to divisional command, and he retired in 1981 as a four-star general. He held several appointive cabinet-level posts in the early 1980s, then entered electoral politics as a national assemblyman and chairman of the National Justice Party in 1985. He became president of the Republic of Korea in February 1988. He is married to Kim Ok Sook; they have two children. He attended the Korean Military Academy.

FURTHER READING

"Roh. . . ." Bradley Martin. *Newsweek*, June 18, 1990.
"Roh faces. . . ." Laxmi Nakarmi. *Business Week*, Dec. 19, 1988.
"Roh Tae Woo." *Current Biography*, Feb. 1988.
"A vote for stability. . . ." John Greenwald and Howard Chua-Eoan. *Time*, Dec. 28, 1987.
"A successor. . . ." Bob Levin. *Maclean's*, July 6, 1987.
"Olympian hurdle. . . ." Donald Kirk. *New Leader*, June 29, 1987.

Ronstadt, Linda (Linda Marie Ronstadt, 1946–) Singer Ronstadt returned to her pop roots in late 1989 with a new album, *Cry like a Rainstorm—Howl like the Wind,* reminiscent of her style in the 1970s. This one featured some new songs by Jimmy Webb and four duets with Aaron Neville. The album moved quickly up into the top ten on the charts, as did the Ronstadt-Neville single "Don't Know Much," which later won a Grammy as best duo or group pop vocal. Promoting the album, Ronstadt toured the United States, with the Neville Brothers—Aaron, Art, Cyril, and Charles—as her opening act. She was named the year's outstanding female vocalist at the Bay Area Music Awards in San Francisco. Ronstadt also continued her long-standing interest in mariachi music, often dressed in the brilliant costumes favored on her earlier Canciones de Mi Padre tour. She sang on Cinemax's special "Latino Session"; at the Mariachi USA Festival at the Hollywood Bowl in midsummer; and at the twenty-fifth-anniversary celebration of the Los Angeles–based theater group El Teatro Campesino.

Tucson-born Ronstadt began her recording and touring career in the late 1960s and emerged in mid-1970s as a very versatile popular and country star. Her first hit album was *Heart Like a Wheel* (1974), containing two of her most popular songs: "You're No Good" and "I Can't Help It If I'm Still in Love with You." She went on to record such albums as *Different*

Drum (1974), *Prisoner in Disguise* (1975), *Hasten Down the Wind* (1976), *Blue Bayou* (1977), *Living in the U.S.A* (1978), *Mad Love* (1980), *Lush Life* (1984), *Trio* (1986; with Dolly Parton and Emmylou Harris), *'Round Midnight* (1987), and *Canciones de Mi Padre* (1987). On stage, she starred in *Pirates of Penzance* (1981; on film, 1983) and off Broadway in *La Boheme* (1984).

FURTHER READING

"Skylark." JONATHAN SCHWARTZ. *GQ—Gentlemen's Quarterly*, Feb. 1990.
Linda Ronstadt. MARK BEGO. Eakin, 1990.
"An intimate conversation. . . ." STEVE BLOOM. *Down Beat*, July 1985.
"A stranger to opera. . . ." DAVID HUTCHINGS. *People*, Dec. 17, 1984.
"Diva Linda." LINDA SANDERS. *Saturday Review*, Dec. 1984.

Rooney, Andy (Andrew Aitken Rooney, 1919–) Broadcaster-writer Rooney sparked controversy when reviewing the year 1989, he said on the air, ". . . many of the ills that killed us are self-induced," including "homosexual unions," which "quite often led to premature deaths." In an interview to clarify the comment, a gay-oriented magazine quoted Rooney as slurring homosexuals and saying that "Blacks have watered down their genes," although Rooney denied making a racial slur. Rooney was quickly suspended without pay from CBS and "60 Minutes" for three months, but—at least partly because of a sharp drop in ratings for "60 Minutes"—CBS rather awkwardly reinstated him after only three weeks, with Rooney declaring that he was not a racist and did not intend to hurt homosexuals. Many felt that Rooney had given bigoted views respectability, while others charged that the suspension infringed Rooney's First Amendment rights. In 1990, Rooney also published a new book, *Most of Andy Rooney*, and a paperback edition of his *Not That You Asked Me. . . .*

Born in Albany, New York, Rooney joined the CBS news department in 1959 as a writer and producer. Although he became an Emmy-winning documentary filmmaker in 1960, he became a nationally syndicated columnist and best-selling author only after becoming a regular on "60 Minutes" in 1978. Among his other written works are *A Few Minutes with Andy Rooney* (1981), *And More by Andy Rooney* (1982), and *Pieces of My Mind* (1984). He married Marguerite Howard in 1942; they have four children. He attended Colgate University in 1942.

FURTHER READING

"The lamentations of Rooney." *Newsweek*, Dec. 6, 1982.
"Rooney tunes." *Time*, July 21, 1980.

Roosevelt, Elliott (1910–90) The second son of President Franklin Delano and Eleanor Roosevelt, and great-nephew of President Theodore Roosevelt, has recently been known for his 1980s mystery novels featuring his mother as detective. New York–born and Groton-educated, he went not to college but into advertising and radio before serving as a combat officer in the army air corps during World War II. Afterward he wrote *As He Saw It* (1946), about the wartime summits; worked for the Hearst papers; raised Arabian horses; and wrote 14 books, including *The Untold Story* (1973) about his parents, which caused a breach with his siblings. (d. Scottsdale, Arizona; October 27, 1990)

FURTHER READING

Obituary. *New York Times*, Oct. 28, 1990.

Rose, David (1910–90) Composer, conductor, and arranger Rose began his career in the 1930s as a dance-band pianist in Chicago, moved into arranging, and began his long radio, film, and television career in 1938. A few of his most notable works were the scores of the musical *Winged Victory* (1943) and the film *Wonder Man* (1945; he received an Oscar nomination), and the songs "Holiday for Strings" (1943) and "The Stripper" (1962). (d. Burbank, California; August 23, 1990)

FURTHER READING

Obituary. *The Times* (of London), Aug. 28, 1990.
Obituary. *New York Times*, Aug. 26, 1990.

Rose, Pete (Peter Edward Rose, 1941–) Rose was one of the most celebrated players and managers in the history of baseball, and at the peak of his popularity at the beginning of 1989. In that year, what he was to later call "my addiction to gambling" ruined his career. After a long investigation, followed by several failed legal maneuvers on the part of Rose, baseball commissioner A. Bartlett Giamatti concluded that Rose had bet on baseball games, including those of his own team, the Cincinnati Reds; in August, Rose was permanently banned from baseball. His troubles were far from over, though; in April 1990, he pleaded guilty to two charges of income-tax evasion, in July he was sentenced to a five-month jail term and fined $50,000, and in August 1990 he was imprisoned. In early 1991, baseball's Hall of Fame ruled that anyone ineligible to participate in baseball was ineligible for the Hall of Fame, thus resolving the potentially embarrassing question of whether or not Rose would be elected to the honorary establishment.

Cincinnati-born Rose was one of the leading players of his time. He started his career as 1963 National League Rookie of the Year and went on to bat more hits than any other player in the history of the game; he became the Most Valuable Player in the league in 1973, and played on fifteen All-Star teams. He led the Cincinnati Reds as a player from 1963 to 1978, as player-manager from 1984 to 1987, and as manager from 1987 to 1989, until his time of troubles came. Rose has co-authored several books, including *Countdown to Cobb: My Diary of the Record-Breaking 1985 Season* (1985), *Ballplayer: The Headfirst Life of Peter Edward Rose* (1988), and *My Story* (1989), the latter two with Roger Kahn. He was formerly married to Karolyn Ann Englehardt, married Carol Woliung in 1984, and has two children.

FURTHER READING

"Fields of. . . ." George V. Higgins. *American Scholar*, Spring 1990.

Hustle: The Myth & Life of Pete Rose. Michael Y. Sorolove. Simon & Schuster, 1990.

"Pete Rose can't lose." Eliot Asinof. *Sport*, Apr. 1989.

"A Rose is a Rose. . . ." Tom Callahan. *Time*, Aug. 19, 1985

Pete Rose: "Charlie Hustle." Ray Buck. Childrens, 1983.

Pete Rose: Baseball's Charlie Hustle. Nathan Aaseng. Lerner, 1981.

Ross, Diana (1944–) Singer, actress, and sometime designer Ross continued to reap the double-edged rewards of fame. J. Randy Taraborelli published an exhaustive, unauthorized, distinctly unflattering biography, *Call Her Miss Ross* (1989). That was followed by Mary Wilson and Patricia Romanowski's *Supreme Faith . . . Someday We'll Be Together,* about the Motown singing group, the Supremes, after Ross's departure; it was a sequel to Wilson's 1986 *Dreamgirl*, the first but far from the last to portray Ross as a villain.

Ross appeared in a concert tour during 1989, her first U.S. tour in five years, and on the March 1990 Academy Awards show she sang "Over the Rainbow," although some purists criticized the producers for not running the Judy Garland *Wizard of Oz* clip instead. She was also heard on a notable cut, "No Matter What You Do," paired with Al B. Sure! on his new album, *Private Times . . . And the Whole 9!* Ross is scheduled to appear in a telefilm biography of the late international entertainer Josephine Baker for Ted Turner's TNT; it will be her first film since 1978. (HBO produced a rival Baker film biography that aired in March 1991.)

In 1960, then-teenager Ross and her friends Mary Wilson and Florence Ballard formed The Supremes, with Ross as lead singer. The trio became one of the leading vocal groups of the 1960s. Ross left to go solo in 1969, and has been a popular music superstar ever since, with such albums as *Diana Ross* (1970), *Lady Sings the Blues* (1972; and the film, with Ross in an Oscar-nominated performance as Billie Holiday), *Touch Me in the Morning* (1973), *The Wiz* (1978; she starred in the film version of the play), *Diana* (1981), *Why Do Fools Fall in Love?* (1981), and *Ain't No Mountain High Enough* (1989). Detroit-born Ross has been married twice and has five children.

FURTHER READING

All That Glittered: My Life with the Supremes. Tony Turner and Barbara Aria. NAL-Dutton, 1990.

Diana. J. Randy Taraborrelli and Reggie Wilson. Doubleday, 1985.

Diana Ross: Star Supreme. JAMES HASKINS. Viking Penguin, 1985.
Diana Ross. GEOFF BROWN. St. Martin's, 1983.
Reach Out: Diana Ross Story. LEONARD PITTS, JR. Sharon, 1983.
I'm Gonna Make You Love Me: The Story of Diana Ross. JAMES S. HASKINS. Dial, 1980; Dell, 1982.

Rostropovich, Mstislav (Mstislav Leopoldovich Rostropovich, 1927–) Soviet cellist, pianist, and conductor Rostropovich visited his homeland for the first time in 16 years. In his triumphant return to Moscow in February 1990, Rostropovich opened the Washington National Symphony Orchestra concert with the last work he had conducted before his self-imposed exile, Tchaikovsky's *Symphony No. 6*, the *Pathétique*, symbolically linking past and present. Rostropovich and his wife, the singer Galina Vishnevskaya, had left for the West in 1974, disillusioned with the Soviet system of the time, after incurring official displeasure for aiding dissident Alexander Solzhenitsyn; they were stripped of their Soviet citizenship in 1978. But with the softening that occurred under Gorbachev, they were invited to return; in February 1990, their citizenship was restored and the Soviet legislature also restored their medals and honors. During their visit, they donated a large supply of needles to help the Soviet medical community fight the inadvertent spread of AIDS.

Back in the United States, Rostropovich spoke out strongly and emotionally in testimony at April Senate hearings against censorship by the National Endowment for the Arts. In May he stormed off the stage in midconcert at Rome's Santa Cecilia Academy when he learned that the program was being televised without advance warning. He dislikes being filmed, saying that it breaks his concentration and feeling of intimacy with the public, and was so angry that he left behind his Stradivarius cello, later retrieved. In a lighter vein, in July in San Francisco Rostropovich stole the show at Isaac Stern's celebrity-studded 70th-birthday celebration by dancing on stage arrayed as a ballerina in full makeup, wig, and tutu.

Born in Baku, Rostropovich was a child prodigy who made his debut as a cellist at the age of 13. During the 1950s, he was

generally recognized as one of the world's leading cellists and was a greatly honored Soviet musician, winner of two Stalin Prizes and a Lenin Prize. From 1974, he performed in the West, also moving into conducting. He became music director of Washington, D.C.,'s National Symphony Orchestra in 1977. Rostropovich and Vishnevskaya have two children. He studied at the Moscow Conservatory, graduating in 1948, and taught at the Moscow and Leningrad conservatories.

FURTHER READING

The Great Cellists. MARGARET CAMPBELL. Trafalgar Square, 1989.
"Rostropovich, Mstislav." *Current Biography*, Nov. 1988.
"Musical events; generous spirit." ANDREW PORTER. *New Yorker*, Apr. 6, 1987.
"The words of. . . ." MICHAEL J. WEISS. *Washingtonian*, Sept. 1982.

Rothschild, Nathaniel Mayer Victor (1910–90) The British scientist became the third Baron Rothschild on the death of his father in 1937 while beginning his long career in scientific research at Cambridge. He served in British intelligence during World War II and worked at Cambridge during the postwar period, then became head of research of Royal Dutch Shell throughout the 1960s. He also became chairman of the British government's Central Policy Review Staff (the "Think Tank"). Rothschild was also chairman of his family companies briefly in the mid-1970s. In 1987, he was publicly cleared by the British government of any involvement in the spying activities of Anthony Blunt and Guy Burgess, whom he had known at Cambridge during the 1930s. (d. Britain; March 20, 1990)

FURTHER READING

Obituary. *The Times* (of London), Mar. 22, 1990.
Obituary. *New York Times*, Mar. 22, 1990.
The English Rothschilds. RICHARD DAVIS. University of North Carolina Press, 1984.
"The English Rothschilds. . . ." FRANK J. PRIAL. *New York Times Magazine*, Dec. 5, 1982.

Rushdie, Salman (Ahmed Salman Rushdie, 1947–) British writer Salman Rushdie remained in hiding, under Scotland Yard protection, in the aftermath of the extraordinary controversy and situation that developed after publication of his 1988 novel, *The Satanic Verses*. The book became a worldwide best-seller after many fundamentalist Muslims protested its publication by rioting, publicly burning the book, and threatening the life of its author and publishers. In February 1989, Iran's Ayatollah Khomeini publicly sentenced him to death and offered $1 million to anyone who would murder Rushdie, a threat since repeated by others and taken very seriously then and now. His successor, Ayatollah Khamenei, repeated the death threat in February 1990.

Rushdie continued to deny any intent to insult Muslims while calling for free speech for those would murder him; in July 1990, he opposed a British ban on a film inciting violence against him, and the film was later allowed to be shown in Britain. In spite of his constant danger, separation from his family and friends, and the constricted life he was forced to lead, Rushdie continued to write, in late 1990 publishing *Haroun*, a book of children's stories. He also attempted to soften the attitudes of fundamentalist Muslims by publicly apologizing to any who might have been offended by his book, opposing its issuance in paperback, and affirming his allegiance to Islam. He also "came out" slightly, appearing at a bookstore to sign copies of his latest book. Despite all that, as of this writing the death sentence still stands.

Bombay-born Rushdie is a leading novelist whose works also include *Midnight's Children* (1981), which won a Booker Prize, and *Shame* (1983). He has been married twice and has one child. He attended King's College, Cambridge.

FURTHER READING

"Rushdie. . . ." GERALD MARZORATI. *New York Times Magazine*, Nov. 4, 1990.
"Rushdie wars." DOUGLAS FOSTER. *Mother Jones*, Sept.–Oct. 1990.
Salman Rushdie: Sentenced to Death. W. J. WEATHERBY. Carroll & Graf, 1990.
The Rushdie Affair: The Novel, the Ayatollah, & the West. DANIEL PIPES. Carol, 1990.
The Rushdie File. SARA MAITLAND, ed. Syracuse University Press, 1990.
The Salman Rushdie Controversy in Inter-Religious Perspective. DAN COHN-SHERBOK, ed. E. Mellen, 1990.
"A life in hiding." ANDREW PHILLIPS. *Maclean's*, Aug. 21, 1989.
"Dangerous involvement." DIANE TURBIDE. *Maclean's*, Feb. 27, 1989.
Salman Rushdie and the Third World: Myths of the Nation. TIMOTHY BRENNAN. St. Martin's, 1989.
"Rushdie, Salman (Ahmed)." *Current Biography*, Nov. 1986.

Rusk, Howard Archibald (1901–89) Nicknamed "Dr. Live-Again," Dr. Rusk was a key figure in rehabilitation medicine. Missouri-born Rusk graduated from medical school in 1925 and practiced internal medicine in St. Louis (1926–42). During and after World War II, he developed many techniques and programs to help disabled people, founding the Institute of Physical Medicine and Rehabilitation at New York University in 1948. He spread his ideas through the institute and NYU Medical School (1946–80), longtime columns in the *New York Times,* consultancies to numerous governmental organizations, several books, and work in private organizations, notably the World Rehabilitation Fund (1955–82), of which he was founder and president. (d. New York; November 4, 1989)

FURTHER READING

Obituary. *Current Biography*, Jan. 1990.
Obituary. *New York Times*, Nov. 5, 1990.

Ryan, Nolan (1947–) Baseball pitcher Ryan scored his 300th career victory on August 1, 1990, when his Texas Rangers beat the Milwaukee Brewers 11–3. Pressure had been building since 15 days earlier, when he won his 299th, after which a crowd of some 250 reporters and photographers dogged his steps. Ryan is only the 19th pitcher ever to have reached the milestone, bringing his career record at that point to 300–267.

Texas-born Ryan is far and away the leading strikeout artist in the history of baseball, with over 5,200 strikeouts to his credit; he has pitched a record six no-hitters and holds numerous other records. He pitched for the New York Mets from 1966 to 1971, the California Angels from 1972 to 1979, and the Houston Astros from 1979 to 1988 before moving to the Texas Rangers. He has been a member of six All-Star teams. In 1988, he published *Throwing Heat: The Autobiography of Nolan Ryan,* written with Harvey Frommer. He married Ruth Elsie Holdruff in 1967. He attended Alvin Junior College from 1966–69.

FURTHER READING

"Ryan's song. . . ." Phil Rogers. *Sporting News*, Aug. 13, 1990.
"A great hand. . . ." Ron Fimrite. *Sports Illustrated*, Sept. 29, 1986.
"Nolan Ryan. . . ." Harry Shattuck. *Sporting News*, May 9, 1983.

S

Sabah, Jaber al-Ahmed al-Salem al- (1928–) Until August 2, 1990, the emir of Kuwait was the ruler of less than two million people, fewer than half of them Kuwaiti citizens. Most of them were people from many countries working in oil-rich Kuwait, possessor of the third largest oil reserves in the world—an estimated 100 billion barrels. Sabah was an absolute ruler: his long-dominant family had abolished the beginning of Kuwaiti democracy in 1976. His country was one of the world's richest welfare states, although some loss of national income and welfare benefits had resulted from falling world oil prices.

Kuwait had been neutral in the 1980–88 Iran-Iraq war, although its Sunni Muslim rulers were deeply concerned by the rise of Shiite Muslim fundamentalism, stimulated by Iran. With the end of the war, Iraq became the main threat as Saddam Hussein, deeply in debt because of the war and his continuing military buildup, once again pressed claims to Kuwait—claims that Britain had last rebuffed by sending troops to Kuwait in 1961. On July 17, 1990, Iraq accused Kuwait of depressing world oil prices by overproduction and began to mass troops on the Kuwaiti border. Other Arab leaders, led by Egypt's president Hosni Mubarak, mediated the dispute; Saddam Hussein denied any intention to take military action against Kuwait.

On August 1, Iraq broke off continuing talks with Kuwait after making a series of major, nonnegotiable demands. On August 2, Iraqi forces took Kuwait. Escaping capture, Sabah and other government leaders fled into exile, eventually to be joined by several hundred thousand Kuwaitis; thus began the Persian Gulf Crisis, which was to grow into the Persian Gulf War. From exile, Sabah called for swift military action to retake Kuwait, supplied funds for a wide range of refugee relief and anti-Iraqi activities, and later supplied some of the funds needed for the war.

Sabah is the head of the Kuwaiti royal family in a government that includes many members of the ruling family, including his son Saad, who functions as prime minister while being crown prince; and Saud Nasir al-Sabah, ambassador to the United States, who became a familiar media presence as the Persian Gulf Crisis developed.

FURTHER READING

"Government of Kuwait. . . ." CLIFFORD KRAUSS. *New York Times*, Aug. 16, 1990.

St. Jacques, Raymond (James Arthur Johnson, 1930–90) A trailblazing Black actor in Hollywood films, Hartford-born St. Jacques began his career in Shakespeare in repertory and then worked in the New York theater, most notably in *The Blacks* (1961). He made his film debut in *Black Like Me* (1964) and went on to such films as *The Pawnbroker* (1965), *The Comedians* (1967), *Up Tight* (1968), *Cotton Comes to Harlem* (1970), *The Book of Numbers* (1973; he also produced and directed), *Lost in the Stars* (1974), and *The Evil That Men Do* (1984), while also appearing in many television roles. (d. Los Angeles; August 27, 1990)

FURTHER READING

Obituary. *Jet*, Sept. 17, 1990.
Obituary. *Variety*, Sept. 3, 1990.
Obituary. *The Times* (of London), Aug. 31, 1990.
Obituary. *New York Times*, Aug. 30, 1990.

Sakharov, Andrei (Andrei Dimitriyevich Sakharov, 1921–89) A leading Soviet nuclear physicist and the "father" of the Soviet hydrogen bomb, Sakharov became his country's leading democratic dissenter in the late 1960s and the defender of all the other dissenters then being attacked by the Soviet government. He was awarded the 1975 Nobel Peace Prize but was not allowed to go to Oslo to accept it. In 1980, he was arrested and sent into internal exile in Gorky, accompanied by his wife, Elena Bonner; she described this time in *Alone Together* (1986). Meanwhile a worldwide campaign developed to free them. In 1986, Soviet premier Mikhail Gorbachev invited Sakharov and Bonner to Moscow to participate in the development of a new, democratic Soviet system. Sakharov supported Gorbachev and was elected to the new Soviet Congress in April 1989, supporting democracy in the long argument about democracy and order that was then beginning. Some of his political and philosophical writings were published as *Andrei Sakharov and Peace* (1985), edited with Edward Lozanski. His *Memoirs* (1990) appeared posthumously. (d. Moscow; December 14, 1989)

FURTHER READING

"The struggle. . . ." DAVID REMNICK. *New York Review of Books*, Aug. 16, 1990.
"Special Issue: Andrei Sakharov." *Physics Today*, Aug. 1990.
"Why he ranks. . . ." DENNIS OVERBYE. *Time*, May 14, 1990.
Obituary. *Humanist*, Mar.–Apr. 1990.
Obituary. DAVID HOLLOWAY. *Bulletin of the Atomic Scientists*, Mar. 1990.
"Tribute to Sakharov." ALEXANDER GELMAN, et al. *Soviet Life*, Feb. 1990.
Obituary. DANIEL E. KOSHLAND, JR. *Science*, Jan. 19, 1990.
"Sakharov's. . . ." PETER HEBBLETHWAITE. *National Catholic Reporter*, Jan. 12, 1990.
"At last, a tomorrow. . . ." PATRICIA BLAKE. *Time*, Dec. 25, 1989.
"The living legacy. . . ." *U.S. News & World Report*, Dec. 25, 1989.
"The death of an activist." ANTHONY WILSON-SMITH. *Maclean's*, Dec. 25, 1989.
"Sakharov's visions." *Economist*, Dec. 23, 1989.
Obituary. *The Times* (of London), Dec. 16, 1989.
Obituary. *New York Times*, Dec. 16, 1989.

Salinas de Gortari, Carlos (1948–) Elected to the Mexican presidency in 1988, economist and public financial planner Salinas faced a series of major problems early in his term, including the need to renegotiate Mexico's $100 billion–plus international debt, revive his country's sagging economy, and improve the worsening lot of Mexico's tens of millions of rural and urban poor. He also badly needed to restore confidence in the ruling Institutional Revolutionary Party, which after 61 years in office barely managed to elect him to the presidency in an election also featuring widespread charges of electoral fraud.

Salinas made a determined attempt to reduce Mexico's debt and interest payments, reaching agreement in principle with foreign creditors in July 1989 and signing a debt reduction and rescheduling pact in February 1990. He also made a start at renovation of his party: In September 1990, the Institutional Revolutionary Party adopted a series of new party rules aimed at cutting the power of the party bureaucracy and bringing internal democracy; how the new

rules work out in practice is a matter of interest. He also moved toward reversal of Mexico's long-standing mistrust of its U.S. trading partner; in June 1990 he began free-trade talks with President George Bush and in November he continued those talks, although he still faces great Mexican resistance to Mexican-U.S. free trade.

A continuing irritant was the case of U.S. drug enforcement agent Enrique Camarena Salazar, tortured and murdered by drug traffickers in Mexico in 1985, allegedly with the complicity of high Mexican government officials. Salinas sharply criticized a January U.S. television program on the case and even more sharply criticized the April kidnapping of Dr. Humberto Álvarez in Mexico by Americans masquerading as Mexican police; Álvarez, who was taken to the United States, was one of nineteen Mexicans indicted in the United States in connection with the murder.

Salinas has spent his whole career in a series of increasingly responsible federal government financial-planning posts, beginning with his 1971–74 term as assistant director of public finance in the finance ministry. Before his 1987 presidential nomination, he was from 1982 to 1987 minister of planning and the federal budget. He attended the National University of Mexico and Harvard University.

FURTHER READING

"The man behind the mask. . . ." JOHN MOODY. *Time*, Nov. 19, 1990.
"Salinas takes a gamble. . . ." ROBERT A. PASTOR. *New Republic*, Sept. 10, 1990.
"How do you say. . . ." DICK J. REAVIS. *Texas Monthly*, Oct. 1989
"Salinas de Gortari, Carlos." *Current Biography*, Mar. 1989.
"A Gorbo for Mexico. . . ." MORTON KONDRACKE. *New Republic*, Feb. 20, 1989

Salmi, Albert (1928–90) Veteran character actor Salmi spent the early part of his career on the New York stage, also appearing often in television. His most notable theater role was in *Bus Stop* (1955), and on television it was opposite Paul Newman in *Bang the Drum Slowly* (1956). He also appeared in several television western series, including "Gunsmoke" and "Wagon Train". From the late 1950s, he appeared in many films, including *The Brothers Karamazov* (1958), *Lawman* (1971), and *Brubaker* (1979). His death was reported as a suicide, committed after he murdered his wife Roberta, from whom he was separated. (d. Spokane, Washington; April 23, 1990)

FURTHER READING

Obituary. *Variety*, May 2, 1990.
Obituary. *The Times* (of London), Apr. 26, 1990.
Obituary. *New York Times*, Apr. 25, 1990.

Sampras, Pete (1971–) Sampras became an instant tennis headliner on September 9, 1990, with his surprise win at the U.S. Open, decisively defeating Andre Agassi (6–4, 6–3, 6–2) in the men's final at Flushing Meadow, New York. On the way to the final, he defeated Ivan Lendl in the quarterfinals and John McEnroe in the semifinals. Sampras at 19 became the youngest Open winner of the 20th century. On December 16, he won again, this time defeating Brad Gilbert to win the $2 million first prize at the Grand Slam Cup tournament at Munich.

Maryland-born Sampras grew up in Palos Verdes, California; he dropped out of Palos

Verdes High School in order to turn professional. Before his U.S. Open victory, he was a virtual unknown; afterward, he was an instant world celebrity and ranked sixth in world tennis.

FURTHER READING

"Calm, cool and collecting." CINDY SHMERLER. *World Tennis*, Nov. 1990.
"Open for debate." STEVE FLINK. *World Tennis*, Nov. 1990.
"Focused. . . ." BRUCE NEWMAN. *Sports Illustrated*, Oct. 22, 1990.
"Clean-cut Sampras. . . ." JOE GERGEN. *Sporting News*, Sept. 24, 1990.
"Float like a butterfly. . . ." ANDREW ABRAHAMS. *People*, Sept. 24, 1990.
"Now playing. . . ." TOM CALLAHAN. *U.S. News & World Report*, Sept. 24, 1990.
"Sampras. . . ." JIM MARTZ. *Sporting News*, Sept. 17, 1990.
"Upset time. . . ." ALEXANDER WOLFF. *Sports Illustrated*, Sept. 17, 1990.
"Plan ahead like. . . ." ARTHUR ASHE. *Tennis*, Aug. 1990.
"Inside the junior game." MARK WINTERS. *World Tennis*, May 1988.
"Pete Sampras. . . ." KAREN DAY. *Tennis*, Mar. 1988.

Sandy (1974–90) Sandy was the previously abused mongrel stray dog who became a star in the musical *Annie*. A largely beige terrier, Sandy was about to be put to death by the Connecticut Humane Society when William Berloni, apprenticed to Connecticut's Goodspeed Opera House, discovered and trained him for the summer stock performances of *Annie* (1976). Sandy played in *Annie* on Broadway (1977–83), appearing also in Las Vegas, twice at the Tony Awards, and six times at the White House. (d. Haddam, Connecticut; August 29, 1990)

FURTHER READING

Obituary. *New York Times*, Aug. 30, 1990.

Sarandon, Susan (Susan Abigail Sarandon, 1946–) Late in 1990, Sarandon starred opposite James Spader as waitress Nora Baker in the film drama *White Palace*. A year earlier, in 1989, she had appeared in the *A Dry White Season*, an anti-apartheid film set in South Africa, with a cast that included Donald Sutherland, Marlon Brando, Janet Suzman, and Zakes Mokae. A year before that, she had starred with Kevin Costner and Tim Robbins in *Bull Durham*; the success of the film generated a projected sequel, *Bull Durham II*. Forthcoming is the film *Thelma and Louise*, in which she co-stars with Geena Davis.

New York City–born Sarandon began her film career with *Joe* (1970) and went on to play a wide variety of roles in the next two decades in such films as *The Rocky Horror Picture Show* (1974), *Pretty Baby* (1978), *Loving Couples* (1980), *Atlantic City* (1981), *The Hunger* (1983), *Compromising Positions* (1985), and *The Witches of Eastwick* (1987). She has also appeared in several plays and on television. Her B.A. was from the Catholic University of America. She was formerly married to actor Chris Sarandon and has two children.

FURTHER READING

"Susan Sarandon. . . ." CLAUDIA DREIFUS. *Progressive*, Oct. 1989.
"Sarandon, Susan." *Current Biography*, Sept. 1989.
"Playboy interview. . . ." CLAUDIA DREIFUS. *Playboy*, May 1989.

"Sarandon, seriously." AIMEE LEE BALL. *Mother Jones*, Feb.–Mar. 1989.
"Susan Sarandon. . . ." DIANA MAYCHICK. *Mademoiselle*, July 1988.

Savimbi, Jonas (1934–) As foreign forces began their withdrawal from Angola, Savimbi, president of the National Union for the Total Independence of Angola (UNITA), continued to fight the long Angolan civil war against the government forces of the Popular Movement for the Liberation of Angola (MPLA). Savimbi and Angolan president José Eduardo Dos Santos had negotiated a cease-fire in June 1989, but their agreement did not hold.

Savimbi became active in the anti-Portuguese Angolan revolutionary movement in the early 1960s. In 1966, he founded the UNITA, and he has led it through 25 years of revolution and civil war. From 1975, he led a guerrilla war against the Soviet- and Cuban-backed Angolan government of the MPLA while being substantially helped by Portuguese exiles from Angola and by the South African government. Savimbi was not a party to the 1988 general peace agreement in southwestern Africa and continued the long civil war with American military and economic aid, although seriously hampered by the withdrawal of all or most of his South African support. He attended the University of Lausanne.

FURTHER READING

"Can this man save Africa?" DAVID REED. *Reader's Digest*, May 1987.
Jonas Savimbi: A Key to Africa. FRED BRIDGLAND. Paragon House, 1987.
"Savimbi, Jonas (Malheiro)." *Current Biography*, Aug. 1986.
"Can we trust Savimbi?" PETER WORTHINGTON. *National Review*, May 9, 1986.
"The travels of. . . ." PETER WORTHINGTON. *Maclean's*, Sept. 23, 1985.

Scalia, Antonin (1936–) Justice Scalia voted with the U.S. Supreme Court's conservative majority in most instances during the 1989–90 session; but not always. He joined the liberal minority in *U.S.* v. *Eichman*, striking down the federal law against flag burning.

He wrote the majority opinion in *Holland* v. *Illinois*, stating that there was no constitutional requirement that juries be racially representative, and joined the conservatives on such cases as the *Cruzan* v. *Missouri* "right to die" case, which denied Nancy Cruzan's family the right to remove her from her life-support system; *Spallone* v. *U.S.*, which upset court-imposed fines on Yonkers, New York, elected officials in a housing discrimination case; and *Board of Education of Westside Community Schools* v. *Mergens*, which upheld the right of students to form a Bible club.

He was on the losing side in several key cases won by the liberal minority, most notably including *Rutan* v. *Republican Party of Illinois*, which cut the power of politicians in power to name party sympathizers to most low-level government jobs, and *Metro Broadcasting* v. *FCC*, which supports an affirmative action program in the broadcasting industry.

New Jersey–born Scalia taught law at the University of Virgina from 1967 to 1974, was an asssistant attorney general from 1974 to 1977, and taught law again, at the University of Chicago, from 1977 to 1982. He was appointed to the District of Columbia U.S. Court of Appeals by President Ronald Reagan in 1982 and to the Supreme Court by Reagan in 1986. He married Maureen McCarthy in 1960; they have nine children. Long associated with the American Enterprise Institute, his Supreme Court appointment was widely viewed as a move by Reagan to further the conservative group within the Court. His B.A. was from Georgetown University in 1957, his LL.B. from Harvard in 1960.

FURTHER READING

Eight Men and a Lady. HERMAN SCHWARTZ, ANDREA NEAL, and DAVID SAVAGE. National Press, 1990.
Packing the Courts: The Conservatives' Campaign to Rewrite the Constitution. HERMAN SCHWARTZ. Scribner/Macmillan, 1988.
"What they say it is. . . ." *Time*, July 6, 1987.
"Scalia, Antonin." *Current Biography*, Nov. 1986.
"Distinguished Jesuit Alumnus." *America*, Oct. 18, 1986.
"Nine who decide. . . ." ELIZABETH WARD. *Scholastic Update*, Sept. 8, 1986.
"A conservative. . . ." LEWIS J. LORD. *U.S. News & World Report*, June 30, 1986.
"Reagan's Mr. Right. . . ." EVAN THOMAS and RICHARD LACAYO. *Time*, June 30, 1986.
"A pair for the court. . . ." LARRY MARTZ. *Newsweek*, June 30, 1986.

Scheider, Roy (Roy Bernhard, 1935–) Actor Scheider appeared in his usual range of roles during 1989–90. In mid–1989, he was California college professor Charlie Nichols, driving his student debating team to super-achievement, in Douglas Day Stewart's film *Listen to Me*. In John Frankenheimer's *The Fourth War* (1990), about the continuing Cold War in the hearts of men despite *glasnost*, Scheider was American commandant Knowles on the Czech–West German border, sparring with his Soviet counterpart Valachev, played by Jurgen Prochnow. Then for HBO's made-for-television movie, *Somebody Has to Shoot the Picture*, Scheider played a burnt-out photographer brought in by the condemned man (Arliss Howard) to film his execution, in a fierce and graphic indictment of capital punishment. He also appeared as ambitious CIA man Russell Sheriton opposite Sean Connery and Michelle Pfeiffer in the film of John le Carré's *The Russia House* (1990). Forthcoming is a role as a millionaire with an unruly bunch of sailors running his yacht in Michelangelo Antonioni's *The Crew*, in a cast that includes Yves Montand, Giancarlo Giannini, Matt Dillon, and Greta Scacchi.

Scheider emerged as a film star in the 1970s in strong supporting roles in such movies as *The French Connection* (1971), and *Klute* (1971), and then as the star of the worldwide hit *Jaws* (1975; and the 1978 sequel), as well as *Marathon Man* (1976), *Sorcerer* (1977), *All That Jazz* (1979), *The Men's Club* (1986), and *Night Game* (1989). Earlier he had also appeared in such plays as *The Chinese Prime Minister* (1963), *The Alchemist* (1964), and *Stephen D* (1968), for which he won an Obie Award. His B.A. was from Franklin and Marshall College, in 1955. He has been married twice, and has two children.

FURTHER READING

"Blue Thunder's Roy Scheider. . . ." CHET FLIPPO. *People*, May 23, 1983.
"Recognizing Roy Scheider." PETE HAMILL. *New York*, May 23, 1983.
"Roy Scheider." *Playboy*, Sept. 1980.

Schlesinger, John (John Richard Schlesinger, 1926–) British director Schlesinger had a number-one box-office hit this year with *Pacific Heights*, which he described as a "yuppie nightmare." In it, unsuspecting Melanie Griffith and Matthew Modine are Patsy and Drake, who rent an apartment in their lovingly renovated San Francisco Victorian house to the wildly deranged Michael Keaton, whom one reviewer dubbed the "Renter from Hell." Schlesinger's work was especially noted for its fine balance between terror and laughter. Schlesinger, also an opera director, directed a production of Verdi's *Un Ballo in Maschera* to open the 1989 Salzburg Music Festival, a production thrown into chaos by the sudden death of Herbert von Karajan, who was to have conducted.

Schlesinger has been one of the leading directors of the past three decades, beginning with such films as *Terminus* (1961), *A Kind of Loving* (1962), *Billy Liar* (1963), and *Darling* (1964). His major films also include *Far from the Madding Crowd* (1967); *Midnight Cowboy* (1969), for which he won a Best Director Oscar; *Sunday, Bloody Sunday* (1972); *The Day of the Locust* (1974); *Marathon Man* (1976); and *Madame Sousatzka* (1985). His television work, which began in the late 1950s, most notably included *Separate Tables* (1982) and *An Englishman Abroad* (1983). He has also directed many plays for Britain's National Theatre and several operas. He attended Balliol College, Oxford.

FURTHER READING

John Schlesinger. . . ." FRANK SPOTNITZ. *American Film,* Jan. 1991.
"John Schlesinger." MARY ELLEN HAUS. *ARTnews,* Nov. 1987.
"John Schlesinger." AMERICAN FILM, Nov. 1987.
John Schlesinger. GENE D. PHILLIPS. G. K. Hall, 1981.

Schröder, Gerhard (1910–90) West German politician Schröder began his career as a lawyer in 1933; in that year he also joined the Nazi Party. In 1938, he joined a church group that in some respects resisted Nazi domination, and in 1941 he married into a family classified as "partly" Jewish, incurring some Nazi displeasure. He volunteered for the German Army in 1939 and fought through the final battle of Berlin. After the war, he was an early member of the Christian Democratic Party and close to Konrad Adenauer; he was elected to the federal parliament in 1950, was interior minister from 1953 to 1961, and was foreign minister from 1961 to 1966, retiring from Parliament and politics in 1980. He was an unsuccessful candidate for the West German presidency in 1973. (d. Sylt, West Germany; December 31, 1989)

FURTHER READING

Obituary. *Current Biography*, March, 1990.
Obituary. *The Times* (of London), Jan. 5, 1990.
Obituary. *New York Times*, Jan. 3, 1990.

Schwarzenegger, Arnold (Arnold Alois Schwarzenegger, 1947–) Actor-bodybuilder-writer Schwarzenegger starred in one of 1990's most expensive films, at $70+ million; it was also one of the year's biggest hits, number one at the theatrical box office and then later in the video rental market. The blockbuster was *Total Recall*, a science fiction action-adventure film in which the muscleman goes to Mars. The film was such a success for Carolco Pictures that, for Schwarzenegger's tour of the U.S. for the President's Council on Physical Fitness and

Arnold Schwarzenegger and Maria Shriver.

Sports, the company's chairman loaned him the corporate jet. With many of his previous hits still actively circulating, it is not surprising that the Video Software Dealers Association voted Schwarzenegger their star of the year.

Late in the year, he opened in yet another movie, the comedy *Kindergarten Cop*, in which he played a detective working undercover as a kindergarten teacher; child cast members from the film joined him on the float of Hollywood's 1990 Christmas Parade, of which Schwarzengger was grand marshal. Schwarzenegger also broke into directing, with a 30-minute episode from HBO's "Tales From the Crypt," called "The Switch." with William Hickey; Schwarzenegger said he would rather do that than "fall on my face" by debuting with a big movie. Late in the year, he was shooting a new movie, *Terminator 2: Judgment Day*, a sequel to his 1984 hit.

Success and celebrity breed lawsuits, and Schwarzenegger was recently involved in two. Firms involved in financing the original *Terminator* sued Schwarzenegger along with others in an argument over distribution of the profits. More personally, in late 1989 Schwarzenegger accepted an out-of-court settlement of an undisclosed amount from British newspaper *News of the World*, along with an apology and a promise to desist; they had alleged that Schwarzenegger was a Nazi sympathizer and admirer of Hitler.

Austrian-born Schwarzenegger was a champion bodybuilder from 1969 to 1975, then turned to films. He played in such movies as *Stay Hungry* (1976) and *Pumping Iron* (1977), and emerged as an action-film star in *Conan, the Barbarian* (1982; and the 1983 sequel), then went on to such very popular films as *The Terminator* (1984), *Commando* (1985), *Raw Deal* (1986), *Predator* (1987), *Red Heat* (1988), and *Twins* (1988). He has also written several bodybuilding books. He attended the University of Wisconsin. He married newscaster Maria Shriver in 1986; they have one child.

FURTHER READING

"Box-office brawn. . . ." RICHARD CORLISS. *Time*, Dec. 24, 1990.
"Pumping. . . ." LYNN ROSELLINI. *U.S. News & World Report*, Nov. 26, 1990.
"Brand loyalty." SUZANNE MOORE. *New Statesman & Society*, Aug. 3, 1990.
Arnold Schwarzenegger Portrait. GEORGE BUTLER. Simon & Schuster, 1990.
Arnold: The Unauthorized Biography. WENDY LEIGH. Congdon & Weed, 1990.
"Arnold Schwarzenegger. . . ." RYAN P. MURPHY. *Saturday Evening Post*, Mar. 1989.
"The self-made man. . . ." TERESA CARPENTER. *Premiere*, Jan. 1989.
"Sexy, fun-loving. . . ." TOM BURKE. *Cosmopolitan*, July 1988.
"Arnold Schwarzenegger." JOAN GOODMAN. *Playboy*, Jan. 1988.

Schwarzkopf, H. Norman (1934–)

In early August 1990, soon after the Iraqi invasion of Kuwait, General Schwarzkopf, commanding officer of the Rapid Deployment Force—later renamed the U.S. Central Command—became commander of U.S. forces and then of allied forces in Saudi Arabia. As such, he engaged in the rapid buildup that would ultimately become the massive force that went to war in January 1991. New Jersey–born Schwarzkopf was dubbed all-too-lightly "Stormin' Norman" (an old nickname) by some media people in the early days of the buildup, before the nature and size of the coming war became apparent; the nickname was largely dropped as the buildup to war continued. He became something of a media celebrity for his lively military briefings during and after the war.

An infantry officer for much of his career, Schwarzkopf was a battalion commander in Vietnam, commanded mechanized infantry divisions at home and in Germany during the 1970s and early 1980s, and was deputy commander of American forces during the Grenada invasion of 1983, becoming a leading field commander in the late 1980s. He married Brenda Holsinger in 1968; they have three children. He is a career military officer, whose B.S. was from West Point, in 1956. (For photo, see Colin Powell.)

FURTHER READING

"The Gulf. . . ." LINDA ROCAWICH. *Progressive*, Jan. 1991.
"Like father, like son?" PAUL GRAY. *Time*, Oct. 22, 1990.
"The desert bear." DEAN FISCHER. *Time*, Oct. 15, 1990.
"How the top cop. . . ." RICHARD Z. CHESNOFF. *U.S. News & World Report*, Oct. 1, 1990.
"Holding the line." HARRY BENSON and EDWARD BARNES. *Life*, Oct. 1990.

"'Stormin' Norman'. . . ." *Newsweek*, Sept. 10, 1990.
"As Washington and Baghdad. . . ." BILL HEWITT. *People*, Sept. 3, 1990.

Scorsese, Martin (1942–) Director-writer Scorsese scored another major success with his *GoodFellas* (1990), about the realities of life in the American Mafia, with a cast that included Robert De Niro, Ray Liotta, Paul Sorvino, and Joe Pesci. Scorsese won the Venice Film Festival's Silver Lion Award as Best Director, although some people were upset at what they saw as ethnic stereotyping. Controversy also still surrounded Scorsese's *The Last Temptation of Christ* (1988). In late 1990, the U.S. Supreme Court rejected an appeal by people who construed the movie as blasphemous and hoped to block future showings. In Italy, Scorsese was acquitted of "contempt of religion" by a Rome appeals court. In a national critics' poll conducted by *American Film* magazine, Scorsese's *Raging Bull* (1980) was named best film of the 1980's and Scorsese the best director. PBS's "American Masters" series produced a new documentary on Scorsese.

Meanwhile, he continued his efforts to preserve America's film heritage, acting as co-chair of the American Film Institute's National Center for Film and Video and with seven other top filmmakers founding the Film Foundation. Privately, Scorsese teamed up with Spike Lee to produce television ads about the dangers of drugs and unsafe sexual behavior in the age of AIDS. He also turned actor for a small but key role as Van Gogh in *Akira Kurosawa's Dreams* (1990).

New York–born Scorsese scored his first major success with *Mean Streets* (1973), set on the underside of New York life. He went on to become one of the major directors of the modern period with such other films as *Alice Doesn't Live Here Anymore* (1974), *Taxi Driver* (1976), *New York, New York* (1977), and *The Color of Money* (1986). He has been married four times and has two children.

FURTHER READING

"Blood and pasta." AMY TAUBIN. *New Statesman & Society*, Nov. 9, 1990.
"Martin Scorsese." ANTHONY DECURTIS. *Rolling Stone*, Nov. 1, 1990.
"Made men." KATHLEEN MURPHY and GAVIN SMITH. *Film Comment*, Sept.–Oct. 1990.
"'God's lonely Man'. . . ." RICHARD GEHR. Video magazine, Mar. 1990.
". . . And blood." RICHARD CORLISS. *Film Comment*, Sept.–Oct. 1988.
"Jesus gets the beat. . . ." MARY PAT KELLY. *Commonweal*, Sept. 9, 1988.
"In the name of Jesus. . . ." DAVID GROGAN. *People*. Aug. 8, 1988.
"Martin Scorsese." DAVID ANSEN. *Interview*, Jan. 1987.
Martin Scorsese: A Guide to References & Resources. MARION WEISS. G. K. Hall, 1987.
"Chalk talk." PETER BISKIND. *American Film*, Nov. 1986.
Martin Scorsese and Michael Cimino. MICHAEL BLISS. Scarecrow, 1985.

Scott, George C. (George Campbell Scott, 1927–) Scott continued to bring his striking talents to a wide variety of roles. For the 1989–90 television season, he appeared in a well-reviewed but short-lived new series, "Mr. President." His major commercial film of 1990 was *Exorcist III: Legion*, a sequel revolving about a series of clerical killings in Georgetown, with Scott as police lieutenant Kinderman (played in the original by the late Lee J. Cobb). Then for HBO he made a new telefilm, *Descending Angel*, playing a Rumanian émigré with a well-hidden Nazi past uncovered by his daughter's fiancé. In a different mode, Scott was the voice of drug-pusher Smoke in *Cartoon All-Stars to the Rescue*, an anti–substance-abuse special for children simulcast by the three major networks and on many other stations in the U.S. and internationally.

Forthcoming is the film version of *Curse of the Starving Class*, starring Scott and Olympia Dukakis as Sam Shepard's warring farm couple, and an ABC telefilm, *Mittleman's Hardware* with Hector Elizondo, produced by James Garner and scheduled for the 1990–91 season. Scott also watched the flowering career of his (and Colleen Dewhurst's) son Campbell Scott, who was playing his first *Hamlet* at London's Old Globe Theatre and also appearing in his first major feature film, Bernardo Bertolucci's *The Sheltering Sky*, supporting Debra Winger and John Malkovich.

Virginia-born Scott suddenly emerged as a star in the American theater with his 1957 *Richard III* at the New York Shakespeare

Festival. He went on to appear in Shakespeare, Chekhov, O'Neill, Coward, and several contemporary works, notably as Willy Loman in the 1975 Broadway revival of *Death of a Salesman*, and a year later in *Sly Fox*; he directed both plays. He later appeared in *Present Laughter* (1982), which he also directed, and *The Boys of Autumn* (1988). He played strong supporting roles in such films as *The Hanging Tree* (1959) and *Dr. Strangelove* (1964), moving into leads with his Best Actor Oscar–winning role as *Patton* (1969; he refused the award as a matter of principle) and leads in such other films as *Jane Eyre* (1971), *The Hospital* (1971), *The Day of the Dolphin* (1973), *Movie, Movie* (1978), and *Firestarter* (1984). He has also appeared in many telefilms and in the series "East Side, West Side" (1963–64). Scott attended the University of Missouri. He has been married four times and has six children.

FURTHER READING

"This time. . . ." BILL DAVIDSON. *TV Guide*, Sept. 6, 1986.
"George C. Scott. . . ." JEFF DEROME. *American West*, Nov.–Dec. 1985.
"George C. Scott. . . ." JOAN BARTHEL. *TV Guide*, Dec. 15, 1984.

Scott, William George (1913–89) A leading British painter of the post–World War II period, Scott had his first one-man show in London in 1942. By the early 1950s, he had moved toward the more abstract work for which he is most appreciated, and which hangs in major museums throughout the world. Scott taught at the Bath Academy of Art and the Royal College of Art. (d. Bath; December 28, 1990)

FURTHER READING

Obituary. *The Times* (of London), Dec. 30, 1989.

Scowcroft, Brent (1925–) Lieutenant General Scowcroft, U.S. National Security Adviser, is an old "Washington hand," a career military officer and strategic planner who was President Gerald Ford's national security assistant, was out of the center of power during the Carter and Reagan administrations but returned to the White House with President George Bush. He is to some extent a public figure who appears on television talk shows to defend administration policies, but he is primarily a military planner and sometimes a behind-the-scenes troubleshooter. It was Scowcroft, for example, who went to China secretly in July 1989 and openly in December 1989 to reestablish working relations with a Chinese government that had not long before shocked the world with its Tienanmen Square student massacres.

Scowcroft graduated from West Point in 1947 and went to Washington as an air force strategic planner in the mid-1960s after teaching at West Point and at the Air Force Academy, as well as serving in Belgrade as an air force attaché. He was a White House–based military assistant to President Richard Nixon from 1971 to 1972, was deputy national security assistant from 1973 to 1975, and became President Ford's national security assistant from 1975 to 1977. During the Carter and Reagan administrations, he served on several advisory committees, most notably as a member of the Tower Commission, joining its adverse report on Reagan administration behavior during the Iran-Contra affair. Utah-born Scowcroft was a West Point graduate in 1947; his M.A. and Ph.D. were from Columbia (1953, 1967). He married Marian Horner in 1951; they have one child.

FURTHER READING

"'We won't let. . . .'" KENNETH T. WALSH. *U.S. News & World Report*, Dec. 24, 1990.
"'Even Saddam. . . .'" DOUGLAS HARBRECHT. *Business Week*, Sept. 10, 1990.
"Distrust, but verify. . . ." FRED BARNES. *New Republic*, Mar. 6, 1989.
"Permanent Washington. . . ." RONALD BROWNSTEIN and NINA EASTON. *Esquire*, Sept. 1983.

Selleck, Tom (1945–) The Emmy-winning star of television's long-running "Magnum P.I." focused on films in the late 1980s. In 1989, he starred as Philip Blackwood in *Her Alibi*, in a role that was a change of pace from what had become his normal action-film-hero roles. In late 1990, he co-starred with Ted Danson and Steve Guttenberg in *Three*

Men and a Little Lady, a sequel to their 1987 film comedy *Three Men and a Baby*; Robin Weisman portrayed 5-year-old Mary. In the same year Selleck starred in the title role of the action film *Quigley Down Under*, set in 19th-century Australia. Moving into production, he co-produced the television film *Heat* (1990).

Detroit-born Selleck appeared on stage and screen during the 1970s and emerged as a major star in the title role of "Magnum P.I." (1980–88). His earlier films included *High Road to China* (1983), *Lassiter* (1984), and *Runaway* (1985). He attended the University of Southern California. He has been married twice, last to actress Jillie Mack in 1987, and has two children.

FURTHER READING

"Three men and. . . ." JEFF ROVIN. *Ladies' Home Journal*, Dec. 1990.
"Magnum, P(retty) I(ndecisive)." PAT JORDAN. *GQ—Gentlemen's Quarterly*, Oct. 1989.
"Tom Selleck." MERRILL SHINDLER. Los Angeles magazine, Feb. 1989.
"The devastating appeal. . . ." TOM BURKE. *Cosmopolitan*, Dec. 1988.
"Selleck, Tom." *Current Biography*, Nov. 1983.
Tom Selleck: An Unauthorized Biography. JASON BONDEROFF. NAL-Dutton, 1983.

Selznick, Irene Mayer (1907–90) Brooklyn-born Irene Mayer, daughter of film mogul Louis B. Mayer, grew up in Hollywood at the top of the developing worldwide film industry. In 1930, she married producer David O. Selznick, who went on to produce *Gone with the Wind*. In 1945, she decided to leave Selznick and Hollywood; the couple separated, to divorce in 1948, and she moved to New York City and the theater, where in her late forties she began her own producing career. In the years that followed, and until the early 1960s, she produced such notable Broadway plays as *A Streetcar Named Desire* (1947), *Bell, Book, and Candle* (1950), *The Chalk Garden* (1955), and *The Complaisant Lover* (1961). In 1983, she published the autobiographical *Private View*. (d. New York City; October 1990)

FURTHER READING

Obituary. *Variety*, Oct. 15, 1990.
Obituary. *The Times* (of London), Oct. 12, 1990.
Obituary. *New York Times*, Oct. 11, 1990.
"Irene M. Selznick." STEVEN M. L. ARONSON. *House & Garden*, July 1983.

Sendak, Maurice (Maurice Bernard Sendak, 1928–) In October 1990, the celebrated American children's writer and illustrator announced a new project: The Night Kitchen, a national children's theater. His partner is Arthur Yorinka; start-up money was pledged by Sendak's publisher, HarperCollins. Sendak and Yorinka planned an early production of *Peter Pan*.

Sendak has been a prolific author and illustrator of children's books since the early 1950s, illustrating such books as *A Hole Is to Dig* (1952), *I'll Be You and You Be Me* (1954), *Charlotte and the White Horse* (1955), *Zlateh the Goat* (1966), *In the Night Kitchen* (1970), *Outside Over There* (1981), and *The Love for Three Oranges* (1984), and writing and illustrating such books as *Kenny's Window* (1956), *The Nutshell Library* (1963), and the Caldecott Award–winning *Where the Night Things Are* (1963). He has also written for television and done several stage designs for opera and ballet. He attended the Art Students League.

FURTHER READING

"Reflections." *Life*, Spring 1990.
"Maurice Sendak. . . ." GLENN EDWARD SADLER. Horn Book magazine, Sept.–Oct. 1989.
"Sendak, Maurice (Bernard)." *Current Biography*, June 1989.

Seton, Anya (1904–90) New York City–born Seton was the writer of several novels, some of them biographical and most of them relying greatly on their historical and geographical settings. Her best-known works were *Dragonwyck*, which was adapted into the popular 1946 Joseph L. Mankiewicz film starring Gene Tierney and Vincent Price; and *Foxfire*, which was adapted into the 1955 Joseph Pevney film starring Jane Russell and Jeff Chandler. (d. Old Greenwich, Connecticut; November 8, 1990)

FURTHER READING

Obituary. *New York Times*, Nov. 10, 1990.

Dr. Seuss (Theodor Seuss Geisel, 1904–) Children's author, artist, and filmmaker Dr. Seuss has been the treasured companion of three generations of the world's children. Even so, loggers in Laytonville, California, tried to ban his classic children's book *The Lorax* (1971) in late 1989 for its condemnation of the destruction of a fictional forest. Children and parents rallied, the national media covered the story, and cooler heads prevailed; the book was not banned.

The author, now 86, continues: His recent *The Butter Battle Book* describes a war between two countries that cannot agree about how to eat toast, butter side up or butter side down. In 1990, he wrote a book designed for children that became a best-seller for people of all ages—*Oh, the Places You'll Go!*—and wrote the script and twelve songs for a forthcoming feature film based on the book. In November 1989, he received a special award from the Academy of Motion Picture Arts and Sciences.

Massachusetts-born Theodor Seuss Geisel was an illustrator and editorial cartoonist before becoming Dr. Seuss, author of scores of the most popular children's books ever published, such as *How the Grinch Stole Christmas* (1957), *The Cat in the Hat* (1957), *Yertle the Turtle* (1958), and *Green Eggs and Ham* (1960). He also created such animated cartoons as the Oscar-winning *Gerald McBoing Boing* (1950), and several "Grinch" and "Cat in the Hat" cartoons. On a far more serious note, he created two Oscar-winning documentaries: *Hitler Lives* (1946) and *Design for Death* (1947; with his first wife, Helen Palmer Geisel). He attended Dartmouth College and Oxford University. He has been married twice.

FURTHER READING

"Maurice Sendak. . . ." GLENN EDWARD SADLER. *Horn Book Magazine*, Sept.–Oct. 1989.
"Dr. Seuss." *Life*, July 1989.
Dr. Seuss (Theodore Seuss Geisel). RUTH K. MACDONALD. G. K. Hall, 1988.
"Growing up with. . . ." JOHN SULLIVAN. *American Baby*, Aug. 1984.
"Theodor Geisel." *Time*, Mar. 12, 1984.

Seyrig, Delphine (1932–90) French actress Seyrig became an international star in her first commercial film, Alain Resnais's *Last Year at Marienbad* (1961), and went on to appear in such films as *Accident* (1967), *Stolen Kisses* (1968), *Daughters of Darkness* (1970), *The Discreet Charm of the Bourgeoisie* (1972), *Day of the Jackal* (1973), *The Black Windmill* (1974), and *India Song* (1976). The last was written and directed by Marguerite Duras, and made by Seyrig when she was seeking to make films directed by women as part of the strong feminist commitment of her later years. She studied in France and at New York's Actors Studio in the 1950s and spent much of her career in the French theater. (d. Paris; October 15, 1990)

FURTHER READING

Obituary. *Variety*, Oct. 22, 1990.
Obituary. *The Times* (of London), Oct. 18, 1990.
Obituary. *New York Times*, Oct. 8, 1990.

Shamir, Yitzhak (Yitzhak Yzernitsky, 1915–) As the unsolved Palestinian Intifada (Uprising) went into its second year, Israel drifted further to the right in the process becoming isolated from its allies, even the United States voicing serious criticisms of the Shamir government. But within Israel, support for Shamir's hard-line policies grew; after his National Unity coalition collapsed in March 1990, he emerged in June at the head of the most conservative government in Israeli history.

Shamir continued to encourage Israeli settlement on formerly Arab Palestinian lands in the Occupied Territories, strongly resisting world criticism. He also sharply attacked the Bush administration for opening talks with the Palestine Liberation Organization (PLO) and hailed the breakdown of those talks, restating his opposition to any Israeli-PLO dialogue. On October 8, 1990, Israeli police killed a reported 21 Arab demonstrators on Jerusalem's Temple Mount, drawing worldwide criticism and a UN Security Council censure resolution, backed by the United States. Shamir and his government remained defiant.

In late 1990, as the Persian Gulf Crisis deepened, Israel was not invited to join the U.S.-led alliance in the Gulf, but it prepared for attack, issuing gas masks to its people; Shamir warned of sharp Israeli response should Iraq attack. But when the Iraqi attack came, in the form of SCUD missiles fired into populated areas, Israel withheld military action at the strong request of the United States, which feared some possible Muslim breakaways from the anti-Iraqi coalition if Israel entered the war.

Shamir became a Zionist in his native Poland and emigrated to Israel in 1935. In 1937, he became a member of the terrorist Irgun Zvai Leumi, and in 1940 he left the Irgun with Abraham Stern to become a founder of the terrorist Lehi, better known as the Stern Gang. In 1942, he became chief of operations of the Stern Gang, which was responsible for a great many terrorist operations, most notably including the assassinations of Lord Moyne in 1944 and of UN mediator Folke Bernadotte in 1948. He was a member of Israeli intelligence from 1955 to 1965. He moved into politics with the Herut Party in 1970, was elected to the Israeli parliament in 1973, was foreign minister in the 1980–83 Menachim Begin government, and succeeded Begin as prime minister in 1983. He was foreign minister from 1984 to 1986, and again became prime minister in 1986. Shamir is married, and has two children. He attended Warsaw University and the Hebrew University of Jerusalem.

FURTHER READING

"The view from Jerusalem." *U.S. News & World Report*, Apr. 16, 1990.
"A talk with. . . ." J. ROBERT MOSKIN. *Present Tense*, May–June 1989.
"A talk with Dr. No." JACQUES AMALRIC and ALAIN FRACHON. *World Press Review*, Apr. 1989.
"Saying no to Arafat. . . ." SCOTT MACLEOD. *Time*, Jan. 2, 1989.
"Shamir stands his ground. . . ." *Newsweek*, Jan. 2, 1989.
"Israel's ironman." GEORGE HOWE COLT. *Life*, May 1988.
"The stubborn strength of. . . ." JOEL BRINKLEY. *New York Times Magazine*, Aug. 21, 1988.
"Shamir, Yitzhak." *Current Biography*, Feb. 1983.

Shannon, Del (Charles Westover, 1939–90) Very popular in the early 1960s, rock guitarist, singer, and songwriter Shannon scored his biggest hit with his first record, "Runaway" (1961), followed by such hits as "Hats Off to Larry" (1961) and "Keep Searchin'; We'll Follow the Sun" (1964). Many lesser hit songs followed until the late 1960s, when his popularity declined, although he continued to play and record through the early 1980s. His death was reported by police as a probable suicide. (d. Santa Clarita, California; February 9, 1990)

FURTHER READING

"Did Charles Westover. . . ." MICHAEL TENNESEN. *Los Angeles Magazine*, Sept. 1990.
Obituary. MICHAEL GOLDBERG. *Rolling Stone*, Mar. 22, 1990
"Singer Del Shannon. . . ." CYNTHIA SANZ. *People*, Feb. 26, 1990.
Obituary. *Variety*, Feb. 14, 1990.
Obituary. *New York Times*, Feb. 10, 1990.

Sharon, Ariel (1928–) Sharon reemerged as a major Israeli political figure in 1990, as Israel's isolation deepened, the Intifada (Uprising) remained unsolved, Soviet Jewish immigration into Israel grew, and Israel grew increasingly isolated from its allies, developing a series of sharply critical exchanges with the Bush administration. In February 1990, Sharon resigned from the Shamir government, strongly criticizing Shamir's peace plan and calling for hard-line solutions to many of Israel's problems. In March, after the Shamir National Unity government fell, Sharon failed in a bid to replace Shamir as party leader. In June he was appointed housing minister in the hard-line new Shamir government, the most conservative in Israeli history, and immediately moved to encourage further Israeli settlement on formerly Arab lands in the Occupied Territories. On July 1, with Israel facing a housing crisis due to the influx of Soviet Jews, Sharon was granted emergency powers. In 1990, he also published *Warrior: An Autobiography*.

Sharon, a career military officer, was active in the main Israeli fighting force, the Haganah, from the mid-1940s and fought in the 1948 Israeli War of Independence and accompanying first Arab-Israeli war. He conducted anti-guerrilla actions in the low-level border war that followed and rose to divisional command during the 1967 and 1972 Arab-Israeli wars. He went into politics in 1973 and held several cabinet-level posts during the 1970s. He was appointed defense minister by Menachem Begin in 1981 and was a chief architect of the 1982 Lebanon invasion, but he was forced to resign that post after the Sabra and Shatilla massacres, although he remained in the cabinet through the 1980s. In 1986, he had been involved in a notable libel suit with *Time* magazine. Sharon is married and has two children. He attended Hebrew University.

FURTHER READING

"Never! Never! Never!" Murray J. Gart. *Time*, Apr. 17, 1989.

Blood Libel: The Inside Story of General Ariel Sharon's History-making Suit Against Time Magazine. Uri Dan. Simon & Schuster, 1987.

Reckless Disregard: Westmoreland v. CBS et al; Sharon v. Time. Renata Adler. Knopf, 1986.

"Ariel Sharon. . . ." Matthew Nesvisky. *Present Tense*, Winter 1984.

"Sharon, Ariel." *Current Biography*, Apr. 1981.

Sheen, Martin (Ramón Estevez, 1940–) U.S. actor Sheen focused much of his attention on political issues in 1989–90. In November 1990, he was one of several prominent actors (including Ed Asner) to take place in a street opera–style mock trial of the murderers of six priests, a woman, and her daughter in El Salvador on the 6th anniversary of the killings. Several times in the previous year, Sheen had been among those arrested at the Los Angeles federal building in protests over U.S. policy in El Salvador. He also marched with César Chavez and the United Farm Workers in their fight to keep California-grown table grapes from being sold because of pesticide concerns. For Ted Turner's new cartoon eco-series, Sheen will be the voice of eco-villain Sly Sludge, working alongside other environmentally minded actors. Another of Sheen's concerns is the plight of the homeless. For CBS's "60 Minutes," Sheen took reporters to Los Angeles's Skid Row and to Chrysalis, an organization to aid homeless people. He gave one of the eulogies at the memorial service for Mitch Snyder, the late homeless advocate whom Sheen had played in the 1986 television film *Samaritan: The Mitch Snyder Story*. Sheen also spoke about homelessness in mid-1989 when he received his "star" on Hollywood's Walk of Fame. Late in 1990, Sheen signed to star in two future films for Ashby Productions.

Ohio-born Sheen played on stage with the Living Theatre from 1959, on Broadway in *The Subject Was Roses* (1964; and in the 1968 film version), and at the New York Shakespeare Festival in the late 1960s. On screen, he appeared in such films as *Catch-22* (1970), *Apocalypse Now* (1979), *Gandhi* (1982), and *Wall Street* (1987) and in such telefilms as *The Execution of Private Slovik* (1974), *The Missiles of October* (1974) as Robert Kennedy, *Blind Ambition* (1979) as John Dean, and *Kennedy* (1982) as John F. Kennedy. He married Janet Sheen in 1961; they have four children.

FURTHER READING

"The luster of. . . ." Audrey T. Hingley. *Saturday Evening Post*, Dec. 1983.

"The breaking. . . ." Sharon Rosenthal. *TV Guide*, Nov. 18, 1983.

"Martin Sheen. . . ." Tony Schwartz and J. P. Laffont. *New York*, Sept. 19, 1983.

"Martin Sheen." Emile De Antonio. *American Film*, Dec. 1982.

Shell, Art (1947–) Shell replaced Mike Shanahan as head coach of the Los Angeles Raiders in 1989, becoming the trailblazing first National Football League Black head coach in sixty years. Shell had been offensive line coach under Shanahan; the replacement came when the Raiders were 1–3 so far for the season. Under Shell, the Raiders immediately reversed course, and went very quickly into championship contention; in the 1990–91 season, they went all the the way to the conference finals before losing to the Buffalo Bills.

Shell has spent his entire career with the Raiders, as a star tackle (1968–83; his team won Superbowl XI in 1977) and then as a line coach (1983–89). In 1989 his long career achievement was also recognized; he was inducted into the Professional Football Hall of Fame. Shell attended Maryland State College. He is married and has two children.

FURTHER READING

"Riding the coaching roller coaster. . . ." *Sporting News*, Feb. 18, 1990.
"Wins, not race. . . ." JEANNIE PARK. *People*, Dec. 4, 1989.
"Resurging Raiders. . . ." JAY LAWRENCE. *Sporting News*, Nov. 13, 1989.
"Shell breaks NFL barrier." JAY LAWRENCE. *Sporting News*, Oct. 16, 1989.
"Black named NFL coach. . . ." *Jet*, Oct. 23, 1989.
"Dreams do come true." JILL LIEBER. *Sports Illustrated*, Oct. 23, 1989.
"Blount, Shell and Wood. . . ." *Jet*, Aug. 21, 1989.
"Art Shell." COOPER ROLLOW. *Sporting News*, Aug. 14, 1989.

Shevardnadze, Eduard (Eduard Amvroslyevich Shevardnadze, 1928–) One of the most spectacular of a long series of major events in the Soviet Union and Eastern Europe was the December 1990 resignation of foreign minister Shevardnadze, who warned of the new dictatorship he felt rising in his country. Long associated with Mikhail Gorbachev, Shevardnadze had replaced Andrei Gromyko in 1985 and was Soviet foreign minister throughout the extraordinary period that saw the end of the Cold War, the freeing of Eastern Europe, the unification of Germany, and the resolution of many regional conflicts throughout the world. Both Gorbachev and U.S. president George Bush paid close attention to every significant aspect of foreign policy during 1989 and 1990; Shevardnadze's role, like that of U.S. secretary of state James Baker, was to prepare, negotiate the essentials—often with Baker—and be at the

side of his president on consummation of the historic agreements that have marked the period.

Shevardnadze has spent his whole life in Communist Party and Soviet government work, starting in the late 1940s; he rose through a series of Communist Party positions in his native Georgia through the early 1970s. His first major move came in 1972, when he led an anticorruption campaign in Georgia and replaced the republic's party leader. He was first secretary of the Georgian Communist Party from 1972 to 1985, and became a Soviet Central Committee member in 1976. He attended the Kutaisi Pedagogical Institute. His wife, Nanuli, is a journalist.

FURTHER READING

"The alternative is dictatorship." *Time*, Apr. 16, 1990.
"Falcon of the Kremlin." E. KAYE FULTON. *Maclean's*, Feb. 26, 1990.
"Shevardnadze. . . ." JOHN KOHAN. *Time*, May 15, 1989.
"The boss of Smolensky Square. . . ." JOHN KOHAN. *Time*, May 15, 1989.

Sihanouk, Norodom (1922–) Once king, Sihanouk has for the past five decades has been a centrally important leader of his country. Sihanouk was relatively inactive in Cambodian politics from the time of the Khmer Rouge (Red Khmer) victory in 1975 until the mid-1980s. He became active again during the long Vietnamese occupation of his country and continued to cooperate with the Khmer Rouge and the Chinese as the tangled Cambodian civil war unfolded. He returned to Cambodia from his Beijing exile in February 1990, living in a Thai-Cambodian border zone held by his noncommunist forces and beginning the process of negotiation toward settlement of the long Cambodian wars. In August, Sihanouk attended the twenty-nation Paris peace conference, quitting as head of his forces just before the end of the conference and expressing a pessimistic view of the chances of peace. He called for a UN-sponsored settlement of the many-sided problem; then, becoming head of the entire guerrilla coalition, he moved toward peace with the Cambodian government. By late November, peace seemed closer as Sihanouk and premier Hun Sen seemed near agreement on a UN peace plan.

Sihanouk's life and varying fortunes have mirrored the recent history of his troubled country. He was the king of Cambodia from 1941 to 1955, in that period preparing for the independence that came in 1953 and the democracy that came with his abdication in 1955. He was prime minister of democratic Cambodia in the mid-1950s, was the elected head of his country from 1960 to 1970, and cooperated with the Khmer Rouge and its Chinese allies after the Khmer Rouge victory in 1975. In 1980, he published *War and Hope: The Case for Cambodia*. He is married and has had fourteen children.

FURTHER READING

"The man who would be king again." *Economist*, Sept. 29, 1990.

"The prince presses on." *Time*, Dec. 11, 1989.

"Sihanouk on the high wire. . . ." ADAM PLATT. *Newsweek*, May 15, 1989.

"An exiled leader. . . ." *Insight*, Jan. 20, 1989.

Prince Sihanouk. MADHARI KUCKREJA. Chelsea House, 1989.

"Bonnie Prince Norodom." *Economist*, Nov. 5, 1988.

"Now you see him. . . ." *Time*, July 25, 1988.

"Sihanouk's political circus. . . . " RUTH MARSHALL. *Newsweek*, Feb. 15, 1988.

"Sihanouk's 'open door'. . . ." FAY WILLEY. *Newsweek*, Dec. 14, 1987.

"Prince Norodom Sihanouk." DEBORAH WEINER. *Playboy*, May 1987.

"Prince Norodom Sihanouk." INA GINSBERG. *Interview*, Dec. 1986.

Silber, John Robert (1926–) An outspoken and often highly controversial U.S. academic and politician, Silber made an unsuccessful Massachusetts gubernatorial run in 1990. Before that, however, he was the surprise winner of the Massachusetts Democratic primary, defeating Francis X. Bellotti by a wide margin; Silber ran on a back-to-basics and "throw the rascals out" set of issues and promised Massachusetts voters a conservative new broom to replace outgoing governor Michael Dukakis. Silber lost the general gubernatorial election to Republican William Weld by 76,000 votes out of approximately 2 million votes cast; in a state in which registered Democrats outnumber registered Republicans by a very wide margin, large numbers of independents and Democrats voted for Weld. Silber might well have won, had not quite as many voters been put off by his name-calling style and by his controversial remarks about women, Blacks, and members of other minority groups.

San Antonio–born Silber taught philosophy at Yale (1952–55) and at the University of Texas

(1955–67), and then continued to be a professor philosophy while moving into administration as a college dean at the University of Texas (1967–70) and from 1971 as the outspoken, rather controversial president of Boston University. He has written several books in his field, and in 1989 he wrote the more general *Straight Shooting: What's Wrong with America and How to Fix It*. Silber received his B.A. from Trinity University in 1947, and his M.A. and Ph.D. from Yale (1952, 1956). He married Kathryn Underwood in 1947; they have seven children.

FURTHER READING

"Silber lining. . . ." JOSEPH NOCERA. *Texas Monthly*, Nov. 1990.
"The politics of outrage." PETER M. BECKER. *Inc.*, Nov. 1990.
"Hi, yo Silber!. . . ." SIDNEY BLUMENTHAL. *New Republic*, Oct. 22, 1990.
"To this angry man. . . ." BILL HEWITT. *People*, Oct. 29, 1990.
"A brawler. . . ." SCOTT MINERBROOK and MISSY DANIEL. *U.S. News & World Report*, Oct. 1, 1990.
"Maverick makes. . . ." HENRIK BERING-JENSEN. *Insight*, Feb. 19, 1990.
"Silber bullet. . . ." DAVID P. HAMILTON. *New Republic*, Dec. 4, 1989.
"The ivory tower triggerman. . . ." SAM ALLIS. *Time*, Aug. 28, 1989.
"Crusader. . . ." HELEN EPSTEIN. *New York Times Magazine*, Apr. 23, 1989.
"Silber, John R(obert)." *Current Biography*, Feb. 1984.

Simon, Kate (Kaila Grobsmith, 1912–90) Warsaw-born Simon was a very popular travel-book writer whose personally flavored works were far more than catalogs of monuments and restaurants. Her best-known work was *New York Places and Pleasures: An Uncommon Guidebook* (1959). She wrote four other well-received "Places and Pleasures" books—for London, Paris, Rome, and Mexico City—several other travel books, and three volumes of autobiography: *Bronx Primitive: Portraits in a Childhood* (1982), *A Wider World: Portraits in Adolescence* (1986), and *Etchings in an Hourglass* (1990). Earlier, she had been an editor and book reviewer. (d. New York City; February 4, 1990)

FURTHER READING

Obituary. *New York Times*, Feb. 5, 1990.
"She came from Warsaw. . . ." CONSTANCE ROSENBLUM. *New York Times Book Review*, Feb. 23, 1986.
"Kate Simon." SYBIL S. STEINBERG. *Publishers Weekly*, May 14, 1982.

Simon, Neil (Marvin Neil Simon, 1927–) Simon suffered what is for him an unusual setback in 1990. His new play, *Jake's Women*, starring Stockard Channing as Maggie and Peter Coyote as Jake, closed out of town after its engagement at San Diego's Old Globe Theatre. It was the first of Simon's 24 plays to close on the road before reaching the New York stage. The new stage comedy *Lost in Yonkers*, set in the 1930s, opened in February 1991 and received the Pulitzer Prize in April 1991; a new film, *The Marrying Man*, starring Kim Basinger and Alec Baldwin, opened to poor reviews in April 1991.

New York City–born Simon worked as a radio and television comedy writer in the 1950s, most notably for Phil Silvers and Sid Caesar, and began his long career as a leading playwright with *Come Blow Your Horn* (1961); it was followed by almost a score of other plays, including such hits as *Barefoot in the Park* (1963; and the 1967 film adaptation), *The Odd Couple* (1965; and the 1968 film), *The Star-Spangled Girl* (1966), *Plaza Suite* (1968; and the 1971 film), *Last of the Red Hot Lovers* (1969), *The Prisoner of Second Avenue* (1971; and the 1975 film), *The Sunshine Boys* (1972; and the 1975 film), and *California Suite* (1976; and the 1978 film). Much of his work is to some extent autobiographical, and there are five directly autobiographical plays: *Chapter Two* (1977; and the 1979 film), *I Ought to Be in Pictures* (1980; and the 1982 film), *Brighton Beach Memoirs* (1983; and the 1986 film), the Tony-winning *Biloxi Blues* (1985; and the 1988 film), and *Broadway Bound* (1986). He has also written the books for several musicals, including *Little Me* (1962), *Sweet Charity* (1966), and *Promises, Promises* (1968); and has written several film scripts, most notably the *The Goodbye Girl* (1977), which starred his second wife, Marsha Mason. Simon attended New York University. He has been married three times and has two children.

FURTHER READING

"Simon, Marvin Neil." *Current Biography*, Mar. 1989.
"Hollywood pays tribute. . . ." *People*, Sept. 26, 1988.
"Simon unbound." YAACOV LURIA. *Present Tense*, Mar.–Apr. 1988.
"Still looking for the pieman." MILAN STITT. *Horizon*, July–Aug. 1985.
"With a triple hitter. . . ." ANDREA CHAMBERS. *People*, June 17, 1985.
"Simon says." DAVID KAUFMAN. *Horizon*, June 1985.
"The craft of the playwright. . . ." *New York Times Magazine*, May 26, 1985.
"'I try to walk. . . .'" *U.S. News & World Report*, Apr. 22, 1985.
Neil Simon. ROBERT K. JOHNSON. G. K. Hall, 1983.

Simon, Paul (1941–) It was four years between Simon albums; his huge audience quite clearly thought it was worth the wait. In 1986, singer and songwriter Simon issued the Grammy-winning album *Graceland*. In October 1990, he issued *The Rhythm of the Saints*, an album with a Brazilian beat that quickly became a worldwide hit; over 1.3 million copies had been sold by late November, and the album was still going strong while Simon was beginning to issue singles taken from the album, some accompanied by videos. Simon also announced a multicity American tour, to begin in January 1991, called "Born at the Right Time." Meanwhile Simon continued to sing his old songs. In Prague in June 1990, just before the free Czech presidential election that brought Vaclav Havel to office, Simon sang his classic "Bridge over Troubled Water" to thousands gathered in Old Town Square. The previous year he had toured the Soviet Union with Miriam Makeba, among others.

Newark-born Simon and Art Garfunkel were one of the leading folk-rock groups of the 1960s, beginning with their album *Wednesday Morning 3 A.M* (1965), with Simon's hit song "Sounds of Silence," and ending with the extraordinarily popular Grammy-winning album *Bridge Over Troubled Water* (1970), its title song still a worldwide favorite. Their work together included the albums *Parsley, Sage, Rosemary, and Thyme* (1967), *Bookends* (1968), and the score for the film *The Graduate* (1968), with its Grammy-winning song, "Mrs. Robinson." After 1971, Simon went on alone, creating such albums as *Paul Simon* (1972), *Still Crazy After All These Years* (1975), *Hearts and Bones* (1983), and *Graceland* (1986). He also wrote, scored, and starred in the film *One Trick Pony* (1980). Simon attended Queens College. He was married twice, last to actress and writer Carrie Fisher.

FURTHER READING

"In praise of midlife crisis. . . ." DAVID GATES. *Newsweek*, Jan. 14, 1991.
"Songs of a thinking man. . . ." JAY COCKS. *Time*, Nov. 12, 1990.
"Flying down to Rio. . . ." BRIAN D. JOHNSON. *Maclean's*, Nov. 12, 1990.
Paul Simon: Still Crazy after All These Years. PATRICK HUMPHRIES. Doubleday, 1989.
"Architectural Digest visits. . . ." JUDITH THURMAN and JAIME ARDILES-ARCE. *Architectural Digest*, Sept. 1987.
"The apostle of angst." JENNIFER ALLEN. *Esquire*, June 1987.
"A songwriter's. . . ." ALVIN P. SANOFF. *U.S. News & World Report*, Mar. 2, 1987.
Written in My Soul: Rock's Great Songwriters . . . Talk About Creating Their Music. BILL FLANAGAN. Contemporary, 1986.

Sinatra, Frank (Francis Albert Sinatra, 1915–) In his sixth show business decade, singer and actor Sinatra is still going strong, although his fans no longer riot to get a little closer to him. He continued an active concert schedule throughout 1990, celebrated his 75th birthday in performance on television in December 1990 before a nationwide audience, and began a yearlong world tour in the same month. In July, he issued a book about his other vocation: *A Man and His Art*. And on December 5, he received the Ella Award (after Ella Fitzgerald) from the Society of Singers for lifetime achievement.

Sinatra began his singing career in cabaret, in 1935. He became a popular singer and recording artist in 1940, while appearing with Tommy Dorsey's band. In January 1943, at a four-week engagement at New York's Paramount Theatre, he became the first of the modern teenage idols, whose fans "swooned" and rioted over him. He also became a radio and film star, in *Your Hit Parade* and in such

musicals as *Anchors Aweigh* (1945) and *On the Town* (1949), and won a special Oscar for his role in *The House I Live In* (1945), a plea for tolerance. But he ran into serious throat problems in 1952, and his career all but vanished. He then made an extraordinary comeback as a dramatic actor, winning a Best Supporting Actor Oscar as Maggio in *From Here to Eternity* (1953), and went on to such films as *Guys and Dolls* (1955), *The Joker Is Wild* (1957), *The Manchurian Candidate* (1962), and *The Detective* (1968). His vocal problems eased, as well; he reemerged as one of the leading song stylists of his time. Sinatra has been married four times, and has three children. His second and third wives were the actresses Ava Gardner and Mia Farrow.

FURTHER READING

"Still good and savey. . . ." CHARLES LEERHSEN. *Newsweek,* Dec. 17, 1990.

"Happy 75th. . . ." TIMOTHY CARLSON *TV Guide,* Dec. 15, 1990.

"Under my skin." WILLIAM KENNEDY. *New York Times Magazine,* Oct. 7, 1990.

His Way: The Unauthorized Biography of Frank Sinatra. KITTY KELLEY. *Bantam, 1987.*

Sinatra: The Man and the Myth (An Unauthorized Biography). NAL-Dutton, 1987.

Frank Sinatra, My Father. NANCY SINATRA. Pocket Books, 1986.

Frank Sinatra: Ol' Blue Eyes. ASSOCIATED PRESS STAFF and NORM GOLDSTEIN. Holt, 1982.

Singh, Vishwanath Pratap (1931–)

Singh became the coalition National Front prime minister of India on December 2, 1989, succeeding Rajiv Gandhi. He enjoyed considerable early popularity as a potential healer of India's deep and growing ethnic and religious conflicts, but rapidly lost support late in 1990 as those problems continued to prove intractable and as new problems arose. The civil war in the Punjab grew, as did the level of violence in Kashmir, while Hindu-Muslim violence grew in many other areas.

The issue that directly brought down his government was his loss of the support of fundamentalist Hindus after he opposed the tearing down of a Muslim mosque in the holy city of Ayodhya in order to build a Hindu temple. Hindu fundamentalists rioted throughout the country during October, and thousands attacked the mosque on October 30, forcing military intervention. Singh resigned on November 7, 1990; he was succeeded by Chandra Shekhar. Singh remained leader of the Janta Dal (People's Party).

Singh has spent his entire career in state and national government; he was elected to the Uttar Pradesh assembly in 1969 and moved up to the Indian parliament as a Congress Party representative in 1971. He held several appointive posts in the Indira Gandhi governments of the mid-1970s and then moved back into state politics, becoming head of the Uttar Pradesh state government from 1980 to 1982. He was a key figure in the Rajiv Gandhi governments of the 1980s, as finance minister from 1984 to 1986 and as defense minister during 1986–87, but split with Gandhi and became opposition leader in 1987. Singh married Sita Kumari in 1955; they have two children. He attended Udai Pratap College and Allahabad University.

FURTHER READING

"Singh fails the test." *Time*, Nov. 19, 1990.

"Stirring old hatreds. . . ." CHARLES LANE. *Newsweek*, Nov. 12, 1990.
"Singh strikes." *Economist*, Aug. 4, 1990.
"The politician who. . . ." *Economist*, June 23, 1990.
"Singh, Vishwanath Pratap." *Current Biography*, May 1990.
"The ring around Singh. . . ." Sudip Mazumdar. *Newsweek*, Feb. 5, 1990.
"The rajah who toppled Rajiv." *World Press Review*, Feb. 1990.

Sisulu, Walter Max Ulyate (1912–) and **Sisulu, Notsikelelo Albertina** (1919–) Walter Sisulu ended his 27-year imprisonment on October 15, 1989, as the new Frederik Willem De Klerk government made its first substantial move toward peace and the end of apartheid in South Africa. With Sisulu came six other African National Congress (ANC) leaders and Jafta Masemola of the Pan Africanist Congress. Their release was hailed throughout the world as a sign that the long South African ordeal might be coming to an end.

Sisulu quickly moved back into the active leadership of the ANC, from February 1990 leading the ANC group planning the move back to legal activity in South Africa. He rejoined the ANC executive committee in March and was an ANC representative at the historic government-ANC May 2–4 Cape Town meeting, which began the long peace process.

Walter Sisulu became a leader of the then-nonviolent African National Congress soon after joining it in 1940. He defied the developing system of apartheid during the 1940s and 1950s, was tried for treason in 1956, and was acquitted in 1961. He was sentenced to six years, imprisonment in 1963, jumped bail while his case was on appeal, was rearrested, and was then sentenced to life imprisonment. He married Notsikelelo Albertina in 1944; they had five children.

Notsikelelo Albertina Sisulu became a leader of the South African freedom movement in her own right, and was restricted and sometimes under house arrest from the early 1960s through the mid-1980s. She was sentenced to four years in prison in 1984 but was freed on appeal. She has been Transvaal president of the United Democratic Front since 1983 and was president of the Federation of South African Women in 1984.

FURTHER READING

The Struggle: A History of the African National Congress. HEIDI HOLLAND. Braziller, 1990.
"Sisulu freed. . . ." FRANK DEXTER BROWN. *Black Enterprise*, Jan. 1990.
"Ex-ANC leader talks. . . ." *Jet*, Nov. 6, 1989.
"Freedom at last. . . ." MARY NEMETH. *Maclean's*, Oct. 23, 1989.
"Free at last. . . ." *Economist*, Oct. 21, 1989.
"Sisulu. . . ." SCOTT MACLEOD. *Time*, Oct. 30, 1989.

Skinner, B. F. (Burrhus Frederic Skinner, 1904–90) Psychologist Skinner was a key theorist of behavioral psychology. A literary-minded undergraduate, Skinner later became fascinated by new behavioral theories and obtained a Harvard Ph.D. in psychology, conducting numerous self-designed animal experiments, often using the "Skinner box," and developing theories about how behavior might be deliberately shaped. Though initially much misunderstood, these theories helped lay the groundwork for many modern learning theories and behavior modification techniques. A long-time Harvard professor (1948–74), Skinner wrote several influential books, notably the utopian novel *Walden Two* (1948), *Science and Human Behavior* (1953), and *Beyond Freedom and Dignity* (1971). Among his autobiographical works are *Notebooks* (1982), *Particulars of My Life* (3 vols.), and *Upon Further Reflection* (1987). (d. Cambridge, Massachusetts; August 18, 1990)

FURTHER READING

Obituary. CARSON M. BENNETT. *Humanist*, Nov.–Dec. 1990.
Obituary. *Current Biography*, Oct. 1990.
"Skinner in a box." *New Republic*, Sept. 10, 1990.
Obituary. *The Times* (of London), Aug. 20, 1990.
Obituary. *New York Times*, Aug. 20, 1990.
Dialogue with B. F. Skinner. RICHARD I. EVANS. Greenwood, 1981.

Skinner, Samuel Knox (1938–) U.S. Secretary of Transportation Skinner became highly visible for the first time after the March 1989 *Exxon Valdez* Alaska oil spill, sharply criticizing Exxon and the oil industry for its cleanup efforts. His May 1989 report on the spill and its aftermath included government efforts in that criticism, and charged that industry and government had not prepared at all adequately for such a massive disaster. Through early 1991, Skinner's period in office was most notable for its absence of specific new programs; his March 1990 comprehensive national transportation program stated substantial goals, called for the states to take much more of the financial burden and cut federal costs, and made no large new specific proposals; accordingly it was widely criticized.

Chicago-born Skinnner was an Illinois assistant U.S. attorney from 1968 to 1974. He has long been closely associated with former federal prosecutor and then Illinois governor James R. Thompson. He practiced law in Chicago from 1977 to 1984 and then moved into transportation, in 1984 becoming chairman of the regional transport authority. He was appointed U.S. secretary of transportation in 1989 by President George Bush. His 1930 B.S. was from the University of Illinois, and his 1966 J.D. from DePaul University. He is married and has three children.

FURTHER READING

"America on the Move." *American Legion Magazine*, Oct. 1990.
"Skinner, Samuel Knox." *Current Biography*, Aug. 1989.
"The more airlines. . . ." SHIRLEY HOBBS SCHEIBLA. *Barron's*, Apr. 3, 1989.

Smith, Maggie (Margaret Natalie Smith, 1934–) British actress Maggie Smith won the 1990 Tony as Best Actress in a Broadway play when she came from London to New York in Peter Shaffer's *Lettice & Lovage*. Playing a tour guide in a minor country house, Smith was lauded for the comic versatility of her tour de force opposite antagonist, and later ally, Margaret Tyzack.

Smith has been one of the leading actresses of the English-language theater since the mid-1960s. She was Desdemona to Laurence Olivier's Othello at the National Theater in 1964, and went on to a long series of classic and modern roles, as in *Miss Julie* (1965), *Hedda Gabler* (1970), and *Private Lives* (1972). She won a Best Actress Oscar in the title role of *The Prime of Miss Jean Brodie* (1969) and starred in the film *The Lonely Passion of Judith Hearne* (1987), as well appearing in many key character roles on screen. She has been married twice and has two children.

FURTHER READING

"There's nothing. . . ." GEORGINA HOWELL. *Vogue*, Apr. 1990.
"English accents." MARK MATOUSEK. *Harper's Bazaar*, Apr. 1990.
"There is nothing. . . ." MATT WOLF. *New York Times Magazine*, Mar. 18, 1990.
"Britain's thoroughbred. . . ." JOHN STARK. *People*, Apr. 28, 1986.

Smith, William French (1917–90) A California Republican and practicing lawyer, Smith met future president Ronald Reagan in the early 1960s, backed and advised Reagan during his successful 1966 California gubernatorial run, and became Reagan's personal lawyer and a chief adviser. He went to Washington with Reagan in 1981 as the 74th attorney general of the United States. A political conservative, he carried Reagan administration views into the Department of Justice, changing and in some instances sharply reversing course on a number of important enforcement matters, including civil rights, abortion, and antitrust law, as well as strongly pursuing a "war" on the drug trade. He also strongly supported the nomination of Sandra Day O'Connor, the first woman to be appointed to the Supreme Court. He was attorney general until 1985, then returned to private practice. (d. Los Angeles; October 29, 1990)

FURTHER READING

Obituary. *National Review*, Dec. 17, 1990.
Obituary. *The Times* (of London), Nov. 2, 1990.
Obituary. *New York Times*, Oct. 30, 1990.
"The President's Men. . . ." JEFF STEIN. *Penthouse*, Aug. 1981.
"Smith, William French." *Current Biography*, Jan. 1982.

Snyder, Mitch (Mitchell Darryl Snyder, 1944–90) Snyder was a powerful advocate for the homeless whose shock tactics angered some

but who achieved results that were denied to many. Snyder began his work for the homeless in 1973, when he joined the Washington-based Community for Creative Non-Violence. With Mary Ellen Hombs, he wrote *Homelessness in America: A Forced March to Nowhere* (1983). Snyder became a nationally known figure in 1984 by demanding a government grant for a homeless shelter in Washington and fasting for 51 days, just before the presidential election, until President Reagan promised the shelter two days before the election. Martin Sheen played Snyder in the 1986 television film *Samaritan: The Mitch Snyder Story*. Snyder's death was an apparent suicide. (d. Washington, D.C.; July 5, 1990)

FURTHER READING

Obituary. TOM BETHELL. *National Review*, Aug. 6, 1990.
Obituary. COLMAN MCCARTHY. *Nation*, July 30, 1990.
Obituary. TIFFANY AYERS. *National Catholic Reporter*, July 27, 1990.
"Mitch Snyder saved. . . ." CHARLES E. COHEN. *People*, July 23, 1990.
Obituary. *Jet*, July 23, 1990.
"'I give to people. . . .'" *Newsweek*, July 16, 1990.
"The unsettling. . . ." DAVID WHITMAN. *U.S. News & World Report*, July 16, 1990.
Obituary. *New York Times*, July 6, 1990.
Signal Through the Flames: Mitch Snyder and America's Homeless. VICTORIA RADER. Sheed & Ward, 1986.

Solzhenitsyn, Alexander (Alexander Isayevich Solzhenitsyn, 1918–) In 1989–90, the winds of *glasnost* reached Vermont, current home of Soviet writer Alexander Solzhenitzyn. His massive work on Stalin's forced labor camps, *The Gulag Archipelago*, had led to his 1974 expulsion from the Soviet Union when the first volume was published abroad. But in 1989, excerpts from the formerly banned *Gulag* appeared in print freely for the first time in the Soviet Union, in Moscow's monthly journal *Novy Mir*; the whole was later published in book form. As part of the government's continuing rehabilitation of previously condemned artists, Solzhenitsyn was in 1990 offered a Soviet literary prize for the work. He refused, however, charging that the government's structural changes were insufficient. The Soviet government also offered to restore Solzhenitsyn's citizenship, which had been stripped from him at the time of his expulsion. Solzhenitsyn has said he will not return to his homeland until his books are made freely available. Meanwhile, Solzhenitsyn published in 1989 a revised English-language version of his early best-seller, *August 1914*; the work has nearly doubled in size and is now projected to be just the first volume of a major historical epic.

Solzhenitsyn was one of the great Soviet dissenters; he survived imprisonment and exile to create a body of powerful work that strongly affected Soviet and world thinking, and helped pave the way for the reforms of the Gorbachev era. He was imprisoned in a labor camp from 1948 to 1953, and then internally exiled to Siberia from 1953 to 1957, but he used these experiences to create his novel *One Day in the Life of Ivan Denisovich* (1962), a trailblazing exposé of the Soviet penal system. Denied publication in the Soviet Union, he published his major works abroad; these included the novels *The First Circle* (1968), *The Cancer Ward* (1968), *August 1914* (1971), and *The Gulag Archipelago* (1973–75). Some of his nonfictional reflections have been published in works such as *The Oak and the Calf: A Memoir, East and West: The Nobel Lecture on Literature, A World Split Apart, Letter to the Soviet Leaders, and a BBC Interview with Aleksandr I. Solzhenitsyn,* and *Solzhenitsyn at Harvard: The Address, Twelve Early Responses, and Six Later Reflections* (all 1980). Solzhenitsyn won the Nobel Prize for literature in 1970. He has been married twice and has three children. He attended Rostov University.

FURTHER READING

"Writers. . . ." PETER HEBBLETHWIATE. *National Catholic Reporter*, Oct. 5, 1990.
Solzhenitsyn's Political Thought. JAMES F. PONTUSO. University Press of Virginia, 1990.
"Russia's prophet in exile. . . ." PAUL GRAY. *Time*, July 24, 1989.
"Solzhenitsyn, Aleksandr Isayevich." *Current Biography*, July 1988.
Solzhenitsyn: A Biography. MICHAEL SCAMMELL. Norton, 1986.
Solzhenitsyn in Exile: Critical Essays and Documentary Materials. JOHN B. DUNLOP, RICHARD S. HAUGH, and MICHAEL NICHOLSON, eds. Hoover Institute Press, 1985.
The Solzhenitsyn-Sakharov Dialogue: Politics, Society, and the Future. DONALD R. KELLEY. Greenwood, 1982.
Solzhenitsyn: The Moral Vision. EDWARD E. ERICSON, JR. Eerdmans, 1982.

Sondheim, Stephen (Stephen Joshua Sondheim, 1930–) Sondheim is one of the leading lyricists and composers of the American musical theater. His works continue to play in revival throughout the world, as in the 1990 Arena Stage revival of *Merrily We Roll Along* (1981) and the 1989–90 London stage revivals of *A Little Night Music, Sunday in the Park with George,* and *Into the Woods*. The year 1990 was Sondheim's British year in another way, as well; in January, he began a year-long stay as Oxford University's first visiting professor of drama and musical theater, resident at St. Catherine's College, a position funded by producer Cameron Mackintosh.

New York City–born Sondheim emerged as a leading American musical theater lyricist in the late 1950s with the lyrics for *West Side Story* (1957) and *Gypsy* (1959), and then as a leading composer as well, with both words and music for *A Funny Thing Happened on the Way to the Forum* (1962). As composer and lyricist, he has won five Tonys—for *Company* (1970), *Follies* (1971), *A Little Night Music* (1973), *Sweeney Todd* (1979), and *Into the Woods* (1988)—and a Pulitzer Prize for *Sunday in the Park with George* (1984). Another major work was *Pacific Overtures* (1976). His B.A. was from Williams College in 1950.

FURTHER READING

Art Isn't Easy: The Achievement of Stephen Sondheim. JOANNE GORDON. Southern Illinois University Press, 1990.
"Exploring along with Sondheim." HAP ERSTEIN. *Insight*, Aug. 28, 1989.
"Broadway's age. . . ." MIRIAM HORN. *U.S. News & World Report*, Feb. 1, 1988.
Sondheim & Co., 2nd ed. CRAIG ZADAN. Harper, 1988.
"Master of the musical. . . ." WILLIAM A. HENRY III. *Time*, Dec. 7, 1987.
"The words and music of. . . ." SAMUEL G. FREEDMAN. *New York Times Magazine*, Apr. 1, 1984.

Soupault, Philippe (1897–1990) In March 1919, Soupault, Louis Aragon, and André Breton founded the magazine *Literature*, beginning the movement that would in the early 1920s become Surrealism. Soupault and Breton experimented with "automatic" writing in 1921, attempting to set down immediately what they believed was emerging freshly from their "subconscious" minds. However, for Soupault Surrealism as a formal movement turned out to be a brief commitment; he and Breton parted in the mid-1920s, Soupault going on to write novels and poetry, teach, and work as a journalist. (d. Paris; March 11, 1990)

FURTHER READING

Obituary. *The Times* (of London), Mar. 13, 1990.
Obituary. *New York Times*, Mar. 13, 1990.
The Surrealists Look at Art. PONTUS HULTEN, et al., eds. Lapis Press, 1990.

Soustelle, Jacques Emile (1912–90) Soustelle was an early De Gaulle ally but became key leader of the French resistance to Algerian independence. He was also an expert in pre-Columbian Mexican culture. Born and raised in southern France, Soustelle won a Ph.D. by age 23. In Mexico when World War II started, Soustelle went to London and became head of information services for the Free French, directing secret services in Algeria from 1943. After France's 1944 liberation he held various ministerial posts, becoming governor-general of Algeria (1955–56) and supporting the French settlers against Algeria's anticolonial independence movement. As De Gaulle moved to accept Algeria's independence, Soustelle resigned and, with others in a secret army, attempted coups and assassinations against De Gaulle. Exiled from 1962 to 1968, Soustelle later focused on his academic work. (d. Paris; August 7, 1990)

FURTHER READING

Obituary. *Current Biography*, Oct. 1990.
Obituary. WILLIAM F. BUCKLEY, Jr. *National Review*, Sept. 3, 1990.
Obituary. *The Times* (of London), Aug. 9, 1990.
Obituary. *New York Times*, Aug. 8, 1990.

Souter, David (David Hackett Souter, 1939–) On July 23, 1990, Justice Souter was nominated by President George Bush to replace retiring U.S. Supreme Court Justice William Brennan. He was overwhelmingly confirmed by the Senate on October 2, after Senate Judiciary Committee hearings in September, although pro-abortion groups had strongly opposed his nomination because he had refused to take a position for or against abortion during the hearings. In committee, only Senator Edward Kennedy voted against the Souter nomination. In the full Senate, the vote was 99–9. Souter had also declined to take positions on a wide range of other matters during the confirmation process; as he had expressed his views very little in his previous professional life, he began his Supreme Court career with something very closely resembling a clean slate. During his first settling-in period on the Court, that continued to be so.

Massachusetts-born Souter moved up in the New Hampshire attorney general's office from

1968 to 1976, and was state attorney general from 1976 to 1978. He was a state court judge from 1978 to 1983 and a state supreme court justice from 1983 until his 1989 appointment by George Bush to the U.S. Supreme Court. His B.A. and LL.B. were from Harvard; he was also a Rhodes scholar.

FURTHER READING

"Naturally right. . . ." JEFF ROSEN. *New Republic*, Sept. 24, 1990.
"A retiring Yankee judge. . . ." BILL HEWITT. *People*, Aug. 6, 1990.
"An 18th century man. . . ." MARGARET CARLSON. *Time*, Aug. 6, 1990.
"In search of Souter." DONALD BAER. *U.S. News & World Report*, Aug. 6, 1990.
"An old-fashioned judge." *Economist*, July 28, 1990.

Spewack, Bella Cohen (1899–1990) Spewack was co-author, with her husband Samuel Spewack, of numerous plays and film scripts, including the books for such Broadway musicals as *Kiss Me, Kate* (1949) and *Boy Meets Girl* (1935). Brought to America from Rumania as an infant, Bella married Samuel when both were New York City journalists. They reported together from Europe, an experience that inspired their first hit, *Clear All Wires* (1932)—

later Cole Porter's *Leave It to Me* (1938)—before beginning their long joint career. Among their films were *My Favorite Wife* (1940) and *Weekend at the Waldorf* (1945). (d. New York City; April 27, 1990)

FURTHER READING

Obituary. *Variety*, May 2, 1990.
Obituary. *The Times* (of London), May 1, 1990.
Obituary. *New York Times*, Apr. 29, 1990.

Spielberg, Steven (1947–) Director, writer, and producer Spielberg has been a major figure in world film since *Jaws* and *Close Encounters of the Third Kind* in the mid-1970s. His most recent works include *Indiana Jones and the Last Crusade* (1989; the third in the series) and *Always* (1989; a remake of *A Guy Named Joe)*. He also co-produced *Back to the Future, Part II* (1989). One of his most notable forthcoming movies is his long-planned Peter Pan film, with Dustin Hoffman as Captain Hook and Robin Williams playing Peter as an adult; Spielberg will direct. Another is a feature-length documentary on the life of physicist Stephen W. Hawking, author of *A Brief History of Time*. Also planned is an animated film version of Andrew Lloyd Webber's *Cats*. Another major project is the production of six television films for Turner Network Television (TNT).

Spielberg directed and in several instances produced several of the most successful action-adventure and science-fiction spectacles of the 1970s and 1980s, including *Jaws* (1975), *Close Encounters of the Third Kind* (1977; and co-authored), *1941* (1979), *Raiders of the Lost Ark* (1981), *E.T.* (1982; he also produced), *Indiana Jones and the Temple of Doom* (1984), and *The Color Purple* (1985; and produced). He also co-authored and produced *Poltergeist* (1982) and co-produced *Back to the Future* (1985). Spielberg attended California State College. He was formerly married to actress Amy Irving and has two children.

FURTHER READING

Icons: Intimate Portraits. Denise Worrell. Atlantic Monthly, 1989.
"Steven Spielberg. . . ." *American Film*, June 1988.
The Picture Life of Steven Spielberg. Michael Leather. Watts, 1988.
Steven Spielberg: Amazing Filmmaker. Jim Hargrove. Childrens, 1988.
The Fantastic Films of Steven Spielberg—Master Filmmaker. Robert G. Marrero. RGM Publications, 1987.
Steven Spielberg. Donald R. Mott and Cheryl M. Saunders. G. K. Hall, 1986.
Steven Spielberg. D. L. Mabery. Lerner, 1986.
Steven Spielberg's Amazing Stories. Steven Bauer. Berkley, 1986.
Steven Spielberg: Creator of E.T. Tom Collins. Dillon, 1983.
The Steven Spielberg Story. Tony Crawley. Morrow, 1983.

Springsteen, Bruce (1949–) Singer, songwriter, guitarist, and bandleader Springsteen was largely inactive in 1989–90 but continued to generate great interest. In December 1989, he told the members of his E Street Band that he would not be using them on his next record, but he did continue to work on new material. Springsteen also suspended concert appearances, but on November 16, 1990, he appeared in concert at the Los Angeles Shrine auditorium for the first time in two years. In an anticensorship move, he gave Luther Campbell and 2 Live Crew permission to use his melody from the song "Born in the U.S.A." for its 1990 single "Banned in the U.S.A."

New Jersey–born Springsteen was discovered by legendary record producer John Hammond in 1972. Springsteen's first album, *Greetings from Asbury Park, New Jersey* (1973), was not very well received, although his second, *The Wild, The Innocent and the E-Street Shuffle* (1974), was promising. With his greatly successful third album, *Born to Run* (1975), Springsteen emerged as a rock superstar. He went on to record *Darkness on the Edge of Town* (1978), *The River* (1980), *Nebraska* (1982), the classic *Born in the U.S.A.* (1984), *Bruce Springsteen and the E Street Band Live/1975–1985* (1986), *Tunnel of Love* (1987), and *Chimes of Freedom* (1988), as well as such political and socially aware pieces as *No Nukes* (1979) and *We Are the World* (1985). He was formerly married and has one child, born in 1990 to his companion, singer Patti Scialfa.

FURTHER READING

The Rolling Stone Interviews: The 1980s. St. Martin's, 1989.
"Romancing the boss." SUSAN SCHINDEHETTE. *People*, Oct. 10, 1988.
"The Catholic imagination of. . . ." ANDREW M. GREELEY. America, Feb. 6, 1988.
Bruce Springsteen Here and Now. CRAIG MACINNIS. Barron, 1988.
Dear Bruce Springsteen. KEVIN MAJOR. Delacorte, 1988; Dell, 1989.
Glory Days: The Bruce Springsteen Story Continues. DAVE MARSH. Pantheon, 1987.
Springsteen. ROBERT HILBURN. Scribner/ Macmillan, 1986.
Bruce Springsteen: Blinded by the Light. PATRICK HUMPHRIES and CHRIS HUNT. Holt, 1986.
Picture Life of Bruce Springsteen. GERI BAIN and MICHAEL LEATHER. Watts, 1986.
Bruce Springsteen. KEITH E. GREENBERG. Lerner, 1986.

Stallone, Sylvester (Sylvester Enzio Stallone, 1946–) In 1976, New York City–born Stallone starred in *Rocky*, for which he also wrote the screenplay. The movie won a Best Film Oscar, and was a worldwide hit, and Stallone became a worldwide star. Sequels followed, and in 1990 he did yet another "Rocky" film, this one *Rocky V;* by now, even the making of the film was a major event. While filming the climactic fight scene in Philadelphia in February, the filmmakers decided they wanted a live audience of 10,000; tens of thousands of fans lined up in the cold outside the Philadelphia Civic Auditorium for free tickets to the two days of filming—and after the film company had departed, local Rocky fans demanded (unsuccessfully) that a Rocky Balboa statue temporarily placed at the top of the Philadelphia Museum of Art steps be left there permanently. However, the film did relatively poorly at the box office, making the future of the series uncertain. Other visual arts matters concerned Stallone, as well. He opened his first art exhibition as a painter in Los Angeles in September; as a collector, he sued an art dealer for selling him allegedly overpriced artworks.

Stallone had made three previous sequels to *Rocky*: *Rocky II* (1979; he wrote the screenplay and directed), *Rocky III* (1982), and *Rocky IV* (1985; he directed). He also starred as Rambo in *First Blood* (1982), *Rambo: First Blood Part II* (1985), and *Rambo III* (1988) and in such other action films as *F.I.S.T.* (1978), *Paradise Alley* (1978), *Nighthawks* (1981), *Rhinestone* (1984), *Cobra* (1986), *Over the Top* (1987), *Lock Up* (1989), and *Tango and Cash* (1989). Stallone attended the American College of Switzerland and Miami University. He has been married twice and has two children.

FURTHER READING

"Rocky: the article. . . ." FRANZ LIDZ. *Sports Illustrated*, Nov. 12, 1990.
"Move over, Rambo. . . ." LAURA MORICE. *Mademoiselle*, Feb. 1990.
"Sly Stallone's rocky road. . . ." LEO JANOS. *Cosmopolitan*, Jan. 1990.
"Requiem for a heavyweight. . . ." CAMERON STAUTH. *American Film*, Jan. 1990.
Rocky and the Films of Sylvester Stallone. ED GROSS. Movie Publications Services, 1990.
"Sly's progress." ELIZABETH KAYE. *Esquire*, Feb. 1989.
Sylvester. A. C. CRISPIN. Tor, 1985.
Stallone! JEFF ROVIN. Pocket Books, 1985.
Sylvester Stallone: An Illustrated Life. MARSHA DALY. St. Martin's, 1984.

Stanwyck, Barbara (1907–90) A star of Hollywood's Golden Age, Brooklyn-born Stanwyck began her career as a cabaret dancer in the 1920s, appeared on Broadway in *The Noose* in 1926, and starred in the play *Burlesque* from 1927 to 1929. On screen, she starred in such films as *The Bitter Tea of General Yen* (1933), *Annie Oakley* (1935), *The Plough and the Stars* (1937), *Stella Dallas* (1937), *Golden Boy* (1939), *The Lady Eve* (1941), *Meet John Doe* (1941), *Double Indemnity* (1944), and *Sorry, Wrong Number* (1948), continuing to appear in films through the mid-1960s. She then moved to television, becoming the Emmy-winning star of the long-running "The Big Valley" (1965–69) and later appearing in "The Colbys" (1985–86) and in the 1983 miniseries "The Thorn Birds." (d. Santa Monica, California; January 20, 1990)

FURTHER READING

"Farewell my lovelies." KATHLEEN MURPHY. *Film Comment*, July–Aug. 1990.

"Barbara Stanwyck. . . ." RICHARD SCHICKEL. *Architectural Digest*, Apr. 1990.
Obituary. *Current Biography*, Mar. 1990.
"Barbara Stanwyck. . . ." JOHN STARK. *People*, Feb. 5, 1990.
"Versatile star. . . ." JOSEPH MCBRIDE. *Variety*, Jan. 24, 1990.
Obituary. *The Times* (of London), Jan. 22, 1990.
Obituary. *New York Times*, Jan. 22, 1990.
"Barbara Stanwyck. . . ." GERALD PEARY. *American Film*, July–Aug. 1989.
Stanwyck. JANE E. WAYNE. Morrow, 1986.
Starring Miss Barbara Stanwyck. ELLA SMITH. Crown, 1985.
Barbara Stanwyck: A Biography. AL DIORIO. Putnam, 1984; Berkley, 1985.
The Films of Barbara Stanwyck. HOMER DICKENS. Carol, 1984.

Starr, Ringo (Richard Starkey, 1940–) The legendary Beatle Ringo Starr became a worldwide celebrity in the 1960s as he, Paul McCartney, John Lennon, and George Harrison created a revolution in popular music. After the Beatles years, he went on his own as a soloist and on screen. His recent work includes his first solo tour, the 1989 30-city American "Tour for All Generations," with his "all-Starr band." He was also very well received in December 1990 in the "Shining Time Station Holiday Special" Christmas television show, as the 18-inch-high Mr. Conductor. For charity, he recorded "With a Little Help from My Friends," for the all-star album *Nobody's Child*, whose proceeds would go to the Romanian Angel Appeal. This appeal was organized by Beatle wives Olivia Harrison, Barbara Bach (Starkey), Linda McCartney, and Yoko Ono, together with Elton John, after they learned of the plight of thousands of Romanian children following the 1989 Romanian Revolution. On the personal side, Starr, a recovering alcoholic, won his Atlanta court fight to reclaim fourteen songs recorded in 1987, while he was in impaired condition, that he did not want released.

Liverpool-born Starr played with The Hurricanes from 1959 to 1962 and joined the Beatles in 1962. The rest is at the center of modern popular music history, with such records and albums as "Please, Please Me" (1963), "She Loves You" (1963), "I Want to Hold Your Hand" (1963), "Yesterday" (1965), *Revolver* (1966), and *Sergeant Pepper's Lonely Hearts Club Band* (1967) and such films as *A Hard Day's Night* (1964), *Magical Mystery Tour* (1967), and *The Yellow Submarine* (1968). After the group broke up in 1970, Starr recorded several albums and appeared in such films as *200 Motels* (1969), *Stardust* (1975), *Son of Dracula* (1975), *Caveman* (1981), and *Give My Regards to Broad Street* (1984). He has been married twice, most recently to Barbara Bach, and has three children.

FURTHER READING

Strange Days: The Music of John, Paul, George & Ringo Twenty Years On. WALTER PODRAZIK. Popular Culture, 1991.
"Ringo on the rebound." STEVE DOUGHERTY. *People*, Aug. 28, 1989.
"A Starr is reborn." DAVID WILD. *Rolling Stone*, Aug. 24, 1989.
It Was Twenty Years Ago Today. DEREK TAYLOR. Simon & Schuster, 1987.
The Beatles, 2nd ed. HUNTER DAVIES. McGraw-Hill, 1985.
Yesterday . . . Came Suddenly: The Definitive History of the Beatles. BOB CEPICAN, BOB and WALEED ALI. Morrow, 1984.
Yesterday—the Beatles 1963–1965. ROBERT FREEMAN. Holt, 1983.
The Beatles A–Z: John Lennon, Paul McCartney, George Harrison & Ringo Starr. GOLDIE FRIEDE, SUE WEINER, and ROBIN TITONE. Routledge Chapman & Hall, 1981.
All You Needed Was Love: The Beatles After the Beatles. JOHN BLAKE. Putnam, 1981.

Starzl, Thomas Earl (1926–) Physician, professor, and medical researcher Starzl announced late in 1990 that he would no longer perform the liver-transplant surgery that he had pioneered. He said that he was emotionally drained after the death of 13-year-old Stormie Jones; he had led the team that in 1984 gave her the world's first heart-liver transplant, which her body rejected six years later, necessitating a second liver transplant that failed. He assured reporters that liver transplants have become quite standardized in recent years and that "8 to 10 lead surgeons" are available to continue the lifesaving operations. In fact, Starzl had not personally performed any liver-transplant operations since August 1990, when he had coronary artery bypass surgery.

Starzl is not leaving the arena of his specialty, however. Instead, he will be devoting more time to studying the drug FK–506, which appears to be far more effective than earlier medications at lessening a patient's rejection of a transplant and may be especially useful in multiple organ transplant. Still only in experimental use, FK–506 is licensed by the Food and Drug Administration only for use at Pittsburgh's Presbyterian University and Children's Hospital, with which Starzl is affiliated. He also plans to work for improvements in the system for locating organ donors and delivering the organs to needy patients.

Iowa-born Starzl graduated from Northwestern Univeristy Medical School, with an M.D. and Ph. D. in neurophysiology, in 1952. After additional work in thoracic surgery at several institutions, he returned briefly to join the faculty of Northwestern University Medical School (1958–61), before moving on to the University of Colorado Medical School at Denver in 1962, rising to become chairman of the surgery department (1972–80). While there he led the team that performed the first successful liver transplant in 1967 and helped develop a skilled team for kidney transplants. In 1981, he moved to the University of Pittsburgh, making its hospital–medical school complex one of the world's prime transplant centers; there most surgeons who perform organ transplants learned the proper techniques, generally from Starzl himself, work for which he has received numerous awards and honors. Previously married to Barbara Brothers, he was remarried in 1981 to Joy Conger. He has three children.

FURTHER READING

"Interview: Thomas Starzl." *Omni*, Sept. 1990.

Steber, Eleanor (1914–90) Soprano Steber became a fixture at the Metropolitan Opera during her 22 years with the company (1940–62), while at the same time appearing at major opera houses and festivals throughout the world. She sang in a wide range of roles and was highly regarded for her roles in the works of Mozart and Strauss; she also introduced several roles to world audiences—for example, the title role in Samuel Barber's *Vanessa* at its 1958 world premiere. Steber was an active recording artist, as well, with over 100 albums to her credit and also appeared in television and radio. (d. Langhorne, Pennsylvania; October 3, 1990)

FURTHER READING

Obituary. Harvey E. Phillips. *Opera News*, Dec. 8, 1990.
"Improper diva." Leslie Rubinstein. *Opera News*, Oct. 1990.
Obituary. *New York Times*, Oct. 4, 1990.

Steenburgen, Mary (1953–) Actress Steenburgen had a big hit on her hands with *Parenthood* (1989), the Ron Howard film about modern family life in which she co-starred with Steve Martin and many others. Her recent work also includes a starring role opposite Michael J. Fox and Christopher Lloyd in *Back to the Future Part III*, the film sequel directed by Bob Zemeckis and produced by Steven Spielberg. Forthcoming are a starring role in *Clifford*, opposite Martin Short and Charles Grodin, and a role in *The Butcher's Wife*.

Arizona-born Steenburgen made her film debut in *Goin' South* (1978) and went on to such films as *Ragtime* (1981); *Time After Time* (1979); *Melvin and Howard* (1980), for which she won the Best Supporting Actress Oscar; *Cross Creek* (1983); *Dead of Winter* (1987); and *End of the Line* (1987). She also produced and played a bit role in *The Whales of August* (1987). In addition, she appeared in such telefilms as *Tender Is the Night* (1985) and *The Attic: The Hiding of Anne Frank* (1988). Steenburgen attended Hendricks College and studied at New York's Neighborhood Playhouse. She married actor Malcolm McDowell in 1980; they have two children.

FURTHER READING

"After years on the mommy track. . . ." Mary H. J. Farrell. *People*, Aug. 28, 1989.
"Mary, Mary, quite contrary." Tim Appelo. *Savvy Woman*, May 1989.

Steinbrenner, George Michael, III (1930–) On July 30, 1990, the highly controversial owner of the New York Yankees was permanently barred from active management of the team and ordered to bring his controlling interest in the Yankees to below 50 percent. Baseball commissioner Fay Vincent announced his decision after finding that Steinbrenner's long feud with player Dave Winfield had included a private investigation of Winfield and payment of gambler Paul Spira for information thought to be derogatory to Winfield. In May, Steinbrenner had been fined by the league for improperly interfering with the trade of Winfield to the California Angels. Steinbrenner resigned as general manager of the Yankees on August 20, after his son had refused the general manager's job and theater owner Robert Nederlander had been named general manager of the team.

Ohio-born Steinbrenner is a leading shipbuilding company executive; he has run the American Ship Building Company since 1967. He bought a controlling interest in the New York Yankees in 1973 and quickly became a highly controversial figure, hiring and firing managers again and again and engaging in widely publicized feuds with key players. He married Elizabeth Joan Zieg in 1956; they have four children. His B.A. was from Williams College in 1952.

FURTHER READING

"The many woes. . . ." TOM CALLAHAN. *U.S. News & World Report*, Aug. 6, 1990.

Damned Yankees: A No-Holds-Barred Account of Life with "Boss" Steinbrenner. BILL MADDEN and MOSS KLEIN. Warner, 1990.

Steinbrenner! DICK SCHAAP. Putnam, 1982; Avon, 1983.

The Boss: George Steinbrenner's Story. PETER GOLENBOCK. Crown, 1982.

Stevens, John Paul (1920–) Justice Stevens was generally identified with the liberal wing of the U. S. Supreme Court during the 1989–90 session, voting with the liberals in such key cases as *Rutan* v. *Republican Party of Illinois*, curtailing the power of politicians in power to name party sympathizers to most low-level government jobs; and *Metro Broadcasting* v. *FCC*, supporting an affirmative action program in the broadcasting industry. He was on the losing side in the landmark *Cruzan* v. *Missouri* "right to die" case, which denied Nancy Cruzan's family the right to remove her from her life support system, as well as in a series of cases involving law enforcement and defendant's rights.

Yet he also continued to defy neat classification as "liberal" or "conservative," voting with some conservatives to uphold the federal law against flag burning in *U.S.* v. *Eichman*. He wrote the majority opinion in *Hodgson* v. *Minnesota*, which struck down an Ohio law requiring that both parents of a minor be notified before an abortion is performed, without the right of a minor to instead have a court hearing on the matter.

Chicago-born Stevens practiced law for two decades before being appointed to the Seventh Circuit U.S. Court of Appeals in 1970. President Gerald Ford appointed him to the Supreme Court in 1975. Stevens was thought to be a moderate conservative at the time of his appointment, as was Ford; the estimate was right, for Stevens often functioned as a middle force between the conservative and liberal wings of the court in the years that followed. He was formerly married to Elizabeth Jane Sheeren in 1942, married Maryann Mulholland

Simon in 1979, and has four children. His B.A. was from the University of Chicago in 1941, his LL.B. from Northwestern in 1947.

FURTHER READING

"A voice of reason. . . ." *American Legion Magazine*, June 1990.
Eight Men and a Lady. HERMAN SCHWARTZ, ANDREA NEAL, and DAVID SAVAGE. National Press, 1990.
John Paul Stevens and the Constitution: The Search for Balance. ROBERT J. SICKELS. Pennsylvania State University Press, 1988.
"What they say it is. . . ." *Time*, July 6, 1987.
"Nine who decide. . . ." ELIZABETH WARD. *Scholastic Update*, Sept. 8, 1986.

Sting (Gordon Matthew Sumner, 1951–) British musician, songwriter, and actor Sting continues to explore new artistic possibilities. In November 1989 he made his Broadway debut as Mack the Knife in a revival of *The Threepenny Opera*. His Mack the Knife was not very well received, although many complimented him for trying to master a difficult role in a strange medium. He also continued to pursue environmental concerns: in April 1990, *Rolling Stone* recognized his role in developing the Rainforest Organization, which works to preserve people and ecology of the Amazon basin.

Sting, a former grade-school teacher, became a major rock star of the early 1980s as lead singer of The Police, formed in 1977 with Andy Summers and Stewart Copeland. Although the group continued, he largely went on his own in the late 1980s with such albums as *The Dream of the Blue Turtles* (1985) and *Nothing Like the Sun* (1987). He also developed a substantial film and stage career; his early films included *Quadrophenia* (1978), *Brimstone and Treacle* (1982), *Dune* (1984), and *Plenty* (1985). He was formerly married and has four children.

FURTHER READING

"Twisting Mack the Knife. . . ." JOHN ISTEL. *Mother Jones*, Nov. 1989.
"Sting." RUDY MAXA. *Washingtonian*, Sept. 1989.
"Sting speaks." ART LANGE. *Down Beat*, Sept. 1989.
"Sting. . . ." LOU SALVATORI. *Rolling Stone*, Feb. 11, 1988.
Written in My Soul: Rock's Great Songwriters. . . . Talk About Creating Their Music. BILL FLANAGAN. Contemporary, 1986.
Sting: Every Breath He Takes. BARNEY COHEN. Berkley, 1984.
Sting and the Police. RAY NIKART. Ballantine, 1984.

Stone, Oliver (1946–) Stone's *Born on the Fourth of July* (1989), based on Ron Kovic's best-selling autobiography of the same name, received enormous attention and considerable acclaim, and was a commercial success. Stone garnered a Best Director Oscar and best director awards from the Directors Guild of America and the Hollywood Foreign Press Association's Golden Globes. Stone also co-wrote the Oscar-nominated screenplay, for which he and Kovic also won a Golden Globe, and appeared in the film in a small role as a television reporter. The film itself won a Golden Globe, as did Tom Cruise for his Kovic portrayal. Not everyone was pleased about Stone's depiction of a young soldier's odyssey from reflexive patriot to anti–Vietnam War activist. The Syracuse, New York, police in particular formally protested about misrepresentation of their handling of antiwar demonstrators; in response, Stone sent a letter of apology.

In 1990 Stone was working on a new film for 1991 release, *The Doors*, with Val Kilmer starring as Jim Morrison, the late legendary lead guitarist of the group; rock star Billy Idol co-starred, despite a broken leg suffered in a motorcycle accident that required changing his role. The crew had special permission to shoot part of the movie in the Mitchell Caverns Natural Preserve in the Mojave Desert. However, park officials found to their horror that set decorators had painted about 100 fake pictographs on the cave walls; they strongly protested, and Stone's crew was required to use nontoxic cleansers in attempting to strip the walls of defacing marks, although initial attempts at removal were unsuccessful. As 1990 ended, Stone was preparing a new film about an investigation into the assassination of President John F. Kennedy. He was also reportedly set to co-produce and possibly direct *The Mayor of Castro Street*, based on Randy Shilts's book about Harvey Milk, the openly gay assassinated San Francisco supervisor.

New York–born Stone fought in Vietnam from 1965 to 1966; the experience deeply affected some of his most notable work. Before *Born on the Fourth of July*, he had won two other Academy Awards: the first for his *Midnight Express* (1978) screenplay; the second for his direction of *Platoon* (1986), which he also wrote and which won a Best Picture Oscar. He also co-wrote *Scarface* (1983), and co-wrote and directed such films as *Wall Street* (1987) and *Talk Radio* (1988). He attended Yale University; his B.F.A. was from New York University Film School in 1971.

FURTHER READING

"Oliver Stone." JOHN CLARK. *Premiere*, Feb. 1990.
Icons: Intimate Portraits. DENISE WORRELL. Atlantic Monthly, 1989.
"Cosmo talks to Oliver Stone. . . ." DONNA BRITT. *Cosmopolitan*, Dec. 1988.
"Oliver Stone." MARC COOPER. *Playboy*, Feb. 1988.
"Talking to. . . ." MAUREEN ORTH. *Vogue*, Dec. 1987.
"Oliver Stone takes stock." ALEXANDER COCKBURN. *American Film*, Dec. 1987.
"From Vietnam. . . ." STEVEN RATTNER. *New York Times Magazine*, Aug. 30, 1987.
"Stone, Oliver." *Current Biography*, June 1987.
"For his look back. . . ." Alan Richman. *People*, Mar. 2, 1987.
"Oliver Stone." Chuck Pfeifer. *Interview*, Feb. 1987.
"Point man." Pat McGilligan. *Film Comment*, Jan.–Feb. 1987.

Strand, Mark (1934–) A poet and academic, Strand became poet laureate in 1990 on the death of Robert Penn Warren. Canadian-born Strand has published several volumes of poems, such as *Sleeping with One Eye Open* (1964), *Reasons for Moving* (1968), *Darker* (1970), *Another Republic* (1976), and *The Late Hour* (1978). He has also published a short-story collection, *Mr. Baby and Other Stories* (1985); a book of essays on art, *Nine American Figurative Painters* (1983); and children's books. Strand's B.A was from Antioch, in 1957, his 1959 B.F.A. from Yale, and his 1962 M.A. from the University of Iowa. He has been married twice and has two children.

FURTHER READING

Mark Strand and the Poet's Place in Contemporary Culture. DAVID KIRBY. University of Missouri Press, 1990.
"Bleak is beautiful." LEE GROVE. *Boston Magazine*, Mar. 1981.
"New voices in American Poetry." *New York Times Magazine*, Feb. 3, 1980.

Streep, Meryl (Mary Louise Streep, 1949–) Long known for her range of looks and accents, Streep has recently stretched in a new direction: toward comedy. In Susan Seidelman's *She-Devil* (1989), she was rich, beautiful, pink-ruffled romance novelist Mary Fisher opposite Roseanne Barr as the unattractive wife dumped by her husband. Although the film overall had little success with either the critics or the public, Streep's comic timing was lauded. Another highly praised quasicomic portrayal was her drug-dependent Hollywood actress Suzanne Vane, opposite Shirley MacLaine's actress-mother, in Mike Nichols's film *Postcards from the Edge;* Carrie Fisher wrote the screenplay from her own semiautobiographical novel, growing up as the daughter of Debbie Reynolds and Eddie Fisher. Unlike *She-Devil*, *Postcards* was successful critically and commercially, rising to the top of the box-office charts. During 1990, Streep shot a new romantic comedy, *Defending Your Life*, opposite Albert Brooks, released early in 1991.

In *American Film* magazine's end-of-the-decade survey of critics, Streep was named best actress of the 1980s, and at the 1990 People's Choice Awards she was voted favorite motion picture actress. At the 1990 Grammy Awards, she presented Paul McCartney with his Lifetime Achievement Awards. Privately, Streep continued to support social causes, especially relating to the environment, testifying before Congress and appearing on television to discuss the danger of pesticides, as on ABC's *Earth Day Special*. She was keynoter at the Screen Actors Guild's first National Women's Conference, speaking about the gender gap in the film industry, particularly women's declining roles both on and behind the screen and their low income relative to men.

New Jersey–born Streep was quickly recognized as a major dramatic star from the late 1970s in such films as *The Deer Hunter* (1978), *Manhattan* (1979), *Kramer vs. Kramer* (1980; she won a Best Supporting Actress Oscar), *Sophie's Choice* (1982; and another Best Actress Oscar), *Silkwood* (1983), *Out of Africa*

(1985), and *Ironweed* (1987). She married sculptor Donald J. Gummer in 1978; they have three children. Her B.A. was from Vassar in 1971; her M.F.A. from Yale in 1975.

FURTHER READING

"Meryl Streep. . . ." WENDY WASSERSTEIN. *Saturday Evening Post*, July–Aug. 1989.
"Ms. Streep goes. . . ." BONNIE JOHNSON. *People*, Mar. 20, 1989.
"Streeping beauty." WENDY WASSERSTEIN and BRIGITTE LACOMBE. *Interview*, Dec. 1988.
"Magnetic, magnificent Meryl." BRAD DARRACH. *Reader's Digest*, Mar. 1988; Canadian version, Apr. 1988.
Meryl Streep: A Critical Biography. EUGENE E. PFAFF, JR., and MARK EMERSON. McFarland, 1987.
Meryl Streep: The Reluctant Superstar. DIANA MAYCHICK. St. Martin's, 1984.
The Meryl Streep Story. NICK SMURTHWAITE. Beaufort, 1984.
"Streep, Meryl." *Current Biography*, Aug. 1980.

Charles and Carol Stuart.

Strout, Richard Lee (1898–1990) A long-time Washington journalist, Strout was famed for his liberal-minded column written by "TRB." New York–born and Harvard-educated, Strout worked his way across the Atlantic and began his journalistic career in England in 1919, returning to the United States to start his 63-year career with the *Christian Science Monitor* in 1921. After receiving a master's in economics from Harvard in 1923, Strout moved to Washington, D.C., reporting for the *Monitor*'s Washington bureau and writing his TRB column for *The New Republic* (1943–83), in the process covering 12 presidents. (d. Washington, D.C.; August 19, 1990)

FURTHER READING

Obituary. *Current Biography*, Oct. 1990.
Obituary. *New Republic*, Sept. 10, 1990.
"An irreplaceable man." *New Republic*, Apr. 18, 1983.

Stuart, Charles (1959–90) and **Stuart, Carol DiMaiti** (1958–89) On October 23, 1989, in Boston, seven months pregnant Carol Stuart was murdered; her husband, Charles Stuart, was shot. His call for help over his car radio, accusing a Black gunman of having forced his way into their car at gunpoint and later shooting them both, was later widely broadcast; this helped to foster a climate in which Boston police, media, and White residents joined to create what many described as a "reign of terror" in Boston's Black community.

Stuart was hospitalized with his wounds; after he left the hospital he identified William Bennett, a Black man with a criminal record, as having been the murderer, picking him out of a police lineup. Broadcasters and publications continued worldwide coverage of the murder and of Black inner-city crimes against Whites, complete with pictures of pregnant, bloody, murdered Carol Stuart being pulled out of her car and of her premature child, who died after a 17–day fight to save its life.

Carol Stuart and her baby were murdered; their tragedy was very real. None of the rest was true; all of it was a lie, created by Charles Stuart. His brother Matthew Stuart, who knew the truth, contradicted Charles Stuart's story on January 3, 1990. It was Charles Stuart who had murdered Carol Stuart; then he shot himself and called for help, at least partly in order to collect on substantial insurance policies taken out on Carol Stuart's life. Shortly after her death, he received over $80,000 in life insurance payments. On January 4, 1990, Charles Stuart committed suicide, jumping off a bridge into Boston harbor.

Carol DiMaiti had graduated from Boston College (1981) and Suffolk University Law School (1986), and worked as a tax lawyer at Cahners Publishing Company outside Boston. Charles Stuart had briefly attended Salem State College (1979) and worked as a salesman in a Boston fur salon. The two had been married for four years, to outward appearances happily, and lived in Reading, a suburb of Boston.

FURTHER READING

"After the lies. . . ." S. Avery Brown. *People*, Oct. 29, 1990.
"A case of wife murder. . . ." *Esquire*, June 1990.
"The perfect marriage. . . ." Marianne Jacobbi and Rosalind Wright. *Good Housekeeping*, May 1990.
"The Stuart case. . . ." Andrew Kopkind. *Nation*, Feb. 5, 1990.
"The race is on. . . ." Bill Hewitt. *People*, Jan. 29, 1990.
"A cold killer's chilling charade." Bill Hewitt. *People*, Jan. 22, 1990.
"Presumed innocent. . . ." Margaret Carlson. *Time*, Jan. 22, 1990.
"A murderous hoax. . . ." *Newsweek*, Jan. 22, 1990.
"Hero, suspect, suicide. . . ." Margaret Carlson. *Time*, Jan. 15, 1990.
"A dark night of the soul. . . ." Montgomery Browers. *People*, Nov. 13, 1989.

Styron, William Clark (1925–) In 1990, novelist Styron produced a stunning memoir focusing on his bout with near-suicidal depression. In *Darkness Visible: A Memoir of Madness* he describes the horror of depression after his body rejected a longtime dependence on alcohol, and how it led him so far as to write a suicide note before he checked himself into a hospital for treatment and regained the will to live. Labeling *Darkness Visible* the "personal account of a survivor," he said the book held out hope for others facing depression and thoughts of suicide. Privately, Styron continued his activities within the literary community, notably as secretary of the American Academy and Institute of Arts and Letters.

With his first novel, *Lie Down in Darkness* (1951), Virginia-born Styron was recognized as a leading American author. His *Confessions of Nat Turner* (1967), a fictional re-creation of the celebrated 19th-century American slave revolt, won a Pulitzer Prize. His *Sophie's Choice* (1979) won an American Book Award; in the film version, Meryl Streep won an Academy Award portraying a European refugee in post-war New York. Styron married Rose Bergunder in 1953; they have four children. His B.A. and Litt.D. were from Duke University in 1947 and 1968.

FURTHER READING

"William Styron." *People*, Dec. 31, 1990.
"William Styron. . . ." Kim Hubbard. *People*, Aug. 27, 1990.
"Out of his system." Laurel Graeber. *New York Times Book Review*, Aug. 19, 1990.
"Trading on pain. . . ." Philip Gold. *Insight*, Sept. 17, 1990.
William Styron. Judith Ruderman. Ungar, 1987.
"Styron's choices." Philip Caputo. *Esquire*, Dec. 1986.
"Styron, William (Clark, Jr.)." *Current Biography*, June 1986.
Conversations with William Styron. James L. West, III. University Press of Mississippi, 1985.
The Achievement of William Styron. Robert K. Morris and Irving Malin, eds. University of Georgia Press, 1981.

Sullivan, Louis Wade (1933–) Sullivan was confirmed as U.S. secretary of health and human services by the Senate on March 1, 1989, after publicly stating his general opposition

to abortion, other than in exceptional instances; earlier he had run into conservative opposition when seeming to back away from denouncing abortion. The only opposing vote came from Senator Jesse Helms. Once in office, however, Sullivan focused far less on abortion than on some of the other pressing health and health-related matters facing his department. He strongly opposed misleading cigarette advertising and urged new federal and state action against smoking. He also strongly supported improved food labeling.

Sullivan supported the use of the medication AZT to fight AIDS, including its use to treat children, and agreed that experimental drugs needed quicker introduction; but in June 1990, AIDS activists who felt the federal government was not doing enough to fight the disease booed his San Francisco speech to the sixth international conference on AIDS. He opposed the 1990 congressional repeal of the catastrophic medical care bill but also opposed national health insurance. In a highly publicized incident, Representative Pete Stark of California called Sullivan, who is Black, a "disgrace to his race" for that opposition; Sullivan demanded an apology and got one.

Atlanta-born Sullivan, a leading doctor and educator, went to Washington after a long and distinguished career that included teaching positions at Harvard Medical School, the New Jersey College of Medicine, and Boston University; he is an internist and hematologist. He was dean of Morehouse College Medical School from 1975 until his cabinet appointment in 1989. He married Eve Williamson in 1955; they have two children. His B.S. was from Morehouse College, his M.D. from Boston University.

FURTHER READING

"How to keep America healthy." *American Legion Magazine*, July 1990.

"Louis Sullivan finds. . . ." MARIA WILHELM. *People*, Mar. 26, 1990.

"Sullivan, Louis Wade." *Current Biography*, July 1989.

Sununu, John (John Henry Sununu, 1939–) Far from being a behind-the-scenes power broker, conservative White House chief of staff Sununu was a highly visible figure throughout the first two years of the Bush administration, defending administration policy on a very wide range of matters, including its antiabortion position, the Panama invasion, the Persian Gulf Crisis buildup, the "war on drugs," and what was seen by most environmentalists as a go-slow approach to the solution of pressing environmental problems. He was even loaned to the Soviet Union for some weeks, to advise the Gorbachev government on the development of sound administrative organizations and practices. Sununu was also a prime administration figure in the complex set of negotiations with Congress that resulted in the budget crises and compromises of 1989 and 1990.

Havana-born Sununu began his career as an engineer and educator; he founded the Astro Dynamics company in 1960 and taught mechanical engineering, then became associate dean of engineering at Tufts University from 1966 to 1982. He moved into politics as a member of the New Hampshire legislature in 1973, ultimately becoming governer of his state from 1983 to 1989. He was a key member of the Bush presidential campaign staff in 1988 and after the election became the president-elect's chief of staff. He married Nancy Hayes in 1958; they have four children. His B.S. was from the Massachusetts Institute of Technology, in 1961, as were his 1962 M.S. and his 1966 Ph.D.

FURTHER READING

"Beasts of the beltway. . . ." FRED BARNES. *New Republic*, Dec. 24, 1990.
"John Sununu. . . ." ROWLAND EVANS and ROBERT NOVAK. *Reader's Digest*, Nov. 1990.
"Big bad John." MICHAEL KELLY. *Playboy*, Nov. 1990.
"Big bad John Sununu. . . ." DAN GOODGAME. *Time*, May 21, 1990.
"The clean, mean political jab." DANIEL WATTENBERG. *Insight*, Mar. 12, 1990.
"John Sununu." CRAIG UNGER. *People*, Mar. 12, 1990.
"A talk with. . . ." LEE WALCZAK, et al. *Business Week*, Feb. 5, 1990.
"Sununu, John Henry." *Current Biography*, May 1989.
"If U knew Sununu." PHILIP WEISS. *Manhattan, inc.*, Feb. 1989.
"The great right hope." PETER OSTERLUND. *National Review*, Mar. 24, 1989.

Sutherland, Donald (Donald McNichol Sutherland, 1934–) In 1989, veteran Canadian actor Sutherland starred as the White South African schoolteacher drawn into the anti-apartheid struggle in *A Dry White Season*, with a cast that included Marlon Brando, Janet Suzman, Susan Sarandon, and Zakes Mokae. His films that year also included Hugh Hudson's *Lost Angels*, set in a psychiatric hospital, and a starring role as a vicious prison warden, opposite Sylvester Stallone's victimized convict in *Lock Up*. In 1990, Sutherland appeared with Geraldine Chaplin in a museum setting in an alternately surreal and slapstick movie directed by German performance artist-sculptor-filmmaker Rebecca Horn, called *Buster's Bedroom*, which takes place largely in Nirvana House, an asylum housing classic film comedians such as Keaton (the Buster of the title) and Chaplin (Geraldine's father). Sutherland's forthcoming films include a starring role opposite Kenneth Branagh and Emma Thompson in the thriller *Dead Again*, directed by Branagh; the arsonist's role in Ron Howard's *Backdraft*; and a starring role in Werner Herzog's *Scream of Stone*, about a mountain-climbing team in Argentina.

Sutherland began his film career in the mid-1960s and emerged a star in the Hawkeye Pierce role in *M*A*S*H* (1970). He went on to a wide variety of dramatic roles, many of them chosen primarily for their quality, in such films as *Klute* (1971), *The Day of the Locust* (1975), *1900* (1976), *Casanova* (1976), *Ordinary People* (1980), *Eye of the Needle* (1981), and *Gauguin* (1986). He attended the University of Toronto. He has been married three times and has five children, including actor Kiefer Sutherland.

FURTHER READING

"Donald Sutherland and. . . ." GERMANO CELAND and BRIGITTE LACOMBE. *Interview*, Sept. 1990.
"Donald Sutherland's. . . ." BARBARA GRAUSTARK. *American Film*, Apr. 1984.
"Sutherland, Donald." *Current Biography*, Feb. 1981.

Swayze, Patrick (1954–) Trained for ballet, Swayze began his career as a dancer and danced and acted a lead in *Grease* for two years on Broadway before emerging as a leading film player late in the 1980s. His breakthrough role was as Johnny Castle in *Dirty Dancing* (1987). It was followed by a starring role opposite his wife, Lisa Niemi, in the fantasy-action film *Steel Dawn* (1987); the bouncer's role in the action film *Road House* (1989); the police drama *Next of Kin* (1989); and the extraordinarily popular Jerry Zucker film *Ghost* (1990), in which Swayze, playing opposite Demi Moore and Whoopi Goldberg, became a major film star in the title role. In 1990, Swayze also appeared in the television miniseries "North and South," and he has appeared in several other television films. In December 1990, Swayze and Whoopi Goldberg received the Golden Apple Awards of the Hollywood Women's Press Club as Stars of the Year.

FURTHER READING

Patrick Swayze." *People*, Dec. 31, 1990
"Patrick Swayze. . . ." KATHRYN CASEY. *Ladies' Home Journal*, Aug. 1990.
"A wild and Swayze guy." BILL ZEHME. *Cosmopolitan*, Aug. 1989.
"Going Swayze." LAURA MORICE. *Mademoiselle*, June 1989.
"A wild and Swayze guy." BILL ZEHME. *GQ—Gentlemen's Quarterly*, Feb. 1989.
"Patrick Swayze. . . ." DEAN LAMANNA. *Ladies' Home Journal*, Feb. 1989.
"Patrick Swayze. . . ." NANCY MILLS. *Cosmopolitan*, Apr. 1988.
"Patrick Swayze. . . ." *Teen*, June 1988.
"Swayze does it." HAL RUBENSTEIN. *Vogue*, July 1988.
Patrick Swayze. MITCHELL KRUGEL. St. Martin's, 1988.
The New Breed: Actors Coming of Age. KAREN HARDY and KEVIN J. KOFFLER. Holt, 1988.

Swenson, May (1913–90) Utah-born Swenson was a highly regarded poet, much of whose light poetry was published by *The New Yorker*. She lived and worked in New York City from the late 1930s, making her living in the early years as an editor. The first of her nine volumes of poetry was *Another Animal* (1954), which brought considerable recognition and some foundation grants. She won the Bollingen Prize in 1981 and a MacArthur Foundation fellowship in 1987. (d. Ocean View, Delaware; December 4, 1990)

FURTHER READING

Obituary. *New York Times*, Dec. 5, 1990.
"Eleven American poets." HARRIET HEYMAN and ANNIE LEIBOVITZ. *Life*, Apr. 1981.

Sydow, Max von (Carl Adolf von Sydow, 1929–) The work of Max von Sydow on film has been celebrated throughout the world since his 1950s creation of several classic roles in Ingmar Bergman films; he has long been recognized as one of Sweden's leading stage actors and has been associated with the Royal Dramatic Theater since 1960. He played a Catholic priest working in Hiroshima in the television film *Hiroshima: Out of the Ashes*, which premiered on August 6, 1990, the 45th anniversary of the atom bombing of city. His forthcoming work includes the film *A Kiss Before Dying*, a remake of the 1956 film based on the Ira Levin novel.

The classic Bergman films in which he made his greatest impact include *The Seventh Seal*, (1957), *The Magician* (1958), *The Virgin Spring* (1960), *Through a Glass Darkly* (1961), and *Winter Light* (1962). He also starred on television in two linked sagas of 19th–century Scandinavian-American immigration: *The Emigrants* (1969) and *The New Land* (1969). His large body of later work includes such films as *Three Days of the Condor* (1975), *Hannah and Her Sisters* (1985), and *Pelle the Conqueror* (1986). Sydow attended Stockholm's Royal Dramatic Theater School. He married Christina Olin in 1951 and has two children.

FURTHER READING

"Scandinavia-hopping Von Sydow. . . ." LAWRENCE COHN. *Variety*, Dec. 21, 1988.

T

Tagliabue, Paul John (1940–) Lawyer Tagliabue became National Football League commissioner in November 1989 and has since dealt with several highly visible major issues. One of the most difficult was the continuing matter of drug testing and use. While continuing to support infrequent testing for illegal drugs, as previously decided by arbitration, the league tested for steroid use frequently and on a random basis, and league executives and senior staff people began periodic testing in July 1990. Tagliabue also considered the case of Dexter Manley, barred for life, who may be allowed to return within a year or two.

In addition, Tagliabue dealt with two serious matters of alleged sexual harassment. In October, he fined Cincinnati Bengals coach Sam Wyche one-seventeenth of his salary, or nearly $30,000, for barring "USA Today's" Denise Tom from the team's locker room after an October 1 game. This occurred after an earlier incident involving the New England Patriots on September 17. In late November, he fined New England Patriot player Zeke Mowatt $12,500, players Michael Timpson and Robert Perryman $5,000 each, and the club a total of $50,000 because of a locker room incident in which sexual harassment was allegedly directed at *Boston Herald* reporter Lisa Olson. On another controversial matter, Tagliabue also stated that Phoenix should not be the site of the 1993 Super Bowl if the state continued to refuse to declare Martin Luther King's birthday a state holiday.

After graduating from law school in 1965, Tagliabue worked at the defense department in Washington until 1969 and then for twenty years as a lawyer at Covington and Burling, becoming a partner in 1974. He became commissioner of the National Football League in 1989. Tagliabue's B.A. was from Georgetown University, in 1962; his J.D. was from New York University, in 1965. He is married and has two children.

FURTHER READING

"The face of. . . ." Rick Telander. *Sports Illustrated*, Sept. 10, 1990.

"NFL commish's torch passed. . . . " *Sporting News*, Feb. 18, 1990.

"Tagliabue. . . ." Paul Attner. *Sporting News*, Feb. 12, 1990.

"Tagliabue plans. . . ." STEVE HUBBARD. *Sporting News*, Dec. 4, 1989.
"A new quarterback. . . ." *U.S. News & World Report*, Nov. 6, 1989.
"In a blink. . . ." VITO STELLINO. *Sporting News*, Nov. 6, 1989.
"The NFL's new boss." PETER KING. *Sports Illustrated*, Nov. 6, 1989.

Tambo, Oliver (1917–) African National Congress (ANC) president Tambo saw the historic freeing of Nelson Mandela and other key political prisoners, the legalization of the ANC, and the full cease-fire agreement of August 7, 1990, from afar. Long in self-imposed exile in Zambia, he suffered a stroke in August 1989 and was flown to Great Britain and then to Sweden for treatment. In February 1990, ANC leaders conferred with him in Sweden, and in March, one month after his release from prison, Nelson Mandela visited Tambo in Sweden. Tambo was able to return home to South Africa in late 1990.

Tambo became active in the South African freedom movement in the early 1950s; he was then a solicitor in Johannesburg. He was banned and otherwise penalized during most of the 1950s, and indicted for alleged treason in 1956, although the charge was dropped in 1957. He became a deputy president of the then-nonviolent African National Congress in 1958. He left South Africa in 1960 to lead the Zambia-based external forces of the ANC. After the Sharpeville Massacre of 1960, the outlawing of the ANC in 1961, and the series of trials that resulted in life imprisonment of Nelson Mandela and many other freedom movement leaders, Tambo and the ANC moved into the long guerrilla war that ended three decades later. In 1988, he published *Oliver Tambo Speaks: Preparing for Power*. He attended the University College of Fort Hare. He is married and has three children.

FURTHER READING

Mandela, Tambo, and the African National Congress: The Struggle Against Apartheid, a Documentary Study, 1948–1990. SHERIDAN JOHNS and R. HUNT DAVIS, JR., eds. Oxford University Press, 1991.
"Return of the native son." *Time*, Dec. 24, 1990.
The Struggle: A History of the African National Congress. HEIDI HOLLAND. Braziller, 1990.
"Bound by blood." ROGER WILKINS. *Mother Jones*, May 1989.
Oliver Tambo and the Struggle Against Apartheid. E. S. REDDY. Apt Books, 1988.
"Oliver Tambo's war cry." HILARY MACKENZIE. *Maclean's*, Sept. 7, 1987.
"Tambo, Oliver." *Current Biography*, April 1987.

Tandy, Jessica (1909–) British-American actress Tandy became, at 80, the oldest person ever to win an Academy Award with the 1990 Best Actress Oscar for her performance in *Driving Miss Daisy* (1989), which also won the Oscar for Best Picture. Her portrayal of a feisty Southern dowager who grows old along with her chauffeur (Morgan Freeman) and son (Dan Aykroyd) was also honored abroad, winning Italy's Best Actress in a Foreign Film "David of Donatello" Award. With her husband, Hume Cronyn, Tandy was one of twelve people to be awarded the National Medal of the Arts presented by President and Mrs. George Bush at a White House ceremony in September 1990. Privately, Tandy testified before Congress about the need for the National Endowment of the Arts to be free from a "climate of fear."

London-born Tandy appeared in London and New York during the 1930s, although mainly in London and in the classics, most notably as Ophelia to John Gielgud's *Hamlet* (1934). Far more notable was her creation of the Blanche Du Bois role in Tennessee Williams's *A Streetcar Named Desire* (1947). After she and Hume Cronyn married in 1942, the couple created a lasting theater partnership, appearing together in such plays as *The Fourposter* (1951), *A Delicate Balance* (1966), and *Foxfire* (1982; and the 1987 television version). She has also appeared in strong character roles in several films, although *Driving Miss Daisy* was by far her most important film role. Tandy's first husband was British actor Jack Hawkins, with whom she had a daughter. She and Cronyn have two children. She attended the Ben Greet Academy of Acting from 1924 to 1927.

FURTHER READING

"Two lives, one ambition. . . ." GERALD CLARKE. *Time*, Apr. 2, 1990.

"Happily ever after." JEANNE MARIE LASKAS. *Life*, Apr. 1990.
"She oughta be in pictures. . . ." NINA DARNTON. *Newsweek*, Jan. 1, 1990.
"Driving Miss Daisy. . . ." ROBERT SEIDENBERG. *American Film*, Jan. 1990.
"Two for the road." MARK MATOUSEK. *Harper's Bazaar*, Jan. 1990.
"Two for the road." HENRY ALFORD and PAULA BULLWINKEL. *Interview*, Nov. 1989.
"Theater's first couple." ELLEN STEIN. *Horizon*, May 1987.
"Jessica Tandy and. . . ." Andrea Chambers. *People*, June 2, 1986.
Actress to Actress. RITA GAM. Lyons & Burford, 1986.
"Tandy, Jessica." *Current Biography*, Aug. 1984.

Tayback, Vic (Victor Tabback, 1930–90) U.S. character actor Tayback was by far best known as Mel, the cook in the film *Alice's Restaurant* (1975); he continued to play the role in the long-running television series "Alice" (1976–85). Tayback appeared onstage in supporting roles from the 1950s and onscreen from the late 1960s in such films as *Bullitt* (1968), *Lepke* (1973), and *Papillon* (1973). (d. Glendale, California; May 25, 1990)

FURTHER READING

Obituary. *Variety*, May 30, 1990.
Obituary. *The Times* (of London), May 28, 1990.
Obituary. *New York Times*, May 26, 1990.

Taylor, A. J. P. (Alan John Percival Taylor, 1906–90) British historian, journalist, writer, and television personality Taylor was both a serious scholar and a popular figure. He taught at Manchester University (1930–38), and then at Oxford (1938–76), and published such works as *The Course of German History* (1945), *The Struggle for Mastery in Europe, 1848–1918* (1954), *The Origins of the Second World War* (1961), *English History, 1914–45* (1965), and *Beaverbrook* (1972). In the 1950s, he also became a well-known television figure and newspaper columnist. In 1983, he published *A Personal History*; in 1988 his wife published *A Life with Alan: The Diary of A. J. P. Taylor's Wife Eva from 1978 to 1985*. (d. London; September 7, 1990)

FURTHER READING

Obituary. *Current Biography*, Nov. 1990.
"Puck of Magdalen." *Economist*, Sept. 15, 1990.
Obituary. *The Times* (of London), Sept. 8, 1990.
Obituary. *New York Times*, Sept. 8, 1990.
"A. J. P. Taylor. . . ." PAUL KENNEDY. *History Today*, Mar. 1986.
"Taylor, A(lan) J(ohn) P(ercivale.)" *Current Biography*, Nov. 1983.

Taylor, Elizabeth (1932–) A film star for over four decades, and late in her career a stage star as well, Taylor from the middle 1980s has used her worldwide celebrity to further humanitarian causes, most notably the fight against AIDS. Since 1987, she has been chairperson of the American Foundation for AIDS Research and a highly visible public figure in the fight against the disease and for humane, nondiscriminatory treatment of those afflicted by it. One of her many contributions has been development of the Art Against AIDS fund-raising program, which features performances by many artists.

Taylor appeared in October 1989 on television in Tennessee Williams's *Sweet Bird of Youth*, but her work in 1990 was limited by a series of health problems, including a near-fatal case of pneumonia in the spring of 1990. Her illness made her the target of a great many media explorations of alleged personal problems; as a result, she filed a $20 million lawsuit against the *National Enquirer* in September. She made news of another kind when her Vincent van Gogh painting, *View of the Asylum and the Chapel at Saint-Remy*, did not make its minimum price at auction and had to be withdrawn from sale.

London-born Taylor began her film career as a pre-teenager with *Lassie Come Home* and *Jane Eyre*, both in 1943, and became a star at the age of 12 in *National Velvet* (1944). She went on to star in such films as *A Place in the Sun* (1951), *Giant* (1956), *Raintree Country* (1957), *Cat on a Hot Tin Roof* (1958), *Suddenly Last Summer* (1959), *Butterfield 8* (1960; she won a Best Actress Oscar), *Cleopatra* (1962), *Who's Afraid of Virginia Woolf?* (1966, and a second best actress Oscar), *Under Milk Wood* (1971), and *The Blue Bird* (1975). She has starred on Broadway in revivals of *The Little Foxes* (1979) and *Private Lives*

(1983). She has been married seven times, twice to actor Richard Burton, and has four children. Her husbands have also included socialite Nicky Hilton, actor Michael Wilding, producer Mike Todd, singer Eddie Fisher, and Senator John Warner.

FURTHER READING

Elizabeth: The Life of Elizabeth Taylor. Alexander Walker. Grove Weidenfeld, 1991.
"Elizabeth triumphant." LANDON Y. JONES. *People,* Dec. 10, 1990.
"Elizabeth Taylor's. . . ." DAVID WALLACE. *Ladies Home Journal,* Sept. 1990.
Elizabeth Taylor: A Celebration. SHERIDAN MORLEY. Viking Penguin, 1990.
"Still reigning. . . ." SUSAN SCHINDEHETTE. People, Mar. 13, 1989.
"My daughter, Elizabeth Taylor. . . ." (two parts). SARA TAYLOR. *Good Housekeeping,* Mar. and Apr. 1989.
The Films of Elizabeth Taylor. JERRY VERMILYE and MARK RICCI. Carol, 1989.
The New Elizabeth. MARIANNE ROBIN-TANI. St. Martin's, 1988.
"Taylor, Elizabeth." *Current Biography,* Oct. 1985.

Taylor, Lawrence (1959–) One of the leading defensive players in the history of football, outside linebacker Taylor in the 1990–91 season led his team, the New York Giants, to victory over the San Francisco 49ers in the conference championships and over the Buffalo Bills in the Super Bowl. Virgina-born Taylor was a star football player at the University of North Carolina, an All-American who was the first pick of the Giants in the 1981 draft. That year, he was both Rookie of the Year and Best Defensive Player of the Year. He went on to become the only player in National Football League history to be named to the Pro Bowl for nine consecutive seasons. In the 1986–87 season he was named the Most Valuable Player in the National Football League. Along the way, in 1986, he triumphed over a serious drug problem that threatened both family and career. In 1987, he published *LT: Living on the Edge,* written with David Falkner. He married Linda Cooley in 1981; the couple have three children.

FURTHER READING

"Taylor, Lawrence." *Current Biography,* July 1990.
"Taylor. . . ." PETER KING. *Sporting News,* Mar. 3, 1986.
"L.T. and the home team. . . ." JOHN ED BRADLEY. *Esquire,* Dec. 1985.
"Sport interview. . . . " BARRY STANTON. *Sport,* Nov. 1985.
"Search and destroy. . . ." MICHAEL SHAPIRO. *New York Times Magazine,* Aug. 26, 1984.

Terris, Norma (Norma Allison, 1904–89) Terris was best known by far for originating the role of Magnolia in the classic Oscar Hammerstein II-Jerome Kern musical *Show Boat* (1927); she introduced such songs as "Why Do I Love You?" and "Only Make Believe" opposite Howard Marsh as Gaylord Ravenal. She played the role again in the 1932 New York revival, with Paul Robeson as Joe singing "Ol' Man River." Terris had made her Broadway debut in the 1920 *Ziegfeld Follies,* toured in vaudeville, and appeared in several musicals during the 1920s before her big break in *Show Boat.* During the 1930s and 1940s, she starred with the St. Louis Muncipal Opera Company and also appeared in several films. (d. Lyme, Connecticut; November 15, 1989)

FURTHER READING

Obituary. *Variety,* Nov. 22, 1989.
Obituary. *The Times* (of London), Nov. 21, 1990.
Obituary. *New York Times,* Nov. 19, 1990.

Terry-Thomas (Thomas Terry Hoar Stevens, 1911–90) British actor and comedian Terry-Thomas appeared in a wide range of roles in theater and variety in the late 1930s, and made his first breakthrough onstage in *Piccadilly Hayride* (1946), also appearing in early television in the series "How Do You View?" (1950). From the mid-1950s, he was a leading film comedian, usually as a "silly ass," in such movies as *Private's Progress* (1956), *I'm All Right, Jack* (1959), *School for Scoundrels* (1960), *Those Magnificent Men in Their Flying Machines* (1965), *How to Murder Your Wife* (1965), and *Don't Look Now* (1968). Although he continued to appear in films through the late 1970s, he was from the early 1970s increasingly crippled by Parkinson's disease and unable to work. (d. Surrey; January 8, 1990)

FURTHER READING

Obituary. *Current Biography*, Mar. 1990.
Obituary. *The Times* (of London), Jan. 9, 1990.
Obituary. *New York Times*, Jan. 9, 1990.

Tharp, Twyla (1941–) An innovative, highly regarded, often jazz-based dancer and choreographer, Tharp is now exploring new affiliations. She resigned as associate choreographer of the American Ballet Theatre after Mikhail Baryshnikov resigned in June 1988, although continuing to work with that and other companies. Her new ballet *Brief Fling* premiered with the American Ballet Theatre in San Francisco in February 1990. Tharp had disbanded her own company after joining Baryshnikov and did not immediately re-establish another company. But in April she established a relationship with Chicago's Hubbard Street Dance Company, the first with a modern dance company since she had disbanded her own. Called The Tharp Project, it began with an agreement to give Hubbard Street the right to produce four of Tharp's works: *The Fugue* (1970), *Sue's Leg* (1975) and either *Eight Jelly Rolls* (1971) or *Baker's Dozen* (1979).

Indiana-born Tharp was a member of the Paul Taylor dance company from 1963 to 1965, and then developed her own company, also choreographing for other companies. Much of her work is developed around jazz and other contemporary themes, as in her *Tank Dive* (1965), *Re-Moves* (1966), *Forevermore* (1967), *The Bix Pieces* (1972), *As Time Goes By* (1974), *Eight Jelly Rolls* (1971), and *Push Come to Shove* (1976). She also choreographed the films *Hair* (1979), *Amadeus* (1984), and *White Nights* (1985). Tharp attended Pomona College, Barnard College, and the American Ballet Theatre School, and studied with many leading dancers. She was formerly married and has one child.

FURTHER READING

"Tharp's new shtick." JOAN ACOCELLA. *Connoisseur*, Feb. 1989.
"Twyla Tharp Dance." MINDY ALOFF. *Nation*, Mar. 28, 1987.
"Twyla Tharp's return." HOLLY BRUBACH. *Atlantic*, Mar. 1987.
"The world according to Tharp." LOIS DRAEGIN. *Savvy*, Feb. 1987.
"Dancing is dancing." SHARON BASCO. Boston magazine, Mar. 1985.
"Guest in the house." ARLENE CROCE. *New Yorker*, July 2, 1984.
"Don't fence her in." GEORGE O'BRIEN. *New York Times Magazine*, June 3, 1984.
"Twyla Tharp . . . ." David Vaughan. Dance Magazine, May 1984.

Thatcher, Margaret (Margaret Hilda Roberts, 1925–) The former British prime minister began to encounter serious political problems in the spring of 1989 as adverse electoral results and unfavorable opinion poll results showed rising popular support for the Labour Party. The polls showed her personal popularity to be slipping as well. Particularly damaging were her often-voiced objections to several aspects of the planned European monetary system, which caused the resignation of Exchequer Chancellor Nigel Lawson in October 1989; and the extremely unpopular new poll taxes, called community charges, which went into effect on April 1, 1990, preceded by mass protests that turned into rioting in London and several other cities. She continued to slip in the polls, as Neil Kinnock and the Labour Party gained the support of many of her moderate supporters and as her personal style was seen by many to be increasingly abrasive and autocratic.

Thatcher was ultimately unable to rally her party around her, even with her strong support of American action in the late-1990 Persian Gulf Crisis and her dispatch of powerful British forces to the area, including a strong naval force and a full armored division. Running 15–20 points behind Labour in the polls, in November she was challenged for Conservative Party leadership by former defense secretary Michael Heseltine. She fell short of the number of Conservative parliamentary votes needed to win on a first ballot, lost many of her supporters at that point, and then withdrew before a second-round ballot. She was succeeded as party leader and prime minister by longtime supporter John Major, chancellor of the exchequer.

Thatcher was a chemist and then a barrister before beginning her political career with her 1959 election as a Conservative member of parliament. She became Conservative education spokesperson in 1969 and when her party came to power again was education and science minister from 1970 to 1974. In 1975, she succeeded Edward Heath as Conservative leader, becoming the first woman to lead any major British political party. In 1979, she became Britain's first woman prime minister, succeeding Labour prime minister James Callaghan, and became Britain's longest-serving prime minister of the century before her downfall.

The Thatcher era was marked by the privatization of several industries nationalized under post–World War II Labour governments and of several long-established public responsibilities, such as water supply. Her government also conducted the 1982 Falklands war, gaining great prestige from victory, and continued the long involvement in the continuing low-level civil war in Northern Ireland; she personally survived several IRA assassination attempts. She married Denis Thatcher in 1951; the couple have two children. She attended Somerville College, Oxford.

FURTHER READING

"She gave Britain. . . ." DANIELLE PLETKA. *Insight*, Dec. 17, 1990.

"Life at the top. . . ." *Maclean's*, Dec. 3, 1990.

"A legacy of revolution. . . ." BRUCE W. NELAN. *Time*, Dec. 3, 1990.

"'The staunchest ally'. . . . " KENNETH AUCHINCLOSS and DANIEL PEDERSEN. *Newsweek*, Oct. 8, 1990.

Maggie: An Intimate Portrait of a Woman in Power. CHRIS OGDEN. L. J. Kaplan, 1990.

Margaret Thatcher: Britain's Prime Minister. DOROTHY HOLE. Enslow, 1990.

Margaret Thatcher: First Woman Prime Minister of Great Britain. LEILA M. FOSTER. Childrens, 1990.

Margaret, Daughter of Beatrice: A Politician's Psychobiography of Margaret Thatcher. LEO ABSE. Random House, 1990.

Margaret Thatcher. MARIETTA D. MOSKIN. Messner, 1990.

"Thatcher, Margaret Hilda." *Current Biography*, Nov. 1989.

Madam Prime Minister: A Biography of Margaret Thatcher. LIBBY HUGHES. Dillon, 1989.

The Iron Lady. HUGO YOUNG. Farrar, Straus & Giroux, 1989.

Margaret Thatcher. KENNETH HARRIS. Little, Brown, 1988.

Tho, Le Duc (Phan Dinh Khai, 1913–90) A founder of the Indochinese Communist Party in 1929, Tho was imprisoned by the French from the early 1930s through 1936 and from 1939–44, then becoming an increasingly important Communist leader under Ho Chi Minh during the long Vietnam wars. He was chief North Vietnamese peace negotiator from 1970, ultimately negotiating the 1973 cease-fire and withdrawal of American troops with Henry Kissinger. He and Kissinger were awarded a joint Nobel Peace Prize; Tho refused his portion, as the agreement had not ended the long wars. After the North Vietnamese victory in 1975, Le Duc Tho was an important, though not central figure in the North Vietnamese leadership until 1986. (d. Hanoi, Vietnam; October 13, 1990)

FURTHER READING

"A taste of glory." *Economist*, Oct. 20, 1990.
Obituary. *The Times* (of London), Oct. 15, 1990.
Obituary. *New York Times*, Oct. 14, 1990.

Thomas, Isiah (Isiah Lord Thomas, 1961–)
A leading basketball player, Thomas led the Detroit Pistons to their second consecutive National Basketball Association championship, in June 1990 with play-off wins against Indiana, New York, Chicago, and Portland; Thomas was named the Most Valuable Player in the play-offs. In 1989, he had led the team to a win over the formerly dominant Los Angeles Lakers. He described the season in *Bad Boys! An Inside Look at the Detroit Pistons' 1988–89 Championship Season* (1989), written with Matt Dobek. But he had an injury-plagued 1990–91 season, in late October requiring a minor operation for an injured tear duct and in mid-January fracturing his wrist.

Chicago-born Thomas turned professional after two years as a star guard at Indiana University, joining the Detroit Pistons in 1981. He has spent his whole playing career with the Pistons, becoming team leader and ultimately taking the team to their back-to-back 1989 and 1990 National Basketball Association championships. He was a key figure in basketball throughout the 1980s and an eight-time All-Star (1982–89). He returned to Indiana University later in the 1980s, graduating in 1987.

FURTHER READING

"Thomas, Isiah." *Current Biography*, Aug. 1989.
"No longer a doubting. . . ." Roland Lazenby. *Sporting News*, Nov. 1, 1988.
"The importance of being Isiah." David Bradley. *Sport*, May 1988.
"'I have got to do it right'. . . ." William Nack. *Sports Illustrated*, Jan. 19, 1987.
Isiah Thomas: Pocket Magic. Bert Rosenthal. Childrens, 1983.

Thornburgh, Richard Lewis (1932–)
Thornburgh went to Washington in July 1988 as Ronald Reagan's last attorney general and was reappointed by president-elect George Bush. As the administration's chief legal officer, he has been involved in a wide range of activities; a few of the most notable and highly visible of these have been the "war on drugs" of 1989–90, with its multiple probes and prosecutions; the Noriega prosecution of 1990, following the Panama invasion; the massive Housing and Urban Development scandal prosecutions; the even more massive savings and loan crisis investigations and prosecutions; and the continuing war against the Mafia and other organized-crime groups.

Thornburgh had previously been a practicing attorney in Pittsburgh from 1959 to 1969, and was with the Department of Justice in western

Pennsylvania and then in Washington from 1969 to 1977. He then moved into electoral politics and was governor of Pennsylvania from 1979 to 1987. During the 1988 presidential campaign, while then-candidate George Bush was attacking the American Civil Liberties Union, Thornburgh publicly declared that he had been a member of the ACLU but had resigned. Pittsburgh-born Thornburgh married Virginia Judson in 1963; they have four children. His engineering degree was from Yale, in 1954, and his LL.B. from the University of Pittsburgh, in 1957.

FURTHER READING

"ACLU too, buddy. . . ." JAMES BENNET. *New Republic*, Oct. 17, 1988.
"Thornburgh, Richard Louis." *Current Biography*, Oct. 1988.
"Pulling up our socks. . . ." *U.S. News & World Report*, July 25, 1988.
"Republican Richard Thornburgh." *Inc.*, July 1987.

Thorndike, R. L. (Robert Ladd Thorndike, 1911–90) Thorndike was a leading U.S. educational psychologist who focused on the measurement and evaluation of scholastic aptitudes and achievements. He is best known for his work with Irving Lorge in creating the widely used Lorge-Thorndike Intelligence, or Cognitive Ability, tests. He taught briefly at George Washington University before joining Teachers College of Columbia University in 1936, and wrote several books and many articles in his chosen area. He was the son of psychologist Edward Lee Thorndike. (d. Olympia, Washington; September 21, 1990)

FURTHER READING

Obituary. *New York Times*, Sept. 25, 1990.

Thorpe-Bates, Peggy (1914–89) The British actress was best known to worldwide audiences as Hilda Rumpole, opposite Leo McKern as "Rumpole" in John Mortimer's very popular television series. British audiences enjoyed her work in the theater for fifty years in a very wide range of roles, beginning with her mid-1930s appearances in repertory and including a great many classic and modern roles in the London theater. (d. December 26, 1989)

FURTHER READING

Obituary. *The Times* (of London), Jan. 2, 1990.

Throckmorton, Peter (1929–90) A pioneering U.S. underwater archeologist, Throckmorton led expeditions that discovered and explored some of the oldest sunken ships known. In 1960, off the coast of Turkey, he discovered a wreck dating from 1300 B.C.; it was one of the earliest great discoveries of the then-new field of underwater archaeology. Fifteen years later, off the Aegean island of Hydra, he discovered a wreck dating from 2500 B.C. He wrote several books and many articles in his field, including the trailblazing *The Lost Ships* (1964). (d. Newcastle, Maine; June 5, 1990)

FURTHER READING

Obituary. *New York Times*, June 11, 1990.

Tognazzi, Ugo (1922–90) Long one of Italy's favorite character actors, largely in film comedies, Tognazzi became an international star with his role as the homosexual nightclub owner in the Eduardo Molinaro film *La Cage aux Folles* (1979); he also starred in the 1980 and 1985 sequels. Tognazzi also appeared in such films as *The Fascist* (1961), *The Conjugal Bed* (1963), *The Ape Woman* (1964), *Barbarella* (1968), and *Pigsty* (1969). (d. Rome; October 27, 1990)

FURTHER READING

Obituary. *Variety*, Nov. 5, 1990.
Obituary. *The Times* (of London), Oct. 31, 1990.
Obituary. *New York Times*, Oct. 29, 1990.

Travolta, John (1954–) After some lean years, Travolta came back as a star of the comedy hit *Look Who's Talking* (1989) opposite Kirstie Alley and the voice of Bruce Willis as Mikey, the baby in the film. Travolta and Alley also starred in the 1990 sequel, *Look Who's Talking Too*, with the voice of Willis again as Mikey and joined by the voices of Roseanne Barr, and Damon Wayans.

New Jersey–born Travolta became a well known actor on television in "Welcome Back, Kotter" (1975–79). On screen, he emerged as a star in the hit *Saturday Night Fever* (1977), followed by other popular starring roles in *Grease* (1978), *Urban Cowboy* (1980), and *Staying Alive* (1983). He has also made several records.

FURTHER READING

"Look who's talking. . . back." SUSAN SQUIRE. *Premiere*, Mar. 1990.
"John Travolta. . . ." SCOT HALLER. *People*, June 24, 1985.
"John Travolta. . . ." *People*, Mar. 5, 1984.
"John Travolta." NORMA MCLAIN STOOP. *Dance Magazine*, Aug. 1983.

Trump, Donald John (1946–) Trump was a highly visible billionaire celebrity until he became an at-least-equally-visible financier in trouble in 1990, running into some very difficult personal and financial problems. In February, his marriage to Ivana Trump broke up, and she announced plans to seek a substantial share of his fortune. In May and June it became clear that his heavy bank- and junk-bond-interest payments called for much more cash than his properties were generating; he had invested heavily in three Atlantic City casino-hotels and high-priced corporate acquisitions and had less-than-expected revenues from his other properties in a very weak real estate market.

When Trump failed to meet major mid-June debt payments, he was able to arrange more short-term financing but was clearly in very great difficulty. On June 26, he arranged additional short-term financing, but lost effective control of his properties to the bankers who had funded his expansion, agreeing to cut back on his expensive life-style and seeking buyers for many of his properties. However, in the much-changed financial climate of the time, buyers at any acceptable price proved very hard to find; by late autumn, the lenders had supplied additional financing and had deferred interest payments while Trump continued to buy time and seek ways out his multiple problems. His 1990 book, *Trump: Surviving at the Top*, written with Charles Leerhsen, was on the best-seller lists but was selling far fewer copies than had been anticipated by its publisher.

Trump became a major real estate developer during the 1970s, ultimately owning such properties as the Plaza Hotel, the Trump Shuttle (formerly the Eastern Airlines shuttle), and several Atlantic City casinos and hotels. He also became a celebrity author with the best-selling *The Art of the Deal* (1987), written with Tony Schwartz. New York–born Trump married Ivana Zelnicek in 1977; they have three children. His B.A. was from the Wharton School in 1968.

FURTHER READING

"Trouble with a big T. . . ." CHRISTINE GORMAN. *Time*, June 18, 1990.
"Manhattan's favorite. . . ." RICHARD L. STERN and JOHN CONNOLLY. *Forbes*, May 14, 1990.
"Playboy interview. . . ." GLENN PLASKIN. *Playboy*, Mar. 1990.
"New York's new power brokers. . . ." *Manhattan, inc.*, Sept. 1989.
"The Trumps. . . ." MARGO HAMMOND. *McCall's*, Feb. 1989.
"Flashy symbol of an acquisitive age." OTTO FRIEDRICH.
Time, Jan. 16, 1989.
Manhattan Passions: True Tales of Power, Wealth & Excess. RON ROSENBAUM. Morrow, 1987.
"Trump, Donald J(ohn)." *Current Biography*, Feb. 1984.

Tune, Tommy (Thomas James Tune, 1939–) Actor-director-dancer-choreographer Tune won two 1990 Tonys, as Best Director of a Musical and as Best Choreographer, for *Grand Hotel* (1989), which won three Tony other awards as well. During the year, Tune was one of several Broadway professionals called in "as friends" to try to help salvage *Annie 2*, a troubled Washington production intended for Broadway. Composer John Kander and lyricist Fred Ebb were also working on a new musical, *Auditions*, which Tune was set to direct. As a dancer, Tune did a special salute to Fred Astaire and also several benefit programs to support AIDS education and counseling programs in the gay community. In late 1990, he played opposite Ann Reinking in a revival of *Bye Bye Birdie* on the road. He also appeared on the televised America's Dance Honors of the new National Academy of Dance.

Texas-born Tune danced on Broadway and on screen from the mid-1960s, in such shows as *Baker Street* (1965) and *How Now Dow Jones* (1967) and such films as *Hello, Dolly* (1968) and *The Boy Friend* (1971), and won a Tony for *Seesaw* (1974). He then also became a leading Broadway choreographer and director; he directed and choreographed *The Best Little Whorehouse in Texas* (1978), won directing Tonys for *A Day in Hollywood/A Night in the Ukraine*(1980) and *Nine* (1982), and won choreography and acting Tonys for *My One and Only* (1983). He also directed several musicals off Broadway and *Stepping Out* on Broadway in 1987. His B.F.A. was from the University of Texas in 1962.

FURTHER READING

"Mr. Musical. . . ." MICHAEL PHILLIPS. *Connoisseur*, July 1990.

"Calling the tune." JOSEF ASTOR and VICTORIA HAMBURG. *Interview*, Oct. 1989.

"Two-part harmony. . . ." JESSE KORNBLUTH. *Architectural Digest*, Aug. 1985.

"Tommy kicks into high gear." *Harper's Bazaar*, April 1985.

"Tune, Tommy." *Current Biography*, Jan. 1983.

Turner, Kathleen (1954–) Turner came back to the New York stage in 1990 and scored a notable Broadway success with her Tony-nominated "tough, sexy, and even funny" performance as Maggie the "Cat" in the revival of *Cat on a Hot Tin Roof*. The slip that constituted her main costume also won attention and, when donated to an auction for charity,

Kathleen Turner and Danny DeVito.

brought $1,200. Late in the year, she moved back to films, shooting *V. I. Warshawski*, in which she played the Chicago private eye of Sara Peretsky's mystery novels, with a cast that included Charles Durning, her "Big Daddy" in *Cat*, and Jay O. Sanders as her journalist-lover; the movie is scheduled for 1991 release.

Turner continued to be among the most popular actresses in the world. The American Video Association's Spirit Awards named her the top actress of the 1980s; she was among the top vote-getters in the People's Choice category of World Favorite Motion Picture Actress; and American college students, in *Movieline* magazine's annual poll, placed her among the top ten female stars. Turner also spoke out strongly against censorship by the National Endowment for the Arts, appearing in a series of radio and print advertisements for the liberal political-action group, People for the American Way, who gave her their Spirit of Liberty Award for her work in preserving free expression and civil liberties.

Missouri-born Turner moved from the theater into films in the early 1980s and quickly emerged as one of the leading movie stars of the 1980s in such films as *Body Heat* (1981), *Romancing the Stone* (1984), *Prizzi's Honor* (1985), *Jewel of the Nile* (1985), *Peggy Sue Got Married* (1986), *Switching Channels* (1988), *The Accidental Tourist* (1988), and *The War of the Roses* (1989). She was also the voice of the sexy cartoon figure Jessica in *Who Framed Roger Rabbit* (1988). She married Jay Weiss in 1984; they have one child. She attended Southwest Missouri State University and received her M.F.A. from the University of Maryland.

FURTHER READING

"Kathleen Turner. . . ." MALCOLM MACPHERSON. *Premiere*, Nov. 1989.
"A new role for. . . ." JENNY CULLEN. *Ladies Home Journal*, July 1988.
"Hot in Hollywood." CAROL KRAMER. *McCall's*, Sept. 1987.
"Joining ranks. . . ." *People*, Jan. 5, 1987.
Kathleen Turner. REBECCA STEFOFF. St. Martin's, 1987.
"The new queen of the screen." LIZ SMITH. *People*, Nov. 3, 1986.
"Kathleen Turner. . . ." JOAN BARTHEL. *Cosmopolitan*, Oct. 1986.
"Some like her hot." LIZ SMITH. *Vogue*, Sept. 1986.
"Kathleen Turner." DAVID SHEFF. *Playboy*, May 1986.
"Turner, Kathleen." *Current Biography*, June 1986.

Turner, Ted (Robert Edward Turner III, 1938–) Financier and yachtsman Turner encountered serious financial problems in the mid-1980s, but in the late 1980s he emerged as a world communications industry leader, at the head of the Turner Broadcasting System (TBS), the Cable News Network (CNN), and the very successful new Turner Network Television (TNT). TNT began broadcasting its combination of old movies, sports, original television movies, and a potpourri of other programming in October 1988, and has in over two years grown into a major asset. During 1989 and 1990, CNN grew into a worldwide broadcast news network with hundreds of millions of viewers, with its 24-hour coverage of such massive events as the Tiananmen Square demonstrations and massacre, the San Francisco earthquake, the tearing down of the Berlin Wall and the massive continuing events in Eastern Europe and the Soviet Union, the Palestinian uprising, and the Persian Gulf War. Personally, Turner and actress Jane Fonda were often companions in 1990, late in the year announcing their plans to marry.

Turner began building what ultimately became a set of major enterprises in the 1960s and emerged as a leading American industrial and sports figure during the 1970s. His holdings also include the Atlanta Hawks and the Atlanta Braves. A leading yachtsman, he won the America's Cup in 1977. He sponsored the Goodwill Games in Moscow in 1986 and in Atlanta in 1990, and has been active in environmental issues. He has been married twice and has two children. He attended Brown University.

FURTHER READING

"Terrible Ted. . . ." IVOR DAVIS. *Los Angeles Magazine*, Aug. 1990.
"Captain planet. . . ." JOHN MOTAVALLI. *Interview*, June 1989.
"Ted Turner. . . ." GREG DAWSON. *American Film*, Jan.–Feb. 1989.
The Alexander Complex: Six Businessmen and the Empires They Built. MICHAEL MEYER. Random House, 1989.
"Once more, with cheek." GWENDA BLAIR. *Business Month*, July–Aug. 1988.
"Adventurer in cable TV." JULIA BENNETT. *Maclean's*, Apr. 11, 1988.
"Turner's windless sails. . . ." BILL POWELL. *Newsweek*, Feb. 9, 1987.
The Corporate Warriors. DOUGLAS K. RAMSEY. Houghton Mifflin, 1987.

Turner, Tina (Annie Mae Bullock, 1938–) A classic rock singer, Turner made a tremendous comeback in 1989–90, beginning with her first album in three years, *Foreign Affairs* (1989), featuring such singles as "Steamy Windows" and "The Best." From April–November 1990, she went on a six-month European tour, appearing in 19 countries before audiences totaling an estimated 3 million—and then announced that she was taking a year or so to rest. Her former partner and ex-husband, Ike Turner, continued to encounter drug-related problems; in February 1990, he was sentenced to a four-year prison term in California.

Tennessee-born Turner joined Ike Turner's band in 1956; the couple were married in 1958 and, after her hit recording of "A Fool in Love" (1960), they emerged as leading rock figures of the 1960s and early 1970s. After their parting in the mid-1970s, Tina Turner went on to become a very popular soloist of the 1980s with such albums as *Private Dancer* (1984) and *Break Every Rule* (1986). She sang (with many others) *We Are the World* (1985) in the USA for Africa benefit. She has also appeared in several films, including *Tommy* (1975) and *Mad Max: Beyond Thunderdome* (1985). In 1986, she published *I, Tina*, written with Kurt Loder. She has four children.

FURTHER READING

"Tina Turner. . . ." *Jet*, July 9, 1990.
"Rich, free and in control. . . ." LYNN NORMENT. *Ebony*, Nov. 1989.
"Lisa, it's for you. . . ." LISA ROBINSON. *Vogue*, May 1987.
"Tina Turner. . . ." ELIZABETH SPORKIN. *Ladies' Home Journal*, Apr. 1987.
Picture Life of Tina Turner. GENE BUSNER. Watts, 1987.
Tina Turner. D. L. MABERY. Lerner, 1986.
T I N A. BART MILLS. Warner, 1985.
Tina Turner. LAURA FISSINGER. Ballantine, 1985.
Tina! STEVEN IVORY. Putnam, 1985.
Tina Turner. PHILIP KAMIN. H. Leonard, 1985.
"Turner, Tina." *Current Biography*, Nov. 1984.

Tutu, Desmond Mpilo (1931–) Archbishop Tutu, the leader of the Anglican Church in South Africa, continued to play a major role in the South African freedom movement. He quickly welcomed prime minister De Klerk's February 2, 1990, legalization of the African National Congress (ANC) and other organizations, along with a series of other moves to relieve tension, and continued to encourage the negotiations that led to the historic full cease-fire of August 7, 1990. He also attempted, without much early success, to help stem the Inkatha-ANC civil war that grew in Natal and spread throughout the country during 1990 while blaming right-wing terror groups for much of the violence in Johannesburg, Cape Town, and other cities from the summer of 1990. He later helped develop the ANC-Inkatha truce of January 1991. In 1990, he also published a second edition of his *Crying in the Wilderness*: *The Struggle for Justice in South Africa*; in 1989, his daughter Naomi Tutu edited *The Words of Desmond Tutu*.

Since his ordination as an Anglican minister in 1961, Tutu has become South Africa's leading apostle of nonviolence within the South

African freedom movement and an immensely respected world figure, as was Martin Luther King in the 1950s and 1960s. Tutu was awarded the Nobel Peace Prize in 1984. He rose steadily within his church and has led the Anglican church in South Africa as archbishop since 1986. He was secretary of the South African Council of Churches from 1979 to 1984, and since 1987 he has been president of the All-Africa Council of Churches. Among his other published works are *Hope and Suffering: Sermons and Speeches* (1984). He married Leah Nomalizo Tutu in 1955; they have four children. He attended St. Peter's Theological College and the University of London.

FURTHER READING

"'No one will stop us. . . .'" *UNESCO Courier*, June 1990.
"South Africa. . . ." Richard Bautch. *America*, May 13, 1989
"A skeptical view." John Bierman. *Maclean's*, Mar. 13, 1989.
"Desmond Tutu. . . ." Hans J. Massaquoi. *Ebony*, June 1988.
Desmond Tutu: The Courageous & Eloquent Archbishop Struggling Against Apartheid in South Africa. David Winner. Gareth Stevens, 1989.
Desmond Tutu. Dennis Wepman. Watts, 1989.
The Rolling Stone Interviews: The 1980s. St. Martin's, 1989.
Archbishop Tutu of South Africa. Judith Bentley. Enslow, 1988.
Tutu: Voice of the Voiceless. Shirley Du Boulay. Eerdmans, 1988.
Desmond Tutu: Bishop of Peace. Carol Greene. Childrens, 1986.
"Tutu, Desmond (Mpilo)." *Current Biography*, Jan. 1985.

Twitchell, David (1955–), **Twitchell, Ginger** (1956–), and **Twitchell, Robyn** (1983–86) On April 8, 1986, in Boston, Massachusetts, two-and-a-half-year-old Robyn Twitchell died after a five-day illness. His illness was later diagnosed as an operable bowel obstruction and his death therefore entirely preventable. His parents, Christian Scientists David and Ginger Twitchell, who later said that they had not realized how serious the illness was, had called in a Christian Science practitioner who prayed for the child, as prescribed by their religion; but no medical doctor had seen Robyn Twitchell at any time during his painful, fevered illness. Christian Science does not prohibit resort to medical doctors but calls for their use only as a last resort. Both adult Twitchells were indicted for manslaughter in a case that attracted unusual attention, as Boston is the site of the founding church and the world headquarters of Christian Science. It was established at the trial that, although both adults

David and Ginger Twitchell.

were devout believers, both had been medically treated during their lifetimes.

On July 4, 1990, both Twitchells were convicted of manslaughter and two days later were sentenced to ten years' probation. They were also ordered by the judge to see to it that their three remaining children received regular medical attention. The case was part of a trend that gained strength in the 1980s as adult Christian Scientists were forced by law to supply medical protection for their children; a considerable variety of charges have been made against those who failed to do so.

The Twitchells were both born in Christian Science families, David in Long Island, New York, and Ginger in Maine. He had atteneded Principia College, the only Christian Science college in the United States, and later worked as administrator in a Christian Science retirement home.

FURTHER READING

"Convicted of relying on prayer. . . ." ALAIN L. SANDERS. *Time*, July 16, 1990.
"Post-mortem. . . ." *U.S. News & World Report*, July 16, 1990.
"Neglect versus creed." Economist, July 7, 1990.
"A test of faith." ALAN J. CUSHNER. Boston Magazine, Dec. 1988.
"Spiritual healing. . . ." STEPHEN GOTTSCHALK. *Christian Century*, June 22, 1988.
"'Manslaughter' medicine." *U.S. News & World Report*, May 9, 1988.

Tyson, Mike G. (1966–) For boxer Tyson, it was a roller-coaster year. In Tokyo in February 1990, after a lackluster 10 rounds,the man they once called "Iron Mike" was decked by a virtually unknown contender, James "Buster" Douglas, and lost his heavyweight title. With that shocking loss, the boxing world wondered whether Tyson was past his peak at 24 years old; whether he had lost his concentration, discipline, and desire. Stories abounded about erratic attention to training. But in December Tyson gave the only answer that really matters in his trade. He knocked out opponent Alex Stewart 2½ minutes into the first round of a scheduled 10-round bout, bringing his overall record to 39–1, with 35 knockouts.

Tyson's next fight was scheduled for spring 1991, against Donovan "Razor" Ruddock, but whether it would be a fight for a title was a complicated question to be settled by the American Arbitration Association. Evander Holyfield, who took the heavyweight championship from Douglas in October, was scheduled to first fight ex-champion George Foreman. Under International Boxing Federation rules, the winner of that fight must fight Tyson by October 25, 1991. Tyson's future bouts will likely not appear on his long-time broadcaster, Home Box Office; his promoter, Don King, ended Tyson's relationship with HBO in favor of pay-per-view television contracts.

Brooklyn-born Tyson turned professional in 1985 and quickly became a leading heavyweight contender. From 1986 to 1988, he successively defeated several other boxers, the last of them Michael Spinks in June 1988, to become sole world heavyweight champion, a title he held until his defeat by Douglas. He was formerly married to actress Robin Givens.

FURTHER READING

"Is he back?" DAVID MILLER. *Sport*, Oct. 1990.
"Mike Tyson. . . ." RICHARD REGEN and MICHEL CONTE. *Interview*, Oct. 1990.
"Mike Tyson. . . ." ROBERT E. JOHNSON. *Jet*, June 25, 1990.
Mike Tyson. JOHN HENNESSEY. Smith, 1990.
Bad Intentions: The Mike Tyson Story. PETER HELLER. NAL-Dutton, 1990.
"Fire and fear. . . ." JOSÉ TORRES. *Playboy*, Aug. 1989.
Blood Season: Tyson and the World of Boxing. PHIL BERGER. Morrow, 1989.
Fire and Fear: The Inside Story of Mike Tyson. JOSÉ TORRES. Warner, 1989.
Serenity: A Book About Fighters: Why They Fight and How It Feels to Be One. RALPH WILEY. Holt, 1989.
"Tyson, Mike." *Current Biography*, April 1988.

U

Ullman, Tracey (1959–) British actress and entertainer Ullman, notable for the variety of comedy characters she created as the star of the Emmy-winning "Tracey Ullman Show," played her first starring role in 1990, opposite Kevin Kline in Lawrence Kasdan's *I Love You to Death*; the film was neither commercially nor critically successful. She also won a 1990 Emmy for best individual performance in a variety or musical program in "The Best of the Tracey Ullman Show;" the show won a total of thirteen Emmy nominations. In March, she was named funniest female performer in a television series at the American Comedy Awards. Ullman also very notably returned to the theater: In June 1990, she played Katherine to Morgan Freeman's Petruchio in a New York production of *The Taming of the Shrew;* and in November, after cancellation of her long-running television show, she was seen in Miami in a one-woman show, *The Big Love.*

Ullman has been on stage since the mid-1970s; she attracted notice in the Royal Court Theatre production of the comedy *Four in a Million* and emerged as a star of British television comedy in the early 1980s. She became a comedy star in American television in her own "The Tracey Ullman Show" (1987–90); the series won a Best Comedy Series Emmy in 1989. She also appeared in supporting roles in several films, including *Plenty* (1985). She has recorded the album *You Broke My Heart in Several Places*, with its hit single "They Don't Know." She is married to Allen McKeown; they have one child.

FURTHER READING

"Tracey Ullman. . . ." Jerry Lazar. *New York Times Magazine*. Oct. 15, 1989.
"Tracking Tracey." Michael Dare and Matthew Rolston. *Interview*, Jan. 1989.
"Ullman, Tracey." *Current Biography*, Oct. 1988.
"Tracey Ullman." Bill Zehme. *Playboy*, Sept. 1988.
"Enter Tracey Ullman. . . ." Louise Farr. *TV Guide*, Feb. 20, 1988.
"Tracey Ullman." *People*, Dec. 28, 1987.
"Tracey Ullman Goes. . . ." Michele Kort. *Ms.*, Sept. 1987.
"Foxy lady. . . ." Bill Zehme. *Rolling Stone*, Aug. 27, 1987.
"Will the real. . . ." Harry F. Waters. *Newsweek*, July 13, 1987.

Updike, John (John Hoyer Updike, 1932–) Novelist Updike killed off his most famous character, Harry "Rabbit" Angstrom, in the fourth and final book in the series, *Rabbit at Rest,* published by Knopf in 1990 and hailed as one of his finest novels; it earned Updike his second Pulitzer Prize in April 1991. After three decades of chronicling American civilization through the life of his WASP antihero, Updike decided that Rabbit was "tired of everything" and had to go. It was *Rabbit Run* (1960)—the first book in the series and his second published novel—that first established Updike as a major writer; it was made into a not-very-successful film in 1970. This was followed by *Rabbit Redux* (1977) and the Pulitzer Prize–

winning *Rabbit Is Rich* (1981). Earlier in 1990, Fawcett published in paperback Updike's personal memoir, *Self-Consciousness: Memoirs.* Late in the year, Updike said his next novel would be a "paradise lost" sort of novel, set in the pre-AIDS America of the 1970s.

Pennsylvania-born Updike has also written several other highly regarded novels, including the National Book Award–winning *The Centaur* (1963), *Couples* (1968), *Bech: a Book* (1970, and its 1972 sequel), and *The Witches of Eastwick* (1984), made into the 1987 film. He has also written short stories, many of them published in *The New Yorker*, as well as essays, poetry, and a play. Formerly married to Mary Pennington, he married Martha Bernhard in 1977 and has four children. His B.A. was from Harvard in 1954.

FURTHER READING

John Updike. Judie Newman. St. Martin's, 1988.
John Updike. Harold Bloom, ed. Chelsea House, 1987.
"Writers 'are. . . .'" Alvin P. Sanoff. *U.S. News & World Report*, Oct. 20, 1986.
"Pigeon feathers. . . ." Rebbie Kinsella. *Christianity Today*, Mar. 7, 1986.
John Updike Bibliography. E.A. Gearhart. Bern Porter, 1985.
"Updike, John (Hoyer)." *Current Biography*, Oct. 1984.
John Updike. Robert Detweiler. G. K. Hall, 1984.
John Updike. Suzanne H. Uphaus. Ungar, 1980.

V

Van Cleef, Lee (1925–89) On stage professionally from 1948 and on screen from 1950 (his debut a small role in *High Noon*), Van Cleef played supporting roles for fifteen years and then found fame playing villainous second leads to Clint Eastwood in Sergio Leone's "spaghetti westerns" *For a Few Dollars More* (1965) and *The Good, the Bad, and the Ugly* (1967). He continued as a movie bad man in such films as *Death Rides a Horse* (1967), *Sabata* (1969; and its 1971 sequel), and *Take a Hard Ride* (1975). (d. Oxnard, California; December 16, 1989)

FURTHER READING

Obituary. *Variety*, Dec. 20, 1989.
Obituary. *The Times* (of London), Dec. 18, 1989.
Obituary. *New York Times*, Dec. 18, 1989.

Van Heusen, Jimmy (Edward Chester Babcock, 1913–90) From the 1940s through the 1960s, Van Heusen was one of Hollywood's most successful songwriters, working with lyricists Johnny Burke from 1940 to 1953 and Sammy Cahn from 1954. He worked very closely with singers Bing Crosby and Frank Sinatra, with Burke writing the scores of several Crosby films and numerous songs for Sinatra. Van Heusen won four Oscars, for "Swinging on a Star" in *Going My Way* (1944); "All the Way" in *The Joker Is Wild* (1957); "High Hopes" in *A Hole in the Head* (1959); and "Call Me Irresponsible" in *Papa's Delicate Condition* (1973). (d. Rancho Mirage, California; February 7, 1990)

FURTHER READING

Obituary. *Down Beat*, June 1990.
Obituary. *Current Biography*, Apr. 1990.
"High on the list." *People*, Mar. 19, 1990.
Obituary. *Variety*, Feb. 21, 1990.
Obituary. *The Times* (of London), Feb. 10, 1990.
Obituary. *New York Times*, Feb. 8, 1990.

Vargas Llosa, Mario (1936–) The celebrated Peruvian writer Vargas Llosa became a leading Peruvian politician in the late 1980s. In 1987, he led a protest movement that developed into the powerful Libertad Party, and in the autumn of 1988 he became his party's presidential candidate. After spending much of the next two years mounting a long, complex campaign while giving up his writing in that period, he ultimately lost the 1990 presidential election to Japanese-Peruvian economist and agronomist Alberto Fujimori. Then it was back to writing, with a pledge never to reenter politics; his next published work was the novel *In Praise of the Stepmother* (1990), written before his political involvement. Another novel, *Aunt Julia and the Scriptwriter* (1978), was made into a film called *Tune in Tomorrow* in 1990, with Peter Falk playing a flamboyant 1950s soap opera writer hired to revive the flagging fortunes of a New Orleans radio station.

Vargas Llosa is a leading Latin American literary figure and social critic, long active in socialist causes, although he has long also been an outspoken foe of totalitarianism. He is a world figure for such powerful novels as *The Time of the Hero* (1962; more closely translated as *The City and the Dogs*), *The Green House* (1965), *Conversation in a Cathedral* (1969), and *The War of the End of the World* (1984). He attended Lima's San Marcos University and the University of Madrid. He is married to Patricia Vargas Llosa; they have three children.

FURTHER READING

"Mario Vargas Llosa." MIRIAM HORN. *U.S. News & World Report*, Nov. 5, 1990.
"From books to ballots. . . ." MARK BUDGEN. *Maclean's*, Apr. 9, 1990.
"Mario Vargas Llosa. . . ." TINA ROSENBERG. *People*, Apr. 9, 1990.
"Vargas Llosa rewrites Peru." GUY MARTIN. *Esquire*, Apr. 1990.
"The fox and the hedgehog. . . ." GUSTAVO GORRITI. *New Republic*, Feb. 12, 1990.
"The temptation of Mario." ELIZABETH FARNSWORTH. *Mother Jones*, Jan. 1989.
"The real life of. . . ." MICHAEL TIGHE and DAVID RIEFF. *Interview*, Sept. 1988.
Interviews with Latin American Writers. MARIE-LISE GAZARIAN-GAUTIER. Dalkey Arch, 1989.
Mario Vargas Llosa. RAYMOND L. WILLIAMS. Ungar, 1987.
Mario Vargas Llosa. DICK GERDES. G. K. Hall, 1985.

Vaughan, Sarah (Sarah Lois Vaughan, 1924–90) Celebrated jazz and popular singer Vaughan began her career in New York in 1943 as a singer and pianist with Earl (Fatha) Hines's band. She joined Billy Eckstine when he broke off to form his own band in 1944 and became a soloist late in 1946. Her first hit recording was "Tenderly" (1947), and her second and greatest hit was her recording of "It's Magic" (1947). She then went to become a worldwide celebrity on records and in concert, singing bebop with Dizzy Gillespie and Charlie Parker in the late 1940s and with many of the leading jazz musicians of the following decades. In later years, her concerts always included "Misty" and "Send in the Clowns," which became her signature song. (d. Los Angeles; April 3, 1990)

FURTHER READING

"Psalms for. . . ." JAMES T. JONES IV. *Down Beat*, Jan. 1991.
"Giants." WHITNEY BALLIETT. *New Yorker*, Oct. 1, 1990.
Obituary. JOHN MCDONOUGH. *Down Beat*, June 1990.
Obituary. *Current Biography*, May 1990.
"One of the glories. . . ." *People*, Apr. 16, 1990.
"The wondrous warbles. . . ." *U.S. News & World Report*, Apr. 16, 1990.
Obituary. *Variety*, Apr. 11, 1990.
Obituary. *The Times* (of London), Apr. 5, 1990.
Obituary. *New York Times*, Apr. 5, 1990.

Vaughan, Stevie Ray (1956–90) Dallas-born Vaughan began his career as a blues and rock guitarist, singer, and composer in the mid-1970s and in 1981 organized Double Trouble, a rock-oriented band. Their first hit record was *Texas Flood* (1983) and their second and much greater hit was the album *Couldn't Stand the Weather* (1983), followed by another hit, *Live Alive* (1986). Vaughan encountered serious drug and alcohol problems in the late 1980s but overcame them. In 1989, Double Trouble's album *In Step* won a Grammy as best contemporary blues recording. On August 27, 1990, Vaughan appeared with guitarists Jimmy Vaughan (his brother) and Eric Clapton at the Alpine Valley Ski Resort in East Troy, Wisconsin. Stevie Ray Vaughan and four others died in a helicopter accident after that concert, on their way back to Chicago.

FURTHER READING

Obituary. TERRI HEMMERT. *Down Beat*, Nov. 1990.
Obituary. JEFFREY RESSNER and ROBERT WILONSKY. *Rolling Stone*, Oct. 18, 1990.
Obituary. JOHN SWENSON. *Rolling Stone*, Oct. 4, 1990.
"A Wisconsin helicopter. . . ." STEVE DOUGHERTY. *People*, Sept. 10, 1990.
Obituary. *U.S. News & World Report*, Sept. 10, 1990.
"Stevie Ray Vaughan." *Variety*, Sept. 3, 1990.
Obituary. *The Times* (of London), Sept. 1, 1990.
Obituary. *New York Times*, Aug. 28, 1990.
"Stevie Ray. . . ." MATT RESNICOFF and JOE GORE. *Guitar Player*, Feb. 1990.
Great Guitarists: The Most Influential Players in Jazz, Country, Blues & Rock. RICH KIENZLE. Facts on File, 1986.

Vidal, Gore (1925–) Vidal is one of America's best-known literary gadflies, puncturing pretensions, ruthlessly exposing the hard reality under his subject's cloak of rhetoric, and occasionally showering vitriol on one and all. Much of his recent work is in the form of essays, reviews, and letters in the main English-language newspapers and journals, often sparking a lively correspondence between supporters and detractors. A paperback collection of Vidal's writings—*At Home: Essays 1982–1988*—was brought out by Vintage. Vidal's major recent full-length work, *Hollywood: A Novel of America in the 1920s* (1989), was the latest in his string of historical novels. Although critical response varied, Vidal's *Hollywood* was honored in his current country-of-residence, Italy, with the Forte dei Marmi Prize for literature. A sometime playwright and screenwriter, he also headed the jury for the Venice Film Festival.

Born at West Point, New York, Vidal is one of the most prolific novelists, satirists, and social critics of the last four decades. His celebrated series of related novels on American historical themes includes *Burr* (1972), *Lincoln* (1984), and *Empire* (1987). He has also written several novels set in the Greco-Roman world, including *Julian* (1964), *Myron* (1974), and *Creation* (1981). His many other works include the novel *Myra Breckenridge* (1968), the plays *Visit to a Small Planet* (1957) and *The Best Man* (1960), several screenplays, occasional nonfiction works such as *Vidal in Venice* (1987), and a wide range of essays. A liberal, he was twice an unsuccessful candidate for public office and in 1971–72 was head of the short-lived New Party. He graduated from Philips Exeter Academy in 1943.

FURTHER READING

"Through the looking glass." HOWARD MEANS. *Washingtonian*, Feb. 1990.
"Tug of war." COLIN WRIGHT. *New Statesman & Society*, Nov. 3, 1989.
"The chore of being Gore." ANDREW KOPKIND. *Interview*, June 1988.
"Gore Vidal's. . . ." EDWARD ALEXANDER. *Society*, Mar.–Apr. 1988.
"Gore Vidal." DAVID SHEFF. *Playboy*, Dec. 1987.
"Vidal, Gore." *Current Biography*, June 1983.
Gore Vidal. ROBERT F. KIERNAN. Ungar, 1982.

Vincent, Fay (Francis Thomas Vincent, Jr., 1938–) Vincent, the current U.S. baseball commissioner, became assistant commissioner of baseball in 1989. He was brought in by his friend, then–newly appointed commissioner A. Bartlett Giamatti, and spent much of his early term in office investigating the Pete Rose scandal. Vincent was appointed commissioner when Giamatti died suddenly, shortly after banning Rose from baseball. As commissioner, Vincent was very quickly faced with the San Francisco earthquake of October 17, 1989, which occurred a few minutes before the start of the third game of the 1989 World Series; the impact of the quake was televised around the world at

the moment it happened. Before the beginning of the 1990 season, he was called upon to informally mediate the labor dispute and owners' lockout of players that ultimately forced cancellation of many preseason games and set season opening back by a week.

On July 30, 1990, Vincent acted in the highly publicized case of New York Yankees owner George Steinbrenner, who had been previously fined for improperly interfering with the trade of player Dave Winfield to the California Angels. Steinbrenner was permanently barred from active management of the Yankees and ordered to bring his controlling interest in the team to below 50 percent; he later resigned as general manager of the team.

Before joining major league baseball, Connecticut-born Vincent was a corporate lawyer and executive, a former president of Columbia Pictures, and vice-president of Coca-Cola. He married Valerie McMahon in 1965; they have three children. His B.A. was from Williams College in 1960, and his LL.D. from Yale in 1963.

FURTHER READING

"Baseball's unlikely. . . ." Tom Callahan. *U.S. News & World Report*, Oct. 15, 1990.
"Fay Vincent. . . ." Richard Sandomir. *Manhattan, inc.*, May 1990.
"Vincent. . . ." Dave Nightingale. *Sporting News*, Feb. 12, 1990.
"After the death. . . ." Ken Gross. *People*, Sept. 18, 1989.

Vishniac, Roman (1897–1990) Russian-born photographer Vishniac was trained as a biologist in Russia and Germany and lived in Berlin between the two world wars. It was there that he became a skilled photographer as well. From 1932–40, in a series of picture-taking trips through Eastern Europe and Germany, he made a unique photographic record of Jewish life before the Nazis murdered millions of Jews in the Holocaust. After emigrating to the United States in 1942, he worked with camera and microscope to become a leading microphotographer. But it was the early photographs that made him a world figure, published in *Polish Jews: A Pictorial Record* (1942; reprinted 1987) and with great impact in *A Vanished World* (1983). (d. New York City; January 22, 1990)

FURTHER READING

"Two more titans fall." *Popular Photography*, May 1990.
Obituary. *Current Biography*, Mar. 1990.
"The saved faces. . . ." *U.S. News & World Report*, Feb. 5, 1990.
Obituary. *The Times* (of London), Jan. 27, 1990.
Obituary. *New York Times*, Jan. 23, 1990.

Walesa, Lech (1943–) Since 1980, Polish political leader Walesa has been the leader of the Polish trade confederation, Solidarity, and the Polish freedom movement; Solidarity was legalized under his leadership in 1989 as Poland and the other nations of Eastern Europe moved toward freedom. He led the negotiations that resulted in the Communist Polish government's turn toward democracy and to the free elections of June 1989; Solidarity won the elections, and Solidarity leader Tadeusz Mazowiecki became Poland's first democratically elected premier since 1948 and the first democratically elected noncommunist to replace a Communist leadership. Walesa refused the Polish presidency at that point, but in June 1990 he decided to run for the presidency. Walesa then defeated Mazowiecki and Stanislaw Tyminski in a three-way vote and in the December runoff defeated Tyminski 3–1.

Walesa became an electrician at the Lenin Shipyard in Gdańsk in 1966; fired after leading the 1970 strike, he continued to organize Poland's developing labor movement. In 1980, he led the successful Lenin Shipyard strike, which sparked a nationwide series of largely successful strikes, and in September 1980 he was a founder and first president of the Polish trade union confederation, Solidarity. He was imprisoned for a year after Solidarity was outlawed in 1981 but continued to be underground leader of the union and the movement. Walesa was awarded the 1983 Nobel Peace Prize. As the Gorbachev era developed, he and Solidarity emerged openly once again. In 1987, he published *A Way of Hope: An Autobiography*. He married Danuta Walesa in 1969; they have eight children.

FURTHER READING

"Lech-luster. . . ." VICTORIA POPE. *New Republic*, Dec. 3, 1990.

"Walesa answers. . . ." MARTIN POLLACK. *World Press Review*, Aug. 1990.

"Walesa's war. . . ." ANNA HUSARSKA. *New Republic*, July 23, 1990.

"Walesa's drive. . . ." PETER HEBBLETHWAITE. *National Catholic Reporter*, June 1, 1990.

Lech Walesa: The Leader of Solidarity and Campaigner for Freedom & Human Rights in Poland. MARY CRAIG. Gareth Stevens, 1990.

"A symbol of hope." PHIL SUDA. *Scholastic Update*, Oct. 20, 1989.
"The struggle for solidarity. . . ." BARRY CAME. *Maclean's*, Apr 17, 1989.
Lech Walesa. TONY KAYE. Chelsea House, 1989.
Crystal Spirit: Lech Walesa and His Poland. MARY CRAIG. ABC-CLIO, 1987.
Lech Walesa and His Poland. MARY CRAIG. Continuum, 1987.
The Book of Lech Walesa: A Collective Portrait. SOLIDARITY FRIENDS & MEMBERS. Simon & Schuster, 1982.
"Walesa, Lech." *Current Biography*, Apr. 1981.

Wallace, Irving (1916–90) Chicago-born Wallace, a best-selling novelist for three decades, began his writing career in the late 1930s, moved from freelance articles to screenwriting in the 1950s, and co-wrote several films. In 1960, he scored with his first best-seller, *The Chapman Report*, and went on to publish fifteen more novels, most of them worldwide best-sellers, although none of them were well received by the critics. *The Chapman Report* and his second novel, *The Prize,* were adapted into films. He also edited, with his wife, daughter, and son, the three *People's Almanac* best-sellers. (d. Los Angeles; June 29, 1990)

FURTHER READING

Obituary. *Current Biography*, Sept. 1990.
Obituary. *Variety*, July 4, 1990.
Obituary. *New York Times*, June 30, 1990.

Wang, An (1920–90) An inventor and computer entrepreneur, An Wang was the star of a modern rags-to-riches story. Born and educated in Shanghai, China, Wang emigrated to the United States in 1945 and received a Harvard doctorate in physics by 1948, the same year he invented the computer memory core he patented and later sold to IBM. Three years later he founded his own company, an electrical fixtures store atop a Boston garage, which he built into a computer giant, making him by 1984 one of America's richest men. He was also an active philanthropist. In 1988, he published *Lessons: An Autobiography*, written with Eugene Linden. (d. Boston, Massachusetts; March 24, 1990.)

FURTHER READING

Obituary. *Current Biography*, May 1990.
Obituary. *The Times* (of London), Mar. 27, 1990.
Obituary. *New York Times*, Mar. 25, 1990.
"An Wang. . ." KAREN BERNEY. *Nation's Business*, Dec. 1987.
"Wang, An." *Current Biography*, Jan. 1987.

Washington, Denzel (1954–) Washington emerged as a major film figure in the late 1980s, winning a 1990 Best Supporting Actor Oscar for his role in *Glory* (1989) as Trip, the runaway slave who became a Union soldier in the 54th Massachusetts regiment. This regiment, which launched a suicidal frontal assault on South Carolina's Fort Wagner, made it very clear that Blacks could make a major fighting contribution to the Union cause. In August 1990, Washington opened in two vastly different works: in the title role of *Richard III* at the New York Shakespeare Festival in Central Park, and as jazz trumpeter Bleek Gilliam in Spike Lee's film *Mo' Better Blues*, set in today's Brooklyn. Roles in *Mississippi Masala* and the action film *Ricochet* are forthcoming; Washington is also reportedly set to play the title role in Norman Jewison's film biography of Malcolm X.

Washington emerged as a strong stage player from the mid-1970s, at the New York Shakespeare Festival and in several off-Broadway plays, one of them the Negro Ensemble Company's *A Soldier's Play*; he re-created this role in the 1984 film *A Soldier's Story*. He became a television star in the 1980s as Dr. Otis Chandler in "St. Elsewhere" (1982–88). His films include *Cry Freedom* (1987), as South African journalist Steve Biko; *For Queen and Country* (1989); *The Mighty Quinn* (1989); and *Heart Condition* (1989). He attended Fordham University and studied at San Francisco's American Conservatory Theater. He is married to singer Paulette Pearson; they have two children.

FURTHER READING

"The glory days of. . . ." LAURA B. RANDOLPH. *Ebony*, Sept. 1990.
"The mo' better Denzel." ELVIS MITCHELL. *California*, Sept. 1990.
"Days of glory. . . ." PHOEBE HOBAN. *New York*, Aug. 13, 1990.
"Denzel delivers." SHARI ROMAN. *Video Magazine*, Aug. 1990.
"Denzel in the Swing." THULANI DAVIS. *American Film*, Aug. 1990
"Denzel Washington." VERONICA WEBB and HERB RITTS. *Interview*, July 1990.
Filming with Attenborough. DONALD WOODS. Holt, 1987.
"Denzel." KHEPHRA BURNS. *Essence*, Nov. 1986.

Wasserstein, Wendy (1951–) After modest off-Broadway successes in the late 1970s and early 1980s, playwright Wasserstein scored a major success with *The Heidi Chronicles* (1988), the story of a modern woman attempting to find herself in a difficult world, a semi-autobiographical theme and set of situations common to most of her work. The play won a 1988–89 season Tony for best play and a Pulitzer Prize. In 1990, she also published her first book of essays, *Bachelor Girls*, exploring similar themes. Wasserstein also writes a column for the magazine *New York Woman*.

New York City–born Wasserstein emerged as a promising new playwright with *Uncommon Women and Others* (1977), the story of a group of women undergraduates facing the same questions of self-development, with a cast that included Glenn Close, Swoosie Kurtz, Ellen Parker, and Jill Eikenberry. In the 1978 telefilm version, Meryl Streep replaced Close. Wasserstein's later work included the play *Isn't It Romantic?* (1981). She attended Mt. Holyoke College and Yale Drama School.

FURTHER READING

"Wendy Wasserstein. . . ." KIM HUBBARD. *People*, June 25, 1990.
"Wasserstein, Wendy." *Current Biography*, July 1989.
"Chronicler of frayed feminism." WALTER SHAPIRO. *Time*, Mar. 27, 1989.
"Some uncommon . . . ." PATRICIA BOSWORTH. *Working Woman*, Aug. 1984.
"Isn't it romantic? . . . ." *People*, Mar. 26, 1984.

Watkins, James David (1927–)
Admiral Watkins retired in 1986 as chief of U.S. naval operations. In 1987, he began an entirely different kind of public career when appointed head of the national AIDS advisory commission by President Ronald Reagan; he then became a prime mover in the issuance of the landmark 1988 commission report, which considerably helped to focus national attention on the fight against the disease and especially on AIDS-connected discrimination. Watkins was appointed secretary of energy by president-elect George Bush in January 1989. His first two years in office did not yield a plan for a comprehensive national energy policy, but it did yield a tough, open, and honest new look at the shocking safety and environmental pollution records of several atomic energy

plants, most notably including the Hanford, Washington, and Rocky Flats, Colorado, plants.

Watkins was a career naval officer who in 37 years moved up through a series of line and staff positions to become commander of the U.S. Sixth Fleet in 1978; vice chief of naval operations in 1979, the year he became an admiral; and commander-in-chief of the Pacific Fleet in 1981. From 1982 until his retirement in 1986, he was chief of U.S. naval operations. California-born Watkins married Sheila Jo McKinney in 1950; they have seven children. His B.S. was from the U.S. Naval Academy at Annapolis in 1949, his M.S. from the Naval Postgraduate School in 1958.

FURTHER READING

"Hands-on Energy leader." WILLIAM LANOUETTE. *Bulletin of the Atomic Scientists*, May 1990.
"The heat is on!. . . ." THOMAS A. LEWIS. *National Wildlife*, Apr.–May 1990.
"James D. Watkins. . . ." WILLIAM LANOUETTE. *Bulletin of the Atomic Scientists*, Jan.–Feb. 1990.
"The new broom." *Economist*, Dec. 23, 1989.
"Admiral Watkins's. . . ." STEPHEN J. HEDGES. *U.S. News & World Report*, Aug. 14, 1989.
"Energy czar. . . ." VICKY CAHAN, et al. *Business Week*, July 24, 1989.
"Watkins, James David." *Current Biography*, Mar. 1989.
"The metamorphosis of. . . ." LYNN ROSELLINI. *U.S. News & World Report*, July 4, 1988.

Watson, Elizabeth M. (1950–) On January 19, 1990, career police officer Watson was named police chief of Houston, Texas; it was the largest American city to have a woman chief of police, her force numbering over 4,000. Watson joined the Houston force in 1972 and rose steadily through the ranks, becoming a detective in 1976, a lieutenant in 1981, and Houston's first woman captain in 1984 and first deputy chief in 1987. She succeeded Lee P. Brown, who left to become New York City police commissioner. During her first year in office, she won a long-overdue raise for her department and further developed the concept of community policing, essentially a move toward decentralization aimed at making her department more responsive to the needs and views of people in Houston's several communities.

Watson graduated from Texas Tech University in 1971. She married Robert Watson, also a Houston police officer, in 1976; they have three children.

FURTHER READING

"Reforming our image. . . ." WALTER SHAPIRO. *Time*, Nov. 26, 1990.
"Cosmo talks to. . . ." BARBARA HUSTEDT CROOK. *Cosmopolitan*, Oct. 1990.
"To each her own. . . ." WENDY COLE. *Time*, Fall, 1990.
"Pregnancy and the chief." *Time*, June 18, 1990.
"Pistol-packin' mama." *Time*, Feb. 19, 1990.

Weaver, Sigourney (Susan Weaver, 1949–) Weaver stood up for her rights this year. She, along with the director and producers of *Aliens* (1979), took the 20th-Century Fox film studio to court, claiming that they had not received their due shares of the net profits from the movie. She also took her case to the public in the July issue of *Glamour* magazine, by blasting the sexist pay scales of Hollywood, noting specifically that the studio was resisting her demands to be paid as much as a male star would make for the scheduled sequel, *Aliens III*. In England, CBS/Fox released a new version of the original *Aliens* containing 17 minutes of previously cut material, much of it dealing with the motivations of Weaver's character Ripley; release of the new version was planned for the U.S. as well. Weaver's recent work includes the blockbuster fantasy-comedy *Ghostbusters II* (1989). Late in 1990, she acted on the London stage, joining Redgrave sisters Lynn and Vanessa in a production of Chekhov's *The Three Sisters* directed by their brother Corin Redgrave, with a cast including his daughter Jemma Redgrave and also Christopher Reeve.

New York City–born Weaver acted on stage from the mid-1970s, most notably in *Hurlyburly* (1984) and *The Merchant of Venice* (1987) although she is best known for such films as *Aliens* (1979; and its 1986 sequel), *Eyewitness* (1981), *Deal of the Century* (1983), *The Year of Living Dangerously* (1983), *Ghostbusters* (1984; and its 1989 sequel), *Gorillas in the Mist* (1988) in the Oscar-nominated role of Dian Fossey, and *Working Girl* (1988). She attended Stanford University and Yale Drama School. She married James Simpson in 1984; they have one child.

FURTHER READING

"Weaver, Sigourney." *Current Biography*, Mar. 1989.
Sigourney Weaver. T. D. MAGUFFEE. St. Martin's, 1989.
"Sigourney weaves. . . ." JESSE KORNBLUTH. *Cosmopolitan*, Dec. 1988.
"Dream Weaver. . . ." CHRISTOPHER DURANG and ROBERT MAPPLETHORPE. *Interview*, July 1988.
"Sigourney takes control." MARCIA PALLY. *Film Comment*, Dec. 1986.
"Sigourney Weaver. . . ." MICHAEL SMALL. *People*, Sept. 8, 1986.
"Sigourney Weaver." *Playboy*, Aug. 1986.
"The years of. . . ." RICHARD CORLISS. *Time*, July 28, 1986.

Wedemeyer, Albert Coady (1897–1989) General Wedemeyer was one of the key U.S. military planners of World War II. During the 1930s, he was an army officer in China, and in the late 1930s he was the only American graduate of the German general staff school in Berlin; both the Chinese and German experiences were to prove invaluable during and after World War II. He served in War Plans under future general Dwight D. Eisenhower and General George C. Marshall in 1941, and in 1943 powerfully supported the American buildup in Britain and cross-channel invasion on D-Day that spelled the beginning of the end for the Nazi war machine. In 1943, he was transferred to Southeast Asia, and in 1944 he succeeded General Joseph Stillwell as commander of American forces in China. After the war against the Axis ended, he urged strong support for Chiang Kai-shek and a military buildup in South Korea, lost both arguments, and retired from the army in 1951. (d. Fort Belvoir, Virginia, December 17, 1989.)

FURTHER READING

Obituary. *Current Biography*, Feb. 1990.
Obituary. *The Times* (of London), Dec. 22, 1989.
Obituary. *New York Times*, Dec. 20, 1989.
"Cheers." *National Review*, May 3, 1985.
"The man who. . . ." KEITH EILER. *American Heritage*, Oct. 1983.

Wheeler, Lyle (1905–90) One of Hollywood's leading art directors from the mid-1930s through the mid-1970s, Wheeler won Oscars for *Gone With the Wind* (1939), *Anna and the King of Siam* (1946), *The Robe* (1953), and *The Diary of Anne Frank* (1959) and received twenty more Oscar nominations as well. His first film was *The Garden of Allah* (1936), his last *Posse* (1975). He also designed for such classics as *Rebecca* (1940), *My Darling Clementine* (1946), *Gentlemen's Agreement* (1947), *The King and I* (1956), and *South Pacific* (1958). (d. Woodland Hills, California; January 10, 1990)

FURTHER READING

Obituary. *Variety*, Jan. 17, 1990.
Obituary. *The Times* (of London), Jan. 15, 1990.
Obituary. *New York Times*, Jan. 13, 1990.
"His Oscars gone. . . ." SUSAN REED. *People*, Mar. 27, 1989.

White, Byron Raymond (1917–) During the 1989–90 session, Justice White continued on in the moderate role he has pursued during his three decades on the U.S. Supreme Court. Three decisions in which he wrote the majority opinions, all issued on the same day, June 18, illustrate his role: In *Ohio* v. *Osborne*, he upheld an Ohio law that made it a crime to possess pornographic photographs of children, a law lauded by conservatives and seen as an attack on free speech by the Court's liberal minory. In *Missouri* v. *Jenkins*, he made it legal for a federal judge to order special local taxes to further school desegregation even though the state did not permit such taxes; his decision was lauded by civil rights advocates and attacked by conservatives. And in the 7–2 *Minnesota* v. *Olson* decision, he called the warrantless arrest of a man who was a guest in a friend's apartment overnight unconstitutional, a position taken by most of his colleagues, liberal or conservative.

Colorado-born White was football star "Whizzer" White in the late 1930s. After World War II, he practiced law in Denver until 1960. He then campaigned for John F. Kennedy in 1960; as president, Kennedy appointed him a deputy attorney general in 1961 and then a Supreme Court justice in 1962. He is married to Marion Stearns; they have two children. His B.A. was from the University of Colorado in 1938, his LL.B. from Yale in 1945.

FURTHER READING

"Byron White leads. . . ." DAVID A. KAPLAN. *Newsweek*, Apr 30, 1990.
Eight Men and a Lady. HERMAN SCHWARTZ, ANDREA NEAL, and DAVID SAVAGE. National Press, 1990.
"What they say it is. . . ." *Time*, July 6, 1987.
"Nine who decide. . . ." ELIZABETH WARD. *Scholastic Update*, Sept. 8, 1986.
"White's flight. . . ." NATHAN LEWIN. *New Republic*, Aug. 27, 1984.
"When judges become targets." *U.S. News & World Report*, July 26, 1982.

White, Patrick (Patrick Victor Martindale White, 1912–90) White was the most celebrated Australian writer of the twentieth century and the first to win worldwide recognition, receiving the Nobel Prize for literature in 1973. Although his large body of work includes short stories, screenplays, and plays, his major work is to be found in his powerful, often painful and abrasive novels, such as *Happy Valley* (1939), *The Living and the Dead* (1941), *The Tree of Man* (1955), *Voss* (1957), *The Solid Mandala* (1966), *The Eye of the Storm* (1973), and *The Twyborn Affair* (1979). In 1982 he published the autobiographical *Flaws in the Glass: A Self-Portrait*. (d. Sydney; September 30, 1990.)

FURTHER READING

Obituary. *Current Biography*, Nov. 1990
Obituary. *The Times* (of London), Oct. 1, 1990.
Obituary. *New York Times*, Oct. 1, 1990.
Patrick White. MAY-BRITT AKERHOLT. Humanities, 1988.
Patrick White. JOHN COLMER. Routledge Chapman & Hall, 1984.
Patrick White. BRIAN KIERNAN. St. Martin's, 1980.

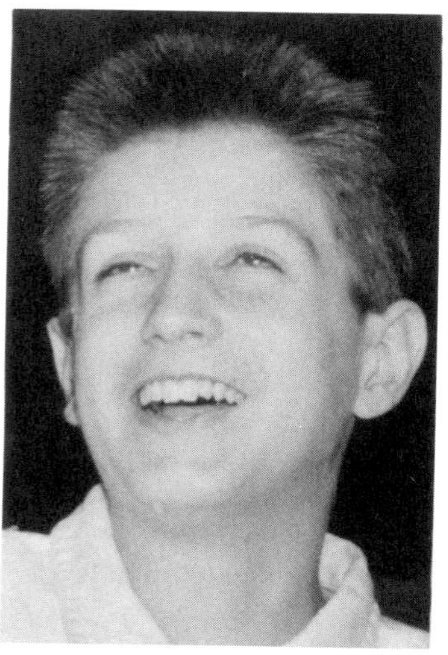

White, Ryan (1972–90) A hemophiliac, White contracted AIDS through a blood transfusion while in his early teens. In 1985, in the extraordinarily fearful climate of that time, he was barred from attending school in Kokomo, Indiana. His struggle for the right to attend school like any other normal teenager touched off a major national debate that helped many to overcome their fears and learn to treat AIDS victims with dignity and compassion. Ryan White won his court fight to attend school, but he and his family were then treated so badly in Kokomo that they were forced to leave that city, moving to the small farming town of Cicero, Indiana. There, treated with decency and with growing support from shocked and angered people all over the country, including many celebrities and politicians, Ryan White was able to attend school unafraid and to live out the rest of his life in dignity. On April 8,

1990, in Indianapolis, Indiana, 18-year-old Ryan White died of complications caused by AIDS. His *Ryan White: My Own Story*, written with Ann M. Cunningham, was published posthumously in 1991.

FURTHER READING

"'I don't want. . . .'" Ann Marie Cunningham. *Ladies' Home Journal*, Aug. 1990.
"'What happens. . . .'" Ray Probasco. *Saturday Evening Post*, July–Aug. 1990.
"Candle in the wind." Bill Shaw. *People*, Apr. 23, 1990.
"The 'miracle' of. . . ." *Time*, Apr. 23, 1990.
"Beloved pariah." *U.S. News & World Report*, Apr. 23, 1990.
Obituary. *New York Times*, Apr. 9, 1990.
"The quiet victories of. . . ." Jack Friedman. *People*, May 30, 1988.
"The happier days for. . . ." Cory SerVaas. *Saturday Evening Post*, Mar. 1988.

Wilder, L. Douglas (Lawrence Douglas Wilder, 1931–) On November 7, 1989, Wilder won the Virginia gubernatorial election, becoming the first Black governor in the history of the United States. The historic "first" was accomplished by a razor-thin 50.1 percent win over Republican candidate J. Marshall Coleman. Wilder survived a recount and was inaugurated on January 13, 1990. During his first year in office, Wilder encountered very serious deficit problems in Virginia as tax revenues were far less than forecast; he introduced large budget cuts and a series of austerity measures, developing a quite conservative financial stance. At the same time, he came forward strongly as a liberal Democrat on the national scene, his many speeches around the country suggesting to many that he had 1992 presidential ambitions.

Richmond-born Wilder came to the governorship after a long career in state government. He was a Democratic member of the Virginia Senate from 1969 to 1985, and was lieutenant governor of his state from 1986 to 1989. Richmond-born Wilder has three children. His B.S. was from Virginia Union University in 1961, his J.D. from Howard University in 1959.

FURTHER READING

"Mild Wilder. . . ." Fred Barnes. *New Republic*, Aug. 13, 1990.
"Wilder, Lawrence Douglas." *Current Biography*, Apr. 1990.
"The first Black elected governor. . . ." Laura B. Randolph. *Ebony*, Feb. 1990.
Wilder: Hold Fast to Dreams: A Biography of L. Douglas Wilder. Donald P. Baker. Seven Locks, 1990
Claiming the Dream: The Victorious Campaign of Douglas Wilder of Virginia. Margaret Edds. Algonquin, 1990.
"Doug Wilder. . . ." Matthew Cooper. *U.S. News & World Report*, Nov. 20, 1989.
"The Wilder side. . . ." Fred Barnes. *New Republic*, Nov. 13, 1989.

Williams, Robin (1952–) Actor-comedian Williams scored a major hit as the freedom-affirming English teacher in *The Dead Poets Society* (1989), receiving a Best Actor Oscar nomination. In the same year, he appeared on the New York stage opposite Steve Martin in a revival of Samuel Beckett's *Waiting for Godot*, and was the star of the film *Cadillac Man*. He, Whoopi Goldberg, and Billy Crystal co-hosted the fourth annual *Comic Relief* benefit for the homeless. In late 1990, Williams scored still another hit as Dr. Oliver Sacks in Penny Marshall's film *Awakenings*, opposite Robert De Niro as his catatonic patient in a cast that includes Max Von Sydow and John Heard. Forthcoming is a role as the adult Peter Pan in Steven Spielberg's long-awaited film opposite Dustin Hoffman as Captain Hook. Also forthcoming is a starring role opposite Jeff Bridges in Terry Gilliam's *The Fisher King*.

Chicago-born Williams began his career as a comic in cabaret, playing many West Coast clubs, and then moved into television in variety and then as the star of *Mork and Mindy* (1978–82). He became a leading film star of the 1980s in such movies as *The World According to Garp* (1982), *Moscow on the Hudson* (1984), *Good Morning Vietnam* (1987), and *The Adventures of Baron Munchausen* (1989). He was formerly married to Valerie Velardi, married Marsha Garces in 1989, and has two children. He attended Claremont College, Marin College, and the Juilliard School.

FURTHER READING

"Talking with. . . ." CARSON JONES. *Redbook*, Jan. 1991.
"Robin Williams. . . ." JOE MORGENSTERN. New York Times Magazine, Nov. 11, 1990.
"Robin Williams has. . . ." LISA GRUNWALD. *Esquire*, June 1989.
"Actor. . . ." *Life*, Spring 1989.
"The zany world of. . . ." JOHN CULHANE. *Reader's Digest*, Apr. 1988; Canadian version, June 1988.
"Robin's morning glory." LOUISE BERNIKOW. *Cosmopolitan*, Apr. 1988.
To Be Somebody. ROBIN WILLIAMS. Carlton, 1989.
"A comic's crisis. . . ." BRAD DARRACH. *People*, Feb. 22, 1988.
"Robin Williams. . . ." BONNIE SCHIFFMAN. *Rolling Stone*, Feb. 25, 1988.
"Black humor. . . ." MICHAEL REESE. *Newsweek*, Jan. 4, 1988.

Williams, William Appleman (1921–90) A leading historian, Williams was president of the American Historical Association in 1980–81, and was throughout his career a sharp critic of American foreign policy from a New Left point of view. Williams described himself as a socialist. A "revisionist," his work questioned many until-then majority views in American history. His many books include *American-Russian Relations, 1784–1987* (1950); *The Tragedy of American Diplomacy* (1960), *The United States, Cuba and Castro* (1962), *The Great Evasion* (1964), *The Roots of the Modern American Empire* (1969), *History as a Way of Learning* (1975), *America Confronts a Revolutionary World: 1776–1976)* (1976), and *Empire as a Way of Life* (1980). He taught at the University of Wisconsin (1960–68) and Oregon State University (1968–86). (d. Newport, Oregon; March 5, 1990)

FURTHER READING

Obituary. MIKE WALLACE. *Nation*, Apr. 9, 1990.
Obituary. *New York Times*, Mar. 9, 1990.

Willis, Bruce (Bruce Walter Willis, 1955–) Building on the success of his 1988 action film *Die Hard*, Willis returned in 1990 as detective John McClane in the extremely popular *Die Hard II*, set during an attempted airport takeover by terrorists, with a cast that once again included Bonnie Bedelia and William Atherton. In late December, he starred opposite Melanie Griffith and Tom Hanks in Brian De Palma's film *The Bonfire of the Vanities*, based on the Tom Wolfe novel. His voice, along with those of Roseanne Barr and Damon Wayans, was featured in the *Look Who's Talking Too*, a comedy starring John Travolta and Kirstie Alley. Forthcoming is the action film *Hudson Hawk*.

German-born Willis worked in the New York theater from the late 1970s and appeared in several small film roles in the early 1980s. He emerged as a star on television in the long-running series "Moonlighting" (1985–89) and with *Blind Date* (1987) moved into starring roles in films. He went on to star in *Sunset* (1988) and then in the greatly popular action film *Die Hard* (1988). *In Country* (1989), though unsuccessful at the box office, showed him in a more serious light. Willis attended Montclair State College. He married actress Demi Moore in 1987; they have one child.

FURTHER READING

"Bruce on the loose." ANTHONY HADEN-GUEST. *Vanity Fair*, Jan. 1991.
"Bruce Willis. . . ." FRED ROBBINS. *McCall's*, June 1989.
"Bruce Willis. . . ." *Video Review*, Feb. 1989.
"Playboy interview. . . ." LAWRENCE GROBEL. *Playboy*, Nov. 1988.
"Bruce Willis. . . ." DENNIS WATLINGTON. *Cosmopolitan*, Sept. 1988.
"Bruce Willis. . . ." AUDREY LAVIN. *Redbook*, Aug. 1988.
"Riding for a fall?. . . ." SUSAN PETERS. *Life*, Nov. 1987.
"Willis, Bruce." *Current Biography*, Feb. 1987.

Wilson, August (1945–) The celebrated playwright, who has so far set all of his work during different decades of the Black 20th-century American experience, introduced a major new play in 1990: *The Piano Lesson*. The work, set in his home city of Pittsburgh in the 1930s, starred Charles S. Dutton as Willie Boy opposite S. Epatha Merkerson as his sister Berniece; Lloyd Richards directed. Wilson won a second Pulitzer Prize for the play (his first was for *Fences*) on May 14, a few days before it opened to excellent reviews on Broadway. *The Piano Lesson* was also chosen as best play of the season by the New York Drama Critics Circle. In January, Wilson stirred dispute with his request (not as a matter of contractual right) that Paramount secure a Black director for the forthcoming film adaptation of *Fences*. Forthcoming is the play *Two Trains Running*.

Playwright and poet Wilson emerged as a major figure in the American theater during the 1980s; his plays also include *Jitney* (1982), *Ma Rainey's Black Bottom* (1984), and *Fences* (1987), which won a best play Tony and a Pulitzer Prize and in which James Earl Jones won a Best Actor Tony. Wilson was formerly married.

FURTHER READING

"An elegant duet. . . ." RACHAEL MIGLER. *GQ—Gentlemen's Quarterly*, Apr. 1990.
"Fine-tuning. . . ." MEL GUSSOW. *New York Times Magazine*, Sept. 10, 1989.
"The light in August." CHIP BROWN. *Esquire*, Apr. 1989.
"On Broadway. . . ." CHARLAYNE HUNTER-GAULT. *Vogue*, Aug. 1988.
"Exorcising the demons. . . ." WILLIAM A. HENRY III. *Time*, Apr. 11, 1988.
"August Wilson. . . ." ALEX POINSETT. *Ebony*, Nov. 1987.
"Wilson, August." *Current Biography*, Aug. 1987.
"August Wilson." Brent Staples. *Essence*, Aug. 1987.

Wilson, Richard (1934–90) Wilson, head of the Oglala Sioux Tribal Council in the early 1970s, was sharply criticized by dissenting Sioux for lack of militancy and a too-cooperative approach in dealing with the U.S. government. In 1973, to dramatize a set of demands, an estimated 300 members of the American Indian Movement occupied Wounded Knee, South Dakota, site of the historic 1890 massacre of the Sioux by U.S. troops. They were ultimately removed only after a pitched battle with U.S. marshals, with many wounded and two Sioux dead. Wilson was elected to a second term as tribal council head in 1974. (d. Rapid City, South Dakota; February 2, 1990)

FURTHER READING

Obituary. *New York Times*, Feb. 4, 1990.

Winfield, Dave (David Mark Winfield, 1951–) A leading baseball player, Winfield carried on a long feud with Yankee owner George Steinbrenner that led to his 1990 trade to the California Angels. Baseball Commissioner Fay Vincent, finding that Steinbrenner had made a private investigation of Winfield and had paid gambler Paul Spira for information thought to be derogatory to Winfield, on July 30, 1990, permanently barred Steinbrenner from active management of the Yankees and ordered him to bring his controlling interest in the team to below 50 percent. Winfield stayed with the Angels and had a good, though not spectacular, year.

Minnesota-born Winfield has been a star outfielder in both major leagues; he played with the San Diego Padres from 1973 to 1980 and with the Yankees from 1980 until the 1990 trade to the Angels. His disagreements with Steinbrenner began early, with Winfield's court case to force Steinbrenner to make what he alleged were agreed-upon payments to

Winfield's charitable foundation. In 1988, he published *Winfield: A Player's Life*, written with Tom Parker. He attended the University of Minnesota.

FURTHER READING

Dave Winfield. JUDY MONROE. Crestwood House, 1988.
"Winfield, Dave." *Current Biography*, Jan. 1984.
Dave Winfield: The $23 Million Man. GENE SCHOOR. Scarborough House, 1982.
Picture Story of Dave Winfield. HOWARD LISS. Messner, 1982.

Winfrey, Oprah (1954–) Broadcast journalist, producer, and actress Winfrey has become a world celebrity, as a result of the success of her daytime television talk and interview show. Coupled with her control over its production, it has made her one of the highest paid and most visible of the world's broadcast journalists, closely followed by millions of fans, who are greatly interested by even such matters as Winfrey's highly publicized years-long struggle to control her weight. Beyond the daytime series, in 1989 she starred as Mattie Michael, a poor Black woman attempting to survive in an inner city ghetto, in the television miniseries "The Women of Brewster Place," based on the Florence Naylor novel. In May 1990, she developed the role as the center of the short-lived television prime-time series, "Brewster Place." In 1990, she received the NAACP's Image Award, as entertainer of the year.

Mississippi-born Winfrey began her broadcasting career in 1972, as a reporter for WVOL radio while still in school and then for WTVF-TV (both in Nashville), then moved to Baltimore's WJZ-TV as co-anchor in 1976. Becoming co-host of the station's morning show, she began a new career; she scored a major success as the host of *AM Chicago* for Chicago's WLS-TV, which was renamed "The Oprah Winfrey Show" in 1984 and became a nationally syndicated hit show. She also heads her own production company. She has appeared in several films, including *The Color Purple* (1985) and *Native Son* (1986). She attended Tennessee State University.

FURTHER READING

Oprah Winfrey. GERALDINE WOODS. Dillon, 1991.
"A brain for. . . ." MATTHEW SCHIFRIN and PETER NEWCOMB. *Forbes*, Oct. 1, 1990.
"Oprah Winfrey tells. . . ." *Jet*, Sept. 17, 1990.
Oprah Winfrey: TV Talk Show Host. MARGARET BEATON. Childrens, 1990.
Oprah Winfrey: Talk Show Host & Actress. LILLIE PATTERSON and CORNELIA H. WRIGHT. Enslow, 1990.
Oprah Winfrey: Media Success Story. ANNE SAIDMAN. Lerner, 1990.
"Oprah Winfrey. . . ." LARKIN WARREN. *Esquire*, Dec. 1989.
"The importance of. . . ." BARBARA GRIZZUTI HARRISON. *New York Times Magazine*, June 11, 1989.
"Simply . . . Oprah!" JULIA CAMERON. *Cosmopolitan*, Feb. 1989.
"Oprah Winfrey. . . ." JOHN CULHANE. *Reader's Digest*, Feb. 1989.
"Winfrey takes all." MARCIA ANN GILLESPIE. *Ms.*, Nov. 1988.
Everybody Loves Oprah!: Her Remarkable Life Story. NORMAN KING. Morrow, 1988.
"Winfrey, Oprah." *Current Biography*, Mar. 1987.
Oprah! ROBERT WALDRON. St. Martin, 1987.

Winger, Debra (1955–) Winger began 1990 with *Everybody Wins,* a film that on paper showed much promise. The screenplay was by Arthur Miller (his first since *The Misfits* in 1961); the director was Karel Reisz; cinematographer, score, and cast, including Nick Nolte playing private eye to Winger's shady lady, were all top-notch. But for reasons not entirely clear to the critics, the film simply did not work and sank almost without a trace. She moved on from that to another project of enormous promise: Bernardo Bertolucci's *The Sheltering Sky*, based on Paul Bowles's best-selling novel, a post–World War II existential tale of a "caravan of horrors." The film was shot in the Sahara late in 1989 and opened late in 1990. Here Winger fared far better; her performance as Kit Moresby, opposite John Malkovich's Port, drew special praise.

Cleveland-born Winger began her career in television, most notably in *Wonder Woman* (1976–77), and then quickly moved into films. She emerged as a highly regarded dramatic actress in the late 1970s in such films as *French Postcards* (1979), *Urban Cowboy* (1980), *Cannery Row* (1982), *An Officer and a Gentleman* (1982), *Terms of Endearment* (1983), *Legal Eagles* (1986), *Black Widow* (1987), and *Betrayed* (1988). She attended California State University. She was formerly married and has one child.

FURTHER READING

"Straight shooting star." LYNN HIRSCHBERG. *American Film*, July–Aug. 1988.
"The taming of Debra Winger." ARTHUR LUBOW. *Cosmopolitan*, May 1987.
"Debra Winger. . . ." NANCY COLLINS. *Esquire*, Dec. 1986.
Debra Winger: Hollywood's Wild Child. M. J. CAHILL. St. Martin's, 1985.
"Winger, Debra." *Current Biography*, July 1984.
"For her family and fans. . . ." *People*, Feb. 6, 1984.

Wonder, Stevie (Steveland Judkins Morris, 1950–) Singer, composer, and instrumentalist Wonder is one of the leading popular musicians of the past three decades, his extraordinary accomplishments made even more so because of his lifelong blindness. His recent work has largely been in performance, for many of the social causes he has made a major part of his life and work, as in his summer 1990 appearance at the third annual Los Angeles *That's What Friends Are For* AIDS benefit concert; his participation in the album *Nobody's Child: Romanian Angel Appeal*, a benefit for Romanian orphans; and in the video *Raise Your Voices: Lift Up Every Voice and Sing,* benefiting the NAACP, the United Negro College Fund and sickle cell anemia research.

Wonder was a child prodigy, a multitalented musician who sang and played harmonica, piano, organ, and drums and later composed much of his work for the synthesizer. His first record, for Motown, was *Little Stevie Wonder, the 12 Year Old Genius* (1967). He went on to become one of the most popular musicians of the next three decades. Many of his songs have become American and worldwide standards, such as "My Cherie Amour" (1969), the Grammy-winning "You Are the Sunshine of My Life" (1972), "Superstition" (1973), "Living for the City" (1975), and the Oscar-winning "I Just Called to Say I Love You" (1984). His many records include such works as the Grammy-winning *Innervisions* (1973), the Grammy-winning *Songs In the Key of Life* (1976), *Journey Through the Secret Life of Plants* (1979), *In Square Circle* (1986), and *Characters* (1987).

FURTHER READING

"Stevie Wonder." MICHAEL GOLDBERG. *Rolling Stone,* Nov. 5, 1987.
Twenty Years of Rolling Stone. JANN S. WENNER. Friendly Press, 1987.
"The secret dreams of. . . ." *Ebony, Dec. 1986.*
"Stevie Wonder's world. . . ." CLAUDIA DOWLING. *Life,* Oct. 1986.
"Stevie Wonder." MARTIN TORGOFF. *Interview,* June 1986.
"The timeless world. . . ." MICHAEL GOLDBERG. *Rolling Stone,* Apr. 10, 1986.
Stevie Wonder. JOHN SWENSON. *Harper*, 1986.
Stevie Wonder. JEFFREY PEISCH. Ballantine, 1984.
Mr. Wonderful: Stevie Wonder. LEONARD PITTS, JR. Sharon, 1984.

Woods, James (1947–) Actor Woods won a 1990 Emmy as Bill Wilson, an alcoholic and then recovering alcoholic who was a co-founder of Alcoholics Anonymous, opposite James Garner as co-founder Dr. Robert Smith, in *My Name Is Bill W* (1989); Daniel Petrie directed. In 1989, Woods also starred as the ex-radical lawyer in *True Believer* and in *Immediate Family* opposite Glenn Close. Forthcoming is *The Boys*, a television film about two long-term friends (John Lithgow is the other lead) who face a terminal illness together. *The Hard Way*, with Woods as a New York detective and Michael J. Fox as the film actor studying him for a role, opened in early 1991.

Utah-born Woods appeared on the New York stage and in films in the early 1970s and emerged as a leading player in such films as *The Onion Field* (1979), *Fast Walking* (1982), *Split Image* (1982), *Videodrome* (1983), *Once Upon a Time in America* (1984), *Against All Odds* (1984), *Joshua Then and Now* (1985), *Best Seller* (1987), and *Cop* (1987). He has also appeared in many telefilms, winning an earlier Emmy for *Promise* (1986). He attended the University of California and the Massachusetts Institute of Technology. He has been married twice.

FURTHER READING

"James Woods. . . ." *American Film*, May 1990.
"Woods, James." *Current Biography*, Nov. 1989.
"Fighting his way. . . ." RICHARD B. WOODWARD. *New York Times Magazine*, Aug. 20, 1989.
"James Woods. . . ." NEIL HICKEY. *TV Guide*, Apr 29, 1989.
"Arresting appeal. . . ." BETSY BORNS. *Harper's Bazaar*, Feb. 1989.
"The winning new world. . . ." TOM GREEN. *Cosmopolitan*, Nov. 1987.
"Out of the Woods." EVE BABITZ. *American Film*, May 1987.

Woodward, Joanne (1930–) Beginning in late 1990, film audiences had the very rare treat of seeing actress Joanne Woodward and her husband Paul Newman appear together onscreen, playing the title roles in James Ivory's *Mr. and Mrs. Bridge*, based on the Evan S. Connell novels. Although some critics found the film overly decorous, Woodward garnered widespread praise for her luminous, sensitive performance as India Bridge, the unfulfilled wife of an affluent mid-20th-century Midwest attorney. The portrayal won her the New York Film Critics Circle's award as best actress of the year and several other nominations, including the Golden Globe, National Film Critics Circle, and the Academy Awards (at the end losing to others in all). Privately, Woodward continued working against drug addiction, through the Scott Newman Center in Los Angeles, named for Newman's son, whose death was drug-related; in particular she focused on the problem of babies born with drug or alcohol addictions. She also spoke out against censorship by the government through the National Endowment for the Arts.

Georgia-born Woodward has been a leading actress for over three decades, since her Best Actress Oscar–winning role in *The Three Faces of Eve* (1957); she went on to star in such films as *The Long Hot Summer*, (1958), *The Sound and the Fury*, (1959), *The Fugitive Kind* (1960), *The Stripper* (1963), *A Fine Madness*, (1965), *Rachel, Rachel* (1968), *Summer Wishes, Winter Dreams* (1973), *The Drowning Pool* (1975), and *The Glass Menagerie* (1987). She has also played in some notable television films, such as *Do You Remember Love* (1985). She married Paul Newman in 1958; they have three children. She attended Louisiana State University from 1947 to 1949, and studied at the Neighborhood Playhouse.

FURTHER READING

"Paul Newman and. . . ." MAUREEN DOWD. *McCall's*, Jan. 1991.
"Mr. and Mrs. Bridge." GRAHAM FULLER. *Interview*, Nov. 1990.
"Joanne Woodward. . . ." BETH WEINHOUSE. *Redbook*, Jan. 1990.
Paul and Joanne: A Biography of Paul Newman and Joanne Woodward. JOE MORELLA and EDWARD Z. EPSTEIN. Delacorte, 1988.
"Joanne Woodward. . . ." MARY CANTWELL. *Vogue*, Nov. 1987.
Actress to Actress. RITA GAM. Lyons & Burford, 1986.

Wyeth, Andrew (Andrew Newell Wyeth, 1917–) For five decades Wyeth has been a leading American painter whose work is prized by museums and collectors and studied throughout the world. He unveiled a great surprise in 1986—a collection of 240 previously unknown oil paintings, watercolors, and drawings done from 1971 to 1985, all of them of his Chadds Ford, Pennsylvania neighbor Helga Testof, some of them major additions to his known body of work. A volume of the works was published in 1987. In November 1989, the works made news again when sold at auction, along with another group of his works (the Olson collection), for an estimated $40–45 million. The specific price and the buyer were undisclosed, although the works toured Japan during 1990. In November 1990, Wyeth received a congressional gold medal from President George Bush at the White House; the medal was developed from a portrait of Wyeth by his son, Jamie Wyeth.

Wyeth was born in Chadds Ford, the setting for much of his work; he is a celebrated American realist who has exhibited since 1937 and whose body of work includes some of the best-known paintings of his time, including the signature *Christina's World* (1948), *Evening at Kuerner's* (1970), and the Helga pictures. He married Betsy Merle James in 1940. They have two children, Nicholas and James; the latter is also a painter. Andrew Wyeth is the son of illustrator N. C. Wyeth.

FURTHER READING

"Wyeth since Helga. . . ." THOMAS HOVING. *Connoisseur*, Dec. 1990.
Wyeth People: A Portrait of Andrew Wyeth as Seen by His Friends and Neighbors. GENE LOGSDON. Taylor, 1988.
"Heavily hyped Helga. . . ." JOHN UPDIKE. *New Republic*, Dec. 7, 1987.
"From the Wyeth house. . . ." MICHAEL ENNIS. *Texas Monthly*, Oct. 1987.
"Wyeth's world. . . ." RICHARD MERYMAN. *Life*, June 1987.
An American Vision: Three Generations of Wyeth Art. JAMES H. DUFF. Bulfinch, 1987.
"Andrew Wyeth's. . . ." RICHARD CORLISS and RICHARD ZOGLIN. *Time*, Aug. 18, 1986.
"Andrew Wyeth." *Current Biography*, Nov. 1981.

Wyeth, Nathaniel (Nathaniel Convers Wyeth, 1912–90) The brother of artist Andrew Wyeth and the son of illustrator N. C. Wyeth, Nathaniel Wyeth chose an entirely different career. He was an engineer and inventor who worked at E. I. Du Pont de Nemours & Company through the mid-1970s. His best known invention was a kind of plastic bottle (made of PET, or polyethylene terephthalate) that became widely used throughout the world. (d. Glen Cove, Maine; July 4, 1990)

FURTHER READING

Obituary. *New York Times*, July 7, 1990.

Wynne, Paul (1943–90) A broadcast journalist, Wynne worked as a reporter, usually covering entertainment, at local television stations in San Francisco from 1979–84. Afflicted by AIDS, he returned to broadcasting in January 1990 with his unique, shocking, and moving *Paul Wynne's Journal*, a trailblazing broadcast diary of his descent to death, toward the end taped from his hospital bed. (d. San Francisco; July 5, 1990)

FURTHER READING

Obituary. *Variety*, July 11, 1990.
Obituary. *New York Times*, July 6, 1990.
"Humanizing AIDS." ANNA PRODANOU. *Maclean's*, May 7, 1990.
"Using the time. . . ." WILLIAM PLUMMER. *People*, Feb. 12, 1990.

Xu Xiangqian (1901–90) Marshal Xu was one of the last of the leaders who took Chinese Communism through the civil war, the Long March, and the war with Japan. He was a graduate of the first class at the Huangpu Academy, joined the Communist Party in 1927, survived the 1934 retreat north known as the Long March, and finished the war against Japan and then the revolution as an army commander in north China. He held several positions in the new government, including that of army chief of staff, was briefly out of power from 1967–69, and was minister of defense from 1978 to 1981. (d. Beijing; September 21, 1990.)

FURTHER READING

Obituary. *The Times* (of London), Sept. 24, 1990.
Obituary. *New York Times*, Sept. 22, 1990.

Yeltsin, Boris (Boris Nikolayevich Yeltsin, 1931–) Yeltsin, a former supporter of Mikhail Gorbachev, moved into opposition in 1987, becoming a leader of those who felt that reform was not proceeding quickly enough. In 1989, he won the Moscow elections to the Congress of People's Deputies by an overwhelming majority. He was at first denied election to the Supreme Soviet by the Communist majority but then elected after a major reformist protest and became an opposition leader in the Soviet parliament.

In March 1990, Yeltsin somewhat changed his political focus when he also won election as a delegate to the Russian Federation's Supreme Soviet. On May 29, he was elected president of the Russian Federation and began a campaign to secure greater Russian autonomy from the central government, sometimes calling it a fight for Russian independence. At the same time, he became a leader of those criticizing Gorbachev's economic reforms as inadequate. In July, he also resigned from the Communist Party. In early August, Yeltsin and Gorbachev agreed in principle on radical economic reform, although not on all the specifics. But in early September, Yeltsin introduced his own "500 day" crash economic plan for the Russian Federation; in late September he opposed the granting of emergency powers to Gorbachev and in late October he criticized the Soviet emergency economic plans as inadequate. By early 1991, he led those opposed to central government intervention in the Baltic Republics and to growing curbs on freedom of expression and dissent. In 1990, Yeltsin published his autobiographical *Against the Grain*.

Yeltsin worked as an engineer from 1955 to 1968, then took up Communist Party work in his home city of Sverdlovsk. During the early 1980s, he strongly supported and was close to Mikhail Gorbachev; Yeltsin moved into far higher party positions in 1985, when

Gorbachev came to power. He was mayor of Moscow from 1985 to 1987 and secretary of the Communist Party Central Committee in 1985–1986. Yeltsin attended the Urals Polytechnic Institute.

FURTHER READING

"Yeltsin . . . ." John Kohan. *Time*, Jan. 7, 1991.
"New Yeltsin . . . ." JEFF TRIMBLE. *U.S. News & World Report*, Dec. 31, 1990.
"The 'Cassandra of . . . .'" STEPAN KISELEV. *World Press Review*, Nov. 1990.
"What makes . . . ." MIKHAIL ZARAEV. *World Monitor*, Aug. 1990.
"'Yeltsin was . . . .'" JEFF TRIMBLE. *U.S. News & World Report*, Oct. 22, 1990.
"Boris Yeltsin . . . ." BILL KELLER. *New York Times Magazine*, Sept. 23, 1990.
"Yeltsin's challenge . . . ." TOM MATTHEWS. *Newsweek*, June 11, 1990.
"Yeltsin spoils . . . ." EUGENE H. METHVIN and VLADIMIR SHLAPENTOKH. *National Review*, March 19, 1990.
"Boris Yeltsin explains." VALENTIN YUMASHEV. *World Press Review*, Jan. 1990.
"Yeltsin, Boris Nikolayevich." *Current Biography*, Jan. 1989.

Young, Andrew (1932–) On August 8, 1990, former Atlanta mayor Young lost the Georgia Democratic gubernatorial primary runoff to Lt. Governor Zell Miller, ending his bid to become Georgia's first Black governor. On September 18, he won a different kind of campaign, as co-chairman of Atlanta's Olympics committee, which won its bid to host the 1996 Summer Olympics.

New Orleans–born Young has been a historic figure ever since his deep involvement in the civil rights movement of the 1950s and 1960s. He was a leader of the Southern Christian Leadership Conference from 1961 to 1970, and a key associate of Martin Luther King, Jr. In 1972, he became the first Black Georgia congressman since Reconstruction. From 1977 to 1979, he was U.S. ambassador to the United Nations, then from 1982 to 1989 was mayor of Atlanta. He married Jean Childs in 1954; they have four children. His B.D. was from the Hartford Theological Seminary in 1955, the year he was ordained as a Congregational minister.

FURTHER READING

"Peach state politicking." BILL WHALEN. *Insight*, June 11, 1990.
"The great black . . . ." JAMES DODSON. *GQ—Gentlemen's Quarterly*, June 1990.
Voices of Freedom: An Oral History of the Civil Rights Movement from the 1950s Through the 1980s. HENRY HAMPTON and STEVE FAYER. Bantam, 1990.
"Keeping faith . . . ." TIM DARNELL. *American City & County*, Nov. 1989.
""Black mayors . . . ." *Mother Jones*, July, 1984.
Andrew Young: Champion of the Poor. PAUL WESTMAN. Dillon, 1983.
Andrew Young: Freedom Fighter. MAURICE ROBERTS. Childrens, 1983.
Andrew Young: Biography of a Realist. EDDIE STONE. Holloway, 1980.

Z

Zappa, Frank (Francis Vincent Zappa, 1940–) Composer, guitarist, and bandleader Zappa was known as an erratic, sometimes brilliant rock musician in the 1960s. In the 1990s, he is largely an imaginative, creative businessman. He and his wife Gail now operate several music-related businesses and market his old records, while he continues to speak out sharply on a wide range of political and social issues, from censorship to abortion. He has also been very active in seeking cultural and business opportunities in newly free Eastern Europe. As part of the restoration of rock music to official approval in Eastern Europe, Zappa was named in 1990 special cultural ambassador to Czechoslovakia by Czech president Vaclav Havel. In 1989, Zappa published *A Mother of Necessity: The Real Frank Zappa Book,* written with Peter Occhiogrosso.

Zappa became a major rock music figure in the 1960s as founder of the group The Mothers of Invention (1964–77); the group's hit albums included *Freak Out!* (1966), *Absolutely Free* (1967), and *200 Motels* (1971; and the 1971 film). On his own, he made such records as *Hot Rats* (1969), *Apostrophe* (1974), and *Joe's Garage* (1979). His hit singles included "Don't Eat the Yellow Snow" (1974), "Dancin' Fool" (1979), and "Valley Girl" (1982), in which he teamed up with his daughter Moon Unit, then only 14. Zappa's most notable later work tries to join jazz and classical music in such albums as *Boulez Conducts Zappa* (1982, 1987) and *The Perfect Stranger and Other Works* (1985). He married Gail Sloatman in 1967; they have four children. Two of them, Dweezil and Moon Unit, in 1990 became the stars of the television situation comedy *Normal Life*.

FURTHER READING

"Frank Zappa—trading partner." David Corn. *Nation*, March 19, 1990.
"Zappa, Frank." *Current Biography*, Feb. 1990.
"Frank Zappa. . . ." Tim Schneckloth. *Down Beat*, Sept. 1989.
"Frank Zappa. . . ." Steve Dougherty. *People*, May 22, 1989.
"Zappa." Michael Smolen. *Stereo Review*, June 1987.
"Frank Zappa. . . ." Batya Friedman and Steve Lyons. *Progressive*, Nov. 1986.
No Commercial Potential: The Saga of Frank Zappa Then and Now. David Walley. NAL-Dutton, 1980.

PHOTO CREDITS

Wide World Photos: Paula Abdul, Kirstie Alley, Corazon Aquino, Yasir Arafat, Hafez al Assad, Tariq Aziz, Mikhail Baryshnikov, Candice Bergen, Benazir Bhutto, King Birendra, Kenneth Branagh, David Brower, Susan Butcher, John Candy, Jennifer Capriati, Elena and Nicolae Ceausescu, Violeta Chamorro, Tracy Chapman, Dick Cheney, Sean Connery and Harrison Ford, Harry Connick Jr., Bill Cosby, Billy Crystal, Tyne Daly, Daniel Day-Lewis, Deng Xiaoping, Robert De Niro, Sharon Pratt Dixon, David Duke, Dianne Feinstein, Karen Finley, Carrie Fisher, David Foreman, James Garner, Richard Gere, Raisa Gorbachev, Arsenio Hall, Leona Helmsley, Evander Holyfield, Saddam Hussein, Janet Jackson, Judith Jamison, Pope John Paul II, Gary Kasparov, Charles Keating III, John F. Kennedy, Jr., Betsy King, Akira Kurosawa, Vyatautas Landsbergis, Spike Lee, Greg LeMond, Maya Lin, Li Peng, John List, Andrew Lloyd Webber, Paul McCartney, Peter MacDonald, Sr., Madonna, Winnie Mandela, Diego Maradona, Wynton Marsalis, Jackie Mason, Michael Milken, Francois Mitterrand, Elizabeth Morgan and Eric Foretich with Ted Koppel, Rupert Murdoch, Eddie Murphy, Willie Nelson, Manuel Noriega, Oliver North, Deborah Norville, Daniel Ortega, Jane Pauley, John Poindexter, Pol Pot, Veronica Prego, Elizabeth Clare Prophet, Muammar Qaddafi, Bruce Ritter, Mstislav Rostropovich, Nolan Ryan, Emir Sabah, Pete Sampras, Arnold Schwarzenegger and Maria Shriver, Eduard Shevardnadze, John Silber, Mitch Snyder, David Souter, George Steinbrenner, Charles and Carol Stuart, Kathleen Turner and Danny DeVito, David and Ginger Twitchell, Lech Walesa, Denzel Washington, Ryan White, L. Douglas Wilder, Oprah Winfrey, Boris Yeltsin, Andrew Young

Baker-Winokur-Ryder, Public Relations: Danny Aiello

Information Section, Embassy of Japan: Emperor Akihito

Embassy of the Republic of Hungary: Józef Antall

U.S. House of Representatives: Les Aspin, Thomas Foley, Barney Frank, Newt Gingrich

Embassy of Chile: Patricio Aylwin

U.S. Department of State: James Baker, W. Nathaniel Howell

©Capital Cities/ABC, Inc.: Roseanne Barr, Neil Patrick Harris, Peter Jennings, David Lynch, Lynn Redgrave and Vanessa Redgrave

D.C. Office of Communications: Marion Barry

U.S. Senate: Joseph Biden, Alan Cranston, Robert Dole, Sam Nunn, Donald Riegle, Jesse Helms, John Sidney McCain III

National Organization on Disability: James Brady

Carol T. Powers, The White House: Barbara Bush

U.S. Army: George Bush

British Information Service: Prince Charles, John Major

©CBS, Inc.: Connie Chung

©Def American Recordings, Inc.: Andrew Dice Clay

©CBS Records, Photo: Deborah Feingold: Judy Collins

Embassy of El Salvador: Alfredo Cristiani

New York State Governor's Office: Mario Cuomo

Embassy of South Africa: Frederick W. De Klerk

Central Office of Information, London, Photo: Terence Donovan: Princess Diana

James Hamilton: David Dinkins

U.S. Department of Labor: Elizabeth Hanford Dole

Columbia Records, ©Ken Regan/Camera 5: Bob Dylan

New York Knicks: Patrick Ewing

Royal Embassy of Saudi Arabia: King Fahd

National Institutes of Health: Anthony Fauci

Triad Artists, Inc.: Morgan Freeman

National Endowment for the Arts: John E. Frohnmayer

Embassy of Peru: Alberto Fujimori

HarperCollins, Photo: Annie Leibovitz: Philip Glass

Information Department, Embassy of Spain: Felipe Gonzalez Márquez

UN Photo 172543, Y. Nagata: Mikhail Gorbachev

Advantage International, Photo: Carl Newsom: Steffi Graf

Brooks Photography: Alan Greenspan

UN Photo 175587, P. Sudhakaran: Vaclav Havel

Australian Overseas Information Service: Bob Hawke

Bantam, ©Miriam Berkley: Stephen Hawking

©MJJ Productions, Photo: Sam Emerson: Michael Jackson

©CBS Records, Photo: Mark Nanaver: Billy Joel

Los Angeles Lakers: Earvin "Magic" Johnson

Chicago Bulls: Michael Jordan

Embassy of Japan: Toshiki Kaifu

U.S. Department of Housing and Urban Development: Jack Kemp

U.S. Supreme Court, Public Information Office: Anthony Kennedy, Thurgood Marshall, Sandra Day O'Conner, William Rehnquist, Antonin Scalia

U.S. Senate, Photo: Dennis DeSilva: Ted Kennedy

German Information Center: Helmut Kohl

ABC News: Ted Koppel

UN Photo 176005, P. Sudhakaran: Nelson Mandela

Columbia Artists Management: Kurt Masur

Random House, ©Elfriede Riley: James Michener

Egyptian Embassy, Photo: Michele Iannacci: Hosni Mubarak

Canadian Embassy: Brian Mulroney

Harvard University Press, Photo: Rafael Doniz: Octavio Paz

UN Photo 169681, J. Isaac: Javier Pérez de Cuéllar

UN Photo 176968, M. Grant: Thomas Pickering

U.S. Department of Defense: Colin Powell and Norman Schwarzkopf

Office of the Vice President: Dan Quayle

Capitol Records, Photo: Deborah Frankel: Bonnie Raitt

CBS News: Dan Rather

U.S. Environmental Protection Agency: William Kane Reilly

Embassy of the Republic of Korea: Roh Tae Woo

Mexican Embassy, Press Division: Carlos Salinas

Random House, ©Czeslaw Czaplinski: Dr. Suess (Theodore Geisel)

Scoop Management: Frank Sinatra

Random House, ©Stathis Orphanis: William Styron

U.S. Department of Health and Human Services: Louis Sullivan

National Football League: Paul Tagliabue

New York Giants: Lawrence Taylor

London Press Service, Central Office of Information: Margaret Thatcher

U.S. Attorney General's Office: Richard Thornburgh

Turner Broadcasting Service: Ted Turner

Alfred A. Knopf, ©Davis Freeman: John Updike

©CBS Records, Photo: Alan Messer: Stevie Ray Vaughan

Random House, ©Jane Bown: Gore Vidal

Philip Bermingham, Photography: James Watkins

Houston Police Department: Elizabeth Watson

California Angels: Dave Winfield

Index by Occupation

For ease of access, we have indexed the individuals profiled in *People in the News* by occupation or other area of news interest. The main body of the work is of course self-indexed, with individuals listed alphabetically.

Business and Finance

Dance and Choreography

Education

Journalism and Publishing

Law and Court Cases

Literature

Military

Miscellaneous

Music

Politics

Religion

Science, Technology, and Medicine

Social Activism

Social Sciences

Sports and Games

Stage and Screen

Visual Arts